DATE			

IRVING STONE'S JACK LONDON

Books by Irving Stone

BIOGRAPHICAL NOVELS

LUST FOR LIFE
(*Vincent Van Gogh*)
IMMORTAL WIFE
(*Jessie Benton Fremont*)
ADVERSARY IN THE HOUSE
(*Eugene V. Debs*)
THE PASSIONATE JOURNEY
(*John Noble*)
THE PRESIDENT'S LADY
(*Rachel Jackson*)

LOVE IS ETERNAL
(*Mary Todd Lincoln*)
THE AGONY AND THE ECSTASY
(*Michelangelo*)
THOSE WHO LOVE
(*Abigail Adams*)
THE PASSIONS OF THE MIND
(*Sigmund Freud*)
THE GREEK TREASURE
(*Henry and Sophia Schliemann*)

BIOGRAPHIES

SAILOR ON HORSEBACK
(*Jack London*)
THEY ALSO RAN
(*Defeated Presidential
Candidates*)

CLARENCE DARROW FOR THE
DEFENSE
EARL WARREN

HISTORY

MEN TO MATCH MY MOUNTAINS

NOVELS

PAGEANT OF YOUTH

FALSE WITNESS

BELLES-LETTRES

WE SPEAK FOR OURSELVES
(*A Self-Portrait of America*)

THE STORY OF MICHELANGELO'S
PIETÀ

WITH JEAN STONE

DEAR THEO
(*Vincent Van Gogh*)

I, MICHELANGELO, SCULPTOR
(*Autobiographies through letters*)

COLLECTED

THE IRVING STONE READER

EDITOR

THERE WAS LIGHT
*Autobiography of a University
Berkeley: 1888–1968*

LINCOLN: A CONTEMPORARY
PORTRAIT
(*with Allan Nevins*)

BOOKS FOR YOUNG READERS

THE GREAT ADVENTURE OF MICHELANGELO

IRVING STONE'S
JACK LONDON

HIS LIFE
SAILOR
ON HORSEBACK
(A BIOGRAPHY)

AND
TWENTY-EIGHT
SELECTED
JACK LONDON STORIES

1977
Doubleday & Company, Inc., Garden City, New York

Library of Congress Cataloging in Publication Data

Stone, Irving, 1903–
    Irving Stone's Jack London, his life (a biography),
and selected Jack London stories.

    Irving Stone's Jack London originally published in
1938 under title: Sailor on horseback; the biography
of Jack London.
    Includes index.
    1. London, Jack, 1876–1916—Biography.
2. Novelists, American—20th century—Biography.
I. London, Jack, 1876–1916. Selected works. 1977.
II. Title. III. Title: Jack London, his life
(a biography), and selected Jack London stories.
PS3523.046Z9 1977   818'.5'209 [B]
ISBN: 0-385-12797-9
Library of Congress Catalog Card Number 76-53418

CONTENTS

FOREWORD

I had always loved Jack London. I grew up in San Francisco, where I read *Martin Eden* as a young boy, and from it gained the concept that I too could become a writer. All of the summers of my childhood and early youth were spent in the Valley of the Moon, where I walked and rode horseback through its sage and manzanita covered mountains. I knew that one day I would write Jack London's story.

When I began the research and writing of *Sailor on Horseback* in 1936, Jack London had been dead only twenty years. He died at the early age of forty. Nearly everyone who had known him, relatives, friends, comrades from his adventuresome years, were still very much alive and full of memories and reminiscences. It was, for me, essentially a ground-breaking task. Apart from Charmian London's *The Book of Jack London* (1921), little had been written about him since his death; no objective writing had yet been seen in print. Nor had anyone assembled the magnificently rich raw material that lay in the minds of all those who had known him, worked, fought, and played with him. Loved him.

First I had to locate the hundred or more men and women, now somewhat widely dispersed, who had valuable materials to

relate. Second, I had to get down their memories of Jack London
and his times as completely and accurately as possible. Third,
after all the accounts were in, they had to be sifted rigorously to
make sure there had been no tricks of the memory, or the usual
distortion that results from the building up of one's importance in
a famous person's life. Memory is not a mountain, it is a river
which can change its bed several times during the flow of the
years.

In spite of double and triple checking this source material, and
a constant comparing of it with Jack London's own accounts,
through letters, journals, notes, manuscripts, some errors of detail
crept into my original manuscript: Heinhold instead of Heinold;
the sailing of the *Umatilla* for the Klondike in March instead of
July 1897; the payment by the *Saturday Evening Post* for *The
Call of the Wild* of $2,000 instead of the actual $750 paid.

Sailor on Horseback has now been thoroughly corrected and up-
dated, thanks to the publication of materials that had long been
unavailable, such as the Diary of Fred Thompson, who sailed on
the *Umatilla* with Jack London, and shared many of his Klondike
experiences. In his several days of reporting to me, Fred Thompson had failed to consult his diary, and consequently gave me the
March sailing date of the *Umatilla* from San Francisco instead of
the July 25 entry in his diary.

All of my recorded dialogues, notes, correspondence, and varying forms of the manuscript of *Sailor on Horseback* are deposited
in the Department of Special Collections at UCLA. The hundred
or more relatives and friends whom I interviewed are dead now.
So far as I know, no one collected or set down their reminiscences
after my publication. This source material then is invaluable to
the serious scholar for an in-depth portrait of Jack London, his life,
work, and times. Of great value as well is the meticulous research
of Jack London enthusiasts spread throughout the United States.

After Jack London's death in 1916, the reading of his work
went into such a serious decline for half a century that it can literally be called an eclipse. Upon the publication of *Sailor on Horseback* I had considerable difficulty convincing people that Jack
London was anything more than a writer of children's stories, or
stories of wild adventure. This kind of submergence happens to
many if not most writers—Ernest Hemingway and F. Scott Fitz-

gerald excepted—in the years following their death. Yet most serious writers, those who have had something meaningful to say, and have said it with both artistry and technical skill, have had a resurgence of their work.

This is precisely what happened to Herman Melville. It is now happening, in strong measure, to Jack London. He is becoming an American folk hero, for he fits into our times as well as or better than he did into his own. Readers are returning to his superb short stories, novels, hard-bitten social commentaries.

It is my sincere hope that the publication of this book at this time will add importantly to the rebirth of an authentic American genius, and a writer of world-wide significance.

Irving Stone
Beverly Hills
1977

IRVING STONE'S JACK LONDON

BOOK I

Jack London, Sailor on Horseback

A Biography by Irving Stone

To
JEAN
(*Who Collaborates*)

"If you suppress truth, if you hide truth, if you do not rise up and speak out in meeting, if you speak out in meeting without speaking the whole truth, then you are less true than truth."

"Let me glimpse the face of truth. Tell me what the face of truth looks like."

JACK LONDON

JACK LONDON,
SAILOR ON HORSEBACK

1

ON a morning in early June of the year 1875 the people of San
Francisco awakened to read a horrifying story in the *Chronicle*. A
woman had shot herself in the temple because her husband had
"driven her from home for refusing to destroy her unborn infant—
a chapter of heartlessness and domestic misery." The woman was
Flora Wellman, black sheep of the pioneer Wellman family of
Massillon, Ohio; the man was Professor W. H. Chaney, itinerant
Irish astrologer; the unborn child was to become known to millions the world over as Jack London.

The *Chronicle* article, though admitting in its last line that the
story was Flora's as filtered through her friends, is solid invective
against Chaney. He is accused of having been confined in the
Tombs prison; of having laid several former wives to rest, "at their
heads a green grass turf, at their heels a stone"; of having forced
Flora to drudge at the washtubs and take care of other people's
children for hire; of having sold the furniture for which she had
helped to pay; of ordering her out of the house, and abandoning
her when she refused to go. There is as little truth in these accusa-
tions as there is in the heading of the *Chronicle* article: "A Dis-

carded Wife"; for Flora Wellman was never married to Professor Chaney.

Flora had but slight intention of suicide. She inflicted upon herself only a flesh wound. The bullet did far more injury to Chaney than it did to Flora, for the story was reproduced in newspapers all over the country, and the remainder of Chaney's life was spent in bitterness and disgrace. He disappeared from San Francisco shortly after. Jack London never set eyes upon his father.

At the time the *Chronicle* article appeared Flora Wellman was about thirty. She was a small, homely, wiry woman who wore spectacles and a wig of black curls because a bout with typhoid had cost her a good part of her eyesight and hair. She had a big nose, big ears, a sallow complexion, and was without taste in dress. Flora came of good Welsh stock, her grandmother, Mrs. Joel Wellman, having guided her four children across the Allegheny Mountains in midwinter, just after 1800, from Canandaigua, New York, to Wayne County, Ohio, a journey which demanded energy, self-reliance, and courage.

Mrs. Joel Wellman's two sons, Hiram and Marshall, grandfather of Jack London, inherited these traits. While on a visit to Cleveland they went by boat in the late fall to an island in Put-In Bay. The boat failed to stop on its return and last trip for the year and the two boys were abandoned on the desolate island without food or shelter, and winter about to set in. With only such tools as they could make out of rocks and driftwood they constructed a raft of sufficient strength to carry them not only to the mainland, but all the way to Cleveland.

Marshall Wellman settled in Massillon, Ohio, where he built canals, patented inventions, chief among which is the Wellman coal grate, accumulated considerable wealth, and built one of the most beautiful homes in Massillon, in which his daughter Flora was born.

Flora Wellman had all the advantages of her times. She was trained in music, educated at a finishing school, was well read, used good English, and had polished manners. As the daughter of the wealthy Wellman family she could have taken her choice of husbands and settled down, as did her brothers and sisters, to a prosperous and solid life. But somewhere the machinery slipped a cog; clever inventor that he was, Marshall Wellman could not think up a device to keep his daughter in line. She was said by her friends to be a clever and intelligent woman but a neurotic, a woman of unstable emotions who had difficulty in holding herself to any given discipline or direction. The attack of typhus she suffered at the age of twenty is said to have left her mind in a disorderly state.

At the age of twenty-five Flora put her belongings in a suitcase and left Massillon, an unprecedented thing for a young unmarried girl to do. To the end of her days she never communicated with her parents, nor her parents with her. That there was a row is indisputable, but the exact cause of the trouble can only be surmised. The inventive *Chronicle* reporter suggested that "she came to this coast about the time the Professor took the journey overland through the romantic sagebrush"; but Flora did not meet Chaney until three years later, in Seattle. We would give a great deal to be able to follow her trail during those three obscured years in which she traveled from city to city earning her living by giving piano lessons; from the evidence one is led to believe that it would not be a pretty tale.

Professor Chaney writes, "Flora was known as my wife in the same lodging-house where she had passed as the wife of Lee Smith. It was a very respectable place, and one day when I came home I found all the lodgers moving away and great excitement throughout the house. As soon as I entered the room Flora locked the door, fell on her knees before me, and between sobs begged me to forgive her. I said I had nothing to forgive. Finally, after much delay and pleading she confesed about Lee Smith and said the lodgers were leaving on account of her being known as Miss Wellman, Mrs. Smith, and Mrs. Chaney all at nearly the same time. Had I followed my first impression I should have left her then, and it would have saved years of misery. But my own life had been a broken one, and on reflection I forgave her."

Chaney first met Flora Wellman in the home of Mayor Yesler of Seattle, who came from Ohio and knew the Wellman family. Flora was stopping with Mayor and Mrs. Yesler; they confided to Chaney that she came from very respectable people, but that she had done something wrong. This undisclosed something wrong had probably been the cause of Flora's leaving home. Chaney was intimate with the Yeslers; he came often to their house; and when he later encountered Flora in San Francisco they met as old friends.

What kind of man was Jack London's father? Of his antecedents we know little, except that he was a full-blooded Irishman, and was born in a log cabin in Maine. He spent many years of his youth at sea. He was a short, powerfully built man who at the age of sixty was able to knock downstairs a bully who had been sent to beat him up. He spent his life writing, editing magazines, lecturing, teaching, and drawing up astrological nativities. He assembled a comprehensive library on philosophy, mathematics, astronomy, and occult subjects. He was a linguist, an able student of history and the Bible. Among his friends, students, and followers he was known as a remarkable man; among astrologers he was acknowledged to be one of the best. As an old man in Chicago he is said to have devoted his great energies, some sixteen hours a day, to the cause of astrology, in which he had a passionate and genuine belief. He considered it to be an exact science, like chemistry and mathematics, one which could raise humanity from the mire.

Chaney's greatest weakness was women. When reproached by his friends for moral delinquency he would point to his horoscope and cry, "Alas! It is in my nativity." He could quickly be aroused to anger, was not easy to get along with, for he had always to be the headman, the leader, the teacher. He spent most of his life in poverty because he was impractical with money, taught for nothing when his pupils were too poor to pay, and was constantly giving away what little means he had.

His students testify that his lectures always commanded close attention, for he had something to say and said it in a pleasing manner. Yet few were his match in sarcasm and irony. He gave his friends plenty to think about if they were capable of thinking, and if they were not, they did not remain his friends long. In Portland, Oregon, his weekly lectures were popular. The audience sat before a two-foot horoscope on a blackboard while Chaney stood before it with a pointer indicating the various configurations and calling on the class to explain their significance. After an hour-and-a-half lecture he entertained them with amusing stories, for he had a lusty Irish humor.

One of his followers, Joe Trounson of Healdsburg, later a

brother socialist of Jack London's, wrote in 1909, "One charm of his conversation was his habit of saying, 'Ah, that gives me an idea!' and then he would proceed to elaborate a beautiful truth or what appeared to be a fact in nature heretofore overlooked. In mathematics and astrology he was wonderful; he taught me the method by which the ancient writings were deciphered. He was a thorough grammarian, was profound, scholarly, had a wonderful memory, and could write for sixteen hours a day without fatigue. He often lectured just as our socialists do in these more modern times; he spoke of the rich getting richer and the poor getting poorer, and the causes and cures of poverty. He taught me more than all the others put together, and was very versatile. One day he said to me, 'I will teach you to calculate an eclipse or any science you wish to learn.' In short, whenever I wanted to know anything I wended my way to Professor Chaney's."

Trounson does not neglect to mention Chaney's failings. He was idiotic in music; he hated the champions of woman suffrage; he was an unrelenting enemy as well as a true friend, and could hardly give the devil his due after a quarrel; he accepted money from the Freethinkers to lecture against orthodoxy . . . and could not stay away from young widows.

Having joined forces with Flora Wellman, Chaney set up house on what was then First Avenue, between Mission and Valencia Streets. He joined the staff of *Common Sense* magazine, which advertised itself as the only Free Thought magazine west of the Rockies, wrote articles, delivered a series of sociological lectures for the Philomathean Society, and gave private readings in horoscopes.

"The Professor has located permanently in San Francisco for the practice of ASTROLOGY. He will also teach the science to such as may desire to obtain a knowledge of this celestial art, which includes among its pupils and admirers such minds as Galileo and Sir Isaac Newton.—In the long lists of persons advertised in this city under the head of Astrologers, there is not one who knows anything of the science. Those calling themselves Astrologers are simply fortune-tellers who divine through a teacup or pack of cards, and by their charlatanism have done much toward bringing genuine Astrology into disrepute.—Office hours from 10

*to 12 a.m. and from 2 to 4 p.m. Receptions for the evenings may
be secured by special arrangement."*

Chaney was no quack. That he was not consciously racketeering
off the gullible is evidenced by the fact that the greater part of his
life was spent in teaching, writing, and lecturing for the cause
without pay. A few anecdotes will illuminate the position he held
in his field.

"At one time a house burned down. It was evidently incendiary.
The owner consulted Professor Chaney. Chaney said there were
three engaged in it and described them so accurately that the
owner went to them and said Chaney said they did it. They confessed at once. If Chaney said it, it was useless to deny it.

"A middle-aged woman who had apparently not lived too rigor-
ously correct a life went to Chaney to have her horoscope read.
In the middle of the reading she jumped up and fled, exclaiming,
'That man can read God's mind!'"

On Sunday nights Chaney gave lectures on astrology in the
Charter Oak Hall, where Flora sold tickets at the door for ten
cents each. For a time these lectures were well attended, though a
portion of the audience came to scoff and amuse itself.

The best record of Chaney's mind and work to come down to
us is contained in the articles he published in *Common Sense:*
"The Causes and Cure of Poverty," and "What Is to Be Done
with the Criminal?"—subjects on which his son Jack would be
writing heatedly some twenty years later. In "Man Should Be Able
to Predict the Future" he writes, "A false education had taught us
that the future belongs to God, and that it is blasphemous for
man to even attempt to pry into it. Trained from earliest infancy
in this belief, probably nine tenths of the people of the United
States are disposed to doubt when they hear it asserted that the
future can be predicted. They occupy a position similar to the
people before the time of Galileo. Educated in the doctrine that
this earth was flat, they looked with abhorrence upon all who
maintained that it was a sphere, and when Galileo was imprisoned by the Pope and Cardinals for maintaining that it moved in
an orbit, the common people felt that this early martyr to science
was properly punished."

A study of Chaney's articles reveals a clear, forceful, and pleasing literary style, an authentic erudition, courage to speak his

mind, a sympathy for the mass of humanity, and a desire to teach them to better themselves. His point of view is modern and progressive; in his article on criminology he writes that the certainty rather than the severity of the punishment is what deters criminals, and in another article proposes that the Philomatheans organize a Brotherhood and Sisterhood of men, women, and children to hold weekly meetings in which the adults will write and discuss theses, and the children will practise music, composition, and criticism so that they may continue to improve the race until in a few generations vice and crime will almost entirely disappear.

At many points the writing, the attack, the attitudes, the enthusiasms, the very turning of a phrase is so similar to the writings of Jack London that the reader rubs his eyes in amazement.

Flora was not only an astrologer, but an ardent spiritualist as well. She held séances in which the public was invited to communicate with the dead, to send messages to former loved ones, and because of the vantage point of the dead, to receive advice from them on how to conduct their business and love affairs, how to settle quarrels and control their husbands or wives. Spiritualism was very much in vogue in the 1870's; dozens of séances were being conducted all over San Francisco, and the believers went so far as to consult the spirits for approval before they would engage a housekeeper.

Flora and Chaney spent a number of happy months together in San Francisco, Flora keeping house, giving piano lessons, conducting séances, lecturing on spiritualism, and taking tickets at the door of the sawdust-floored tent where Chaney was lecturing on chemistry, astronomy, and occultism. They had friends among the astrologers, were well thought of, occupied a position of leadership in their cult. Flora seems to have loved Chaney, and was eager to be married to him, but Chaney was too busy lecturing to the Philomatheans on "The Phenomena of Physical, Intellectual, Moral, and Spiritual Life" to be bothered with anything so mundane as marriage.

When Jack London was twenty-three years old he wrote to Chaney to ask if he was his father. On June 4, 1899, twenty-four years to the day after the appearance of the *Chronicle* article, Chaney replies to his inquiry, addresses him as "Dear Sir," agrees to "comply with his wish to observe silence and secrecy," and gives his own version of the happenings leading to Flora's attempted suicide. "I was never married to Flora Wellman," writes Chaney, "but she lived with me from June 11, 1874, until June 3, 1875. I was impotent at that time, the result of hardship, privation, and too much brain work. Therefore I cannot be your father, nor am I sure who your father is."

Acceding to Jack's plea to help him determine who his father was, Chaney repeats the gossip that linked Flora's name with two other men in the spring of 1875, but readily admits that he "knows nothing of his own knowledge." He then pens one of the most heartbreaking pages ever written. "There was a time when I had a very tender affection for Flora; but there came a time when I hated her with all the intensity of my intense nature, and even thought of killing her and myself, as many a man has under similar circumstances. Time, however, has healed the wounds and I feel no unkindness toward her, while for you I feel a warm sympathy, for I can imagine what my emotions would be were I in your place. . . . The *Chronicle* published that I turned her out of doors because she would not submit to an abortion. This was copied and sent broadcast over the country. My sisters in Maine read it and two of them became my enemies. One died believing I was in the wrong. All others of my kindred, except one sister in Portland, Oregon, are still my enemies and denounce me as a disgrace to them. I published a pamphlet at the time containing a report from a detective given me by the Chief of Police, showing that many of the slanders against me were false, but neither the *Chronicle* nor any of the papers that defamed me would correct the false statement. Then I gave up defending myself, and for years life was a burden. But reaction finally came, and now I have a few friends who think me respectable. I am past seventy-six, and quite poor."

Unsatisfied, Jack London sent another urgent demand for information. Chaney, still denying that he was Jack's father, wrote one last letter.

"The cause of our separation began when Flora one day said to me, 'You know that motherhood is the great desire of my life, and as you are too old—now some time when I find a good, nice man are you not willing for me to have a child by him?'

"I said yes, only he must support her. No, she must always live with me and be the wife of Professor Chaney. A month or so later she said she was pregnant by me. I thought she was only trying me and did not think she was pregnant. So I made a great fuss thinking to warn her not to make the attempt. This brought on a wrangle that lasted all day and night. After daylight I got up and told her she could never be a wife to me again. She was humbled in a moment, for she knew I was in earnest. She crawled on her knees to me, sobbing, and begged my forgiveness. But I would not forgive her, although I still thought she was merely pretending to be in a family way. But her temper was a great trial, and I had often thought before that time that I must leave her on account of it.

"When she left she went to Doctor Ruttley's house; went out to the back yard, soon returned, a pistol in one hand and a box of cartridges in the other, a wound in the left side of her forehead and the blood running over her face. In reply to Mrs. Ruttley, Flora said, 'This little woman has been trying to kill herself and made a bad job of it.'

"A great excitement followed. A mob of a hundred and fifty gathered, swearing to hang me to the nearest lamp-post."

Although all the copies of the defense pamphlet Chaney published have disappeared, its existence has been verified by people who read it at the time. The detective reported that the pistol was second-hand and had not been discharged since being oiled; that it smelled of oil and not of gunpowder; that a carpenter working within twenty feet of Flora at the time had heard no report of a pistol; that her face would have been filled with powder had she shot as she had said, but there was no mark of powder about her.

What is remarkable about Chaney's effort to prove that Flora was only shamming is that he made no attempt to look at Flora's wound to see if it were real or imaginary, nor did he bring up this point in the defense pamphlet. And for good reason: that Flora carried the wound on her temple has been attested by her stepdaughter, Eliza London Shepard, and by her stepgrandson, John Miller. Chaney was apparently trying to establish that if Flora had wounded herself at all, it was with some instrument far less lethal than a gun—for example, a jagged piece of metal—but even if he had proved his point, he would have been no better off.

This same type of omission is what makes Chaney's denial of

paternity unacceptable. If he had wanted to confound Flora's charge that she was pregnant by him, and he had been truly impotent, all he would have had to say was, "Flora, you and I have had no sexual relations, so how can I be the father of your child?" And if he were impotent, would Flora have been so foolish as to claim that she was pregnant by him? Chaney, with all his education, simply got his words twisted; he meant to tell Jack that he was sterile, and could not create life; for nowhere does he deny that Flora was in point of fact a wife to him.

Why did Chaney deny that he was Jack London's father? Since his denial seems sincere there is reason to believe that he had genuinely thought himself sterile, and was convinced that Flora had been with another man during that critical month. But even if he were not convinced, he was now past seventy and too tired to begin a father-and-son relationship at the very end of his life. He had suffered greatly because of his union with Flora Wellman, and he had no mind to plunge all over again into an affair that had embittered him for so long. Jack London was a stranger to him, an unknown name. All Chaney wanted, in relation to Flora and Jack London, was to be let alone.

It was futile for Chaney to have denied his fatherhood. His writing of the name Jack London on the envelopes of the letters he sent to Jack cannot be distinguished from Jack's own signature. Jack inherited from his father his strong, handsome Irish face, his light hair, high forehead, deep-set mystical eyes, sensuous mouth, powerful chin, and short, husky torso. Doctor Hall, who attended Flora during her pregnancy, testifies that sixteen years later he saw a handsome, heavy-set young boy walk on the ferryboat who was so much the spit and image of Professor Chaney that he knew even before asking his name that it could be none other than Chaney's son. Rarely did a father and son seem more completely alike in temperament and tenor of thought.

After the attempted suicide Flora was taken into the home of William Slocum, a writer on the *Evening Post* and the publisher of *Common Sense*, where she was befriended until the birth of Jack. After his failure to clear himself, Chaney joined the one sister in Portland who had not lost faith in him. Here he lived for many years, collected a fine library, published pamphlets and an astrological almanac, acquired students and followers. Later he went to New Orleans where he published an occult magazine and tutored two young boys for his board and lodging. His last move was to Chicago, where he finally married, named himself principal of the College of Astronomy, and eked out a living by giving oral nativities for one dollar each. In 1902 he passed on, fulfilling to the letter, according to one of his students, a prediction that he would die on a given day and be buried in a blizzard.

Flora Wellman gave public lectures on spiritualism and was active in séances up to the day her son was born. San Franciscans remember her standing on the platform, weirdly dressed, the false black curls reaching her shoulders, crouched over as though there were a hump in her back, her baby sticking straight out in front of her. They were sorry for this frail unmarried woman who was alone in the world; several times collections were taken up to help her.

On the fourteenth of January, 1876, the *Chronicle* once again prints the name of Chaney, but this time more kindly: "Chaney. —In this city, January 12, the wife of W. H. Chaney, a son." The boy was known as John Chaney for only eight months; then Flora married John London.

John London was born in Pennsylvania, of English extraction. He went to country school, and was fond of quoting. At nineteen, when boss of a section of the Pennsylvania-Erie Railroad, he married Ann Jane Cavett. The couple had ten children, and lived together happily. London left the railroad and became a farmer. When the Civil War broke out he fought for the North until an attack of typhus destroyed one lung. After the war he took up a section of government land near Moscow, Iowa, where he farmed, was sheriff, worked as a carpenter and builder. He was a deacon of the Methodist Church, and on Sundays after the sermon brought the parson home for Sunday dinner.

Not long after Ann Jane Cavett's death one of their sons was injured by being struck on the chest with a baseball. The doctor recommended that the boy be taken to California where the climate would help him recover. The doctor failed to mention that within its twelve hundred miles the state had several different kinds of weather. San Francisco being the only town in California that London knew about, he bundled his sick son and two youngest daughters onto a westbound train for that city. After ten days of San Francisco fogs the boy was dead.

London next sent to Iowa for a married couple to come to California and keep house for him and his two daughters. The couple took care of the children for a few months, then went upstate, where the man had been offered a job. Once again left alone with his two girls, London paid to have them kept in the Protestant Orphan Asylum on Haight Street.

John London was then in his mid-forties, a nice-looking man with a full-face beard, kindly, gentle, remembered by everyone as sweet. Still grieving over the loss of his wife and son, he was persuaded by a fellow worker to attend a spiritualist meeting. "Come on, John, and see if you can't get a message from them." Instead of getting a message from his old wife, London got himself a new one.

Whether London met Flora before or after the birth of her son is not a matter of record, but there can be little doubt that he knew Flora had not been married to Chaney. Flora told it herself in public meeting in Charter Oak Hall while in the process of giving the now absent Professor a thorough castigation. At the time most people wondered why London married Flora. Though not in robust health he was well set up, had a pleasant personality, and was liked by the women he took out, particularly the attractive actress who accompanied him on Saturday afternoons to visit his two daughters in the Orphan Asylum.

John London was alone in San Francisco, he was a homebody; he longed for a wife and hearth for himself, and for a home and mother for his daughters. Flora was convivial, she was a good talker, she played the piano for him and filled his lonesome hours. When he once again came down with typhus, she nursed him. Two weeks after John was confined to his bed Flora appeared at the Orphan Asylum during the Saturday afternoon visiting hours, told the girls that their father was ill and that she was to be their new mother. The girls refused to believe her.

On the seventh of September, 1876, Flora Wellman signed herself as Flora Chaney on the marriage license and took her eight-months-old son to live with John London in a small flat in the workingman's section south of Market Street. When the family was settled John went to the Asylum and brought home his two daughters, of whom the oldest was Eliza, a plain-featured, plain-spoken girl of eight, mature and self-reliant for her age. Eliza was shown through the house by her father and told that the baby was her brother. When she looked down at Jack for the first time she saw that there were flies on his face, for Flora had not thought to buy a piece of mosquito netting with which to cover the infant. Eliza asked no questions; she made a fan out of a piece of paper and sat by the cradle keeping the flies off the baby. In that instant the practical-minded girl of eight adopted Jack as her own child, a trust she was to hold sacred to the day she buried Jack's ashes on a high hill overlooking the Valley of the Moon.

Flora had little liking for the job of mother. She was restless, temperamental, moody, too busy with her music and lectures and spiritualism to pay any attention to the boy, who fell ill with bowel trouble. Upon advice of their doctor the London family moved from town to Bernal Heights, a district of farms, where Flora advertised for a wet nurse. Mrs. Jenny Prentiss, a negress who lived across the road and who had just lost her own baby, became Jack's wet nurse, foster mother, and life-long friend. Mammy Jenny was a tall, broad, deep-bosomed woman, black as coal, hard-working, religious, proud of her home and family and her respected position in the community. She took Jack on her spacious lap, sang him Negro lullabies, squandered on him all the impetuous love she would have lavished on her own child had he lived. Between Eliza and Mammy Jenny, little Jack was now well cared for.

After a year the family moved back to the crowded working-man's section, 920 Natoma Street. By this time Jack was toddling and had a little red wagon that he pulled. Eliza would put her doll in it, and Jack would haul it up and down the sidewalk. One day when Eliza returned from school she found her doll had been smashed because Flora had given it to Jack but had neglected to tie it in the wagon.

The Londons lived in a long railroad flat in the three-story frame building for two years. Flora took in a boarder, whose rent money paid for a Chinese servant. John London worked as a carpenter and builder, but the depression of 1876 still had the West in its grip and work was scarce. He got a job opening crates for the IXL Emporium, and later canvassed for the Singer Sewing Machine Company, earning a modest living.

When an epidemic hit San Francisco, Jack and Eliza came down with diphtheria. The two children, who were quarantined in the same bed, were dying. Eliza wakened out of her coma long enough to hear Flora ask, "Can the two of them be buried in the same coffin, doctor, to save expenses?" While Jack's mother was thus arranging her son's funeral, his foster father was rushing about town to find a trained nurse and a doctor who might save the children. Hearing of a doctor in the city of Oakland, across the Bay, who was having marked success with diphtheria cases, John took the first boat across and pleaded with him to come to San Francisco. The doctor came, burned the white cankers off the children's throats, poured sulphur down them . . . and the double funeral was averted.

As soon as Jack and Eliza had fully recovered, the family moved to Oakland, a sun-flooded, sleepy suburb of San Francisco which was trying to become a metropolis on its own. They rented a comfortable five-room cottage on Third Street. Flora was gone from home all day with get-rich-quick business schemes to supplement John London's sporadic earnings. Her chief scheme was selling gold leaf to saloonkeepers with which to gild the frames of the pictures over the bar. When the saloonkeeper refused to be convinced that the frames of his pictures would look better in gilt, Flora stood on the bar and gilded them herself.

Mammy Jenny was a little later to move to Oakland to be closer to her "white child," but in the meanwhile the mothering of Jack fell squarely upon Eliza's shoulders. She either had to stay home with the boy, or take him with her to school. When she explained to her teacher why she had to bring her little brother along, the teacher fixed a box on the platform as a desk for him and gave him picture books to pore over. Jack, then four years old, enjoyed playing in the yard with the other children, who would give Eliza an apple or allow her to wear their rings for the privilege of letting Jack sit with them.

John London next ventured to open a grocery store in the workingman's section of Oakland at Seventh and Peralta Streets. The family lived in the four rooms behind the store. It was here Jack received his first inkling that something was wrong in the family relationship, for in his hand-scrawled notes for an autobiography which he one day hoped to write under the title of *Sailor on Horseback*, he tells of a six-year-old boy overhearing a quarrel in the back of a grocery store, in which the father reproaches the mother for having a child out of wedlock, and the mother defends herself by crying, "I was so young, and he promised me a bed of roses."

The grocery store prospered. John London, who was an excellent judge of produce, traveled among the outlying farms to buy the best in fruits and vegetables, while Flora and Eliza waited on trade and Jack helped himself to candy and nuts every time he tripped through the store. Mammy Jenny settled in a cottage in Alameda, where Jack spent many hours of his day playing with her children, eating at her table, being watched over and nursed and cared for by the kindly woman to whom he was as much a son as her own blood. From her Jack received counsel and comfort; when he tired of playing in the back yard with the other children he would climb onto her lap to hear the lullabies of his baby days, or fairy stories which Mammy Jenny had inherited from her race.

It seems to have been a happy period for the family. Only Flora was discontented, for she did not feel they were going ahead rapidly enough. She introduced John to a man by the name of Stowell, to whom she persuaded her husband to sell a half interest in the store so they could expand and make money faster. Together the London and Stowell families rented a large, modern house on Sixteenth and Woods Streets in a solid residential neighborhood. The store was enlarged, and the business grew so big that John London had to spend all his time in the country buying merchandise. Stowell took charge of the store and the money that came in. London no longer knew what was going on. One day he returned from a trip to find his store stark empty: Stowell had sold out the entire stock and fixtures and absconded with the cash.

Broke once more, John London returned to his one and only love, farming. He leased the twenty-acre Davenport place in Alameda, where he raised corn and other vegetables for the market. Jack writes that it was a forlorn period of his childhood, for he had no playmates and was forced to turn inward on himself.

London was a skilled farmer and would have made a success of it, but Flora was not one to let well enough alone. Because she was supposed to be the smart member of the family John entrusted the business to her hands. He never could figure where she spent the money, for apparently she did not pay her bills. Flora prided herself on being a clever woman; she was always trying to make money out of new ventures, including lottery tickets and stocks. She meant well, but she was fly-by-night. In addition, she insisted that every detail in the running of the household be guided by departed spirits. In spite of the fact that London never went to another spiritualist meeting after his marriage, Flora invited groups of spiritualists to her house. During the séances six-year-old Jack would be laid on a table in the center of a dark room and seven pairs of hands would be placed on the edge of it. Jack and the table would then begin floating about.

As a result of these spooky sessions, of the frightening conversation he had overheard in the back of the Oakland grocery store, and of the emotional instability and lack of control he had inherited from both parents and the shattered nervous system bequeathed to him by Flora, the boy suffered from frequent nervousness and was occasionally on the verge of a breakdown.

Flora was a little thing—she could walk under her husband's outstretched arm—but the scenes she could create were out of all proportion to her size. Besides, she had a "heart." She would have heart attacks at the dinner table, and then the three children would have to help her to the couch and make a great fuss over her. The housework consequently fell upon the shoulders of Eliza, who by the age of thirteen was doing the cooking, cleaning, and washing.

There are numerous anecdotes told about Jack's childhood, but many of them are apocryphal, and one treads among them as on broken glass. Aside from his occasional nervous attacks he appears to have been a normal, wholesome child, good as gold, never malicious. He was blond and had curly hair, blue eyes, and a clear skin. At the least little thing his sensitive mouth would quiver. Here in Alameda he started school, but the better part of his time was spent in the fields paddling about with John London, who was his idol.

On Saturday nights the family went to the Tivoli Theater in

Oakland, where beer and sandwiches were served while plays were given. John set Jack on the table so that he could see the comedy, and the boy would laugh and clap his hands. One weekday, playing in the kitchen where Eliza could keep an eye on him while she scrubbed the floor, he fell against a jagged hole in the sink and cut his forehead from the hairline to his nose. Eliza, remembering how her father had treated a cut on a horse's leg, filled the wound with cobwebs and covered it with tar. The first Saturday after the accident John put a bandage around Jack's head and took him to the theater as always, but the second Saturday Flora refused to take him with the bandage. She told Eliza she would either have to scrape the tar off the boy's head, or stay home with him. Eliza and Jack both wanted to see the show; standing in the middle of the kitchen she picked off the tar and the scab with it. Jack always carried that scar on his forehead.

The Londons now had a cow, plenty of vegetables, and a comfortable house. John culled all his produce, selling only the best to the market, and giving the less desirable vegetables to the poorer families about him. He established a reputation among the produce men for having first-rate goods, and he could have continued to earn a fair living on the Davenport place. Yet before long we find them giving up the farm and moving to San Mateo, a few miles down the coast from San Francisco. The family reports that the Londons moved because they wanted more space to raise horses. It is questionable whether John wanted to leave his farm; perhaps Flora agitated him with a get-rich-quick horse-breeding scheme, or perhaps she simply forgot to pay their bills, and they were forced off the land.

On his seventy-five acres along the fogbound coast John London planted potatoes, put his few horses to graze, and rented out pasture land. Jack attended school on top of a hill below Colma, with the one teacher and four or five grades all in the same room. In their free hours he and Eliza went to the beach to wade and gather clams and mussels. It was desolate, unbeautiful country, with a harsh coastline. Jack spent the dreariest year of his childhood here; he had no playmates, the farms were far apart, and the neighbors were either Italian or immigrant Irish for whose company Flora cared little. The only bright moments came when he and Eliza tramped to a neighboring farm to watch an Italian wedding or dance, or when he rode into San Francisco on the high wagon with his father when John was hauling potatoes to market.

Jack remembered this period as the hungriest of his life. He maintained he was so hungry for the taste of meat that he once stole a piece the size of his two fingers from a girl's lunch-basket, and that when his schoolmates threw chunks of meat to the ground because of surfeit, only pride prevented him from dragging them from the dirt and eating them.

When Jack was eight, John London put a down payment on an eighty-seven-acre ranch in Livermore, in the warm valley behind Oakland, and the family moved into an old farmhouse on the property. He planted a row of olive trees all about the ranch, put in vineyards and orchards, and cultivated his fields. This was the first time since he had been in California that he had bought, and he intended to make this his permanent home. Here Jack began doing the simple chores, hunting eggs, bringing in wood, drawing water from the well. Often he sat on the high seat alongside his father (Jack called him Father and loved him as a father even after he learned there was no blood relation between them) when John drove his produce to the Oakland market. London implanted in the boy's mind an enthusiasm not merely for farming, but for that scientific farming which brings forth only the finest produce from the earth and the finest animals from breeded stock. It was a devotion which Jack mistakenly thought was in his blood.

It was here too the boy discovered the authentic passion of his life, which was in truth passed down to him by Professor Chaney, the one talisman that never failed him, that brought him meaning and direction: the love of books. His teacher loaned him Irving's *Alhambra*; in the homes of neighbors, who possessed books only by accident, he stumbled upon a life of Garfield, Paul du Chaillu's *African Travels*, and most important of all a copy of Ouida's *Signa*, the lyrically written story of an illegitimate son of an Italian peasant girl and a wandering artist, who rose from poverty and hardship to become one of Italy's great composers, a story which in its essentials Jack was to duplicate. Jack writes that reading *Signa* pushed back his narrow hill-horizon, and all the world was made possible if he would dare it. Eliza reports him saying at this time, "You know, Lize, I'm not going to get married until I'm forty years old. I'm going to have a big house, and one room is going to be filled with books." By the time he was forty he had the big house, and several rooms filled with books. . . .

Though Jack enjoyed going into the fields with John, and reading with his sister Eliza, the two years spent in Livermore were also dismal ones. He was not too young to sense that there were several things wrong with his family; the home was rarely a pleasant one in which to live, dominated as it was by Flora's confusion of mind, her scenes and heart attacks and demands. Flora was not cruel to Jack, he loved her as any normal child will love its mother; she simply had no tenderness to bestow upon the boy, who turned to Eliza for affection. However, Flora arranged to board a middle-aged Civil War veteran by the name of Shepard, who had been widowed with three children. To her task of cooking and keeping house and mothering Jack, sixteen-year-old Eliza now had the added responsibility of mothering Shepard's three children, the oldest of whom was thirteen.

By the end of the first year John London had once again established himself in Oakland as a producer of fine vegetables, and there was always a market for his crop. The prospects for the future were so bright that the family bought Jack his first store-bought undershirt, which fairly transported the boy who had never known anything but the coarse homemade shifts. Then Flora, again not satisfied with their rate of progress, hatched a business scheme. She took John across the Bay to San Francisco on numerous trips, brought him into contact with the manager of one of the large hotels, negotiated an agreement whereby John was to start a chicken ranch and the hotel man was to buy all his chickens and eggs.

John London, who knew nothing about chickens, mortgaged his interest in the ranch to build enormous coops and steam-heated brooder houses. For a short time the San Francisco hotel man bought all his eggs and whatever chickens he wanted to sell. Then three calamities hit him at once: Eliza, who took care of the chickens, married Shepard and left the ranch; an epidemic killed off a flock of the hens; and the remainder refused to lay. London's money being sunk in olive trees, orchards, and brooder houses, when the interest on the mortgage fell due he was unable to pay. The bank foreclosed. Once again the Londons were out on the road, their belongings piled high in their potato wagon.

Jack London's mind was like a seismograph that recorded every slight tremor about him . . . and tremors there were aplenty, for the next thirteen years of the family's life were spent in poverty and defeat. He often said that he had had no childhood, that his first memories of life were pinched by poverty, and that the pinch of poverty had been chronic.

Jack was ten years old when John London gave up forever the farming he loved so well and went back to Oakland. Jack was wiry, fair of face, with dark blue eyes, still suffering keenly from the loss of Eliza. He was not a fighter, but at the Garfield School there was the established California custom that every boy fight every other boy, so he soon learned to use his fists. He enjoyed most hunting ducks and fishing along the Alameda sea wall with his father, who gave the boy his own small gun and fishing rod. The constant failure and flight of the family, the horrors of the spiritualist séances to which he was exposed, the presentiment that there was something askew in his paternity made him self-conscious, timid, unassuming. Between the older man and the boy, both suffering from injuries inflicted upon them by Flora, each powerless to right the wrong, there grew an ever-deepening sympathy. They escaped together as often as they could to spend whole days forlornly roaming the waterfront. They loved and trusted each other completely, but it was a love touched by sadness.

In Oakland the family rented a bay-window cottage on East Seventeenth Street. Close by were the California Cotton Mills, which had brought a number of girls over from Scotland to do their work. The manager asked London if he wanted to board the girls. John was now fifty-five, crushed by the knowledge that he would never again get back to the land or be his own master; and there were not many jobs he was still able to fill. He agreed to run the boarding-house.

Flora had brains, and at the beginning of each new cycle she used them to advantage. She sent John, who knew good produce and their prices, to do the marketing while she supervised the cooking. The twenty young Scotch girls were satisfied, the mill management was pleased, and the Londons cleared such a substantial profit that at the end of a few months they were able to make a down payment on their cottage. When the mills imported another group of girls, Flora insisted that she and John buy the lot next door and build a second bungalow to house them.

For a time everything went well. The second bungalow brought them increased profits, for Flora was still managing carefully. Then the inherent emotional instability of her character overcame her. She lost interest; they were not making money fast enough, there was no excitement about a boarding-house . . . there were plenty of enterprises in which a woman as clever as she could make a fortune. She began spending—no one knew on what—and when the payments came due on the two mortgages, there was no cash with which to meet them. The bank took away both buildings, and with them John London's last steady means of earning a living.

While the London boarding-house had been prospering, young Jack had made a great discovery—the Oakland Public Library. During the five years he had been reading he had found but five genuine books; for the rest the barren countryside had afforded him only discarded dime novels and old newspapers. Dimly the child knew that there were other and even more beautiful books, but he had no conception of how to get to them. He had never dreamed that there was such a thing as a public library, a building that held thousands of books, all of them free for the asking. Jack dated his spiritual birth from the moment that he stood, cap in hand, in the doorway of the wooden building, his eyes wide with unbelieving that there could be so many books in the world. From that day on, though he would suffer much, though he would undergo agonies of the brain and soul, though he would be beaten and despised and cast out as a pariah, never again would he be alone. For Professor Chaney's son had come home.

In the public library he met for the first time an educated woman, one who was at home in the world of books. Miss Ina Coolbrith saw the light in his eye as he walked down the rows of books and ran his finger tips lovingly across the bindings. Before she came to his rescue he had stumbled across and read such mature books as Smollett's *Adventures of Peregrine Pickle*, and Wilkie Collins's *The New Magdalen*; Miss Coolbrith soon learned that his greatest desire was for books of adventure, of travel, of sea voyages and discoveries, and she supplied him bountifully. She was a cultivated woman, the poet laureate of California, and Jack came to love her. Each day he tried to read all the volumes she had given him so that he might see her again the next day when he returned them.

The boy gorged himself on the books for which he had been famished; he read in bed, at table, as he walked to and from school, during recess while the other boys played. Possessor of a volatile imagination and nervous system, his feelings were molten and could easily be poured. He enjoyed being able to soar to the heights in vicarious ecstasy, plunging to the depths of despair when the characters with whom he was identifying himself were unhappy or defeated. He consumed so many books in so short a time that he developed the jerks. To everybody he replied, "Go away; you make me nervous." From the tales of old travels and romantic voyages he gained the heady notion that Oakland was just a place to start from, that the world and its exciting adventures were awaiting him just as soon as he was able to escape.

John London was now out of work. The family moved to poorer quarters on San Pablo Avenue near Twenty-Second Street. Mammy Jenny lived not far away, and to her Jack went constantly to tell his troubles and pleasures, to be fed at her table, have his neck scrubbed and his hair combed at her sink, and be sent out into the world again with a reassuring pat on the shoulder. John London tried to find regular employment, but there was nothing available and it became the task of eleven-year-old Jack to furnish food for the family. He got up while it was still dark to call for his bundle of newspapers, which he delivered along a regular route; after school he delivered another route. The job paid twelve dollars a month, which he turned over intact to Flora. He also worked on an ice wagon on Saturdays, and set up pins in a bowling alley at nights and on Sundays. He had little time for reading, for he was learning about life at first hand now, fighting with the other newsboys, watching brawls in saloons, becoming acquainted with the colorful life on the Oakland Estuary, which was filled with whalers from the Arctic, curio-hunters from the South Seas, opium-smugglers, Chinese junks, Yankee sailing ships, oyster pirates, Greek fishing boats, blackened freighters, houseboats, scows, sloops, and fish patrols. Just as he had escaped the London household by way of adventure books when he was ten, so would he escape it by way of the Estuary and the sea when he was thirteen.

John London at length found a job as night watchman at Davies Wharf, but this did not mean that Jack would have the spending of the money he earned. Since he was never permitted to buy such toys as a top or marbles or a knife, he traded his extra papers for the pictures given away with each package of cigarettes —Great Race Horses, Parisian Beauties, Champion Prize Fighters —and when he had completed a set he would swap it for the things he wanted so desperately and the other boys had the money to buy. He developed into a sharp trader, a faculty that was to come in handy when he was exchanging his stories for editors' cash. His sense of values became so acute that other boys called him in to sell their collections of rags, bottles, sacks, and oilcans to the junkman, paying him a commission.

Ina Coolbrith pictures him at this time as coming into the library with a bundle of newspapers under his arm, badly poised, looking poor, shabby, and uncared for, asking for something good to read, and wanting to consume every book that had an interesting title. Miss Coolbrith reports him as having confidence in himself, and feeling sure he would get what he wanted. Thus appears the first fundamental contradiction in Jack's nature: he was timid and shy because of the inferiority and uncertainty he felt over his illegitimate birth and chaotic home; he was confident and sure because he had inherited a forceful brain from Professor Chaney.

There is little to distinguish his years in the public schools. Frank Atherton, his chum from Cole School, reports that when Jack heard the Chinese were paying large sums for wildcat meat to make them strong for their tong wars, he and Frank made slingshots and went hunting wildcats in the Piedmont hills because Jack wanted to earn enough money to leave school and become an author, a typical instance of *after-the-fact* reminiscing. An anecdote that sounds more in character is that the two boys rented a boat on the Estuary to hunt mud hens: Jack's twenty-two-caliber revolver falling overboard, he demanded that Frank, who could swim, dive the five fathoms after it. When Frank refused, Jack threw both oars into the Estuary in a fit of temper, then had to float helplessly for several hours. At the Cole School, where they had community singing every morning, the teacher noticed that Jack remained silent. She asked him why. He replied that she did not know how to sing, that she would spoil his voice because she flatted. The teacher dispatched him to the principal to be punished. The principal sent him back with a note saying that he could be excused, but that he would have to write a composition each morning for the fifteen minutes of singing. Jack ascribed his ability to write a thousand words every morning to the habit formed in this class.

Along with his love for books the greatest love of his life was for the sea. He spent every spare minute around the Yacht Club on the Estuary, hoping for a chance to work on the boats and at the same time earn the additional money he had to bring home. The yacht-owners grew to like him because he was courageous, would crawl out on a boom in the roughest weather, and did not care how wet he got. They paid him small sums for scrubbing down decks and taught him what they knew about small boats. Before long he was able to reef a sail in a stiff breeze.

By the time he was thirteen he had managed to hoard two dollars in nickels and dimes which his conscience left him free from handing over to Flora. With this money he bought an old boat, ran it up and down the Estuary, and attempted short sails on the Bay. Short sails they had to be, for the boat had no centerboard and never stopped leaking. He was constantly swamping his craft, crashing into other boats on the Estuary, capsizing, but by trial and error he trained himself. He was happiest when he could feel the swell of waves beneath his boat, when he could taste the ocean salt on his lips, and cry, "Hard a-lee!"—even though he was alone in the boat—when he wanted to practise the maneuver.

At thirteen he was graduated from the Cole School. He was named class historian, and was selected to give a speech at graduation, but since he owned no reputable-looking suit of clothes in which to appear he never even attended the exercises. There could be no thought of his going on to high school, for John's employment was becoming more and more fitful. Jack continued to carry his paper routes; he also sold papers on the Oakland streets at night, and took any kind of extra job he could find, such as sweeping out saloons at Idora and Weasel Parks after Sunday picnics.

He was a shabbily dressed, hard-working kid with a beautiful flashing smile; a tough fighter, prone to outbursts of temper, and frightfully sensitive.

Over the course of a year, from special odd jobs about which he told Flora nothing, he scraped together the six dollars necessary to buy him freedom in the form of a secondhand skiff. When he had been able to accumulate a dollar and seventy-five cents he painted it a gay color; another month of odd jobs provided him with the two dollars for a sail; and when he finally put together a dollar and forty cents for a pair of oars, the world was wide open for him to explore. He took ever longer sails on San Francisco Bay, going out on ebb tide to Goat Island for rock cod, and coming in on the flood at evening; shipping water in the wake of ferryboats; singing sailor chanties, "Blow the Man Down" and "Whiskey, Johnny, Whiskey" while the winds whitecapped the strong tides and splashed him with spray; and crossing the Bay in his open skiff in a roaring southwester, with the scow schooner sailors telling him he lied because it couldn't be done.

He was not only fearless, he was foolhardy; the worse the weather the greater chances he took, for he was not afraid of the sea. Floundering always in his mind to learn what he was, he liked to tell himself that he was a Viking, descendant of those mighty sailors who crossed the Atlantic in an open boat; that he was an Anglo-Saxon, a member of a fighting race, afraid of nothing. And because he was afraid of nothing, because he seemed to have an affinity for the sea, he became one of the most expert small-boat sailors on the treacherous Bay.

For a year, between selling papers and doing odd jobs, he managed to find an hour or two every day to spend in his beloved boat. But before he was fifteen John London was struck by a train and severely injured. The family lived in an old cottage near the Estuary in what is reported to have been squalor of an aggravated type. Many of the near-by shacks were built from wreckage or dismantled ships and old buildings. Jack's clothes were ragged, his house had no modern sanitation, he suffered from an ever-gnawing hunger of the belly and brain. He got a steady job in a cannery in an abandoned stable by the railroad tracks, at which he was paid ten cents an hour. The shortest day he ever worked was ten hours; on occasion he worked eighteen and twenty. There were weeks on end when he never knocked off earlier than eleven o'clock. Then he had a long walk home because he could not afford carfare. He was in bed at half-after midnight, and at half-past five there was Flora shaking him, trying to strip down the bedclothes to which the sleeping boy clung desperately. In a huddle, at the foot of the bed, he still remained covered. Then Flora braced herself and pulled the bedding to the floor. The boy followed the blankets in order to protect himself against the chill of the room. It seemed as though he would fall head-first to the floor, but consciousness fluttered up in him, he landed on his feet, and was awake.

He dressed in the darkness, went to the greasy sink in the kitchen, and washed himself with soap grim with dishwater and hard to lather. Then he dried himself on the damp, dirty, and ragged towel that left his face covered with shreds of lint, and sat down to the table to eat his bread and drink the hot muddy liquid the Londons called coffee. Outside it was clear and cold; he shivered at the first contact with the air. The stars had not yet begun to pale in the sky, and the city lay in blackness. As he entered the cannery gate he always glanced to the east, where across a ragged skyline of housetops a pale light was beginning to creep.

On January 1, 1891, he began a section in his notebook called "Financial Receipts and Disbursements." For cash on hand he lists fifteen cents. Between the first and the fourth of the month he spent five cents for limes and ten cents for milk and bread, and then could buy nothing more until he received his wage of ten dollars and a half, out of which he paid the rent of six dollars, and bought butter, coal oil, oysters, meats, nuts, ice, doughnuts, and twenty-five cents' worth of pills for Flora. A notation of fifty cents paid out for washing indicates that Flora was not exerting herself to make both ends meet.

As he trudged through the weary months, unable to find time to go to the library, too tired to keep his eyes open over a book at night, he asked himself if this were the meaning of life, to be a work-beast. He had Professor Chaney's short, husky torso, he could stand up to the work physically, but temperamentally he was unfitted for mechanical labor. A son of an intellectual, having inherited his father's active brain and fertile imagination, he found the work deadening, and he revolted against it. If he could have known that he was Professor Chaney's son he might not have tormented himself by demanding why he detested this work so bitterly when the other young boys and girls around him accepted their fate with a kind of heroic phlegm.

He remembered his skiff, lying idle and accumulating barnacles at the boat wharf; he remembered the wind that blew every day on the Bay, the sunrises and sunsets he never saw; the bite of the salt water on his flesh when he plunged overboard. There was only one way to escape the deadening toil, and still support his family—to go to sea. In his own words he was in the flower of his adolescence, athrill with romance and adventure, dreaming of wild life in the wild man-world.

On Sunday afternoons when he took his skiff for a sail, and hung around the waterfront, he became acquainted with the oyster pirates, a hard-drinking crew of adventurers who raided the privately owned oyster beds in Lower Bay, and sold their booty for good prices on the Oakland docks. Jack knew that they rarely made less than twenty-five dollars for a night's work, and that a man who owned his own boat could clear two hundred dollars on a single catch. When he overheard that French Frank, one of the older pirates, wanted to sell his sloop, the *Razzle Dazzle*, Jack's mind was made up. He would buy it! He who had inherited from his father the passionate desire to be quit of the brutish labor of the machines, also inherited from his mother the disregard for that discipline which to his working comrades dictated that they remain fast by their honest if bestial jobs.

But where was he to get three hundred dollars, he who had never known anything but poverty? Straight he ran to Mammy Jenny, who had been working as a nurse. Would she lend him the money? *Would she!* What Mammy Jenny had was his.

The following Sunday Jack rowed out to the *Razzle Dazzle*, joined a party that was going full blaze, and made his offer. On Monday morning he met French Frank in the First and Last Chance saloon, paying over Mammy Jenny's bright twenty-dollar gold pieces. No sooner was the deal wetted down with his first drink of whiskey than he ran all the way to the dock, broke out anchor, and filled away close-hauled on the three-mile beat to windward out into the Bay. The breeze blew its tang into his lungs and curled the waves in midchannel. Before it came the scow schooners, blowing their horns for the drawbridges to open. Red-stacked tugs tore by, rocking the *Razzle Dazzle* in their wake. A sugar bark was being towed from the bone yard to the sea. The sun-wash was on the water, and life was big. There it was, the smack and slap of the spirit of revolt, of adventure and romance.

Tomorrow he would be an oyster pirate, as free a freebooter as the century and the waters of San Francisco Bay would permit. He would outfit his grub and water in the morning, hoist the big mainsail, and beat his way out of the Estuary on the last of the ebb. Then he would slack sheets, and on the first of the flood run down the Bay to Asparagus Island and anchor offshore. And at last his dream would be realized: he would sleep upon the water.

2

TO his amazement Jack found that when he had purchased the *Razzle Dazzle* from French Frank for three hundred dollars he had also inherited Mamie, queen of the oyster pirates. She had been French Frank's girl, and had fallen in love with the handsome open-faced boy the day before when he had boarded the *Razzle Dazzle* to make the deal. Mamie was sixteen, a wild-spirited, good-looking waif. Jack said that she was warm and kind, and that she made him a real home in the little cabin of the *Razzle Dazzle*, the first congenial home he had ever known. Jack was the youngest skipper in the fleet, the only one who sailed with a woman on board. This caused a sensation and not only forced him to fight with several skippers to keep his girl, but nearly cost him his life at the hands of jealous French Frank.

That night Jack took part in his first raid on the oyster beds. A black-whiskered wharf rat by the name of Spider, who had been working on the *Razzle Dazzle*, agreed to stay with him as his crew. Big George, Young Scratch Nelson, Clam, Whiskey Bob, Nicky the Greek, and a dozen other men, big and unafraid, some of them ex-convicts, assembled in sea boots and gear, revolvers strapped about their waists. Having laid their plans, the flotilla set out under cover of darkness. It was the big June run out of the full moon; the fleet lowered its small boats in the Lower Bay and rowed until they hit the soft mud. Jack nosed his skiff up on the shore side of a big shoal, opened his sack, and began picking. In no time the sack was full and he had to return to his boat for a new one. At dawn he raced back for the early morning market in Oakland, sold his oysters to the saloon- and innkeepers, and found that he had made as much in one night as he had by working for three months in the cannery. To the boy's mind it had been a glorious adventure. He paid Mammy Jenny back part of her loan; the balance he turned over to Flora for the household.

As the weeks passed he won his spurs among the toughest of the oyster pirates. When French Frank tried to run him down with his schooner and get Mamie back, Jack stood on the deck of the *Razzle Dazzle*, a cocked shotgun in his hands as he steered with his feet and held her to the course, compelling his fifty-year-old adversary to put up his wheel and keep away. There was the proud morning that he brought the *Razzle Dazzle* in with a larger load than any other two-man craft; the time the fleet raided in the Lower Bay and Jack's was the only craft back at daylight to the anchorage off Asparagus Island; the Thursday night the entire fleet raced to market, and Jack brought the *Razzle Dazzle* in first, without a rudder, to skim the cream of the Friday morning trade.

When police officers came aboard, Jack opened his choice oysters, served them with squirts of pepper, and rushed the growler with a can for beer.

He was a convivial lad. He liked his friends among the pirates, he wanted them to like him. When they drank, he drank; when they got drunk, the fifteen-year-old boy, eager to prove that he was a man, got as drunk as the best of them. Since he had established himself as one of the smartest sailors in the crowd, strong, fearless in a fight, given to gales of gusty laughter, he was accepted as an equal and a pal. But in between raids, when he was tied up to the wharf, he walked to the Oakland Library where he had long talks with Miss Coolbrith, and selected an armful of books to take home to the *Razzle Dazzle*. He locked his cabin door so that his companions wouldn't catch him, lay on his back in his bunk, and lighted one book off the end of the other while he sucked on cannon balls or chewed taffy slabs.

Among the oyster fleet there was constant drinking, fighting, stabbing, and shooting; boats were stolen, sails burned; there were killings among the partners and crew. To Jack, who was still cramming himself with tales of buccaneers and sea rovers, sacks of cities and conflicts of armed men, all this was life raw and naked, wild and free. From the sandpits of the Oakland Estuary where the pirates settled their grievances, where knives flashed and sand was thrown into the eyes of opponents, the way led out to the vastness of adventure of all the world, where battles would be fought for high purposes and romantic ends.

For many months he sailed his *Razzle Dazzle*, repaid Mammy Jenny most of the three hundred dollars he had borrowed from her, supported his family, went on a hundred exciting and perilous adventures among the fisherfolk of the Bay, lived happily with Mamie in the cabin of his boat. Then he teamed up with Young Scratch Nelson, a twenty-year-old daredevil with the body of a Hercules. Jack adored the older boy because he was a blue-eyed, yellow-haired, rawboned Viking. During a drunken brawl in which the entire fleet of pirates participated, Young Scratch was shot through the hand and his boat, the *Reindeer*, beached and ripped open, while Jack got into a fist-fight with Spider, his crew, who set fire to the mainsail of the *Razzle Dazzle* and then deserted. Another crowd of enemy pirates boarded the *Razzle Dazzle* and scuttled, fired, and sank her. Jack and Young Scratch joined forces, repaired the *Reindeer*, borrowed money for an outfit of grub from Johnny Heinold, proprietor of the First and Last Chance saloon, filled their water barrels, and sailed on the *Reindeer* for the oyster beds.,

Young Scratch's greatest joy was to steer to miss destruction by an inch. Never to reef down was another of his manias, blow high or blow low. They barely missed death many times because Young Scratch dared what no one else would think of doing. Jack kept up with his reckless exploits, even attempted to surpass his master, for was he too not a Viking, a fearless one?

They roamed, pirated, and raided up and down the several hundred miles of waterways of the sloughs, straits, and rivers leading into the Bay, making as much as a hundred and eighty dollars for a night's work, but forever broke because the mad devil Young Scratch went on blind drinking bats the moment he reached shore to keep up with the high level of excitement he was enjoying in his race with death and the penitentiary. Here too Jack felt that he had to keep up with his pal, drink along with him whiskey for whiskey, even though he had no innate taste for liquor, nor desire to get drunk.

After a while it was no longer difficult to swallow the vile-tasting raw whiskey. He began to be enamored of the effects of intoxication, the wild laughter and singing, fierce fighting and new friendships, and the maggots crawling in his brain that made him sound brilliant to himself. When times were dull he drank, he got drunk. Ever an extremist, his uncertain poise made him want to do everything better and more mightily than everybody around him. Just as it was necessary for him to become Prince of the Oyster Pirates, so he had to become Prince of the Drunkards. He deserted his hard-pressed family, spending in saloons the money they needed for food and rent. The old-timers around the waterfront, hard drinkers themselves, became disgusted with the fifteen-year-old roustabout who was drinking himself to death at an unprecedented rate of speed; they gave him a year to live.

One night, broke and thirsty, but with the drinker's faith in the unexpected drink, he sat in the Overland House with Young Scratch waiting for something to turn up. Joe Goose dashed in to tell them that there was free booze, as much as they wanted of it, at a political rally in Haywards. All they had to do was wear a red shirt and a helmet and carry a torch in a parade. After the parade the saloons were opened and the Oakland waterfront gang jammed six deep before the drink-drenched bars. Finding this method of securing drinks too slow, Jack and his pals pushed the bartenders aside and took the bottles from the shelves. They went into the street, knocked the necks off the bottles against the concrete curbs, and drank.

Joe Goose and Young Scratch had learned discretion with straight whiskey; Jack had not. He thought that since it was free he should drink all he could hold. During the course of the night he consumed more than two quarts. When it came time to go back to Oakland he was burning internally, in an agony of suffocation. On the train he broke a window with his torch to get air, but this precipitated a gang fight and he was knocked unconscious. He awakened seventeen hours later in a waterfront lodging-house where he had been dumped by Young Scratch, so close to death that he was within an inch of fulfilling the waterfront prediction that he would not last out the year.

Had Jack been like the other pirates he would have continued in his raiding and carousing until a bullet through his head laid him on the coroner's slab in Benicia as it did Young Scratch, or he had drowned or been stabbed to death as were his friends Clam and Whiskey Bob, or ended in San Quentin for greater crimes than oyster pirating, as did Spider and Nicky the Greek. But Professor Chaney's heritage was stirring in his brain, urging him to leave this wasteful life for nobler adventures in more exotic corners of the world. After each bout with Young Scratch he would creep into the cabin of the *Reindeer*, sick from the whiskey, lock the door behind him, and open his beloved books, to be made well again by the new, fresh copies of Kipling's *The Light That Failed*, Melville's *Typee*, Shaw's *An Unsocial Socialist*, and Zola's *Germinal*, which Ina Coolbrith had put away for him when they arrived, still smelling of wet ink, from the publishers in New York.

He was slowly groping toward a break when an accident befell him. He and Young Scratch had made a big haul, and been on a drunk for three weeks, with what Jack called but few intermittent spaces of partial sobriety. At one o'clock in the morning, dead drunk from a bout with a fishing crowd, he tried to stumble aboard his sloop at the Benicia pier, and fell in. The tides which sweep through Carquinez Straits as in a millrace bore him away. He said that the blues were heavy upon him; he decided that drowning would be a splendid culmination to his short but exciting career. The water was delicious, and this was a hero's way to die.

When he passed the Solano wharf, where there were lights and people, he cunningly kept quiet. Clear of interruption, he lifted his voice to the stars in his own dirge and quite enjoyed the thought of saying good-bye to the whole works. He lay on his back in the starlight watching the familiar wharf lights go by, red and green and white, bidding sad, sentimental farewells to each. However, the cold water sobered him; he decided that he didn't want to die, after all. He undressed and struck out, crossing the current at right angles. When daylight broke he found himself in the tiderips of Mare Island where the swift ebbs from Vallejo and Carquinez Straits were fighting each other. He was exhausted and numb with cold; the land breeze was washing waves into his mouth. A few moments more and such great novels as *The Call of the Wild, The Sea Wolf, Iron Heel, Martin Eden, Valley of the Moon, Burning Daylight, Star Rover,* and a hundred superb short stories would have drowned in the flood tide from San Pablo Bay. A Greek fisherman running in for Vallejo hauled him unconscious over the side of the boat. It was the end of his wild drinking for many years to come.

A few days later, while he and Young Scratch were running in a load of oysters at Benicia, they were hailed by a state officer who suggested that they give up the fugitive life of an oyster pirate and become deputies for the Fish Patrol. San Francisco Bay was infested with Chinese shrimp raiders and Greek salmon thieves who were violating the fish laws of the state. These men were not imprisoned when caught; they were fined. Jack was offered fifty per cent of the fines collected from the law violators he captured. Having played one half of the game of Cops and Robbers, he gleefully accepted the job as a deputy of the Patrol.

His first assignment was a raid on the Chinese shrimp catchers who put down nets of such fine mesh that not even the newly hatched fish could pass through. Jack, Young Scratch, and four other patrolmen left the Oakland docks in the *Reindeer* and a salmon boat. They ran down after dark, dropped anchor under the bluff of Point Pinole, and at dawn slanted across the Bay on the land breeze. The shrimp fleet lay spread out in a half-moon, the tips of the crescent three miles apart, each junk moored fast to the buoy of a shrimp net. The Chinese were asleep below.

Jack was ordered to throw Young Scratch and George, one of the patrolmen, each onto a junk, and make fast to a third himself. He ran up under the lee of a junk, shivered his mainsail into the wind, and glided past the stern so slowly that Young Scratch stepped lightly aboard. By now a conch shell was sounding the alarm. The decks were beginning to swarm with half-naked Chinese. Jack rounded the *Reindeer* alongside another junk for George to spring aboard. Then he threw out his mainsheet and drove down before the wind on a junk to the leeward. The boats came together with a crash, the two starboard sweeps of the junk crumpling. An evil-looking Chinaman with a yellow silk bandana tied around his pock-marked face let out a curdling yell of rage, planted a pike pole on the *Reindeer's* bow, and began shoving the entangled boats apart. Jack paused long enough to let go the jib halyards, and just as the *Reindeer* cleared he leapt aboard the junk with a line and made fast.

Alone, unarmed, he stood facing five threatening Chinese, each of whom carried a long knife under his sash. They advanced upon him threateningly, but he stood his ground and put his hand on his hip pocket. The Chinese retreated. He ordered them to drop anchor at the junk's bow. When they refused, he went forward, let go the anchor, and with his hand still on his empty hip pocket forced the Chinese to board the *Reindeer*. He then sailed his boat to the junk on which he had left George, who herded his Chinese on board at the point of a revolver.

The Chinese wearing the yellow bandana brushed against Jack's hip pocket and felt that he had no revolver. He quickly incited his men, who prepared to rush the two patrolmen and throw them overboard. George, the deputy with the revolver, was in a funk and demanded that Jack put the Chinese ashore on the beach at Point Pedro. He refused. George turned his revolver on Jack and cried, "Now will you head for the beach?"

Faced by a gun, and sixteen Chinese with knives, Jack thought of the shame of losing his prisoners. He threw one hand into the air and brought his head down. The bullet went high. He then grabbed George's wrist. The Chinese lunged at him. He swung George's body around to receive their impact, ripped the revolver from George's fingers, and flung him at Yellow Bandana, who stumbled and fell over him to the deck, giving Jack time to cover the prisoners with the gun.

His share of the fines amounted to nearly a hundred dollars.

The ensuing months proffered similar adventures. There was the time he had to run for his life down the Martinez wharf, pursued by a howling mob of fishermen because he had just caught two of their number red-handed and arrested them; the time he came upon two men with an illegal sturgeon line and chased them round and round a wheat ship; the time he was out-sailed by two men who used a Chinese line to trap the sturgeon, and raised their line with over a thousand pounds of sturgeon on the hooks.

He worked for the Fish Patrol for several months, living, fighting, and adventuring with hundreds of men: honest and courageous patrolmen, sailors, gamblers, fishermen, barkeeps, stevedores, navigators, men who had been to every port of the world, seen every sight, committed every kind of crime, loved every kind of woman, and engaged in every kind of adventure. Each time he took the *Reindeer* up or down the Bay he passed the Golden Gate Strait, which led out to the Pacific. Beyond that strait lay the exciting lands of the Orient, the colorful experiences and dramatic ports these men told him about, and that he read about in the pages of the Oakland Library books. He was seventeen now, big and strong and bold, with the feel and look of the man about him. He wanted to see the world, and there was only one way for him to reach it.

Becoming a deep-sea sailor had been implicit in his fate ever since the moment, four years before, when he had bought a leaky skiff for two dollars and sailed it down the Estuary. There were many ships tied up along the San Francisco docks among which he might choose: freighters, schooners, passenger ships. He chose the most romantic of the lot, one of the last sealing vessels to sail out of San Francisco Bay, headed for Korea, Japan, Siberia, and ninety days of harpooning seals—for had he not read over and over again Herman Melville's *Moby Dick?*

The *Sophie Sutherland* was an eighty-ton schooner, built for speed. She carried an enormous spread of canvas, over a hundred feet from the deck to the truck of the main-topmast. The forecastle into which Jack dropped his dunnage bag was lined on either side to a V point by bunks, while on the walls hung oilskins, sea boots, and lanterns.

Though he had never been out of the Golden Gate Strait, he had signed on as an able-bodied seaman because it carried a higher wage. The other sailors were men who had been at sea for years, and had paid with years of suffering to acquire their sea skill. They were mostly rawboned Scandinavians who as boys had served sailors, and as able-bodied seamen expected to be served by boys. They resented this youngster's being signed on as an equal.

Unless Jack could prove that he knew his job he would be forced to suffer seven months of maltreatment such as one can only undergo in a sailing schooner from which there is no escape.

Because he had been around with sailors long enough to know their simple psychology, he resolved to do his work so well that no one would be called upon to do it for him. He never malingered when pulling on a rope, for he knew that the eyes of his forecastle mates were squinting for just such evidence of his inferiority; he made it a point to be among the first of the watch to go on deck, among the last to go below, never leaving a sheet or tackle uncoiled. He was always eager for the run aloft for the shifting of the topsail sheets, nor did it take him long to learn the names and uses of the few new ropes, to box the compass.

On the third day out the *Sophie Sutherland* ran into a storm. It was Jack's trick at the wheel. The captain questioned whether this seventeen-year-old boy could hold the ship on her course in the fierce wind and swift-running sea. After watching him for a few minutes the skipper nodded his approval and went below for his supper. Jack fought the storm while the wind whipped his hair into his eyes, exulting in keeping the vessel on her tack for an hour without another soul on deck, the entire crew leaving its fate in his hands. Nothing he ever was to accomplish made him prouder or gave him more pleasure than this feat.

When the storm had lifted and the *Sophie Sutherland* was once again racing along, Jack noticed that the resentment was gone from the faces of his mates. He had an occasional fight, for the forecastle was narrow and crowded, and his temper did not allow for anyone's trampling on his feet; but for the greater part the voyage was a happy one. After the storm there followed fifty-one days of fine sailing. At night as he lay stretched on his back on the prow, his head pillowed on his interlocked hands, the stars were so sharp and close they seemed strung on a tarpaulin. During the warm days he and his mates stripped on deck and threw buckets of sea water over each other. He made friends with Big Victor and Axel, and for the rest of the cruise they were known as the Three Sports.

He spent enjoyable hours listening to his comrades in the forecastle spin yarns of storms at sea and gigantic catches; when things seemed dull there he went aft to the steerage where the hunters bunked, their guns on the walls, tall tales in their mouths, and a thousand fights in their fists. On nights when he came off his trick at the wheel and the rest of the forecastle was snoring lustily he slipped smoothly into his other life, even as he had when he was an oyster pirate, propping a book against the steel wall of the prow, a history of the Orient, or sea tales by Melville and Jacobs that he had bought out of his *Sophie Sutherland* advance, Flaubert's *Madame Bovary* and Tolstoi's *Anna Karenina*, which Miss Coolbrith had loaned him from her private collection, and holding a lighted wick in a saucer in one hand, turned the pages with the other and read the night out.

At length the *Sophie Sutherland* lifted the volcanic peaks of the Bonin Islands, sailed in among the reefs to the landlocked harbor, and dropped anchor among a score of sea gypsies like herself. Aborigines in outrigger canoes and Japanese in sampans paddled about the bay. After ten years of dreaming, ever since he had read *African Travels* at the age of seven, Jack had won through to the other side of the world; he would see all that he had read about in the books come true. He was wild to get ashore, to climb a pathway that disappeared up a green canyon, emerged on a bare lava slope, and continued to climb among palms and flowers and strange native villages. And at last he would fish from a sampan!

The Three Sports went ashore. Jack was their pal and they each had to buy him a drink, and he was their pal and he had to buy them each a drink. At the bars they met mates from the San Francisco waterfront, friends from other voyages, comrades from the days of oyster pirating. Every reunion meant another round of drinks, for what else had they in the world but good fellowship?

Though the *Sophie Sutherland* remained in the bay of Bonin Islands for ten days, Jack never climbed the path among the flowers and native villages. Instead he made hundreds of friends among the whalers, heard endless yarns, got drunk with his comrades, helped wreck the native village, sang rollicking sea chanties under the stars, was rolled for his money by runaway apprentices, and in general behaved like an old tar.

Having filled her water casks, the *Sophie Sutherland* raced for the north. Jack, who was a boat-puller, spent many days binding the oars and oarlocks in leather and sennit so that they would make no noise when creeping up on the seals. Then one day the lookout raised the coast of Japan, and they picked up with the great seal herd. North they traveled with it, following as far as the coast of Siberia, ravaging and killing, flinging the naked carcasses to the sharks and salting down the skins. After Jack had rowed his hunter back to the ship he went to work with a butcher knife to skin the seals, working each day on decks covered with hides and bodies, slippery with fat and blood, the scuppers running red. It was brutal labor, but to Jack it went under the name of adventure. He loved every hour of it.

After three months, the seal herd having been dispatched, the *Sophie Sutherland* sailed south to Yokohama, a batch of skins in her salt, and a heavy payday coming. At Yokohama Jack drank shoulder to shoulder with the men with whom he had faced death and incredible hardship, smiling to himself when he remembered that only five months before they had thought him a boy who had no right to call himself a seaman.

Back in San Francisco he bought his mates one round of drinks, bade them farewell, and took the ferryboat home to Oakland.

He found his family in debt, trying to live off the few dollars that John London earned as a constable of Brooklyn township. From his *Sophie Sutherland* wages he paid the bills, bought himself a second-hand hat, coat, and vest, some forty-cent shirts, and two fifty-cent suits of underwear. What was left he turned over to Flora.

His infatuation with the Oakland waterfront was now quite dead; he had no more desire for vagrancy. For a few days he soaked himself in books at the library; then it was time to settle down.

He had chosen an unfortunate time to look for work. The financial panic of 1893 had thrown the country into a severe business depression; eight thousand business organizations had failed, many of them banks. All active enterprise had stopped; only the most necessary work was undertaken, and a large proportion of the workingmen were unemployed. The man with any kind of job was considered lucky. In Oakland ten cents an hour was all that could be earned by able-bodied men. This rate of pay caused strikes and lockouts, further decreasing employment.

The only job he could find was in a jute mill at ten cents an hour, one dollar for a ten-hour day. The mill was filled with long rows of machines, their bobbins revolving rapidly. The air was warm, moist, thick with flying lint, and the noise so terrific that he had to shout at the top of his lungs to be heard. At the machines were children from eight years of age up, some crippled, many consumptive, all undernourished and suffering from rickets, earning their two dollars for a sixty-hour week.

At this time he was developing what he liked to call troubling potencies and proclivities, a rather ponderous phrase to describe his interest in young girls. The seventeen-year-old boy who had had Mamie for mate on board the *Razzle Dazzle*, who had had other hardened women up and down San Francisco Bay, was so shy and self-conscious over his rough manners absorbed from rough company that he was in agony whenever he chanced to be in the company of a nice girl. He had been so busy being a man that he didn't know anything about girls.

Since he came from the wrong side of the railroad tracks he had little opportunity to meet the sweet and pretty ones in whom he was now interested. He became chums with Louis Shattuck, a blacksmith's apprentice, whom he describes as an innocently devilish young fellow quite convinced that he was a sophisticated townsboy. Louis became Jack's tutor. After work the boys went home for their supper, washed, put on a clean shirt, and met in a candy store where they bought cigarettes and candy red-hots. They had access to no girls' homes, and they couldn't go to public dances because they both had to pay board at home, and this left them with about seventy-five cents a week spending money. All they could do was stroll the streets in the early evenings. Louis tried to show him how to give a certain eloquent glance of the eye, a smile, a daring lift of his cap; then, hesitancies, giggles, a spoken word. But Jack was timid and bashful. Girls remained strange and wonderful to him, and he failed of the bold front and necessary forwardness when the crucial moment came.

After a time he did make a few friends; occasionally he would take a girl out to Blair's Park, twenty cents for carfare, bang, just like that, ice cream for two, thirty cents . . . and he was broke for the rest of the week. He had a penchant for Irish girls; in his notebook are listed the addresses of Nellie, Dollie, and Katie, factory girls who enjoyed his banter, his vigorous dancing and infectious laughter. Best of all he liked Lizzie Connellon, who worked with a hot fluting-iron in an Oakland laundry. Lizzie had a pretty face and was fast on the saucy comeback; she gave Jack her gold ring with a cameo insert to show that he was her feller.

But at last love came. Her name was Haydee. They sat side by side in a Salvation Army meeting. She was sixteen, wore a tam o'shanter, a skirt that reached her shoe tops, and had a slender oval face, beautiful brown eyes and hair, and a sweet-lipped mouth. For Jack it was love at first sight.

They arranged stolen half hours in which he came to know all the madness of boy and girl love. He knew it was not the biggest love in the world, but he dared to assert that it was the sweetest. He who had been hailed Prince of the Oyster Pirates, who could go anywhere in the world as a man among men, who could sail boats, lay aloft in black and storm, go into the toughest hangouts in sailor town and play his part in any roughhouse that started, or call all hands to the bar, he didn't know the first thing to say or do with this slender chit of a girl who was as abysmally ignorant of life as he thought himself profoundly wise. They never succeeded in managing more than a dozen meetings; and they kissed perhaps a dozen times, briefly and innocently, and wonderingly. They never went anywhere, not even to a matinée, but he always fondly believed that she loved him. He knew that he loved her. He dreamed day dreams of her for a year or more, and the memory of Haydee always remained very dear.

One evening Flora, who well remembered that Jack's father had been a writer, came to him with a copy of the San Francisco *Call* and urged him to write a composition for the contest the paper was holding. Jack hesitated for a moment, recalled a typhoon off the coast of Japan that the *Sophie Sutherland* had battled, sat down at the kitchen table, and began composing. He wrote quickly, smoothly, and painlessly. The following night he finished the story, polished it as best he could, and sent it to the editor of the *Call*. He was awarded the first prize of twenty-five dollars. Second and third prizes went to students connected with the University of California and Stanford University.

A reading of *Typhoon off the Coast of Japan* shows it to be fresh and vigorous after the passage of forty-five years. The imagery is vivid, the element of suspense is never lacking, the prose rolls onward with an authentic rhythm of the sea; and there is music in the sentences of the seventeen-year-old boy who had had only a grammar-school education. The *Call* wrote, "The most striking things is the largeness of grasp and steady force of expression that shows the young artist." Prophetic words.

When the article appeared John London had his happiest moment since he left Moscow, Iowa; Flora chuckled silently at her secret joke; and Jack promptly sat down at the kitchen table to write another sea yarn. However, the editor of the *Call* was not running a fiction magazine, and sent the manuscript back. In his notebook Jack lists at this time an expenditure of thirty cents for stamps and paper wraps, which leads us to believe that he continued to write, and to send his manuscripts to magazines.

If Jack had continued to handle the "Financial Receipts and Disbursements" as he had at the age of fourteen when he worked in the cannery, the family would have fared moderately well. However, he turned his wages over to Flora. Thomas E. Hill of Oakland, in whose sister's home both he and the Londons rented rooms, reports that Flora fell two months behind in her rent, and his sister was forced to ask the family to move.

The jute mill had promised to raise his wage to a dollar and a quarter a day, but after he had worked there for several months they refused to make good their promise. Jack quit. Having observed that manual labor would always keep him at the bottom of the trough, earning ten cents an hour, he decided to learn a trade. The new discovery called electricity looked as though it were going to have a future, so he decided to become a practical electrician. He went out to the power plant of the Oakland Street Railway, told the superintendent that he was not afraid of hard work and that he was willing to start at the bottom. The superintendent put him in the cellar shoveling coal for thirty dollars a month, one day off a month.

His job was to pass coal to the firemen, who fed it to the furnaces. He had to pass the coal for the day and night shifts, so that despite working through his lunch hour he rarely finished before nine at night, making it a thirteen-hour day. This brought his wage under eight cents an hour, less than he had earned at the cannery when he was fourteen. Dripping with sweat from the intense heat of the furnaces, he filled the iron wheelbarrow with coal, ran it to the scales, weighed the load, trundled it to the fire room, and dumped it on the plates before the fires. When he got a little ahead of the day firemen he had to pile the night coal higher and higher, buttressing the heap with stout planks.

Once again he became a work beast. When he reached home in the blackness of night he was too exhausted to eat; it was all he could do to wash and fall into bed. There was no time or energy for books, for nice girls, for anything that smacked of life, for he did not have even a Sunday off. He lost weight, navigated always in a nightmarish fog of coal dust and heat. Once again he could not understand why he suffered so much on this job, he who had worked at more difficult tasks among men older and stronger than himself. This time one of the firemen took pity on him and told him that there had always been two coal-passers, one for the day shift, one for the night. Each of these men had received forty dollars a month. When Jack had come along, young and eager to learn, the superintendent had fired the two coal-passers and put him in to handle both jobs. When he asked why he had not been told before, the fireman replied that the superintendent had threatened to give him his time if he let on.

A few days later the same fireman showed him an article in an Oakland newspaper which told how one of the former coal-passers, whose place Jack had unwittingly taken, and who had a wife and three children to feed, had killed himself because he could not find work. Jack flung aside his shovel.

The result of this work orgy was to sicken him with manual labor. Apparently a man had to be either a slave or a vagabond; there was no visible middle ground. He was young and strong and loved life. The call of adventure ran wild in his blood. Wasn't it better to royster and frolic over the world than break his fine young body on the wheel of other people's greed?

By the time he reached this conclusion, in April, 1894, the amount of unemployment in the United States had grown to staggering proportions. In Massillon, Ohio, Flora's birthplace, a man by the name of Coxey was organizing an army of unemployed men to march on Washington and demand that Congress issue five million dollars in greenbacks with which to put men to work on the building of public roads. The newspapers gave Coxey's Army of the Commonwealth so much space that detachments sprang up spontaneously in a number of American cities. In Oakland a man by the name of Kelly organized the unemployed into military companies and arranged with the railroads to provide his men with free transportation in boxcars.

When Jack heard of General Kelly's detachment he jumped at the chance to join the Army and go to Washington. Such an adventure was too good to resist. That he was walking out on Flora and John London, who were in sore need of his wages, did not deter him any more than it had deterred him when he quit the cannery for the dubious life and dubious income of an oyster pirate. Neither Flora Wellman nor Professor Chaney had ever been adepts at discipline or sacrifice, or sticklers for the fulfilment of moral obligations.

Kelly's Army was scheduled to leave Oakland on Friday, April 6. When Jack and his chum, Frank Davis, reached the freight yards that afternoon they found the Army had left early in the morning. Jack cried, "Come on, Frank, I know all about this tramp business; we'll beat our way east on the freights until we catch up with Kelly's Army." Within the hour he had found a train that was ready to pull out. He slid open the side door of an empty boxcar and climbed in behind Frank. He closed the door. The engine whistled. Jack was lying down, and in the darkness he smiled.

He had not been exaggerating when he told Frank Davis that he knew all about the tramp business, for this was not the first time he had gone on The Road. Three years before, when he had been fifteen, there had come a lull in oyster pirating; his boat lay at the end of Steamboat Wharf at Benicia and he sat on deck in the warm sun, the fresh breeze on his cheeks, the flood tide swirling past. He spat over the side to gauge the speed of the current, saw that he could run the flood nearly all the way to Sacramento, cast off his moorings, and hoisted sail.

At Sacramento he went swimming in the river, and fell in with a bunch of boys who were sunning themselves on the sandbar. They talked differently from the fellows he had been herding with. They were road-kids. The yarns they told had made Jack's oyster pirating look like thirty cents. A new world was calling to him in every word spoken, a world of rods and gunnels, blind baggages and side-door Pullmans, bulls, shacks, chewin's, pinches, getaways, strongarms, bindlestiffs, punks, and profesh. With every word they uttered the lure of The Road laid hold of him more imperiously. He joined the push, or crowd.

He was given the monica of Sailor Kid. The ringleader, Bob, took him in hand and turned him from a gay-cat or tenderfoot into a punk, or road-kid. They taught him how to batter the main stem for light pieces, that is, beg for money on the main street. They showed him how they rolled drunks, preyed upon bindlestiffs, and successfully taught him how to steal a five-dollar Stetson stiff-rim from the head of a prosperous Sacramento Valley Chinese. Arrested in a whopping street fight, he had served three days in jail.

Jack had soon heard expounded the law of The Road, that no kid was a road-kid until he had ridden the blinds over the Sierra Nevadas. One night Jack and French Kid, who had just joined the push, waited in the darkness ahead of the Central Pacific Overland and when it went past nailed the blinds. French Kid slipped, fell under the wheels, and had both legs amputated.

Bob had warned Jack to deck her, or ride the top of the car, until the train passed Roseville, where the constable was reputed to be "horstyle," and then to climb down to the blind behind the mail car. But Jack had held down the deck the whole night, clear across the Sierras, through the snow sheds and tunnels and down to Truckee on the other side, in a funk over climbing down the swiftly moving express train. He never confessed his disgraceful conduct to the push, which welcomed him back to Sacramento, renamed him Frisco Kid, and made him a full-fledged road-kid.

After a few weeks he had tired of Sacramento and rode a freight back to Oakland. Now, three years later, he was once again "mate to the wind that tramps the world."

Jack and Frank Davis left their side-door Pullman at Sacramento, only to learn that the Army had departed for Ogden at four that afternoon. They caught the Overland Limited and held her down until Truckee, where they were ditched, or thrown off. That night they tried to take the Overland east; Frank made her out, but Jack was left behind. He caught a freight train instead, and slept so soundly in spite of the cold that he was sidetracked at Reno without waking. He spent the day in Reno watching the unemployed congregate on street corners as they made up a detachment to start east; all along the line he met hundreds of unemployed chasing the first detachment of the Industrial Army.

Intent on catching up with Frank, he left Reno before the company was formed, traveled all night and all day in a boxcar, and at Wadsworth slept in an engine cab in the yards until four in the morning when the wipers routed him out. He caught an early morning freight and rode the blind, or space behind the coal car. A spark from the engine landed in his overcoat pocket and suddenly burst into flame. The train was going forty miles an hour, and it was difficult to put out the fire. His overcoat and coat were ruined and had to be thrown away.

That night in Winnemuka he caught up with Frank. They decided to wait for the Reno detachment and travel with it, but a freight train came through and the temptation was too great: they boarded her and rode east. Two days later Jack and Frank once again parted company. Jack notes in his boyish scrawl, "The Road has no more charms for Frank. The romance and adventure are gone and nothing remains but the stern reality of the hardships to be endured. Though he has decided to turn west again I am sure the experience has done him good, broadened his thoughts, given him a better understanding of the low strata of society, and surely will have made him more charitable to the tramps he will meet hereafter when he is in better circumstances. He starts west and I start east tonight. I am going to break coal on the engine from here to Carlin."

For Jack the greatest charm of tramp life was the absence of monotony. In Hobo Land the face of life was an everchanging phantasmagoria where the impossible happened and the unexpected jumped out of the bushes at every turn. Each day was a day apart, with a record of swiftly moving pictures all its own. At nights he rode the freight and express trains, at meal times he "threw his feet," that is, begged at back doors for a handout, or panhandled along the main street. He encountered hundreds of hoboes with whom he beat the trains, pooled his money and tobacco, boiled up, cooked mulligan in the jungles, battered the main stem, played cards, swapped yarns, and fulfilled the dictates of the profesh, to keep going on the fastest trains.

Ditched in the Nevada Desert, he had to walk all night to a junction. It was early in the year, and cold in the upland pastures where snow lay on the mountains and a miserable wind blew; priding himself on being a blowed-in-the-glass tramp, he carried no blanket. Oftentimes he would "throw his feet" for hours without getting a scrap of food at a back door, or land in a strange town at midnight without a penny in his pocket, and nothing to do but sit in the jungle by the tracks and shiver the night through. Other nights he spent on the pilot behind the engine, where he tried to doze off to the coughing of the engine, the screeching of the wheels, and the rain of hot cinders. Once when he was ravenously hungry he was given a big handout wrapped in newspaper. He ran to a near-by lot to devour the meal . . . and found it to be soggy cake which the people at the party the night before had refused to eat. He sat on the ground and wept.

It was while "throwing his feet" that he developed the art of spontaneous story-telling, for upon his ability to tell a good story depends the success of the beggar. The instant a back door is opened he must size up his victim and tell a story that will appeal to the peculiar personality and temperament of that victim. In Reno a kindly, middle-aged mother opened her back door. Jack instantly became an innocent, unfortunate lad. He couldn't speak . . . never before in his life had he asked anyone for food . . . only the harsh pangs of hunger could compel him to do so degraded and ignoble a thing as beg. The good woman had to relieve his embarrassment by telling him that he was hungry and urging him to come into the kitchen for a set-down, the tramp's delight.

Later in Harrisburg, Pennsylvania, he knocked on a back door just as two maiden ladies were about to sit down to their breakfast. They invited him into the dining-room to share their buttered toast and eggs out of egg cups. The two maiden ladies had never looked upon the bright face of adventure; as the Tramp Royals would have it, they had worked all their lives on one same shift. Jack was hungry, he had been riding the blinds all night; while the servant brought him more and more eggs, and more and more toast and coffee, he thrilled the ladies with wild yarns, bringing into the sweet scents and narrow confines of their existence the large airs of the world, freighted with lusty smells of sweat and strife and danger. Jack never forgot that breakfast, and one is safe in assuming that the maiden ladies never forgot his hair-raising fiction stories.

When the going got too tough, when middle-class doors remained locked, when the big house on the hill refused him scoffings and he could no longer stand his hunger, he would go to the poor section of the town, to the shack with its broken window stuffed with rags and its tired-faced mother broken with labor. Here he could always find something to eat, for the poor never withheld from what they needed for themselves. From these experiences Jack later said that a bone to the dog is not charity; charity is the bone shared with the dog when you are just as hungry as the dog.

Best of all Jack liked the exciting and dangerous contests with the train crews, for he was out to prove that he was the greatest Tramp Royal on The Road, the Prince of Hoboes. He would run ahead of the crack Overland in the darkness before it left the depot and when the first blind came past jump on. The crew has seen him. The train is stopped. He jumps off and runs ahead into the darkness. This time the brakeman rides the blind, but there is no entrance to the train from the blind; before it is going very fast he must drop off and catch a rear car. Jack stays so far ahead of the train that the brakeman has dropped off the blind by the time it reaches him and he can safely jump on; safely, providing he doesn't slip and kill himself. He thinks he is secure, but in a few moments another brakeman who has ridden the engine comes after him. The train is stopped. Jack jumps off. He runs ahead. This time when the train comes past the brakeman is riding the first blind, so Jack jumps on the second one. The brakeman drops off the first and jumps on the second. Jack drops off the opposite side and sprints ahead for the first blind. The brakeman pursues him, but the train is picking up speed and the brakeman cannot catch up. Once again Jack thinks he is safe . . . until the fireman plays a stream of water on him . . . the train is stopped . . . he sprints ahead into the darkness . . .

He is mighty proud that he, a poor hobo, has four times stopped the Overland with its many passengers and coaches, its government mail, its two thousand steam horses straining in the engine. So the game goes on through the night; in order to escape the ever-pursuing brakemen he decks her, straddles the ends of two cars, goes underneath and rides the rods. By now he has the engineer, conductor, fireman, and two brakemen after him, but to the eighteen-year-old boy who prides himself on being at the top of the profesh, the fun of the game is enhanced by the terrible price he would pay if he lost.

He took incredible risks, jumped off trains that were going at full speed, at one time traveling so fast through the air that he knocked down and stunned an officer who was standing on a street corner watching the train go by. He rode the rods on bad lines, lines on which the brakemen were known to take a coupling pin and length of bell cord to the platform in front of the car under which the tramp was riding, and let the coupling pin strike against the rails, beating the tramp to death. He was afraid of nothing; the greater the risk, the greater the fun. Was he not a Viking who had crossed San Francisco Bay in an open skiff in a howling southwester?

Routed out of a boxcar in the mountains during a snow storm, he gave up Lizzie Connellon's ring to a brakeman who was shaking him down for money. When the nights were too cold for travel he went to the roundhouse and slept in an engine cab, and several times went to the electric-light works where he slept on top of the boilers in the terrific heat. In the afternoons he would go to the town library to read; at night he always tried to catch the blind baggage of the express. With great delight he writes, "I was determined to hold her down all night, and pursued by the train crew I rode the blinds, the tender of the engine, the cow-catchers, the pilots of the double-header, the decks and the platform in the middle of the train." The nights were so cold and the days so hot that his face began to peel, and he describes himself as looking as though he had fallen into a fire.

All these details and a thousand others he writes meticulously in his notebook. The seventy-three-page diary of The Road reveals him to be a well-bred and gentle boy in spite of his rough background, nefarious activities, and cutthroat associates. The notebook is filled with character sketches of the men he met, stretches of dialogue he overheard, notes on individual stories of how they came to be tramps, railroad and tramp vocabularies, descriptions of towns and scenes and adventures. Though the diary was scrawled in pencil in boxcars, roundhouses, jungles, and saloons, the writing is literate and lyrical, the charming unstudied flow of a natural-born writer.

For the greater part the notebook is robust and joyous, the picturings of a vigorous young man in love with all the startlingly new and fascinating phenomena of life; but he cannot keep himself upon this high plane of evowal, sustain this eternal Yea! Suddenly his nerves are shattered, he becomes depressed; in his notebook he will scrawl a passage on the right to commit suicide which takes us back to the night four years before when he fell off the Benicia pier and decided that drowning was a hero's death. For him his own life always had a strong death appeal.

Caught in a blizzard at the summit of the Rockies, where he was freezing in an open blind, a friendly brakeman told him that on the opposite track was the Reno detachment of Kelly's Army. When Jack climbed into the boxcar he found eighty-four men stretched out, two feet of straw under them, keeping each other warm. Since there was no available straw upon which to step, he stepped on the men, who promptly put him through their threshing machine, bandying him from one end of the car to the other until he found an unoccupied bit of straw. Thus was he initiated into the Industrial Army.

They were a jolly crowd; some of them were unemployed who really thought they would get work from Congress, others were tramps just going along for the ride, and still others were young boys like himself out on the adventure trail. While the car rode through the blizzard they instituted a Scheherazade in which every one of the eighty-five men had to tell a good story. The penalty for failure was the threshing machine. Jack says that he never sat through such a marvelous story-telling debauch.

For twenty-four hours the Reno detachment rode out the storm, locked in their car without a bite of food. When they reached the plains of Nebraska they took up a collection and wired the authorities of Grand Island, which they would reach at noon, that eighty-five healthy, hungry men would arrive at meal time and wanted something to eat. When the freight train stopped at Grand Island the police and special reception committees marched the detachment to the hotels and restaurants, fed them, and marched them back to the train, which had been ordered to wait for its passengers.

When they arrived in Omaha at one in the morning they were met by a special platoon of policemen who guarded them until they were shipped across the river to Council Bluffs. Ordered to march in a torrential rain the five miles to Chautauqua Park where General Kelly was encamped, Jack and his new pal, Swede, a six-foot towhead mechanic, slipped through the police lines and sought shelter. They found a saloon propped on big timbers where Jack spent the most miserable night of his life. The building, perched in the air for the purpose of being moved, was exposed in a multitude of places through which the wind whistled. Soaked to the skin, Jack rolled under the bar, where he shivered and prayed for daylight. At five in the morning, blue with cold and half dead, he caught a freight back to Omaha and begged his breakfast. He saw the sights, then started out for Camp Kelly but was stopped at a toll bridge A sympathizer gave him a quarter to ride all the way to Chautauqua Park. Arriving there he reported to General Kelly and was assigned to the last rank of the rear guard.

The railroads operating between Omaha and Chicago were hostile, afraid to give the Army free boxcar transportation for fear of setting a precedent. They filled their trains with armed Pinkerton detectives to ward off Kelly's men. For two days and nights Jack lay with the Army beside the railroad tracks, pelted by sleet, hail, and rain. Then two young ladies of Council Bluffs induced a boy to steal his father's engine, and a committee of Omaha sympathizers threw together a train of boxcars. When the train reached Kelly's encampment it was found to be too small to accommodate the Army, and was regretfully returned.

After a number of unsuccessful skirmishes General Kelly decided to walk his Army to Washington, where he would join General Coxey. Taking to the road with twelve wagons loaded with food and campstuffs donated by the people of Omaha and Council Bluffs, the Army made an imposing array with flags and banners and General Kelly at its head astride of a fine black horse presented by an enthusiastic Council Bluffs citizen. After two days the soles of Jack's shoes were off, and he was walking on his socks. He went to the commissary, but they claimed they had no shoes for him. The next day he had such a crop of blisters that he could hardly walk; as a gesture of protest he walked in his bare feet . . . which promptly brought shoes from the commissary.

The state of Iowa was friendly and hospitable; when the Army arrived at a town the entire population lined the main street with flags and banners. As soon as the men were encamped the crowds moved out there to have community sings, listen to political speeches, and watch the town nine play baseball against the Army team. Jack remarks in his notebook that the ladies mingled their sweet voices with those of the boys all hoarse from the cold weather. He also notes with pride that everybody expressed a good opinion of the Army, and many were surprised at the gentlemanly bearing and honest appearance of the boys.

Still a non-conformist, finding discipline intolerable, and with a desire to know everything about the country through which he was traveling, Jack ran the Army pickets every night to look the new town over. He again developed blisters and determined to ride the freights, but the marshals provided wagons to get the non-walkers out of town. Just before the Army reached Des Moines the wagon rides ran out, and Jack vowed to go to jail rather than walk another step on his festering feet. He went down to the railroad station, and "playing on the sympathy of the people, I raised a ticket."

When the Army reached Des Moines the men swore their feet were sore and refused to walk any further. Stuck with two thousand itinerants, Des Moines put up the Army in an abandoned stove works and fed it six thousand meals a day, while the officials tried to persuade the railroads to carry it on to the next stop. The railroads declined. Jack rested, played baseball, caught up on his sleep and food. Then the town took up a subscription and the Army built rafts to float itself down the Des Moines River.

Sailor Jack and nine other men from his company, all of whom he termed hustlers, picked a good boat and went down the river on their own. They were always half a day to a day in advance of the Army. When they approached a small town they raised their American flag, called themselves the advance boat, and demanded to know what provision had been made for the Army. When the farmers brought forth the supplies, Sailor Jack and his pals took the cream: the tobacco, milk, butter, sugar, canned goods. They were not altogether heartless, they left for the Army the sacks of beans and flour and slaughtered steers, but as Jack remarked, they were living fine. They even disdained to use coffee boiled in water; they boiled it in milk. Jack admitted that this was hard on the Army, but then, the ten of them were individualists, they had initiative and enterprise, and ardently believed that grub was for the man who got there first.

General Kelly was outraged. He sent a light skiff to head off the "advance boat" and when this failed, sent out two men on horseback to warn the countryside. After that Jack and his comrades were met with "the icy mitt," and were forced to go back to the regular Army. In Quincy, Illinois, which someone told Jack was the richest town of its size in the United States, he "threw his feet" for a whole day and returned with enough underwear, socks, shirts, shoes, hats, and suits to clothe half his company. He had told a thousand stories to the people of Quincy, and every story a good one. When he came to write for the magazines he regretted the fecundity of fiction he lavished that day.

However, that was the end of opulence for the Army. For thirty-six hours the farmers provided no free food. The sun came out hot and strong, spring was at hand, the scents in the air were intoxicating . . . and the Industrial Army began to desert by whole squads and platoons. Jack jotted in his notebook, "Am going to pull out in the morning, I can't stand starvation." All nine of his boat comrades deserted with him. General Kelly pushed on and with a few men finally reached Washington, but by the time he got there he found General Coxey in jail. Coxey, who was a few administrations ahead of his time in demanding federal projects to create work for the unemployed, had been arrested by Capitol police for walking on the grass!

Jack rode the Cannonball into Jacksonville, the Kansas City passenger into Mason City, caught a cattle train, and rode it all night into Chicago. At the post office he found mail from home, with four one-dollar greenbacks from Eliza. He located the second-hand district where he bought shoes, a hat, pair of pants, shirt, and overcoat. That night he went to a theater, saw the sights, and slept in a fifteen-cent bed, the first he had lain in since leaving Oakland. The next day he took a boat across the lake to St. Joseph, Michigan, where Flora's sister, Mary Everhard, lived with her husband and children. Jack stayed for several weeks in the comfortable Everhard home, wrote many pages of notes, made up for lost meals, enjoyed being spoiled by his Aunt Mary, did a little farm work, and told the Everhards exciting stories of The Road.

By midsummer he had ridden the rails into New York City. He got into the habit of begging for food in the mornings, and spending the afternoons in the little park by the City Hall, where he could escape the sweltering heat. For a few cents each he bought current books that had been injured in the binding, and lay on the cool grass reading and drinking penny glasses of ice-cold milk.

One afternoon he joined the throng watching a group of youngsters playing pee-wee. Suddenly one of the boys yelled "Chickey for the bulls!" and the crowd broke up. Jack was sauntering toward the park with a book under his arm when he saw an officer coming toward him. Jack paid him no attention. The policeman hit him over the head with a club and knocked him down. Dizzy and sick, he managed to scramble to his feet and run, for if he had not escaped it would have meant thirty days on Blackwell's Island for resisting an officer.

Two days later he rode into Niagara Falls in a boxcar, and headed straight for the Falls. Entranced by the spectacle, he remained all afternoon without eating. Eleven o'clock that night still found him watching the dark water under the moonlight. He then headed out into the country, climbed a fence, and slept in a field. At five o'clock he awakened and returned to the Falls. As he walked through the sleeping streets he saw three men coming toward him. The men on either side were hoboes, the one in the middle a fly-cop who demanded the name of the hotel at which he was staying. Unable to conjure up the name of a hotel, he was arrested as a vagrant and taken to the Niagara Falls jail. In the morning sixteen prisoners were brought into the dock. The judge, acting as his own clerk, called out the names of the vagrants and promptly sentenced each of them to thirty days at hard labor.

Jack was handcuffed to a tall negro, a steel chain was run through the links of the handcuffs, and the eight pairs of men were chained together and walked through the streets of Niagara Falls to the railroad station. On the train he shared his tobacco with the man behind him, who had been in many prisons and knew the ropes, and they became friends. They were taken to the

Erie County Penitentiary, where Jack's head was shaved and he was put into prison stripes. Early the next morning he joined the lock-step and marched out to the yard to unload canal boats.

After two days of hard manual labor on bread and water—meat was served once a week, and then not until all the nutrition had been boiled out—Jack's friend from the train came to his rescue. The man had found former prison pals among the trusties, had been appointed a hall man, and in turn had secured Jack's appointment as a hall man. It was his duty to serve the prisoners their bread and water, to keep them in order. Jack bartered the pieces of bread that were left over for books and tobacco, or for suspenders and safety pins which he would swap with the long-timers for meat.

Once he had become a trusty the halls were open for him to watch what went on. He saw prisoners throw fits, go mad; be whipped down eight tiers of stone steps; beaten to death; indescribable horrors in a torture chamber of helpless derelicts. He became friendly with other trusties, guards, short-timers, long-timers; he came to know hundreds of men, to hear their stories, record their dialects, grasp their philosophies, integrate their backgrounds. And all the time, in order to keep his job as a trusty, he stayed in solid with his pal. They spent many warm and comradely hours together planning the burglaries they were going to pull when they got out.

At the end of the thirty days the two men were released, begged pennies on the main drag of Buffalo, and went into a saloon for "shupers" of beer. With the foaming beer in front of him, Jack excused himself from his crony, went to the rear of the saloon, jumped the fence, and ran all the way to the railroad station. A few minutes later he was on board a freight headed west.

It took him several months to beat his way across the three thousand miles of Canadian railroads. A number of times he kept himself out of jail only by his ability to invent tales which convinced the police that he was anything but a vagrant. Often he went hungry because he couldn't speak French, and the Canadian peasants were afraid of tramps. He rode nights in freezing boxcars and in the mornings he was barely able to crawl out and beg his food. But he enjoyed his adventures, particularly the time he rode the same coal car for a thousand miles, begging his food in town each time the train stopped, returning to his coal-bed to eat it while he watched the Canadian countryside slip past. At last he reached Vancouver, signed on the *Umatilla* as a sailor, and worked his way back to San Francisco.

3

SEARCH the records as one may, one cannot find that Jack London thought a socialistic thought or uttered a socialistic sentiment prior to the year spent among what the sociologists termed the submerged tenth. He had been what he later learned to call a rampant individualist; an individualist who, with his nine cronies in the fastest boat of the fleet, victimized his comrades of Kelly's Army out of their food because "we had initiative and ardently believed that grub was for the man who got there first"; an individualist who as hall man at the penitentiary had not distributed the surplus bread among the unfortunate prisoners, but had made them pay for it from their scant supply of tobacco, books, and meat. He had good health, hard muscles, and a stomach that could digest scrap iron; he exulted in his young life and was able to hold his own at work or fight. He saw himself raging through life without end, conquering by sheer superiority and strength. He was proud to be one of nature's strong-armed noblemen.

What changed his mind was the startling manner in which he found the submerged tenth had been recruited. Before going on the road he had imagined that the men who were tramps were tramps by choice, because they wanted to roam and adventure without responsibility, or because they were loafers, lunatics, dullards, or drunks. Though he realized that a certain portion of these men would be waste material under any economic order, he soon saw that the greater part of them had once been as good material as himself, just as blond-beastly: sailormen and laboring men wrenched and twisted out of shape by toil and hardship and accident, then cast adrift like so many old horses, tramps on the road without a blanket or spare shirt or meal to their names. As he battered the drag and slammed back gates with them, or shivered with them in boxcars and city parks, he listened to life stories that had begun under auspices as fair as his own, and which had ended in the shambles in the bottom of the social pit.

They were men who had been injured and maimed at unguarded machines, and abandoned by their bosses; men who had sickened because of fourteen hours a day of toil in airless factories, and been let out as useless; men who had grown old in the harness and been replaced by younger and stronger ones. They were men whose industries had been killed off by changing times, and who had been unable to find or adjust themselves to new ones, who had been supplanted by machines, who had been replaced by women and children at lower wages, who had been thrown out of work by depression and had never been re-employed. They were men who had not been sufficiently skilled to handle new technical equipment; migratory laborers whose very jobs forced them to be idle from a third to a half of each year; the inefficient, the mediocre, the discouraged workers; slag of competitive and uncontrolled industry who had chosen vagabondage in preference to the slums. They were men who had gone on strike against long hours and low pay, had had their jobs taken by scabs, and been blacklisted by employers.

Jack saw that in five, ten, twenty years he too would be replaced by a younger and stronger man, would perforce become part of the slums of the city or the slums of The Road. He learned two things, first that he would have to educate himself so that he could work with his brain instead of his easily replaceable brawn; and second, that there was something wrong with an economic system that took from a man the best years of his working life, then cast him on the junk heap to starve and rot, a tragedy for the individual and his family, brutalizing and wasteful for society.

By the time he got back to Oakland he knew his thinking and attitude toward life had changed, that he believed in something new. He was not quite certain what this something was. He went to the books to find out. From workers and wanderers on The Road, some of them educated and trained men, he had heard a good deal about trade unions, socialism and workers' solidarity, which provided a clue as to where to begin his search.

He learned at once that modern socialism was only about seventy years old, so contemporary that it had been born but a few years before his own mother; he had the feeling that he was amazingly fortunate to be alive at the very beginning of the movement, to be almost a charter member. The very timeliness lent an added zest to his discovery. His next step was to perceive that economic conditions and not men breed revolutions. France, the mother of modern socialism, had revolted against a corrupt and burdensome monarchy only to find an equally burdensome bourgeoisie strapped to her back. The coming of machine production brought long hours, low wages, and cyclical unemployment, and the condition of the mass of workers became worse than it ever had been under the profligacies of Louis XIV and Louis XV. Another revolution, economic in nature instead of political, was needed, and from this need arose the Utopian Socialists who were led to socialism by observing that the few were surfeited with riches while the many, who worked ceaselessly, lived in poverty.

He went to the work of Bebeuf, Saint-Simon, Fourier, and Proudhon, where he found the first recorded attacks on private property and the first differentiation of the economic classes; the insistence that the basis of private property was labor; the demand for the abolition of unearned income and inheritance of wealth; and the revolutionary conception that social reform was a function of government. Jack bought a five-cent brown paper tablet at the stationery store and in his undisciplined scrawl wrote down the aims of these pioneers who tried to visualize an industrial society wherein no man would live off the labor of his fellows, where every man had to work and work was guaranteed to all. He noted that although these men had broken ground for the revolution, they had not been able to provide a mechanism by means of which the socialist state was to be achieved; they had hoped that the masters would give the workers socialism out of the Christian goodness of their hearts.

A wandering philosopher of The Road had told him about a pamphlet called *The Communist Manifesto*. Jack secured a copy of *The Communist Manifesto*, and reading it avidly found that it was as though his own heart and brain had suddenly become magnificently articulate. He capitulated utterly to Karl Marx's reasoning, for here he found the method whereby man not only could achieve the socialist state, but under historical imperatives would be compelled by economic force to embrace it. In his notebook Jack jotted down, "The whole history of mankind has been a history of contests between exploiting and exploited; a history of these class struggles shows the evolution of economic civilization just as Darwin's studies show the evolution of man; with the coming of industrialism and concentrated capital a stage has been reached whereby the exploited cannot attain its emancipation from the ruling class without once and for all emancipating society at large from all future exploitation, oppression, class distinctions and class struggles."

Pushing onward in *The Communist Manifesto* Jack found scientific socialism demanding the abolition of private property in land; abolition of all rights of inheritance; factories, means of production, communication, and transportation to be owned by the state; and all wealth, except consumption goods, to be owned collectively. With his heavy pencil he underlined in the *Manifesto* the call of socialism to the workingmen of the world: *"The socialists disdain to conceal their aims and views. They openly declare their ends can be attained only by a forcible overthrow of all existing conditions. Let the ruling classes tremble at the socialistic revolution. The proletarians have nothing to lose but their chains. They have a world to gain. Working men of all countries, unite!"*

It was not long before Jack was to proclaim that socialism was the greatest thing in the world.

Having decided that he would live by his brain rather than his brawn, Jack settled upon the kind of work he wanted to do. He had kept a notebook during his year on the road, and he knew for a certainty that his life could have meaning and he could be happy only as a writer of the stories that charged through his brain. For him to have reached this decision at so early an age is not difficult to understand; the thousands of astrological divinities Professor Chaney had written were short stories, pure creations of fiction. Jack came legitimately by his passion to spin yarns for a living.

He also settled upon the University of California in Berkeley, a streetcar ride from his home, as the place where he would derive the ultimate in education. However, he had never attended high school and had three years of routine work ahead of him before he might be admitted.

He was nineteen when he entered the freshman class of Oakland High in a much-worn, wrinkled, and ill-fitting dark blue suit and woolen shirt without a tie. He was strong and rugged looking, his face sunburned, his tawny hair disheveled as though he always ran his fingers through it. He was still chewing tobacco, a habit he picked up on The Road and continued when he returned to Oakland because it anesthetized the pain of the numerous cavities in his teeth. When Eliza offered to have his cavities filled and to replace the extracted teeth with false ones if he would give up chewing tobacco, he readily assented. Pleased with his shining new teeth, Jack invested in the first toothbrush he had ever owned.

He was slouchy in manner, a habit acquired during the months of begging, and leaned back at his desk with his feet stretched out in front of him, his hands in his pockets, looking off into space. He turned his head first one way, then the other; at short intervals a shadow would pass over his face, then he would pull himself together and the smile would come back. When called upon to recite he raised himself with apparent difficulty to a half-upright position, keeping both hands on his desk as though to steady himself. His recitation was always in a low voice, soft, almost inaudible, his answers as curt as possible. When finished he would sit down quickly and abruptly, as though exhausted.

The boys and girls around him were fourteen and fifteen years old; most of them came from protected homes, had never been farther away than San Francisco. To Jack they seemed babies. He had the feeling too that although education was the gateway to a better life, the lessons he had to go through in French, Roman history, and algebra were childish. He made no attempt to conceal from his classmates that he was bored, that he considered the work trivial, that he was interested in the world of maturity into which they had not yet been initiated.

He wanted to be one with his class, yet couldn't. He would stand by and listen eagerly to the general conversation, but if spoken to by one of the boys or girls would show irritability and leave abruptly. Once again was manifested the fundamental contradiction in his nature first noticed by Ina Coolbrith: his supreme self-confidence existing side by side with his strangulated shyness and sense of inferiority. To the students he seemed resentful about something, as a result of which he was often gruff when they wanted him to join their activities. They were sorely pressed to understand him. One of his classmates, Georgia Loring Bamford, reports that at times his face beamed and showed the character of a beautiful child, at other times he looked like a waterfront loafer and seemed proud of it. He kept his cap stuffed in his coat pocket and when school was over pulled it out, stuck it on his head, and dashed out of the building swinging his arms sailor fashion.

He would have had little time for social life even if Oakland High had accepted him. John London had found employment as a special depot guard during the railroad strike, but Jack still had to support himself. On Saturdays and Sundays he solicited odd jobs, mowed lawns, beat carpets, ran errands. From her modest income Eliza bought his supplies and books and provided him with a bicycle to ride to school. He was always pressed for cash. When the janitor of Oakland High needed an assistant, Eliza got her brother the job. After school was over Jack remained to sweep the floors and scrub the lavatories. Years later he proudly wrote his daughter that he had washed every window in the building where she was attending high school.

A group of girls, seeing him go into a saloon on Broadway with a couple of tramps he had known on The Road, spread the word that he associated with rough companions and was accustomed to violence. With Jack becoming the school janitor the chasm between him and the other students became even more unbridgeable.

However he had discovered the student literary magazine, *The Aegis*, and when they accepted his article, "Bonin Islands," he decided that he was going to like the school after all. The article, which ran in January and February of 1895, is written with verve, with a freshness and vitality that keeps it enjoyable even at this distance. The pictures of the whaling fleet and the Islands are vivid, the characters are warmly human and lovable, and above all the prose has a music of words. Seeing his article in print taught Jack more about writing than all the criticisms scrawled over his manuscripts by the English teacher who abhorred his informal style, his spontaneity, his gusts of eagerness and delight with nature. In March *The Aegis* published "Sakaicho Hona Asi and Hakadaki," then came two stories from his experiences on The Road, called "Frisco Kid" and "And Frisco Kid Came Back," both rich in dialect and showing insight into the psychology of road-kids.

The railroad strike was settled, John London lost his job, and it was up to Jack to provide for the family. He had to find more outside jobs, work harder. Since he could no longer spend any money on himself his classmates noted that he became more and more shabby. He was always overworked, on edge, going without sufficient food or sleep. Because he wrote honestly about himself the students came to know that he had been a sailor and a tramp. The girls would have nothing to do with him. The fact that he was a writer not only did not make his eccentricities acceptable, but made him the more a creature apart. He enjoyed writing his stories in his spare hours at night, he enjoyed the great number of books he took out of the public library on the six family cards, but there was little in his days to bring him personal happiness: friendship, love, a place in the sun . . . he had none of these. Then he joined the Henry Clay Debating Society.

The Henry Clay Debating Society was the one rallying point for intellectuals in Oakland. To it belonged young schoolteachers, doctors, lawyers, musicians, university students, socialists, all interested in the world about them. More than any other group in Oakland they judged a man by the quality of his mind rather than the clothes on his back. Jack sat quietly during a meeting or two, then entered the discussions. The club appreciated the clear and logical manner in which his mind worked; they enjoyed his robust Irish humor, his lively stories of the sea and the road, thought him good fun and jolly company. They were moved by his burning passion for socialism and the fund of knowledge he had already acquired on the subject. But most important of all for Jack at this point, they liked him, they accepted him as an equal and a friend. In the warm glow of their acceptance Jack shed his ill poise, his moroseness, his self-consciousness; he kept his head up, expressed himself fully and with ease. He had found a place among his contemporaries.

Of all the members Jack liked best Edward Applegarth, a slim, brown-haired, brown-eyed boy who came from a cultivated English family that had settled in Oakland. Applegarth had a keen wit and an incisive habit of thinking. The two young men were of the same age; they stimulated each other to swift, sound thought. They began spending their spare hours together on long walks and friendly talks. To Applegarth Jack was not an ill-dressed, crude-mannered boy from the wrong side of the railroad tracks; he was an intelligent, roguish, well-traveled chap who happened to be poor at the moment, but who was on his way up.

Applegarth brought Jack into his home and introduced him to his sister Mabel. Jack had no more than crossed the threshold when he fell in love with all the speed and spontaneity of his forceful nature.

Mabel Applegarth was an ethereal creature with wide, spiritual blue eyes and a wealth of golden hair. Jack likened her to a pale gold flower upon a slender stem. She had a beautiful speaking voice and tinkling laughter which to him was the most musical sound in the world. Mabel was three years his senior, an honest woman without pretense or coquetry. She was a student at the University of California, taking special courses in English. Jack marveled at all the knowledge that was so neatly stored in her pretty head. Her manners were flawless; she had a profound sense of breeding; art and culture were her constant companions. Jack loved her as a goddess to be worshipped but not to be touched. To his delight she accepted him as an equal and a friend; had the boy only known it, she was as much drawn to his warm strength and crude manliness as he was to her delicacy.

Jack became a frequent visitor at the home of the Applegarths, who lived in a rambling house filled with books and paintings. They loaned him their books, their knowledge and training in fields he had not yet invaded; he watched them carefully, their gestures, their speech. Before long the rough words began to drop out of his vocabulary, the sailor's roll from his walk, the crudeness from his manners. He was invited to the homes of other members of the Henry Clay Society where he met other cultivated young ladies whose dresses reached the ground, and with whom he discussed poetry and art and nuances of grammar over cups of tea. His brusqueness dropped away and his handsome, flashing smile more and more adorned his clean-cut face. He gave himself to his new friends with a full and deep love. When it was enthusiastically reported back to the students of Oakland High that Jack London was a charming and remarkable young man who surely had a brilliant future, they glanced over at their badly dressed and bored classmate and wondered what had gone wrong with the judgment of their elders.

The members of the newly formed Socialist Party of Oakland, one of the first on the Pacific coast, invited Jack to join their Local. Here he met such men as Austin Lewis of the British Socialist-Labor Party, German Socialists who had been exiled from their Fatherland by the ban against socialists, mature and well-trained men who served as whetstones for the nineteen-year-old to sharpen the tools of his mind. The Socialist Local in Oakland was more a cultural than an economic group; they met of evenings for music and a glass of beer and to study and orate on political economics. They were intellectuals, theoreticians not directly involved in the class struggle, for no workingman had as yet joined the party. Grateful as he was for this company and training, Jack did not believe that socialism belonged to the intellectuals. He believed that it belonged to the workingman and the unions that were destined by the processes of history to carry on the class war, fight the revolution, and establish the proletarian world state which Karl Marx had taught him was the next step in the development of civilization.

He began attending workingmen's meetings, talked about socialism at labor unions, listened to speeches in City Hall Park. One afternoon, feeling moved, he got up on a bench and told the large crowd of listeners that capitalism was a system of organized robbery which had the laborers by the throats and was choking the last dollar of labor out of them before flinging them aside. He had not been talking more than ten minutes when there was a clatter of horses' hooves on Broadway, a black patrol wagon drew up alongside the park, and two officers clapped him under arrest. They escorted him through the crowd to the patrol wagon, rode him behind locked steel doors through the Oakland streets, and threw him in jail. When Jack protested that this was America where they had free speech, and that socialism was no crime, the desk sergeant replied, "Maybe not, but speaking without a license is."

The Oakland papers ran the story under huge streamers, calling Jack "The Boy Socialist," a name that was to stick to him for years.

What made Jack London a socialist? He was raised in poverty, he knew hunger and deprivation, he had learned harrowing lessons about the fate of the laboring man. But hundreds of thousands of Americans of his time who had grown up in hunger and deprivation believed in the capitalist system and went out to corner their share of wealth. Just as he had been wise enough to understand that a certain number of the men on the road would be waste material under any civilization, he also realized that only a portion of the hardships of his youth were a result of the unsocial structure of American capitalism, that a major part of his hunger had been caused by his mother's unbalanced business schemes that had prevented John London from earning a living.

Professor Chaney was inherently a socialist before Jack was born. He had an intense though intellectual interest in the working class and a belief in the willingness of men to work hard and to work together. For many years he lectured and wrote articles on the causes and cures of poverty. This sympathy with and interest in the worker is, for those who are not workers themselves, a matter of temperament, tied up with a warm human nature, a sensitivity to the hardships of others, a personal liberality, and an imagination sufficiently vivid to project one's self into the sufferings of conscientious men whose wives and children are starving. Professor Chaney had all these attributes; they made him a socialist; similar traits made his son a socialist.

Chaney was an Irishman; so was Jack. They both were endowed with the characteristics that go to make up the genius of the Irish: compassion for the sufferings of others; liberality with their own possessions; the love of a fight such as the Class War between capital and labor; and the courage to plow in with both fists flying.

Would Jack London have been a socialist if Flora had kept her hands out of John London's affairs, and the family had prospered? The answer would seem to be yes, though he more likely would have developed into an intellectual or utopian socialist rather than a workingman's socialist, and would have been content to let socialism filter slowly through the centuries by means of the ballot, instead of rising up and demanding militantly that the workingmen Unite! Throw off their chains! Wipe out by force the ruling predatory class!

To Jack, socialism was a system of human, historical, and economic logic, as irrefutable as the multiplication table. Though he had as yet accumulated only a limited *content* of thought he had the apparatus for a scientific *method* of thought, the perseverance to follow a given line of reasoning, and the courage to accept its conclusions no matter how they might violate his preconceived notions.

Then too, he had an inexhaustible quarrel with the world: his illegitimacy. Since he could not fight with his mother about it, rectify the wrong that had been done him, nor bring it out into the light, it festered in the subterranean darkness of his unconscious. The only quarrel in the external world which had the epic proportions to match in magnitude his internal quarrel was the overthrowing of the predominant class of society by the subservient class, of which he was a member.

The Chamber of Commerce and a section of the established Oakland society were outraged at his preaching destruction of the existing order; and in the public City Hall Park! They agitated to have him sent to prison. When the case came up the judge recommended that Jack's youth be considered a mitigating circumstance, and let him off with a warning that if he ever did it again he would be sent away. After Jack's death Mayor Davies of Oakland dedicated an oak tree to him in City Hall Park on a spot not too far distant from where he had been arrested for his first fiery speech.

The position he had begun to establish for himself was shattered by the arrest and unfavorable publicity. The Socialist Local stuck by him, as did Edward and Mabel Applegarth and a few of the other Henry Club debaters, though Jack complained at this time that really decent fellows who liked him very well drew the line at his appearing in public with their sisters. A number of the homes that had been opened to him through the Henry Clay Society were now closed. For the rest of Oakland he had merely strengthened the impression of being a none too savory character. He had been known to be an outlaw; in his pirating days he had been seen drunk along the waterfront and in questionable company; he had been a tramp; he came from a poverty-stricken, déclassé family living in the worst part of town. The people of Oakland believed that being a socialist not only proved that there was something wrong with a man's mind, but with his morals as well. So rare a phenomenon was a socialist that reporters were sent to interview him. When Jack boldly took a stand for the municipal ownership of public utilities he was branded a red-shirt, a dynamiter, and an anarchist. The interviews when published were pathological studies of a strange and abnormal specimen. Jack shuddered when he thought what the newspapers would have called him if he had admitted that he believed in the public ownership of all means of production.

Although Mabel Applegarth was shocked by Jack's arrest and was displeased at the derogatory newspaper interviews, the incident made no difference in their relationship. They were perfect complements, Jack robust, vital, crude; Mabel delicate, cultivated, and polished. They took bicycle rides together, ate picnic lunches in the deep golden poppy fields of the Berkeley hills overlooking the Bay, went for long sails in his skiff. One Sunday afternoon in early summer they were drifting down the Estuary with Mabel sitting primly in the prow in a fluffy white gown and picture hat. She was reading to him from Swinburne's poetic pessimism in such a soothing voice that Jack fell asleep. The tide went out and left them stranded. Because she knew how little rest he got, Mabel did not disturb him. When he awakened he had to roll his one good pair of trousers above his knees and carry her through the mud to shore. It was the closest he had as yet gotten to the young lady.

Jack had received a B average in his courses for his first semester. After working during the summer to help the family and to get a few dollars ahead for his school needs, he returned to

Oakland High to continue his preparation for the University. *The Aegis* continued to publish his articles and stories, running ten in all. The short stories, such as "One More Unfortunate" and "Who Believes in Ghosts?" show an innate sense of story structure. "One More Unfortunate" tells of a promising young musician who went forth to conquer the world, as did Ouida's Signa, learned over a period of difficult years that he had but a small talent, was overjoyed to find refuge as a fiddler in a cheap beer garden, and one night killed himself because he realized how far he had fallen from his childhood dreams.

In "The Run Across," taken from his sailing experiences on the whaler *Sophie Sutherland*, his eye exults because each moment new beauties appear: he follows the gulls, solemn and graceful, watches the glorious sunrises at sea, the schools of porpoises and a whale blowing to the leeward, at night the dim form of the helmsman and the sails lost to view in the black vault. To his ear nothing is harsh or discordant, everything harmonizes. The creaking of a block is music, the groan of the towering canvas, the dash of water from the dancing stem, the splutter of flying fish against the sails. He exults when nature is angry, when the sky is overcast with black storm clouds, the air is a howling unseen demon, and the decks are a flood of churning water. The joy of combat sends his blood leaping when the bellying sails are overcome or the reluctant rope is forced to yield; and the chants of the seamen make sweet music in his ear as men conquer Mother Nature in the fierce struggle to subsist.

He loved Nature tenderly for all the beauties there were in her, but above all he loved her for her force, the terrific strength with which she dwarfed all mankind.

That the Oakland High School *Aegis* had a liberal editorial policy is evidenced by the fact that they published his socialist article, "Optimism, Pessimism and Patriotism," in which he accused the "powers that be" of keeping the masses from education because education would make them revolt against their slavery. He charged capitalism with long hours, sweat systems, and steadily decreasing wages, conducive to nought but social and moral degradation, and cried out to "ye Americans, patriots and optimists to awake! Seize the reins of a corrupted government and educate the masses."

Because he was a convincing talker Jack was appointed one of the debaters for the Christmas week graduation exercises. One may safely assume that the subject of the debate was a goodly distance from socialism, but Jack had been talking only a minute or two when he came to a pause, shifted his weight to the other foot, and began assailing the dressed-up audience of students, their parents and friends with what has been reported by one listener to have been the most truculent socialistic diatribe she ever heard. He told them that the time had come when existing society had to be destroyed, and that he was ready to break it down with any means or force. He talked with such passion that the audience felt he had lost himself and was already clutching at the throats of his enemies in the class struggle. Some were frightened, others thought it a joke, others maintained that it was pitiful, that the boy was not responsible, that he was a superegoist and a latent paranoiac. Members of the Board of Education demanded drastic treatment.

It seems possible that Jack had seized this opportunity to fire his parting shot, for he never returned to Oakland High. It would have taken him two more years to graduate, and since he had just turned twenty he felt that he could not spare the time. Instead he went to a cramming school in Alameda, called the University Academy, to prepare for the fall entrance examinations to the University. Eliza gave him the money for tuition. He made such swift progress that at the end of five weeks, or at least so Jack reports, the owner returned the money and told him he would have to leave because his school would be discredited if the University found out that two years' work could be covered in the four months that it was going to take him.

His five weeks at the cramming school had been useful not only for what he had learned in facts, but for what he had learned about method. For the next twelve weeks he locked himself in his room at Flora's, where he cracked open book after book with a sledgehammer method of acquiring knowledge. At approximately the same time that Professor Chaney is reported as sitting at his desk in the College of Astronomy in Chicago for nineteen hours a day, studying science and writing nativities, his son Jack is sitting at his desk in Flora Wellman's house in Oakland for nineteen hours a day, studying mathematics, chemistry, history, and English. He gave up the Henry Clay meetings, the socialist meetings, even sacrificed his treasured visits to the home of Edward and Mabel Applegarth. His body and brain began to fag, and his eyes to twitch, but he never faltered.

At the end of the twelve weeks he rode the streetcar to Berkeley, where he spent several days taking the examinations. Confident that he had passed he borrowed a sailboat, stowed a roll of blankets and some cold food into its cabin, and drifted out of the Estuary on the last of an early morning tide. He caught the first of the flood up the Bay, and raced along with a spanking breeze. Carquinez Straits were smoking as he left astern the old landmarks he had first learned with Young Scratch Nelson on the unreefed *Reindeer*. At Benicia he made fast and hurried up among the arks. Here he found his pals from the Fish Patrol. When the word got around that Jack London had returned, the fishermen dropped in to talk over old times and drink his health. Jack, who had not touched a drop of liquor in over a year, got roaring drunk.

Late that night his former chief of the Fish Patrol lent him a salmon boat. Jack added charcoal and a fisherman's brazier, a coffee-pot and frying-pan, coffee and meat and a fresh black bass, and cast off his painter. The tide had turned and the fierce ebb, running in the teeth of a fiercer wind, kicked up a stiff sea. Suisun Bay was white with wrath and sea-lump. Jack drove his salmon boat into it and through it. Cresting seas filled her with a foot of water, but he laughed as he sloshed about and sang "Treat My Daughter Kind-i-ly," "Come All You Rambling Gambling Men," celebrating his admission to a world where men worked and conquered with their brains.

After a week of sailing he returned refreshed to enter the University. James Hopper describes him at this time as a strange combination of Scandinavian sailor and Greek god, made altogether boyish by the lack of two front teeth, lost cheerfully somewhere in a fight. Hopper writes that the word "sunshine" leapt to his mind the first time he saw Jack on the campus. He had a curly mop of hair which seemed "spun of the sun's gold"; his strong neck in a loose, low, soft shirt was bronzed with it; his eyes were like a sunlit sea. His clothes were flappy and careless, the forecastle had left the suspicion of a roll in his broad shoulders. He was full of irrepressible enthusiasms and gigantic plans. He was going to take all the courses in English, nothing less, and most of the courses in the natural sciences, history, and philosophy. Hopper concludes by saying that Jack's personality shed as much warmth as the sun itself, that he was intrepid, young and touching, pure and vibrant.

One of the girls from Oakland High who had been repulsed by his appearance and conduct the year before met Jack on the campus, and to her surprise found him neat and clean, happy, well fitted into his surroundings, without the slouch or gloom or sense of embarrassment that had so strangled him among the youngsters of the high school. He spent many hours on the campus with Mabel Applegarth. Here also were his associates from the Henry Clay Society. He already possessed a reputation among the students as one who had done wild and romantic things; he had many friends and was respected and well liked.

The University of California had a good library and faculty. Jack enjoyed his work heartily. Though he had letters on economics and political subjects printed in the Oakland *Times*, and stories published in such local magazines as *Evenings at Home* and *Amateur Bohemian*, he does not appear to have submitted any material to *The Occident*, the University literary publication. He continued to do odd jobs around Oakland, and when completely broke again went to Johnny Heinold, proprietor of the First and Last Chance saloon where he had had his first drink of whiskey when he bought the *Razzle Dazzle*, and borrowed forty dollars.

Though Jack had known since before he was six that John London was not his father, he had never had a clue as to who his real father might be. At this time he somehow came in possession of the Chaney evidence. He never revealed the source of his information, but there were several sources available. John London, realizing that he was nearing the end of his life, might have told Jack so that he could know the truth and understand himself better. He might have heard the talk of old-timers around San Francisco and Oakland, many of whom knew his paternity. His attention might have been drawn to the *Chronicle* article about Flora and Chaney, or he might have been prompted to look up the announcement of his birth and have found that he had been born under the name of Chaney. Lastly, Flora always kept her marriage certificate, which was dated eight months after the *Chronicle* announcement of Jack's birth, and on which she signed herself as Flora Chaney, in a wooden box which did not lock.

Jack confided his secret to Edward Applegarth while they were walking in the warm sunshine past the old St. Mary's College on Broadway. Applegarth reports that Jack was terribly cut up, and asked permission to use his address when he wrote to Chaney; he did not wish to hurt his mother by any sign that he knew of her troubled background, nor did he want Flora to intercept Chaney's answer. He asked Chaney for information on the three questions that were to torment and torture him to the end of his days: *Who was my father? Was my mother known as a loose woman? Was my mother diseased?*

He received grades of A and B for his first semester, worked during the Christmas vacation, and returned to the University. However, in a few weeks he saw that it was a hopeless struggle. It has long been rumored that he left the University because he submitted a short-story manuscript to an English professor who scrawled across the margin the Greek equivalent for the word "junk." The real reason is more prosaic: John London, who had been granted a peddler's license because he was a Civil War veteran, and who was peddling pictures from door to door in Alameda, was in frail health and could not earn a living for himself and Flora. Jack undertook the responsibility. If it had not been for the lack of money there is reason to believe that he would have continued to study at the University, that he would have published articles and stories in *The Occident*, perhaps even have had the patience to fulfill the academic requirements and graduate.

Despite the fact that the family was in desperate need, he took a last gamble before he went out to seek another manual-labor job. He decided that since he eventually was going to be a writer, the best thing he could do was sit down and write. Maybe he would sell something. Maybe he would be able to support his family, earn more than the current dollar a day being paid in the labor market. For five years he had been reading widely, discussing widely, filling and firing his brain, formulating his ideas, seeing unforgettable pictures of nature in beauty and stress and storm, working and adventuring shoulder to shoulder with men from all nations. The time had arrived to give back some of his treasure trove.

Once again he locked himself in his room. He composed steadily for fifteen hours a day, day after day, pouring out ponderous essays, scientific and sociological tracts, short stories, humorous verse, tragic blank verse, and elephantine epics in Spenserian stanzas. In the flush of his first creative fervor he forgot to eat; he said that there never was a creative fervor such as his from which the patient escaped fatal results.

He sent his manuscripts East as soon as he had typed them, using his remaining cash for stamps. When they came back rejected he sold his books and clothing for small sums, borrowed wherever he could, and continued to write. But when the household had used its last dollar, and there was no more food, Jack set aside his pencil and found a job in the laundry of the Belmont Academy, where Frank Norris had been a student. His board and lodging was provided, so that he could turn over the thirty dollars a month wage, after taking out tobacco money, to Flora. His job was to sort, wash, starch, and iron the white shirts, collars, cuffs, and white trousers of the students and professors and their wives.

He sweated his way through long weeks at a task that was never done, working nights under electric lights to keep up with the soiled laundry. The trunk of books he had taken with him so hopefully remained unopened, for when the day's work was done he had his supper in the kitchen of the Academy, and fell into bed. On Sundays all he could do was lie in the shade, read the comics, and sleep after the eighty-hour work week. Occasionally on a Sunday, if he was not too exhausted, he would pedal his bicycle down to Oakland to spend a few hours with Mabel Applegarth. He knew that he was trapped in a blind alley, but he did not know where to turn. Should he quit and take another job? But jobs were all alike; when a man labored for wages there was no time for leisure, for reading and thinking, even for living. He was just another machine into which was poured sufficient food and sleep to do the next day's work. He asked himself how long he would have to toil thus meaninglessly, and where the road lay that would lead him to the life he wanted.

Fate presented him with the answer. Gold was discovered in the Klondike, and when the first great rush started in the spring of 1896, Jack was in the vanguard. The fact that Flora and John London had been living on his thirty dollars a month, that he had given up both the University and his writing to earn it for them, did not detain him. Adventure called.

Once again faithful Eliza came to the rescue. Her husband, now past sixty, had also caught the Klondike fever. Eliza put a thousand-dollar mortgage on her home and took five hundred dollars out of her savings to outfit the two men. Jack and Shepard went across to San Francisco, which was doing a land-office business in Alaskan outfits, and bought fur-lined coats, fur caps, high boots, red flannel shirts, blankets, a tent, stove, runners, thongs, and tools with which to build dog sleds and boats, and a thousand pounds of grub apiece.

On July 25, 1897, they sailed on the *Umatilla*, the same ship on which Jack had reached San Francisco at the end of his tramping days. Once again he was the youngest of a motley crowd, a husky, handsome, blue-eyed, affable youngster who could handle himself with the best of them in a discussion, a fight, or a day's work. There was no guile or malice in him; he liked everybody and everybody liked him. On the *Umatilla* Jack became friendly with Fred Thompson, with Jim Goodman, a miner, and Sloper, a carpenter. These four men were to remain fast friends during the difficult days to come.

The *Umatilla*, jammed to the gunwales with venturesome gold-seekers, took the inside passage and anchored off Juneau, where they joined other prospectors standing amidst their tons of supplies against the Arctic winter, bargaining frantically with Indians to haul them to Dyea Beach and Skagway. When Jack and Shepard left San Francisco the quoted rate for Indians to portage over Chilkoot Pass had been six cents a pound. They left Juneau August 5. By the time they reached Dyea Beach so great was the demand for porters that the Indians had raised their rates to thirty and forty cents a pound, and when a dumbfounded miner hesitated for a moment, jacked the price to fifty.

If Jack and Shepard had paid this rate they would have been left without a dollar, and the Northwest Mounted, or Yellow Legs, who demanded that every prospector carry five hundred dollars in cash in addition to his thousand pounds of food, would have turned them back at the Yukon. Many of the prospectors who could not afford to pay these rates, and who were not strong enough for the back-breaking trail over Chilkoot Pass, sailed back with the *Umatilla* to San Francisco, defeated. Shepard went with them, leaving Jack with Thompson, Goodman, and Sloper.

Though it was only August 7, they had two months of hard work ahead if they hoped to cross the Pass, portage the twenty-five miles to Lake Linderman, cross the lake, shoot the rapids, travel the hundreds of miles up the Yukon, and pack into Dawson, close to which flowed the gold-laden Klondike, before winter froze down on them and made further travel impossible. Jack, as the sailor of the crowd, was sent out to buy a small boat, which the men carefully loaded with provisions and pulled up the Dyea River, or Lynn Canal, against the current. The trip was seven miles to the foot of Chilkoot Pass; arriving there the men unpacked the boat, cached the gear, and rode the spring current back to Dyea to fill up again. After many weeks of labor, their bodies straining forward against the ropes, the three thousand pounds of supplies had been moved to the foot of the Pass.

Chilkoot Pass is reputed to be one of the world's toughest for portage. It is all rocks, and goes very nearly straight up. Jack loaded a hundred pounds of grub on his back and started the climb; the trail, which is 3,500 feet high, was a solid stream of men from top to bottom. Strewn along the sides were older men, weaker and softer men, men from offices who had never lifted anything heavier than a pencil, fallen in exhaustion . . . who would take the next boat back to the States. When the summer sun got too hot Jack peeled off his coat and shirt in the middle of the Pass and startled the Indians by plunging upward in his red flannels. It required ninety straight days for Jack, Goodman, Thompson, and Sloper to get their four thousand pounds over the top. More than any book he was to write, Jack derived pleasure from the fact that he started at the bottom of the trail with Indian packers, none of whom was carrying more than he, and often beat them to the top.

On the shores of Lake Linderman another contingent of adventurers was turned back because no boats were available. Jack's party once again cached their supplies and each morning walked eight miles upriver to where Sloper had set up a crude sawmill.

They chopped down a number of trees, hung them, and whip-sawed the lumber by hand. Sailor Jack was called upon to design two flat-bottomed boats. He named them *Yukon Belle* and *Belle of the Yukon,* and wrote a poem about each the day they were launched.

He cut and stitched canvas sails and sailed the boats across the lake in record time, thus increasing their chances of getting into Dawson before the freeze. Linderman behind them, the party pulled into the headwaters of the Yukon and prepared for the final dash. When they reached White Horse Rapids they found nearly a thousand boats lining the shore, and thousands of men standing by frustrated because every party that had tried to shoot the rapids had drowned. Thompson said, "Jack, you go look at the rapids, and if they're too dangerous . . ."

Jack tied the two boats ashore. A throng of men, most of whom had never been in a boat before, gathered about to assure him that the rapids were certain suicide. Jack took a look at White Horse, came back, and said, "Nothing to it. The other boats tried to fight the current to keep off the rocks. We'll go with the current and it'll keep us clear."

While the crowds of men lined the banks and cheered, Jack nailed his canvas sails over their provisions, stationed Sloper on his knees in the prow with a paddle, put Thompson and Goodman in the center with instructions to give him plenty of speed, and sat himself in the stern to steer. By following the main force of the water they shot the rapids safely, tied up in calm water, and walked back for their second boat.

Instantly Jack was deluged with offers to take other boats through. He took only the Ret boat because he had become friends with the husband and wife, but refused to charge them anything.

Even so they had delayed too long. At the mouth of the Stewart River, seventy-two miles from Dawson, winter fell with a thunderous clap of white snow, and they could go no further. They took possession of an abandoned cabin on the bank of the Yukon, cut down spruce trees for firewood, and dug in for a long siege. Between fifty and seventy men were caught at Stewart, among them a doctor, a judge, a university professor, an engineer.

There were high hills sloping back from the river, buttressed by an occasional ridge that had been cleft by the stream. All around were forests of spruce and a mantle of snow four feet deep. All men coming over the long trail had to pass Jack's cabin, and the smoke rising white and lazily from the chimney was a temptation, for it spoke of warmth and rest and comfort. To this cabin came Burning Daylight, Louis Savard, Peacock, Keogh, Prewitt, Stevens, Malemute Kid, Del Bishop; trappers, Indians, Yellow Legs, *chechaquos*, seasoned sourdoughs, men from all over the world who were to gain immortality in Jack London's gripping tales of Alaska.

Here Jack spent a delightful winter. The company was congenial and varied; there were some books in camp, of which Jack had carried over Chilkoot Pass Darwin's *Origin of Species*, Spencer's *Philosophy of Style*, Marx's *Capital*, and Milton's *Paradise Lost*. One old Alaskan prospector who had been caught in a fierce storm stumbled into camp half dead, threw open the door of Jack's cabin, and found it thick with pipe smoke and men all trying to talk at once, bellowing at each other and waving their arms. The prospector reports that when he heard what the crowd was arguing so fiercely, he thought that in his struggles to escape the storm he had lost his mind. The subject of the argument? Socialism.

One night W. B. Hargrave, who occupied an adjoining cabin, listened in on a heated discussion over a Darwinian theory between Judge Sullivan, Doctor B. F. Harvey, and John Dillon. Jack lay in his bunk also listening, and making notes. When his friends became tangled in a moot point, he called out, "The passage you fellows are trying to quote runs about as follows . . ." and gave the passage. Hargrave went to another cabin where the *Origin of Species* had been borrowed, brought it back, and said, "Now, Jack, give that spiel again, I'll hold the copy on you." Hargrave reports that Jack quoted it word for word.

Hargrave says that the first time he entered Jack's cabin, Jack was sitting on the edge of his bunk rolling a cigarette. Goodman was preparing a meal and Sloper was doing some carpentry work. Jack had challenged some of Goodman's orthodox views, and Goodman was doggedly defending himself against the rapier thrust of Jack's wit. Jack interrupted the conversation to welcome the stranger. Hargrave writes that his hospitality was so cordial, his smile so genial, his fellowship so real that it instantly dispelled all reserve. He was at once invited by Jack to join in the discussion.

Hargrave records that Jack was intrinsically kind, irrationally generous, a prince of good fellows to be with. He had a gentleness that survived the roughest associations. In argument when his opponent had caught himself in the web of his own illogic, Jack threw back his head and gave vent to infectious laughter. Hargrave's parting estimate of Jack is too genuine to be tampered with. "Many a long night Jack and I, outlasting the vigil of the others, sat before the blazing spruce logs and talked the hours away. A brave figure of a man he was, lounging by the crude fireplace, its light playing on his handsome features. He had the clean, joyous, tender, unembittered heart of youth, yet he displayed none of the insolent egotism of youth. In appearance older than his twenty years; a body lithe and strong; neck bared at the throat; a tangled cluster of brown hair that fell over his brow and which he was wont to brush back impatiently when engaged in animated conversation; a sensitive mouth, but lips nevertheless that could set in serious and masterful lines; a radiant smile, eyes that often carried an introspective expression; the face of an artist and a dreamer, but with strong lines denoting will power and boundless energy. An outdoor man, in short a real man, a man's man. He had a mental craving for truth. He applied one test to religion, to economics, to everything: *What is truth?* He could think great thoughts. One could not meet him without feeling the impact of a superior intellect. He faced life with superb assurance, and faced death serenely imperturbable."

Fred Thompson bought a sled and a team of dogs and took Jack prospecting up the various creeks that fed into the Yukon. Thompson testifies that Jack was an expert at out-of-doors life, that he could kindle a fire in a storm, make delicious flapjacks and bacon, sling a tent so they could sleep warmly in a temperature of thirty degrees below zero. Jack would have said that all this was apple pie to a Tramp Royal who had spent a year sleeping in the open without a blanket and cooked his food in tin cans over a railroad jungle fire.

Jack and Thompson began prospecting on the Henderson, which emptied into the Yukon a mile below Stewart Camp.

Where the swift water kept the ice at bay they thrust their shovels into the creekbed and brought them up with shining dust in the bits of gravel clinging to the blades. Breathlessly they staked out their claims, mushed behind their dogs at a swift clip to get back to Stewart, and spread the word. Every last man in camp set out on foot or behind his dogs to stake a claim. Thompson told Jack that they were worth a cool quarter of a million. What dreams Jack must have dreamed of bringing his sacks of gold back to Oakland, of supporting Flora and John London in style, repaying Eliza for her many kindnesses, claiming Mabel Applegarth for his wife, and having the leisure to become a writer.

The dreams did not last long; the old sourdoughs who had dashed out to Henderson Creek came in with a loud laugh. Jack's pure gold dust had proved to be mica! Thompson says that Jack did not seem to be too greatly disappointed; going up on the *Umatilla* he had told Thompson that he was not going to Alaska to mine, but to gather material for books. Still, he could not have been altogether indifferent to that "cool quarter of a million."

The best account of Jack to come out of Alaska is given by Emil Jensen, from whom Jack fashioned his Malemute Kid, and whom he later described as a noble man. Jensen writes that Jack gave him the first word of welcome he heard on the cold, inhospitable riverfront. Jack greeted him by saying, "I can tell that you are a sailor and a Bay man by the way you landed your boat without a jar in spite of the current and the drift ice."

Jensen writes that the smile on Jack's lips was boyishly friendly and his eyes sparkled as they looked straight into his. He was consistently cheerful, always likable, always a staunch friend. When people disagreed with his socialism Jack would say, "You are not ripe for it yet, but it will come."

According to Jensen, the London cabin was the center of attention, for Jack ranked first in versatility and in chaining the interest of his listeners. When men sometimes told tales that seemed a little too tall, and the others withdrew in incredulity, Jack only dug in deeper to extract the last of the details. The little as well as the big things in his daily camp life held for him a stimulus that made his every waking hour worth living. To him there was in all things something new, something worthwhile, be it a game of whist, an argument, or the sun at noonday glowing cold and brilliant above the hills to the south. Whether silent in wondering awe as on the night he saw the snows aflame beneath a weird sky, or in the throes of excitement while he watched a mighty river at flood tide, he was ever on tiptoe with expectancy.

Jensen tells the amusing anecdote of how Jack loaned him the *Origin of Species.* When Jensen complained that the book was too complex for his simple vocabulary, Jack gave him a copy of Haeckel's *Riddle of the Universe* for lighter reading. This still proving too complex, Jack dug out of his blankets his most valued possession, Milton's *Paradise Lost.* Jensen confessed that he didn't like poetry and couldn't read *Paradise Lost.* Jack set out for a cabin down the Yukon where he had heard it rumored there was a copy of Kipling's *The Seven Seas,* returned to Jensen's cabin with the book, entreating him to read just a few pages so that he might see that poetry was beautiful; and when Jensen read straight through the book, Jack felt he had scored a major triumph.

Jensen's written tribute to Jack also deserves to be given intact. "Jack's companionship was refreshing, stimulating, helpful. He never stopped to count the cost or dream of profits to come. He stood ever ready, were it a foraging trip among the camps for reading matter, to give a helpful hand on a woodsled, or to undertake a two days' hike for a plug of tobacco when he saw us restless and grumpy for the want of a smoke. Whether the service was big or little, asked or unasked, he gave not only of himself but of his belongings. His face was illumined with a smile that never grew cold."

Jack spent many hours in his bunk reading and making notes on Alaska, writing down the stories he had heard, the arguments in which he had engaged, the dialects, philosophies, personalities, and characters of the men who came into the cabin. As late as 1937 Thompson grumbled that sometimes he couldn't get Jack to split wood because the boy was too busy extolling the virtues of socialism. A number of old-time Alaskans have testified that the favorite topic of conversation in Stewart Camp that winter of '97 was socialism, for Jack was by no means alone in believing in its economic philosophy. The miners were not aware of the irony of these rampant individualists, out gold-hunting to establish private fortunes, spending their spare hours praising collective socialism. Jack would have answered that there was nothing so strange in the picture, for these were brave men, pioneers, the kind that took chances on exploring strange, dangerous, and far-off lands, and strange, dangerous, and far-off theories.

When spring finally came Jack duplicated the stunt of his grandfather, Marshall Wellman, who had constructed a raft and floated it from Put-In Bay to Cleveland on another frontier. Jack and Doctor Harvey dismantled Harvey's cabin, and Jack lashed the logs together into a raft and floated it down the river to Dawson, where they sold the logs for six hundred dollars.

Jack found Dawson to be a carnival tent city with fifty thousand people and a muddy main street lined on either side by saloons in which men not only drank but ate, slept, bought their provisions, arranged business transactions, danced with the dance-hall girls, and lost their gold dust to professional gamblers. Food was scarce, ham and eggs sold for three dollars and a half a portion, laborers were paid an ounce of gold a day, worth about seventeen-fifty. In the town were collected some of the world's greatest adventurers and adventuresses. The prostitutes gathered in such great numbers that the Mounted Police corralled them across the river in a space called Louse Town. There was a bridge across the river a block long, hung on ropes; Jack noted that few of the miners considered the bridge too dangerous to cross.

Thompson says that Jack "never done a tap of work" in Dawson. It appears that he did put in a few days finding logs in the river and towing them by rowboat to the sawmill. However, there was little reason for him to work when he could go everywhere without money. He was welcome at the bars, where the miners bought him drinks for the privilege of spinning long yarns to him; he was good at drawing people out, helping them to talk and tell their stories, which he wanted far more than he did their bad whiskey. The women liked him because he was good-looking and a good talker; even though he had no money, he had fun. When there were no stories to be heard he would sit on the sidewalk and entertain the crowd with tall tales of his own. His nights he spent in the gambling houses watching and making notes. By listening to the right men, the trappers and sourdoughs who had been in Alaska before the Klondike strike, he gathered the first authentic history of the early days of the country. He knew what kind of material he wanted, and he knew how to get it, for he was evolving a scientific method of inquiry which was to enrich his later work.

There being no green foods in Alaska, Jack came down with the scurvy. His face became covered with sores and his few remaining teeth weakened in the gums. He was taken into the Catholic Hospital, where Thompson says he paid a small sum for Jack's keep. Here he was given treatment until he was able to travel. In June, Charley Taylor, a Kentuckian, John Thorson, and Jack left Dawson in a small open boat to make the nineteen-hundred-mile trip down the Yukon and along the Bering Sea. Jack did the steering. They traveled in intense heat at midday and at night tied up and made camp on shore. They crossed the Yukon Flats with its millions of mosquitoes, ran the rapids, watched Anglo-Saxons dancing with Indian girls in native villages.

Despite the fact that the scurvy had Jack almost entirely crippled from the waist down, and his right leg was so drawn that he could not straighten it, he went shooting wild fowl at midnight while his companions slept. He wrote in his notebook every day. After describing the robins singing in the islands, partridges drumming, the discordant cries of gulls and loons, the flight of plover and wild geese, the beauty of the night while they drifted downriver, he would note in the margin that the material would go well in *Outing Magazine* or *Youth's Companion*.

It took Jack's party nineteen days to cover the nineteen hundred miles. Without a mishap they sailed along the shore of the Bering Sea and tied up at St. Michael's. Jack got a job stoking the furnace on a ship going from St. Michael's to British Columbia, and from there traveled steerage to Seattle. From Seattle it was an easy matter for a blowed-in-the-glass tramp to beat his way down to Oakland on the freights.

He arrived home without a penny in his pocket, yet he who had never mined an ounce of gold in Alaska was to make more money out of the gold rush than any sourdough who staked a claim on Bonanza Creek.

4

WHEN Jack reached his home at 962 East Sixteenth Street in Oakland he found that John London had died. Jack was deeply grieved, for he had had from his foster father only kindness and companionship.

Up to this time John London had been the apparent head of the household; he had earned a dollar whenever his advanced years and frail health would permit. But now Jack was the man of the family. To increase his responsibility, Flora had adopted little Johnny Miller, grandson of John London, by Ida, the younger of the two daughters he had brought to California. Flora became a devoted mother to the five-year-old boy, lavishing on him all the tenderness that had not been forthcoming during Jack's barren childhood.

There was only one thing in the world Jack London wanted to become: a writer. His decision was not reached arbitrarily, because he wanted notoriety or fame or wealth or the sight of his name in print. It had come from within, had been forced upon him by the imperious dictates of his nature and talents. In his notebook he had jotted down character sketches while on The Road, descriptions of the Alaskan countryside, snatches of dialogue and integrations of plot that had poured unbidden through his mind because he had been born with the gifts of perception and sensitivity and a command over words with which to convey emotion. The decision had been strengthened by his learning that his father, Chaney, was an educated man, part of the world of books and writing. In the nineteen-hundred-mile trip down the Yukon, in the ship that carried him from St. Michael's to Seattle, he had planned and organized the stories he would put on paper when he reached home. He had seen sights and witnessed struggles in the Klondike that were hammering at the gates of his brain to be written.

Jack's sense of obligation moved in cycles. When he had been a newsboy and when he had worked in the cannery he had turned over every cent he earned for food and rent and pills for Flora; then he abandoned his steady earnings to become an oyster pirate. For a time he supported his family on the money taken from pirating, then began squandering it on wild drinking bouts. When he returned with his *Sophie Sutherland* wages he bought only a few second-hand garments before turning his pay over to his mother; when he had worked at the jute mill, the electric plant, the laundry, he had kept for himself only seventy-five cents a week. Then after monotonous months of dutiful conduct the springs of responsibility had run down and he had lit out for the adventure trails of The Road and the Klondike. Now, at the age of twenty-two, caught in the focus of a directed impulse to do something constructive with his life, he might for the first time have found some justification for walking out.

Instead he resolutely shoved into the background the stories clamoring for expression. After sixteen months of adventuring the clock of responsibility was rewound; he was not willing to expose his mother and her adopted grandson to privation during the months that it would take to get his stories down on paper and sell them to the magazines. Their needs were immediate; his finding of work would have to be immediate.

Times were hard. The financial depression of 1893 which had forced him into the jute mill at ten cents an hour five years before was still paralyzing the Far West. Muttering to himself that times were always hard in an acquisitive society, Jack tramped the streets and docks for many days, finding even the meanest of man-

ual labor no longer available. Trained in laundry work, he tried
for a job in every Oakland laundry. He spent two of his last dollars to advertise in the newspapers. He answered advertisements
of elderly invalids in need of companions, hawked sewing machines from house to house as had John London in San Francisco
twenty years before. He felt that he was a bargain in the labor
market; he weighed a hundred and sixty-five pounds stripped,
every pound of which was hardened for toil, but all he could find
were the same odd jobs that had sustained him at Oakland High:
mowing lawns, trimming hedges, washing windows, beating carpets in back yards. The days were rare in which he managed to
earn a whole dollar.

Mabel and Edward Applegarth gave a dinner to welcome him
home. They invited a number of his old friends from the Henry
Clay Debating Society who wrung his hand, slapped him on the
shoulder, and told him how glad they were to have him back in
Oakland. Jack was touched by this warm reception, regaled them
with tales of the Klondike . . . and got each of them off in a
corner to ask if they knew where he might find a job. No one
knew.

After his absence of sixteen months and the rough life among
the prospectors of Stewart Camp and Dawson, Jack found Mabel
more delicately beautiful than ever. When the debaters had
finally made their adieus and Edward had discreetly withdrawn to
his room, Mabel turned the lights low, took him gently by the
hand and led him to the piano, where she played and sang the
songs she had sung when he first came into the house and she had
been both attracted and repelled by his male crudity and strength.
She saw the love shining out of his eyes as he leaned opposite her
in the bay of the piano enthralled by the music and her fragile
scent; and he felt her love for him giving body to the thin sweet
voice as she confessed to him in the words of the sentimental ballad that she loved him too. Yet he knew that this was not the moment to speak; he could not take her out of a cultivated home of
books and paintings and music until he had something better to
offer than second-hand clothing and starvation.

The next morning he saw a notice in an Oakland newspaper
that examinations were being held for the mail service. He rushed
down to the central post office, took the tests, and passed with a

grade of 85.38. If there had been an opening he would soon have been pounding a beat on the Oakland streets with a mail pouch slung over his shoulder.

The odd jobs he was able to find did not fill his days, nor did they provide sufficient money for his family. Reading in a Sunday supplement of the San Francisco *Examiner* that the minimum rate paid by magazines was ten dollars for each thousand words, and having half a dozen exciting articles pulsing on the tips of his fingers, he sat down at the rough wooden table Flora had put in his eight-by-ten bedroom and wrote a thousand-word narrative about his trip in the open boat down the Yukon. That afternoon he mailed it to the editor of the San Francisco *Examiner*. He had no idea that he was beginning a literary career; he was simply trying to earn ten dollars to stave off the landlord until the mail-carrier appointment came through. He decided that his attack upon the literary world would have to be postponed until he could manage to put away a few hundred dollars in savings, or he no longer had other mouths to feed.

Once his writer's brain got a taste of writing he could not turn himself off. He immediately plunged into a twenty-thousand-word serial for *Youth's Companion*, making the chapter lengths conform to those in serials he had read in that magazine at the library. Before he realized what he was doing he had dashed off seven of the Alaskan stories that were formulated in his mind. He had opened the floodgates but the slightest crack and was being overcome by the torrent.

No appointment came from the post office. The *Examiner* not only did not send him the ten dollars, but did not even acknowledge receipt of the manuscript. Left without a coin with which to buy food, Jack pawned the bicycle Eliza had given him to ride to Oakland High; when the landlord said pay or get out, he pawned the watch Eliza's husband had given him as a gift, then the mackintosh John London had left him as his sole legacy. When a former waterfront comrade came along with a dress suit wrapped in newspapers, for the possession of which he had no convincing explanation, Jack swapped him some Alaskan souvenirs for it and pawned the dress suit for five dollars, spending the better part of it for stamps and envelopes to send his mounting manuscripts to the magazines. He still had no idea that he was becoming a professional writer; he was simply a man in desperate straits, unable to find work, utilizing his lone talent in a wild effort to earn food money until he was appointed to the civil service.

Winter came on. He was still wearing his light-weight summer suit. The grocer on one corner allowed him credit up to four dollars, and then was adamant; the butcher on the other corner went as high as five dollars before shutting down. Faithful Eliza brought to the London house whatever food she could spare from her own table, and gave Jack enough change to supply him with writing paper and the smoking tobacco without which he could not exist. Jack lost weight, hollows appeared in his cheeks, he became nervous and jumpy, and would no longer have been a bargain in the labor market. Once a week he had an opportunity to eat a hearty meat meal at Mabel's, but with an effort he restrained himself at table so that the girl he loved might not know how hungry he was. Yet his hopes were bright because he remembered that the magazines paid ten dollars per thousand words, and the stories and articles he had sent out ran from four to twenty thousand words, the sale of any one of which would rescue the family. Always in the back of his mind, holding him up as a tentpole holds up a tent, was the hope that maybe he would have several stories accepted. Then he would see his way clear to earn a living from his literary work; he would not be forced by the exigencies of circumstance to become a postman. He did not ask for great rewards or a deal of money; the most he hoped to earn from his work was ten dollars a thousand words, which, even if he sold every line he wrote, could not bring him more than three hundred dollars a month, and more than likely would bring about one hundred and fifty dollars.

He became so immersed in his stories, fighting for that one slim chance of an acceptance, that he found it difficult to stop his writing to mow a lawn or beat a carpet. The family fell into miserable straits; only because Flora was a tough and wiry woman with a twenty-year training in intermittent starvation was she able to stand the privation. Jack became weak and then ill from lack of nourishment. He was so shabby and distrait that he gave up the one evening a week he had been spending with Mabel. At the end of his tether, he was willing to take back the coal-passer's job at thirty dollars a month. As the days passed and he became sicker in body and mind, not only over the starvation but over the uncertainty of his future, his thoughts turned once again to self-destruction, as they had the night he had fallen off the Benicia pier, and when he had grown melancholy on The Road. He says that if he had not been unwilling to desert Flora and little Johnny, the chances were in favor of his suicide. Frank Atherton, Jack's boyhood chum, reports, "Jack penned farewell letters. There came a friend to say good-bye, who had also decided to end it all." Jack's arguments in dissuading his friend from suicide were evidently so eloquent that he convinced himself as well.

Then one cheerless morning toward the end of November he received a thin, oblong envelope from the *Overland Monthly,* a literary magazine with a national reputation that had been founded in San Francisco by Bret Harte in 1868. It was an acceptance of one of his Alaskan stories! He had sent them "To the Man on Trail," and they were publishing it! Like lightning his mind calculated figures . . . the manuscript was five thousand words . . . they paid ten dollars a thousand . . . the enclosed check was for fifty dollars . . . he was rescued! . . . he would be able to go on writing. He sank down on the edge of his bed and with trembling fingers tore open the envelope just as his trembling imagination was tearing open the bright vistas of the future.

There was no check. There was only a formal note from the editor saying that he found the story "available," and would pay five dollars for it upon publication. Five dollars for a manuscript that had taken five days to write! The same old dollar a day he had earned as a laborer in the cannery, the jute mill, the electric plant, the laundry. His eyes glazed, his mind stunned, his body too weak to move, he sat there shivering. He had been a credulous fool. He had been duped. He had believed a Sunday supplement article. The magazines didn't pay the fair wage of a penny a word; they paid a penny for ten words. No man could subsist on that rate of pay, let alone support a family. Even if he wrote great masterpieces, and sold everything that came from his thick, scrawling pencil, there was no hope for him. Only the rich could afford to be writers; he would have to crawl back to the lawnmower and the rug-beater, hang on somehow until the post-office appointment came through.

That very afternoon, by a coincidence that Jack's life could get away with but his fiction never, he received another thin, oblong envelope, this time from a magazine in the East called *The Black Cat*, to which he had sent a story written in that brief, hectic period between the University of California and the Belmont Academy steam laundry. *The Black Cat* was owned and edited by a man by the name of Umbstaetter who had done a great deal to encourage young American writers. Umbstaetter wrote Jack that his story was "more lengthy than strengthy," but if Jack would give him permission to cut the four-thousand-word manuscript in half, Umbstaetter would promptly send him a check for forty dollars.

Give permission! It was equivalent to twenty dollars a thousand words, or double the rate he had believed. He hadn't been duped. He hadn't been a fool. He would be able to earn a living for his family by doing the kind of work he loved. He wrote Umbstaetter that he could cut the story in two halves if only he would send the money along. Umbstaetter sent the forty dollars by return mail. And that, says Jack, is precisely how and why he stayed by the writing game.

He went to the pawnbroker and took his bicycle, watch, and mackintosh out of hock. He paid the grocer his four dollars, the butcher his five dollars. He stocked the house with food, paid twelve dollars for two months' rent, bought a second-hand winter suit, some typewriter paper, and a sheaf of pencils, and rented a typewriter. That night he put up a picnic lunch in Flora's kitchen, and the next morning called for Mabel Applegarth. Side by side they rode through Oakland on their bicycles, then climbed to their favorite knoll in the Berkeley hills. It was a clear, beautiful day with hazy sun and wandering whisps of breeze. Filmy purple mists that were fabrics woven of color hid in the recesses of the hills. San Francisco lay like a blur of smoke upon her heights. The intervening bay was a dull sheen of molten metal whereupon sailing craft lay motionless or drifted with the lazy tide. Far Mount Tamalpais, barely seen in the silver haze, bulked by the Golden Gate, beyond which the Pacific was raising on its skyline tumbled cloud masses that swept landward.

Here, lying in the deep grass by the side of the first woman he had ever loved, he told Mabel of his acceptances by the *Overland Monthly* and *The Black Cat*. Remembering how far Jack had come in three short years, Mabel cried out her joy and happiness for him. Jack's arm began to steal behind her and around her, and drew her to him slowly and caressingly. She put a hand on either side of his warm, sunburned neck; his strength seemed to pour into her fragile body.

Mabel Applegarth was the complete antithesis of Jack London. Where he was robust, she was frail. Where he flouted convention, she lived by it. Where he had been exposed to the hardship and cruelty of a man's world, she had been carefully nurtured and protected. Where he broke the rules, she obeyed them. Where he was boisterous, teeming with vitality, she was quiet, retiring. Where he was controlled by no man, she was completely under the dominance of her mother, a selfish, dictatorial woman who controlled her daughter's every move. Jack knew that Mrs. Applegarth had high aspirations for Mabel, that she intended marrying her to a man with wealth in order to recoup the family fortune which Mr. Applegarth had brought over from England and invested in a land colonization scheme that had failed.

Jack had no fear of Mrs. Applegarth. At worst she could be no more difficult to manage than the unreefed *Reindeer*, the wheel of the *Sophie Sutherland* during a storm, the blinds of the Overland Express, or White Horse Rapids.

Munching the thick sandwiches he had put up the night before, the sweethearts agreed that they should be engaged for a year, at the end of which time Jack would have established himself so solidly that they would be able to marry. They would open a little home of their own where they would have shelves of books and paintings on the walls and a piano for Mabel to play and sing to him, and a workroom where he would write gripping short stories and novels, and his wife would correct his manuscripts for occasional errors in grammar; they would make a good living and have intelligent, amusing friends, and raise children and travel and be very, very happy. They sat on through the passing glory of the day, marveling at the wonder of love and at destiny that had flung them so strangely together. The cloud masses on the western horizon received the descending sun and the circle of the sky turned to rose. Holding herself in his arms Mabel softly sang "Good-Bye, Sweet Day." When she had finished he kissed her again, and hand in hand, their fates entrusted to each other, they wandered down the hills and rode their bicycles back to Oakland.

Jack had exactly two dollars left out of his forty dollars from *The Black Cat*. This he invested in stamps to send out the manuscripts the Eastern magazines had returned and he had tossed under his table because there was no postage with which to send them out again. Once more he plunged into his writing, mailing the manuscripts as soon as he had finished typing them. But it had been a false dawn. His stories came back with standard rejection slips. The food slowly disappeared from Flora's shelves. The watch, bicycle, mackintosh, and finally the warm winter suit went back into pawn. The magazines might pay a penny a word, or a dollar a word; what good did it do him when he couldn't even sell a sentence?

On the sixteenth of January, 1899, a letter summoned him to work at the post office. The job would be steady, would last all the days of his life. It paid sixty-five dollars a month. He could have plenty to eat, a suit of clothes that was new instead of second-hand, a luxury the twenty-three-year-old boy had not yet attained. He would be able to buy the books and magazines for which he was starved. He would be able to take care of Flora and little Johnny, and if Mabel would be willing to move in with his family for a time, they could be married at once.

Jack and Flora faced the situation squarely. If he continued with his writing they would have to suffer more years of hardship. But if he became a postman what would be the good of his plentiful food and new clothes and books and magazines? He had not been put on earth merely to feed and clothe his body and amuse his mind; he had been put here to create, to contribute great stories to literature. He would be able to endure the privations of the artist because he would be taking a primal ecstasy from his work which would make all other possible pleasures, such as eating and possessing material objects, seem dull and inconsequential. But what would there be to sustain Flora? If she had made a scene, staged a heart attack, cried, or pleaded, Jack might have gone down to the post office and taken the job. But this mother who had borne him out of wedlock, deprived him of love and tenderness, made poverty, bitterness, and chaos the portion of his youth, now firmly told him that he must go on with his stories, that he had it in him to succeed, and that she would stand by no matter how long it took. For if Jack became a successful writer, Flora Wellman, black sheep of the Wellman family of Massillon, would be vindicated.

Now that the decision was irrevocable Jack tackled his job with all the impetuous fire and ardor of his resolute nature. In order to become a writer there were two things he had to acquire: knowledge and the ability to write. He knew that if he thought clearly he would write clearly, for if he were badly educated, if his thoughts were confused and jumbled how could he expect a lucid utterance? And if his thoughts were worthy so would his writing be worthy. He knew that he must have his hand on the inner pulse of life, that the sum of his working knowledge would be the *working philosophy* by which he would measure, weigh, balance, and interpret the world. He felt that he had to educate himself in history, biology, evolution, economics, and a hundred other important branches of learning because they would broaden his thought, lengthen his vistas, drive back the bounds of the field in which he was to work. They would give him a working philosophy which would be like unto no other man's and force him to original thinking, provide him with something new and vital for the jaded ear of the world. He had no intention of writing trivia, of administering chocolate-coated pills to constipated minds.

And so he went direct to the books and laid siege to the citadel of their wisdom. He was no college boy cramming sufficient facts to pass an examination, no casual passerby warming his hands at the great fires of knowledge. He was a passionate wooer and to him every new fact learned, every new theory absorbed, every old concept challenged and new concept gained was a personal victory, a cause for rejoicing. He questioned, selected, rejected, submitting everything he read to a searching analysis. He was not blinded or awed by reputations. Great minds made no impression upon him unless they could present him with great ideas. Conventional thinking meant little to this man who had broken every convention he had met; an image-breaker himself, iconoclastic thinking on the part of others did not frighten or repulse him. He was honest, he was courageous, he could think straight, and he had a profound love for truth, four indispensables for the scholar.

Though he was short on education he had the feeling that he was a natural student. Education seemed to him like a chartroom. He had no fear of unknown books, he knew that he didn't get lost easily, and he had already spent enough time in it to know what coasts he wanted to explore. When he met a book he used no delicate pick covertly to pry open its lock and steal the contents. Jack London about to tackle a new volume upon which he had stumbled in a wilderness trail was like an abysmal brute, a starving wolf poised to spring. He sank his teeth into the throat of the book, shook it fiercely until it was subdued, then lapped up its blood, devoured its flesh, and crunched its bones until every fiber and muscle of that book was part of him, feeding him its strength.

He went back to the father of economics, Adam Smith, and read *The Wealth of Nations,* then worked forward through Malthus's *Theory of Population,* Ricardi's *Theory of Distribution,* Bastiat's *Theory of Economic Harmonies,* the early German theories of value and marginal productivity, John Stuart Mill's *Shares in Distribution* . . . straight down through the historical corollaries until he came to the founders of scientific socialism and was on familiar ground. For his science of politics he went back to Aristotle, followed Gibbon through the rise and fall of the Roman Empire, traced the conflict between Church and State in the Middle Ages, the influences of Luther and Calvin on the Reformation political structure, to the beginning of modern political conceptions in the books of the Englishmen Hobbes, Locke, Hume, Mill; the emergence of the republican form of government to meet the needs of the Industrial Revolution. In metaphysics he read Hegel, Kant, Berkeley, Leibnitz. In anthropology he read Boas and Frazer, in biology he had already read Darwin, Huxley, Wallace, and went back to them with greater understanding. He consumed all the books he could find on sociology: unemployment, business cycles and depressions, the causes and cures of poverty, slum conditions, criminology, charity; burrowed deeper and deeper into trade unionism.

He made careful notes on everything he read, and started a card-catalogue system so that he could lay his hands on his material when he wanted it. But it was not until he struck Herbert Spencer's *First Principles* that he found his long-sought method of correlating the varied trends of thought he had assimilated into a working philosophy. His meeting with the mind of Herbert Spencer was perhaps the greatest single adventure in a life fraught with adventures. One night, after long study-bouts with William James and Francis Bacon, and after writing a sonnet as a night-cap, he crawled into bed with a copy of *First Principles*. Morning found him still reading. He continued reading all the next day, abandoning the bed for the floor when his body tired. He perceived that he had been merely skimming over the surface of things, observing detached phenomena, accumulating fragments, making superficial generalizations, with everything unrelated in a capricious and disorderly world of whim and chance. Here was the man Spencer organizing all knowledge for him, reducing everything to a unity, presenting to his startled gaze a universe so concrete of realization that it looked like the model of a ship that sailors made and put into glass bottles. There was no caprice; everything was inescapable law. Jack was more thrilled by this discovery than he had been at the discovery of gold on Henderson Creek, for he knew that Spencer's monism could never turn out to be mica.

Herbert Spencer made him drunk with comprehension. All the hidden phenomena were laying their secrets bare. In the meat on his plate that night at dinner he saw the shining sun and traced its energy back through all the transformations to its source a hundred million miles away, traced its energy ahead to the moving muscles in his arms that enabled him to cut the meat, and the brain wherewith he willed the muscles to cut the meat, until with inward gaze he saw the sun shining in his brain, both made of the same substance, both part of each other. Herbert Spencer had shown him that all things were related to all other things from the farthermost stars in the waste of space to the myriads of atoms in the grain of sand under one's foot, and that mankind, man the individual, was just another form of squirming, proto-plasmic matter.

Jack's four intellectual grandparents were Darwin, Spencer, Marx, and Nietzsche. His working philosophy, German and English, stemmed directly from these four great minds of the nineteenth century. In 1899 it took intestinal fortitude to read these bitterly attacked and maligned revolutionaries; it also took clarity, intelligence, and penetration to understand them. Jack had the requisite courage and the intelligence; his four masters enriched his life and philosophy. They deepened his healthy skepticism, his love of truth for its own sake, swept away the mental garbage of the Dark Ages, and gave him a ruthless scientific method for the pursuit of knowledge. In his turn, Jack was to dramatize and pass on their teachings.

Frederick Nietzsche had perhaps the greatest emotional effect upon Jack because their experiences were more closely akin. Exposed as he had been to the horrors of spiritualism during his childhood, just as Nietzsche, as a clergyman's son, had been exposed to excesses of piousness, Jack revolted against all manifestations of religion, belief in supernatural powers, in a life after death, and a God-controlled universe. "I believe that with my death I am just as much obliterated as the last mosquito you or I smashed." He believed the entire Christian religion to be a mass of empty ritual and incredible fact. He was convinced that religion, any and all religion, was mankind's greatest enemy because it anesthetized the brain, doped it with dogma, made men accept blindly instead of thinking for themselves, kept them from asserting themselves as masters of the earth upon which they trod, and hence from bettering their lives. In Nietzsche, Jack found justification for everything he felt about the shams, hypocrisy, and falsity of religion, stated with such brilliance that he was certain Nietzsche had dug a grave for Christianity.

In Nietzsche too he discovered the theory of the superman who was bigger and stronger and wiser than all his fellows, who could conquer all obstacles and rule the slave mass. Jack found the philosophy of the superman much to his taste, because he conceived of himself as a superman, able to conquer all obstacles, a giant who would end by ruling (teaching, leading, directing) the masses. The fact that his philosophy of the reign of the superman over the slave masses made Nietzsche detest socialism as a government of the weak and inefficient, and led him to cry down trade unions as making the workers dissatisfied with their lot, did not seem to disturb Jack. He was going to believe in the superman and socialism at one and the same time, even if they were mutually exclusive. All his life he remained an individualist and a socialist; he wanted individualism for himself because he was a superman, a blond-beast who could conquer . . . and socialism for the masses who were weak and needed protection. For a number of years he was to be successful in riding these two intellectual horses, each of which was pulling in an opposite direction.

In addition to becoming learned, Jack had on hand the more immediate and prosaic problem of earning a living. He spent long hours in the free reading-room of the library critically studying the current magazines, comparing the stories to those that were tumbling off his own typewriter, wondering what secret trick had enabled them to sell. He was amazed at the enormous amount of printed stuff that was dead: no light, no life, no color shot through it. He was puzzled by the countless short stories written lightly and cleverly but without vitality or realism. Life was so strange and wonderful, filled with an immensity of problems, dreams, and heroic toils, yet these printed fabrications dealt with the sentimental commonplaces. He felt the stress and strain of life, its fevers and sweats and wild insurgences—surely this was the stuff to write about! He wanted to glorify the leaders of forlorn hopes, the mad lovers, the giants who fought under stress and strain, amid terror and tragedy, making life crackle with the strength of their endeavors. These magazine writers, typified by Richard Harding Davis (*Soldiers of Fortune, Princess Aline*), George Barr McCutcheon (*Graustark*), Stanley Weyman (*Gentleman of France, Under The Red Robe*), Margaret Deland (*John Ward, Preacher*), Clara Louise Burnham (*Doctor Latimer, Wise Woman*), seemed afraid of real life, of its profounder truths and realities. They prettified, evaded, threw a spurious veil of romance over their characters, avoiding anything that cut deep.

The dominant reason for this attitude, he decided after a searching analysis, was fear: fear of shocking or displeasing their editors, fear of alienating their Mid-West public; fear of antagonizing the newspapers, the vested interests, the capitalist-controlled pulpit and educational system; fear of the vigorous, the brutally true; above all fear of the unpleasant. They were stodgy and puny, these fictionizers, with no guts in their bellies or genitals between their legs. They had no originality, no working philosophy, no true knowledge; all they had was a formula for saccharine romance. They were impoverished minds impoverishing literature. He recognized them to be pigmies; only giants dared cross swords with authentic literature. He would make the editors and the public accept him on his own ground.

He turned to the writers whom he judged had truly blazed their own trails: Scott, Dickens, Poe, Kipling, George Eliot, Whitman, Stevenson, Stephen Crane. He burrowed into what he named the triumvirate of geniuses, Shakespeare, Goethe, and Balzac. From Spencer, Darwin, Marx, and Nietzsche he had learned how to think; from his literary parents, Kipling and Stevenson, he learned how to write. He felt that now that he had a working philosophy of scientific determinism with which to focus the characters he drew, and a lucidity of literary expression for the thoughts he uttered, his work would be sane, fresh, and true.

To Jack one of the greatest things in the world was words, beautiful words, musical words, strong and sharp and incisive words. He read the heavy and learned tomes always with a dictionary at hand, wrote down words on sheets of paper and stuck the sheets into the crack between the wood and mirror of his bureau where he could memorize them while he shaved and dressed; he strung lists of them on a clothesline with clothespins so that every time he looked up or crossed the room he could see the new words and their meanings. He carried lists of them in every pocket, read them while he walked to the library or to Mabel's, mumbled them as he sat over his food or prepared for sleep. When the need came in a story for a precise word, and out of the hundreds of lists sprang the one with the exact shade of meaning, he was thrillled to the core of his being.

But how could he get his stories past the stone barricade of editors who protected their genteel publics from the onslaughts of barbarians from the West? There was no one to help him, to give him a word of advice. He did not know an editor or writer or anyone who had ever attempted to write. He was fighting the battle alone, in the dark, with nothing but his strength, his determination, his convictions, and his feel for narrative to sustain him. He poured his soul into his stories and articles, folded them just so, put the proper amount of stamps inside the long envelope, sealed it, put more stamps on the outside and dropped it into a mailbox. It traveled across the continent and after a lapse of time the postman returned it. He was convinced that there was no human editor at the other end but a cunning arrangement of cogs that changed the manuscript from one envelope to another and stuck on the stamps.

Time! Time! was his unending plaint, time to learn, to master his craft before the lack of money for food and rent destroyed him. There weren't enough hours in the day to do all the things he wanted. It was with regret that he tore himself away from his writing to study, with regret that he tore away from serious study to go to the library and read the magazines, with regret that he left the reading-room to go to Mabel's for the only hour of recreation he permitted himself. Hardest of all was to put aside his books and pencil and close his burning eyes for sleep. In his great passion he limited himself to five hours' sleep a night. He hated the thought of ceasing to live even for so short a time; his sole consolation was that the alarm clock was set for five hours ahead, the jangling bell would jerk him out of unconsciousness, and he would have before him another glorious nineteen hours of work. He was a soul enchanted, a soul inflamed.

At last, in January, "To the Man on Trail" was published in the *Overland Monthly.* It was Jack's début as a professional writer. The editor had not only failed to send him the five dollars promised on publication, but did not even bother to mail him a copy of the magazine. Jack stood in front of a newsstand on Broadway gazing wistfully, for he did not have ten cents in his pocket with which to buy a copy and see how his story looked in print. He walked uptown to the Applegarth house, borrowed a dime from Edward, walked downtown again . . . and bought his copy.

The Oakland newsdealers quickly sold out their supply of the *Overland Monthly,* for Jack's friends in the Henry Clay Society had spread the good word. One of the Oakland newspapers, which had mocked and ridiculed him as the Boy Socialist, now ran a respectful and proud little article about Mr. Jack London, the Boy Author, having a story published in the venerable *Overland Monthly.* Though Jack was in the grip of destitution, still dressed in oddly matched second-hand clothes and living on forced-march rations, he felt a decided change in the attitude of the people about him; if he really were going to succeed as a writer, then they would have to forgive him his eccentricities of dress and manner and thought.

"To the Man on Trail" is not the best of Jack's Alaskan tales, for the emphasis is more on plot than characterization of nature. Yet from the moment Malemute Kid rises with cup in hand, glances at the greased-paper window where the frost stands three inches thick, and cries: "A health to the man on trail this night; may his grub hold out, may his dogs keep their legs; may his matches never miss fire," the reader, gripped and rushed headlong to the end of the story, is aware that a new, youthful, and vigorous voice has arisen in American letters.

The *Overland Monthly* had offered him the princely sum of seven dollars and a half for any additional stories they might buy; in spite of the fact that they had not yet sent him the five dollars for the first story, Jack mailed them "The White Silence," which they promptly accepted and published in their February issue. Jack felt the story to be one of his best, and that he ought to get at least fifty dollars for it, but he was prompted to let it go for the dubious seven-fifty for a number of reasons: he hoped that the critics and magazines editors of the East would see the story and be struck by it; he wanted to keep justifying his work to Mabel; and the seven-fifty, if he could collect it, would feed his family roughly for a month.

"To the Man on Trail" had led Oakland to suspect that Jack London might become a successful author. "The White Silence," one of our imperishable classics of the frozen country, made them realize that he could write. The story, told with tenderness, depth of feeling, and magnificent imagery, brings one pity and terror and that exultation which can be realized only through experiencing a perfectly conceived art form. Jack had been reading and copying hundreds of poems into his notebooks; he had been writing them every day for facility of expression and because words sang in his brain the same way that musical notes sing in a composer's brain. In "The White Silence" he proves that he is what we least would have expected from a boy of his background: a true poet. "Nature has many tricks wherewith she convinces man of his finity—the ceaseless flow of the tides, the fury of the storm, the shock of the earthquake—but the most tremendous, the most stupefying of all is the passive phase of the White Silence. All movement ceases, the sky clears, the heavens are as brass; the slightest whisper seems as sacrilege and man becomes timid, affronted at the sound of his own voice. Sole speck of life journeying across the ghostly wastes of a dead world, he trembles at his audacity, realizes that his is a maggot's life, nothing more. Strange thoughts arise unsummoned, and the mystery of all things strives for utterance."

Jack believed that dig could move more mountains than faith ever dreamed of. He set himself a quota of fifteen hundred words a day, refusing to stop work until he had set them down in his undisciplined scrawl and had transferred them to the typewriter. He wrote everything in his mind before setting it down on paper, after which nothing could persuade him to make changes other than the substitution of a word or two. With the bicycle, watch, mackintosh, and winter suit in hock again, whole weeks passed in which the family subsisted on beans and potatoes, the diet relieved only when Eliza brought them food from her own table. In desperation Jack began writing triolets and jokes, hoping to earn a dollar from the humorous magazines.

Twice more that spring the Oakland post office summoned him to work, once when there was not a five-cent piece or a slice of bread in the house. He borrowed ferry fare from Eliza, buckled on his fighting armor, and rode across the Bay to the office of the *Overland Monthly* which had ignored his pleading letters and re-fused to send him the five dollars for "To the Man on Trail" or the seven-fifty for "The White Silence." The moment he entered the office he realized that it was not the prosperous magazine of national importance he had imagined. It was on its last legs finan-cially, being kept alive to support the assistant editor and business manager, Roscoe Eames and Edward Payne, who were to move into Jack's life through this chance meeting and were never to move out again. Eames and Payne were delighted to meet Jack London; they saluted his genius in glowing terms . . . and prom-ised to mail him five dollars the very first thing in the morning. Only the threat of physical violence from the starved author brought forth five dollars in small change from the pockets of the two literary gentlemen.

Sunk in the middle of a crater of debts, Jack's family lived off that five dollars for the month of March. The *Overland Monthly* asked for another story for their April issue; Jack refused to supply it until they remitted for "The White Silence." After consid-erably more dunning they paid, and he sent them "The Son of the Wolf." In April he also had published one of his humorous triolets, "He Chortled with Glee," in San Francisco's *Town Topics*. Flora and Jack were so harassed by their creditors and landlord that he offered to sell five-thousand-word stories for a dollar, anything to get a few cents in his pocket. Though his confidence was being sustained by the work he was doing, there were periods when he suffered severe nervous attacks; all the uncertainties buried deep in his system would rise to tell him that the odds were too great, that he could never succeed.

May was his first big month. *Town Topics* published a poem, "If I Were God One Hour," the *Overland Monthly* ran the fourth of his Alaskan tales, "The Men of Forty Mile," a lusty yarn, estimable for its rough Irish fighting and humor, *Orange Judd Farmer* ran "On Furlough," and Mr. Umbstaetter of *The Black Cat* finally printed "A Thousand Deaths." Jack sat in his cramped, poorly lighted bedroom with the four magazines opened at his contributions, running fingers like a comb through his tousled hair, his gray-blue eyes sparkling with happiness. What did it matter if the house were cold from lack of heat, the larder empty, if his cheeks were sunken and his clothes so shabby that he no longer dared go into the Applegarth home for fear Mabel's mother would see his destitution? He and Flora had a long tradition of starvation; they were sinewy people who could endure on it where softer families would be destroyed. The steel of his character had been tempered by hard usage; he had goaded himself into laughing in the teeth of incredible hardship and dangers as a boy. Should he as a grownup be any the less a Viking? He had set himself the most difficult task that any man could conceive; all the more reason, then, to conquer it, for no adversary less than the most formidable of all adversaries did he deem worthy of his prowess. As a boy he had forced himself to invite and enjoy danger, yet it had not been an unnatural forcing. He was in the true sense of the term a brave man, even if he sometimes did have to romanticize that bravery. Or so he told himself as he sat over his month's literary haul in the hummingwall silence of his bedroom, a man alone with his work.

June saw him published in an Eastern newspaper, the Buffalo *Express* printing "From Dawson to the Sea," the account of his nineteen-hundred-mile trip down the Yukon in the open boat. *Home Magazine* ran his "Through the Rapids on the Way to Klondike," and the *Overland Monthly* continued its Alaskan series with "In a Far Country." However, he had to wait until July to achieve really professional status, for in this month he had stories and articles appearing in five periodicals, a miracle for a twenty-three-year-old who had been writing for only nine months. The *American Journal of Education* published two of his articles on language and the use of verbs, indicating how far he had come in his self-education, while *The Owl, Overland Monthly*, and Tillotson Syndicate released short stories.

Finding this gala month as much a cause for celebration as the sale of his first two stories, Jack took his bicycle out of pawn, called for Mabel, and rode with her into the hills. This time when he laid his triumphs at her feet he noticed that his sweetheart seemed sad. In answer to her direct question he confessed that all five of the sales had netted him only ten dollars in cash, with the possibility of another seven dollars and a half from the *Overland Monthly*, which still owed him for two back stories. Mabel broke down and wept with her head in his lap. The year of their engagement was already half over, and to Mabel's mind Jack's lean earnings from his successful stories only proved that they could never marry or live on his income as a writer. She herself would have been willing to share his poverty, but Mrs. Applegarth had made it forcefully clear that she could not marry Jack until he was making a substantial living.

Jack had brought along a number of his new manuscripts, which he read to her eagerly to prove that it was only a matter of time before the rich Eastern magazines would begin buying. In the face of his booming confidence that his work was true and strong, that it was unlike anything being written in America, Mabel at last garnered the courage to tell him that she did not like it, that the stories were crude, indelicate, bestial in their depiction of raw life, suffering, and death . . . and that the public would never accept them. She loved him more than ever . . . she flung her arms about his neck and kissed him warmly to prove it . . . she would always love him . . . she would marry him right away . . . only wouldn't he be sensible and take a position in the post office . . . or try to get a steady job as a reporter on a newspaper?

Jack was saddened by Mabel's lack of faith in his work, but it did not lessen his love for her. Like the hothouse editors in the East, she had been bred in a genteel and anemic tradition. Well, he'd show them. He'd blast them out of their complacency! He'd teach them what a short story really was!

He returned to his rough wooden table, rolled himself an unending line of bumpy cigarettes, and dug in harder than ever. He wrote blistering articles about the Class War on the same typewriter ribbon with adventure stories for children; gripping tales of death and heroic struggles against fate in the frozen North on the same notepaper with jokes for *Town Topics*. He attacked his books with renewed vigor, making copious notes on war, international trade, graft in government and the courts, the wastes of competitive industry, strikes, boycotts, the woman's suffrage movement, criminology, modern medicine, the progress of engineering and modern science, building file after file of material into his own well-organized reference library. No day passed with less than sixteen hours of study and writing; whenever his physical condition permitted he forced himself to work for nineteen hours, and seven days a week. *Dig can move more mountains than faith ever dreamed of.*

During the months of intense application he had had little time for friends or social activity. Mabel and her mother had moved to San José, a small town in the Santa Clara Valley. Now he began to feel that he had cut himself off from people too much; one of the first needs of his nature was for genial and interesting companionship. When the newly formed Ruskin Club, composed of the cream of the Bay area liberals and intellectuals, invited him to join, he accepted with enthusiasm. A few nights later he went unannounced to a meeting of the Socialist Local, where he was given a noisy and heartwarming reception. Urged to speak to the members, Jack walked up to the platform and talked about "The Question of the Maximum," in which he tried to show that when capitalism reaches its maximum development it must inevitably become socialized. He had written an article on the subject only a week before. "The Question of the Maximum," which was bought by an Eastern magazine but never published, established Jack as an economist, for it showed not only a complete grasp of the economic interpretation of history, but indicated the extent of his research in international political economy.

Pleased by the way the Local received his talk, Jack agreed to give several Sunday night lectures in the educational series it was proposing. After his first Sunday talk he was amazed to find the Oakland press writing up his remarks in a serious, friendly fashion. Socialism and Jack London had become respectable together!

In September, October, and November Jack cracked three new magazines—*Conkeys*, *The Editor*, and *Youth's Companion*. His friends in the Ruskin Club and the Socialist Local considered him a successful writer. Sundays when he wasn't lecturing at the Socialist Local he bicycled the forty miles to San José to visit with Mabel; during the week he spent several evenings at meetings, lectures, and discussions. In the company of Jim Whitaker, a Canadian pioneer turned novelist, and Strawn-Hamilton, he rode across the Bay one night to hear Austin Lewis lecture on socialism at the Turk Street Temple. Here he met Anna Strunsky, an ardent socialist whom Jack described as an emotional genius. She was doubtless the most brilliant woman he was to encounter.

Anna Strunsky, a student at Stanford University, was a shy, slender, sensitive girl with dark brown eyes and curly black hair. She came from one of the pioneer families of San Francisco, her parents' home being an outstanding cultural center of the city. Miss Strunsky writes that Jack was pointed out to her as a comrade who spoke on the streets of Oakland and who earned his living writing stories. When she was introduced to him after the lecture, she says that it was as though she were meeting in their youth Lassalle, Marx, or Byron, so instantly did she feel that she was in the presence of a historical character. Objectively she says that she confronted a young man with large blue eyes fringed with dark lashes, and a beautiful mouth which, opening in its ready laugh, revealed an absence of front teeth. The brow, the nose, the contour of the cheeks, the massive throat were Greek. His body gave the impression of grace and athletic strength. He was dressed in gray and was wearing a soft white shirt with color attached, and black necktie.

Between Jack London and Anna Strunsky there began a tempestuous friendship fraught with terrific arguments on affairs so-

cial, economic, and feminine. Jack shocked Miss Strunsky by telling her that although he was a socialist he was going to beat the
capitalists at their own game. People thought that socialists were
failures, weaklings, and incompetents, but he was going to prove
that a socialist could succeed with the best of them, and by so
doing he would be serving a propagandistic service to The Cause.
Miss Strunsky was repelled by this dream of his, and warned him
that real socialists would be incapable of harboring it; to pile up
wealth and success—surely anybody who was a beneficiary of the
Old Order must belong to it to some extent in spirit and fact?
Jack laughed good-naturedly and replied that the Eastern editors
who were starving him now would pay handsomely for stories
when they wanted them later; that he was going to extract every
last dollar from capitalism he could get.

Aside from family debts and money worries Jack was now enjoying his life. He was earning between ten and fifteen dollars a
month; he was being published in a slowly widening circle of magazines; he liked to write, to think, to study, to correlate, to understand. On Sunday nights he lectured to the Socialist Local on
such subjects as "The Expansionist Policy"; he went to dinners
given by the Ruskin Club, where he now numbered among his
friends young instructors from the University of California, professional men, the new Oakland librarian, who had replaced his
old friend and inspirator, Ina Coolbrith. Week-ends he spent as
the guest of the Applegarths in San José, reading his new manuscripts to Mabel, weighing her criticisms, stealing a few lover's
kisses as they picnicked in the woods or sat on the Applegarth
sofa. Completely as he loved Mabel, he never tried to fit her into
his tumultuous life in Oakland. It was heresy even to think of her
in the smoke and din of a socialist meeting. No, she was the cool
goddess who remained above the strife and turmoil of the world;
after they were married she would be a gracious hostess to his less
rambunctious friends and argufiers, and when he returned from
his boisterous meetings, all excited and sweated up, her arms
would be a quiet harbor in which he could relax, be quiet, know
peace. She had the qualifications for a superman's wife.

At last, a short while before the end of the century, the big
break came for Jack London, as he inevitably knew it had to come
for all men who had "faith, dig, and talent." In the weeks just

passed he had written a long story called "An Odyssey of the North," which he had had the sheer presumption to send to Boston to the *Atlantic Monthly,* the most blue-blooded, stiff-necked, unapproachable literary magazine in the United States. By all precedent the *Atlantic Monthly* should have sent the manuscript back with a horrified little note. Instead Jack received one of those long, flat envelopes, the arrival of which suffocated him; the editor praised the story, asked him to cut three thousand words out of the opening sections, and offered to pay one hundred and twenty dollars for the publication rights. Once again Jack sank to the edge of his bed, trembling, his eyes glazed, as on that morning the thin envelope arrived from the *Overland Monthly.* A hundred and twenty dollars! Enough to lift the family debts, take his possessions out of pawn, fill the larder, pay the rent for six months in advance! With a terrific leap he sprang off the bed, flung open the door of his bedroom, ran to the kitchen, grabbed Flora, and spun her around with her feet in the air crying: "Mother, look! look! I did it! The *Atlantic Monthly* is publishing my big story. All the Eastern editors will see it. They'll want to buy, too. We're on our way up!"

Flora Wellman nodded her head and smiled grimly behind her narrow steel-rimmed spectacles as she kissed her only son.

Jack's predictions proved truer than even he had dared hope. The publishing firm of Houghton Mifflin, which was associated with the *Atlantic Monthly* in Boston, and had seen the manuscript of "An Odyssey of the North" and Jack's other Alaskan tales appearing in the *Overland Monthly,* agreed to bring out a volume of his short stories in the spring. Houghton Mifflin's first reader's report when they were considering publication of the group of short stories is probably the first professional criticism of a collection of Jack's work. "He uses the current slang of the mining camps a little too freely, in fact he is far from elegant, but his style has freshness, vigor, and strength. He draws a vivid picture of the terrors of cold, darkness, and starvation, the pleasures of human companionship in adverse circumstances, and the sterling qualities which the rough battle with nature brings out. The reader is convinced that the author has lived the life himself."

No longer would he have to accept seven dollars and a half for a short story, a seven dollars and a half he was having increasing difficulty dunning from the *Overland Monthly*. On December 21, 1899, the contract was signed, and Boston, stronghold of the English stranglehold on American culture, was pledged to sponsor a California-Alaska frontier revolution in literature. With a conservative Boston publishing house backing his radical innovations, his work had a chance for a fair hearing, it would be judged on its merits rather than its departures.

A few nights later Jack sat in his bedroom surrounded by his manuscripts, files, books, and notes for a hundred future stories. In a few hours the twentieth century would be born. He had the feeling that at midnight he too would be born; that he and the new century would be launched together.

A hundred years ago this night humanity had wandered shatter-brained in the miasmic fogs of the Dark Ages, conceiving the world to be preordained, unchangeable; credulously believing that the forms of government, economic structure, morality, religion, and all other aspects of life had been set forever in one unbreakable mold by the Lord God, not the slightest tenet of which might be tampered with or altered. Hegel, rebellious German philosopher, had broken up this rigid concept, which had been forced upon the unthinking mass by king and clergy. Out of the ignorance, the fear, the hypocrisy and sham also had arisen Darwin and Spencer to free mankind from the shackles of religion, and Karl Marx to supply a mechanism with which it might burst its bonds and create a civilization to fit its needs. A hundred years ago this night humanity had been slaves; one hundred years from this night would they be masters? They now had the means and the equipment with which to free themselves; the world could be anything and everything men wanted it to be; all they lacked was the will. He was determined to play his part in providing that collective will.

Quietly, reflectively, he made an estimate of himself, his work, his age, and his future. He had a strong gregarious instinct, he liked to rub against his own kind, yet in society he saw himself as a fish out of water. Because of his background he took to conventionality uneasily, rebelliously. He was used to saying what he thought, nothing more nor less. The hard hand of adversity, laid upon him at the age of ten, had left him sentiment but destroyed sentimentality. It had made him practical so that he was sometimes known as harsh, stern, and uncompromising; it had made him believe that reason was mightier than imagination, that the scientific man was superior to the emotional man. "Take me this way," he wrote to Anna Strunsky in the early days of their acquaintanceship, "a stray guest, a bird of passage splashing with salt-rimmed wings through a brief moment of your life—a rude blundering bird, used to large airs and great spaces, unaccustomed to the amenities of confined existence."

He had no patience with show or pretense. People had to take him as he was, or leave him alone. He wore a sweater most of the time, and paid calls in a bicycle suit. His friends passed the stage of being shocked, and no matter what he did, said, "It's only Jack." He catered to no one, played up to and sought favors from no man, yet he was loved and sought after because, as Anna Strunsky put it, "To know him was immediately to receive an accelerated enthusiasm about everybody." His words and laughter and attitudes vitalized those with whom he came in contact; his presence in a group brought that group sharply to life. He had an electric quality that sent a current through people, shocking them into wakefulness so that their bodies and brains came alive when he entered a room.

Perhaps the greatest passion of his life was for exact knowledge. "Give me the fact, man, the irrefragable fact!" is the motif that runs through all his days and all his work. He believed in the physical basis for life because he had seen the hypocrisy, fraud, and insanity behind the spiritual basis. He wanted scientific knowledge to replace unreasoning faith; only through accurate and penetrating reason could the God of the Dark Ages be taken off the backs of men, could He be dethroned and Mankind set up in His place. An agnostic, he worshipped no god but the human soul. He had learned how vile man could be, but he also had seen the mighty heights to which he could aspire. "How small man is, and how great he is!"

He demanded virility in a man, first and always. "A man who can take a blow or insult unmoved, without retaliating—paugh! I care not if he can voice the sublimest sentiments, I sicken." A man without courage was to him despicable. "Enemies! There is no necessity. Lick a man when it comes to the pinch, or he licks you, but never hold a grudge. Settle it once and for all, and forgive." He had an open-handed generosity with his friends; he gave himself to those he loved without reservation, did not abandon them when they hurt him or made mistakes. "I do not feel that because I condemn the deficiencies of my friends is any reason why I should not love them."

The backbone of his life was socialism. From his belief in the socialized state he derived strength, determination, and courage. He did not look for the regeneration of mankind in a day, nor did he think that men had to be born again before socialism could attain its ends. He would have liked socialism to filter through gradually, without open revolution or bloodshed, and he was eager to do his part in educating the masses to take over their own industry, natural resources, and government. But if the capitalists made this evolutionary process impossible then he was ready to fight at the barricades for The Cause. What new civilization had ever been born without a baptism of blood?

Organically related to his socialism was his philosophic adherence to a combination of Haeckel's monism, Spencer's materialistic determinism, and Darwin's evolution. "Nature has no sentiment, no charity, no mercy. We are puppets at the play of great unreasoning forces, yet we may come to know the laws of some of these forces and see our trend in relation to them. We are blind factors in the action of natural selection among the races of men. . . . I assert, with Bacon, that all human understanding arises from the world of sensations. I assert, with Locke, that all human ideas are due to the functions of the senses. I assert, with Laplace, that there is no need of a hypothesis of a creator. I assert, with Kant, the mechanical origin of the universe, and that creation is a natural and historical process."

In his writing he hoped to follow in the footsteps of his master, Kipling. "Kipling touches the soul of things. There is no end to him, simply no end. He has opened new frontiers of the mind and of literature." He announced his revolt against "that poor young American girl who mustn't be shocked or given anything less insipid than mare's milk." The decade in which he had matured, the last decade of the century, had been its low point, a period of sterility and vacuousness in which the forces of Victorianism had ossified into control. Literature was bounded on all four sides by a Mid-West morality; books and magazines were published for a public that considered Louisa May Alcott and Marie Corelli great writers. Original work was difficult to do, only respectable middle-class or rich people might be written about, virtue always had to be rewarded and vice condemned; American authors were commanded to write like Emerson, to see the pleasant side of life, to eschew the harsh, the grim, the sordid, the real. The American literary leaders were still the pleasantly poetic voices of Holmes, Whittier, Higginson, W. D. Howells, F. Marion Crawford, John Muir, Joel Chandler Harris, Joaquin Miller. American editors, who dwelt in the rarefied and chilly atmosphere of the high places, paid unheard-of prices for Barrie, Stevenson, Hardy, even went so far as to print the daring revelations (editorially castrated, of course) of Frenchmen and Russians, yet demanded of their American authors a repetition of the pseudo-romance formula with only a change in backdrop permitted.

A revolution was being carried on in Russia by Tolstoi and the realists; in France by Maupassant, Flaubert, Zola; in Norway by Ibsen; in Germany by Sudermann and Hauptmann. When he read the stories written by Americans, and compared them to the works of Hardy, Zola, Turgenev, he no longer wondered why on the Continent America was considered a nation of children and savages. The *Atlantic Monthly*, high priestess of American Letters, had been printing the fiction of Kate Douglas Wiggin and F. Hopkinson Smith. "It was all perfectly quiet and harmless, for it was thoroughly dead." Well, "An Odyssey of the North" would be out in a few days now; neither the *Atlantic Monthly* nor American fiction would be harmless and dead any longer. He determined to do for literature in his own country what Gorky was doing for the art form in Russia, Maupassant in France, and Kipling in England. He would take it out of the Henry James high society salon and place it in the kitchen of the mass of people where it might smell a little occasionally, but at least it would smell of life.

In American literature of the day the three unmentionables were atheism, socialism, and a woman's legs. He would play his part in destroying organized religion, in destroying organized capitalism, and in converting sex from something vile, ugly, and unmentionable into the scientific play of selective forces engaged in the perpetuation of the species. Nor did he intend to become a mere pamphleteer; he was above all a writer, a maker of literature. He would train himself to tell stories so adroitly that propaganda and art would be indissolubly wedded.

In order to accomplish his fourfold purpose he decided that he would have to make himself one of the best educated men of the dawning century. To calculate what kind of start he had in his Herculean task, he looked at the books spread out on his desk and bed, all of which he was in the process of studying and annotating. Yes, he was on the right track: Saint-Amand's *Revolution of 1848*; Brewster's *Studies in Structure and Style*; Jordan's *Footnotes to Evolution*; Tyrell's *Sub-Arctics*; Bohm-Bawerk's *Capital and Interest*; Oscar Wilde's *The Soul of Man under Socialism*; William Morris's *The Socialist Ideal—Art*; William Owen's *Coming Solidarity*.

The clock in his mother's room struck eleven. There was only one hour left to the perishing century. He asked himself what kind of century it had been, what it had left behind for America, the America that had started in 1800 as a group of loosely affiliated agricultural states, had spent its early decades pioneering in the wilderness, its middle decades developing machinery, factories, spanning the continent, its closing decades amassing the greatest wealth the world had ever known . . . and along with its wealth and technological progress had chained the mass to their machines and their poverty.

But the new century, ah! that would be a great time to be alive. The resources, the machines, the scientific skill would be made to serve mankind instead of enslaving it. The human brain would be educated in natural laws, taught to face the irrefragable fact instead of being anesthetized by a religion for the weak and a morality for morons. Literature and life would become synonymous. The true soul of man would emerge in his art and literature and music, niceties which the triple monster of frontier, religion, and capitalism had strangled in childbed.

What a magnificent America would his sons' sons see one hundred years from this night as they sat at their desks and surveyed the century that had just passed! It would be his fortune to help bring about that new America. He would cast off the shackles of the dark century now closing; he would refuse to wear the ugly high stiff collars that dug into men's flesh, and the ugly high stiff ideas that cut into their brain and made them miserable. He would turn his back on the antiquated ideology of the nineteenth century and resolutely face the twentieth, unafraid of what it might bring. He would be a modern man and a modern American. One hundred years from this night his sons and his sons' sons would think back to him with pride.

Flora's clock tolled midnight. The old century was gone. The new one was beginning. He sprang up from his desk, donned a turtle-necked sweater, put clasps about his trousers at the ankles, took out his bicycle, and pedaled the forty miles through the dark night to San José. What better way to begin the century than by marrying the girl he loved on its opening day? If his sons' sons and their sons were to think back to him with pride one hundred years from this night, then he had no time to lose!

5

MRS. APPLEGARTH had never wanted Jack for a son-in-law. She had not opposed the engagement too strenuously because she knew the marriage to be predicated on Jack's ability to support a wife by his writing, an eventuality of which she had little fear. When he walked into the cottage on the corner of Elm and Asbury Streets and showed Mabel and her mother his advance copy of "An Odyssey of the North" as a good omen of what a happy New Year it was going to be, Mrs. Applegarth changed her mind abruptly. Yes, she would consent to their being married, yes, that very day . . . on one condition. Jack either had to step into the Applegarth house in San José as its provider—Mr. Applegarth was dead, Edward no longer lived at home—or take his mother-in-law with them to Oakland and promise that he would never separate her from her daughter.

Jack, who only a few days before had written to a friend that "he already had a family to support, and that was hell for a young man," was less appalled at the prospect of taking on the responsibility of an entire second family than at the unmistakable manner in which Mrs. Applegarth had dug iron claws into her daughter. A scene ensued. Jack insisted that Mrs. Applegarth had no right to stand in the way of her daughter's happiness. Mrs. Applegarth informed Jack that Mabel was a dutiful child, that she was grateful for all her mother had done for her and would not abandon her in her old age—all this in spite of the known fact that Mrs. Applegarth was twice as strong as Mabel, that she had tyrannized the girl into playing nursemaid to her, and even now was demanding of her daughter that she serve her breakfast in bed.

Mabel sat between the two people she loved, pale and distraught, lashed by the mounting quarrel, unable to take sides. She always had been dominated by her mother, and that domination had taken root in the bone. This frail woman who was so weak that she could not lift her voice against her mother, had the astounding strength to sit silently as her life was being destroyed, as she watched her dreams of love, a husband, and children be shattered.

When Jack reached Oakland that night, thwarted and disconsolate, fresh troubles were added to his burden. Flora informed him that the last of the *Atlantic Monthly* money was spent. In the morning he rode the familiar route to the pawnbroker with John London's mackintosh on the handlebars of his bicycle; when he emerged he had a few dollars in his pocket, but he had to walk home. His journey to the pawnbroker coming on top of Mrs. Applegarth's ultimatum served to show him what an impossible situation he faced. For Mabel to come into his house and share his bed and board would mean but little added expense; their love would enable them to fight their way through hardship. But it would be years before he would earn enough to support his mother-in-law. The idea of bringing her to live with Flora was fantastic; the two women would be at each other's throat inside of twenty-four hours. And even when he was able to maintain two establishments, would he be master in his own home? Wouldn't Mrs. Applegarth run his house just as she would run his wife? Mabel would have to be a daughter to Mrs. Applegarth first, and in her spare time a wife. Such a condition would be intolerable!

His brain churned with frustration at Mrs. Applegarth's domination. At the height of his rage he remembered Mabel, caught between two strong personalities, having her very life squeezed out between them. His anger vanished in the face of his tenderness and concern for her, and he resolved that no matter what the obstacles he would not abandon her to the mercies of her mother; that he would marry her and handle Mrs. Applegarth when the need arose. Quieted, happy in his determination to make everything right, consciousness flooded back, forcing him to realize that every victory he might gain over Mrs. Applegarth in the establishing of a normal marriage would be paid for a hundredfold by Mabel out of her slender fund of health. Again he would decide that he would not allow Mabel to be sacrificed, that as soon as he was earning enough money he would set up a separate establishment and let Mrs. Applegarth rule his household, that nothing he might suffer under her domination would be worse than what he and Mabel were suffering now. Then the torturous cycle started all over and he realized that this surrender too would destroy them, for how could a marriage be a happy one when the wife's body and spirit were in bondage to her mother?

He was undergoing his greatest disappointment. His love for Mabel was a well-rounded love; it would have made a good marriage. He admired and respected her for all the niceties of cultivation he lacked; because of her ethereal quality and the delicacy of her health he would have protected her and exercised care not to hurt her. Mabel in her turn had never loved anyone before Jack, and was never to love anyone after him. She would have made a devoted wife and given him the kind of home he had longed for all the years of his youth. He was intensely unhappy, not only because he was losing his dreams of a wife and home and children, but because the woman he loved was caught in a senseless tragedy he was powerless to right, a tragedy which would not only destroy their relationship, but Mabel as well.

January proved to be a gala month even though his rising sun as yet shed little financial warmth. "An Odyssey of the North" was released in the *Atlantic Monthly,* which ran only one or two short stories a month; "Economics in the Klondike" appeared in the *Review of Reviews,* and "Pluck and Pertinacity" in *Youth's Companion.* "An Odyssey of the North" tells the story of Naass, headman of Akatan, a modern Ulysses who searches the world over for his wife, Unga, who had been stolen from him on his wedding night by a yellow-haired Viking. As with "The White Silence," the reading of this story fills one with tragic ecstasy. It was received in the East with huzzahs of praise, for brave work inspires courage in others. An Oakland newspaper ran an article about the growing literary importance of Oakland, of which Mr. Jack London was the outstanding figure. His friends, remembering the hardships he had endured, were not consumed with jealousy and envy as are most friends when one of their circle rises above the prescribed limit of success; they gave a party for him, and everyone was happy for his sake.

Toward the end of the month he borrowed five dollars from a friend to take his bicycle out of pawn, and pedaled to San José. With the passage of the days he had laid out his arguments with so much clarity and precision he was convinced that Mabel would not be able to resist them, that she would establish her independence. Mabel hardly understood his words; she kept murmuring in a sort of cataleptic trance: "Mother needs me. She couldn't get along without me. I couldn't desert her." As late as 1937 Edward Applegarth said sadly, "Mother was always a selfish woman; Mabel spent her whole life taking care of her."

He did not altogether give up hope; he loved Mabel as much as ever. But he turned to other women for companionship. He saw a good deal of Anna Strunsky, at whose dinner table there were always several extra places for friends who might drop in . . . and Jack dropped in often. Anna was also writing short stories and sociological essays. They criticized each other's work, argued fiercely about every subject under the sun, admired each other. "Anna, don't let the world lose you, for insomuch that it does lose you, insomuch have you sinned." There was a San Francisco newspaper woman by the name of Ernestine whose picture shows her to have had an exquisite profile and a devilish gleam in her eye; she and Jack went on what he called "far from conventional jaunts."

Despite the fact that he had had such a brilliant January, he could sell not a line in February. The *Atlantic Monthly* money had paid off debts, bought reputable-looking clothes for Flora and Johnny and himself, and books and subscriptions to the current magazines he needed. Now without a penny in the house, he became hugely disgusted. The economic indignities of his childhood, which he had come to feel no human being should have to endure, taught him to think that pauperism was as objectionable as great wealth. He decided that he would be frankly and consistently brutal about money, that only fools despised it. "It's money I want, or rather the things money will buy; and I can never possibly have too much. As to living on practically nothing, I propose to do as little of that as I possibly can. It's the feed not the breed that makes the man. More money means more life to me. The habit of getting money will never become one of my vices, but the habit of spending money, ah God! I shall always be its victim. If cash comes with fame, come fame; if cash comes without fame, then come cash."

So saying, he pawned his books and magazines, the new suit of clothes of which he had been so proud. As always, his first stop after he left the pawnshop was the post office where he bought stamps to send his manuscripts on their way again. When *The Editor* magazine offered him five dollars for a seventeen-hundred-word article he was insulted, but he took the money anyway. He went back to his work with double incentive. He had been writing a thousand words a day, six days a week, and made it a rule to make up the next day any amount he fell behind. Now he increased his stint to fifteen hundred words, then to two thousand, but beyond that he refused to go.

"I insist that good work cannot be done at the rate of three or four thousand words a day. Good work is not strung out from the inkwell; it is built like a wall, every brick carefully selected." The fact that he wanted lots of money, quick money, did not make him careless in his methods or sleazy in his thinking; nor did it change his mind about the type of story he wanted to write. He declared that if the magazines wanted to buy him body and soul they were welcome if they could pay the price, yet all the time he was not writing he spent studying Drummond on evolution, Hudson on psychology, and all the books he could find on anthropology, the inescapable fact that the magazines would not pay ten cents a ton for evolution and anthropology deterring him not at all.

Craving money to release him from his perpetual slavery, he wrote passionate articles on socialism which he knew he couldn't possibly sell, lectured for the Socialist Party in Alameda, San José, and other small towns without pay. He was strangled by the lack of cash, yet his friends of this period report him traveling any distance to get into a group where he could start a heated discussion on anthropology. When he encountered Weismann's radical theory that acquired characteristics cannot be inherited, he was so greatly exercised he dropped all work and made the rounds of his friends, open book in hand, to let them share the great discovery. He who maintained that he would write rot if someone would pay him for it, then proved himself brutally inconsistent by writing about the things he believed in, revolutionary articles and stories whose spiritual brothers were even then reposing on the floor under his desk. He wanted money, but the price the magazine editors demanded for their money was too high for him to pay! "I am firm. Everybody who has had a chance to know me well has noticed that things come my way even though they take years. No one sways me, save in the little things of the moment. I am not stubborn but I swing to my purpose as steadily as the needle to the pole. Delay, evade, oppose secretly or openly, it's all immaterial, the thing comes my way. Life is strife, and I am prepared for that strife. If I had not been an animal with a logical nature I would have stagnated or perished by the wayside."

In February, within a very few days of each other, occurred two events, each apparently insignificant when happening, which was to determine the external pattern of his life. He accepted an invitation to luncheon in San Francisco from Mrs. Ninetta Eames, wife of the business manager of the *Overland Monthly*. And Fred Jacobs, a classmate from the University who had enlisted for the Spanish-American War, and had died on board a transport from eating canned meat provided by the ubiquitous war profiteers, was returned to Oakland for burial. Mrs. Eames's luncheon came first; although it took a little longer to exert its influence, that influence was the more lasting.

Mrs. Ninetta Eames was a sweet, mincing, childless woman of forty-seven. Known always as "poor Netta," she was a shrewd and clever person whose purpose rarely appeared on the surface, a clinging vine with flexed fingers of steel beneath her softness and sentimentality. Her husband being a pretentious weakling, Mrs. Eames had taken over the affairs of the family, and attained her ends in the only ways open to women of the eighties and nineties who had to control and energize their husbands without the world suspecting.

The purpose of the interview was an article which Mrs. Eames proposed to write about Jack for the *Overland Monthly*. To this luncheon Mrs. Eames also invited her niece, whom she had raised from infancy, Clara Charmian Kittredge, a fairly good replica of her aunt. Clara Charmian Kittredge, vivacious, quick-tongued, with a slender but sensuous figure, was twenty-nine years old and still unmarried; it is not impossible that Mrs. Eames hoped Jack and her niece might become interested in each other. Miss Kittredge, however, sniffed at Jack's shabby clothes and was indignant when Mrs. Eames paid the check; she showed emotion only when Mrs. Eames told Jack that her niece was a typist in an office close by. Miss Kittredge promptly kicked her aunt in the shin for revealing that she had to work for a living.

On the twentieth of February Jack excitedly finished reading proofs on *Son of the Wolf*, his first stories to appear in book form, and mailed them back to the publisher. The following day he attended the funeral of Fred Jacobs, where he met Bessie Maddern, Jacobs's fiancée, a handsome, Junoesque Irish girl whom Jack had known while at the University of California. She was well liked and highly regarded by her associates, who were sympathetic over her bereavement. The next morning Jack received a letter from Mabel Applegarth, an old friend of Bessie's, asking him to call upon Bessie and do what he could to lighten her burden. He called at the home of the Madderns that evening.

Bessie Maddern, who was a cousin of Minnie Maddern Fiske, the famous actress, had graduated from Girls' High in San Francisco. At the time of Fred Jacobs's death she was privately coaching in mathematics delinquent grammar-school children, and high-school students who wanted to enter the University. She was a strong woman physically, stolid, phlegmatic, riding her bicycle from house to house in Oakland and Alameda to her various pupils. She was a little older than Jack, had warm, sad eyes, an aquiline nose, a large but well-cut mouth, a strong chin, and black hair with a narrow streak of gray running straight back from her forehead, the result of an accident when she was eighteen. There was a well-poised, quiet assurance about her, and she was entirely forthright in nature.

Miss Maddern was grieving over the loss of Fred Jacobs; Jack was grieving over the hopelessness of his engagement to Mabel Applegarth. They found each other's company pleasant and salutary; they felt comfortable together. Before long Jack found himself spending many evenings with Miss Maddern. She coached him in mathematics and physics, in which he was untutored, while he went back to the beginnings of English literature and reviewed its history for her. On Sundays they took their bicycles across to Marin County, where they wandered through Muir Woods and cooked their dinner of broiled steak, baked sweet potatoes, crab, and coffee over hot coals. On other nights, if Jack had a little money, they would have dinner in one of San Francisco's North Beach Italian restaurants and then go to the opera.

He continued to bicycle the forty miles to San José each week, but his meetings with Mabel left him saddened and disillusioned. It was with relief that he returned to Bessie's cool, undemanding company. She was correcting all his manuscripts by now, polishing down the occasional awkward phrase; she liked his work and believed implicitly that he would become one of the world's great writers, a faith that never wavered.

Jack's rooms on Sixteenth Street had become a meeting-place for the people he knew, for they had begun to clamor for his company. "I have the fatal faculty of making friends, and lack the blessed trait of being able to get rid of them." There was nothing he liked better than playing host, but the bicycles began tinkling so frequently outside his house that he often had to do his writing with three or four men sitting on the bed, smoking, talking over old times, arguing whether a belief in materialism necessarily brought about pessimism. Jack could not let his guests go unfed; when a few lonely dollars arrived from the *Overland Monthly* for "The Impossibility of War," or from the *National Magazine* for "A Lesson in Heraldry," he bought a supply of steaks and chops to keep in the icebox.

Friends from the Ruskin Club dropped in for a smoke and a chat, his comrades from the Socialist Local to ask him to address a meeting, old pals from the Yukon, from the Fish Patrol, the oyster pirates, his brother tramps of The Road. "That's one of the drawbacks of my present quarters, everybody comes dropping in, and I haven't the heart to turn them away."

Because his house was becoming too small to hold all his books, his friends, and his work, and because he expected *Son of the Wolf* to earn him royalties, Jack decided to move to larger quarters. He and Flora found a two-story house at 1130 East Fifteenth Street, just a few blocks away, in which there was a large living-room with bay windows, and a good-sized bedroom that could be fitted up to make a workroom and den. Eliza did most of the work of decorating the seven rooms, but Bessie Maddern helped to make Jack's den cozy and colorful. On the night before the family was to move in, Eliza and Miss Maddern were hanging curtains in the den while Jack lay stretched out full length on the rug, his fingers interlaced behind his head, as he had lain so many nights on the prow of the *Sophie Sutherland*. Eliza turned about to pick up a curtain rod and noticed Jack studying Bessie with a curious expression on his face. In a flash she saw a decision settle in his eyes; this sister, who had been more mother than sister, knew at once what that decision was. She was not surprised the next morning when Jack informed her that he was going to marry Bessie Maddern.

Jack had been determined to marry Mabel Applegarth not only because he loved her, but because he was in a marrying mood. He had lived a good deal more than his twenty-three years bespoke; he had a strong feeling for fatherhood, so strong that even as a tramp on The Road he had written in his notebook of his longing for children. "Divers deep considerations have led me to do this thing; but I shall override just one objection—that of being tied. I am already tied. Though single, I have had to support a household just the same. Should I wish to go to China the household would have to be provided for whether I had a wife or not. As it is, I shall be steadied, and can be able to devote more time to my work. One has only one life, after all, and why not live it? My heart is large, and I shall be a cleaner, wholesomer man because of a restraint being laid upon me in place of being free to drift wheresoever I listed."

Jack and Bessie were honest with each other. They did not profess to be passionately enamored in the romantic tradition; they knew that Bessie still loved Fred Jacobs and that Jack still loved Mabel Applegarth. But both had had their hearts set on marriage. They liked and respected and enjoyed each other, felt they could build a good marriage and a solid home, and raise fine children. They agreed that although love was one of the smallest words in the language, it was sufficiently elastic to admit of many definitions. Miss Maddern considered the proposal for a day or two, then accepted.

Unwilling to marry under a name that was not legally his, because of the equivocal position in which it might place his children, Jack told the Madderns the circumstances of his birth. Together he and Bessie went to see an Oakland judge who was a friend of the Maddern family; he assured them that since Jack had been living under the name of London all his life, and had published under it, his right to it was legally established.

On a Sunday, one week after he had made his decision, Jack and Bessie were quietly married. Flora was outraged and refused to attend the ceremony. The newlyweds rode off on their bicycles for a three-day honeymoon in the country, then returned to Oakland to set up house and dig into work. The Ruskin Club staged a dinner in their honor; the Oakland *Enquirer*, writing up the marriage, said, "The bride is a beautiful and accomplished young woman," a compliment which Oakland agreed was well deserved.

During the day Bessie continued her coaching of backward students, earning enough to keep the house going when Jack's income could not. At night she corrected his manuscripts and typed them, read the new books in which he was interested so that she might discuss them with him, copied onto sheets of paper poems he had enjoyed, binding hundreds of them between red cardboard covers, collected and bound magazine articles for him on economic and political subjects, set up a dark room and showed him how to develop his own pictures. On Sundays they took long bicycle rides through the fertile San Leandro Valley, where Jack told Bessie stories of his early days on John London's farm. One weekend they went to Santa Cruz, where they swam in the ocean and frolicked on the beach. If they achieved no ecstasy, they did have fun together, and honest, dependable comradeship. Jack gave every evidence of being pleased with his choice, and pleased with his marriage. Bessie said in 1937, "I did not love Jack when I married him, but I very soon came to love him."

The marriage seems to have brought its own good luck, for in May, Jack at last cracked an Eastern short-story magazine, *McClure's*, which published action stories for men. There began a honeymoon period between Jack and the publisher, S. S. McClure, who gained immortality by paying high prices for stories from unknown writers on the grounds that "the boys have to eat." McClure bought "The Grit of Women" and "The Law of Life," writing to Jack, "We are greatly interested in you and want you to feel that you have the warmest kind of friends right here in New York. I wish you would look upon us as your literary sponsors hereafter. If you will send us everything you write we will use what we can, and what we cannot we will endeavor to dispose of to the best possible advantage."

There was no more heartening message a young writer could receive. Taking McClure at his word, Jack gathered together a boxful of manuscripts, then dug in to write fresh ones that had been formulating in his mind. McClure bought "The Question of the Maximum," paying him three hundred dollars in all for the three pieces of work, the largest amount of money Jack had ever possessed. The material McClure could not use he sent to other magazines with his recommendation; when the manuscripts became too numerous for him to handle, he turned them over to a reputable literary agent. With his sales to McClure, and McClure's sponsorship among the editors of the New York literary world, the name of Jack London began to be known.

When *Son of the Wolf* was released in the spring of 1900 it met with instantaneous critical success. The book was like a time-bomb blowing open the new century. With the exception of an occasional antiquated phrase there was no element of the now-dead nineteenth century in it. The short stories spoke vigorously of the new century. The scientific attitudes toward evolution and the strife among species, the amoral values of people who lived without fear of being excommunicated by the parson, the bold approach to life's cruelty and ugliness and grimness as well as the beautiful and the good, the introduction of whole classes of characters who had never before been admitted into the polite society of the short story, the orgiastic action, brute conflict, and violent death that had been forbidden to the story-teller—all tolled the death knell of the anemic, the sentimental, the evasive, the hypocritical, that marked nineteenth-century literature.

Many of the critics of the day picked up the gage for Jack. *The Literary World* of Boston said, "The author's spade goes down into the root of things"; the *Atlantic Monthly*, "The book produces in the reader a deeper faith in the manly virtues of our race." Other critics wrote: "Full of fire and feeling; a natural born story teller; virility and forcefulness throughout; all outward signs of genius; great artist, powerful. . . ." One commented, "His stories are imbued with the poetry and mystery of the great North. The dominant note is always tragedy (in contrast to the formula of happy endings), as it always is where men battle with the elemental forces of nature. He has brought to the comedy and tragedy of life in the Klondike much of the imaginative power and dramatic force of Kipling. But he has the tenderness of sentiment and a quick appreciation of the finer sentiments of heroism that are seldom seen in Kipling."

His first published book, and already he was being compared favorably to his beloved master! Elated as he was with the reviews, he found time to be angry with the critics for not realizing Kipling's true greatness, and dashed off a sizzling article on the subject.

The issuance of *Son of the Wolf* marked the beginning of the modern American short story. It had antecedents in Edgar Allan Poe, Bret Harte, Stephen Crane, and Ambrose Bierce, who had all broken with the conventional pattern to write authentic literature, but Jack was the first to bring the story home to the common people, to make it entirely understandable and enjoyable. Up to this time the bulk of short stories had been written for maiden ladies; Jack's stories were for every class of Americans except maiden ladies—and they gobbled them up behind drawn blinds and locked doors. He was also the first to imbue the form with the scientific attitude of the twentieth century, and to give it the force and vitality that Americans had used to conquer the continent and build gigantic industries.

For a long time he had been wanting to try his hand at a novel; since a novel takes from six months to a year to write, during which time there can be no income from the work, the possibility of his getting sufficiently ahead to do a sustained piece of work seemed remote. Now he wrote McClure about his predicament. McClure answered post-haste, "We will back your novel on your own terms. We will send you a check each month for five months for $100, and if you find that you need $125, why we will do that.

I am confident that you can make a strong novel. At any time when you feel in need of any sort of help, please let us know."

Then, with his career sailing like the *Razzle Dazzle* before the wind, Bessie brought him the news that she was pregnant. Jack was overjoyed and knew at once that it would be a son. Kind as he had been before, he now became gentle as a child, tenderly solicitous of her health and well-being. The knowledge that he was soon to be a father touched off the spark, and within a few hours of Bessie's revelation he had begun work on his first novel, *A Daughter of the Snows*.

Though he had figured to a nicety the details of already being tied down, and having a household to support, Jack had failed in a typically masculine fashion to realize that no kitchen has yet been built that is large enough to hold two women. Flora was raising hell with his wife.

She had been deeply hurt by what she termed her son's desertion at the moment when he was beginning to earn a little money. Having suffered without complaint during the months of want, she now felt she was entitled to her reward—instead of which Jack had brought a strange woman into the house. She had cooked for him and taken care of him, and now Bessie wanted to do the cooking; she had been the hostess when his friends came to call, now Bessie was the mistress. Flora did not like being superseded in Jack's affections; she assumed that she was being shoved into the background. As she brooded about her troubles the old neurasthenia returned. She quarreled constantly with Bessie, made things as unpleasant for her as she could. Twenty years after Jack's death, Bessie commented: "I should have catered to Flora and petted her and made her the boss, and we would all have gotten along fine. But I was young, and wanted to do things for my husband. So we clashed!"

Oftentimes when Jack was trying to concentrate on the difficult structural problems of his first novel, the angry voices of the two women would fill the room in which he was working, driving out of his mind *A Daughter of the Snows*. He would stand it as long as he could, then dash out of the house, walk at top speed to Eliza's, and implore her to go to his house and quiet them. When he returned home an hour or two later Eliza had the situation in hand, and he would go back to work.

With better facilities for entertaining his friends, Jack began gathering about him an interesting circle, encouraging them in their habit of dropping in on Wednesday nights. Chief among them was tall, athletic, exquisitely sensitive George Sterling, of whom Jack wrote, "I have a friend, the dearest in the world." Sterling had abandoned his studies for the priesthood of the Catholic Church to become one of those rare poets who weave beauty, tenderness, and a passion for truth into his work. An esthete grounded in the classics, he was a split personality, torn between his love for socialism and the conception of "art for art's sake," which had been drilled into him by Ambrose Bierce, with whose philosophy of defeatism Jack disagreed violently. Possessing a mind rich in imagery and the music of words, Sterling's loyal comradeship, flaming spirit, and penetrating literary criticism did much to smooth down Jack's rough edges. James Hopper, the husky, powerful football player whom he had known at the University, and who was also trying to write short stories, became an intimate, as did Jim Whitaker, who had seven children and had given up his job security to write novels, and Xaviar Martinez, the Spanish-Indian painter. Frederick Bamford, assistant librarian of Oakland and founder of the Ruskin Club, brought his precise goatee and precise bishoplike culture to Jack's board. Anna Strunsky came over from San Francisco, also Strawn-Hamilton, the philosophical anarchist, Austin Lewis, the Social Democrat, and other Bay region radicals. Mrs. Ninetta Eames visited frequently, bringing her literary friends and progress reports of her niece's tour of Europe. Everyone came for supper, after which manuscripts were read, and the new books and plays discussed. Later the men played poker or red dog for small stakes, high excitement, and big laughter. Soon these Wednesday night parties became known as Jack's open house.

Cloudesley Johns, a handsome, lovable young chap, rode up from his post office in a small Southern California town to spend a week. Johns had been the first person to write enthusiastically to Jack when "To the Man on Trail" was published in the *Overland Monthly;* they had been corresponding ever since. Tramps from The Road, sailors, former waterfront cronies, all liked to show up at Jack's house for a glass of sour Italian wine, a friendly chat. "Every once in a while some old shipmate turns up . . . just re-

turned from a long voyage . . . big payday coming . . . 'Say Jack,
old boy, can you lend me a couple of dollars until tomorrow?'"
Jack scaled them down to half, gave them the money, and let
them go. He was supremely happy in being able to dispense hospitality; he always liked a crowd of his friends in his house when he
had finished the day's work.

Though the hundred and twenty-five dollars from *McClure's* arrived regularly each month, it was no longer sufficient to fill the
needs of his family, his rising standard of living, and the influx of
friends. He began doubling his working time, devoting the mornings to his serious literature, the afternoons to writing pot-boilers.
As a result he sold an article to the Boston *Transcript* on how he
had slept on the Common and told the arresting officer tales
about Japan to keep out of jail; an article on "The Husky," the
Alaskan sled dog, which *Harper's Weekly* bought; another on "Expansion," which the San Francisco *Wave* ran as an editorial; two
domestic narratives, "Their Alcove," published by *Woman's
Home Companion*, and "Housekeeping in the Klondike," by
means of which he crashed *Harper's Bazaar*; a triolet to *Town
Topics*:

> He came in
> When I was out
> To borrow some tin
> Was why he came in,
> And he went without;
> So I was in
> And he was out.

And Jack was in one dollar!

He worked so steadily at his typewriter and books that sometimes for days he did not go out the front door except to pick up
the evening paper from the porch. He lost weight, grew soft,
found that he was growing timid in proportion as he grew soft,
that he was becoming afraid to write the things in which he
believed, was asking himself if this manuscript would sell, or that
one would please the public. It had always been his conviction
that a sickly body could not harbor a healthy brain, so he bought
a pair of dumbbells with which he exercised every morning in

front of an open window before sitting down to compose—rarely later than six A.M.—and after work went hunting behind the Berkeley hills or fishing on the Bay. His body hardened, and with it his nerve and courage. In a burst of renewed vitality he wrote "Jan the Unrepentant" and "The Man with the Gash." They were his first humorous tales of the Klondike, written with the diabolical sense of humor of the Irishman at a wake who plays tricks with the corpse.

In spite of its good critical press, *Son of the Wolf* sold but moderately well. Nor was he getting anything better than wages from magazines other than *McClure's*, twenty dollars being a high price for a manuscript. His name was not yet known to the reading public; he would have to keep writing for that one smash hit which would put him over. In the meanwhile he continued to pick up a few dollars wherever he could; when *The Black Cat* ran a story contest, and he could think of no major plot with which to win one of the big prizes, he wrote the ironic "Semper Idem," the idea for which he got out of his evening newspaper, and won a fifty-dollar prize. When *Cosmopolitan Magazine* ran a contest on "Loss by Lack of Cooperation," he took a million-to-one shot and wrote a revolutionary article for them called "What the Community Loses by the Competitive System"; he won the first prize of two hundred dollars, which caused him to comment that he was the only man in America making money out of socialism.

After months of interminable wrangling between his wife and mother, Jack rented a small cottage on the street just back of his house and moved Flora and Johnny into it. This excommunication made Flora furious; now she was being put out of her son's home, discarded! Jack achieved little by the maneuver except added expense, for she not only came into his house and caused an even greater amount of confusion, but began rehearsing her grievances with the neighbors, who started unfortunate gossip. Imagining that she was on her own again, Flora began dipping into small business ventures, spending the money Jack gave her no one knew where, running up debts which her son had to cover.

Through the summer and fall Jack continued to work on his novel, lectured for the Socialist Local at mass meetings in San Francisco, attended meetings when other lecturers spoke, joined the Ibsen circle, took fencing and boxing lessons in his back yard, and on Wednesday nights played host to his friends. He was a long way from being a melancholy intellectual—one of the best times he had during the fall was watching California trounce Stanford at football—yet his most consistent adventure of the period was the discovery of great books, to which he gave himself with the whole-hearted abandon of the ragged, uncared-for newsboy, a stack of papers under his arm, who had wandered into the Oakland Library fourteen years before and asked Miss Coolbrith for something good to read. He writes to Anna Strunsky: "I have been sitting here crying like a baby, for I have just finished reading *Jude the Obscure*. With Jude and Tess to his name, Hardy should die content." He vowed that he too would die content if he could create one or two books that might stand shoulder to shoulder on the shelves with the books that had so enriched his life.

Between Jack and Anna Strunsky there was developing a curious relationship. That their minds were magnificently mated they had at length come to realize, even though they still were arguing violently over biology, materialism, and socialism. By July Jack's letters to her begin to acquire a tender note. "For all the petty surface turmoil which marked our coming to know each other, really, deep down, there was no confusion at all. We were attuned somehow, a real unity underlaid everything. The ship, new launched, rushes to the sea, the sliding ways rebel in creaks and groans; but sea and ship hear them not. So with us when we rushed into each other's lives."

He submitted his serious work to Anna Strunsky, who brought to her criticism a mind finely attuned to spiritual values. In turn he urged her to continue with her own writing. "Oh Anna, if you will only put your flashing soul with its protean moods on paper! You make me feel as though some new energy has been projected into the world. Anna, read your classics, but don't forget to read that which is of today, the new born literary art. You must get the modern touch; form must be considered; and while art is eternal, form is born of the generations. Oh, Anna, don't disappoint me."

By the end of 1900 he was writing, "A white beautiful friendship?—between a man and a woman?—the world cannot imagine such a thing, would deem it as inconceivable as infinity." Nor had Jack himself conceived it as possible; if he had he might have done his courting in San Francisco instead of Oakland when he was discouraged over Mabel Applegarth. He meant no disloyalty to his wife, yet his mind came to love the mind of Anna Strunsky. He and Bessie had plumbed certain depths together, they had known companionship and created life, and for these things he loved her. But he and Anna had plumbed other depths, depths of the mind and spirit, and for these things he loved Anna.

With Bessie all swollen and big with child, Jack began to torment himself over his feelings for Miss Strunsky, whom he describes as "a Russian Jewess who happens to be a genius." Yet no word had been uttered between them about their feelings for each other. "Ah, believe me, Anna, the things unsaid are the greatest. A happiness to me? Why, you have been a delight, dear, and a glory." He had married for emotional stability, for a solid, permanent position in society, but ". . . just when freedom seems opening up for me I feel the bands tightening and the rivetting of the gyves. I remember now when I was free, when there was no restraint and I did as the heart willed."

That he was feeling a genuine emotion for Miss Strunsky there can be no doubt, but mixed in with it are the fears and misgivings, the yearnings for freedom of the young man who is about to become a father, to have further and permanent responsibilities strapped to his back. Yet what would have happened if Mrs. Applegarth had not issued her ultimatum until Jack was writing to Anna, "A happiness to me? Why you have been a delight, dear, and a glory"?

He continued to write poems for exercise in fluency; to read omnivorously in modern fiction to get well in hand the modern touch; to perform many experiments, not for sale, but to extend his range; to write long criticisms on the technique of story writing; to let no sentence pass in his manuscript in which the words were not smooth and beautiful to his ear. When he thought he was getting too cocky about his work he dug out a batch of old stories and he would settle down. He and Cloudesley Johns, who had had an academic training, exchanged blistering criticisms in the margins of each other's manuscripts. Johns, who was writing a book called *The Philosophy of The Road*, sent it to Jack for correction. Jack's answer contains his literary credo. "You are handling stirring life, romance, things of human life and death, humor and pathos, but God, man, handle them as they should be. Don't you tell the reader the philosophy of The Road. HAVE YOUR CHARACTERS TELL IT BY THEIR DEEDS, ACTION, TALK. Study Stevenson and Kipling and see how they eliminate themselves and create things that live, and breathe, and grip men, and cause reading lamps to burn overtime. Atmosphere stands always for the elimination of the artist. Get your good strong phrases, fresh and vivid; write intensively, not exhaustively or lengthily; don't narrate —paint! draw! build! CREATE! Better one thousand words that are builded than a whole book of mediocre, spun-out, dashed-off stuff. Damn you! Forget you! And then the world will remember you!"

By the time he reached the home stretch of *A Daughter of the Snows* he knew it was a failure. There was enough good material in it to make two good novels, with sufficient bad material left over to make still a third, bad novel. From *A Daughter of the Snows* emerge his two great weaknesses, implicit here in this beginning, explicit after he had published forty volumes: his conception of the supremacy of the Anglo-Saxon race; and his inability to transcribe to a flesh-and-blood reality on the printed page any woman above the working class.

In Frona Welse Jack tried to create a twentieth-century woman who would be an antithesis of the nineteenth-century woman: strong without being hard, intelligent without being flat-chested, courageous without losing her charm or femininity, able to work and live and fight and think and hold the trail with the best of men. From her character he eliminated everything he detested in womankind: sentimentality, slovenly thinking, coquetry, weakness, fear, ignorance, soft vampirish clinging, hypocrisy. He tried to conceive of a woman who would be a worthy mate for his twentieth-century man; though he was sailing in dangerous, unchartered waters he very nearly makes Frona credible. If he could have gone on from here he might have created in his later work an image that would have served as a model for the new womankind. . . .

Frona appears at her worst when she talks like one of Jack's sociological essays, expounding the chauvinistic fallacy—which Jack had swallowed whole-hog from Kipling—of the supremacy of the white race, of their destiny to rule supreme forever over the red, the black, and the yellow, a gullibility of which he was eagerly guilty because of his own Viking complex. "The sharp-beaked fighting galleys, and the sea-flung Northmen, great muscled, deep-chested, sprung from the elements, men of sword and sweep . . . the dominant races come down out of the North . . . a great race, half the earth its heritage and all the sea! In three score generations it rules the world!"

Jack permitted his Anglo-Saxon myopia to corrupt his thinking about socialism, the one subject above all others in which he wanted to be honest and accurate. When he was writing about the dominant races come down out of the North, he wrote to Cloudesley Johns, "Socialism is not an ideal system devised for the happiness of all men; it is devised for the happiness of certain kindred races. It is devised so as to give more strength to these certain kindred favored races so that they may survive and inherit the earth to the extinction of the lesser, weaker races." Thus did Nietzsche speak through Kipling to pervert Karl Marx.

He had bravely turned down the material luxury of a postman's wage for the uncertainties of a writer's career. Now a hundred and fifty dollars a month, an undreamed-of sum less than a year before, was not sufficient to keep him. By the time a check arrived there was a long line of people waiting to cash it. A list of his financial activities between Christmas and New Year's includes a loan to Jim Whitaker; footing the bills for a friend who had had both ankles broken in an accident; paying forty-one dollars of Flora's pressing back debts, giving Mammy Jenny, who was about to lose her home, enough cash to pay the interest on her mort-gage, and her delinquent taxes; and, the only unpleasant task in the series, refusing to lend Cloudesley Johns money to leave his desert post office, because he, Jack, had had to go out and borrow money to run his house. And with Bessie expecting to be confined in a week!

Bessie says that she continued her coaching right up to the morning the baby arrived. For a time it looked as though the child might be born on January 12, Jack's twenty-fifth birthday, but Bessie did not go into labor until the morning of the fifteenth. When she knew that her moment had arrived she sent for the doctor, who came in such haste he forgot to bring an anes-thetic. Jack was dispatched to buy a bottle of chloroform. On his way home he rode his bicycle so hard and fast he fell off, broke the bottle, and cut his hand. Bessie was delivered of a nine-pound girl, but the afterbirth was botched and Bessie was ill for a long time. Jack was not able to hide from his wife his disappointment that it was not a boy.

Despite the fact that McClure decided against publishing *A Daughter of the Snows* in his magazine, he continued to send Jack the monthly check of a hundred and twenty-five dollars. "Being a married man, and knowing that it costs money to buy potatoes, I am enclosing . . ." The novel finished, Jack devoted himself to a series of short stories. With the passing of the weeks the disappointment at not having a son was allayed somewhat; he grew attached to his daughter, Joan, who favored him strongly in looks. Mammy Jenny moved into the London house to take care of Joan, just as she had cared for Joan's father on Nob Hill, twenty-five years before.

One of the avowed reasons Jack had married Bessie was because he had believed she would breed strong children; nor was he mistaken. He had married her on an impulse, to fill an empty space in both their lives, to plunge them into the swift stream of living. Bessie was everything she had appeared to be: loyal, devoted, gentle, intelligent, willing to work with him, share his hardships. He enjoyed being a father, and felt a strong sense of gratitude toward her. Yet sometimes in his fatigue his mind turned against his wife for those very qualities for which he valued and had selected her. He was mercurial of nature, he had fire in his veins, he liked to burn and exult, to live wildly and fiercely, to soar to the heights in exultation, to drag the depths of despair. In these spiritual debauches Bessie would not accompany him; she was emotionally stable, placid, stolid, even of temper and mood. When he was working and accomplishing all the things he had set out to accomplish he was thankful to her, but when the work was done there were moments of revolt when he longed to slip his moorings and beat out to the Bay on the early morning tide. Then he would sigh for his old freedom, for the right to move on to another place, another woman. It was the first time he had not been able to chuck his obligations and strike out for Adventure Road.

At such times he would write to Anna Strunsky, "Surely sitting here, gathering data, classifying, arranging, writing stories for boys with moral purposes insidiously inserted, hammering away at a thousand words a day, growing excited over biological objections, thrusting a bit of fun at you and raising a laugh when it should have been a sob, surely this is not all? Were ever two souls, with dumb lips, more incongruously matched?"

They decided to write their spiritual and intellectual feelings into a book. They would call it *The Kempton-Wace Letters,* Jack to be Wace, and Anna to be Kempton, in which Anna would defend the poetic or spiritual wellsprings of love against the attacks of Jack's biological and scientific evolution. Thus would they enjoy the passions and poetries of each other's mind without hurting anyone or violating any codes. Thus would Jack defend his marriage to Bessie, even while escaping it.

While doing double duty at his desk he also had found time to lecture for the Alameda Socialist Party on "The Tramp," and at the San Francisco Academy of Science on "Competitive Waste." The local press reported his lectures respectfully. When the moment arrived to nominate a candidate for Mayor of Oakland, the first candidate the young Socialist Party had dared put in the field, to whom should the honor go but to their best-known member, Mr. Jack London. In accepting the nomination Jack said, "It is we, the Socialists, working as a leaven throughout society, who are responsible for the great and growing belief in municipal ownership. It is we, the Socialists, by our propaganda, who have forced the old parties to throw as sops to the popular unrest certain privileges."

He campaigned in Oakland on the premise that socialism was the hair shirt of capitalism, the irritant which would bring forth from the vested interests certain soothing lotions in the form of better wages, hours, working conditions. He urged the unions and unorganized workers to vote the Socialist ticket so that their display of strength would give them greater bargaining power with their employers.

The workers turned a deaf ear to his economic reasoning. Only the "intellectual proletariat" stood behind him. To the citizens of Oakland and Alameda he was able to sell but two hundred and forty-five votes in his mild Utopia.

In May there appeared in *Pearson's* magazine "The Minions of Midas," as revolutionary a departure in American literature as had been "An Odyssey of the North" the year before. There was no such phenomenon as a socialist fiction writer in the United States, nor had there ever been one. But Jack had never cast about for the approbation of precedent; he was determined to be a socialist writer in the days when it took as much courage to be a socialist writer as it does nowadays not to be one. In this story he first conceives of a world-wide organization of proletariats so powerful that it cannot be downed by the police, the state militia, or the national government, an organization which is taking over by force the wealth of the world. If "The Minions of Midas" is not the first proletarian story to have been published in America, it seems to have been the first to appear in a magazine of national importance and distribution. Not that *Pearson's* committed the heresy of buying the story for its socialism; Jack was such a consummate story-teller that *Pearson's* published it for its horror-entertainment value, calculating its socialism to be so farfetched the readers would think of it as a Jules Verne fantasy.

Jack followed "The Minions of Midas" with "The Dream of Debs," which predicted the San Francisco general strike of 1934, and "The Iron Heel," which predicted the rise and current terror of Fascism. After his death the critics were able to agree about few things in his work, but on one point there is little controversy: Jack London is the father of proletarian literature in America. In 1929 the *New Masses* was to say in simple and true words, "A real proletarian writer must not only write about the working class, he must be read by the working class. A real proletarian writer must not only use his proletarian life as his material; his writing must burn with the spirit of revolt. Jack London was a real proletarian writer—the first and so far the only proletarian writer of genius in America. Workers who read, read Jack London. He is the one author they have all read, he is one literary experience they all have in common. Factory workers, farm hands, seamen, miners, newsboys read him and read him again. He is the most popular writer of the American working class."

His Wednesday gatherings remained the high spot of his week. His friends now began dropping in about midafternoon; Jack being an inveterate puzzle-worker, they brought pull-aparts, unhookers, mechanical riddles, boards on which marbles or ball bearings had to be rolled into cups and slots. Bessie hunted the magazines assiduously, cutting out the coupons for all advertised puzzles, games, and practical jokes. By suppertime fifteen or twenty people had assembled, and were playing Animals, Statues, Charades, trying to separate interlocking steel rings, drinking water from glasses that had a small hole near the bottom and sprung a stream onto their neckties, or finding a furred mouse in their pocket. The laughter was continuous and uproarious; Jack kept it uproarious because he loved to laugh, and was eager to fill his belly with all the laughter it could hold. He had not had a joyous childhood; he was going to make up for it in simple fun.

Across his big round supper table the arguing was always furious; he knew each man's vulnerabilities, and taunted them with pseudo-serious comments until the battle royal started. A number of young women journalists, musicians, writers had joined the group; after supper there was music, singing, and dancing. Mrs. Ninetta Eames's niece, Charmian Kittredge, was back from Europe. She was an accomplished pianist, and Jack liked to sit on the bench beside her while she played and sang.

After the music, when the crowd was in a quiet mood, Jack brought forth the manuscripts he had written during the week. Seated in a leather chair in the now darkened room, the pages illumined only by the flickering light of the open fire, he read to his friends while they listened attentively. This was followed by an hour or two of solid literary discussion, and then Jack once again started the fun, bringing out the cards and arranging those games in which the most laughter and excitement could be evoked. He laughed lustily at every turn of luck, and at the winning or losing of a pot would become as excited as a child. Men who attended these Wednesday open houses still remember them as the most delightful and stimulating nights of their lives.

There was always a gallon of sour red Italian wine for those who wanted to drink it, but no whiskey. It had been eight or nine years since Jack had done any serious drinking. When going into the Klondike he had carried a quart of Scotch over Chilkoot Pass; six months later he pulled the cork for the first time, so that the whiskey might be used as an anesthetic, half of it going down the throat of Doctor Harvey, the other half down a man whose leg the doctor was amputating. The patient lived.

Early in the year McClure had suggested that Jack now had

published enough stories to put out a second collection of his Alaskan tales. In May *The God of His Fathers* appeared. Though there is no single story in it to equal the brilliance of "An Odyssey of the North," the volume has a more consistent level of excellence than his first. Jack carried further his revolution in storytelling, making a rigid elimination of nonessentials, of the gingerbread façade. He stripped the form to fit the action. In these stories he proved that death-appeal in literature is more powerful than sex-appeal. Though some of the critics did not like the second volume as well as the first, most of the press was highly enthusiastic. *The Commercial Advertiser* said, "The stories ought to be read, and widely read, because they represent one of the most encouraging tendencies in contemporary American fiction"; while *The Nation* reported in July, 1901: "The stories in *The God of His Fathers* are vivid, concise, dramatic. They are sometimes coarse, generally disagreeable, always cynical and reckless. But if anyone wants to be interested, amused, and thoroughly stirred, he cannot do better than read this volume." Other papers commented: "Strongest short-story writer to arise in this country since Poe." . . . "A new Kipling come out of the West." . . . "Does for Alaska what Bret Harte did for California." . . . "We are held spellbound." . . . "Power and force . . . true to life . . . first-class raconteur . . . natural-born storyteller . . . realistic, keen observation . . . swift, clean, virile . . . full of healthy optimism . . . gives us new faith in the strength of our race." The dissenting voices called the stories brutal, vulgar, and unpleasant, written without polish, delicacy, or refinement.

The San Francisco *Examiner* sent a reporter and photographer to the home of Felix Peano, into whose amazing house Jack had moved his family a short time before, to get material for a big spread and pictures of Jack and his study. Felix Peano was an eccentric Italian sculptor who had adorned his house with plaster arabesques, urns, sculptured fawns, angels, devils, dryads, cherubs, centaurs, and lusty nude female torsos reclining under bowers of grapes—all of the rococo ornamentation against which Jack was revolting in literature. Falling upon hard times, Peano had turned over the greater part of the house to Jack rent-free, in return for his board. The inside of the house was large and comfortable even if the outside was incredible.

As a result of the article in the *Examiner* Jack found himself definitely famous in the Bay area, although his local fame did him little good financially. Fan letters began to come in. Women in particular seemed stirred by his writing and his pictures, and wrote asking all manner of favor. There was the woman who gave her minister as a character reference, then proposed that Jack be the father of her child so that the child would inherit a magnificent body and brain. Although he heartily approved of the lady's biological thesis, he managed to turn down the proposal.

He was severely in debt: to the stores, to the pawnshop, to his friends. The royalties from *The God of His Fathers* were charged against his advances from McClure, so that no cash was forthcoming. Any check that was due was spent a month before it arrived; though he sold a number of stories and articles to small magazines he could not collect his money. The business of literature was a wretched one; editors took months to decide whether they wanted a story, more months to publish it, and still more months after publication to pay for it. Jack fumed against this system, crying out that if a man bought shoes or vegetables he paid cash, so why shouldn't editors pay cash for stories? This shabby treatment of a man who needed his wages to buy the necessities of life for his family made him the more determined eventually to make editors pay him high prices.

By summer, when he was hopelessly in debt, the San Francisco *Examiner* summoned him to write special articles for the Sunday supplement, the section for which he had written his first article, four years before, in an attempt to earn the requisite ten dollars to feed Flora, Johnny Miller, and himself until the appointment from the post office came through. He reported prize fights, wrote a hysterical article about the arrival of the *S.S. Oregon*, which brought down on him the wrath of the local literati, did articles on "Girls Fighting Duels," the Washoe Indians coming to civilization, and finally spent ten straight days reporting the German *Schuetzenfest*. He forced himself to make the articles red-blooded, virile, as the *Examiner* had promised its readers they would be; as a result they sound forced and artificial, but the food they bought for his family was very real indeed.

In August a calamity hit. After reading a number of short stories written over a period of months, among which were

"Moon Face" and "Nambok, the Unveracious," and rejecting them all, McClure lost faith in him. "Your work seems to have taken a turn which makes it impractical for this magazine. Of course I understand that you must follow the lead of your genius . . . but unless there is a possibility of our securing the material we can use, do you not think it would be better for us to drop the salary after September or October?" Six people to support, and his only reliable source of income cut off!

McClure suggested that if he would turn back to the kind of story he had written before, the magazine would pay him high prices. If he obeyed McClure, made a laborious effort to copy his early material or write according to formula, he could make good money; if he obeyed the dictates of his probing mind, which demanded that he continue to explore new and revolutionary fields of human conduct and artistic form, he and his dependents would once again face starvation. To this man who claimed that he wanted money passionately, who said that the magazines could buy him body and soul if they would pay the price, who had vowed to be "frankly and consistently brutal about money," only one decision was possible. He threw McClure overboard and went ahead writing the things he felt deeply, that he knew had to be written.

He had two months before McClure was to cut off his hundred-and-twenty-five-dollar salary. If he worked desperately, wrote furiously, surely he could sell something, crack open a new field?

6

"FOR me the New Year begins full of worries, harassments, and disappointments." He was three thousand dollars in debt, one of his greatest liabilities being that people liked and trusted him and consequently gave him too much credit; he was unable to earn enough to support his growing list of dependents; he was dissatisfied both with the rate of progress he was making in his work and with the speed at which he was becoming known. Yet the greater part of his distress was caused by his recurrent bouts of despondency, the cyclical nature of which had manifested itself early in his youth. "I dined yesterday on canvasback and terrapin, with champagne and all manner of wonderful drinks I had never tasted before warming my heart and brain, and I remembered the sordid orgies of my youth. [In more vigorous moods he recalled these orgies as romantic adventures.] We were ill-clad, ill-mannered beasts, and the drink was cheap and poor and nauseating. And then I dreamed dreams, and pulled myself up out of the slime to canvasback and terrapin and champagne, and learned that it was solely a difference of degree which art introduced into the fermenting."

Disillusioned words, sick words, but only momentarily meant, the relapse-mood of the rampant individualist who spends most of his energy conquering the world. Caught in the grip of his dejection he wrote, "What is this chemical ferment called life all about? Small wonder that small men down the ages have conjured gods in answer. A little god is a snug little possession and explains it all. But how about you and me who have no God? There's damned little satisfaction in being a materialistic monist."

From a professional viewpoint he had little cause to feel despondent, for on the twenty-seventh of December, George P. Brett, president of the Macmillan Company, one of the most vigorous publishing houses in America, had written to tell him that his stories represented the very best work of the kind that had been done in the country, and expressed a keen desire to publish him in America and England. In reply Jack had sent Brett a group of Alaskan-Indian stories under the title of *Children of the Frost.* Only five days after he had penned his melancholy sentences about this chemical ferment called life, Macmillan accepted *Children of the Frost,* and agreed to his request to advance him two hundred dollars. His weariness disappeared as he wrote to Brett, "I don't know whether *Children of the Frost* is an advance over previous work, but I do know that there are big books in me, and that when I find myself they will come out."

In February began Jack's migration to the hills. He found a house in Piedmont on five acres of ground, in a clump of magnificent pines, half the ground in bearing orchard, the other half in golden poppies. There were a large living-room and a dining-room finished in redwood, and in the pines a small cottage for Flora and Johnny Miller. "We have a most famous porch, broad and long and cool, and our view commands all of San Francisco Bay for a sweep of thirty or forty miles, and all the opposing shores such as Marin County and Mount Tamalpais, to say nothing of the Golden Gate and Pacific Ocean . . . and all for $35 a month!"

The house was always full of people; rarely were the spare beds unoccupied. Writers on a visit from the East were promptly brought to Jack's house, socialists on lecture tours, actors, musicians, intelligent friends of other friends. Since everyone was welcome and made to feel wanted, Jack's circle grew apace . . . as did his entertainment bills. The *Examiner* continued to give him spe-

cial assignments such as interviewing Governor Taft when he returned from the Philippines, but Jack groused to Cloudesley
Johns: "Lord, what stacks of hack I'm turning out. I wonder if I'll
ever get clear of debt?" When an Oakland grocer wrote him asking for a hundred and thirty-five dollars due, he answered in a fit
of temper with a scorching letter in which he upbraided the
tradesman for annoying and insulting him, told him to be courteous and wait his turn and he would be paid, that if he attempted
to blacklist him or make trouble, he would forfeit his turn among
the creditors. The grocer turned the letter over to the newspapers
for its advertising value, and the papers played it up with great
glee, the picture of a debtor putting a creditor in his place being
too delicious to resist. The article was syndicated all over the
country, and should have taught Jack not to write tempestuous
letters . . . a lesson he was never able to learn.

He was invited to speak before the Women's Press Association
of San Francisco, and told them he would lecture on Kipling, who
was still thought of by a considerable portion of the American
public as a crude and vulgar barbarian. The subject was widely advertised, the combination of Jack London and Rudyard Kipling
drawing a large and distinguished audience. When Jack mounted
the platform he announced that unfortunately he found he had
sent his article on Kipling to an English magazine in the hope of
selling it, and since he could not speak without his material, he
would give them instead his lecture on "The Tramp." The cold
waves generated by the rigidly circumspect group of San Francisco
women would have frozen anyone less impervious to his audience.
However, the women did not remain frigid at the end of the lecture, in which Jack justified the tramp, and blamed his position
on society; they attacked him with such vehemence that the
chairlady had to bang on the table with her gavel and adjourn the
meeting to prevent a free-for-all.—Of course the papers ran the
story.

Already known as an odd and colorful character around the
Bay, his reputation for eccentricity now became national in scope.
A reporter sent to interview him from *The Reader* magazine
writes, "Jack London is one of the most approachable of men, unconventional, responsive, and genuine, with a warmth of hospitality which places the visitor on an immediate footing of a

friend. He is boyish, noble, lovable; primitive, free, and unhack-
neyed." Jack is reported as saying, "Any style I have has been
acquired by sweat. Light out after it with a club, and if you don't
get it you'll get something that looks remarkably like it." The San
Francisco *Chronicle,* which first had begun to publicize him when
he was but a month in his mother's womb, gave a full-page spread
to the Piedmont Literary Colony, with pictures of Jack and his
home in the pines acknowledged to be its center.

In addition to the numerous hack articles he was writing a
novel for juveniles called *Cruise of the Dazzler,* a group of adventure stories for *Youth's Companion* under the title of *Tales of the
Fish Patrol,* serious Alaskan stories, and *The Kempton-Wace Letters* with Anna Strunsky. *The Kempton-Wace Letters,* a brilliant
philosophical analysis of the realist versus the romantic attitudes,
continued to be a curious defense by both of their position in
their love for each other. Jack, who had married Bessie on what
he liked to call the basis of reason, wrote: "Considered biologi-
cally, marriage is an institution necessary for the perpetuation of
the species. Romantic love is an artifice, blunderingly and unwittingly introduced by man into the natural order. Without an
erotic literature, a history of great loves and lovers, a garland of
love songs and ballads, a sheaf of spoken love tales and adventures
—without all this man could not possibly love in the way he does."
Anna Strunsky, the poet, insisted that "the flush of roselight in
the heavens, the touch of a hand, the color and shape of fruit, the
tears that come for unnamed sorrows are more significant than all
the building and inventing done since the first social compact.
You cannot explain the bloom, the charm, the smile of life, that
which rains sunshine into our hearts, which tells us we are wise to
hope."

By March they had fifty thousand words written, and Jack was
convinced the book would go. In order that their work might be
expedited he invited Anna to come and stay in his home. Two
years later she was to tell inquiring newspaper reporters: "I received a letter from Mr. London asking me to come to his house
in Piedmont to revise the manuscript. His wife and mother added
their requests. During the first days of my stay there Mrs. London
was cordial and manifested great interest in our work, but after a
stay of five days I became convinced that she had begun to dislike

me. [In 1937 Bessie London confided that she had come upon Miss Strunsky sitting on Jack's knee in his study, their heads glued together over the manuscript; no great breach, but upsetting to a woman of Mrs. London's strict sense of the proprieties.]

"She did nothing of any importance to make me feel out of place, but judging from several little occurrences I decided it was best for me to leave. I left very much against Mr. and Mrs. London's will. The farewell between Mrs. London and myself was that of two acquaintances between whom existed a mutual liking. Mr. London and I treated each other as friends, no more. Besides, Mr. London is hardly the man to make love to another woman in his own house. His behavior was most circumspect to me, and always has been. My observation at the time served to convince me that he was blindly in love with his wife."

That Miss Strunsky, a woman of the highest integrity, was telling the simple truth is confirmed by Jack, who wrote about her, "It was her intellect that fascinated me, not her womanhood. Primarily she was intellect and genius. I love to seek and delve in human souls, and she was an exhaustless mine to me. Protean, I called her. My term for her of intimacy and endearment was what? a term that was intellectual, that described her mind."

McClure still owned the rights to *A Daughter of the Snows*. Though he did not like the manuscript well enough to publish it himself, he made every effort to sell it to another house for book publication. At length he was successful, Lippincott's accepting it and paying an advance against royalties of seven hundred and fifty dollars. After McClure deducted what was still owed him, there remained a hundred and sixty-five dollars in cash for Jack. Jack wanted to withdraw the manuscript, but he was powerless to do so; besides, though it was a small sum of money, it enabled him to meet the demands of his more pressing creditors. When galley proof began to arrive for correction he was heartbroken; each batch seemed the worst, until the next batch came, and finally he commented that it was futile to try to doctor a sick thing.

On July 21 he received a telegraphic offer from the American Press to go to South Africa to report the Boer War. He was still three thousand dollars in debt; Bessie was pregnant again, and that would mean more expense; and it was the call of Adventure. He accepted by telegraph within the hour, packed his bag that night, and the following morning kissed Bessie and his daughter good-bye at the Oakland mole—where eight years before, when pursuing Kelly's Industrial Army, he had crawled into an empty freight car. On the train bound for Chicago he encountered a woman whose accidental presence served to accelerate the development of his own life plot. "Let me tell you a little affair which will indicate the ease with which I let loose the sexual man. You remember when I started for South Africa. In my car was traveling a woman with a maid and a child. We came together on the jump, at the very start, and had each other clear to Chicago. It was sexual passion, clear and simple. Beyond being a sweet woman, she had no charm for me. There was no glamour of the mind, not even an overwhelming intoxication of the senses. Nothing remained when our three days and nights were over."

Nothing but the memory of pleasure; for he had always enjoyed women for their entertainment value. He had no horoscope to which he might point and cry, "Alas! It is my fate," as had Professor Chaney, even though he had inherited in full measure his father's predatory instincts. "The flesh, in my cosmos, is a little thing. It is the soul that is everything. I love the flesh as the Greeks loved it, and yet it is a form of love that is almost, if not quite, artistic in nature." A little later his men friends were to call him, with pride, the Stallion.

Despite the fact that he writes, "I easily went the limit in those days," this affair on the train seems to have been the first time he let himself go in the two years of his marriage. Nor was it until he returned from England that his "little affair which will indicate the ease with which I let loose the sexual man" developed its full psychological consequences.

Once again he arrived in New York in the full heat of summer. This time he did not "batter the main stem for light pieces" with which to buy glasses of iced milk and imperfect copies of new books to read while lolling in the grass of City Hall Park; instead he went straight to the Macmillan Company, where for the first time he was able to clasp hands with a publisher. George P. Brett was an astute editor, a liberal and honest man with a deep love for literature; he was in addition a staunch friend who was to be Jack's guardian angel through many stormy years, and a lifelong Jack London admirer. Jack had a boat to catch and there was little time for negotiating, but the two men agreed that when Jack returned from South Africa they would enter into a permanent relationship under which Macmillan would publish all the books Jack wrote. Jack told Brett about *The Kempton-Wace Letters*, which he accepted at once for publication.

When he reached England, where he was supposed to interview British generals for their views on the future in the Transvaal before sailing for South Africa, Jack found a cable canceling the engagement. His round-trip transportation had been paid, and a small amount of advance money which he had already spent. Here he was in London, seven thousand miles from home, without resources, and without a job to do.

Always a man of swift adaptability, he decided to go into the East End of London, which his extensive reading in sociology had taught him was one of the worst hell holes for humanity in the western world, and investigate conditions. It did not occur to him that this was a daring and difficult task, that it took almost foolhardy courage for an utter stranger, an American who had been on English soil only forty-eight hours, to attempt to understand, analyze, and then confound a nation with one of its major economic problems. His first volume of short stories had already been released in England, and had received, from a usually conservative press, surprisingly good notices. His publishers were friendly; he could have spent an amusing few weeks among the English literati, enjoyed a vacation. Instead he found a second-hand store on Petticoat Lane, bought a pair of well-worn trousers, a frayed jacket with one remaining button, a pair of brogans which plainly had seen service where coal was shoveled, a thin leather belt, and a very dirty cloth cap, and plunged into the heart of the East End. He rented a room in the most congested district of the slums, then ventured forth to become acquainted. His publishers had been horrified, had told him that it was impossible, that he would be murdered in his sleep. Jack was a son of the people; he laughed at their fears.

He was taken for an American sailor who had been ditched at port. Once again he became Sailor Jack, slipping into the rôle as easily as though he had never left it. He was no outsider, no research man looking down from academic heights; he was one of them, a seafaring man down on his luck. The people of the East

End accepted him, trusted him, and talked to him. What he learned about this human shambles he put into a book called *The People of the Abyss*, which is fresh and vigorous and true today, one of the world's classics about the underprivileged.

"I took with me certain simple criteria with which to measure. That which made for more life, for physical and spiritual health, was good; that which made for less life, which hurt, dwarfed, and distorted life, was bad." From the basis of these "simple criteria" he found that life in the Abyss, where lives one tenth of London's population, was a prolonged, chronic starvation, families of father, mother, and children working long hours and every day, and earning enough to afford only one room in which the entire family had to cook, eat, sleep, and discharge all the duties of intimate living. He found disease, despair, and death the inseparable companions of the People of the Abyss, saw homeless men and women, guilty of no crime but ill health and poverty, pushed about and maltreated as though they were loathsome animals. That some of these people were congenital loafers and wastrels, he soon found out, but just as from his experiences on The Road in America, he discovered that ninety per cent of the East-Enders had been conscientious workingmen until old age, sickness, or business slack had thrown them out of their jobs. Now, unemployed, or at best making sweat-shop products in their rooms, they and their families were left by the City of London to rot away until providential death cleaned them off the streets.

"The London Abyss is a vast shambles; no more dreary spectacle can be found. The color of life is gray and drab, everything is hopeless, unrelieved, and dirty. Bathtubs are a thing totally unknown; any attempts at cleanliness become howling farce. Strange, vagrant odors come drifting along the greasy wind; the Abyss exudes a stupefying atmosphere of torpor which wraps about the people and deadens them. Year by year rural England pours in a flood of vigorous young life that perishes by the third generation. At all times four hundred and fifty thousand human creatures are dying miserably at the bottom of the social pit called London."

On the coronation day of Edward VII Jack walked up to Trafalgar Square to watch the majestic medieval pageant. For company on his walk he had a carter, a carpenter, and a sailor, old now and out of work. He saw that from the slimy sidewalk they were picking up bits of orange peel, apple skin, and grape stems and eating them; stray crumbs of bread the size of peas, apple cores black and dirty, these things the men took into their mouths and chewed and swallowed. "It has been urged that the criticism I have passed on things as they are in England is too pessimistic. I must say in extenuation that of optimists I am the most optimistic. I measure manhood less by political aggregations than by individuals. For the English I see a broad and smiling future, but for a great deal of the political machinery, which at present mismanages them, I see nothing less than the scrap heap."

He rented a room in the home of a London detective which he could use as a place of refuge to bathe, change his clothes, do his reading, and write his book without becoming suspect. In the course of three months he studied hundreds of pamphlets, books, and government reports on poverty in London, interviewed countless men and woman, took pictures, tramped miles of streets, lived in workhouses, paupers' homes, stood in bread lines, slept in the streets and parks with his newly made friends, and in addition wrote a complete book—a triumph of energy, organization, and burning passion for his subject.

He arrived in New York in November with the manuscript of *The People of the Abyss* in his suitcase. He hoped that Macmillan would publish it, but he well knew that he could not make money from his sociology. The man who had told Anna Strunsky he was going to extract every last dollar from his writing, who had written to Cloudesley Johns that the magazines could buy him body and soul if they paid the price, again gave the lie to himself. He was a writer first, a socialist second; the man who wanted to earn money ran a very poor third.

A friend who met him at the dock writes, "He wore a wrinkled sack coat, the pockets of which bulged with papers and letters. His trousers bagged at the knees. He was minus a vest, and his outing shirt was far from immaculate. A leather belt around his waist took the place of suspenders. On his head he wore a dinky little cap." George P. Brett, however, had eyes only for Jack's manuscript. He thought *The People of the Abyss* a penetrating job, made some trenchant sociological criticisms, and accepted it at once. Jack told him, "I want to get away from the Klondike. I have served my apprenticeship at writing in that field, and I feel that I am better fitted now to attempt a larger and more generally interesting field. I have half a dozen books, fiction all, that I want to write. I have done a great deal of thinking and studying in the last two years, since I wrote my first novel, and I am confident that I can today write something worthwhile."

Brett was equally confident, and acceded to Jack's plea that Macmillan pay him a hundred and fifty dollars a month for two years. In return they were to publish all the books he wrote during that period. In part Brett gave him what was perhaps the best single piece of advice he was ever to receive. "I hope that your work from this time on will show the marks of advancement which I found so strong in your earlier books, but which is not so marked in the last volume or so, these showing signs of haste. There is no real place in the world of literature for anything but the best a man can do." To which Jack replied, "My hope, once I am on my feet, is not to write prolifically, but to turn out one book, a good book a year. Even as it is, I am not a prolific writer. I write very slowly. The reason I have turned out so much is that I have worked constantly, day in and day out, without taking a rest. Once I am in a position where I do not have to depend upon each day's work to keep the pot boiling for the next day, where I do not have to dissipate my energy on all kinds of hack, where I can slowly and deliberately ponder and shape the best that is in me, then, at that time, I am confident that I shall do big work."

On the train headed west Jack spread opposite him on the Pullman seat his three books that had been published in October, just a few weeks before he returned to New York: *A Daughter of the Snows, The Cruise of the Dazzler,* and *Children of the Frost.* He realized that the publication of three books by one man in a single month was not only a record, but also a foolhardy piece of business, the one for which Brett had chided him. He resolved that now that he had "settled down with one publishing house" he would manage his affairs better. Along with the books, he spread out clippings from the newspapers to see how his work had fared. About *A Daughter of the Snows,* which had been put out by Lippincott, the press made many incisive criticisms, accused him of making Frona Welse unbelievable, and of not handling his construction problems; but for the rest the critics were tolerant, spoke enthusiastically of his strong, graphic style, and predicted that he would do better with his second novel. Jack, who had anticipated a lashing, blew a sigh of relief. *The Cruise of the Dazzler*, which was released by the Century Company, received only the mild reception that he could expect from a novel for juveniles. The most important of his three books, *Children of the Frost*, the Alaskan-Indian stories that were Macmillan's first publication, established him as the dominant figure in the American short story.

Sitting back in his seat pleasedly musing over the past few crowded years as the landscape flashed by unseen, he mingled his memories of his determination to recreate the American short story with the lines of praise the critics had lavished on *Children of the Frost*: ". . . has few superiors as a story-teller . . . a domain which is his by right of conquest . . . marvelous literary development, will last . . . will win fame both wide and permanent." Though he was happy and proud of himself he realized that he had gained merely the bottom rung of the ladder, that the fight had only begun. Mulling over his ideas and plans, he vowed to do for the American novel what he had already done for the short story. Since Herman Melville there had been no great sea novels in American literature; he would write great sea novels. There were as yet no great proletarian novels in American literature; he would not only write great proletarian novels and make the critics and public like them, but he would also hasten the socialist revolution. He had his work cut out for him; it would take a full twenty years to accomplish everything he had in mind. He determined to fulfill every demand of his program before his time on earth was up.

When Jack reached Piedmont he found that Eliza had been living with Bessie for some six weeks, keeping peace and quiet between Bessie and Flora. His reunion with his family was a joyous one; on November 21, 1902, in writing to Brett a brief survey of his life, Jack said: "Finding myself anchored with a household, I resolved to have the compensations of a household, so I married and increased the weight of my anchor. But I have never regretted it. I have been well compensated."

More than ever he found that he had become a busy literator, for not only had he his new work to write, but proofs to read on

The Kempton-Wace Letters, and corrections and additions to make to the manuscript of *The People of the Abyss.* He so relished being immersed in the welter of books and stories and publications that he went back to his schedule of nineteen hours a day of work, with five hours of sleep. The only time spent in relaxation was during his Wednesday open house, when his old friends gathered and new friends came into the fold, when he played poker and practical jokes, and initiated his cronies into the intricacies of the English puzzles he had packed into his suitcase.

When Bessie came out of her travail she found that she had once again presented her husband with a daughter. Jack's hand was not cut this time; what was cut was the lifeline of hope that he would have a son to whom he could hand down not only his name but his literary tradition. He made himself miserable and ill with frustration; his disappointment made Bessie ill, too.

After wandering about disconsolate for a number of days, a fresh idea shook him out of his lethargy. It was a dog story, which he intended to do in four thousand words, a companion-piece to another dog story he had written the year before. At the end of four days he had written his four thousand words and discovered to his surprise that he had barely begun, that the story was taking on motivation and scope of which he had never dreamed. He decided that he would name it *The Call of the Wild,* and let it grow however it willed, for the story was master now and he the servant writing it; it had taken hold of his imagination and fired him as no other yarn he had ever tackled. For thirty glorious, labor-laden days he wrote with his thick pencil on the rough scratch paper, made his few word corrections, and transferred the material to the typewriter. He neglected everything else—friends, family, debts, the new baby, galley proof arriving in daily batches from Macmillan; living only with his dog Buck, half Saint Bernard and half Scotch shepherd, who had been a country gentleman on a ranch in the Santa Clara Valley until he was kidnapped and shipped into the primitive wilds of the Klondike.

Then at a Wednesday open house Jack made good his neglect of his friends. He settled himself in the comfortable lounging chair by the fire while his guests placed themselves in the window seats and on cushions on the floor. With a grave look in his gray-blue eyes, one hand combing fondly through his hair, he read to them the story of the great dog Buck, who remained faithful to his love of man until the call of the forest and the recollection of wild wolves drew him back to primitive life. There were no card games that night, no wild laughter or practical jokes. Jack read until one in the morning, the silence growing ever deeper about him. When he had finished, his usually loquacious friends could say little, but he saw their thoughts in their shining eyes. His three years of writing Alaskan tales had been at last justified; he had expressed himself in an art form so flawlessly and completely that for these few hours his listeners shared with him the ecstasy he had known in its creation.

The following morning he put the manuscript into an envelope, stamped it, enclosed another stamped envelope to bring it back to him, and sent his story to the *Saturday Evening Post,* the most popular and highest paying magazine in the world. He knew no one on the staff; they had never been hospitable to his work, and he had little expectation of selling them the story. But the "cunning arrangement of cogs that changed a manuscript from one envelope to another," against which he had inveighed so strongly four years before when he had been a novice, failed to function. The *Saturday Evening Post* did not use the stamped return envelope with which he had provided them. Instead they sent him a flat, oblong one, in which he found a glowing letter of acceptance, and a check for seven hundred and fifty dollars.

Seven hundred and fifty dollars for a month's work! He had always said that serious literature could pay dividends. He had always said he would write his own way, and make the editors like it. Seven hundred and fifty dollars . . . enough to pay the doctor bills for his second daughter, Bess, the accumulated doctor bills for Flora and for the mother of Johnny Miller, to pay his debts to insurance companies, department stores, grocers, butchers, druggists, clothing, typewriter, and stationery stores, to help all his friends who needed assistance . . . enough to buy those new glass bookcases he wanted, and to order that list of forty books from the East. Not since he had sold "An Odyssey of the North" had he known such an overflowing measure of exultation. Had he not justified everything he stood for? Had he not, within sixty days of his heroic resolution on the train from New York, begun his revitalization of the American novel? When those friends who had listened to the reading of *The Call of the Wild* thronged back into the house to congratulate him, to wring his hand and slap him on the back, had he not to send down for another gallon of sour Italian wine and get tipsy dreaming more roseate dreams for the future?

Now that things were better for him he engaged a second servant to help Bessie, who was having a difficult time recovering her strength, and entertained more widely. Into his house came many attractive women; after his successful siege of work Jack began to avail himself of them. There perhaps had been an insufficient sexual compulsion in his marriage, but even if that were not so, there was the burden of Bessie having been pregnant for eighteen and recovering from her deliveries for at least another six of the thirty-two months of their marriage. A man of vigorous appetites, accustomed to sexual satisfaction since the days of Mamie on the *Razzle Dazzle*, this had worked a hardship on him; his three days and nights with the woman on the train to Chicago remained strong in his memory. Less than three years after he had written, "My heart is large, and I shall be a cleaner, wholesomer man because of a restraint being laid upon me in place of being free to drift wheresoever I listed," he renounced all obligations to abstinence.

"You know my sexual code," he later wrote, "you know the circumstances of the period, you know I had no compunction of dallying along the primrose path." Dally he did, to the fullest extent of his opportunities, yet for him, outside of his marriage, there was no emotion tied up with the sexual act; it was a purely sensory experience, giving pleasure to both parties and hence, since he was a hedonist, a deed of virtue in direct proportion to the harmless pleasure incurred. "Though I have roved and ranged and looted, I have never looted under false pretense. Never once have I said, 'I love you' for the gain it might often have brought me. I have been fair, and fastidiously so, in my dealings with women, demanding no more than I was willing to give. I bought, or took in fair exchange, and I never lied to get the best of a bargain or to get the bargain that was otherwise beyond me." And, in an effort to justify himself: "Man can pursue his lusts, without love, simply because he is so made. Mother Nature cries compellingly through him for progeny, and so man obeys her urging, not because he is a wilful sinner, but because he is a creation of law."

Jack had not mentioned *The Call of the Wild* in the list of books he outlined to Macmillan because he had not known he was going to write it. He sent the manuscript to Brett, who replied on March 5, saying that he did not like the title. "I like the story very well indeed, although I am afraid it is too true to nature and too good work to be really popular with the sentimentalist public which swallows Seton-Thompson with delight." Brett then made him an offer of two thousand dollars for immediate publication on an outright sale basis, instead of contracting for it on a royalty basis and postponing publication for a year or two. "I would like to try an experiment in relation to this book, putting it out in a very attractive typographic form and spending a very large sum of money in endeavoring to give it a wide circulation and thus assist the sale of not only your already published books, but of those still to come. But don't let me overpersuade you in the matter. The decision is entirely in your hands and if you decide not to accept the cash offer we will publish the book in due course under the terms of our agreement."

He had already spent the seven hundred and fifty dollars from the *Saturday Evening Post;* the Macmillan hundred and fifty dollars a month was inadequate to support his family of six, two servants, and Mammy Jenny. No book of his had ever earned one thousand dollars in royalties, let alone two thousand dollars, and there was no reason to believe this one would be an exception. Even if the book were to earn two thousand dollars, he would have to wait at least two years for his royalties, and then the money might well have been absorbed by his advance hundred and fifty dollars a month. This was two thousand dollars clear, right now, and money in the hand was money that could be spent . . . particularly for that trim little boat called the *Spray* he had his eye on. He accepted Brett's proposition and sold out all interest in *The Call of the Wild.*

The *Spray* was a sailing sloop with a good-sized cabin in which he could cook and sleep two persons. He bought her not only because he longed once again to live upon the water, but because he had been contemplating a sea novel, and he wanted the feel of a ship under him before he began writing. It was nine years since he had come off the *Sophie Sutherland;* his gear had gone rusty. "It will be almost literally a narrative of things that happened on a seven months' voyage I once made as a sailor. The oftener I have thought upon the things that happened during that trip, the more remarkable they appear to me." Brett replied, "I feel very great hopes for your sea story. So few sea stories are appearing, and none of these good for anything, that a really good sea story at the present time would without question achieve a very remarkable success."

With Brett's encouraging words ringing in his ears, he provisioned the *Spray* with food and blankets and went for a week's sail on the Bay, retracing the trips he had made up the sloughs and straits when he had been a daring oyster pirate and member of the Fish Patrol. At the end of a week, with the sea salt in his nostrils and the feel of sail-ropes in his calloused hands, he returned home, sat down at his desk and wrote *The Sea Wolf,* Chapter One. Whenever the interruptions proved too great, the friends about him too many, he put food on board the *Spray* and pushed off by himself, writing his fifteen hundred words each morning as he sat on the hatch and let the early spring sun warm his body to the pitch that his thoughts about the Sea Wolf were warming his brain. Later in the day he went sailing, shot ducks on the Sacramento River, fished for his supper. On Saturday afternoons and Sundays he sometimes took Bessie and his two daughters, Eliza and her son, and a crowd of his friends for a sail.

It was a busy and exhilarated period. *Wilshire's,* a socialist magazine, published *The People of the Abyss* serially, which put him in the front rank of American socialists; he wrote "How I Became a Socialist" for *The Comrade,* and a series of critical articles for the *International Socialist Review. Wilshire's* paid him a modest sum for *The People of the Abyss,* but for the socialist newspapers he wrote always without pay. He also composed two new lectures to give to the socialist locals about the Bay, "The Class Struggle," and "The Scab," both of which were published in the socialist press. Fellow socialists began to write to him from all parts of the country; invariably they began their letter, "Dear Comrade" and ended it "Yours for the Revolution." Jack answered every letter himself, beginning "Dear Comrade" and ending "Yours for the Revolution."

With the spread of his name and fame, Jack's home in Piedmont became an intellectual center of the Bay area. No less than a hundred people a week walked through his front door, enjoyed his hospitality. Even with two servants, and Mammy Jenny to care for the children, there was a great deal of work to be done. Bessie was not always in the mood for more and more company and more and more work; for one Wednesday night open house she is reported as purposely preparing less food than would be necessary to feed the horde of people that would be coming in. Nor was she too pleased at the way the women were flocking about her Jack—Jack of the warm, golden smile and booming laugh—flinging themselves at his head. She grew jealous. Jack wanted Bessie to buy beautiful clothes for the many formal affairs to which he was now invited; Bessie declined to buy them. Eliza shopped with her and showed her how stunning she looked in a long velvet gown and a velvet hat with a plume, but she insisted upon wearing blouses, sailor skirts, and sailor hats, even to such affairs as the dinner at the swank Bohemian Club in San Francisco at which Jack was the guest of honor. Jack felt badly about this; he admired Bessie's figure and wanted to show her off to her best advantage. That she was far from well, and had little desire to be out at all, is part of the explanation; the other part is that Fred Jacobs had probably admired her in blouses and sailor skirts.

In spite of these minor frictions, Jack and Bessie got along well together. The one complaint he voiced to her was that he wished she would read more, so they could discuss the new books. Bessie replied that there was nothing she would like better to do, but that she was awakened at six by the baby, and from that moment until ten at night it was an unending round of routine tasks. Jack patted her hand sympathetically, said yes, he knew, and that when the children grew a little older she would have more time for her reading. Though people attest, thirty-five years later, that they appeared an incongruous couple—Bessie seemed middle-aged and matronly, Jack a vivacious young boy—everyone agrees that they lived together harmoniously. Eliza London Shepard, who saw a great deal of them at the time, often staying in their house, attests to this most strongly. Apparently the only criticism Jack made against his wife in his own mind—as reflected by the notes he kept at the time—is that Bessie was literal-minded, that "she had a narrow band around her forehead." In all fairness to his wife he also acknowledged that he had always known this, that the emotional stability it gave her was something he sorely needed, and had attracted him to her in the first place. It is at this very time, March, 1903, that Jack wrote to Cloudesley Johns, who at Jack's wedding had said, "I will withhold my congratulations until your tenth anniversary": "By the way, I think your long deferred congratulations upon my marriage are about due. I have been married nearly three years, have a couple of kids, and think it's great. So fire away. Or, come and take a look at us, and at the kids, and then congratulate."

He swung along vigorously on *The Sea Wolf*, the creating of which was bringing him far greater joy than had even *The Call of the Wild*. In his spare hours he wrote such excellent Alaskan tales as "The One Thousand Dozen," "Gold Hunters of the North," and a dozen others. In addition to the *Spray* he bought a horse and rig to cart his family and friends around the countryside, for warm weather was coming on and he liked to take a crowd into the hills to picnic and play games, swim in the reservoir, and broil steaks over wood fires. Late in April he was thrown from the buggy and had the tip of one of his thumbs cut off. "It feels as though it had a heart beating at the end of it," he complained, but the accident did not prevent him from writing his thousand words a day on *The Sea Wolf*, the main character of which was based on Captain Alex McClean, of whose amazing exploits he had heard while he was on the *Sophie Sutherland*. He continued to sail the *Spray* for relaxation and privacy, once having his sails cut to ribbons in a surprise storm, and finding it difficult to make the Estuary.

In June *The Kempton-Wace Letters* was published anonymously, receiving a good press. "Unusual . . . thoughtful, frank . . . sure to have a wide reading . . . has much of the enquiring spirit of today . . . good meat for the mind . . . a new departure in novel writing . . . piquant, clever, original philosophy." The San Francisco *Argonaut* recognized one of the authors by the "evolutionary deductions," and the news spread so rapidly that when Macmillan was printing its second edition it asked Jack's permission to acknowledge the authorship. *The Kempton-Wace Letters* sold only moderately well, having too little action, plot, and swiftness for the general public, but Jack and Anna Strunsky exchanged letters between Piedmont and New York, where she was now living, congratulating each other on an important job well done.

Late in June, desiring to take her two children to the country for the summer, Bessie rented a cabin in a grove of cabins which had been put up by Mrs. Ninetta Eames as a summer resort at Glen Ellen, in Sonoma County in the Valley of the Moon. Jack wanted to continue to sail the *Spray* and concentrate on *The Sea Wolf*, so he remained in Piedmont. One night toward the end of the month when he was crossing the hills in his buggy with George Sterling and some other men friends, the buggy ran off the road and plunged into a ravine. Jack's leg was badly hurt. Charmian Kittredge came frequently to nurse him. At the beginning of July, as soon as he was able to walk, Jack left for Glen Ellen to join his family. Charmian Kittredge also went to Glen Ellen, to join her aunt.

The *Overland Monthly* was having difficulties. Roscoe Eames and Edward Payne were out of work. Edward Payne and Mrs. Eames had built an octogan-shaped house called Wake Robin on the banks of a stream opposite which Payne, who was a Unitarian minister without a pulpit, had put together picnic tables and log seats to hold revival meetings and philosophical discussions. In order to make money out of the project, Mrs. Eames had built the cabins and put up tents, which she rented out to families.

When Jack reached Glen Ellen he found his family comfortably entrenched in a cabin with a canvas top, located in a grove of wine-colored manzanita and madrone. The campers lived as a communal group; everyone cooked their meals in a common kitchen by the river bank, and ate on long picnic tables. Jack spent a few dollars to dam the clear, cool stream where it flowed along a sandy beach, and the entire camp collected to swim and sun itself. Here Jack spent his afternoons playing with the youngsters, teaching them to swim. In the mornings he went to a shaded and secluded spot on the bank of the stream where, on the sawed-off-trunk of an oak tree, he scrawled his thousand words a day. And one night toward the end of July the entire camp assembled, even the small children, snugly wrapped in blankets, to hear him read the first half of *The Sea Wolf*. He read the manuscript as it rested on the tree trunk on which he had written it, flanked on either side by candles, the campers and neighbors spread out on the ground at his feet. Dawn was beginning to mottle the sky over Sonoma Mountain when he turned the last page. The people alive today who heard Jack London read *The Sea Wolf* by the bank of that stream in Glen Ellen, in late July, 1903, still remember it as one of the most beautiful and moving experiences of their lives.

And then, within a few hours, came the explosion that shattered the existence of the London family. It would perhaps be best to have Bessie tell the story in her own words.

"One day toward the end of July, after lunch, Jack and I stayed down by the stream and talked. He wanted to get away from Oakland for a time, because there were too many interruptions to his work. He said that he had been thinking about buying a ranch on the Southern California Desert, and asked if I would mind going down there to live. I told him, not at all, as long as there would be modern conveniences for the children. [Bessie was mother first, wife second.] Jack promised, and we made plans to leave in the fall.

"At about two o'clock I took my two babies back to the cabin to put them to sleep. Miss Kittredge had been waiting around, and I saw them walk over to a big hammock at the side of Mrs. Eames's house and begin to talk. I thought nothing of it. I put the two children to sleep and worked around the cabin straightening up. Miss Kittredge and Jack sat in that hammock for four solid hours and talked.

"At six o'clock Jack walked up to the cabin and said, 'Bessie, I am leaving you.' Not understanding what he was talking about, I asked, 'You mean you're going back to Piedmont?' 'No,' replied Jack, 'I'm leaving you . . . separating. . . .' Stunned, I sank to the edge of a cot and stared at him for a long time before I could stammer, 'Why, Daddy, what do you mean . . . you've just been talking about Southern California. . . .' Jack kept repeating doggedly that he was separating from me, and I kept crying, 'But I don't understand . . . what has happened to you?' He refused to tell me another word."

No one, least of all Bessie, knew that Charmian Kittredge had happened to Jack. Of all the women of whom she might have been jealous, it had never entered her mind to be jealous of Miss Kittredge, who was between five and six years older than Jack, not attractive-looking, the subject of a good deal of biting talk and comment among the Piedmont crowd who knew her well. She had been around Jack a good deal, but Bessie was accustomed to that from the house in Piedmont. Jack apparently had not been seeing more of her than of anyone else at the camp. Besides, he had said a number of uncomplimentary things about her to his wife; Bessie knew that he did not care much for her.

In June, 1903, a month before the separation, Miss Kittredge was writing to Jack, "Oh, you are wonderful—most wonderful of all. I saw your face grow younger under my touch. What is the matter with the world, and where do I belong? I think nowhere, if a man's heart be nowhere." In the same month Jack writes to her: "My arms are about you. I kiss you on the lips, the free frank lips I know and love. Had you been coy and fluttering, giving the lie to what you had already appeared to be by manifesting the slightest prudery or false fastidiousness, I really think I should have been utterly disgusted. 'Dear man, dear love!' I lie awake repeating those phrases over and over."

On July 7 Charmian Kittredge writes to Jack: "I am growing frightened about one thing. I am afraid that you and I will never be able to express what we are to each other. The whole thing is so tremendous and all human modes of expression too inadequate." A few days later she typewrites from her business office in San Francisco: "You are a poet and you are beautiful. Believe me, oh my dear, my dear, that I never was so GLAD, so genuinely, satisfyingly GLAD over anything in my life. To feel that the man who is the greatest of all to me, has not found me wanting."

In the canvas-covered cabin at Glen Ellen, with his two children sleeping peacefully, Jack spent what was probably the most wretched and confused night of his life. He was above all a gentle, kindly person. Sensitive himself, knowing the nature of pain, he had shrunk from hurting others. It had always been his great joy to help people, to share with them everything he had. Yet he was caught in the grip of such a shattering compulsion that he was walking out on his wife and babies just as he had walked out on Flora and John London when he was younger and emotionally unstable. A tender human being, a socialist who had compassion for all of humanity, who was willing to give the best in him, without hope of reward, to better the lot of the masses, his social and moral consciousness was shoved aside by the conflicting Nietzschean ideal, the strange but constant bedfellow of his socialism, which told him that he was the superman who could wrest from life whatever he wished, that he had no need to concern himself with slave morality, or the feelings of the slave-mass, of which Bessie was an unfortunate member.

In the morning Jack returned to Piedmont, moved his possessions out of the house he had written about so proudly to his friends, and rented a room from the family of Frank Atherton. Within a few days the newspapers had the story of the separation splashed over the front page. Since Jack refused to talk to the reporters, they blamed his separation on *The Kempton-Wace Letters,* for in it Jack had written, "The emotion of love is not based on reason." This sentiment was alleged to have hurt Bessie so deeply that it had caused a break-up of their marriage.

7

JACK'S relationship with Charmian Kittredge started on a high plane of avowal and mounted ever higher. On September 1 she writes to him: "You are my very OWN, and I adore you, just as blindly and madly and passionately and unreasonably as ever girl loved before." The next day she continues: "Ah, my love, you ARE such a man. And I love you, every bit of you, as I have never loved, and shall never love again!" Two days later: "Oh, you are my dear Love my Own Man, my very, actual, true Heart Husband, and I love you so!" In her next letter she says: "Think of me tenderly and lovingly and madly; think of me as your dear dear friend, your Sweetheart, your Wife. You are all the world to me, and I shall live on the thought of your face, your voice, your mouth, your masterful and tender arms—all the whole, sweet Man—until we meet again. Oh, Jack, Jack! You're so booful!"

Not to be outstripped in protestation or literary expression, Jack replies, "You cannot know how much you mean to me. As you say, it is inexpressible. The moments when first I meet you, and see you, and touch you, are unspeakably thrilling moments. When I receive your letters you are with me, in the flesh before me, and

I am looking into your golden eyes. Ah, dear heart, my love for woman did begin with you and will end with you."

For fear of the scandal that would descend upon them when the cause of his separation became known, the lovers met secretly once or twice a week. During the days when they could not be together they released a torrent of letters to each other. From her business office in San Francisco Miss Kittredge wrote daily letters ranging from one thousand to five thousand words; the many hundreds of pages she composed and typed to Jack during the ensuing two years would be the equivalent of half a dozen normal-sized novels. Her letters are artful and coquettish, fluttery and flowery, but beneath the façade of verbiage can be detected the hand of a shrewd and clever woman. Pictured through her letters their love becomes the greatest love of all times. She tells him that she always knew she was intended for some extraordinary destiny. "Oh, Jack, dear, dear Love, you are my idol, and you cannot know how I love you," until he comes to believe that he is loved as no man since the beginning of time has ever been loved, and he answers, convinced, "I doubt if I can ever love you enough, so greatly do you love me." The way in which he takes her cues, letter by letter, is almost automatic; since he is the literary one of the relationship, can he write any the less gallantly, avowedly, passionately?

"Nay, nay, dear Love," he writes, "not in my eyes is this love of ours a small and impotent thing. That I should be willing to live for you or die for you is proof in itself that it means more to me than life or death. That you should be the one woman to me of all women; that my hunger for you should be greater than any hunger for food I have ever felt; that my desire for you should bite harder than any desire I have ever felt for fame and fortune— all, all goes to show how big is this, our love."

Under the spell of Miss Kittredge's thousands of words beating daily against his eyes, he begins to sound like a fifth-rate Marie Corelli. Mesmerized by her literary style, he replies in her own florid-purple nineteenth-century effusion, a manner against which he had asserted his revolt since the days of his earliest writing; a style of effervescing about love from which he was never to recover, and which was to mar so many of his books. Jack, who in *The Kempton-Wace Letters* had been the antagonist of sentimental and poetic love, the advocate of the theory that love is just a biological urge, suddenly becomes "God's own mad lover, dying on a kiss." If Anna Strunsky could have read over his shoulder and seen how completely he had reversed his position, she might have enjoyed an ironic laugh while confronting him with his own line, "Without an erotic literature man could not possibly love in the way he does."

Writing from Stockton on November 10, 1903, he reaches the heights of his profusion. "Know, sweet love, that I never knew how greatly you loved me until there came the free and utter abandonment, the consent of you and your love and of every fibre of you. When you sealed with your dear body all that your soul had told me, then I knew! I knew!—knew that the last of you and all of you were mine. Had you loved me as you do, and yet withheld, you would not have been quite so great a woman to me. My love and worship of you would not have attained the sheer pitch that they have. If you will go over my letters I am sure you will find that I was never utterly *mad* until after you gave greatly. It was *after* you gave greatly that I became your 'slave,' expressed willingness to die for you, and all the rest of the delicious hyperbole of love. But it is not hyperbole, dear, not the hyperbole of the silly sentimentalist. When I say I am your slave, I say it as a *reasonable* man—which goes to show how really and completely mad I am."

In 1890, when she was nineteen years old Charmian Kittredge was, in her own words, "a rosy-cheeked girl whom many people call pretty, generally in good spirits except when jealous." By 1903, at thirty-two, she was not considered pretty; she had thin lips, narrow eyes, and drooping lids, but she carried herself with an air of exciting bravado. In many ways she resembled Frona Welse, whom Jack had created to stand as a model for the twentieth-century woman. Forced by the death of her parents to earn her own living in the days when it was not considered genteel for a girl to work, she had made herself into a competent secretary "earning the small and insufficient salary of thirty dollars a month." She was well read, unconventional in thought; when Jack first met her, in 1900, she had already begun to collect a library of the more modern and daring novels the Oakland Public Library was banning. She had a genuine love for music, sang pleasingly, and even while working six days a week had had the force and discipline to train herself to become an accomplished pianist.

She had a sexually rich and stimulating voice with a wide tone range, laughed a great deal, even though the point of humor might be obscure, and was an indefatigable talker, being known to speak from four to seven hours without interrupting herself. She could carry on an intelligent and logical discussion, for she had a varied flow of words and phrases. A woman of great physical courage, she was the first to ride astride a horse into the hills when few women were riding at all, and those who dared were riding English side-saddle on the Golden Gate Park bridle paths. She had a deep love of horses. Ambitious, both socially and intellectually, she worked hard to advance herself, had saved her money with which to take a trip through Europe, did a little painting on China dishes, tried hard to make progress each year over the last.

However, as reflected by her frothy language and frilly lace caps, by her fluttering manner, in anything relating to love and sex she was a perfect blooming of the nineteenth-century woman, the exact opposite of Frona Welse. Many facets of her complex nature are revealed in her diary: her saccharine, sentimentalist approach to romance; every man she meets, no matter how casually, instantly becomes in her mind the source of a great romance. Every man looks at her either admiringly or passionately, and cannot tear his eyes from her. She has little use for her own sex; every woman is jealous of her and she is jealous of every woman. When there were men about she dramatized herself with verve, with gusto, making a conscious bid for the focus of attention. People who knew her disclose that she was no respecter of private property as far as men were concerned. Because of her preoccupation with the snaring of a husband, young women who were keeping company or were married were suspicious and afraid of her.

There is a continuous string of men who come into her life and are soon gone. One is hard-pressed to understand why so attractive a young woman was not able to achieve marriage. Miss Kittredge, too, is stumped. Auntie, who demands immediately if each new man's intention is marriage, is getting nervous as the years pass by and all the other girls marry but her niece somehow always misses out.

Miss Kittredge had been a frequent visitor at the London house in Piedmont on her return from Europe, and in his vagrant mood Jack went on the make. "I confess what you already know, what you knew from the very first moment. When I first broke silence it was with the intention of making you my mistress. You were so frank, so honest, and not least so unafraid. Had you been less so, in one touch, one pressure, one action, one speech, I think I should have attempted to beat down your will to mine. . . . I remember when we rode side by side on a back seat, and I suggested 'Haywards' and you looked me in the eyes, smiling, not mocking, with no offended fastidiousness in your face, no shock, no fear, no surprise, nothing but good nature and sweet frankness —when you looked me thus in the eyes and said simply, 'Not tonight.' "

Two months after his separation from Bessie, Jack writes, "Sometimes I wonder why I love you, and I am compelled to confess that it is not for your beautiful body or mind that I love you, but for the flash of spirit that runs through all of you, that makes you carry your clothes, that makes you game, that makes you sensitive; that makes you proud, proud in yourself, proud of your body, and that makes your body in itself and apart from you, proud."

There can be little doubt but that he had become entangled with Miss Kittredge during the month of June, when he was alone in the house in Piedmont, and that his suggestion to Bessie that they move to Southern California, leaving behind the San Francisco Bay he loved so dearly, was an attempt to escape from the situation in which he found himself. It apparently took Miss Kittredge four hours of solid talk to change his mind.

"If either of his two daughters had been a son," observed one of Jack's closest friends, "no force on earth could have torn him away from his family."

Charmian Kittredge was genuinely convinced that Jack was mismated; she believed she could be the kind of wife he needed, one who would roam and adventure and dare with him, and not be tied down to a home and routine. Abetted by her Aunt Netta, who harbored the lovers from the very beginning, she appears to have been the motivating force behind the break-up in the London family, yet the fact that Jack was vulnerable is evidenced by the completeness with which he gave his mind's love to Anna

Strunsky, and his body's love to the woman on the train to Chicago. It is likely that if not for the advent of Miss Kittredge with her particular background, Jack would have remained married to Bessie, using his home for headquarters while he traveled and adventured by himself. There is always the possibility, however, that if Miss Kittredge had not been successful in capturing him, the next woman, or the tenth from the next, might have. . . . As Jack had written so often in his stories, this was a world of dog eat dog, with the wolves devouring those who fell behind; if Bessie were too weak to hold her husband, that was no concern of Miss Kittredge; she had the right to fight for what she wanted and to take all she could get. Where Jack would be hurting three of the people he loved most, two of whom he had caused to be brought into the world, she would be hurting no one she loved.

In order to allay suspicion, Miss Kittredge went frequently to Bessie's house and accepted Bessie's confidences about her marital difficulties. On September 12, 1903, she writes to Jack, "Last night I went to see Bessie. She was lovely to me—so lovely it made me sick. She begged me to come and stay all night with her, any time. She was so sweet and hospitable that it seemed as if all the trouble and tearing apart might be a dream. Sometimes I have to fight off a feeling of actual WICKEDNESS, when I think of it all, but my reason enters and helps me out; but oh!!!" Five days later she continues: "I have about given up thinking Bessie really suspects me, though I would not be surprised at ANYTHING she did! She is deep, and I do not understand deceitful people." Miss Kittredge played her part so adroitly that on October 2 Jack was able to write to her, "All goes well with Bessie, so far as you and I are concerned. She told me last night she wouldn't know what she would do if it weren't for you. In fact you were exalted above all people."

Though Bessie was stricken, she was too proud to fight, to cause scenes. Completely in the dark as to her husband's motives, she sat quietly and wondered why the man who had insisted that she marry him, who had insisted that she bear him children, who had accepted her financial help during the first year of their marriage and her assistance on manuscripts, notes, and the assembling of material, who had lived with her in peaceful comradeship for three years, should suddenly, without warning, discard her.

In her troubles she found one friend: Flora London. For three years Bessie and Flora had quarreled, driving Jack to distraction, but Flora had learned the meaning of motherhood through her love for little Johnny Miller; she now turned against her son for abandoning his family. Bitter at what he termed his mother's treachery, Jack's mind fell into chaos. He developed a persecution mania, charging that everyone was against him, that the world was conspiring to keep him from his "love-woman." On September 22 from the *Spray* he writes to Miss Kittredge, "By every human right I should not have ridden off into the dark. You were mine, mine, and the world had no right to drive me away. And yet I was driven, ignobly driven, from the woman I love dearer than life."

His thoughts became so confused that in spite of the magnificent critical reception of *The Call of the Wild*, which the press agreed was a "classic enriching American literature," he could not do a stroke of work. He decided that the only way he would ever finish *The Sea Wolf* was to escape the churning currents about him by slipping his cables. He had the *Spray* overhauled, then sent transportation money to Cloudesley Johns, who lived in Southern California and knew little of his troubles. The two men headed for the mouth of the Sacramento River; in the mornings they worked at their books, in the afternoons they swam, shot ducks, fished. After his woman-complicated world—though he himself had made the complications—he found the companionship of a man salutary. "The more I see of Cloudesley, the more I like him. He is honest and loyal, young and fresh, understands the discipline of a boat, and is a good cook, to say nothing of being a good-natured and genial companion."

Man fashion, he shoved his troubles out of his mind and wrote his thousand words on *The Sea Wolf* every morning. The only trouble he could not successfully ignore was that by September 14 he was again without funds. He wrote to Miss Kittredge, "Bessie makes out to you that I am almost destitute. I feel pretty close to it, when all I have between me and pauperism is a bare $100, and an unexpected doctor bill comes in for $115." He put aside *The Sea Wolf* to write a story for *Youth's Companion*, plotting a whole month of hack work in order that he might get a little ahead.

Every few days he called in at a small town, Stockton, Antioch,

Vallejo, for his mail. One day he received a letter from Bessie telling him that Joan was down with typhoid. He raced back to his daughter and was at her bedside constantly, in anguish lest the child die. When the doctor reported that she was sinking, Jack felt it was retribution being visited upon him. He vowed that if only the child would get well he would give up his great love and return to his home. The newspapers reported that the Londons had been reconciled at the bedside of their daughter. However, when Joan began to recover, Jack was like the shipwrecked man who fell on his knees on the raft and prayed, "Dear God, if you will only send me a ship I promise to be good for the rest of my life . . . never mind, God, I see a sail." When Joan was up and about again, he went back to the *Spray*.

Though the present might be muddled he had done good work in the past and that good work brought its reward. *The Call of the Wild* caught the popular favor, and because of its universal theme was selling to all classes and ages of people. By November it was number three on the best-seller lists, topped only by *The Bar Sinister* and *The Little Shepherd of Kingdom Come*, and leading such favorites as *Mrs. Wiggs of the Cabbage Patch*, *Rebecca of Sunnybrook Farm*, and *Pigs in Clover*. In November *The People of the Abyss* was released to very nearly solid praise, the critics claiming that as a sociological document the book stood unequalled, that if he had never written anything besides *The People of the Abyss*, Jack London would deserve to be famous, and that it would make a smugly complacent civilization sit up and wonder if it had been making the best use of its opportunities. The English press, which might have been expected to consider him an unqualified intruder, accused him of exaggeration and of tackling his subject with an axe, but also admitted that no one had succeeded as he had in getting close to the heart of the London slums.

Jack had sent Brett the first half of *The Sea Wolf*. Brett was so excited by the tale that he sent it to the editor of *Century* magazine with a glowing recommendation. When he heard what Brett had done Jack shook his head in perplexity, for he knew the *Century* to be a staid and conservative family organ. It was unthinkable that it should run the vigorous and bitterly real *Sea Wolf*. The editor of *Century* was thrilled with the manuscript, agreeing that if he were given the right to blue-pencil the latter half, on which Jack was still working, if the man and woman when left alone on the island would do nothing to offend his subscribers, he would pay four thousand dollars for the serial rights.

Four thousand dollars! For the magazine rights alone! More money than he had received for the total rights to *The Call of the Wild.* He spread full canvas and sailed at top speed down the Bay and through the Estuary to his dock. Immediately on landing he telegraphed the editor of *Century* that he could blue-pencil to his heart's content, that he "was absolutely confident the American prude would not be shocked by the second half of the book." The deal was closed and Jack dug in with renewed vitality and concentration, completing the book in thirty feverish days of writing. The *Century* magazine was already blazoning his name to the four winds in advertisements astounding in size and vigor as they told the whole world that Mr. Jack London, author of the popular *The Call of the Wild*, would have his new book, *The Sea Wolf*, published in the pages of *Century*.

Within a few months he was to be the possessor of four thousand dollars in cash. In the meanwhile, just one week before Christmas, he found himself practically penniless. He had exactly $20.02 in the bank, and no Christmas presents bought. "I wonder if on the strength of the sale of *The Call of the Wild* Brett is going to give me an honorarium for a Christmas present? It would come in handy." *The Call of the Wild* was having what the publishers termed a runaway sale, but Brett did not send him the honorarium. This does not appear to have been stinginess on his part, for he was liberal with his star author over a period of exacting years. Brett felt that Jack had made a bargain and that if he sent him an honorarium he would be breaking the agreement and setting a precedent. If Jack had kept his rights to *The Call of the Wild* the royalties during the next few years would have earned him close to a hundred thousand dollars—assuming that Brett would have invested as much money in promotion under the changed conditions. Jack never regretted his bargain; Brett had spent a fortune in advertising his name, and he knew the worth of advertising to his future career.

By New Year's Day of 1904 it appeared certain that Russia and Japan would go to war. Jack did not want this to happen; as a socialist he was against all war because he knew that in war the working people of the world were shot down to further or protect the moneyed interests. However, if war did begin he wanted to be on the spot to see it. He had studied military tactics and equipment for destruction, was interested to observe what modern warfare could do to destroy civilization. He also had a lot of theories about the Yellow Peril to investigate. In addition he felt that if he made his reputation as a war correspondent he would always be able to earn money. It was Adventure Road once again, offering an escape from his marital and love complications.

Magazines and newspapers began sending their correspondents to Japan. Jack received offers from five syndicates, and accepted the one that bid the most money, the Hearst chain. In the first week of January he went to the offices of the *Examiner* and had his picture taken on the roof of the building. Wearing a workingman's dark suit and high shoes and needing a haircut, he looked as though he had just come off a shift at the Belmont Steam Laundry. The pictures reveal the stress and anxiety of the six months since he had separated from Bessie in their cabin at Glen Ellen; the look of boyishness has been dissipated, he appears troubled and harassed.

He ordered Macmillan to send his monthly check to Bessie, asked Eliza to give Miss Kittredge anything she might need, the first intimation Eliza had of what was going on, then commissioned George Sterling to edit *The Sea Wolf* before Macmillan sent it to press. On the seventh of January, 1904, five days before his twenty-eighth birthday, he crossed on the ferry to the Embarcadero and sailed on the S.S. *Siberia* for Yokohama.

On board the *Siberia* was a jolly group of newspapermen, which promptly named itself the Vultures. On the first day out from Honolulu, while playing jumping games on deck, Jack landed on a round stick and sprained his left ankle. His right ankle being weak from a spill off an express train when a Tramp Royal, this accident crippled him. "For sixty-five sweaty hours I lay on my back. Yesterday I was carried on deck on the back of an English correspondent." He had little time to brood over his ill fate, for the Vultures thronged his cabin, regaling him with yarns of other wars and other assignments.

When he docked at Yokohama he had a drink at each of the

bars where as a boy of seventeen he had drunk shoulder to shoulder with Big Victor and Axel when they had been the Three Sports of the *Sophie Sutherland*. Then he took the train for Tokyo, where he found correspondents assembled from all over the world, awaiting permission from the Japanese Government to go into the field. Because war had not been formally declared the Japanese officials were evading the requests, providing the correspondents instead with sightseeing trips, sumptuous banquets, diverting entertainment.

Jack had not come to Japan to attend banquets. After two days of encountering exquisitely polite evasions he did a little sagacious interviewing and learned what the other correspondents did not yet suspect, that the Japanese Government had no intention of allowing the newspapermen anywhere near the firing line. He realized that if he wanted to report the war he would simply have to go out and find it. Without breathing a word to any of the Vultures he slipped out of Tokyo on a train for Kobe and Nagasaki, where he hoped to catch a boat for Chemulpo in Korea, where the Japanese forces were being rushed to the front.

After a few days of hunting up and down the coast he found a vessel going to Chemulpo on February 1. He bought his ticket, thinking of how he would be with the Army in Korea while the other correspondents were still being fed sumptuous dinners in Tokyo. To fill his spare hours he went into the streets to take photographs of coolies loading coal and bales of cotton. Within a few moments he saw the inside of a Korean jail and later suffered a series of military restrictions that must have made him long for the comparative security of the hall man's job at the Erie County Penitentiary: for the Japanese officials had arrested him as a Russian spy! He was put through eight hours of grilling, moved the next day to a larger jail for more questioning, and finally released . . . too late to catch his boat.

Learning that soldiers were being called from their homes in the middle of the night, he frantically searched the coastline for another ship bound for Chemulpo. Finally on the eighth of February he secured passage on the *Kieogo Maru*, but the Government confiscated the vessel just before it was to sail. Outraged at the thought that he might not be at the front to report the first battle, he made a wild dash in a steam launch for a small steamer going to Fusan, a port en route to Chemulpo, catching it amid such confusion that one of his trunks was lost overboard. It was a native ship, with not a bite of white man's food aboard; in spite of the fact that it was alternately snowing and sleeting, he had to sleep on the open deck, reminding him of the nights he had lain shivering in the railroad jungles without a blanket.

At Fusan he made connections with a second boat, but when they reached Mokpo the Government seized the vessel and un-ceremoniously dumped passengers and baggage ashore. The speed with which the Japanese were shipping soldiers to Korea con-vinced him that war was about to be declared, yet here he was, several hundred miles from Chemulpo, and no ship to be had. He was being paid to write up the war, and by God! he was going to write it. But how was he going to get to it? The voice of Marshall Wellman, his maternal grandfather who had built a raft at Put-In Bay and floated it back to Cleveland, told him in clear and unmis-takable terms. Charter an open native junk and sail it across the Yellow Sea, then along the Korean coast until he reached Che-mulpo!

The thermometer read fourteen degrees below zero, but he had endured sixty below in the Klondike; the wind was howling over the Yellow Sea, but not any worse than it had howled over Lake Linderman; it was a magnificently courageous, foolhardy thing for him to try, but no more foolhardy or courageous than for the twelve-year-old lad to have sailed a leaky catboat across treach-erous San Francisco Bay in a lashing southwester. That his jour-ney would be as difficult and dangerous as that made by the Vikings who crossed the Atlantic in an open boat only made it the more appealing. He purchased what he considered a sea-worthy junk, engaged three intrepid Koreans to help him man it, and set sail for Chemulpo.

"The wildest and most gorgeous thing ever! If you could see me just now, a captain of a junk with a crew of three Koreans who speak no English. Made Kun San at nightfall, after having carried away a mast and smashed the rudder. We arrived in the driving rain, with the wind cutting like a knife. You should have seen me being made comfortable—five Japanese maidens helping me un-dress, take a bath, and get into bed, passing remarks about my beautiful white skin."

For the next six days and nights he was out in freezing weather, the tiny boat tossed by a fierce gale, in danger every moment of going under. There was no heat except from a charcoal burner, the fumes of which poisoned him even worse than the native food upon which he had to subsist. Both ankles being weak, he sailed the junk in a crippled state. His condition when he reached Chemulpo is described by R. L. Dunn, a *Collier's* photographer who had arrived there on the last boat to clear.

"When London arrived at Chemulpo I did not recognize him. He was a physical wreck. His ears were frozen, his fingers were frozen, his feet were frozen. He said he didn't mind his condition so long as he got to the front. I want to say that Jack London is one of the grittiest men it has ever been my good fortune to meet. He is just as heroic as any of the characters in his novels."

Jack bought several horses, learned to ride, engaged servants and a *mapu*, or horse-boy, and started north across Korea in the direction of the Russian troops. The roads were covered with mud and ice, and by nightfall each day they had to beat the Japanese soldiers to the next village in order to find a place to sleep.

After several weeks of forced march during which he endured incredible hardship, he finally got to Ping Yang, the farthest point north to be reached by any war correspondent. Here he was held in jail for a week on a complaint lodged with the Japanese Government by the correspondents who were still being entertained in Tokyo, and whose papers were sending sizzling cables demanding to know why Jack London could send dispatches out of Korea when they couldn't. Ordered back to Seoul, two hundred miles behind the front, he was thrown into a military prison on orders from Tokyo because he had no permit to accompany the Army.

The Japanese Government then decided to make a friendly gesture to the other nations. "Fourteen of us correspondents, who had refused to remain pickled in Tokyo, were allowed to travel with the Army, but it was like a party of Cook's tourists with the supervising officers as guides. We saw what we were permitted to see, and the chief duty of the officers looking after us was to keep us from seeing anything. We did see part of the battle of the Yalu from the walls of Wiju, but when one Japanese company was annihilated, we were ordered back to camp."

With the arrival of spring weather the correspondents were permitted to cross the Yalu River; in a grove beside a temple the Army built each of them a magnificent little camp. Jack swam, played bridge and other games, but his movements were limited to a radius of a mile and a half . . . while the Japanese were out bombarding the Russian entrenchments.

It was difficult to work when held captive forty miles behind the line of action, yet he did his best. He made a careful estimate of the Japanese Army: "The Japanese soldiery and equipment command universal admiration." He wrote analyses of the military tactics and maneuvers of both armies. He took photographs, utilizing the training Bessie had given him with a camera, of the Army on the march, digging trenches, making camp, caring for the wounded, the first war pictures to reach America. Though he sent out nineteen dispatches and hundreds of photographs, he had to wait until he got back to San Francisco to learn if the *Examiner* had received them. "I am disgusted!" he cried. "I'll never go to a war between Orientals again. The vexation and delay are too great. Never were correspondents treated in any war as they have been in this." By June he was ready to go home, for he knew that he was wasting his time. "I am profoundly irritated by the futility of my position in this Army and sheer inability to do any decent work. The only compensation for these months of irritation is a better comprehension of Asiatic geography and character."

A threat of court martial gave impetus to his desire to leave. One day his *mapu*, reporting to Army headquarters for feed for his master's horses, was prevented from getting his full share by a Korean whom Jack had long suspected of robbing him. When Jack accused the Korean of this, the man made a threatening gesture with his knife. Jack knocked him down with a blow of his fist. He was promptly commanded to report to General Fuji, who threatened drastic punishment. When news reached Richard Harding Davis, splendidly marooned in Tokyo, that Jack London was in danger of being executed, he burned the cables to President Roosevelt, who in turn sent angry protestations to Japan. General Fuji was ordered to release him. Jack packed his kit and made his way back to Tokyo where he found the correspondents he had left behind four months before, still awaiting official permission to join the Army. Davis rode with him to Yokohama to see him off, swearing that as soon as he heard a shot fired he was returning home, but after having waited all these months he couldn't leave without hearing that one shot!

"Only in another war, with a white man's army," mourned Jack, "may I hope to redeem myself." He need not have felt badly; he had gotten out more dispatches than any other correspondent, had given his paper several scoops, especially with the war photographs, and they were well enough pleased with his work. Not the least important aspect of his Oriental junket was that the newspaper chain had given his stories flaming headlines. What with the success of *The Call of the Wild*, and the spectacular advertising *Century* had given *The Sea Wolf*, by the time he reached San Francisco the name of Jack London was becoming more widely known than that of any other American writer.

He confidently expected that when his ship tied up at the Embarcadero he would be greeted by Miss Kittredge's outstretched arms; instead he was greeted by the outstretched hand of a process server with a copy of Bessie's divorce complaint. Bessie had put an attachment on the earnings still due him as war correspondent for the *Examiner*. He flinched under the blow, but what stunned and made him heartsick as he read further in the complaint was that Bessie had named Anna Strunsky as the cause of her marital troubles!

Jack had been eager for Bessie to begin her divorce proceedings, but to involve Anna in a scandal, Anna whom he had not seen for two years . . . ! When he was able to blink the mist out of his eyes he saw to his relief that Bessie had not accused Anna of wrongdoing; she had merely charged that their collaboration over *The Kempton-Wace Letters* had caused her husband to become cold and indifferent to her.

There was no sign of Miss Kittredge anywhere on the dock. When Eliza, who had come down to greet him, handed him his mail, he found a letter from Newton, Iowa, where she was staying with an aunt. He read, "I fear you will be disappointed that I am not in California. The terror of all my dear ones, the scandal, makes me sicker every time I think of the possible happenings during the next few months. I am not writing coldly, dear; indeed there never was a moment since we loved each other that I was madder for you than right now, but I am forced for the sake of others, as well as my own, to be level-headed."

Jack was hurt, angry, disgusted. When he went up to Piedmont to greet Bessie and to hold his two daughters in his arms, the thought came to him, "If I was brave enough to sail the Yellow Sea in a sub-zero gale, in an open junk, then why am I not brave enough to stand by my wife and obligations even though I have fallen in love with another woman?"

The next morning the news flashed across the continent that Jack London's wife was divorcing him, and naming Anna Strunsky. The San Francisco papers announced it in bold streamers; from that moment forward Jack found that he would live the smallest and most intimate details of his life on the front page of the newspapers. Cornered by reporters he cried, "The only feature of the case that stirs me up is that Miss Strunsky's name should be mentioned, for she is an extremely sensitive person." Miss Strunsky told the newspapermen: "I am astonished. I have seen Mr. London only twice in the past two years, for I have been in New York and Europe. My visit to the London house occurred two years ago, and at that time there was not a breath of rumor to the effect that their married life was not a happy one." Asked in 1937 why she had named Miss Strunsky, Bessie said that she regretted her mistake. "I knew that Jack would never have left me except for another woman, and I couldn't think who it might be, except Anna Strunsky."

It took Jack but a short time to convince Bessie that Anna Strunsky had nothing to do with their separation; once convinced, she withdrew Anna's name from the case. He then pointed out that if she stuck to her lawyer's advice to keep an attachment on his earnings, the lawyers would get most of the money and there would be little left for the children. Quite gray now, saddened, bitterly wounded, Bessie asked if he would build her a house in Piedmont so that she would always have a secure roof over her children's head. When he agreed, she withdrew the attachment, amended the suit to simple desertion. Jack wrote to Miss Kittredge, "It has taken all the resolution I could summon to prevent my going back, for the children's sake. I have been sadly shaken during the last forty-eight hours—so shaken that it almost seemed easier to sacrifice myself for the little ones."

Instead he told Bessie that Charmian Kittredge was the other woman. Bessie received the news in stony silence, her only comment being that she never cared to see Miss Kittredge again.

In July he went up to Glen Ellen, rented a cottage from Ninetta Eames, and waited for Miss Kittredge to come back to him. When she wrote that she needed money for transportation he sent her a check for eighty dollars. Still she kept writing that she was afraid to come home for fear of the scandal. At length Jack burst out: "Am hugely disgusted. Somebody is not playing fair. I talked it over with Netta and Edward and both were satisfied that there was nothing to apprehend from Bessie. I wrote a check, which Edward cashed and mailed to you . . ." after which follows ten tumultuous pages of how "hugely disgusted" he was with Ninetta Eames and Edward Payne, the first of a long series of disgusts that were to extract their toll on his psyche.

The only pleasure he derived from the hot summer weeks was taking the *Spray* for long sails. The boys along the banks of the creeks recognized him and cried out, "Hello, Jack, how's every little thing in Korea?" When Manyoungi, the loyal and devoted Korean boy who had served him so well, and to whom he had given transportation money, arrived, Jack rented a roomy flat at 1216 Telegraph Avenue, where he installed Flora as his chaperon. Happy to have her son to herself once again, Flora forgot about her quarrels with Jack when he had left Bessie, and settled down to become a charming hostess, with Manyoungi keeping the house clean and cooking for "Master." Later he bought a house for Flora, Mammy Jenny, and little Johnny.

Jack entered one of the most unhappy and unproductive periods of his life. He was unhappy about losing his two children; he was unhappy about hurting Bessie and Anna; he was unhappy about Charmian not standing by; he was unhappy about having squandered his time and health in Korea and producing no good work; he was unhappy because his thoughts were dry and brittle, because no big ideas came to him, no internal force to conceive and execute big projects. At the bottom of his despair he wrote to Anna Strunsky, "I wander through life delivering hurts to all that know me. And I am changed. Though I was a materialist when first I met you, I had the saving grace of enthusiasm. That enthusiasm is the thing that is spoiled."

The Faith of Men, his fourth collection of short stories, which had been released by Macmillan in April, was selling so well that it had to be reprinted in June, and now again in August, but even this did not hearten him. He agreed with the critic of *The Nation* who regretted that a man with his powers should spend all his time in the frozen North. Both his body and mind went soggy and stale. He came down with the grippe; when he recovered he developed a nervous skin itch that put him through torture. He could not exercise, his weight fell off, he became thin, soft, jumpy. Because of his physical affliction and the low state of his mind he lived as a recluse.

In August he paid sixteen hundred dollars for a lot at 519 Thirty-First Street in Piedmont, called in an architect, let Bessie say what kind of house she wanted, and watched the work begin. When he had returned from Korea he had four thousand dollars in the bank from the *Century* and the *Examiner*; every dollar of it, plus a good-sized mortgage, went into the building of the house, leaving him once again without funds. Determined not to let his melancholia disrupt his discipline, he plunged into work. He read the dozens of books he had missed while in Korea; wrote articles, such as "The Yellow Peril," for magazines and newspapers; began a short prize-fight novel called *The Game*; lectured to every socialist organization in the vicinity; spoke free of charge to clubs and churches in order to make converts to socialism and thus hasten the revolution. He began work on his first play, *The Scorn of Women*, based on one of his Alaskan tales, gave readings in *The People of the Abyss* and *The Class Struggle*. His skin ailment receding, he again entertained his friends on Wednesday nights, went on swimming parties at the Piedmont Baths and on picnics in the hills. He worked hard and played hard because he did not want to have time to realize how wretched he felt. Yet he did not fool himself about the quality of the work he was doing. "Still plugging away at *The Game*. Believe it is a failure, but the work is good for me. *The Scorn of Women* is not a big effort, I wouldn't dare a big effort."

His one sustaining force was Brett of Macmillan. On the strength of the advance sale of *The Sea Wolf*, which reached twenty thousand by the beginning of October, Brett increased the monthly allowance to two hundred and fifty dollars. He assured Jack that it was a truly great book, and finally, at the beginning of November, communicated the magnificent news that *The Sea Wolf*, Jack's tenth publication in less than four years, had sold forty thousand copies to the bookstores before its release. In December he sent Jack a check for three thousand dollars, which Jack had figured he would need to get him out from under his load of insurance, mortgage, and personal debts.

The Sea Wolf shot onto the market like a thunderbolt, became the rage overnight, was on everybody's lips to be praised or cursed. Many readers were insulted and offended by its attitudes; others valiantly took up the cudgels in its defense. Part of the press called it cruel, brutal, and revolting, but the greater part agreed that it was "rare and original genius . . . raises the quality of modern imaginative literature." It marked another milestone in American literature, not only because of its realism and vigor, the wealth of characters and situations unknown to American literature, but also because it heightened the intellectual tone of the modern novel. Where before had Americans encountered such dread suspense, such authentic death-appeal as found in the conflict of the spiritual versus the materialistic as took place on board the *Ghost* between Wolf Larsen and Peter Van Weyden? Where before had they been presented with mature philosophy, had they found it made exciting, something to fight about? Jack had taken the scholar's revolution of the nineteenth century, dramatized it, popularized it, made it thrilling and intelligible to the great mass of people who had never even heard of evolution, biology, or scientific materialism. Darwin, Spencer, Nietzsche stalk through the book, its unseen protagonists. In dramatizing the teachings of his beloved masters he made the battles of the mind as exciting as the Irish bricklayers' free-for-all in Weasel Park in his later novel, *The Valley of the Moon*, no mean accomplishment.

Toward the end of the book Jack introduces its only woman character and thereby marred what was, and is still, a nearly perfect example of the novelist's art. When the literary critics declared that the woman was unbelievable, Jack cried, "I was in love with a woman, and I wrote her into my book, and the critics tell

me that the woman I love is unbelievable." He had not only written Miss Kittredge into the book but also the poetic-hysteric manner of writing about her which he had absorbed while answering
her letters. In everything pertaining to the woman and the love between her and Peter Van Weyden, *The Sea Wolf* shows the
worst of the rococo nineteenth century; on all other counts it is a
forerunner of the best in twentieth-century literature.

A few weeks after its release it ran fourth to such raspberry-
syruped sawdust as *The Masqueraders* by K. C. Thurston, *Prodigal Son* by Hall Caine, *Whosoever Shall Offend* by F. Marion
Crawford, and *Beverly of Graustark* by George Barr McCutcheon.
Three weeks later it was leading the best-seller lists, far out in
front, and the twentieth century at last had thrown off the
shackles of its predecessor. *The Sea Wolf* is as thrilling today, as
profound a reading experience, as it was in November, 1904. It
dates very little. Many critics consider it London's most powerful
work; readers who pick it up again are enthralled by it.

Miss Kittredge returned from Iowa; they had several rapturous
though fugitive engagements in Oakland and San Francisco, then
she left for Glen Ellen to live with Ninetta Eames. There followed an occasional impassioned meeting, Jack penned a few
rhapsodic messages, but for the most part his letters became
newsy and casual. He is no longer God's own mad lover dying on
a kiss. Once again his fancy roamed. Miss Kittredge tells of the
development. "I know that your thoughts and interests for the
past few weeks have been taken up by another woman. You're
only a boy, after all, dear Man, and transparent enough. But the
shock you gave me the night of your 'Scab' lecture in the city,
made me very thoughtful. I saw you watch for her in the audience
when you were through speaking; I saw you wave to her; I saw her
backing and filling and fluttering after her manner. I saw you
come together in the light of your cigarette, and I knew that you
had been together the evening before. It isn't the mere fact of
your unfaithfulness—you haven't that kind of integrity, very few
men have, and I have faced the probability of your infidelity for a
long time, and accepted it in a way. You have been very happy of
late, and I knew I was not responsible for your light-heartedness.
Somebody was, of course, and so . . ."

The year 1905 was one of headlines for Jack; everything he did excited the press. He began the year peacefully enough with a trip to Los Angeles, where he had been invited to address the local socialists. Julian Hawthorne wrote of him in the Los Angeles *Examiner:* "It is pleasant to look upon Mr. London. He is as simple and straightforward as a grizzly bear. Upon his big, hearty, healthy nature is based a brain of unusual clearness and insight. His heart is warm, his sympathies wide, his opinions are his own —independent, courageously expounded." He had no sooner returned to Oakland than he was invited by the liberal-minded president of the University of California to address the student body, an honor for a man who had been forced to leave the University only seven years before to work in a steam laundry. Jack harangued the young people with one of the most fiery speeches he had ever made, telling them that the greatest revolution the world had known was in the making before their very eyes, that if they did not wake up it would descend upon them in their sleep. After the lecture, when he complained to a professor of English that the students were given literary pap to feed upon, the professor replied, "I wouldn't say that, Mr. London. A chapter of *The Call of the Wild* is included in our new reference book." The circle of faculty members laughed, Jack flushed, murmured something about being canonized, and subsided. The following day the president of the University was attacked for permitting Jack London to preach revolution. He replied calmly, "It is the man we invite, not the subject. London has earned his right to appear before us."

It was at Stockton, where Jack accepted his first invitation to speak to a club of businessmen, that he got into his initial embroilment of the year by an art comparable in its foolhardiness and courage with crossing the Yellow Sea in a howling gale, or descending into the slums of London to write *The People of the Abyss*. The report of the Stockton paper, though a little biased, is a vivid one: "He lectured the club of businessmen as though they were unruly schoolchildren; he demanded to know what each of them knew about the subject of socialism; he informed them that they had read little and seen less; he pounded the table and puffed out volumes of cigarette smoke—all of which so alarmed and befogged his auditors that they subsided into embarrassed silence."

They did not remain silent for long; at the close of his talk Jack horrified the businessmen of Stockton by telling them that the socialists in Russia who had participated in the 1905 uprising and killed several of the Czarist officials were his brothers! The audience jumped to its feet, storming at him. The next morning headlines screeched across the country: "JACK LONDON CALLS RUSSIAN ASSASSINS HIS BROTHERS." A furor arose, retractions were demanded, editorials flamed out against him, one of the papers cried, "He is a fire-brand and red-flag anarchist, and should be arrested and prosecuted for treason." Jack stood his ground. The Russian revolutionists were his brothers, and no one could make him repudiate them.

Society had persistently tried to lionize him as California's one literary genius, saying, "Socialism is his hobby. A little extreme, but he's so young and original. His socialistic theories are only a fad, he'll get over them." Now the gates were locked against him as tightly as though he were still a tramp on The Road. No longer was he invited to what he called pink teas, or to formal dinners where he wore his soft white shirt and flowing tie in a sea of starched linen; for society at last concluded that he had been serious when he had so charmingly told them over their dinner tables that as a class they were a parasitic fungus growth.

The scandal had no sooner died down than Jack gave another lecture in which he mentioned that William Lloyd Garrison had said, "To hell with the Constitution!" when he was condemning slavery in 1856, and that General Sherman Bell had said it more lately in putting down strikers. The next morning he was once again the man of the hour, with hundreds of newspapers from California to New York shouting: "JACK LONDON SAYS TO HELL WITH THE CONSTITUTION." He did his best to explain that he was not the author of the phrase, but newspapers are rarely interested in the aftermath of a flash story.

If the freedom of the press allowed bigots to tear a man to shreds, it also permitted wiser men to speak their piece. In the San Francisco *Bulletin*, by no means a radical paper, he read, "The hot sincerity and hatred of wrong that burns in the revolutionary heart of young Jack London is the same spirit that characterized the tea-overboard party in Boston Harbor. It is the spirit that will ultimately reserve for the Republic all that is best, for it is the opposite of the dull spirit of slavish respect for the Established, which slavishness is composed of abasement of mind, and selfishness of character."

A few days later he was invited to speak by the debating society of his own Oakland High School. When the principal learned about it he refused them the use of the school building. Once again the papers played up the story, and every man and woman in the state discussed the merits of the case. The San Francisco *Post* remarked caustically, "Socialism may be all that is urged against it, but the best way to propagate its doctrines is to forbid their propagation."

Jack was delighted at the nation-wide publicity that socialism was earning through his efforts. Besides, the free advertising, which would have cost him thousands of dollars if he had had to buy it, was booming his work. *The Call of the Wild, The Sea Wolf, The People of the Abyss* were being widely bought, and even more widely read and discussed. People might disagree with his ideas for an economic democracy; they might quarrel with the manner in which he was revolutionizing American literature; but it was no longer possible to gainsay the fact that he was the leading young writer in America. And his enemies had helped him arrive!

In the midst of the furor over his socialism, Macmillan released his *War of the Classes*. The book aroused so much interest that it had to be reprinted in June, October, and November, an astounding accomplishment for a collection of revolutionary essays in a country which denied vehemently that there was such a thing as a war between the classes, where socialism was ridiculed and despised, accused of being a Hydra-headed monster that devoured its young. His was a voice crying in the wilderness, but more and more people were coming to hear that voice, particularly the generation just growing up, just throwing off the shackles of a restricted pioneer mentality, and beginning to count the human costs of large-scale industrialism. Jack London was a great name to this generation; it went to his books with burning faith. All over America one still meets people who relate with pride that Jack London turned them into socialists; the fact that their socialism did not always stick is perhaps not Jack's fault.

In March he once again agreed to run for Mayor of Oakland on the Socialist ticket, receiving 981 votes, exactly four times as many as he had received in 1901. In April he and Manyoungi went to Glen Ellen, where he paid Ninetta Eames six dollars a week for a cabin at Wake Robin. Mrs. Eames gave out the report that "Jack had come home to Mother because of troubles in Oakland." The trusting farmers of the neighborhood suspected nothing.

Spring in Sonoma County was beautiful. He regained his good spirits and full working force; the melancholia of the winter was forgotten. Having sold a story to *The Black Cat*, he spent two hundred and fifty dollars of the three-hundred-dollar check for a saddle-horse which the indefatigable Miss Kittredge rode the twenty-two miles from Petaluma to Glen Ellen. They rode horseback among the groves of redwood and pine on Sonoma Mountain, over the trails through the wine-colored manzanita and madrone. The air was clear, fragrant, and intoxicating, and when the full moon rose the valley was filled with a luminous white mist. "Now I know why the Indians named this place the Valley of the Moon," commented Jack.

His creative force in full flower again, he wrote *White Fang*, a sequel to *The Call of the Wild*, the story of how White Fang, instead of going from civilization back to the call of the primitive, comes out of the wilds to live with mankind. Although the book does not rise to the heights of *The Call of the Wild*, it is a beautiful and moving dog story, carrying with it the thrill of first-rate literature. He did several full-page articles and book criticisms for the Hearst chain, outlining the existing struggle between labor unions and employers when he reviewed *The Walking Delegate*, giving the sweat-shop system a blasting when he praised *The Long Day*, which told of the privations of a factory girl in New York. The Intercollegiate Socialist Society was organized in the East by Upton Sinclair and J. G. Phelps-Stokes, and Jack was elected president at the first meeting of the executive committee. When Macmillan published his first story, *The Game*, and the critics condemned it as trivial and unbelievable, he sent them news clippings to prove that a fighter could smash in the back of his skull when falling to the mat from a hard blow.

The heat of summer coming on, he again spent a few dollars to have the creek damned. Here his neighbors collected to swim. He worked in the mornings, swam in the afternoons, and enjoyed himself . . . except that he missed his two children. Then one hot afternoon, when he was riding across the mountains inhaling the sage scents that beat upward from the slope, he stumbled onto the Hill Ranch, one hundred and thirty acres of majestic land leading up from the floor of the valley to Sonoma Mountain. "There are great redwoods on it, some of them ten thousand years old. There are hundreds of firs, tan-bark and live-oaks, madrone and manzanita galore. There are deep canyons, streams of water, springs. It is one hundred and thirty acres of the most beautiful, primitive lands to be found anywhere in America."

He went wild about the place and decided at once that he must own it, a sentiment in which Miss Kittredge heartily encouraged him; only by getting him away from the city and from contact with other women would she avoid the danger of losing him, as she had almost lost him a few months before. Jack rode into the small village of Glen Ellen where he learned that the land was for sale and that the price had been set at seven thousand dollars. That afternoon at five he was at the home of the Hills, excited as a schoolboy, ready to buy. "I hear you set the price of the land for Chauvet at seven thousand dollars," he said to Mr. Hill. "Yes," replied Hill, "that was the price I set him ten years ago." "I'll buy it!" cried Jack. "Not so fast," said Hill, "you'd better go home and think it over for a few days."

After Jack left, Mr. Hill told his wife that he had asked seven thousand dollars of Chauvet because Chauvet had wanted to utilize the water rights, but since Jack expected to farm the piece, five thousand dollars was all he could ask. The next day Jack dashed in more excited than ever; he had been unable to sleep for the planning of his beautiful ranch. "Now I want to talk to you about the price . . ." began Hill. Jack leapt out of his chair, his face reddened, and he shouted in a burst of anger, "You can't do that to me! I won't stand for it! You can't raise the price! Everybody around here is trying to do me. Seven thousand is the price you agreed to and that's the price I'm going to pay!" Unable to break into the torrent, Hill waited until he had subsided, then said quietly, "All right, Mr. London, take it at your price."

Years later, when Jack and the Hills had become close friends, Mr. Hill told him how he had done himself out of two thousand dollars. Jack laughed heartily, said that it ought to teach him to control his temper.

That night he and Miss Kittredge laid their plans. There was a ramshackle barn on the Hill Ranch that could be remodeled to house their horses and hired man. While Jack was away that fall on a lecture tour of the country, the hired man could clear a number of the acres, plant hay and corn, build pigsties and chicken houses, and get the ranch in working order against the day when Bessie's divorce would be granted and they could marry.

Jack wrote to Brett for the seven thousand dollars with which to buy the Hill Ranch. Brett replied, "I am doubtful as to the advisability of any man who has a part to play in the world tying himself down to the purchase of real estate in any part of the country, no matter how beautiful and productive." Jack wrote back, "I was careful to buy a piece out of which no profit could be made. I'll never be bothered with a profit or loss account, but in twenty years it will be worth one hundred and twenty thousand dollars. I am anchoring good and solid, and anchoring for keeps." Resignedly, Brett sent him the seven thousand dollars against the *Sea Wolf* royalties, and Jack exultantly became owner of the Hill Ranch. He then hired a farm hand, bought several horses, a colt, a cow, a plow, a barrow, a wagon, a buggy, harnesses, chickens, turkeys, and pigs.

When he finally came out of the wild buying spree he found that he did not have a dollar left, and that no money would be due from Macmillan for a long time. "All this buying was unexpected, and has left me flat broke. Also I am expecting to receive, and dreading to receive, a notice from Bessie that she wants several hundred dollars with which to buy a horse and surrey. I've taken all the money I could get from Macmillan to pay for the land, and haven't enough left to build a barn with, much less a house. Am writing some short stories in order to get hold of some immediate cash."

By October 4 he had overdrawn so heavily from Macmillan that they asked him to pay interest on the new advances. His bankbook showed $207.83 to his credit, while among the immediately necessary outlays were $75 to Bessie, $55 to his mother, $57.60 for ranch tools, $24 for rent at Glen Ellen, $50 for store bills. "I must pay my way and Manyoungi's way to Chicago; Charmian follows in twenty-four hours, and there are her expenses. My mother wants me to increase her monthly allowance. So does

Bessie. I have just paid hospital bills of over $100 for Johnny Miller's mother. I have promised $30 to pay for printing of appeal of Joe King, a poor devil who had a fifty-year sentence hanging over him and who is being railroaded. There is a bill for over $45 for the hay press, and in November I must meet between $700 and $800 in insurance. So you see I am not only sailing close into the wind but that I am dead into it and my sails flapping."

During his lifetime, in the course of which he earned well over a million dollars from his writing, he was almost never the owner of his money when it reached him. He always spent first, then split his head trying to figure where the necessary money was to come from. As Emil Jensen had said in the Klondike, he was never one to count the cost. It apparently never occurred to him that if he didn't spend his money until he had earned it he would not only keep out of debt, but out of trouble as well. "The habit of spending money, ah God! I shall always be its victim!"

In October he started on his lecture tour attended by Man-youngi. Miss Kittredge returned to her aunt in Newton, Iowa, so that she could be closer to him. The tour, which included most of the large cities of the Mid-West and the East, was carried out in a blaze of publicity, for he was rapidly becoming one of the most romantic figures of the period. In addition to being the voice of socialism, the voice of scientific evolution, the voice of a new and robust realism in American literature, he also represented the youth and courage of the world. The women's clubs liked his virile figure, his smoke-puffing masculinity, his passionate sincerity on questions of social reform, his golden smile and infectious laughter. He made several hundred dollars a day, found amusing and intelligent company in each town, and was treated with friendliness by the newspapers. "Jack London is a personality of unusual magnetic attraction. If it had been possible to spoil him he would have been spoiled by the regiment of adorers who beset him. He has been subjected to the same experiences as the matinée idol. However, he is without personal vanity."

Then, on Saturday, November 18, he received a telegram in Chicago that Bessie's final divorce decree had been granted. He wired Miss Kittredge to come on at once from Newton to be married. She reached Chicago Sunday afternoon at five, but Jack had no marriage license. The bureau of course was closed, so he engaged a carriage and drove at top speed through the Chicago streets to enlist the aid of influential friends. The first two visits proving fruitless, a third friend was taken from his dinner table because he knew a city official. After another long drive they reached the home of the official, who said that he would be glad to do anything to help Jack London, but what was his blistering hurry, anyway? Why couldn't he wait until morning when the license bureau would be open and he could do everything in apple-pie order? Jack refused to wait, brought all his considerable force of argument to bear, ended by persuading the official to get into the carriage and drive with them to the south side of town, where the marriage-license clerk was routed out of bed. The clerk was dumbfounded, but under Jack's determined will he dressed and accompanied the party to the City Hall, opened his office, and made out the license. After several vain attempts they located a justice of the peace, Mr. Grant, who married Jack to Charmian Kittredge in the library of his home.

The following morning, November 20, 1905, the press of the nation was shocked by what they termed the "indecent haste" of his marriage. Up to this time people had assumed that his separation from Bessie was caused by internal differences which made it mutually desirable. By his terrific sweat to remarry Jack showed that he had broken up his home for another woman . . . and that put an unpleasant face on affairs. Friendly as the press had been up to Saturday, on Monday it turned against him, not only its anger and indignation, but its ridicule as well. On Tuesday morning the nation was informed "JACK LONDON'S MARRIAGE INVALID," for the new divorce laws of Illinois, which were still in confusion, declared that no marriage could be valid unless it took place a year after the granting of the final decree. Cornered by reporters, Jack, once again feeling that he was being persecuted, cried out in impetuous ardor, "If necessary I'll get married in every state in the Union, as fast as I can get from one to the other!" Many witty stories were written about the much-marrying Mr. London.

Had he waited until he returned to California, had he waited a few circumspect months he could have avoided the entire scandal. His marriage would have passed with brief notice. Instead he laid himself open to attack from every quarter. Sermons against him were preached from pulpits; the towns of Pittsburg and Derby banned his books from the public library, suggesting that other cities follow their lead; syndicated dispatches were released urging the women's clubs to cancel his lectures; many papers commented that it was strange that persons who were unable to regulate their own domestic affairs set themselves up as teachers of humanity at large. Articles were written questioning the mystery and haste of his second marriage. Miss Kittredge was attacked for breaking up his marriage to Bessie.

Because of the conduct of their leader, the socialists of America took severe punishment. The capitalist press utilized the weapons at hand: "There's socialism for you! Deserts its wife and babies . . . sanctions immorality . . . would bring about chaos . . . socialism is anarchism, would destroy our civilization . . ." It was bootless for his comrades to protest, "You cannot blame London's erratic conduct on socialism! Socialism disapproves of this sort of thing as vigorously as does capitalism!" Their leader had violated certain codes, and their Cause consequently had to suffer. Accused by his comrades of retarding the socialist revolution in America by at least five years, he smilingly replied, "On the contrary, I believe I still have accelerated the revolution by at least five minutes."

Just what motivated his theatrical rush to have that belated ceremony performed, to flaunt a new marriage in the face of the public? Part of it was a romantic gesture for Miss Kittredge. Part of it was rash, impetuous thoughtlessness, the act of a man who doesn't stop to question what the world will think. Part of it was sheer bravado, the act of a thick-skinned Irishman who doesn't care what it thinks. Lastly, the immediate taking of another wife was an appeasement to his conscience for the wrong he had done Bessie, and hence all wives.

The attacks against him in press and pulpit continued for several weeks. The seriousness of his work was injured in the minds of many readers, but in return the blazing publicity extended his public. It remained for the fashionable Averill Women's Club to administer the crowning blow, and close the discussion. At an open meeting the ladies passed a resolution approving free textbooks for public schools, and resolutions denouncing college football and Jack London.

8

IN January of 1906 the lecture tour finally brought Jack to New York, where he was met by Doctor Alexander Irvine, handsome Irish idealist, minister of Pilgrim's Church in New Haven and head of the New Haven Socialist Local. Doctor Irvine had come to New York to persuade him to lecture at Yale University. Jack heartily concurred that the opportunity of launching a bolt of socialism at three thousand Yale students was too good to pass up. Doctor Irvine took the next train back to New Haven, where he then proposed to the Yale Debating Club that they sponsor the lecture. The members nervously agreed to present Jack London the following evening—on condition that he was not to say anything radical.

Elated, Doctor Irvine went that night to a socialist painter by the name of Delfant, who made ten posters on which were drawn a likeness of handsome Jack in his turtle-necked sweater, and under it a mass of red flames with the title of the lecture, "REVOLUTION." Just before dawn Delfant and Doctor Irvine went about the campus tacking up the posters on trees. Yale was aghast when it awakened and saw the glaring announcements. A faculty member immediately summoned the chairman of the Debating

Club and informed him that the meeting would have to be canceled, that if it were not, he would have permission to use Woolsey Hall revoked. There would be no revolution preached at Yale University! The club was about to obey when Doctor Irvine urged its members to go to the younger professors and see if they couldn't raise support against the reactionaries. The first professor to whom the chairman presented his problem was William Lyon Phelps, who asked, "Is Yale a monastery?"

The rebuke was so adroitly yet gently put that it silenced the opposition. At eight o'clock that evening three thousand students and three hundred faculty members, nearly the entire university, jammed Woolsey Hall. Jack was given a warm reception as he walked onto the stage, and was listened to attentively as he told of seven million men in all countries of the world who "are fighting with all their might for the conquest of the wealth of the world, and for the complete overthrow of existing society. They call themselves comrades, these men, as they stand shoulder to shoulder under the banner of revolt. Here is tremendous human force, here is power; the revolutionists are swayed by a great passion, they have much reverence for humanity but little reverence for the rule of the dead." After an hour of dissecting the capitalist system with an economic scalpel he concluded with the challenge, "The capitalist class has failed in its management, and its management is to be taken away from it. Seven million men of the working class say that they are going to get the rest of the working class to join with them, and take that management away. The revolution is here, now. Stop it who can!"

In spite of the fact that he "shocked them out of their socks," as Doctor Irvine put it, and that not twenty students in the audience agreed with a word he uttered, he received an ovation when he finished. Yale University sportingly refused to take any rent for the Hall, and the entire gate, at twenty-five cents a head, went into the treasury of the New Haven Socialist Local, a windfall.

After the lecture Jack, Doctor Irvine, and a hand-picked group of a dozen of the best debaters at the University went to Old Mory's for beer and solid talk. It was Jack against the field; from all reports of the rough-and-tumble discussion, in which he tried to prove that private property is based on either seizure or theft, Jack held his own even if he did not make any converts. When he and

Doctor Irvine reached the latter's home at four o'clock in the morning they found a group of workingmen waiting to thank him for his lecture. At eight o'clock the next morning the doorbell was rung by a gangling, red-headed reporter from the Yale *News* who wanted a personal interview with Jack London because it would help his chances on the paper. The reporter's name was Sinclair Lewis.

By January 19 he was back again in New York after two weeks of lecturing to speak on "The Coming Crisis" for the first open meeting of the Intercollegiate Socialist Society, of which he had been named president. Reports of how many people crowded into the Grand Central Palace vary from four to ten thousand, but every socialist on the Atlantic coast who could scrape up the fare to New York was present. In spite of the title of the organization, there were probably not a hundred college students scattered among the thousands of working people. On his way north from a lecture in Florida, Jack's train was late. Upton Sinclair, who was just having published a book about the Chicago stockyards titled *The Jungle*, and who was the organizing force and brains behind the Intercollegiate Socialist Society, kept the crowd interested by telling them that they could help bring economic democracy to America. At ten o'clock, when Jack appeared in a black cheviot suit, with a white flannel shirt and white tie, and well-worn patent leather pumps, his hair flying, the crowd thronged to its feet to give him the greatest reception of his life: Eugene V. Debs was their giant, but Jack London was their fighting young leader and prophet. Upton Sinclair says that the audience cheered and waved tiny red flags for fully five minutes before Jack had a chance to make himself heard. When he predicted the downfall of capitalist society by the year 2000, the crowd went delirious with delight even though not a soul among them would be present to witness that great Judgment Day.

He remained in New York for a week. New York always had a strange effect upon him; it excited him physically and depressed him nervously. He told Doctor Irvine that every time he found himself entering the city he wanted to cut his throat. The day following his lecture for the Intercollegiate Socialist Society he met Upton Sinclair at luncheon to discuss plans for the Society. Sinclair, who was an ardent prohibitionist, reports that Jack had been drinking before he arrived, that his eyes were excitedly bleary, that he continued to drink straight through the luncheon. Before reaching New York Jack had written a glowing review of *The Jungle* which now sent that muckraking classic and its author on their way to fame.

On February 3, when lecturing in St. Paul, he fell ill and his mouth became covered with cold sores. He canceled the balance of his lectures to return to Glen Ellen, where he rented part of Wake Robin from Ninetta Eames and Edward Payne, the joint owners. It was here he hatched his plans for an adventure which was to make all other adventures of his thrill-packed life seem pale by comparison.

The summer before, while sunning himself on the beach at the swimming hole at Glen Ellen, he had read to the group of vacationers from Captain Joshua Slocum's book *Sailing Alone Around the World.* Captain Slocum's boat had been thirty-seven feet long; Jack mentioned jokingly that he would not be afraid to sail around the world in a small boat, say forty feet long. Now, back at Wake Robin, having had his fill of crowds and cities and adulation, sensitive to the fact that he was being attacked from many corners and for many reasons, that the people of Glen Ellen were hostile because of the haste and circumstances of his second marriage, he once again began talking about the voyage around the world. He had long planned just such an expedition to the South Seas; it was one of the great dreams of his life, kindled by the romantic tales of Stevenson and Melville. Charmian, whose forte was adventure, encouraged him, as did Ninetta Eames and Edward Payne, who hoped Roscoe Eames would become captain of the ship.

"I had a house to build on the ranch, also an orchard, a vineyard, several hedges to plant, and a number of other things to do. We thought we would start in four or five years. Then the lure of adventure began to grip us. Why not start at once? Let the orchard, vineyard and hedges be growing while we were away. After all, I'd never be any younger." Always impetuous, swift of decision, heedless of cost, he resolved that he too was going to circle the globe in a small boat.

Ten days after his return to Wake Robin he wrote to half a dozen of the leading Eastern magazine editors in an attempt to get them to underwrite his adventure with hard cash. "The boat is to be forty-five feet long. It would have been a bit shorter had I not found it impossible to squeeze in a bathroom otherwise. I sail in October. Hawaii is the first port of call; from there we shall wander through the South Seas, Samoa, New Zealand, Australia, New Guinea, and up through the Philippines to Japan. Then Korea and China, and on down to India, the Red Sea, Mediterranean, Black Sea and Baltic, across the Atlantic to New York, and then around the Horn to San Francisco. I shall certainly put in a winter at St. Petersburg, and the chances are that I shall go up the Danube from the Black Sea to Vienna. I'll go up the Nile and the Seine; there is no reason at all why I shouldn't come up to Paris and moor alongside the Latin Quarter, with the bow line out to Notre Dame, and a stern line fast to the Morgue. I shall not be in a rush; I calculate that seven years at least will be taken up by the trip."

Although there were several seaworthy boats on San Francisco Bay that could be bought for a reasonable price, Jack discarded this idea; he would sail no man's boat but his own. There were expert ship architects in San Francisco, but he would sail in no vessel but one that had been fashioned in his own mind. There were competent shipbuilders with yards on the Bay, but he would be master of no boat but the one he had built himself.

He decided to design a boat that would be a departure in sailing vessels, even as everything in his life design had to be a departure. He hit upon the idea for a "ketch," a compromise between a yawl and a schooner which would retain the virtues of both, but he frankly admitted that he had never seen a ketch, let alone sailed one, that the whole thing was a theory in his mind. He sunk himself in the details of boatbuilding, pondering such problems as whether a two-, three-, or four-cycle engine would be best; whether he should use a make-and-break or jump spark for ignition; what was the best kind of windlass; whether the rigging should be set up with lanyards or turn buckles. Always a swift and penetrating student, in a few weeks he taught himself a great deal about modern shipbuilding.

Roscoe Eames in his palmier days had sailed small boats around San Francisco Bay. On the basis of this experience Jack hired him at sixty dollars a month to take the plans down to San Francisco and supervise the building of the *Snark,* an arrangement which pleased everyone concerned and gave to the aging and cantankerous Roscoe the first wage he had earned in years. Jack decided to call his boat the *Snark* after an imaginary animal in *The Hunting of the Snark. Cosmopolitan* had suggested that he name it after their magazine; Jack agreed that if they would pay the cost of building the boat he would not only name it *Cosmopolitan Magazine,* but would also take subscriptions along the way. He calculated the *Snark* would cost seven thousand dollars to build and, so calculating, said to Roscoe, "Spare no money. Let everything on the *Snark* be of the best. Never mind decoration; pine board is good enough for me. Put the money into construction. Let the *Snark* be as staunch and strong as any boat afloat. Never mind what it costs to make her staunch and strong; I'll go on writing and earning the money to pay for it."

Having dispatched Roscoe with the boat plans and an open check book, Jack cast about for his next serious project. It was four months since he had done any creative work. Among the many books he had ordered from England by catalogue was Stanley Waterloo's *Story of Ab,* one of the first attempts to recreate in literature the life of man when he was still more animal than human. Waterloo had put in ten years of study and work on his book; the result was erudite but unexciting. Jack saw his opportunity: here was a mechanism with which he could bring life to Darwin's theory of evolution! That afternoon he formulated his outline, leaning heavily on Waterloo's book, and the next morning he began to write *Before Adam,* illustrative of his talent for conceiving titles. By using the simple device of a modern boy who dreams at night that he is growing up as a primitive child, he contrasts the two periods with telling effect. The writing is so warm and honest that the reader believes this is how man really lived after having taken his historic step forward from the ape. "It is going to be the most primitive story ever written!" exulted Jack.

Conceived in the dark days when organized religion was fighting the theory of evolution as a diabolical concoction of sacrilegious souls, before the methods of scientific investigation had made much headway against the stone wall of ritualistic dogma, *Before Adam* was a brave attempt to popularize Darwin and Wallace, to bring the meaning of their work to the masses so they might better understand their antecedents. He was a superb story teller, and this book about primitive people is as absorbing as any of his Alaskan tales. Though *Before Adam* misses being first rate literature because of the tumultuous haste in which it was poured out, it makes delightful and illuminating reading, particularly for young people just beginning to sharpen the teeth of their mind.

Roscoe bought supplies, hired workmen, rented space in a ship-building dock, then informed Jack that the keel of the *Snark* would be laid on the morning of April 18, 1906. On the eve of the eighteenth Jack talked for hours about his trip, recalling that "when I was a small boy I read a book of Melville's called *Typee*, and many long hours I dreamed over its pages. I resolved then and there, mightily, come what would, when I had gained strength and years I too would voyage to Typee." In the very early morning, awakened by the floor shaking under his bed, he assumed that he had been dreaming of the valley of Typee and had tossed in his sleep in excitement. When dawn finally came he saddled Washoe Ban, rode to the top of Sonoma Mountain, and saw San Francisco in flames. He returned at top speed to Wake Robin, caught a train to Oakland, and then a ferry across to San Francisco, where he took photographs and dashed off a telegraphic story for *Collier's*.

Among the many major tragedies brought on by the San Francisco earthquake and fire, there was the minor tragedy that the keel of the *Snark* could not be laid. Supplies that had been paid for were burned; there were no workmen to be had; the iron-works had been razed, equipment ordered from New York could not be brought into the city. There could be no lick of work done on the *Snark* for many weeks. Jack left Roscoe behind to get construction under way again just as soon as possible, and returned to Glen Ellen to write some of his finest Klondike stories, among them "Love of Life," "The White Man's Way," "The Story of Keesh," "The Unexpected," "Negore," "The Coward"; he had begun to suspect that the *Snark* might cost a little more than his original estimate of seven thousand dollars to build.

In June the keel of the *Snark* was at last laid. Jack also conceived the motif for the novel based on the economic life of the people, for which he had long been casting about in his mind. "I am deep in the beginning of a socialistic novel! Am going to call it *The Iron Heel.* How is that for a title? The poor futile little capitalist! Gee, when the proletariat cleans house some day!" Again his vigorous imagination, which just two months before had invented a device to plunge a story backward in time some tens of thousands of years, now created a device to project *The Iron Heel* forward by seven hundred years: the finding of the manuscript of Ernest Everhard where it had been hidden just after the Second Revolt of the People had been bathed in blood by the Oligarch. Anatole France, who called Jack the American Karl Marx, wrote in an introduction to *The Iron Heel,* "Jack London has that particular genius which perceives what is hidden from the common herd, and possesses a special knowledge enabling him to anticipate the future."

Another trait he shared with Professor Chaney was his ability to predict the future, nearly always accurately. In *The Iron Heel* Jack once again proved that ideas can be more exciting than action, and that they control the world; just as in *The Sea Wolf* and *Before Adam* he had paid his debt to his masters, Spencer, Darwin, and Huxley, he now paid his debt to his master, Karl Marx, popularizing his teachings, dramatizing socialism and the revolution, making it intelligible to the masses. Karl Marx would have been pleased with *The Iron Heel.*

In writing his book Jack went to the extensive files and catalogues he had studiously compiled over a period of years, drawing from them sufficient factual material to make it one of the most scathing indictments against capitalism ever conceived. Economics was not only considered dry and dull and boring by Americans, but any discussion of the principles underlying private property and distribution of wealth was as tabu as discussions of evolution. Industrialists and bankers ruled by what had been known before the republican revolution as the Divine Right of Kings; workmen were told to be grateful for the labor and bread provided them through the wisdom and goodness of their employers. The Church, as exemplified by Jack's contact with it in Chicago while on his lecture tour, when the only two allegedly liberal ministers in the city refused to speak at the funeral of former Governor John P. Altgeld because he had pardoned the men railroaded in the Haymarket Riot, was a pot-bellied handmaiden of industry, as was the so-called higher education in the colleges, which taught only what its paymasters permitted.

All this he documented and wrote into one of the most terrifying and beautiful books ever written; if *The Iron Heel* is not his greatest contribution to the realm of literature, it is certainly his greatest contribution to the economic revolution. In it he not only predicted the coming of the now current Fascism, but detailed the methods by means of which it would murder all opposition and wipe out existing culture. *The Iron Heel* reads as though it were written yesterday . . . or ten years from today. In all contemporary literature there is no chapter more exciting than the one in which Ernest Everhard faces the Philomath Club (note the resemblance of the club name to the one Chaney invented, the Philomatheans), whose members formed the wealthiest Oligarch on the Pacific coast. Nor was there ever a more prophetic paragraph than the one in which the leader of the Oligarchs answers Everhard, who has just laid bare the waste and rapine of the profit system, and predicted the taking over of industry by the working people. "When you reach out your vaunted strong hands for our palaces and purple ease, we will show you what strength is. In the roar of shell and shrapnel and the whine of machine-guns will our answer be couched. We will grind your revolutionists down under our heel, and we shall walk upon your faces. The world is ours, we are its lords, and ours it shall remain. As for labor, it has been in the dirt since history began, and in the dirt it shall remain so long as I and mine have the power."

In the extensive bibliography on communism, Bukharin lists only one book by an American author, *The Iron Heel*.

Compared in scope as an adventure of the mind to his seven-year plan of sailing a forty-five-foot boat around the world, *The Iron Heel* makes the contemplated *Snark* voyage seem like a ferry ride across San Francisco Bay. He wrote the book in full consciousness that it would make him bitter and powerful enemies; he wrote it in full knowledge that it would injure his career, that it might hurt his past books and kill any new ones he might write. He wrote it in full awareness that Macmillan might be forced to refuse to publish it, that no magazine would dare serialize it, that there was no way to make enough money from it to pay for the food he consumed during the months of writing it.

All of which was even more courageous in view of what was happening to his bank account over the building of the *Snark*. Fulfilling his own command, "Never mind what it costs to make her staunch and strong," he ordered the most expensive Puget Sound planking for the deck so that there would be no butts to allow leakage; built four watertight compartments so that no matter how large a leak the *Snark* might spring, only one compartment could fill with water; sent to New York for a costly seventy-horse-power engine; bought a magnificent windlass and had castings specially made so that the engine could transmit power to the windlass to haul up the anchor. He built a dream of a bathroom, with schemes, devices, pumps, levers, and sea valves. He bought a rowboat, and then a small launch with a motor in it. He had a bow built on the *Snark* that cost a small fortune, but over which no sea could break, the most beautiful bow he had ever seen on a boat. Reporters sent to interview him wrote that he became "all boy" when the subject of the cruise was mentioned, that it was a new toy and he was going to have a lot of fun playing with it.

By midsummer he found that he already had ten thousand dollars in the *Snark*, and that she was not half finished. The ten thousand dollars had taken from him every dollar he could command; royalties and advances from Macmillan and his English publishers, the four hundred dollars he got from McClure who had bought *Love of Life*, the money he had received from other stories he had written after completing *Before Adam*. In addition to building his boat, he supported Flora, Johnny Miller, and Mammy Jenny in the house he had bought for Flora; Bessie and his two daughters in the house he had built for Bessie; Charmian, Roscoe Eames, and in part, Ninetta Eames and Edward Payne in Wake Robin; and had a foreman and hired men on the Hill Ranch who were planting and clearing, buying equipment and materials.

The editors to whom he had sent his excited letters in February were turning a cool cheek to his plea for advances against articles about the voyage. The acquiring of enough money to support his list of fourteen relatives, dependents, and workmen, and in addition to pay wages to the workmen on the *Snark*, became known as London's monthly miracle. Common sense told him to abandon the *Snark*, for the present at least, as he could not foot the bills. Or, if he wanted to continue pouring money into the *Snark*, to give up writing on *The Iron Heel*. He was a poor one for compromise. He continued his impassioned thousand words a morning on *The Iron Heel*, and in the afternoons, Sundays, and holidays turned out stories, articles, essays, anything to earn the hundreds and hundreds the *Snark* was consuming. In addition to buying a series of articles about the days when he had been a tramp on The Road, *Cosmopolitan* at last sent him a thousand dollars against an article he was to write about the *Snark before* he sailed; apparently *Cosmopolitan* entertained serious doubts about the forty-five-foot boat ever reaching another port.

By October 1, the date on which he had planned to cast off, he had fifteen thousand dollars in the *Snark*, and it was only half finished. He had poured into it the two thousand dollars from *Everybody's* magazine for the serialization of *Before Adam*, the thousand dollars from *Cosmopolitan*, the two thousand dollars from the *Woman's Home Companion* which it had agreed to advance him against articles on the domestic life of the aborigines, and at least another two thousand dollars earned by the batch of Alaskan tales, but he found that if he wanted to continue work on the boat he would have to borrow against the house he had bought for Flora. And at last he perceived that Roscoe Eames was a tragic error. Eames was quarrelsome and could get little work out of his men; he was inefficient, the workmen were duplicating their efforts; he was so garrulous and chaotic-minded that he was paying three prices for gear, buying materials for which he had no use, giving checks for equipment no one bothered to deliver. Uncompromising in his demands upon himself that he master any field of knowledge or endeavor before he wrote about it, Jack had not thought to make such demands of the people he employed, accepting them on their self-evaluation.

To complicate matters further, *Cosmopolitan*, which had had to be bludgeoned for a thousand-dollar advance, ran full-page advertisements that they were sending Jack London around the world in the *Snark* to write stories for them. "Everywhere prices have been raised, and stuck into me, and broken off, all upon the understanding that I wasn't spending my own money, but the money of a rich magazine."

In addition to this false advertising, which hurt Jack doubly because it put his voyage in a different light, making him look like an employee rather than an adventurer, *Cosmopolitan* also mutilated his first article about the *Snark*. Jack was never in better form than when he was writing angry letters to people whom he felt had taken advantage of him. "You're treating me scurvily. This is that first squabble I've ever had with a magazine. I hope it will be my last, but I'll make it hum while it lasts. Either we're going to work together, or we're not. Frankly I'd like to call the whole thing off. If you can't find a fair and square basis for treating me, then on your head be it. I'll neither give nor take quarter. You want to know when my next article will be sent to you. There are a few things I want to know first or else you will never know when that second article will be sent to you. You'll think the Day of Judgment will be a whole lot quicker in coming than that second article. I weave my stuff, you can't cut out parts of it and leave mutilated parts behind. Who in the dickens are you, anyway, to think that you can better my work? Do you think that I'll write my heart, my skilled professional heart into my work to have you fellows slaughtering it to suit your journalistic tastes? I refuse flatly and definitely to collaborate with anyone in your office!"

What vexed him more than the wasteful expenses were the prolonged delays. The *Snark* was promised for November 1, then November 15, then December 1. In desperation he moved to Oakland, sent Roscoe home to study navigation, and undertook supervising the completion of the boat himself. He hired fourteen men, paid them earthquake wages, and a dollar a day bonus for working fast. In order to do this he had to mortgage the Hill Ranch. By December 15 in spite of the tremendous outlay of cash, he saw that the *Snark* was as far from completion as it had been on October 1; once again he had to postpone his announced sailing date.

The newspapers began to publish satiric rhymes about the procrastinating Mr. London; the *Woman's Home Companion*, upset because *Cosmopolitan* beat them to publication with an article about the *Snark*, protested against his not sailing and demanded an article on the aborigines while he was still in San Francisco; his friends bet with him against his sailing date.

His foreman at the Hill Ranch collected the first bet on New Year's Day, 1907, and this amount was added to the twenty thousand dollars invested in the *Snark*. "After that the bets came fast and furious. My friends surrounded me like a gang of harpies, making bets against every sailing date I set. I was rash, and I was stubborn. I bet and bet, and continued to bet, and paid them all."

So well had the voyage of the *Snark* been publicized by the newspapers and magazines that he received thousands of letters from all over the country, the writers pleading to be taken along. Ninety per cent were willing to work in any capacity, and ninety-nine per cent were willing to work without pay. "Physicians, surgeons and dentists in large numbers offered to come along without pay; there were reporters, valets, chefs, illustrators, secretaries, civil engineers, machinists, electricians, retired sea captains, schoolteachers, university students, ranchers, housewives, sailors, riggers." Only one of them was Jack unable to resist, a seven-page letter from a young lad in Independence, Kansas, by the name of Martin Johnson. Jack wired him, "CAN YOU COOK?" and Martin Johnson telegraphed back "JUST TRY ME," then rushed out to get a job in the kitchen of a Greek restaurant in Independence. By January the future African explorer was in Oakland, ready to sail on the *Snark*, but the *Snark* was not ready for him. Because Jack insisted upon paying a fair wage to everybody who worked for him, Martin Johnson's wage was added to the roster.

Despite the fact that he now knew Roscoe to be incompetent, Jack did not fire him and engage one of the many available accredited sea captains to command his ship, any one of whom he could have had for the same one hundred dollars a month he was to pay Roscoe after they sailed. Nor did he accept the offer of any of the able-bodied seamen who begged to come along, with or without pay. Instead he hired for his lone engineer and sailor a Stanford University student by the name of Herbert Stolz, who was a husky and willing young man. That was to be his crew: Jack, Charmian, Roscoe Eames, Martin Johnson, Herbert Stolz, and a Japanese cabin boy, not one of whom, aside from Jack, knew how to reef a sail or haul up an anchor.

Having completed *The Iron Heel* he read the first two chapters to the Ruskin Club. An Oakland newspaper commented that he always tried out his socialistic ideas on Oakland because he knew that if they went there, they would go anywhere. He then sent the manuscript to Brett, who predicted that the newspapers would ignore it, or come down on the head of the author and publisher, but claimed that it was good work and agreed to publish it regardless of the consequences, a brave decision. His only request was that Jack delete a footnote which Brett was sure would land them both in jail for contempt of court. Jack replied, "If they find me guilty of contempt I'd be only too glad to do six months in jail, during which time I could write a couple of books and do no end of reading."

He had good reason to yearn for the comparative peace and quiet of a jail, for the *Snark* had landed him in a veritable bedlam. In February, one year after he had written his enthusiastic letters to the editors, the *Snark* had been so long in the building that she was breaking down faster than she could be repaired. The boat became a farce, London's folly. The newspapers laughed openly. Nobody took her seriously, least of all the men who were working on her. "Old sea dogs and master sailors by the score have made pilgrimages to the *Snark* and gone away shaking their heads and voicing misgivings of many sorts." Sailors said the *Snark* was badly planned and badly rigged, and would founder at sea. Bets were laid against the *Snark* ever reaching Hawaii. Manyoungi, the Korean boy who had served "Master" faithfully for three years, was so sure he would never reach Hawaii that he forced Jack to fire him by demanding, "Does God wish his coffee now?" Day and night the boat was surrounded by a crowd of curious jeering spectators.

Realizing that "the stage was set against him," that he could never complete the boat in San Francisco, Jack decided to sail her to Honolulu as she was and finish her there. His decision was no sooner made than the *Snark* sprang a leak that took days to repair. When he finally was able to start her for the boatways, she was caught between two barges and severely crushed. The workmen moved her to the ways and started her for the water, but the ways parted and the *Snark* dropped stern-first into the mud. Twice a day for a week, at high tide, two steam tugs pulled and hauled at the *Snark*, trying to get her out of the mud. When Jack tried to help by using the windlass, the specially made castings shattered, the gears ground and the windlass was put permanently out of commission. In despair he turned on the seventy-horse-power motor, but it shattered the cast-iron bedplate that had come all the way from New York, reared up in the air, smashed all connections and fastenings, and fell useless on its side.

By now Jack had twenty-five thousand dollars sunk in the sunken boat. His closest friends advised him that he was whipped, that he had better leave the *Snark* where she was and abandon the voyage. They assured him that to sail in her, if he could ever get her to sail, was courting suicide. Jack cried, "I can't quit!" Day after day he spent in a rage against the incompetent workmen, the defective materials that had been sent him, the merchants dunning him with bills, the newspapers that were openly ridiculing him. If he admitted defeat now he would be the laughing-stock of the country; he would never be able to live down the shame and disgrace! He was a man of his word. He'd sail that boat to Hawaii if it was the last thing he did. Better to die a hero's death in the deep Pacific than be jeered at by the working-men and merchants who had mulcted him, the newspapers that had satirized him, the crowds of onlookers who had laughed and called him crazy, that had raised the odds against his ever reaching Honolulu to twenty to one, with no takers!

"By main strength and sweat we dragged the *Snark* off the wrecked ways and laid her alongside the Oakland City Wharf. The drays brought the outfit from home, books, blankets, and personal luggage. Along with this, everything else came on board in a torrent of confusion—wood and coal, water and water tanks, vegetables, provisions, oil, the lifeboat and launch, all our friends and those who claimed to be their friends, to say nothing of some of the friends of the friends of the crew. Also there were reporters and photographers, and strangers, and cranks, and finally, over everything, clouds of coal dust from the wharf."

But at last the long, heart-breaking travail was over; they were to sail on Saturday, April 20, 1907. On Saturday morning Jack went on board with a check book, fountain pen, and blotter, and nearly two thousand dollars in cash, all he had been able to collect in advances from Macmillan and the magazines, and waited for the balances due the hundred and fifteen firms whom he felt had delayed him so long. Instead of the merchants coming on board for their pay, a United States marshal arrived and tacked a notice on the *Snark's* mast that she was labeled for debt by S. H. Sellers, a ship chandler, to whom he owed $232. The *Snark* was a prisoner and could not move; Jack thrashed about the town trying madly to find his creditors, the sheriff, the mayor, anyone to get clear. Everyone was away for the week-end.

On Monday morning he sat once again on the *Snark* pouring out greenbacks, gold, and checks to his creditors, so blinded with anger and frustration that he could not even itemize the bills, make sure he owed the money, or that he hadn't paid the bill before. When he added it all up he found that the *Snark*, whose seventy-horse-power engine was lashed down for ballast, whose power transmission was a wreck, whose lifeboat leaked and motor launch wouldn't run, whose one coat of paint had already worn off, had cost him thirty thousand dollars.

Robbed, ridiculed, cried over, given up for a hopelessly romantic idiot, Jack hoisted Jimmy Hopper's California football sweater to the top of the mast, and raised his anchor by hand. Then, with a navigator who couldn't navigate, an engineer who couldn't engineer, and a cook who couldn't cook, the *Snark* limped down the Estuary, crossed the Bay, and sailed out the Golden Gate Strait into the Pacific.

Though his lack of practicality started his troubles, those troubles were usually compounded by the cupidity of the people around him. When he came to inspect the forward beams, which had cost him seven dollars and a half each because they were supposed to be oak, he found that they were pine, worth two-fifty each. The special planking brought from Puget Sound spread, and the deck leaked so badly it flooded the bunkrooms, ruined the tools in the engine room and the provisions in the galley. The sides of the *Snark* leaked, the bottom leaked, and then the expensive watertight compartments began leaking into each other, including the one in which the gasoline was stored. The ironwork broke off in his hand, particularly the portion used in the rigging. Every gadget in the dream bathroom went out of order within twenty hours. When he came to inspect the provisions he found that the oranges had been frozen before being put on board, that the apples and cabbages, having been put on for one of the earlier announced sailings, were spoiled and had to be thrown overboard, that kerosene had spilled on the carrots, the beets were woody, the kindling wouldn't burn, and the coal had spilled out of the rotting potato sacks and was being washed through the scuppers.

Not until they were several days at sea did Jack discover that Roscoe Eames had failed to learn anything about navigating during the months when he was being paid to do so, that Roscoe couldn't take an accurate bearing, and that the *Snark*, leaking like the proverbial sieve, was lost somewhere in the Pacific! He dug out the navigation books and studied them, then drew his charts and took a shot at the sun. "Navigating by observation of the sun, moon, and stars, thanks to the astronomers and mathematicians, is child's play. One whole afternoon I sat in the cockpit, steering with one hand, studying logarithms with the other. Two afternoons, two hours each, I studied the general theory of navigation and the particular process of taking a meridian altitude. Then I took the sextant, worked out the index error, and shot the sun. Proud? I was a worker of miracles. I had listened to the voices of the stars and they had told me my place upon the highway of the sea."

They ran into heavy weather that sent Martin Johnson and Tochigi, the cabin boy, into their bunks with acute cases of seasickness; in addition to his other duties Jack stood knee-deep in water in the galley trying futilely to manage a hot meal. Charmian not only took her regular trick at the wheel, but two four-hour tricks in a row, holding the course in rough and black seas while the five men slept securely below deck. Roscoe, who had put aboard hundreds of dollars worth of specially canned health foods, at Jack's expense, sat in his cabin eating the health foods. When Jack asked why he didn't scrub down the decks and make some attempt to keep the boat clean, Roscoe replied that he couldn't work because he was constipated.

In the midst of the dirt, danger, and confusion, with his world almost literally sinking beneath him, Jack sat down on the forward hatch and began writing *Martin Eden*, perhaps the finest novel he ever wrote, and one of the greatest of all American novels. The original ink-scrawled manuscript shows few changes, indicating the tremendous powers of organization he had developed, and the concentration with which he pitched into his work. After a week the sun came out, Martin Johnson and Tochigi climbed weakly from their bunks, and Herbert Stolz, without a captain to command him, did his best to keep the *Snark* before the wind. Jack wrote his thousand words a morning, pushing forward into the autobiographical story in which he tells of his own struggles to overcome his lack of book-learning, to turn himself from a rough sailor into a cultivated man and a successful author in the short period of three years. The main characters are himself, Mabel Applegarth and her family, and George Sterling as the poet Brissenden. Ruth Morse, the name Jack gave his heroine, is convincing because she is taken from a life model, the only woman above the working class he ever made believable. Warm, crude, vital, *Martin Eden* is strikingly prophetic; the poet Brissenden warns Martin Eden that he must tie himself to socialism or when success comes he will have nothing to hold him to life. Martin renounces his socialism, and then, sated with success, drowns himself.

When the book was published two years later, the San José Women's Club invited a book-reviewer by the name of Mira MacClay to review *Martin Eden* for them. In the course of her review Mrs. MacClay lashed the heroine for being a coward and a weakling, for ruining Martin Eden's life as well as her own. She had no way of knowing that the pale, ethereal, spinsterish-looking woman in the front row, gazing up at her with death in her eyes, was Mabel Applegarth.

After twenty-seven days of sailing, during which the magnificent prow of the *Snark*, into which Jack had poured so much love and money, proved not only useless but dangerous because she would not heave to in rough weather, land was sighted. Jack was chagrined over his navigation; according to his charts the nearest land should have been a hundred miles distant. It soon proved to be the summit of Haleakala, towering ten thousand feet above the sea, and fully a hundred miles away. Always prouder of his physical than his intellectual accomplishments, he was more elated than he had been since he held firm the wheel of the *Sophie Sutherland* in the typhoon off the coast of Japan.

Early the following day they drifted around Diamond Head and into full view of Honolulu. A launch of the Hawaiian Yacht Club came out to meet the *Snark*, bringing with it newspapers with cable dispatches from the States that the *Snark* had foundered. The commodore of the club bade them welcome to Hawaii, led the way to Pearl Harbor, and took them home for a hot bath and *poi* cocktails; a friend by the name of Tom Hobron placed a cottage on the Island of Hilo at their disposal. Each morning Jack was awakened by mynah birds. He walked the few steps to an emerald-colored lagoon for a swim, sat down to breakfast at a table under the trees that Tochigi had strewn with red hibiscus and glassy coral peppers, and after breakfast worked in a blue kimono at an improvised desk set up on the lawn. He wrote the details of his difficulties in getting the *Snark* built and launched into "The Inconceivable and Monstrous"; told of the thousands of letters he had received from people who had wanted to join his adventure in *Adventure,* and the story of how the *Snark* was lost because Roscoe Eames couldn't navigate, and how he had taught himself to navigate in "Finding One's Way About." He was in desperate need of funds, the articles were amusing, and they sold to the magazines. He wrote one short story, *To Build a Fire,* an Alaskan tragedy of epic proportions.

For the first twelve days the *Snark* was in Pearl Harbor he did not go aboard. On the thirteenth when he rowed out to the boat he found that the decks had not been hosed down even once, that along with the exposed gear, they were rotting under the tropical sun. He promptly fired Roscoe Eames and Herbert Stolz and sent them back to California. The newspapers told the American public that there had been quarreling and dissension on the *Snark.* Because Jack did not want to hurt Ninetta Eames by exposing Roscoe, he made no attempt to defend himself. He then sent transportation money to Eugene Fenelon, a friend of George Sterling, to join the *Snark* as its engineer. Fenelon, who, as the newspapers commented, "gained his knowledge of the sea while traveling as strong man of the circus, and while studying for the priesthood," arrived, spent several months attempting to put the *Snark* in shape, and returned to Carmel leaving the equipment in worse condition than ever.

Not only was Hawaii "a sweet land, but the people were sweet people." The editors of the *Star* and the *Pacific Commercial Traveler* gave a dinner in their honor, they were invited to a reception for Prince Kalamanaole and Her Majesty, Liliuokalani; everywhere they were entertained and shown the majesty of the islands. Every day held a new and dramatic adventure: he fished by torchlight with Prince Kalamanaole, went to native *luaus*, or moaning feasts, swam in the bright, warm moonlight, lived on the Haleakala Ranch on the Island of Maui. The manager, Louis von Tempsky, took him to watch cattle drives, colt-breakings, and brandings, and on the ride of incredible beauty and danger eight thousand feet up the sides of mountains, and across shaky hempen bridges which spanned great gorges, to Haleakala crater, from the crest of which he saw all of the islands and the sea beneath them. Out of this adventure came the article, "The House of the Sun."

He spent a week on the leper island of Molokai, where he and Charmian lived and mingled with the lepers on terms of physical equality, sitting side by side with them at their shooting club and standing in the rifle boxes, shooting with rifles still warm from their hands, or attending the horse races they staged. The lepers pleaded with him to write an article which would tell the truth about the maligned Island of Molokai so that the world might know that they lived well and happily, and in "The Lepers of Molokai," written as soon as he returned to his bungalow in Hilo, Jack fulfilled his promise with a tender and tragically beautiful description of his stay there. Alexander Hume Ford, authority on surf-riding, taught him to ride the breakers; although he received a sunburn that kept his sensitive skin blistered for two weeks, he wrote an article called "A Royal Sport" which did much to popularize surf-riding among Americans. He loved the easy, beauty-drenched life of the islands, and worked well on *Martin Eden*, in addition to his other writings.

When the series of tramp articles appearing in the *Cosmopolitan* were ready to be issued in book form, Brett wrote to Jack asking if he would still be willing to publish *The Road* if he, Brett, could prove that the book would hurt him with his public. Jack replied, "In *The Road*, as in all my work, I have been true. As my character has developed through my work there have been flurries of antagonism, attacks, and condemnations. But I pulled through them all. I have always insisted that the cardinal literary virtue is sincerity. If I am wrong in that belief, if the world downs me on it, I'll say, 'Good-bye, proud world,' retire to the ranch, and plant potatoes and raise chickens to keep my stomach full. It was my refusal to take cautious advice that made me."

There was one piece of cautious advice that he did take, one that probably saved his life: in mid-October he set sail from Hilo for the Marquesas with a registered sea captain and a Dutch sailor on board. Captain Warren had been paroled from the Oregon penitentiary on a charge of murder; Hermann had once captained his father's fishing ketch off the coast of Holland. If he had had the caution to hire experienced seamen while building the *Snark*, or before sailing her to Hawaii, he could have saved himself twenty thousand dollars and endless aggravation. The only one from his original crew to prove himself a worthy adventurer was six-foot, handsome Martin Johnson, who was promoted from cook to mechanic, and thereafter was an asset to the *Snark*. During the two years of its adventuring, Charmian too proved her worth to Jack. She was dead game, a woman of inexhaustible courage, cheerful in the face of hardship, as staunch as a man companion when bucking danger. Whether it was spending the week among the lepers of Molokai, recruiting among the head-hunters of the Solomon Islands, riding a horse over hempen bridges and across tropical canyons, traversing a portion of the Pacific that no sailboat had ever attempted, she had spunk and resourcefulness. She was calm in troubled times, a joyous companion in good times. If Jack had wanted someone to roam side by side with him, in Charmian he found that woman.

Several days out of Hilo Jack opened his book of sailing directions for the South Pacific Ocean, and read that not only had no sailing-boat in recorded history made the cross from Hawaii to the Marquesas, but that, owing to the equatorial currents and the position of the southeast trade winds, it was considered impossible to fetch the Marquesas. "The impossible did not deter the *Snark*," commented Jack, and continued merrily on his way, fetching the Marquesas by a stunning feat of navigation and sailing, escaping death only because the larger fates said that the man called Jack London had a number of books in him that had to be written before he could be killed off.

They found themselves wedged between the trade winds and the doldrums, with the *Snark* standing motionless for days. They were buffeted by storms of wind, rain, and sea, by squalls that time and again seemed as though they would snap the tiny, leaking *Snark* like a matchstick. In sixty days they sighted no sail or steamer's smoke; they lost half their water overboard and were saved from perishing of thirst by a providential rain. To Jack, death-appeal was the greatest of all thrills; he was living as ecstatically as a young boy. He navigated the *Snark* through unchartered waters, fished for dolphins and sharks and sea turtles, stretched out on the hatch with the sea-salt in his nostrils and the roll of the ocean caressing his body, wrote his thousand words every day on *Martin Eden*, and exciting articles such as "A Pacific Traverse." On warm days he sat on deck and read to Charmian, Captain Warren, Martin Johnson, Hermann, Nakata, the jovial Japanese cabin boy who had replaced Tochigi, and Wada, the cook, from Stevenson's books on the Marquesas and Tahiti, from Conrad's *Typhoon* and *Youth* and Melville's *White Jacket*, *Typee*, *Moby Dick*. The troubled background of the *Snark* was forgotten as he fulfilled his promise to the romantic boy of thirteen who had read every travel book Miss Coolbrith could find for him in the Oakland Public Library.

Two months of sailing brought him to Nuka-hiva, in the Marquesas. "The trade blew out of the northwest, while we steered a steady course for the southwest. Ten days of this, and on the morning of December 6, at five o'clock, we sighted land just where it ought to have been, dead ahead. We passed to leeward of Uahuka, skirted the southern edge of Nuka-hiva, and that night, in driving squalls and inky blackness, fought our way in to an anchorage in the narrow bay of Taiohae. The anchor rumbled down to the blatting of wild goats on the cliffs, and the air we breathed was heavy with the perfume of flowers."

In Nuka-hiva it was a source of pleasure and gratification to him to rent the clubhouse in which Robert Louis Stevenson had spent frequent afternoons when he lived in the Marquesas. On the second day, as soon as they were able to ride, the entire crew set out for Melville's magnificent valley of Hapaa, which Melville had pictured in *Typee* as peopled by a strong and warlike tribe living in the midst of a tropical and fertile garden. Alas for the disillusionments of youth's dreams: by the time Jack rode through the valley of Hapaa it had become an untenanted, howling, tropical wilderness, with the few Marquesans who had escaped the ravages of the diseases brought in by the "inevitable white man" dying in their wretched huts of galloping consumption. He wrote a heart-broken article about the extinction of this glorious race, which he named, in deference to Melville, "Typee."

"All the strength and beauty has departed, and the valley of Typee is the abode of some dozen wretched creatures afflicted by leprosy, elephantiasis and tuberculosis. Life has rotted away in this wonderful garden spot."

After twelve colorful days in the Marquesas, during which he hunted wild goats, and witnessed native festivals, dances, and feasts, he hoisted anchor and sailed through the Paumotan Islands for Tahiti, where he was to pick up his mail. Here he learned that the *Snark* had once again been given up for lost, that the San Francisco sailors were recalling their prophecies that she was badly planned and badly rigged. Many of the papers ran stories of genuine regret over the loss of so able a young writer; others accused him of staying lost merely to get publicity, and one editorial even charged him with employing a very clever press agent who had secured for him free advertising worth more than the cost of the boat.

Though he had been gone only eight months, an examination of the many boxes of accumulated mail showed him that when the master is away his affairs soon fall into chaos. The Oakland bank, convinced that he was on the bottom of the South Pacific, had foreclosed the mortgage on Flora's house. A number of checks he had issued in Hilo, totaling eight hundred dollars, had been returned by another Oakland bank marked "Not sufficient funds," causing an uproar in the press.

When Jack left Glen Ellen he had given Ninetta Eames his power of attorney and made her his agent and business manager. She had set her own salary at ten dollars a month, which she now raised to twenty dollars a month, in addition to the forty dollars a month she was charging as rent for the rooms at Wake Robin he was not occupying. Poring over the bills, Jack learned that she had spent a thousand dollars to build an annex to the barn on the Hill Ranch so that the foreman might live there with his wife; fourteen hundred dollars in the month of December to take care of Flora, Johnny Miller, Mammy Jenny, Bessie, and the two girls, to pay wages, buy supplies and equipment for the ranch, to pay insurance, and keep up Wake Robin. Another bill totaling a thousand dollars was a three-page list of equipment for the *Snark*, including everything from a thousand gallons of gasoline to a hundred boxes of Jack's special Egyptian cigarettes and a dozen boxes of candy. All of these myriad expenses in addition to the thousands a month it was costing him to man and run the *Snark!* Despite the fact that in December Macmillan had paid him fifty-five hundred dollars in royalties; Reynolds, his occasional agent in New York, had sold *To Build a Fire* to *Century* for three hundred and fifty dollars; Ninetta Eames had sold *The Lepers of Molokai* to *Woman's Home Companion*, *Finding One's Way About* and *The Inconceivable and Monstrous* to *Harper's Weekly*; that money had come in from English magazines and English publishers, from his Scandinavian, German, French, and Italian publishers, he learned that in the first week of the year 1908 he had exactly sixty-six dollars in the world, and no immediate promise of anything more.

When he had arrived in Honolulu on May 28 of the previous year, almost the first thing he had said was, "I am bankrupt and shall probably have to stay here until I raise some money." He had then written a number of articles about the voyage and stories about Hawaii which had brought from three hundred to five hundred dollars apiece. It was only four and a half years since the success of *The Call of the Wild*; he had earned enough to spend forty thousand dollars on the *Snark*, eleven thousand on the Hill Ranch, ten thousand on Bessie's home, eight thousand on Flora's home, and about thirty-five thousand more to support his ever-growing entourage. It was now costing him three thousand dollars a month to navigate, yet here he was stranded in Tahiti with sixty-six dollars in the world!

The S.S. *Mariposa* was scheduled to sail from Tahiti for San Francisco. Jack decided to leave with her, to go home and try to straighten out his affairs. How he got together the money to buy the tickets for himself and Charmian remains a mystery. He left the *Snark* in the hands of Captain Warren and the crew, and returned to California. His horde of anxious relatives, who had hoped to receive mail on the *Mariposa* to assure them that he was safe, were stunned when they learned he was in San Francisco. The newspapers broke out the boldest headlines yet to herald his arrival. One reporter stated, "The smile that won't come off doesn't half express the London smile. This is hearty and soulful, of wide expanse, and good to look upon." Many accused him of abandoning his voyage. When he told everyone that he was returning with the *Mariposa* when it sailed a week later, those of his friends who did not laugh at him in disbelief tried to persuade him against it, urging that since he had demonstrated he could do it, he should let well enough alone and remain home. They evidently did not believe his statement to the reporters that the days spent on board the *Snark* were among the happiest of his life.

He immediately wired Macmillan for an advance against the almost completed *Martin Eden*, with which he lifted the mortgage on Flora's house and paid the ever-mounting bank interest on the Hill Ranch. He arranged with *Harper's Weekly* to publish a series of the *Snark* articles, using the money to pay his most pressing debts and to give Flora her fifty-two-dollar check for February, Bessie her seventy-five-dollar check, Mammy Jenny her fifteen dollar . . . By glancing at the back files of the *Woman's Home Companion* he learned why he had been charged double prices in Hawaii and Papeete: the *Companion*, to whom he had transferred his contract because *Cosmopolitan* had broadcast the news that they were sending him around the world, had found that identical piece of false advertising too juicy to resist.

The year 1907 had seen three of his books published, equaling his record for 1902. He was but thirty-one years old and he had published nineteen books, for he was as profligate with the great riches of his mind as he was with the riches they earned for him.

Before Adam, his dramatization of evolution and primitive life, is still read with delight by Americans. *The Road*, though it received scant attention when released, is now recognized as one of our few genuine source books on tramp life. *Love of Life* includes some of his most finely wrought Alaskan tales. Written for the cash he needed to pour into the *Snark*, the excellence of these tales indicates that some men who write for literature, with nary a tarnishing thought of money in mind, can create trash, while others who write for money can create literature. A man's gifts, and not what he plans to do with the rewards of those gifts, are the determining factors. Jack had a love of truth, an ability to think straight, a vigorous education, a deep understanding of people, and the courage to say what he felt and thought. Coupled with this richness and integrity of mind was a native story-teller's gift whipped into shape by hard and intelligent work. The fact that he needed money had not caused him to give short measure or sabotage his craft; his career was founded on the belief that good work deserved good money.

Brett's prediction about *The Iron Heel* proved accurate; the majority of newspapers did not mention its publication; the few that did declared that "the hand of the law should descend heavily upon him." Ignored, unfavorably reviewed, the book received no recognition and no sale except among the handful of Marxian socialists in America. Ten years later it was to emerge as one of the world's great classics of revolution, and to make of Jack London a veritable God to the Russian people. Bitter as was the capitalist press against *The Iron Heel*, the socialist press, which the year before had berated him for walking out on a luxurious yacht when there was so much work to be done at home, was even more bitter. He was accused of betraying the Cause, of antagonizing the public by preaching bloodshed, of alienating the party membership, which was peaceful and wanted socialism to filter through gradually by means of education, legislation, and the ballot, and not by death at the barricades. Though the capitalist and socialist presses united in calling him a menace, by April, three months later, the socialists had forgiven him sufficiently to suggest that he run for the presidency of the United States on the Socialist ticket.

He fulfilled his promise and returned with Charmian on the *Mariposa* to continue his seven-year voyage around the world. On April 9 he sailed in the *Snark* from Tahiti to Bora Bora, gem of Polynesia. In Bora Bora he joined the native stone fishers; in Raiatea he lived with the aborigines amid a wealth of food and gifts showered upon him in a profusion unknown to more civilized countries; in Pago Pago he was entertained by a native king. Sailing onward to Suva in the Fiji Islands the *Snark* was buffeted by storms and lost for days because the chronometer went out of order. They reached Suva, capital of the Fijis, in June. Here Captain Warren, who had grown melancholy during the month of May and twice gone berserk, went ashore, leaving the *Snark* badly in need of repairs, and did not return. Jack had his possessions sent after him, and from that time forward captained his vessel himself without mishap. He cruised through the Solomon Islands, lived on the copra plantations in the bush "as near the rawest edge of screaming savagery as any place to be found on this earth." At Malaita, where many white men lost their heads to the savages, he joined friends on the *Minota* and went recruiting with them among the bushmen for slave labor for the plantations. He was attacked from ambush by cannibals, by natives on board the boat who wanted to loot and scuttle her and *kai-kai* the white crew. When it looked as though the ship would pile up on the reef he was shot at with poisoned arrows, was attacked by tribes of screaming black natives. "When the *Minota* first struck there was not a canoe in sight; but like vultures circling down out of the blue, canoes began to arrive from every quarter. The boat's crew, with rifles at the ready, kept them lined up a hundred feet away with a promise of death if they ventured nearer. There they clung, black and ominous, holding their canoes with their paddles on the perilous edge of the breaking surf." Here indeed was adventure worthy of the boy who had sailed the *Razzle Dazzle* without reefing, who had four times stopped the Overland Express, who had shot White Horse Rapids, and sailed a native junk across the Yellow Sea. "I'm having the time of my life!" he cried.

He made copious notes, took photographs, at each island collected native canoes, paddles, shells, wood carvings, spears, calabashes, bowls, mats, tapa cloth, jewels, coral, and aboriginal ornaments that formed a complete South Seas museum when he took them back to Glen Ellen. And everywhere he went, Fiji, the Marquesas, Samoa, wherever he could gather together ten white men, he gave his lecture on revolution!

Living as he did in the midst of leprosy, elephantiasis, malaria, ringworm, gari-gari (a horrible skin itch), Solomon sores, or yaws, skin ulcers, and a hundred other jungle diseases, the *Snark* was converted into a hospital ship. Every time a member of the crew bruised himself on board or cut his leg while beaching the boat or treading through the jungle, a yaw developed which spread over his body, the individual ulcers becoming big as silver dollars. In the Solomons the entire crew contracted malaria, sometimes as many as five of them being down with it, leaving the sixth to sail the *Snark* through fair weather or foul. Jack had so many bouts of malaria that for months he was as much on his back as he was on his feet, doped with forty grains of quinine. On the way to Fiji he scratched some mosquito bites and his body became covered with yaws. Even these hardships he enjoyed because they seemed to him the romantic hardships of the explorer, the intrepid and inevitable white man who conquered the world. He liked to call himself an Amateur M.D.; he pulled teeth, treated Charmian's and Martin Johnson's open yaws with corrosive sublimate, slammed quinine down the throat of Wada, who had contracted blackwater fever and with Oriental fatalism had given over to dying.

Except when down with malaria, he kept rigidly to his routine of composing a thousand words every morning. Charmian, equally faithful to her duties, typed his manuscripts and took dictation for the replies to his voluminous correspondence. His one novel to come out of the South Seas, *Adventure*, which took him many months of painstaking labor, was laid on a copra plantation he had visited on the Solomon Islands. When the critics complained about his "screaming savagery," Jack defended himself on the ground that he had portrayed only what he had seen with his own eyes. Veracity of reporting, however, does not make convincing literature; *Adventure* is adequate escapist entertainment, but no better than could have been done by a dozen of his contemporaries. It was serialized by *Popular Magazine*, whose readers had a low literacy quotient, and when published in book form died a quick death.

His articles about the voyage, later collected in *The Cruise of the Snark*, are colorful and dashing journalism, told in the warm, infectious, friendly style of narrative which so precisely reflects his character; but he would have been the last to imagine they had any solid literary value. On board the *Snark*, and in the years to come, he was to write thirty short stories laid in the South Seas; while some of them, such as "The House of Mapuhi," "The Heathen," "Koolau," "The Leper," "Chun ah Chun," "Yah! Yah! Yah!" are good yarns, the reader sits apart in wonderment, as though watching some aboriginal sideshow. The stories of the "inevitable white man" who tames the blacks and farms the world are exciting and exotic, but they have little of the universal in them. The reader is rarely able to identify himself with the main character, to live and fight and die with him, as he does with Jack's Alaskan heroes, with his native American protagonists. His South Seas adventures could be important to no one but himself. His socialist comrades had criticized him for going away when there was so much work to be done at home. They were right in a profounder sense: Jack's simplest writings about his own people and customs and conflicts create literature, stay with us to enliven our memories and broaden our concepts, and our love of the printed page.

The voyage of the *Snark* repaid him many times over in adventure; if as an investment in literary materials it was not to prove profitable, Jack would not have been concerned over this aspect of the bargain. He loved to cry, "I have always stood for the exalting of the life that is in me over art, or any other extraneous thing."

In addition to maintaining rigid discipline in his work, he strove valiantly to keep his business affairs in order. Wanting some guest houses built near Wake Robin to accommodate his friends when he returned, he wrote Mrs. Eames a nine-page letter of instructions containing a mass of technical information about building. While thousands of miles away in the Solomon Islands he detailed which way each door should swing, where the washbowl should stand in relation to the toilet. He wrote beautifully clear, logical, comprehensive letters to his business associates, but the more instructions he wrote the greater confusion his affairs fell into; he had not yet come to realize that any man who earns between twenty thousand and thirty thousand dollars a year is running a big business and has to remain close to the factory. His agent in New York would sell a short story to an English magazine while Ninetta Eames was in the process of selling the same story to an American magazine; after Jack had spent the money the American magazine had paid, it would irately demand a refund because it had been cheated out of the English copyright. His American and English book publishers were quarreling over who owned the distribution rights in the Colonies, which resulted in publications being held up; editors who would have bought stories and articles if certain details could have been adjusted, returned the manuscripts because it took too many months to negotiate through the Solomon Islands. His value in the market had gone up, he had been receiving five hundred and six hundred dollars for a manuscript from such magazines as *Cosmopolitan* and *Collier's*; when the editors stopped buying, Ninetta Eames began hawking stories and articles as though they were fish, demanding, "How much will you give for this Jack London story?" and taking any price offered. The editors soon began to sense that the London material was being sent out under panic conditions; they refrained from buying altogether, the market became glutted with his manuscripts, his income halted abruptly.

The hundreds upon hundreds of typewritten pages Ninetta Eames sent to Jack during this period constitute an amazing document. In sentiment as well as language they bear a family resemblance to the hundreds of typewritten pages sent to Jack by Mrs. Eames's niece five years before. Fluttery, flowery, bathed in saccharine protestations of undying love and sacrifice and devotion, the steely fingers are visible beneath every line. Ninetta Eames built an annex to her Wake Robin home; when Jack returned to Glen Ellen she charged him rent to occupy the rooms his money had built. For a second time she raised her own salary, this time to thirty dollars a month, back-dating the raise, and demanding to know of Jack if he were not willing to pay her a living wage. Anguished by this attack, Jack protested, "One of the things I have prided myself on since I have had a dollar to spend has been that everybody who ever did anything for me has always been well paid." After months of crying about her poverty, her hardships, her inability to repay Jack the loan he had made her at Wake Robin before he left on the *Snark*, he finally wrote, "My money on deposit at the Bank of Oakland is earning me no interest; help yourself to it for whatever you need." An examination of the check books today reveals that Ninetta Eames took him at his word: there are hundreds of checks to sanitariums, doctors, drugstores; there are checks for clothing, furniture, repairs to Wake Robin, and for grocery bills that would have fed a large-sized institution.

If all of this was without Jack's knowledge, it was at least with his overt permission. What he did not know was that he was getting about twenty-five cents' worth for every dollar being spent on the Hill Ranch. He was paying to have a solid stone wall built in the new barn he had ordered, but a few years later when an earthquake hit Glen Ellen, the walls cracked and he discovered that they were not only hollow but that the workmen had thrown into them the tin cans and refuse from their lunches. There was the matter of the bathroom equipment bought for the foreman's house, for which he paid full price, but which proved to be second-hand when it was deposited at the Glen Ellen railway station. However, the worst blow to Jack was that Mrs. Eames stopped sending him his monthly accounts. In an agonized letter written to her from Penduffryn, in which he tries to set her straight on a score of business complications, he complains that although he received mail from her every month of the year 1908, she had sent him accounts for only February and May.

Then, in the midst of the chaos, Ninetta Eames concluded an astute business deal and Jack forgave her everything. She sold the serial rights of *Martin Eden* to the *Pacific Monthly*, for the princely sum of seven thousand dollars, which covered his debts and put him a few thousand dollars ahead.

Adjoining the Hill Ranch in Sonoma Valley was the Kohler vineyard property of eight hundred acres and the Lamotte Ranch of one hundred and ten acres. For many months Ninetta Eames kept reminding Jack that the Kohler property was for sale for thirty thousand dollars and a great bargain, and repeatedly informed him that the Lamotte Ranch could be bought for ten thousand dollars. There was no reason for him to buy either of these ranches; he already owned a hundred and thirty acres of magnificent land on which he had not yet passed a single night; there remained another five years in which he intended to sail around the world; and the seven thousand dollars he had just received from *Martin Eden* had saved him from imminent bankruptcy. But he remembered the rolling hills and redwoods of the Lamotte Ranch, the happy hours he had spent riding down its canyons and across the trails through the vineyards and madrone. By return mail he ordered Mrs. Eames to buy the Lamotte Ranch for him. She paid about three thousand dollars down, and mortgaged the balance. Sailing a ketch among the Solomon Islands,

headed for Japan, India, and the Suez Canal, uncertain whether
he could sell tomorrow's story or meet next month's bills, Jack
was now owner of two hundred and forty acres of the most beautiful foothill country in California. . . .

By September 18, 1908, the fun of playing the Amateur M.D.
was gone; his hands began to swell with dropsy; only by the most
painful effort could he close them. Then the skin began to peel
off, first one layer, then two, then five and six layers. He was in
constant agony. No one could diagnose the strange disease he had
contracted. A nervous affliction seized his whole body; at frequent
intervals he became helpless, unable to stagger about the deck for
fear of being forced to clutch something with his hands. The nervous disturbance began to affect his mind; his persecution mania
returned, there was a conspiracy against him, people were trying
to prevent him from completing his voyage around the world.

Danger nor hardship had been able to deter him, expense and
ridicule had only whetted his determination. But illness at last
conquered him. Helpless with pain, he arranged for a retired captain to watch over the *Snark*, then engaged passage for himself,
Charmian, Martin Johnson, and Nakata on the S.S. *Nakomba* for
Sydney.

The night before he was to sail he went alone aboard the *Snark*.
A full moon lighted the deck of the ship that had grown under
his own brain and his own hand. He loved every part of her, even
her weaknesses and faults, for they too had been of his making.
She was worth every dollar he had poured into her, every ounce of
energy he had expended in her behalf, all the abuse and ridicule
he had borne in her creation. At times she had been errant and
self-willed, at others weak and incompetent, but she had served
him well, she had been faithful to him, had carried him safely
over thousands of miles of ocean at his bidding, had brought
him great happiness and heroic adventures, had provided his mind
with rich and exotic scenes upon which his memory might feed in
leaner, duller days. Together they had faced death unflinching,
had battled stormy seas, been lashed by wind and rain, lay quies-
cent in the doldrums; been warmed and made joyous by the
strong clean sun and the salt sea sir. The *Snark* had been a good
friend to him, and in separating he ran a pain-racked hand fondly

across her railings and riggings and gear, shedding an honest, sentimental tear, as he felt all true friends should at parting.

After twelve wretched days at sea he entered a hospital in Sydney, and stayed five weeks there on a white cot. His malady baffled the Australian specialists, appeared to be unknown in the history of medicine. "I am as helpless as a child. On occasion my hands are twice their natural size, with seven dead and dying skins peeling off at one time. My toenails, in twenty-four hours, grow as thick as they are long."

Finding that they could do him no good in the hospital, Jack spent the next five months in Sydney hotels and apartments, hoping for a cure that would enable him to return to the *Snark*. He was unable to write, and in such pain that he was hardly able to read. The only job he turned in was a report of the Burns-Johnson fight in Australia. What a newspaper reporter had described only a year before as "the smile that won't come off" was now completely gone. He was sick, discouraged.

By the beginning of March, 1909, he realized that if he did not go home to California he would leave his bones in the tropics just as surely as he would have if the bushmen of the New Hebrides had cut off his head and "*kai-kai'd*" along him." He sent Martin Johnson with a navigator to the Solomon Islands to bring the *Snark* down to Sydney. "I left the *Snark* in charge of a drunken master, and when she was brought back to Sydney she had damned little left upon her. I am still wondering what became of my automatic rifles, of my ship's stores, of my naturalist's shotguns, of my two cameras, of my three thousand French francs." He took his personal possessions off the *Snark*, then offered her up for sale. She fetched three thousand dollars, and was put into recruiting slave labor among the Solomon Islands, an ironic end for a ship built by one of the world's leading socialists.

Arriving in San Francisco on July 23, 1909, after more than two years of wandering, he told newspapermen at the dock, "I am unutterably weary, and I have come home for a good rest." He was under a staggering load of debt, his health was badly undermined, the newspapers of the country were either hostile or disinterested, the magazine editors had seen so little real material from him in the past year that they suspected he was through; even the public was tiring of his recent work, in which he was fulfilling too well the accusation that Jack London began a story with three characters and ended by killing four of them. By poor navigating he had piled his craft on a tropical coral reef, where it was slowly breaking up under heavy seas.

9

JACK'S health had improved on the voyage from Sydney which he made in leisurely stages by way of South America and Panama; once home, the temperate California climate soon brought him back to normal. When he stumbled on a book called *Effects of Tropical Light upon White Men,* and learned that his baffling affliction had been nothing more sinister than the ultraviolet rays of the tropical sun tearing at his skin, his psychological recovery was completed. By August he was swimming in the creek he once again dammed, riding Washoe Ban across the Hill and Lamotte Ranches, inhaling the hot curative scents of sage and pine and baking native earth.

Construction never having been begun on the guest houses about which he had written Mrs. Eames from the Solomon Islands, he once again moved into Wake Robin, occupying the annex that had been built during his absence. Not a man to harbor past injuries, he gave Ninetta Eames an honorable discharge, bought the seventeen-acre Fish Ranch so that she would have a meadow to pasture her cow, and when she divorced Roscoe Eames and married Edward Payne, gave her a five-hundred-dollar gift in addition to her wedding outfit.

With the intelligent Nakata to cook and care for him, and Charmian guarding his privacy, he set to work in deadly earnest to straighten his affairs. His first move was to recall every manuscript from the market, and to inform the editors that he was home to stay, that he had magnificent new material, that there would be no more confusion in the marketing of his wares. For a period of three months not a line appeared in a magazine under the by-line of Jack London, the first time he had been missing from the reading world of America since the appearance of "An Odyssey of the North" at the opening of the century. These months he devoted to heroic labor, nineteen hours of concentrated work a day, seven days a week, the identical schedule he had imposed upon himself in his novitiate: for he knew it to be more difficult for a man to climb to favor a second time than a first. Editors and critics were saying that he had shot his bolt, that the public was tired of him; he knew that he had barely scratched the surface of the fine and moving stories he had to tell.

When *Martin Eden* was released, though it deserved the finest reception of all his books, the novel was so neglected or abused by the unfriendly press that Brett could find no laudatory lines from the reviews to quote in his advertisements. Jack complained that the critics had not understood him, that the reviewers were accusing him of abandoning his socialism and making individualism sound alluring, whereas he had written the book as an indictment of the Nietzschean superman philosophy. On the fly leaf of the copy he sent to Upton Sinclair, he wrote, "One of my motifs in *Martin Eden* was an attack on individualism. I must have bungled, for not a single reviewer has discovered it." He had not bungled; he had merely written such a gripping human life story that his conflicting philosophies had fallen by the wayside. If he could have known that *Martin Eden* was going to inspire an entire generation of American authors, if he could have known that thirty years later *Martin Eden* would be considered by thousands of fiction lovers as the greatest of American novels, he would not have been so heartbroken over the treatment afforded what he always called his best book.

The deeper he was in debt the better he worked; the greater the odds against him, the more passionately he attacked his adversaries. He began work on the boldly conceived *Burning Daylight,* a novel of the Klondike and San Francisco; he wrote four of his best South Sea tales; he wrote "Samuel" and "The Sea Farmer," two stirring dialect yarns laid on the coast of Ireland. Anger had always been one of his most potent motivations; he burned at white heat, for he was madder'n hell at having almost destroyed himself, at the critics for saying he was washed up. The sheer ecstasy of creative writing having palled after the publication of twenty volumes, pressure helped him to turn out his daily stint. For the following seven years that pressure remained so heavy and constant one comes to suspect he knew he had to keep himself in debt in order to get his work done. "I am swinging along a thousand words a day on a novel, and I wouldn't break it off for anything short of the trumpets of doom."

By November he had worked so faithfully and so well that he sold the best of his prize-fight stories, "A Piece of Steak," to the *Saturday Evening Post* for seven hundred and fifty dollars, and received a contract to supply them with twelve stories the following year. When *Burning Daylight* was completed he sold the serial rights to the New York *Herald* for eight thousand dollars. Having acquired the privilege of selling the reprint rights to as many newspapers as would purchase them, the *Herald* wrote glowing, promotional articles about Jack London and *Burning Daylight* which were reproduced in the hundreds of newspapers buying the serialization. This favorable publicity offset much of the abuse and ridicule he had been enduring.

Burning Daylight ranks with *Call of the Wild, Sea Wolf, Iron Heel, Martin Eden, John Barleycorn, Valley of the Moon,* and *Star Rover* as important American novels. The first third, in which Jack portrays the history of Alaska before the Klondike gold strike, and Burning Daylight's dash with the mail from Circle City to Dyea, is the most stirring writing to come out of the frozen North; in the last third the descriptions of the beauties of the countryside at Glen Ellen reveal him to be a lover of nature to whom nature in turn reveals her beauties and subtleties; but the real accomplishment of *Burning Daylight*, which purports to be an action and adventure story, is the manner in which he wove his socialism into the middle third, making it such an integral part of the action and suspense that the reader unsuspectingly drinks it in as a necessary development of the tale. Burning

Daylight, a Nietzschean blond-beast buccaneer, while raiding the business pirates of San Francisco, muses, "Work, legitimate work, was the source of all wealth. Whether it was a sack of potatoes, a grand piano or a seven passenger touring car, it came into being only by a performance of work. Where the bunco came in was in the distribution of these things after labor had created them. By hundreds of thousands men sat up and schemed how they could get between the workers and the things the workers produced. These schemers were business men. The size of the whack they took was determined by no rule of equity, but by their own strength and swinishness. It was always a case of 'all the traffic could bear.'"

Rank heresy to unawakened America of 1910, this was authentic proletarian writing; because the sentiments were not superimposed upon the story, because they appear to be a necessary part of Daylight's observations and conclusions about the local scene, they become at one and the same time proletarian writing and art. When *The Iron Heel* had been published Jack had been accused of destroying a good novelist to become a mediocre propagandist; he had replied that he could weld propaganda and art so that the reader could never see where they had been joined. In *Burning Daylight* he was successful at this most difficult of all writing tasks. With millions of people thrilling to the exploits of Burning Daylight, he was reinstated in favor with both the bourgeois and socialist publics.

Confirmed in his knowledge that he had lost none of his powers, and desirous of firing a twenty-one-gun salute in honor of Charmian's announced pregnancy, Jack began the fulfilment of another of his great life dreams. He started work on the house in which he planned to live for the rest of his life, choosing for its site a magnificent spot in a canyon of the Hill Ranch, surrounded by redwoods, vineyards, prune orchards, and forests of manzanita. Here he would have room for his library of four thousand volumes, for the stacks of broad white cardboard boxes in which he arranged his government reports, socialist pamphlets, newspaper clippings, national dialects, names and customs, the poems he still bound together between red covers. Here he would have room for his steel files, crammed with business and personal correspondence, for his thirty-high rows of narrow black boxes in which he treasured his souvenirs from The Road and Alaska, from his trips to Korea and the South Seas; in which he kept his hundreds of jokes, puzzles, games, pull-aparts, water pistols, coins with both sides the same, decks of strange cards. Here he would be able to make his guests comfortable, provide them with such modern conveniences as electricity and running water in their rooms; build a huge playroom in the cool basement for men only, in which they could hatch political schemes, tell stories, play billiards and poker, bowl, concoct any amount of noisy nonsense. Here he would have a beautiful music room in which Charmian and his many musician friends could play, a huge dining-room where he could seat fifty people for good food and good talk, a redwood-lined bedroom for himself in which there would be space for an ingeniously devised night table to hold the accouterments Nakata deposited for Master at bedtime, and on which he wouldn't be so crowded he would forever be spilling his iced drink on his books. Here he would at last have an adequate workroom with provision for a dictaphone and space set aside for a professional secretary.

He maintained that he was building his "historic home." The Indians of Alaska had called the conquering white man "Wolf"; that one word had come to dominate much of Jack's thinking, for he always thought of himself as the conquering Wolf. He used it in such titles as *Son of the Wolf* and *The Sea Wolf*, signed himself as Wolf in his letters to George Sterling, and now he was building the Wolf House of the great white chief. He hoped with all his considerable might that Charmian would give him a son so that he could start a London dynasty that would live forever in the Wolf House.

He determined that it must be the most beautiful and original home in America; to achieve that end he was willing to spend any amount of money. The house must be constructed of the huge red stones the Valley of the Moon grew more plentifully than any other crop; the two-to-three-thousand-year-old redwoods must be cut down for timber. He called in San Francisco architects and spent many happy hours mulling over blueprints, arranging the rooms, designing the exterior to fit indigenously into the hills. In Santa Rosa he found as Italian master stonemason by the name of Forni, whom he ordered to build a house that would stand through the centuries. Every inch of rock had to be washed with water and scrubbed with a steel-wire brush; more cement had to be used, and less lime, so that the walls would stand forever; one workman had to spend all his time keeping the walls wet so the cement wouldn't harden too fast and turn to powder; there had to be two floors between each stage, and sometimes three; the inside walls had to be of solid timber, the outside logs bolted into the inside studs for double security; copper had to be used for the roof gullies and copper for all lead-in pipes.

As a rampant individualist he was going to build himself a rustic redwood mansion. As a socialist he was going to give working-men good jobs, and devote more than half of the twenty-three rooms to guests. In order to expedite construction he had Forni put thirty men to work.

In the spring of 1910 he made one of his wisest moves: he invited Eliza London Shepard to live with him permanently and take care of his ranches. Mrs. Shepard was now forty-three years old, separated from her seventy-one-year-old husband; she had suffered hardship and spiritual adversity since leaving John London's ranch in Livermore, and had developed into a sympathetic woman. She was still plain of face and manner, honest, capable, hard-headed, having trained herself to become a lawyer so that she might help her husband in his legal work. Without froth, frill, or pretense, she was loved by everyone who came in contact with her. She had been faithful to Jack through the years, loving him as devotedly as she did her own son, Irving.

Jack's first move, now that he had Eliza to manage for him, was to complicate her task by buying the Kohler vineyards about which Ninetta Eames had so often written him when he was away on the *Snark*, eight hundred acres of land joining the Hill, Lamotte, and Fish Ranches. The Kohler vineyards cost him thirty thousand dollars, very little of which he had in his possession, for the Wolf House had already been started and was also scheduled to cost thirty thousand dollars. What prompted him to buy that additional eight hundred acres when he had no money with which to pay for them, when he already had so much beautiful land to live upon, cultivate, and enjoy? Thirty thousand seemed a cheap price for so much fine land, it would connect his other two ranches, make him monarch of all he surveyed. . . . But he always insisted that there was no explaining the why of "I Like."

"When philosophy has maundered ponderously for a month tell-ing the individual what he must do, the individual says in an in-stant, 'I like' and philosophy goes glimmering. It is 'I like' that makes the drunkard drink and the martyr wear a hair shirt; that makes one man pursue fame, another gold, another love, another God." He liked the Kohler vineyards, and so he bought them.

By June of 1910 he was once again sending frantic letters East for money. "I have a pressing need of money on account of a ten-thousand-dollar payment I have to make in buying some land. By throwing myself on others' mercy I had the time extended to June 26, but if I do not pay then I stand to lose not only the land but the advance payment."

Charmian left for Oakland to prepare for the coming of her baby. Jack set a corps of men to work clearing a new riding path which would join his ranches and circle the site of the Wolf House, a surprise for her against the day he would bring her back to the ranch with her son: for he was positive this time it would be a son. He dreamed away pleasant hours thinking of the great moment when he would be able to put his boy on a pony and have the lad ride by his side through the eleven hundred acres which would one day be his domain.

On June 19, Charmian gave birth to a daughter. The baby lived only thirty-eight hours. Eliza took care of the burial. Grieving, in-consolable, Jack wandered into a saloon near his old waterfront haunts at Seventh and Webster Streets, a bunch of newspapers under his arm. Muldowney, the proprietor, accusing him of want-ing to paste circulars on the walls, started a fight in which four of his hangers-on joined. Jack was severely beaten before he man-aged to escape. He had Muldowney arrested, but the judge dismissed the case, implying it had been a drunken brawl in which the court had no concern. Police court reporters sprayed the story of the "drunken brawl" over the nation's papers, heaping double invective upon him for getting drunk with his wife in the hospital, and his baby just dead. When well-wishers wrote him that the judge had not vindicated him because he owned the premises upon which the saloon was located, Jack sent a raging letter to the judge, copies of which he mailed to the press syndi-cates, in which he reviewed the case and ended with, "Someday, somewhere, somehow, I am going to get you, and I shall get you to the full hilt of the law." He then inserted an advertisement in those Bay papers that would carry it, asking for information concerning any political, judicial, or social corruptiveness of the judge who owned the land occupied by Muldowney's tenderloin resort. The false charges of drunken brawling had been wretched business, but when his letter to the judge was reproduced all over America, people shook their heads in amused despair. The only revenge he was to enjoy was in the form of the writer's perennial revenge: he wrote a story about the affair called "The Benefit of the Doubt," in which he thrashed the judge . . . and then sold it to the *Post* for seven hundred and fifty dollars.

Several days later, with a swollen and purple eye, he departed for Reno, where he spent ten days writing up the training camps and the Johnson-Jeffries fight for the New York *Herald*. He enjoyed prize fights; the ten days at the training camps with the other correspondents, most of whom were friends from other campaigns, provided him with an escape from the bitterness of having lost his child. He now had the prescience that he would die without ever having bred a son, a conviction that made him feel dry and barren despite the twenty-four books he had begot.

Back in Oakland he spent the money he had just earned to buy the *Roamer*, the fourth of his sailboats in which to cruise about the Bay. As soon as Charmian had recovered they went together for a vacation on the water, working, sailing, fishing for their supper. When he returned to Glen Ellen, his neighbors, thinking to hear romantic tales of the South Seas, invited him to lecture in the local Chauvet Hall. Since he declined to speak from the stage, the chairman went to the grocery next door and brought back a soap box for him to stand upon so that the audience might see him. The farmers of Glen Ellen heard not one word about his adventures in Tahiti, Fiji, or Samoa; instead he spent the hour trying to prove Eugene V. Debs's theory that "So far as the class struggle is concerned there is no good capitalist and no bad workingman. Every capitalist is your enemy and every workingman is your friend."

The passage of the summer months healed the wounds of the loss of the baby, and the Oakland trouble. His greatest pleasure was to call his favorite dog, Brown Wolf, and ride Washoe Ban across the fields to the Wolf House to note its daily progress and talk with Forni and the workmen; to observe with gratification that the workmen were coming to love the house as much as he loved it, to feel that it was a great work of art they were helping him create. The workmen lived in tents on the ranch, and after work they would climb to the highest knoll with a jug of wine and an accordion and sing sentimental Italian songs to the warm, close stars. Often of a clear evening Jack came to sing with them, to drink a glass of their sour red wine and discuss the building problems that had arisen during the day. Forni says, "Jack was the best human man I ever met. He was kind to everybody, never saw him come on job without smile. Was very good Democrat—very noble gentleman, a man for family love and for the workingman. Never heard a word from him in four years that we was working bad or too slow." When the workmen were ready for sleep he would shake hands with each of them, wish them a good night, and then walk with Brown Wolf through the prune orchard with the smell of the plums and the leaves and the rich, exuding earth in his nostrils.

He was completely devoted to Charmian. With Nakata they took a driving trip behind four spirited horses through the wilds of Northern California, Oregon, and Washington. She was still game for any adventure, rode and swam and sailed with him, played the piano and sang for him, typed his manuscripts and took dictation on his mail. He also maintained friendly relations with Bessie, going to the house in Piedmont several times a month to visit the children, play with them, take them to the theater or the circus. Bessie told newspaper reporters, "Mr. London is doing all he possibly can for his two daughters. He loves them devoutly. He comes here often to see them when he is in Oakland, and they consume hours playing and talking together. They love their father and there is no reason why they should not. There is no bitterness in my heart toward him. In doing for the children as he is, he is doing for me far more than he can realize." There was always a touch of the tragically noble in Bessie Maddern's character.

Flora, with the encroachment of old age, was growing more erratic than she ever had been in the early days with John London. Despite the fact that Jack had bought her the house in which she lived, that he had put Mammy Jenny into it to look after her, and sent her a fifty-five-dollar check every month of his life, she went about to her neighbors in Oakland telling them that Jack London wasn't supporting her, that she needed money to live on, and wouldn't they buy the home-made bread she was about to go into the business of baking? Profoundly distressed by such callous treatment of an aging mother by a wealthy and famous son, the neighbors signified their willingness to buy a loaf of home-made bread daily. Flora then bought a stove and began baking. The story was quickly spread by word of mouth, and Oakland was horrified. At his wit's end to know how to control his mother, Jack wrote her the most patiently tender but pathetic letter he ever penned. "Dear Mama: I just want to give you the figures and reasoning in your bread-making. In your most prosperous month you have cleared $7.50. You paid $26 for the stove. If, for three months, you devoted your total profits of $7.50 to paying for the stove, you will have worked those three months with no profit to yourself, and at the same time, since you say you are no longer able to do your share of the housework, you will have to hire somebody else to do your share of the work, and that will cost you at least the $7.50 profit you are making on the bread. . . ." He knew his mother too well to appeal to her on the grounds that she was hurting his name in Oakland; only by appealing to what she liked to think was her business sense could he dissuade her.

The letter worked; Flora gave up bread-making. Needing some business on which she could expend her manifold energies, she next started to open a newsstand on Broadway. He spiked that activity just in time. Soon collectors began arriving at the ranch with bills for articles Flora had bought, and for which she had no earthly use, chief among which was an item of six hundred dollars for diamonds. Jack was always gentle with her, as each new book appeared he sent it to her with a loving inscription, never did he let on that she was hurting him with her eccentricities, but he was forever afraid of the new scheme she would hatch behind those tight, peering eyes and narrow, steel-rimmed spectacles. In time he was to begin brooding over the horrible possibility that his mother had never been altogether sane. Yet so strange is the sum total of human attributes that Johnny Miller remembers Flora as the finest woman he ever knew, a gentle, loving, and altogether rational mother and friend to him; while people who took piano lessons from her at this time remember her as a sweet and kindly old lady.

The *Post* was now paying him seven hundred and fifty dollars for all the stories he could supply, *Collier's* offered one thousand dollars, the *Herald* offered seven hundred and fifty dollars for a short Christmas story, he signed a contract with *Cosmopolitan* to supply them with a series of stories at seven hundred and fifty dollars apiece about a character whom he called Smoke Bellew. Macmillan released *Lost Face*, a collection of short stories, *Revolution*, a collection of essays, and *Burning Daylight*. *Lost Face* earned him a deservedly warm press, for "Lost Face," "Trust," "That Spot," and "The Passing of Marcus O'Brien" are successful humorous Alaskan tales, while *Flush of Gold* and *To Build a Fire* are intensely wrought dramatic tales. Not since *Son of the Wolf* and *God of His Fathers*, his first two volumes of short stories, had he maintained such a high standard of excellence. *Revolution*, a heterogeneous and uneven collection of essays, was received apathetically, but *Burning Daylight* received the exciting reception everyone had anticipated.

By a combination of force, driving power, concentration, and sheer talent he had accomplished what only giants can accomplish: in less than a year he had catapulted himself from the frightening abyss of death and destruction to the greatest heights ever enjoyed by an American author.

In June of 1911, heartily sick of living in makeshift accommodations at Wake Robin, and seeing that the Wolf House would not be completed for at least another two years, he made a move that brought him the happiest and richest years of his life: he bought the ten acres in the middle of the Kohler vineyards upon which stood an abandoned winery, a broken-down ranch house, and some barns. He put stonemasons and carpenters to work adding a comfortable dining-room with a huge fireplace, and a broad lounging verandah, then enlarged the kitchen and renewed the bedrooms and sleeping porches. One of the bedrooms he converted into a workshop, lining the walls with shelves for his books and papers and cardboard reference boxes. His small, screened sleeping porch overlooked a secluded tropical garden in front of the house, the rear lounging verandah overlooked a spacious yard and huge barn, part of which he turned into nine comfortable guest rooms for his friends. Nakata became general manager, employing two more Japanese to cook and keep the house clean.

The ranch house was a success from the beginning; it was informal and people could have fun in it. When living at Wake Robin he had filled the cabins, tents, and every spare cot with his friends and intimates: George Sterling, Cloudesley Johns, James Hopper, his socialist and anarchist friends, newspapermen, sailors, tramps, and comrades that fitted into no apparent category. Now that he had adequate accommodations he began inviting the wide world; every day became Jack's Wednesday night open house. Nearly everyone in the artistic, professional, or thinking world that came West spent a few days at what he called his Beauty Ranch. In all the tens of thousands of letters he sent out from the ranch, and a goodly portion were to people who were quarreling with him, attacking, or abusing him, he never failed to put at the end, "The latchstring is always on the outside at the Beauty Ranch, and there are always blankets and grub for our friends. Come visit us, and stay as long as you like." So many accepted that he had to have circulars printed giving directions to Glen Ellen from San Francisco and Oakland. Rarely were there fewer than ten guests around the elastic dinner table; often there were twenty and more. One dinner party included Hyhar Dyall, founder of the Dyallist movement in India against the British, an American novelist, a Stanford University professor of mathematics, a neighboring farmer, an engineer, Luther Burbank, a sailor just back from Penang, Princess Ula Humphrey, an actress who had been in the Sultan's harem, three tramps, and a lunatic who was going to build a house from San Francisco to New York. No matter from what walk of life they came, visitors were stunned by their fellow guests. Some of his brilliant non-working friends who lived on the ranch for months at a time smelled so badly from hardly ever taking a bath that he built a special house for them in the woods; however, everyone ate at the same big table in the stone dining-room. Writers, artists, politicians, European statesmen and philosophers, churchmen, convicts, business magnates, engineers, housewives, thousands of people were to be his guests during the following five years. Tired of traveling, he now let the world come to him. Never a train pulled into Glen Ellen station but was met with a wagon from the Beauty Ranch to haul the visitors up the winding dirt road over which so many tons of grapes had been hauled before them.

He thrived and gloried in being the host, the benevolent patriarch, the squire, in seeing his friends and associates enjoy themselves as they ate at his table, rode his horses across his mountains, slept in his beds. But best of all he liked to probe the people who came to his ranch, to find out "what made them tick," to derive sustenance from the color of their character, the wisdom of their mind, the foibles of their weaknesses, the flavor of their dialogue and the yarns of their background. What astounded and delighted his visitors, as hundreds of them have testified, was the clarity of his mind, the speed and accuracy of his thinking, the depth and range of his knowledge, and above all, the celerity with which he extracted and then absorbed the knowledge the world-renowned specialists brought to his table. No matter how small a fund of information a guest brought with him, by the time he left the ranch Jack was in possession of that knowledge. Always he talked the other man's subject, asking adroit questions, discussing heatedly, challenging fundamental concepts, correcting his own impressions, information, concepts, thinking methods, sometimes besting his opponent in intellectual dispute even though he might be disputing the other man's specialty. He relished a battle of wits; one of his favorite exclamations was, "I'll take either side!"

He had the profound intellectual curiosity of the true scholar; he had amassed one of the finest collections of socialist books, pamphlets, reports, magazine and newspaper articles in America; the walls of his workroom were lined to the ceiling with the books he ordered constantly from New York and England. "I for one can never have too many books, nor can my books cover too many subjects. I may never read them all, but they are always there, and I never know what strange coast I am going to pick up in sailing the world of knowledge." The consistency with which topnotchers glowingly attested that Jack London had the richest brain they ever encountered is a tribute to the boy who had to go to work in a cannery at the age of thirteen because he could not afford to attend high school.

Alexander Irvine says that Jack talked softly, that he had the mellifluous, whispering voice of a gentle lady. He practised unfailing courtesy, even in the face of bigotry, ignorance, and fool-

ishness, and since he was inviting hordes of absolute strangers to
be his guests, he encountered these qualities, too. Men and
women whose philosophies he despised, whom he regarded as enemies of civilization, would come to his ranch, sleep in his beds,
ride his horses, eat at his table; no matter how long they stayed
they never suspected that he harbored such sentiments about
them. Human beings from every school, standard, income group,
and background passed through his house . . . and into the tex-
ture of his work he wove their variegated richness of character. He
took from his guests all they had to give, of wisdom and ignorance, of character and weakness, of viciousness and fun. Never
trying to shout down his opponent, to beat him by brute strength,
he was interested in the meat of the discussion, not the victory.

Everyone speaks of the force of his dynamic personality. Janet
Winship, daughter of his friends from Napa, says that when he
entered a room where a group of visitors would be sitting slumped
in their chairs, silent, dull, uninterested, an electric current would
shoot through them and they would come instantly to life, not
only their bodies, but their minds and spirits. His tremendous vitality was only part of the cause; he had such a warm, vibrant,
glowing quality of being alive that he invested everyone he met
with a radiance, a spirit of well-being. Irvine summed it up for
many of Jack's friends when he said, "Jack London was a mountain in life."

Before Jack retired at night, usually at eleven o'clock, Nakata
fixed his night table with notepaper, pencils, galley proof, the
books and pamphlets he was reading, manuscripts from aspiring
authors sent to him for correction and criticism, some light food
to nibble on to fight off sleep, a box of cigarettes and pitchers of
an iced drink which he kept sipping to hydrize his mouth,
parched from incessant smoking. The lamp burned deep into the
humming silence while the man alone on the sleeping porch studied, made notes, smoked, sipped his iced drink, pored over printed
words, words of wisdom and falsity, words of justice and man's
inhumanity to man . . . until fatigue gathered like specks of dust
under his burning eyelids. He drove himself continuously to acquire knowledge, not only because he loved knowledge, but for
fear he might be missing something new or important in the
world. And always on that night table, never to be moved until

after his death, was a two-volume work by Paul du Chaillu, whose *African Travels* had been the first adventure book to fall into his hands when he had been eight years old, living on the ranch in Livermore. The two-volume work was called *The Viking Age*.

About one o'clock in the morning he would place a match in his book to mark his place, then set the hand on the cardboard time-dial hanging outside his door to show Nakata at what hour he wished to be awakened. He rarely allowed himself more than five hours of sleep; the latest time indicated on the dial is six o'clock. Generally at five Nakata would awaken him with his coffee, after which he would lie abed revising the previous day's manuscript, which Charmian had typed, reading the various government reports and technical studies for which he had sent, correcting the latest batch of galley proofs from his publishers, making notes for the day's work or future stories. By eight he was at his desk composing his original thousand words, glancing occasionally at the poem tacked on the wall:

> Now I get me up to work,
>   I pray the Lord I may not shirk;
> If I should die before the night,
>   I pray the Lord my work's all right.

His stint of the thousand words completed by eleven o'clock, he dug into his staggering piles of business and personal mail. He was now averaging ten thousand letters a year, the very least of which he answered fully and courteously. Many days he read and dictated replies to a round hundred letters.

All guests were notified that the mornings were reserved for quiet and work. At one o'clock, having already turned in an eight-hour day, he would wander onto the back porch, his hair mussed, his white shirt open at the throat, a green eyeshade slanted across his forehead, a cigarette between his lips, and a sheaf of papers in his hand. With a broad smile he would exclaim, "Hello, folks!" and the room was full of him, full of his magnetic warmth, his clean-cut, boyish lovability, his richly alive and contagious humanness. His entrance marked the beginning of the day's fun.

After lunch, which lasted a couple of hours if the conversation was good and the banter amusing, saddle-horses were brought to the yard between the ranch house and the barn. When the party was mounted he led the way to the top of Sonoma Mountain and across the crest of the range overlooking San Francisco Bay; if the sun was out he galloped them up the lake, which he had formed for irrigation purposes by building a stone dam across a pond fed by running springs. Here in a bathhouse made of fresh-cut logs they changed into their bathing suits, swam, went boating in the warrior canoes he had brought back from the South Seas, sunned themselves on the dock, played leap frog and jousted, Indian-wrestled and boxed, dumped into the lake men who went boating in their street clothes. At dusk he led his party through the forest of redwood, spruce, and manzanita on the trail that ran past the Wolf House, dismounted, and guided it among the scaffoldings, telling how beautiful the Wolf House would be, pointing with pride to the flawless stone masonry, explaining that he did not need fire insurance because he was fireproofing his house with asbestos-covered pipes, fireproof paint over the woodwork, stone walls, and tile roofing.

Back at the ranch house they dressed, became acquainted with the new arrivals, had a good dinner, discussed world politics and philosophy. Cards were his favorite form of relaxation, and soon they were playing red dog or pedro for twenty-five cents a hand. He was still inventing all sorts of ridiculous practical jokes. Whenever anarchists such as Emma Goldman visited the ranch, Jack set on their dinner plate a book with the title *A Loud Noise* printed in bold letters across its cover. When the unsuspecting anarchist opened the book it would explode in his hands from the firecracker concealed in it. He always used their fright and consternation to show them that they really wouldn't overthrow the world by force even if they had the chance. The water glass with the hole in the side was reserved for lay visitors who were so stunned by the fact that they were actually sitting at the dinner table of the great Jack London that they could hardly breathe, let alone eat.

Finn Frolich, a Norwegian sculptor and sailor with the most tremendous, booming laugh ever vouchsafed to mortal, whom Jack had made his court sculptor and jester, says: "When I came up there I found they were playing like children, playing tricks and all kinds of funny games. When the joke was on Jack he would laugh more than any of us." A favorite trick was to place a man against the dining-room door to measure his height, and then hit the back of the door at the head height with a mallet. The joke that got the best laugh was practised on prissy people: holes were bored through the floor of the guest's room, and rope interlaced between the holes and the bedposts. After the guest was asleep the jokesters would begin heaving on the ropes, which would rock the bed violently. The guest would tear out into the yard in his nightclothes crying, "Earthquake! Earthquake!" In Chop and Stop the newcomer would be seated on the ground; as water was poured between his spread legs it was his task to keep chopping up mud to make embankments. When the victim had enough water collected, and was working frantically to keep it from running over, his feet would be seized and he would be pulled forward into the puddle of his own making. "Jack was just an overgrown kid," says Carrie Burlingame, a neighbor from Sonoma. "He did everything with full force; even when he relaxed and had fun he did it with all his might." He would go so far for fun and laughter that one night when his guests had scouted his story of eating raw fish in the Solomons, he offered to eat a live goldfish from the bowl in the center of the table if he chanced to pull the lowest card of the draw. The other men agreeing, the cards were cut; the lowest fell to a visiting bridegroom. He thrust his hand into the bowl, extracted a goldfish by the tail, and swallowed it . . . eliciting laughter and applause, and the cry from his bride that she would never kiss him again.

Jack enjoyed his ranch doubly because of the fun he could have on it with his guests. His most constant companion was George Sterling with his sharp Indian features and receding forehead slanting back at an angle from his eyebrows, that he carefully kept hidden by combing his hair down in bangs; a magnificently ugly man with beauty in his sensitive, transparent face, and an intense feeling for the pain of life. Much of his poetry was brilliantly written, much of it was bombastic, loaded with biblical references and meaningless pageantry. Though his wife, Carrie, was a beautiful Junoesque woman in the Bessie Maddern tradition, though he was so gentle of nature he would not allow a spider caught in his house to be killed, he had no compunction over wounding his wife when his fancy was caught by another woman. Unlike Jack, he was protected by a wealthy uncle, knowing little of the proletarian base of life; a successful Don Juan and hard drinker, he was an almost perfect example of the vanishing Bohemian poet.

The story ran that every time George Sterling lost a hand at red dog or pedro he took a drink of Jack's liquor to make up the loss, and every time Jack lost he wrote a word to earn back the twenty-five cents. There was a sideboard in the dining-room with an array of bottles, the guests were invited to help themselves to as many drinks as they wanted, but for weeks at a time Jack did not join them even in a before-dinner cocktail. Aside from an occasional drink for sociability in his hours of relaxation, he did no drinking on the ranch.

Glen Ellen was at that time a sporting village, its main street lined with saloons. Whenever he wanted to get away from his family, his heavy load of obligations and work, his ever-present friends, he harnessed four horses to his buggy, put his special bells on the horses' collars, and drove like mad down the winding dirt road to town. When Glen Ellen heard those bells, the village awakened from its hot torpor. "Jack London's coming down the hill!" a native cried, and within an instant word had spread through the town, people thronged the streets wearing broad grins, bartenders got out bottles and polished glasses with new animation. As Jack drove down the main street everyone cried, "Hi, Jack!" and when he saw someone he knew he would shout, "Hello, Bill!" and wave his sombrero in the air. He tied his horses to the first hitching post and went into the nearest saloon, where, as in his sailor days, "he called all hands to the bar." No one else was allowed to show the color of his money. The crowd would kid him, laugh at his yarns, let him know what they thought of his latest publications, and tell him their new jokes, particularly the Jewish stories which he loved above all others. After a few minutes and a few drinks he would move on to the next saloon, where its particular clientèle was waiting to slap him on the back, wring his hand. Once again the drinks were on him, and there would be much loud masculine laughter and good fellowship. There were perhaps a dozen saloons in town; by nightfall he had visited them all, consumed a quart of whiskey, rubbed elbows, talked and bantered with a hundred men. Then he would walk back to his rig, untie the horses, and while Glen Ellen gathered to cry, "So long, Jack! Come see us again soon!" he would drive his horses up the long dirt road through his orchards, vineyards, and rolling hills. Glen Ellen people tell that the brightest days in the year were the days when they heard those bells high up on the hillside, and Jack London, in a ranger's hat, bow tie, and white shirt, came dashing down the road behind his four spirited horses, a happy smile on his lips, a friendly salute for everybody.

One afternoon a week he would harness two of his fastest horses and drive at top speed the sixteen miles to Santa Rosa, the county seat and center for the hops, grapes, and wine industry; a hard-drinking town, but so reactionary in its politics that the residents did not think Jack merely mistaken to believe in socialism, they thought him insane. He would dash down the main street, his harness bells jingling, draw up in front of Ira Pyle's real estate office, shout, "Hey, Puh-hyle! Let's go!" and the two men would ride over to the Hotel Overton bar, where Jack took up his leaning station in the last niche of the bar with his back to the rest of the room, and ordered a quart of Scotch. He drank his whiskey out of a twelve-ounce water tumbler; he always poured Pyle's first two drinks, after that Pyle could drink as much or as little as he wished.

Introduced as Jack's drinking partner, Pyle exclaimed, "I could never claim that title! No one could. Jack stood in a class by himself. He was really two-fisted; he took four or five drinks to my one. Funny thing, though: eighty-five per cent of his conversation at the bar was about socialism. He came into Santa Rosa because he could get the best arguments there. People didn't like him because he would say things in the presence of judges, chamber of commerce executives and business men about how corrupt the capitalist system was. In all the years he came into Santa Rosa, I never heard anyone agree with him. When I asked him a stickler about the new socialist state, he would think for a moment, shake his head, say, 'Wait until I get another drink under my belt, and then my mind will flow more freely.' The next drink always did it, and he would be off on a discourse about how little commodities would cost the consumer when they were produced for use and not for profit."

When he wasn't with Pyle he would walk into the Overton bar, take a quick look around, go to his nook, have a drink or two, then motion for somebody to come over and talk. He would start off with, "Now, that point you made the other day about socialism destroying personal incentive, I've been thinking it over and I've got some new ideas. . . ." Friends who drank with him remember his discussing war, poverty as the cause of crime, biology, labor organization, Freud's psychoanalysis, judicial corruption, literature, travel, and the coming utopia. At six o'clock, having polished off a bottle of Scotch with whoever had joined him, he got into the buggy and drove home. He never had trouble with his horses, but when he had been drinking he liked to drive fast. Billy Hill, who was his bartender at the Overton bar, and later at Fetters and Boyes Springs, says, "Jack could handle more liquor than any other man, but it never fazed him. He always stood up straight, always had his dignity on. When he pulled out of a place he pulled out like a gentleman. When he'd had enough, he'd had enough. I never saw him ugly or quarrelsome; he always remained jovial and pleasant, stayed out of arguments unless it was somebody who could really argue, but he was so much smarter than anybody he'd meet that he always won the argument." Pyle says he never saw Jack drunk. He had the Irishman's capacity for absorbing whiskey. Drinking removed his fatigue and nerve strain, loosened his tongue, lubricated his brain, gave him a vacation, a change, and a rest.

Out of his drinking arose the idea for a book that was to win him more fame and infamy than any he published. *John Barleycorn* is an autobiographical novel; as far as it goes it tells the truth about his drinking, but like most autobiographical books, "The only trouble about *John Barleycorn* is that I did not put in the whole truth. I did not dare put in the whole truth." He omitted the fact that in certain periods of his life he suffered from despondency, that when he was low in spirits the knowledge of his illegitimacy, which he could forget or shrug off as unimportant when he was in good form, poisoned his mind and his thoughts, made him melancholy; that he often drank to drown that most indestructible of all bitter herbs. He exercised the utmost care to keep concealed from everyone these recurrent depressions. The attacks came too rarely, not more than five or six a year, to make him the manic depressive that is most every creative artist, yet when they gripped him he loathed his writing, his socialism, his ranch, his friends, his mechanistic philosophy, brilliantly defended man's right to suicide. At such times the load he was carrying seemed too heavy for his shoulders, he vowed he could carry it no further; at such times when drinking heavily, he became thickjawed, insensitive, unsympathetic, quarrelsome. But the attacks passed, often in a single day.

The value of *John Barleycorn* as literature does not depend upon its conformity to the pattern of his life. *John Barleycorn* reads like a novel, is fresh, beautifully honest, simple and moving, contains magnificent writing about the White Logic, and remains as a classic on drinking. Were it wholly fiction it would still be convincing, first-rate fiction. Published in the *Saturday Evening Post*, and later in book form, it was read by millions of people. Ministers seized upon it as a moral lesson against drinking; temperance unions, prohibition organizations, anti-saloon leagues claimed the book as their own, reprinted material from it in pamphlets which they scattered by the hundreds of thousands. Educators, politicians, newspaper and magazine men, lecturers, organizations that would not be linked together for any other cause on earth, joined hands over *John Barleycorn* to fight the liquor interests. A motion picture was made of the book, which the distilleries offered huge sums to have suppressed. So tremendous was the tumult and shouting that hundreds of thousands who had not opened a book since they left grammer school avidly consumed *John Barleycorn.* Though he had portrayed his victory over alcohol, the public which garbles so much of what it reads set him down for a habitual drunkard.

John Barleycorn, because of the new and focused energy it released, was one of the leading factors in bringing Prohibition to the United States in 1919. The picture of a man who often drank to numb the cyclical pain of his illegitimacy, of a man who had had a great deal of fun, excitement, and comradeship from drinking, who had not the slightest intention of giving up liquor providing the ammunition with which the reformers brought upon the United States the horrors of the Prohibition Era, is one of the major ironies in a life crowded with mordant ironies.

The seasons passed, he watched his fields plowed and sowed with seed in the spring, grow green and then yellow in the late summer, a deep russet brown from the burning sun of the long dry autumn, then deluged with the winter rains. He took pride in his writings, in his newly cleared, revitalized land, in his countless friends. With everything in his life going well, "the smile that won't come off" was never missing from his handsome Irish face. Finn Frolich says, "I never saw a man with so much beautiful magnetism. If a preacher could have that much love in his make-up the whole world would go religious. When Jack talked he was marvelous; his eyes were big, and his mouth was just as sensitive and full of expression, and the words came out of him just rippling. It was something inside him, his brain ran sixty miles a minute, you couldn't keep up with him. No matter what he talked about his lips would go up, the humor would come out, you would have to laugh your head off."

He was happy, everyone loved him, his work went forward with magnificent strides.

When he had first bought the Hill Ranch he had written to Cloudesley Johns, "I am not going ranching; the only cleared ground on the place will be used for growing hay." But he found that his interest in farming and ranching was growing apace, that every development led him into new operations. He subscribed to agricultural newspapers and magazines, wrote to the agricultural departments of the University of California and the state government for information and advice. With the passage of the months he realized that agriculture and ranching were exciting subjects, and that he was becoming fascinated. Tired of adventuring abroad, he now began to adventure at home; farming became his hobby. Giving himself to the new activity with his accustomed zeal, before long he found he had acquired sufficient knowledge to constitute himself something of an authority.

The more he studied agriculture in the State of California the more he found wrong with it, the more he decided that the entire agricultural system was a counterpart of the economic system, haphazard, wasteful, needing a sharp reconstruction with scientific methods. He had the land, he had the money, he had the knowledge and determination; he decided to put them together to rescue California farming. Slowly, as he continued with his studies and delved more deeply into his subject, there formed in his mind a vision of the type of model farm his foster father, John London, had wanted to build in Alameda and then Livermore. This

model farm he would build through the years would point the
way to a higher type of agriculture throughout the country, would
enable the farmers to get a higher quality produce out of their
land and stock.

He learned that the Kohler and Lamotte Ranches were worn
out, useless because the former owners had tilled the land for
forty years without feeding it fertilizer, without allowing it to lie
fallow. He found the stock of the countryside had degenerated;
scrub bulls without pedigree were being used for the mount; the
horses, pigs, and goats were all of inferior breed. The fertile hills
of California were being wasted; "we must develop scientific
methods to turn the slopes into productive areas." He reasoned
that if he rehabilitated the land and reinvigorated the stock, if he
threw overboard the wasteful, destructive methods of the farmers
who were failing all about him, if he farmed for only the highest-
grade produce he could save that section of the state for agriculture. To achieve this end he and Eliza threw all their resources,
energy, and capability into the task. Jack planned everything with
Eliza, who then gave the orders and supervised the work.

"At the present moment I am the owner of six bankrupt
ranches, united in my possession. The six bankrupt ranches represent at least eighteen bankruptcies; that is to say, at least eighteen
farmers of the old school have lost their money, broken their
hearts, lost their land. The challenge to me is this: by using my
head, my judgment, and all the latest knowledge in the matter of
farming, can I make a success where these eighteen men failed? I
have pledged myself, my manhood, my fortune, my books, and all
I possess to this undertaking."

On his cleared fields he planted vetch and Canadian peas, for
three years plowing under his crop to enrich the soil. Across from
his ranch house were uncultivated hill slopes; he set men to work
to clear and terrace them as he had seen hills terraced in Korea.
He set twenty-two men to work in the vineyards to prune and
sucker the vines. He told Eliza the grapes would have to begin to
pay their own expenses, then rode Washoe Ban into Glen Ellen
to vote for local prohibition because he believed the saloons were
a menace to the families of workingmen. Convinced that national
prohibition would come within a few years, and in addition learning that the soil in the vineyards was too exhausted to give him a

good crop, he had his men tear out seven hundred acres of the vines, fertilize the fields, and replant them with eucalyptus trees because his studies had led him to the conviction that the eucalyptus tree, which produced what was called Circassian walnut, would be greatly in demand as hardwood for decoration and building. The first year he put in ten thousand trees, the second year twenty thousand more, until he had a hundred and forty thousand eucalyptus trees, at a planting cost of $46,862, growing on his land. "I'll just plant them now, and twenty years from now they'll be worth a fortune, without my being forced to do anything with them." He figured his investment was as safe as money in the bank, and in addition would be earning him thirty per cent interest.

In other fields he planted beets, carrots, red oats, grain, barley, hay, and alfalfa, on the raising of which Eliza had taken correspondence courses from the University of California; everything he felt he would need for the first-rate stock ranch he was in the process of creating. When Luther Burbank brought some of his new spineless cactus from his experimental gardens in Santa Rosa, Jack, game to try anything once, planted a field of it for feed.

As the foundation of his horse stock he bought a prize Shire stallion for twenty-five hundred dollars, then bought four pedigreed Shire mares for seven hundred dollars apiece. Because he believed that big workhorses were coming back he bought up all the mares used by the drayers in San Francisco that had developed sore feet on the cobblestones. When he needed more draft horses to clear and plow his fields, and couldn't find the kind of animal he wanted, he took a buying trip to Southern California. When he couldn't find the kinds of cows and heifers he wanted, he advertised in the agricultural journals, went to the stock show at Sacramento and purchased the blue-ribbon animals: a prize shorthorn bull for eight hundred dollars to sire his herd, and eight good heifers for three hundred and fifty dollars apiece. He went into the market and bought the finest pedigreed pigs and a herd of eighty-five angora goats. After a few seasons of scientific breeding he planned to sell some of his stock to the neighboring ranchers at low prices so the quality of their herds would be improved. He also planned to cull his beef and swine, just as John London had taught him to cull vegetables, selling only the very best meat to the San Francisco hotels. To house his rapidly growing stock he built new barns, new pens, bought a complete blacksmith's shop in Glen Ellen and moved it up to the ranch. To house his ever-growing list of laborers he built accommodations for the men and their families.

He wrote articles on the new agriculture, made notes for a "back to the soil novel," exchanged countless letters with agricultural societies and experimental farms, gave interviews to the curious newspaper reporters on his new activity. While on a stock-buying expedition to Los Angeles, where he stayed in the home of his old sculptor friend, Felix Peano, he told interviewers: "I began studying the problem of why the fertility of this California land had been destroyed in forty or fifty years while land in China had been tilled for thousands of years, and is still fertile. I adopted the policy of taking nothing off the ranch. I raised stuff and fed it to the stock. I got the first manure-spreader ever seen up there. I set men to work clearing the brush and turning the brush land into tillable fields. Here is the desperate situation in this country which makes correct farming certain of good returns: in ten years the mouths to feed in the United States have increased by sixteen millions. In that ten years the number of hogs, sheep, dairy cows, and beef cattle have actually decreased on account of the breaking up of large ranches into small farms. The rancher who gets good stock and who conserves and builds up his soil is assured of success."

By working his eleven hundred acres he was able to give men jobs, to enable them to earn a living. He instructed Eliza that on no condition was she to turn away any man looking for work until he had earned three or four days' wages, and eaten three or four days' square meals. If there was no work for the man, she was to make work, to set him clearing stones off the hillsides, or building fences between fields. To Forni, supervising the building of the Wolf House, he said, "Forni, never let any man go away without three or four days' work, and if he's a good man, keep him." Convicts in Folsom and San Quentin prisons who could be paroled if they had a job to go to wrote him asking to be hired. He nearly always advised the prison authorities that he would give the paroled man a job, refusing only when he had no bed or corner of a cottage to provide. One applying convict who was refused wrote back saying, "You don't have to be afraid to let me work around the house. I wouldn't steal anything, I'm only a murderer." Most of the time there were ten paroled convicts working and living on the ranch.

By the time his ranching activities reached their height in 1913, his payroll had reached the staggering figure of three thousand dollars a month. He was employing fifty-three men for farm work and thirty-five on the Wolf House, providing a living for nearly a hundred men and their families, or a round five hundred human souls. On payday he rode Washoe Ban across the fields and hills, paying the men in gold from money bags strapped around his waist, the same gold pouches he had carried in the Klondike. The knowledge that he was making work for men brought him profound and unending pleasure, as great as the pleasure he was deriving from his farming experiments and the thought that he was the savior of California agriculture. He farmed more than he wrote.

The farmers of the neighborhood jeered at him for plowing three crops under, laughed at what they called the "eight-hour socialists" working on the ranch. When he had been laughed at for building the *Snark*, just as he was being laughed at now for building a model ranch, he had complained, "A man picks out a clean, wholesome way to make and spend money, and everybody jumps on him. If I went in for horse races or chorus girls, there'd be no end of indulgent comment." To people who cautioned him against sinking such huge sums of money in experiments he answered, "I earn my money honestly, and not off the backs of labor. If I want to spend it to give employment, to rehabilitate California ranching, why have I not the right to spend my money for my own peculiar kind of enjoyment?"

And enjoy himself he did. Each new guest was proudly escorted to the dairy barn to be shown the milking records being kept on each cow, the rich alfalfa and corn his fields were growing, the improved breeds of beef cattle, hogs, and goats he had started. When one of the animals won a blue ribbon at a stock show he was enormously set up. When away for a sailing trip on the *Roamer*, or on a four-horse driving trip with Charmian and Nakata, he wrote constant letters of advice and instruction to Eliza, who in turn wrote telling him every detail of what was happening on the ranch. He writes to her, "See that the pigs in the pasture are fed. How did the barley fields get flooded? Don't forget to work the stallion. Are the engine and water hose shaded from the heat of the sun? I'm heartbroken that the pigs have cholera. Have the foundations of the twenty-stall barn repaired. Now is the time to see that every horse working, and every colt, is fed in addition to pasturage. In making the stone wall alongside the orchard, be sure the men haul only the large stones so they will make a beautiful stone wall." Everything had to be the biggest and best: the Wolf House, the stone wall, the alfalfa and corn, the Shire horses, the cows, the hogs, the goats . . . always his vigorous and full-blooded Rex complex made him feel he must be a king among men (the last shall be first, the bastard shall be king); and his equally vigorous Messianic complex made it necessary for him to free American literature, American economics, and now American agriculture from destruction and decay.

He was earning seventy-five thousand dollars a year from his writing and spending a hundred thousand. Everything he owned was heavily mortgaged, including his future. On the first of each month he and Eliza sat at the desk in the corner of the dining-room, their heads glued together over the account book, sore beset to know how they were going to juggle their money to meet their obligations. At one time he was so broke Eliza had to put a five-hundred-dollar mortgage against her house in Oakland to buy feed for the stock. His letters East form a continuous wail for money. "Please send the $2000 you owe for stories, as I am building the first stone silo in California. . . ." "You must let me have another $5000 against book publication, as I have to build a new dairy barn." . . . "I need $1200 right away to buy a rock crusher." . . . "You must send me $1500 immediately as I have to put in a tile drainage system to keep my rich top soil from being washed away by floods." . . . "If you will contract in advance for this series of stories you will enable me to buy the adjoining Freund Ranch of four hundred acres for the reasonable price of $4500." He gave his Eastern editors a liberal education in scientific ranching, but sometimes they would cry out in exasperation, "Mr. London, we simply can't help it if you have to buy a new litter of pigs," or "We don't feel that the clearing of your new fields should be our responsibility!" One of them even had the temerity to tell him that "it's all right for a writer to own a farm, providing he doesn't try to farm it." There were delays, vexations, disputes, anxious and sometimes angry flurries of telegrams, but always he earned the money, always the thousands poured in with which to build not one stone silo to store his corn, but two; to build his dairy barn; to buy the rock crusher; to put in miles of irrigation pipes; to buy the Freund Ranch, which now brought his holdings to fifteen hundred acres; to put a twenty-five-hundred-dollar tile roof on the Wolf House, the cost of which, after three years of labor, had risen to seventy thousand dollars and much work remaining to be done. The faster the money came in, the faster it slipped through Eliza's often unwilling fingers, for more money meant to Jack that he could hire more men, clear more fields, add new stock, new irrigation and drainage systems. At no time was he less than twenty-five thousand dollars in debt; more often it was fifty thousand.

In addition to the workingmen for whose support he now was responsible, there was the ever-increasing coterie of relatives, relatives of his relatives, friends, friends of his friends, guests, charity cases, hangers-on, parasites of all descriptions. Generosity was as natural to him as breathing. Every tramp in America knew that the most illustrious of their former comrades was good for a meal, a drink, and a bed, and most of them included the Beauty Ranch in their itinerary. Jim Tully, who like Jack had risen to fame as a novelist after being a tramp on The Road, reports that one night in Los Angeles when a bum panhandled Jack for the price of a bed, Jack thrust a five-dollar gold piece into the man's hand. Johnny Heinold reports him walking into the Last Chance saloon, taking one drink from a full bottle of whiskey, then leaving a five-dollar gold piece on the bar, saying, "Johnny, tell the boys Jack London was in, and to have a drink on him."

Convicts sent him handwoven bridles for which he had no use. He sent them twenty dollars apiece, unable to turn down an imprisoned man who was trying to earn a few dollars.

Nearly all his friends borrowed money, not once but continuously. Never was one dollar returned. He received thousands of requests for money through the mail, most of which he complied with. Writers, complete strangers, wrote asking to be subsidized while they completed a novel; he mailed them monthly checks. When socialist and labor newspapers were in financial trouble, which was almost always, he sent them subscriptions for all his friends, free articles and stories; when socialists or labor organizers were arrested, he sent money for their defense. When strikes were failing for lack of funds, he sent money for soup kitchens. When he heard of an Australian woman who had lost both sons in the World War, he sent her fifty dollars a month, unasked, for a long period of time. When an old woman from the mountains of New York wrote him tortured letters of poverty, and he had not one dollar in the bank, he sent Brett stricken letters imploring him to send the woman money and take it out of his future earnings. When San Francisco wanted to start a school of the opera, he pledged himself to pay so much a month. When a socialist comrade from Oregon, whom he did not know, wrote that he was bringing his pregnant wife and four children to stay on the ranch while he went to Arizona to cure his tuberculosis, Jack wired back that he had no cottage or beds in which to put them up. The family had already left Oregon; when they arrived on the ranch Jack said nothing about his wire, found them a cottage, fed and cared for the family, had the wife delivered of her fifth child, and gave the family back to the father when he returned from Arizona, six months later.

Socialist comrades wrote by the thousands for the chance to come and live on the ranch. "Just give me one acre and some chickens and I'll make a go of it."—"Couldn't you spare me a couple of acres, and a cow? That's all my family needs." He would order Eliza not to employ any more people, then a workingman with his wife and children would wander onto the ranch, having heard that a man could always find work there, and he would hire him himself. Eliza, who kept the books, says that half of all the money Jack earned was given to other people. If one adds the money he paid for labor for which he had no legitimate use, the figure would rise to nearly two thirds of his income. Anybody could touch him who told a good story, but half the time he sent money without being asked. Rarely did he refuse to give help; the wife of Bob Fitzsimmons, the prize fighter, wired him that she needed a hundred dollars immediately but gave no explanation of what she needed the money for. Racking his brain to find three thousand dollars with which to pay his insurance and interest on mortgages, he wired back that he was broke. Two days later he read in the newspaper that Mrs. Fitzsimmons had been operated on in the charity clinic of a county hospital. He never forgave himself; after that when people asked him for money he didn't have, he went out and borrowed it.

He spent little on his personal needs, eating and dressing simply. On his friends and hospitality he spent a fortune, rarely accepting hospitality in return. When he did go out for dinner he would eat half a pound of raw hamburger before leaving home because he did not care for other people's cooking. So fastidious was he about money matters that no guest was allowed to give another guest an I.O.U. over his card table. He took the I.O.U., paid out the money to the winner, then put the note of indebtedness into a cigar box. One day when Frolich was passing Jack's study a shower of white papers flew out the window. Picking up a few scraps, he saw that Jack had just torn up another box of the I.O.U.'s.

With his life he was painting a portrait of a native Californian, that unusual specimen of humanity indigenous to the soil of the state, to be found nowhere else in the same form. A modest megalomaniac, like most native Californians, he was simple, genuinely unpretentious with his friends and associates about his success and accomplishments, but to himself fiercely sure, positive. On the notes for the hundreds of short stories, articles, and novels he planned to write in the future one invariably finds scrawled: "Great Short Story," "Tremendous Novel," "Terrific Idea," "Magnificent Labor Material," "Colossal Yarn." Like most native Californians he was robust, hearty in manner, with strong physical appetites, worshipping the beauty, strength, skill and pleasures of the body, which in turn led him to admire the arts and the fruits of culture. He was childlike in his desire to play, to have fun. Above all he wanted to laugh, not gently or delicately, but uproariously. Like most native Californians he was informal, hated starchy people and starchy ideas and preconceived prejudices, was intolerant of the bonds of tradition, enjoyed being a vigorous iconoclast. Like California's Spanish predecessors' his home was a sanctuary, open to all wayfarers, high or humble; no man was turned away without a meal, a drink, a night's lodging. Like these

Spanish predecessors he wanted space about him, could not stand to be cramped, had to be lord of a domain.

Like the gold miners who opened up California he despised money because it could be made so easily and in such large quantities, and squandered it to show the world how little he was its slave. He was prodigal with the riches of his land, his brain, his purse, his friendship. Like most Californians he wanted to do everything at the top of his might: work, play, laugh, love, relax, conquer, create. He was independent, self-willed, difficult to lead around by the nose; moody, volatile, often ornery, pig-headed, tempestuous, sadistic. Like most native Californians he despised mental and physical cowardice, had great personal courage. "He had the guts of a bear," said Ira Pyle; "he would plow into anybody or anything." Like most native Californians he thought himself a pioneer, a trail-blazer, a creator of a new and better civilization. Since everything around him was so strong and so vast and so rich, he had boundless confidence in himself, positive that everything that sprang from the California soil was the greatest on earth.

Living in so fertile and spontaneous a countryside he too was spontaneous, flaring quickly to new ideas, new enthusiasms, to love or anger. He worshipped beauty and nature because he was surrounded by magnificent natural beauty. Impatient, reckless, charged with impetuosity, swagger, and exaggeration, he had in him a love for primitive crudity and emotion; but living in the midst of romantic scenery and opulence his red-blooded violence was crossed with an almost feminine sensitivity to beauty and to pain. He was bluff, honest, often noisy and crude; he harbored no suspicion of his fellow man, believed every man honest until he proved himself otherwise. As a result he was often credulous, gullible, easily hoaxed. In his fearlessness, his toughness, his hardness to kill he resembled the grizzly bear which stood on the state flag as its emblem. Constant in his faiths and friendships, openhandedly generous, bitter only against human poverty and injustice, he was a true pagan, pantheistic in his worship of God in the natural beauty and forces that surrounded him. An unquenchable optimist, believing in human progress, he was willing to devote his life to bringing to mankind an intelligent civilization.

By the spring of 1913 he was the highest-paid, best-known, and most popular writer in the world, filling the position Kipling had occupied at the opening of the century. His stories and novels were translated into Russian, French, German, Swedish, Norwegian, Danish, Dutch, Polish, Spanish, Italian, Hebrew. His photographs were reproduced so constantly that his youngish, handsome, clean-cut face was known and loved by millions.

Rumors and anecdotes about him spread as far as the wilds of Tartary. Every word he uttered, every move he made was rehearsed in the newspapers; when he did nothing that produced copy, the reporters made up news. "I remember that on a single day three news dispatches went out concerning me: The first dispatch stated that my wife had quarreled with me in the city of Portland, Oregon, had packed her Saratoga trunk, and departed on a steamer for San Francisco, going to her mother. The second lie was that in the town of Eureka, California, I had been beaten up in a saloon row by a millionaire lumber man. The third lie was that in a mountain resort in the State of Washington, I had won a $100 bet by catching a perfectly uncatchable variety of lake trout. On the day in question my wife and I were deep in a forest reserve in southwestern Oregon, far from railroads, automobile roads, telegraph wires, and telephone lines."

Though he never answered or defended himself against these journalistic fictions, he was often hurt and disgruntled. "Do you know that when a university girl wandered into the hills in back of Berkeley and was attacked by a tramp the papers said it must have been Jack London?" Never once had he been invited to the Press Club of San Francisco, but when its members decided to build a clubhouse, they asked him to contribute two thousand dollars; it is the only time he derived pleasure from refusing a request.

Worse than these false and usually slanderous stories were the articles and pamphlets distributed with his name as the author. A single printed sheet called *The Good Soldier* caused him the most trouble. "Young Man: the lowest aim in your life is to be a good soldier. The 'good soldier' never tries to distinguish between right and wrong. If he is ordered to fire on his fellow citizens, on his friends, on his neighbors, he obeys without hesitation. If he is ordered to fire down a crowded street where the poor are clamoring for bread, he obeys and sees the gray hairs of age stained with red and the life tide gushing from the breast of woman, feels neither remorse nor sympathy. A good soldier is a blind, heartless, soulless, murderous machine."

The article is cleverly concocted, for in both sentiment and language it sounds startlingly like Jack. The United States Army officers raised an uproar at the insult to its enlisted men. Protests were lodged with Congress. The Post Office Department decided they had a criminal case against him for distributing the circulars through the mails. Jack's vehement denial of authorship stopped the prosecution, but attacks against him because of the "military canard" hounded him until his death.

Doubles sprang up all over America, wearing his well-known ranger's hat, bow tie, and sack coat, doubtless giving rise to many of the newspaper yarns. They lectured in his name, sold manuscripts purported to have been written by him, led revolutionary forces against Diaz in Mexico, signed his name to spurious checks, and lastly, made love to women as the red-blooded, primitive Jack London. Letters came in constantly from people who told about meeting him in places he had never been. All of this amused him until a double turned up in San Francisco who began to make love to a lady by the name of Babe. Babe sent open-faced postcards to Glen Ellen asking, "Don't you love me any more?" signing them, "Your sweetheart." Because of the uncertainty of his antecedents, strangers claimed him as their son, brother, uncle, cousin. One story emerged from a family in Oswego, New York, that Jack London was in reality Harry Sands, who had run away from home at the age of fourteen. Newspapers printed the pictures of Harry Sands and Jack London side by side so the public might be given an opportunity to detect a resemblance.

Mingled with his good reviews and favorable stories were frequent literary attacks against him. There was the accusation of falsifying life in Alaska, of not knowing about what he was writing. Fred Thompson, with whom Jack had packed into the Yukon, and who remained in Alaska for twenty years, chuckled at these reports as he remembered the sourdoughs of Alaska waiting impatiently for Jack's tales of the Klondike, considering them the most authentic material written about them.

Plagiarism suits were so frequent he was almost never without one. As far back as 1902 he had been accused of stealing a short story from one Frank Norris had published. When it was learned that still a third man had published a story on the identical subject, the matter was investigated and it was found that the three writers had been stirred by the same report of an occurrence in Seattle. Stanley Waterloo, upon whose *Story of Ab* Jack had based his *Before Adam,* caused an international scandal after the publication of the book. Jack replied by acknowledging his debt to Waterloo, then insisted that primitive man was in the realm of public domain. Frank Harris, erratic writer and editor, from one of whose articles Jack had taken for *The Iron Heel* a speech purportedly made by the Bishop of London, now earned publicity for himself by quoting his article side by side with Jack's, showing Jack to be a literary thief. To quiet the uproar Jack could only answer, "I am a sucker, not a plagiarist; I thought Harris was quoting from an historical document."

To keep up with his expenditures, as well as the vast operating costs of the ranch and the Wolf House, he turned out an unending stream of stories that would sell. If he had dared to stop for a breather his whole superstructure of obligation and indebtedness would have come crashing down over his head. His surest sale was for Alaskan tales; he kept grinding them out, groaning, "I'm still trying to dig myself out of the Klondike." His mind was alert, rich, vigorous, and in spite of the strain on him to make everything salable, many of the Alaskan stories are well done, as are such South Seas yarns as "The Seed of McCoy" and "The Inevitable White Man" in *South Seas Tales,* and "The House of Pride" and "The Sheriff of Kona" in *The House of Pride.* Only the Smoke Bellew stories were fabricated so they would earn him money. The other tales he had put on paper had been clamoring in his mind for expression; the need for money was the immediate incentive required to get them down. The Smoke Bellew stories were his first hack work, of no literary value; they provided cement and lumber and copper for his home. For these commodities he gave honest, solid commodities in return. "I didn't like the job of writing the thirteen Smoke Bellew stories, but I never hedged from my best in writing them."

His short stories began to fall off in excellence, partly because he was tired of the short form, found it too limiting in scope. He wanted to write only novels. The two he created during this period, *John Barleycorn* and *Valley of the Moon,* are not only among the best he has done but stand shoulder to shoulder with the finest novels written in America. Aside from the third section, which deals with his agricultural observations and which should have been made into a separate book, *Valley of the Moon* contains the greatest thinking and writing to be found in the heart and brain of Jack London. His portraits of Saxon, the laundry girl, and Billy, the teamster, are done with utter conviction; the description of the Bricklayers' Union free-for-all at their picnic in Weasel Park, where as a boy Jack had swept out the saloon on Sunday afternoons, is a classic of Irish-American folklore; and the drama and tragedy of the railroad strike in Oakland remains twenty-five years later the model for strike literature in the United States.

Sometimes he had to cast about in desperation for suitable plots for the magazines. It was in one of these periods of pressure that he received a letter from Sinclair Lewis, the gangling, red-headed chap who had wanted an interview for the *Yale News*, and who was now trying to become a writer. Lewis sent him the outlines of several plots which he suggested Jack might be able to use . . . at seven dollars and a half apiece. After studying them, he selected "The Garden of Terror" and one other, sending Lewis a check for fifteen dollars. Lewis replied post-haste, thanking Jack and telling him that the fifteen dollars was now part of an overcoat against the wintry New York winds.

Later, while working on *The Volta Review* of the American Association to Promote the Teaching of Speech to the Deaf, Lewis sent him another group of twenty-three plot outlines on what he called "a very businesslike INVOICE OF GOODS shipped as per yrs. of the steenth with prices of same," signing himself "Sinclair Lewis, otherwise Hal, alias Red." In the accompanying letter he hoped Jack would be able to take a considerable part of the plots, for if he did, it would finally give Lewis the chance to get back to his freelance writing, claiming that what writing he had been doing had been done only at the cost of sleep—which was too cheap and instructive an amusement, was sleep, to be wasted. Jack bought Lewis's "House of Illusion" idea for two-fifty, the list price, the "Prodigal Father," "Guilt of John Avery," "Explanations," "Recommendations," "The Gallant Gentleman," and "Woman Who Gave Soul to Man" for five dollars each; "The Dress Suit Pugilist," and "The Common Sense Jail" for seven-fifty each; and "Mr. Cincinnatus" for ten dollars, sending Lewis a check for fifty-two dollars and fifty cents. Whatever else Lewis may have used the money for, he proudly wrote Jack that he was keeping up his Red, or Socialist, card. From these plot ideas Jack wrote the short story "When All the World Was Young," which he sold to the *Post*, and the short novel, *The Abysmal Brute*, serialized in the *Popular Magazine*. When he wrote Lewis that for the first time in his life he was disgusted with a story, and didn't know what to do with Lewis's "Assassination Bureau," Lewis, his professional pride aroused, sent Jack at no extra charge a long synopsis of how the plot should be reconstructed.

His greatest generosity was to the aspiring writers who descended upon him in staggering numbers, their manuscripts darkening his sky like a locust plaque. Not a day of his life passed without his receiving a manuscript from a hopeful author, asking him to criticize, rewrite, sell it. These manuscripts, which ranged from a one-page poem to eight-hundred-page novels and treatises, he read with the utmost care, then sent the authors long criticisms embodying the literary technique he had worked out over a period of years. To these strangers he gave the best he had in him, sparing himself neither time nor energy. If he thought the work was good he tried to sell it to a magazine or publisher; if he thought it bad, he told the author why he thought so. Often his honest criticisms brought forth violent recriminations; the knowledge that he almost certainly would be called unpleasant names did not deter him from pointing out to these writers just where their work was bad, and how it could be improved. One author, to whom he had sent a trenchant criticism when returning the unsolicited manuscript, wrote back a praticularly vilifying letter. Jack sat up the better part of the night, allowing himself only three hours of the sleep for which his brain was crying, in order to write a brilliant and patient letter to the aspiring author, a letter of seven pages, the length of a short story that could have fetched him five hundred dollars, in which he pleaded with the man to learn how to take criticism so that he might better his work.

The only writers with whom he grew angry were those who wanted him to provide them with short cuts to literary success. To these writers Jack said, "The man who dreams of artistry, and yet thinks it necessary for somebody else to lick him into shape, is a man whose art is doomed to mediocrity. If you're going to deliver the real goods, you've got to do your own licking into shape. Buck up! Kick in! Get onto yourself! Don't squeal. Don't tell me, or any man how good you consider anything you've done, and that you think it is as good as somebody else's. Make your work so damned well better that you won't have time or thought to compare it with another's mediocrity."

In his files are letters from nearly every successful writer of his time, telling him of their needs, their troubles, their mental and spiritual anguish. To them all he gave of his sympathy, his encouragement, his love and understanding of their work, steeling them to believe in themselves, in literature, in the world they were trying to comprehend. When a publishing house had a book with social significance they sent him a copy; he read it faithfully and telegraphed back the praise needed to launch it.

In his business dealings with editors and publishers he was equally generous and honest. He always liked to play things "the big way" and was constantly distressed at the business men at the other end "playing things the small way." He was gentle, courteous, and easy to get along with—until he decided that someone was cheating him or injuring his work. Then he descended upon the offender with the ferocity of an enraged grizzly.

Since 1910, the year in which *Burning Daylight* had been released, he had given Macmillan a play called *Theft*, the collection of South Seas articles called *The Cruise of the Snark*, and four volumes of short stories, none of which was selling well. Now Brett informed him that the market for collections of short stories was being wiped out by the pulp paper magazines appearing by the dozens and carrying good imitations of the action stories that had made Jack famous; that he felt himself unable to meet his constant demands for advances, few of which were under five thousand dollars. After ten years of successful association he parted company with Brett and Macmillan in 1912. He then signed a contract with the Century Company, which published *Smoke Bellew, The Night Born,* and *The Abysmal Brute,* but refused to finance the writing of *John Barleycorn* at one thousand dollars a month for three months. Never having been happy at Century, and with *John Barleycorn* headed for his first brilliant success in three years, he sent them a series of sizzling telegrams in an effort to be released from his contract in order to return to Macmillan:

"All publishers agree that you can transfer Barleycorn. The only thing that can prevent you is the hope of big profits. You would sell yourself and your company's good name for a handful of silver. Please remember that I am not a money scavenger, and that the millions who read Barleycorn will later on read about you. The echoes of this will make you apologetic to the world for many a day, and when you are dust in your graves, the echoes in the brains of those yet unborn will stir your dust. I want your answer that you would rather be men than money grubbers. . . . I have sweated through hells you fellows never dreamed existed; I am possessed of a patience of which you fellows are incapable. I have a careless scorn of personal welfare and financial self-advantage that is beyond your shrinking comprehension. At any moment I will be able to look at my face in the mirror and be better pleased with myself than you fellows will be when you look at your faces in the mirror. . . . I raise my eyes and look at my bookshelf on which are the thirty-four books I have written which have already been published. In the whole row of thirty-four books there is only one scrubby volume—*The Abysmal Brute*, published by you just now. Again it is a two-by-four publisher trying to publish the stuff of an eight-by-ten author. . . . Still awaiting reply to my long telegram of May 10, 1913. You have had several days in which to eat Sunday dinner and see your wives and children and be genial and human. Come on, then, and be genial and human with me and let go of me. You know that the one asset I can carry to a new publisher is Barleycorn. Let go the few dollars profit and let me go out from you not entirely naked."

When the Century Company does not reply, he sends one last desperate telegram: "I can understand anger in any man, but sullenness is so abysmally primitive, so like the balky stupid horse, that I cannot comprehend such an attitude on the part of men who claim to be modern and fairly civilized."

When Century finally refused to give up *John Barleycorn* he wrote, "I have been whipped too many times in my life to hold grudges or bad feeling on account of my being whipped," and cooperated with them fully. However, after *John Barleycorn* was released he went back to Macmillan and ventured forth no more.

He admitted to Brett that he had been something of a brute, himself, in trying to get clear of the Century contract.

During the summer of 1913 he and Charmian spent happy weeks visiting the Sterlings in Carmel, swimming in the surf and sun-bathing on the sand, hunting for abalone and eating abalone steaks cooked over a wood fire on the beach, adding a myriad of verses to the humorous poem for which Sterling, ironically enough, is best remembered:

> Oh! Some folks boast of quail on toast,
> Because they think it's tony;
> But I'm content to owe my rent
> And live on abalone.

On his Beauty Ranch in the cool of the early morning he continued work on his series of long novels, writing *The Mutiny on the Elsinore*, which *Cosmopolitan* serialized under the title of *The Sea Gangsters*. The half of the book that contains the straight line of action is well done, particularly the sea material for which he had been called the American Conrad; the other half, in which the main character talks about the action, is poorly done and injures the book so severely that *The Mutiny on the Elsinore* died a deserved death.

In the afternoons he rode the trails along the fertile fields ripening under the powerful sun, ending the day at the pool in Boyes Springs where he swam with his friends. On the way home he stopped at each of the bars for a drink, a story, a laugh. At dusk he rode to the Wolf House to talk to Forni and the workmen. By August, 1913, he had spent eighty thousand dollars on his almost completed home. The newspapers lashed him unmercifully as an apostate socialist building a castle; the socialists were angry, again felt they had been betrayed. Pyle reports that Jack would "back and fill" when twitted about the magnificence of his home. To newspaper reporters he insisted that no matter how big his Wolf House, he was not a capitalist because he was building it with his own wages; when everyone referred to the Wolf House as a castle, he replied that the magnificent redwoods and red stone had belonged to him, that if the place resembled a palace of Justinian or Caesar, it was a fortunate accident costing him nothing in addition. When Harrison Fisher told him that he had the most beautiful home in America, he knew that all the money and effort spent on his Wolf House was justified.

At last, on August 21, clean-up day arrived. The electricians had completed their wiring, the carpenters and plumbers were finished, Forni's men went about gathering the waste which they had soaked in turpentine to wipe down the woodwork. Within two or three weeks a crew of men would begin moving Jack and Charmian into their new home. That night Forni worked with Jack at the ranch house until eleven, then tramped past the Wolf House to his own cabin. Just before two in the morning he was awakened by a farmer dashing in and crying, "Forni, it's burning! The Wolf House is burning!" When Forni reached the canyon the Wolf House was a mass of flames.

Within a few minutes Jack came running, out of breath, his hair flying. He stopped abruptly on the knoll where he had sat with the Italian workmen singing and drinking wine. Before him was a roaring inferno, every part of the house burning at once. It was mid-August, there was no water. He could do nothing but stand with tears running down his cheeks and watch one of his greatest life dreams be destroyed.

Every piece of woodwork was burning; even the window sills, burning with an unnatural blue flame. Lying out beyond the ring of redwoods that surrounded the house was a pile of finished redwood with which Jack's sleeping quarters were to have been trimmed. The ring of redwoods had not caught fire, but the pile of wood beyond them was ablaze. Many people were accused of the firing, a good part of them in anonymous letters sent to Jack. Shepard, whom Eliza was divorcing, had quarreled with Jack that very day; he was accused. A workman whom Jack had thrown off the ranch for beating his wife was seen in the vicinity; he was accused. An ill-tempered foreman was accused. Forni was accused, jealous socialists were accused, disgruntled tramps were accused. Forni feels the fire was a result of spontaneous combustion; the turpentine-saturated waste with which the woodwork had been rubbed down might have burst into flame. This would not explain the entire house burning at once. If the fire had started in any one room it could not have spread through the stone walls. Defective electrical wiring, if the current had been turned on, might have fired all the rooms simultaneously . . . but no wires extended to the pile of redwood outside the house, beyond the redwood ring. . . .

Jack was convinced that the house had been fired, if not by the hand of man, then by the hand of a fate that did not want him to enjoy the fruits of his labor, that did not consider it meet for a socialist to dwell in a castle. During the long, bitter night he spoke only twice. While the flames were at their height he murmured, "I would rather be the man whose house was burned, than the one who burned it." At dawn, when only the outer stone shell that had been put together for the centuries was left standing, he said quietly, "Forni, tomorrow we will start to rebuild."

He never did rebuild the Wolf House. Something in his heart burned out that night and was destroyed forever.

10

FOR four days he lay in bed on the screened sleeping porch overlooking the tropical garden. Every illness he had contracted, from the earliest days of The Road and the Klondike through Korea and the Solomon Islands, rose up to smite him. Convinced that the Wolf House had been fired by someone he had befriended, he wrestled with a searing disgust. It was not merely the gutting of his house that crushed him; it was the loss of the love and faith in humanity that had dominated his hours and his character. His eyes were suddenly opened to much that he had not seen before, or, having seen, had passed as unimportant. The burning of the Wolf House appeared symbolic of the manner in which everything he had tried to do for socialism and literature would be destroyed. He aged considerably during those four days.

His first move when he climbed out of bed was to ride Washoe Ban across the fields to the Wolf House. Gazing forlornly at the skeleton of magnificent red stone jutting its nude towers into the blue Sonoma sky, he named it The Ruins. Though he could have declared himself bankrupt, he paid the contractors in full. Seventy thousand dollars was dead loss, as was the time and energy he had spent writing the Smoke Bellew stories . . . which again led him to wonder if there might be a moral hidden somewhere in the ashes. He wrote that he was now one hundred thousand dollars in debt; the weight of the money was not heavy upon his shoulders, but the thought of the creative work he was going to have to produce to earn it sat like a stone on his brain.

He repeated to Forni and Eliza that he was going to rebuild the Wolf House; he had Forni clear the débris from the ruins, and had Eliza cut down more redwoods to season. But deep in his mind he was discouraged . . . the house would only be burned again. When *Cosmopolitan* sportingly sent his monthly two thousand dollars ahead of time because of his loss, he built an extension to his overcrowded study, and here, under a cool, spreading oak, he moved his roll-top desk, his wire baskets loaded with papers and mail, his steel files with their records of accomplishment, his cardboard reference boxes with the notes for hundreds of stories, and his writing supplies. Here he spent the working hours of the last three years of his life.

He slipped back into his routine; everything was the same as it had always been, yet everything appeared different. When he rode about the ranch he could no longer fail to note that the laborers were soldiering on the job, putting out as little as they could for their wages. By a little discreet inquiry he learned that they considered the ranch a rich man's hobby, no more to be taken seriously than the workmen had taken the *Snark* seriously. His mechanics too were indifferent to the quality of the work they were turning out; when he jumped off Washoe Ban in front of the blacksmith shop and inspected a shoeing job the smithy had just completed, he saw that the man had rasped off half an inch of the toe of the hoof to make the shoe fit. Studying the ranch bills and feeling they were too high, he rode into town to consult with the merchants. They told him that his foremen demanded a twenty per cent kickback on every dollar of merchandise purchased, and that there was no alternative but to add it to the bills.

In 1900 he had written to Anna Strunsky, "I do not feel that because I condemn the deficiencies of my friends is any reason why I should not love them." Love and tolerance and generosity were the wellsprings of his nature; yet they were growing increasingly difficult to maintain. He asked his friend Ernest, who was in Oakland, to buy him some heavy draft horses. Ernest charged him a commission, added a bill for expenses, then shipped two sick horses and two below the specified weight. When he wrote Ernest that the horses were unsatisfactory, Ernest answered with an angry, insulted letter. Jack replied, "You go bleating around about your hurt feelings, but what about me? Because I have the presumption to dare to tell you that the two work horses, instead of weighing the fifteen hundred pounds you said they did, weighed thirteen hundred and fifty, and the other two were sick and decrepit enough for chicken feed, you go up in the air, raise a roar about being called a grafter. You have stuck my money in a hole, and now you tell me to come and get it out. You feel sore! How many hundreds of dollars sore do you think I feel? Here I am with the only available horse money tied up, and not enough horses to work the ranch with."

As far back as 1904 when his newspaper friend Noel had been out of work, Jack had given him the right to dramatize *The Sea Wolf*, and to keep two thirds of the royalties he might earn from the dramatization. Instead Noel had sold the dramatic rights to someone else and retained the thirty-five-hundred-dollar purchase price. Contracting with Hobart Bosworth to make a motion picture of the book, Jack had to plead among his publishers for the thirty-five hundred dollars needed to buy back those rights. And here was Noel urging him to put money into the Millergraph Company he was organizing to market an improved lithographing process. Resolving not to be changed or made hard by his newly awakened cynicism, he ordered Brett to pay Noel a thousand dollars; when the Millergraph Company needed more funds he again mortgaged Flora's house for four thousand dollars, writing to Noel, "I play with my cards on the table, and put myself absolutely in the trust of my friends." The stock he was supposed to receive was juggled, the company went into bankruptcy.

Charmian told him she had to have three hundred dollars immediately; he sent out pleas to the hundreds of men and women who had borrowed from him an aggregate of more than fifty thousand dollars, vowing they would return every cent. He could collect only fifty dollars. For the first time he wondered if his friends were laughing at him. Had he been marked early for a fall guy, a wild Irishman who spent his money like a drunken sailor? Always it had been a case of one-way traffic: he gave and gave, others took and took. His former bouts of despondence had been self-generated; because of their cyclical nature they had soon passed. Now his thoughts, steeping like tea, became increasingly black and bitter.

For several years he had been urging Bessie to bring the two girls to Glen Ellen during their summer vacations so they would come to love his Beauty Ranch. Only once had Bessie accepted his offer; she had brought Joan and Bess and a group of friends to the ranch for a picnic. No sooner had the lunch been spread than Charmian came galloping by in a red cap and red shirt, spreading a fine layer of dust over the food.—Jack vowed fervently that if Bessie would allow him to build her a cottage on the ranch he would keep Charmian away from her. Bessie declined. Having lost her husband to Charmian, she feared she might also lose her daughters. She told him she did not consider the second Mrs. London a fit moral example to which to expose her growing girls.

His efforts to get a friendly word or gesture from Joan, who was now thirteen, failed. He had hoped she would be old enough to become his companion and friend. On August 24, two days after the burning of the Wolf House, he pleads with her to remember that he is her father, that he has fed her, clothed her, housed her, and loved her since the first moment she drew breath, and then asks, "What do you feel for me? Am I a fool who gives much and receives nothing? I send you letters and telegrams, and I receive no word from you. Am I beneath your contempt in every way save as a meal ticket? Do you love me at all? What do I mean to you? I am sick—you are silent. My home is destroyed—you have no word to say. The world does not belong to the ones who remain silent, who by their very silence lie and cheat and make a mockery of love and a meal ticket of their father. Don't you think it is about time I heard from you? Or do you want me to cease forever from caring to hear from you?"

What hurt most in his awakening was the cruel realization that Charmian, at the age of forty-three, was still a child, preoccupied with infantile details. Her neighbors report that "she told interminable stories about childlike things, trivial things, about her jewels, her antique clothes, her little caps. She wanted to be eternally feminine, to use her wiles and charms." He suffered acutely as he saw his guests try to conceal their embarrassment at her posing and acting, at her coyness, her attempts to play the young and beautiful girl she forever thought herself, at her bizarre, jeweled, red costume-clothing and frilly lace caps dating back to the past century. Charmian's stepsister says that when Charmian was young it was her habit to stick her head around a corner, make a face or say something cute, and then run, expecting to be chased. She was still sticking her head around corners, saying something cute, expecting to be chased. One evening as Jack sat with Eliza at the ranch desk in the dining-room, worried sick over how he was to meet his obligations, Charmian bounced in with an unwrapped bolt of velvet goods draped across her, strutted up and down as she cried, "Look, Mate, won't this make a gorgeous outfit? I've just bought two bolts." There was a long, sad silence after she left the room; then he turned to Eliza and said quietly, "She is our little child. We must always take care of her."

If he could have started out on another South Seas voyage or four-horse driving trip, or any adventure, Charmian would still have been the ideal companion. But he was living at home now, he had grown tired and disenchanted, he wanted a mature woman "to stand flat-footed by his side" in a mature world. He needed a wife who would share his broad bed, whom he could touch with his hand when he awoke in the deep of night, troubled.

Surrounded by friends and relatives, with hundreds of thousands of admirers spread throughout the western world, he felt unutterably alone. He ached as only a man who has started on the down grade toward death can ache for his own flesh and blood, for that son who could be trusted, on whose strong and devoted shoulder he could lean in his older years, who would carry on his name and tradition.

And yet the year 1913 proved to be his most fruitful; in it he reached the climax of his publishing career. Four of his novels were serialized in magazines, among which was *The Scarlet Plague*, which showed how mankind reverted to primitive life when a plague wiped out civilization. In book form there were published *The Night Born*, which contains the stirring tales "The Mexican," "To Kill a Man," and "When the World Was Young"; a short prize-fight novel, *The Abysmal Brute*, based on a Sinclair Lewis plot; and, within sixty days of each other, his two great novels, *John Barleycorn* and *Valley of the Moon*. This record of accomplishment made the publishing world regard him not so much as a man, as a natural force.

Fate, which could deliver shattering blows, could still treat him as its favorite. Toward the end of the year, having completed the exhausting *Mutiny of the Elsinore* and needing a big idea to revitalize him, his friend Ed Morrell was released from San Quentin. After having spent five years in solitary confinement Morrell had been taken out of the disciplinary strait-jacket and black hole to be made head trusty of the prison. For many years Jack had been working to have him pardoned, and at last succeeding, wired Morrell "Congratulations and welcome home." The two men met at the Saddle Rock restaurant in Oakland, where they made fast a friendship that had been begun through correspondence, as so many of Jack's friendships had begun. Morrell spent much of his time on the Beauty Ranch feeding Jack's lifelong interest in criminology and penology, subjects on which Professor Chaney had been writing with intelligence before Jack was born. Before long he had plunged into his eighth and last great novel, *The Star Rover*, powerful in emotional impact when describing the sufferings of the men lashed into canvas strait-jackets, tender in feeling when describing the friendships between the prisoners in their airless cells, bold in imagination when projecting their backward flights into the realm of time. For pure death-appeal, breathlessness of suspense, musical lyricism of writing, and profound human sympathy, *The Star Rover* is a magnificent literary accomplishment.

The work served as a catharsis; such gratification did the writing bring him that his mental and physical illnesses were shoved into the background. As in the early days of Piedmont, he derived pleasure from reading to his guests each new chapter as he completed it. To a young boy who wrote for encouragement he answered, "I have been through the ennui of sixteen as well as twenty; and the boredom, and the blaséness and utter wretchedness of the ennui of twenty-five and thirty. And yet I live, am growing fat, and laugh a large portion of my waking hours." Morrell says of this period, "No matter what he said or did his everpresent kindness held you. He could say the rashest and brashest things, hurt your feelings and make you like it . . . because there was no personal sting. He was one of the most lovable characters of his age."

As a man with a long and successful business career, an increasing portion of his time had to be devoted to promoting and protecting his interests. He had agreed with Hobart Bosworth, the actor, to take a portion of the profits in return for the right to make his books into motion pictures. Bosworth had no sooner begun work than other film companies pirated his stories and made pictures of them, two versions of *The Sea Wolf* playing in theaters on opposite sides of the street. The copyright laws were not only in confusion, but court decisions had been against the author, who found that when he sold material for serialization to a magazine the magazine automatically acquired all rights to that material. Jack learned that any of his work which had first appeared in a magazine belonged to the magazine rather than to him; that the pirating film companies were buying up these copyrights for insignificant sums.

He joined with Arthur Train and the newly formed Authors' League in a fight to have the law revised so that when an author sold a story to a magazine he retained his rights. Into this legal battle, which lasted for several years, he threw his strength, energy, and resources, making trips to New York and Hollywood, retaining lawyers, arguing cases in court, sending out hundreds of impassioned letters and telegrams. If the long and complicated battle was waged at the expense of the literature he might have been creating, he helped make it possible for future generations of American writers to derive the full benefit of their work.

By May of 1914, shortly after he had completed *The Star Rover*, the United States Government took a hand in the Villa-Carranza revolution in Mexico, sending battleships and troops to occupy Vera Cruz. Ever since he had been thwarted in his desire to report the Russian-Japanese War of 1904, Jack had looked forward to the day when he would be able to vindicate himself. Offered eleven hundred dollars a week and expenses by *Collier's*, he departed for Galveston within twenty-four hours, then shipped for Vera Cruz.

Once again he was unable to report the war . . . this time because there was no war to report; having no intention of conquering Mexico and establishing a protectorate, the United States contented itself with the show of arms in Vera Cruz. Once again he hammered out virile articles on "The Red Game of War" and "The Mexican Army," described the United States Army clearing up the pestilence of Vera Cruz, and the revolutionists attacking the foreign oil interests in Tampico. For nearly two months he pursued war news, but all he was able to take out of Mexico was a severe case of amoebic dysentery; the memory of a crap game in which he cleaned out the newspaper correspondents and the ambassadors from France and Spain; and the material for a series of short stories about Mexico which excited him considerably. When the editor of *Cosmopolitan* expressed interest, he began outlining and annotating the stories.

He returned to Glen Ellen ravaged by the dysentery, pale and weak. In an effort to regain his strength he took the *Roamer* for a several weeks' cruise on San Francisco Bay. His recovery was slow, pain-fraught. When the editor of *Cosmopolitan* changed his mind about the newly projected group of stories, deciding that the American public was fed up with Mexico, Jack discarded the material without writing another word. In his fighting days he would have written his Mexican tales and made the magazines like them. If the planned stories would have been the equal of the only one he did write, "The Mexican," he robbed himself and the world of a superb volume.

Ill health was attacking him more steadily; what Cloudesley Johns called his "periods of mental depression when his splendid will to live almost left him" were becoming more frequent; the cycle had begun to accelerate. It was becoming increasingly difficult for him to squeeze out his thousand words daily . . . yet in the fall of 1914 he informed his editor that he had jumped into a new novel that was going to be the biggest, most tremendous thing he had ever written ". . . in a setting that never before in the history of all the literature of the world was ever put into print. A mighty trio in a mighty situation. As I go over this novel I am almost led to believe that it is what I have been working toward all my writing life. It will be utterly fresh, utterly unlike anything I have ever done."

Starting with his apparently genuine conviction and enthusiasm —though in his fatigue and despair he may only have been trying to whip up his own interest as well as that of the editor—he began work on his back-to-the-land novel, *The Little Lady of the Big House*. Ostensibly an agricultural novel based on his ideas for a model ranch and the rehabilitation of California agriculture, it developed into a love triangle written with all the flowery sentimental hyperbole of the nineteenth century, a book so artificial, strained, and exaggerated that the reader is stunned, at a loss to understand how such spurious thinking could have emanated from Jack London.

Only a few months before he had completed *The Star Rover* and such first-rate stories as *Told in the Drooling Ward*, the scene of which was laid in the asylum which adjoined the Hill Ranch, and *South of the Slot*, a proletarian story of power and conviction. His confidence had not run down, his concentration and discipline had not run down, his eagerness to create had not run down, but the powerful machine that was the brain of Jack London, after having produced forty-one books in fourteen years, was at last beginning to tire, to lose its grip.

Deeply as he had felt hurt by Joan the year before, he made another determined effort to win his daughter's allegiance. When Joan, who had just entered high school, sent him a play she had written he was as delighted with it as with anything he had turned out himself. "I like it tremendously, and can hardly believe that I am the father of a girl who is so big that she can write such a play." His business and personal letters of the next few months proudly tell that he is the father of a girl already in high school.

Having formulated his plans, he went humbly to the house in Piedmont, where he laid his proposition before Bessie. If she would permit the children to visit him at the ranch, to become acquainted with their father all over again, and to love the ranch as they rode over its trails with him, he would change his will, which now deeded everything to Charmian, and leave the estate to the two girls. He would build Bessie a home in a protected corner of the ranch, so she could be with them. She could come with them at all times to be sure that Charmian would not intrude. . . . He would do anything she asked, anything, if only she would let him have back his two daughters. Bessie was not tempted.

A few days later he wrote directly to Joan. "Now, Joan, it is a hard proposition to put up to you at your age, and the chances are that in deciding on this proposition I put up to you on Sunday night you will make the mistake of deciding to be a little person in a little world. You will make that mistake because you listened to your mother, who is a little person in a little place in a little part of the world, and who, out of her female sex jealousy against another woman, has sacrificed your future for you. I offer you the big things of the world, the big things that big people live and know and think and act."

Many anxiously pleading letters followed. For a long time Joan remained silent. At last, at his insistence, she wrote him a one-page letter in which she told him that she was perfectly satisfied with her surroundings, that she had no wish to change them, that she would stay with her mother always, that she resented his opinions of Bessie, whom she loved as a good mother. She begged him to let her feel that this would be the last of the awful letters he would force her to write—a closing which was in reality a farewell.

When Charmian tried to take away from him the "philosophic tramps" he kept permanently on the ranch, he said to her in a cry wrung from within, "I get more sheer pleasure out of an hour's talk with Strawn-Hamilton than all of my inefficient Italian laborers have ever given me. He *pays* his way. My God, the laborers *never* have. Please remember that the ranch is *my* problem. What all the various ones who have worked on it have lost for me in cash is a thousand times more than the few meals and beds I've given my bums. I give these paltry things of paltry value out of my heart. I've not much heartthrob left for my fellow beings. Shall I cut this out, too?"

Charmian developed sullen and moody spells, interfered with his management of the ranch, told him what trees he could or could not cut down, hampered the progress of the work by complaining that insomnia kept her awake all night and that the workmen, who reported at seven, were not to be allowed near the ranch house until nine because they might awaken her. When he insisted that they had work to do she picked up her bedding and slept in the barn. Defeated, Jack ordered the workmen to keep away from the house even if they had to stand idle . . . until one morning, when he was crossing his fields at five o'clock, he found her in a haystack with a young guest, watching the sunrise.

The criticisms he had made of Bessie London were that she

dressed badly, that she was not a good hostess, and that she was jealous. By a twist of fate he found these same attributes in Charmian. She made no attempt to be a hostess or to manage the house; the Japanese servants ran everything, and she was simply another guest in his home. When friends arrived, Jack or Nakata showed them to their rooms; one woman guest tells of Jack's embarrassment because Charmian never troubled with the new arrivals, that he had even to show the women where the toilet was. Where Bessie had paid little attention to women unless they threw themselves upon his neck, Charmian was actively jealous of every other female. He was rarely permitted to go anywhere without her; when they were out she played a game which women who witnessed it called "breaking it up." For only two minutes was he allowed to talk to another woman, even though they might be discussing the coming election; at the end of that time she interrupted with a gushing monologue.

Once when his secretary, Jack Byrne, was sending him a telegram to Los Angeles, he added to it the information that a woman whose entire family Jack had known and loved for years would like to see him. Charmian told Byrne to omit this part of the message, as she would be wiring Jack later and would tell him about it. Her wire was never sent. Even at the cost of working herself half to death, she had never permitted Jack to employ a woman secretary. "I wouldn't let anyone else in," she said, "I mustn't take my finger out of it." It was not until Johnny Miller's mother died, and her second husband, Jack Byrne, was out of a job that he was allowed to have the full-time secretary he greatly needed.

From New York she received a telegraphic report that "Jack is spending all his time with a woman who lives in the Van Cortlandt Hotel on Forty-Eighth Street. Amy." Feeling unhappy, restless, he was having affairs with other women. Years before he had written to Charmian, "Let me tell you a little affair which will indicate the ease with which I let loose the sexual man." Yet his promiscuity seems to have resulted from a break-up of the marriage ties rather than any inherent license. He was faithful to Bessie until their marriage, physically, had been disrupted. He was faithful to Charmian for nine years, until their marriage, spiritually, was destroyed.

Though he had drunk to defeat his cyclical depressions, most of his drinking had been for companionship, pleasure, and relaxation. He now began drinking heavily, not to incur pleasure but to ease pain. He had rarely done any drinking on the ranch; now he drank there a good deal. He harnessed his horses and drove to Santa Rosa, not one afternoon a week, but three and four. Ira Pyle reports that he no longer argued for the fun of it; he grew angry, banged his fist on the bar, showed his disgust with people who reasoned from self-interest rather than logic. Except for his wild bouts as a young oyster pirate, he had been able to take his liquor or leave it alone. Only the year before, returning on the S.S. *Dirigo* around Cape Horn from a business trip in the East, he had put aboard at Baltimore one thousand books and pamphlets he wished to study, and forty gallons of whiskey. "When we dock at Seattle either my thousand books will have been studied, or the forty gallons of whiskey will be gone." He left the ship with the thousand volumes annotated, the whiskey untouched. But all this was changed; he had to have whiskey to deaden the long hours, to make them tolerable. His illnesses made him drink, his drinking made him ill. His mental fatigue and depression made him drink, his drinking fatigued and depressed him. No longer well, no longer young, no longer fresh, happy, and working vigorously, he could not handle his quart of Scotch a day. Before, people had seen him drinking; now they saw him drunk.

His disillusionment at the hands of his friends and business associates continued apace. Two friends tasting the grape juice he made from his grapes suggested they form a company to market it. They were to supply the money, Jack his name and the grapes. Before long he had been hauled into court, where they were suing him for thirty-one thousand dollars. After spending thirty-five hundred dollars to get back the dramatic rights to *The Sea Wolf*, and giving the film companies his best stories, he was informed by the producers that there were no profits for him to share. He bought a half interest in an Arizona gold mine which he was never able to locate, a block of stock in the new Oakland Fidelity Loan and Mortgage Company, which kept him in the law courts for two years. Always "a flyer, a white chip on the table, a lottery ticket" brought him grief.

His bitterest blow was the trouble Ninetta and Edward Payne, to whose support he was even yet contributing, stirred up among his neighbors, getting them to sign a petition preventing him from using the water from a second dam he had built high up on his land to control the winter rains, on the grounds that it would divert water from the creek which ran alongside their home. While few of the other neighbors seemed exercised or frightened at the possibility of losing their water, Ninetta and Edward Payne carried through, securing an injunction against him.

He learned that some of his friends who were constantly asking for money were saying that he made it so easily they would be fools not to help him spend it. Even George Sterling, to whom he had just sent one hundred dollars for a plot he did not want, because he knew Sterling was broke, was criticizing him for writing for "Hearst's gold." In his earlier years money had been easier to make, had given him more joy in the making. He had accepted avarice, sloth, and hypocrisy with the cheerful resignation of the man who knows the worst about humanity and goes on from there. Becoming increasingly ill and despondent, he now viewed this abuse of his generosity with bitterness.

In February of 1915, after a number of cold and bleak months, he left with Charmian for Hawaii to finish out the winter. Here in the warm sunlight, with daily swimming and horseback riding, his health improved sufficiently to enable him to begin a new novel, *Jerry of the Islands*, with the last remaining flare of the Jack London spirit. "I assure you in advance that Jerry is uniquely new and different from anything that has appeared in fiction, not only under the classification of dog stories, but under the general classification of fiction. I am making fresh, vivid, new stuff, and dog psychology that will warm the hearts of dog lovers and the heads of psychologists." *Jerry of the Islands* is a delightful story of dog adventure in the New Hebrides. Sitting in a loose kimono at his desk on an open verandah facing the palm-fringed lagoon, his mind journeyed back to snow-covered Alaska, back to Buck of *The Call of the Wild*, the dog that had sent him skyrocketing to fame. It was pleasant to think about dogs and to write about them; they were a loyal species.

By summer he had completed *Jerry of the Islands*, and returned to Glen Ellen. He went to the Bohemian Grove on the Russian River for the High Jinks of the Bohemian Club, where he met a number of his artist friends, argued socialism versus defeatism, swam in the river, and drank heavily. After the Jinks he brought Sterling, Martinez, and a few others back to the ranch; the drinking continued. His uremia became acute, but he was not willing to stop drinking long enough to cure the infection. He worked only on the novelized version of the movie scenario of *Hearts of Three* for which entertainment nonsense the *Cosmopolitan* had offered him twenty-five thousand dollars. Glad of the opportunity to escape serious thinking, he tossed off his daily thousand words in an hour and a half.

He still liked to laugh, but his sporadic gaiety was forced. Finn Frolich says, "He didn't do the sporting things he used to do, wrestle, play, didn't want to go up into the mountains riding horseback any more. The gleam was gone from his eye." He no longer discussed to obtain information, to enjoy a battle of wits. He argued to win, sometimes grew quarrelsome. George Sterling advised Upton Sinclair not to visit the Beauty Ranch, as Jack had changed.

His only peace and pleasure was derived from the ranch itself. Though he was disgusted with a large part of the men who were working for him, he never lost his confidence in the land. "I am that sort of farmer who, after delving in all the books to satisfy his quest for economic values, returns to the soil as the source and foundation of all economics." He continued to clear new fields, to plant new crops, to extend his irrigation systems, to put up new stone buildings for his stock. To Joe King, the printing bill for whose appeal he had paid six years before and whom he was still trying to get pardoned from San Quentin, he wrote, "I have just completed a pig pen that will make anyone in the United States who is interested in the manufacture of pork sit up and take notice. There is nothing like it in the way of piggeries ever built. It cost three thousand dollars to build and will pay twelve per cent in the mere cost of labor. I am running nothing but registered pigs on the Ranch. I plan shortly to build a slaughterhouse and install a refrigerating plant."

He was not exaggerating about his Pig Palace, as the piggery was soon named. There was a private indoor and outdoor suite for each pig family, with two taps of running water. Built by Forni in a perfect circle with a stone house in the center in which to store the feed, it is a work of art, architecturally flawless. He also planned with Forni to build a circular stone barn for his cows which would be equally labor-saving and permanent. To the editor of *Cosmopolitan* he wrote, "Please remember that my Ranch is the apple of my eye. I am working for results and I am going to get results that will take their place in books some of these days."

In his mind he was slowly developing a new idea, an extension of his plan for a model farm. He would establish a select rural community. Weeding out the undesirable laborers, he would employ only those men who had a personal integrity and a love for the land. For each of these men he would build a cottage; there would be a general store at which commodities would be sold for cost; and a little school for the laborers' children. The number of families he would include in his model community would depend solely on the number the land could support. "My fondest hope is that somewhere in the next six or seven years I shall be able to break even on the Ranch." He wanted no profit, no return on his investment of a quarter of a million dollars; he wanted only to break even, to maintain a real community of workers, bound by their common love of the soil.

Misfortune struck his plans almost at once. Though he had gone to the Agriculture Department of the University of California for advice about his piggery, the entire collection of registered pigs caught pneumonia and died. His prize shorthorn bull, the foundation of his stock, slipped in its pen, dug a horn into the earth, fell over it, and broke its neck. The herd of Angora goats were wiped out by disease. The Shire stallion which had won him several blue ribbons, and whom he loved as though it were human, was found dead in the fields. His entire investment in Shire horses proved to be a mistake, for the hair on their legs made it impossible to keep them clean and in working shape during the winter months. His heavy draft horses, too, had been an error in judgment; they were being replaced by lighter equipment, which lighter horses could pull, and by tractors. His one hundred and forty thousand eucalyptus trees, which were to grow by themselves and net him a fortune after twenty years, were suddenly useless for anything but firewood; all interest in Circassian walnut had disappeared.

He was whipped, he knew he was whipped, but he would not admit it. If anyone had come to him and said, "Jack, the ranch is an expensive failure, for your own sake you had better abandon it," he would have cried, as he had cried when he had been urged to give up the *Snark*, "I can't quit!" In order to earn more money to keep the ranch going he eked out his thousand words a day. The act of writing, which had been blood in his veins and air in his lungs, was now poison to him. "The only reason I keep on writing is that I have to. If I did not have to, I'd never write another line. Take that straight."

He was not the only one tiring of his work. The critics and public were also tiring, choked by a plethora. When he finished *Hearts of Three* he wrote, "This yarn is a celebration. By its completion I celebrate my fortieth birthday, my fiftieth book, my sixteenth year in the writing game." A few days later he groused, "I have not seen a best seller of my own for a weary time. Is the work of other authors better than mine? Is the public souring on me?" *The Valley of the Moon* had been his last book to be favorably received; though *The Strength of the Strong* contains his best proletarian and prophetic stories, and represents the finest cross-cut of his variegated genius, it passed as just another collection of Jack London tales. To a lone friendly reviewer he wrote, "You are the only man in the United States who has cared a whoop in hell for *The Star Rover*. The rest of the reviewers have said that *The Star Rover* is my regular red-blood, up-to-the-neck, primeval gore sort of stuff, too horrible for women to read, and too horrible for men to read, except degenerates. If my stories are fierce, then life is fierce. I think life is strong not fierce, and I try to make my stories as strong as life is strong."

He had his five-year contract with *Cosmopolitan* to provide them with two novels a year, but the failing giant was now so completely enchained that his secretary Byrne wrote to a man who wanted Jack to collaborate on a new idea, "The class of work he must turn out is indicated to him by his publishers, to whom he is under contract for several years to come." At the age of twenty-four he had revitalized the magazine world, made his own rules. Now he replied to an aspiring author, "If you want to write for the magazines you must write what the magazines want. Magazines have their own game. If you want to play their game you must play it their way!"

No longer could he awaken himself to combat. To a woman high-school teacher in a small town in California who wrote to him for help against a corrupt political machine, he answered, "It is a good many years since I jumped into the battle to right political affairs, to give all men and women a square deal. Really, I feel a sort of veteran when I think over the long years of the fight. I am not exactly a beaten veteran, but unlike the raw recruit I do not expect to storm and capture the enemy's position by the next sunrise. I am the veteran who neither hopes to see the end of the campaign, nor any longer forecasts the date of the end of the campaign." To another friend who wanted him to join in a concerted attack on religion, he wrote that "the battle over religion seems so far away, a little and forgotten battle still being waged off somewhere in a secret corner of the world. I think you are fighting an antagonist already, intellectually, beaten." To Mary Austin, who complained to him that her finest writings were being misunderstood, he replied, wearily, "The best efforts of my heart and head have missed fire with practically everybody in the world who reads, and I do not worry about it. I go ahead content to be admired for my red-blood brutality, and for a number of other nice little things that are not true of my work at all. Those who sit alone must sit alone. As I remember it, the prophets and seers of all times have been compelled to sit alone except at such times as they were stoned or burned at the stake."

He retired to his study like an injured grizzly bear into a cave to lick his wounds. When he received hurt, angry, and disillusioned letters from his followers about *The Little Lady of the Big House* —for they were flinging copies of the magazine into the fire, begging him to come down to earth again—he lashed out at them, sensitive and stung. "Let me tell you right now that I am damned proud of The Little Lady."

What no one except Eliza knew was that he was torturing himself with the fear of going insane. His brain was too exhausted to work, to create, and yet he had to write every day of his life. He was afraid that his mind would break under the constant and heavy pressure, a fear intensified by his conviction that his mother was not rational. Time and again he begged, "Eliza, if I go insane, promise that you won't put me in an institution. Promise!" Nor could Eliza minimize his fears. Each time she had to assure him solemnly that she would not put him in a public institution, that she would take care of him.

He held out only one hope for himself: that he would find a mature, genuine woman whom he could love, who would love him, and give him a son. He knew Charmian would never give him the son for whom he hungered. So grieved was he that he would go sonless to his death, he who had been so fruitful in creating human beings on the printed page, that he vowed "he was going to have a son, and he didn't care how he got one. He was going out to find a woman who would give him a son, and bring her to the Ranch." There is ample evidence that he found the woman he was looking for, that he loved her deeply, and that she loved him. But he did not carry out his determination. He could not bring himself to hurt Charmian. He was gentle with her as one is gentle with a child, continued to write glowing inscriptions into her copy of his books . . . for she had given him years of companionship, and he was grateful.

Charmian was greatly upset, nervous; she knew that he was being unfaithful to her, that she was in grave danger of losing him. Rumors of divorce flew about Oakland. She suffered constantly from insomnia, told everyone at the ranch that the night after Jack's death she enjoyed her first sleep in many months.

He knew himself to be caught in an impasse. With his various distresses tearing at his mind, he drank constantly. His writing had by now become little more than the reflex of a once powerful organism. In 1915, beside *The Little Lady of the Big House*, he had published only one short story, "A Hyperborean Brew," both of which had been written the year before. On December 1, 1914, he had written, "Yesterday I finished my last novel, *The Little Lady of the Big House*; tomorrow I begin to frame up my next novel, which I think will be entitled, 'The Box Without a Lid.'" This book was never written. "The Assassination Bureau" he abandoned in the middle as hopeless.

In January of 1916, hoping the sun would once again cure his illnesses, he and Charmian sailed for Hawaii. At the very beginning of his career he had cried out exultantly, "Socialism is the greatest thing in the world!" Only a month before he had been heading his letters "Dear Comrade" and ending them with "Yours for the Revolution." Only a few months before he had written a fervent introduction to Upton Sinclair's anthology, *The Cry for Justice,* that was an indictment of the "unfairness, cruelty, and suffering" that existed in the world. He had not allowed the betrayals of his friends or untrustworthy laborers to injure his belief in the socialized state; more militantly than ever he believed in the economic philosophy and human logic of socialism. Now, sitting in his stateroom he wrote, "I am resigning from the Socialist Party because of its lack of fire and fight, and its loss of emphasis on the class struggle. I was originally a member of the old, revolutionary, up-on-its-hind-legs, fighting Socialist Labor Party. Trained in the class struggle, I believe that the working class, by fighting, by never fusing, by never making terms with the enemy, could emancipate itself. Since the whole trend of socialism in the United States of recent years has been one of peaceableness and compromise, I find that my mind refuses further sanction of my remaining a party member. Hence my resignation."

He had done a great deal for the Cause, and the Cause had done a great deal for him. It made no difference that he thought he was quitting to go farther Left; by his resignation after fifteen years of loyal service he dealt the party a severe blow, and himself a death blow. In *Martin Eden* he had had Brissenden warn Martin that he had better tie himself to socialism, or when success came he would have no reason to continue living. In December, 1912, he had replied to an admirer, "As I said in *John Barleycorn,* I am Martin Eden. Martin Eden died because he was an individualist, I live because I am a socialist and have social consciousness."

This time Hawaii healed neither his mind nor his body. He wrote "Michael, Brother of Jerry," a few feeble Hawaiian stories, and began work on a novel about an Eurasian girl named Cherry which he never completed. He drank hard to drown his uncertainty and unhappiness . . . but they would not drown. When he returned to Glen Ellen his friends hardly knew him. Eliza said he was not the same man. He had grown fat, his ankles were swollen, his face bloated, his eyes lackluster. He who had always looked so boyish now looked many years past his age. He was morose, despondent, in pain. Only occasionally did he invite his cronies up to the ranch for a pressed duck dinner. Drifting, completely off balance, he was seen drunk in Oakland.

Shortly after his return he went to Bessie's home in Piedmont, for he at last realized that he had been cruel, that the loss of his children had been his own fault. In return for two small endowment policies which would not fall due for several years, he offered to double her allowance. Bessie accepted. The former husband and wife had a tender meeting in which he said, "If you ever need me, and I am at the end of the earth, I will come back to you." Bessie answered, "I don't think I will ever need you, Jack, but if I ever do, I will send for you."

Aside from Eliza there was only one human being he loved and trusted completely: "Nakata, for six or seven years you have been with me night and day. You have been with me through every danger over the whole world. Storm and violent death have been common in your and my experience. I remember the times in storms when you stood nobly by. I remember the hours of sickness when you nursed me. I remember the hours of fun when you laughed with me and I laughed with you." Nakata, leaving "Master" to study dentistry in San Francisco, replied, "You sheltered me and fed me, you have stayed up all night to save me when I was helpless with fish poisoning. You took your valuable time and taught me how to write and read. You have introduced me to your guests and friends as your friend and son. You have treated me as your son. This beautiful relationship was made by 'your big heart.'" And so, with Nakata, his Japanese servant, Jack found the only son, the only son's love he was to know. When Eliza said to him, "Jack, you are the loneliest man in the world. The things your heart wanted, you've never had," he demanded, "How the devil did you know?"

He had always said he wanted a short life and a merry one. He had wanted to blaze across the firmament of his age like a white streak of fire, searing the image of his thoughts into every last human mind. He had wanted to burn hard and bright and burn himself out for fear death might catch him unawares with a dollar unspent or an idea uncommunicated. He and George Sterling had always agreed they would never sit up with the corpse; when their work was done, their life spent, they would bow themselves out.

There were books he would still like to write, his "Christ" novel, his *Sailor on Horseback* autobiography, *The Farthest Distant*, a story of the days when the planet was growing cold. When he had been going strong no book had been big enough to hold everything he had had to say on the subject; nor had his fifty books been big enough to hold the force he felt within him. But he was tired. When he passed the rows of white boxes in his workroom in which he had notes for many, many more stories, he once again said to himself that he was no longer the raw recruit, he was the veteran who knew that the enemy's position would not be captured by sunrise, nor a century of sunrises.

He had fought his fight; he had done his share; he had had his say; he had earned his rest. He had made many mistakes and committed innumerable follies, but at least he had the satisfaction of knowing that they had been big ones. He had never played life "the little way." Time now to make room for the younger men who were fighting upward. Like the prize fighters he had written about, his legs were weakening, his wind was gone, he had to give way to what he had so often called "youth unquenchable and irresistible—youth that must have its will, and that will never die."

It was funny, he mused, how people became known for something they did not stand for. The critics charged his work with a lack of spirituality—he whose writing had been permeated with philosophy and the love of mankind. He had always written with two motifs—the superficial running motif, and the deep underlying motif, which only a few had ever glimpsed. When reporting the Russian-Japanese War, an official had come to his hotel and told him that a crowd was gathered in the square below to see him. He had felt enormously set up to think his fame had spread to the wilds of Korea. But when he mounted the platform that had been erected for him, the official asked if he wouldn't take out his bridge of artificial teeth. For half an hour he had stood there taking out his teeth and putting them back again to the applause of the multitude; it was then he had had his first glimpse of the fact that men rarely become famous for the things for which they strive and die.

To a young girl writing for encouragement he answered, "At my present mature age I am convinced that the game is worth the candle. I have had a very fortunate life, I have been luckier than many hundreds of millions of men of my generation have been lucky, and, while I have suffered much, I have lived much, seen much, and felt much that has been denied to the average man. Yes, indeed, the game is worth the candle. As a proof of it, my friends all tell me I am getting stout. That, in itself, is the advertisement of spiritual victory."

The long battle had been even more enjoyable than the victory; sunk by his mother's irresponsibility in the very abyss of poverty, he had fought his way upward, unaided. It had been a good brain Professor Chaney had bequeathed him, and though he had often been miserable over his illegitimacy, it had provided him with an important part of his driving power. He had a feeling that Professor Chaney would be proud of his son.

It seemed to him that the world, too, was growing old. "The world of adventure is almost over now. Even the purple ports of the seven seas have passed away, and have become prosaic." Long ago he had said, "I am an idealist who believes in reality, and who therefore, in all I write strive to be real, to keep my own feet and the feet of the readers on the ground, so that no matter how high we dream our dreams will be based on reality." He had dreamed his dreams, and they had been high dreams; and now he would face the reality that his dreams and his life were over.

Before the end the dying organism reared up for one last show of strength. He wrote "Like Argus of the Ancient Times," one of his most delightful Alaskan stories, and "The Princess," one of his best stories of The Road, flashing back to the wild adventurous days of his youth and his first success. He ordered Forni to begin work on the circular stone dairy barn, and had the sacks of cement hauled up the long road. He would send to San Francisco the very finest J.L. milk, butter, and cheese . . . and old John London too would be proud of his son. He went with Eliza to Sacramento to attend the state fair, told her they would go forward with all their plans for the ranch, that they had three of their fences built and soon they would have the fourth one built and would be self-supporting. From three different catalogues he sent to New York and England for copies of *The Siege of Rochelle, Racial Decay, Conjugal Happiness,* a copy of Dreiser's *The Genius,* Stanley's *The Congo,* and a half dozen other books on botany, evolution, California plants, monkeys, the Dutch founding of New York.

He planned to go to the Orient, reserved his steamship tickets, then canceled them. He planned to go to New York, alone, but Ninetta Payne organized the water suit against him, and he had to remain in Glen Ellen. Nearly everyone agreed he had a right to the water. On the concluding day of the trial he testified for four hours, then left the courtroom with Forni, who reports that he was ill with uremia and in great pain. A few days later he invited to luncheon all the neighbors who had signed the petition for the suit; over the friendly table they assured him they had never wanted the injunction put against him.

On Tuesday, November 21, 1916, he completed his plans to leave for New York the following day, talked quietly and alone with Eliza until nine o'clock. He said he would stop over at the Chicago stock fair, buy some good stock and ship it home. Eliza agreed to go to the fair at Pendleton, Oregon, to see if she could find some shorthorn beef cattle. He told her to put an acre of ground at every laborer's family's disposal, and to build a house on it; to select a site for the community school and to apply for a teacher. She was also to pick a site for the community store. It was his ambition to raise everything on the ranch, to make it self-sufficient, to haul nothing up the hill except flour and sugar.

Ready to retire for the night, they walked together down the long hall to his study. Eliza said, "By the time you come back I'll have the store all built and stocked, and the school all built and the teacher applied for. We'll apply to the government for a post office, and I'll put up a flagpole and we'll have a little town of our own up here, and we'll call it Independence." He put his arm about her shoulder, gave it a rough squeeze, said in deadly earnest, "I go you, old girl," walked through his study and onto his sleeping porch. Eliza went to bed.

At seven o'clock the next morning Sekine, the Japanese servant who had replaced Nakata, came running into Eliza's room with terror on his face, crying, "Missie, come quick. Master act funny, like he drunk." Eliza ran to the sleeping porch, saw at once that Jack was unconscious, telephoned to Sonoma for Doctor Allan Thomson. Doctor Thomson found Jack in a state of narcosis; he had apparently been unconscious for some time. On the floor of the room he found two empty vials labeled morphine sulphate and atropine sulphate; on the night table he found a pad with some figures on it which represented a calculation of the lethal dose of the drug. He then telephoned the druggist in Sonoma to prepare an antidote for morphine poisoning, and asked his assistant, Doctor Hayes, to bring it up with him. The two doctors washed out Jack's stomach, administered stimulants, massaged his limbs. Only once during these treatments did he seem to respond. His eyes opened slowly, his lips muttered what might have been "Hello." He then again relaxed into unconsciousness.

Doctor Thomson reports that grief-stricken Eliza worked with him as a nurse; that "in a conversation with me during the day Mrs. Charmian London [to whom Jack's 1911 will left his entire estate] said it was very important that the now probable death of Jack London should not be ascribed to anything but uremic poisoning. I told her it would be difficult to ascribe it to that alone, as any of the telephone conversations overheard that morning, or any information supplied by the druggist who prepared the antidote, would tend to ascribe his death to morphine poisoning."

Jack died at a little after seven that evening. The following day his body was taken to Oakland, where Flora, Bessie, and his two daughters held services. The whole world mourned his passing. In Europe his death was given more space than that of Emperor Franz Joseph of Austria, who had died the day before him. The grief of America is best pictured by Mrs. Luther Burbank, who picked up a newspaper and cried out to a frolicing group of young friends leaving for the University campus, "Don't laugh! Jack London is dead." Edwin Markham had called him part of the youth and heroic courage of the world; with his passing the world was bereft of a flame.

That night his body was cremated, and the ashes returned to his Beauty Ranch. Only two weeks before, while riding over a majestic knoll with Eliza, Jack had reined in his horse and said,

"Eliza, when I die I want you to bury my ashes on this hill." She put his ashes in a box, dug a hole on the very top of the knoll that was shaded from the hot sun by madrone and manzanita, buried them, and cemented over the top. There she placed the huge red stone that he had named, "The stone the builders rejected."

ACKNOWLEDGMENTS

My greatest debt is to Mrs. Charmian Kittredge London and Mrs. Eliza London Shepard, who turned over to me Jack London's private files, library, account books, papers, correspondence, notes, manuscripts, and family documents; who revoked their order to the Huntington Library that the business correspondence in their possession was not to be shown during their lifetime; and who agreed that I might write and publish about them, in relation to Jack London, anything which in my opinion seemed necessary.

Mrs. Bessie London was at all times sympathetic and helpful. Irving and Mildred Shepard have been unflagging in their efforts to aid me in documenting the life of their uncle.

I wish to express my gratitude to the host of Jack London's friends who gave unstintingly of their time, their material, and their memories: Anna Strunsky, Frank Atherton, Cloudesley Johns, Edward Applegarth, Mr. and Mrs. Johnny Miller, Fred Thompson, James Hopper, Xaviar Martinez, Upton Sinclair, Finn Frolich, Ed Morrell, Janet Winship, Austin Lewis, J. Stitt Wilson, Doctor Jessica Peixotto, Alexander Irvine, Mrs. Robert Hill, Mrs. Carrie Burlingame, Forni, Billy Hill, Ira Pyle, Blanche Partington, Mira MacClay, Thomas Hill, Doctor and Mrs. Allan Thomson.

Thanks are due to Mrs. Charmian Kittredge London's relatives for their courtesy: Mrs. Ninetta Eames-Payne, Mrs. Growall, Beth Wiley and Mrs. Wiley.

It is a pleasure to be able to express my appreciation to the people of Santa Rosa and Sonoma for their co-operation: Ang and Gertrude Franchetti, godparents of this project; Mrs. Byrd Weyler Kellogg and Senator Herbert Slater of the Santa Rosa *Press Democrat*; R. M. Barrett, Mrs. Luther Burbank, Glen Murdock, Fred Kellogg, Mrs. Paramore, and Mrs. Celeste Murphey. To Robert Pickering for his scout work.

To the efficient and courteous staffs of the Bancroft Library of the University of California and the Huntington Library of San Marino, my salutations for making research work a joy; to the public libraries of Massillon, Ohio, and Van Nuys, California, my appreciation for their helpfulness; and to the Huntington Library for turning over to me their Jack London material, my heartfelt thanks.

Presently, I am indebted to Russ Kingman of "The World of Jack London Museum and Bookstore," Glen Ellen, California, for his unflagging efforts to bring *Sailor on Horseback* abreast of modern research.

Mrs. Stone and I read and made copies of the two W. H. Chaney letters to Jack London on the Jack London Ranch during July–August 1937. The original letters have since disappeared.

Eliza Shepard led Mrs. Stone and myself to Charmian's series of diaries, starting in 1898. They were in a safe behind a secret door-panel among the bookshelves of Charmian's library. We made copies of several of these diaries. The early diaries have also since disappeared.

Dr. Allan Thomson gave me one of the morphine sulphate vials, he put it, for safekeeping. It still has four tablets left in it.

Irving Stone

Beverly Hills, California
1937, 1977

BOOK II

Jack London's Stories

INTRODUCTION

Jack London was one of a trio of colorful and similar authors who dominated literature in this country for the first sixty years of our century. The other two were F. Scott Fitzgerald and Ernest Hemingway. All three were handsome, virile, talented storytellers who lived intensely dramatic lives and had a flair for attracting world-wide attention. Since Jack London was the first of the three, since he had to come the longest distance to achieve his craft, as well as his fame, and since he probably had the most explosive effect on our American thinking, he was in many ways the most important of the group.

Jack London was born in a sentimental time. Writers were not supposed to penetrate to the truth of life, but rather to cover it with a caramel icing. To use a different figure of speech, stories were an entertainment and provided escape. What did it matter if what one were reading was romantic nonsense; wasn't that the purpose of storytelling, to gloss over harsh reality?

Not to Jack London. He was a realist and a fighter.

He was also a natural-born storyteller, but he by no means came into the world with the gift perfect or whole. It took years of con-centrated hard writing for his full talent to emerge.

We thought it might be fascinating to present a retrospective of Jack's short stories, to watch his growth from the nineteen-year-old boy who published six stories in the *Oakland High School Aegis*, in 1895, to the fully arrived artist and social thinker who created *The Call of the Wild* in 1903 and *The Apostate* in 1906.

What are Jack London's strengths as a short story writer that enable his work to endure? For he is read around the world in many languages.

There is his narrative drive. The reader turns the page excitedly, wanting to know "What happens next?" His writing is to the point so that the impact on the reader's mind is sharp and clear.

There is his superb sense of form. Every story has a beginning, a middle, and an end, in proportion and on balance. The reader feels an underlying sense of architectural structure.

There is his capacity to observe, *and to enable the reader to see.* We are drawn into the very heart of the setting, the action, the sweep of human drama, and the vagaries of fate.

There is his genius as a naturalist, or more accurately, a nature writer. His descriptions of San Francisco Bay or the terrors of the snow-packed Yukon have rarely been equaled. For the reader, they are simply unforgettable.

There is his innate and indestructible sense of justice, his bitter hatred of ignorance, poverty, enslavement, the "Iron Heel" of those in power grinding the faces of the weak. Without this quality, no writer is worth the salt to keep him alive.

There is his robust and sometimes sardonic sense of humor, or irony, which permeates a number of the stories included here, a talent long neglected by Jack London's critics.

There is his penetrating grasp of man's diverse and chaotic character, and his ability to enable us to understand motives which appear to be hopelessly enmeshed in veils of self-delusion. Because of Jack London's wisdom concerning the human condition, the miracle sometimes happens that we do not merely read his stories, *we live them*, as with *The Story of Jees Uck* or *The Odyssey of the North*. When he is writing about rough-hewn men his language is fittingly rough-hewn; but even in wilderness backgrounds he is sensitive and compassionate.

And finally, Jack London had style, which means that when he sat down at his desk to write, he was in a state of grace. A word or phrase will have become old-fashioned, but the main thrust of his writing is filled with passion, with philosophical and poetic insights, beautifully told.

Each person will have his own favorite stories. The ones that follow, within the available space and copyright restrictions, are my favorites.

Not on the basis of Jack London's best or greatest. I wanted the reader to watch and enjoy the growth of his skills. I have put at the beginning a group of four stories relating his life as a rollicking young adventurer on San Francisco Bay. We don't know precisely when they were written, since he rarely bothered to date his manuscripts. We do know that they were published by 1905. He had been asked to write some stories for young people; he not only reached back into his own youth for the adventures, *he also wrote young*.

The second section of stories is from the Yukon. Here we see Jack London make giant strides toward the mastery of his art and craft. This group has been published between January 1899 and March 1901.

Since it was my desire to afford the reader as much variety as possible, the stories in Section Three move away from the Yukon, and into San Francisco and Oakland; into humor, young love, science fiction, and sociology.

Then it is back, in Section Four, to some of Jack London's greatest stories of men, gold, cold, and the machinations of God and the devil. If we would put together in one book all of Jack London's Yukon stories to be read here, it would constitute an epic novel of the North, with each short story a chapter in the ongoing saga.

Next I have supplied Jack London's finest proletarian story, *The Apostate*, published in 1906. The material for *The Apostate* was derived from Jack London's experience while living in the East End of London in 1902, from which he derived his sociological reportage, *The People of the Abyss*.

But lastly, I wanted the reader to end this volume with an immortal classic, what nearly everyone is agreed upon as his masterpiece, *The Call of the Wild*, published in 1903. This story not only added a new phrase to the English language, it created for us a national hero, Buck, half St. Bernard, half Scotch shepherd, a dog whose intelligence and will power matched his inexhaustible physical strength; one of the best known and best loved dogs in most countries of the world. Buck is Jack London, a Jack London writing about his own life and struggles.

Does this seem strange? Not particularly. Much of our best writing is autobiographical in nature; or at least the good writer sets down those aspects of life he knows the most about. Jack London knew most about struggle, conflict, fighting one's way up in the world, achieving freedom and expression. Through the powerful dog Buck, Jack London tells us what he considers the desirable and heroic qualities in a man. When he has Buck thinking, feeling, suffering, triumphing, he has man thinking, feeling, suffering, triumphing. We are persuaded that there might not be too much difference between the mind and spirit of a man and a great-hearted dog!

Good reading!

I wish to acknowledge my indebtedness to Houghton Mifflin Company for their permission to quote from my Introduction to their Riverside Literature edition of *The Call of the Wild*.

My wife, Jean Stone, collaborated on the selection and arrangement of these stories.

Irving Stone
Beverly Hills
1977

SECTION ONE

THE KING OF THE GREEKS

BIG Alec had never been captured by the fish patrol. It was his boast that no man could take him alive, and it was his history that of the many men who had tried to take him dead none had succeeded. It was also history that at least two patrolmen who had tried to take him dead had died themselves. Further, no man violated the fish laws more systematically and deliberately than Big Alec.

He was called "Big Alec" because of his gigantic stature. His height was six feet three inches, and he was correspondingly broad-shouldered and deep-chested. He was splendidly muscled and hard as steel, and there were innumerable stories in circulation among the fisher-folk concerning his prodigious strength. He was as bold and dominant of spirit as he was strong of body, and because of this he was widely known by another name, that of "The King of the Greeks." The fishing population was largely composed of Greeks, and they looked up to him and obeyed him as their chief. And as their chief, he fought their fights for them, saw that they were protected, saved them from the law when they fell into its clutches, and made them stand by one another and himself in time of trouble.

In the old days, the fish patrol had attempted his capture many disastrous times and had finally given it over, so that when the word was out that he was coming to Benicia, I was most anxious to see him. But I did not have to hunt him up. In his usual bold way, the first thing he did on arriving was to hunt us up. Charley Le Grant and I at the time were under a patrolman named Carmintel, and the three of us were on the *Reindeer,* preparing for a trip, when Big Alec stepped aboard. Carmintel evidently knew him, for they shook hands in recognition. Big Alec took no notice of Charley or me.

"I've come down to fish sturgeon a couple of months," he said to Carmintel.

His eyes flashed with challenge as he spoke, and we noticed the patrolman's eyes drop before him.

"That's all right, Alec," Carmintel said in a low voice. "I'll not bother you. Come on into the cabin, and we'll talk things over," he added.

When they had gone inside and shut the doors after them, Charley winked with slow deliberation at me. But I was only a youngster, and new to men and the ways of some men, so I did not understand. Nor did Charley explain, though I felt there was something wrong about the business.

Leaving them to their conference, at Charley's suggestion we boarded our skiff and pulled over to the Old Steamboat Wharf, where Big Alec's ark was lying. An ark is a house-boat of small though comfortable dimensions, and is as necessary to the Upper Bay fisherman as are nets and boats. We were both curious to see Big Alec's ark, for history said that it had been the scene of more than one pitched battle, and that it was riddled with bulletholes.

We found the holes (stopped with wooden plugs and painted over), but there were not so many as I had expected. Charley noted my look of disappointment, and laughed; and then to comfort me he gave an authentic account of one expedition which had descended upon Big Alec's floating home to capture him, alive preferably, dead if necessary. At the end of half a day's fighting, the patrolmen had drawn off in wrecked boats, with one of their number killed and three wounded. And when they returned next morning with reënforcements they found only the mooring-stakes of Big Alec's ark; the ark itself remained hidden for months in the fastnesses of the Suisun tules.

"But why was he not hanged for murder?" I demanded. "Surely the United States is powerful enough to bring such a man to justice."

"He gave himself up and stood trial," Charley answered. "It cost him fifty thousand dollars to win the case, which he did on technicalities and with the aid of the best lawyers in the state. Every Greek fisherman on the river contributed to the sum. Big Alec levied and collected the tax, for all the world like a king. The United States may be all-powerful, my lad, but the fact remains that Big Alec is a king inside the United States, with a country and subjects all his own."

"But what are you going to do about his fishing for sturgeon? He's bound to fish with a 'Chinese line.'"

Charley shrugged his shoulders. "We'll see what we will see," he said enigmatically.

Now a "Chinese line" is a cunning device invented by the people whose name it bears. By a simple system of floats, weights, and anchors, thousands of hooks, each on a separate leader, are suspended at a distance of from six inches to a foot above the bottom. The remarkable thing about such a line is the hook. It is barbless, and in place of the barb, the hook is filed long and tapering to a point as sharp as that of a needle. These hooks are only a few inches apart, and when several thousand of them are suspended just above the bottom, like a fringe, for a couple of hundred fathoms, they present a formidable obstacle to the fish that travel along the bottom.

Such a fish is the sturgeon, which goes rooting along like a pig, and indeed is often called "pig-fish." Pricked by the first hook it touches, the sturgeon gives a startled leap and comes into contact with half a dozen more hooks. Then it threshes about wildly, until it receives hook after hook in its soft flesh; and the hooks, straining from many different angles, hold the luckless fish fast until it is drowned. Because no sturgeon can pass through a Chinese line, the device is called a trap in the fish laws; and because it bids fair to exterminate the sturgeon, it is branded by the fish laws as illegal. And such a line, we were confident, Big Alec intended setting, in open and flagrant violation of the law.

Several days passed after the visit of Big Alec, during which Charley and I kept a sharp watch on him. He towed his ark around the Solano Wharf and into the big bight at Turner's Shipyard. The bight we knew to be good ground for sturgeon, and there we felt sure the King of the Greeks intended to begin operations. The tide circled like a mill-race in and out of this bight, and made it possible to raise, lower, or set a Chinese line only at slack water. So between the tides Charley and I made it a point for one or the other of us to keep a lookout from the Solano Wharf.

On the fourth day I was lying in the sun behind the stringerpiece of the wharf, when I saw a skiff leave the distant shore and pull out into the bight. In an instant the glasses were at my eyes and I was following every movement of the skiff. There were two men in it, and though it was a good mile away, I made out one of them to be Big Alec; and ere the skiff returned to shore I made out enough more to know that the Greek had set his line.

"Big Alec has a Chinese line out in the bight off Turner's Shipyard," Charley Le Grant said that afternoon to Carmintel.

A fleeting expression of annoyance passed over the patrolman's face, and then he said, "Yes?" in an absent way, and that was all.

Charley bit his lip with suppressed anger and turned on his heel.

"Are you game, my lad?" he said to me later on in the evening, just as we finished washing down the *Reindeer's* decks and were preparing to turn in.

A lump came up in my throat, and I could only nod my head.

"Well, then," and Charley's eyes glittered in a determined way, "we've got to capture Big Alec between us, you and I, and we've got to do it in spite of Carmintel. Will you lend a hand?"

"It's a hard proposition, but we can do it," he added after a pause.

"Of course we can," I supplemented enthusiastically.

And then he said, "Of course we can," and we shook hands on it and went to bed.

But it was no easy task we had set ourselves. In order to convict a man of illegal fishing, it was necessary to catch him in the act with all the evidence of the crime about him—the hooks, the lines, the fish, and the man himself. This meant that we must take Big Alec on the open water, where he could see us coming and prepare for us one of the warm receptions for which he was noted.

"There's no getting around it," Charley said one morning. "If we can only get alongside it's an even toss, and there's nothing left for us but to try and get alongside. Come on, lad."

We were in the Columbia River salmon boat, the one we had used against the Chinese shrimp-catchers. Slack water had come, and as we dropped around the end of the Solano Wharf we saw Big Alec at work, running his line and removing the fish.

"Change places," Charley commanded, "and steer just astern of him as though you're going into the shipyard."

I took the tiller, and Charley sat down on a thwart amidships, placing his revolver handily beside him.

"If he begins to shoot," he cautioned, "get down in the bottom and steer from there, so that nothing more than your hand will be exposed."

I nodded, and we kept silent after that, the boat slipping gently through the water and Big Alec growing nearer and nearer. We could see him quite plainly, gaffing the sturgeon and throwing them into the boat while his companion ran the line and cleared the hooks as he dropped them back into the water. Nevertheless, we were five hundred yards away when the big fisherman hailed us.

"Here! You! What do you want?" he shouted.

"Keep going," Charley whispered, "just as though you didn't hear him."

The next few moments were very anxious ones. The fisherman was studying us sharply, while we were gliding up on him every second.

"You keep off if you know what's good for you!" he called out suddenly, as though he had made up his mind as to who and what we were. "If you don't, I'll fix you!"

He brought a rifle to his shoulder and trained it on me.

"Now will you keep off?" he demanded.

I could hear Charley groan with disappointment. "Keep off," he whispered; "it's all up for this time."

I put up the tiller and eased the sheet, and the salmon boat ran off five or six points. Big Alec watched us till we were out of his range, when he returned to his work.

"You'd better leave Big Alec alone," Carmintel said, rather sourly, to Charley that night.

"So he's been complaining to you, has he?" Charley said significantly.

Carmintel flushed painfully. "You'd better leave him alone, I tell you," he repeated. "He's a dangerous man, and it won't pay to fool with him."

"Yes," Charley answered softly; "I've heard that it pays better to leave him alone."

This was a direct thrust at Carmintel, and we could see by the expression of his face that it sank home. For it was common knowledge that Big Alec was as willing to bribe as to fight, and that of late years more than one patrolman had handled the fisherman's money.

"Do you mean to say—" Carmintel began, in a bullying tone.

But Charley cut him off shortly. "I mean to saying nothing," he said. "You heard what I said, and if the cap fits, why—"

He shrugged his shoulders, and Carmintel glowered at him, speechless.

"What we want is imagination," Charley said to me one day, when we had attempted to creep upon Big Alec in the gray of dawn and had been shot at for our trouble.

And thereafter, and for many days, I cudgelled my brains trying to imagine some possible way by which two men, on an open stretch of water, could capture another who knew how to use a rifle and was never to be found without one. Regularly, every slack water, without slyness, boldly and openly in the broad day, Big Alec was to be seen running his line. And what made it particularly exasperating was the fact that every fisherman, from Benicia to Vallejo, knew that he was successfully defying us. Carmintel also bothered us, for he kept us busy among the shad-fishers of San Pablo, so that we had little time to spare on the King of the Greeks. But Charley's wife and children lived at Benicia, and we had made the place our headquarters, so that we always returned to it.

"I'll tell you what we can do," I said, after several fruitless weeks had passed; "we can wait some slack water till Big Alec has run his line and gone ashore with the fish, and then we can go out and capture the line. It will put him to time and expense to make another, and then we'll figure to capture that too. If we can't capture him, we can discourage him, you see."

Charley saw, and said it wasn't a bad idea. We watched our chance, and the next low-water slack, after Big Alec had removed the fish from the line and returned ashore, we went out in the salmon boat. We had the bearings of the line from shore marks, and we knew we would have no difficulty in locating it. The first of the flood tide was setting in, when we ran below where we thought the line was stretched and dropped over a fishing-boat anchor. Keeping a short rope to the anchor, so that it barely touched the bottom, we dragged it slowly along until it struck and the boat fetched up hard and fast.

"We've got it," Charley cried. "Come on and lend a hand to get it in."

Together we hove up the rope till the anchor came in sight with the sturgeon line caught across one of the flukes. Scores of the murderous-looking hooks flashed into sight as we cleared the anchor, and we had just started to run along the line to the end where we could begin to lift it, when a sharp thud in the boat startled us. We looked about, but saw nothing and returned to our work. An instant later there was a similar thud and the gunwale splintered between Charley's body and mine.

"That's remarkably like a bullet, lad," he said reflectively. "And it's a long shot Big Alec's making."

"And he's using smokeless powder," he concluded, after an examination of the mile-distant shore. "That's why we can't hear the report."

I looked at the shore, but could see no sign of Big Alec, who was undoubtedly hidden in some rocky nook with us at his mercy. A third bullet struck the water, glanced, passed singing over our heads, and struck the water again beyond.

"I guess we'd better get out of this," Charley remarked coolly. "What do you think, lad?"

I thought so, too, and said we didn't want the line anyway. Whereupon we cast off and hoisted the spritsail. The bullets ceased at once, and we sailed away, unpleasantly confident that Big Alec was laughing at our discomfiture.

And more than that, the next day on the fishing wharf, where we were inspecting nets, he saw fit to laugh and sneer at us, and this before all the fishermen. Charley's face went black with anger; but beyond promising Big Alec that in the end he would surely land him behind the bars, he controlled himself and said nothing. The King of the Greeks made his boast that no fish patrol had ever taken him or ever could take him, and the fishermen cheered him and said it was true. They grew excited, and it looked like trouble for a while; but Big Alec asserted his kingship and quelled them.

Carmintel also laughed at Charley, and dropped sarcastic remarks, and made it hard for him. But Charley refused to be angered, though he told me in confidence that he intended to capture Big Alec if it took all the rest of his life to accomplish it.

"I don't know how I'll do it," he said, "but do it I will, as sure as I am Charley Le Grant. The idea will come to me at the right and proper time, never fear."

And at the right time it came, and most unexpectedly. Fully a month had passed, and we were constantly up and down the river, and down and up the bay, with no spare moments to devote to the particular fisherman who ran a Chinese line in the bight of Turner's Shipyard. We had called in at Selby's Smelter one afternoon, while on patrol work, when all unknown to us our opportunity happened along. It appeared in the guise of a helpless yacht loaded with seasick people, so we could hardly be expected to recognize it as the opportunity. It was a large sloop-yacht, and it was helpless inasmuch as the trade-wind was blowing half a gale and there were no capable sailors aboard.

From the wharf at Selby's we watched with careless interest the lubberly manœuvre performed of bringing the yacht to anchor, and the equally lubberly manœuvre of sending the small boat ashore. A very miserable-looking man in draggled ducks, after nearly swamping the boat in the heavy seas, passed us the painter and climbed out. He staggered about as though the wharf were rolling, and told us his troubles, which were the troubles of the yacht. The only rough-weather sailor aboard, the man on whom they all depended, had been called back to San Francisco by a telegram, and they had attempted to continue the cruise alone. The high wind and big seas of San Pablo Bay had been too much for them; all hands were sick, nobody knew anything or could do anything; and so they had run in to the smelter either to desert the yacht or to get somebody to bring it to Benicia. In short, did we know of any sailors who would bring the yacht into Benicia?

Charley looked at me. The *Reindeer* was lying in a snug place. We had nothing on hand in the way of patrol work till midnight. With the wind then blowing, we could sail the yacht into Benicia in a couple of hours, have several more hours ashore, and come back to the smelter on the evening train.

"All right, captain," Charley said to the disconsolate yachtsman, who smiled in sickly fashion at the title.

"I'm only the owner," he explained.

We rowed him aboard in much better style than he had come ashore, and saw for ourselves the helplessness of the passengers. There were a dozen men and women, and all of them too sick even to appear grateful at our coming. The yacht was rolling savagely, broad on, and no sooner had the owner's feet touched the deck than he collapsed and joined the others. Not one was able to bear a hand, so Charley and I between us cleared the badly tangled running gear, got up sail, and hoisted anchor.

It was a rough trip, though a swift one. The Carquinez Straits were a welter of foam and smother, and we came through them wildly before the wind, the big mainsail alternately dipping and flinging its boom skyward as we tore along. But the people did not mind. They did not mind anything. Two or three, including the owner, sprawled in the cockpit, shuddering when the yacht lifted and raced and sank dizzily into the trough, and between-whiles regarding the shore with yearning eyes. The rest were huddled on the cabin floor among the cushions. Now and again some one groaned, but for the most part they were as limp as so many dead persons.

As the bight at Turner's Shipyard opened out, Charley edged into it to get the smoother water. Benicia was in view, and we were bowling along over comparatively easy water, when a speck of a boat danced up ahead of us, directly in our course. It was low-water slack. Charley and I looked at each other. No word was spoken, but at once the yacht began a most astonishing performance, veering and yawing as though the greenest of amateurs was at the wheel. It was a sight for sailormen to see. To all appearances, a runaway yacht was careering madly over the bight, and now and again yielding a little bit to control in a desperate effort to make Benicia.

The owner forgot his seasickness long enough to look anxious. The speck of a boat grew larger and larger, till we could see Big Alec and his partner, with a turn of the sturgeon line around a cleat, resting from their labor to laugh at us. Charley pulled his sou'wester over his eyes, and I followed his example, though I could not guess the idea he evidently had in mind and intended to carry into execution.

We came foaming down abreast of the skiff, so close that we could hear above the wind the voices of Big Alec and his mate as they shouted at us with all the scorn that professional watermen feel for amateurs, especially when amateurs are making fools of themselves.

We thundered on past the fishermen, and nothing had happened. Charley grinned at the disappointment he saw in my face, and then shouted:

"Stand by the main-sheet to jibe!"

He put the wheel hard over, and the yacht whirled around obediently. The main-sheet slacked and dipped, then shot over our heads after the boom and tautened with a crash on the traveller. The yacht heeled over almost on her beam ends, and a great wail went up from the seasick passengers as they swept across the cabin floor in a tangled mass and piled into a heap in the starboard bunks.

But we had no time for them. The yacht, completing the manœuvre, headed into the wind with slatting canvas, and righted to an even keel. We were still plunging ahead, and directly in our path was the skiff. I saw Big Alec dive overboard and his mate leap for our bowsprit. Then came the crash as we struck the boat, and a series of grinding bumps as it passed under our bottom.

"That fixes his rifle," I heard Charley mutter, as he sprang upon the deck to look for Big Alec somewhere astern.

The wind and sea quickly stopped our forward movement, and we began to drift backward over the spot where the skiff had been. Big Alec's head and swarthy face popped up within arm's reach; and all unsuspecting and very angry with what he took to be the clumsiness of amateur sailors, he was hauled aboard. Also he was out of breath, for he had dived deep and stayed down long to escape our keel.

The next instant, to the perplexity and consternation of the owner, Charley was on top of Big Alec in the cockpit, and I was helping bind him with gaskets. The owner was dancing excitedly about and demanding an explanation, but by that time Big Alec's partner had crawled aft from the bowsprit and was peering apprehensively over the rail into the cockpit. Charley's arm shot around his neck and the man landed on his back beside Big Alec.

"More gaskets!" Charley shouted, and I made haste to supply them.

The wrecked skiff was rolling sluggishly a short distance to windward, and I trimmed the sheets while Charley took the wheel and steered for it.

"These two men are old offenders," he explained to the angry owner; "and they are most persistent violators of the fish and game laws. You have seen them caught in the act, and you may expect to be subpœnaed as witness for the state when the trial comes off."

As he spoke he rounded alongside the skiff. It had been torn from the line, a section of which was dragging to it. He hauled in forty or fifty feet with a young sturgeon still fast in a tangle of barbless hooks, slashed that much of the line free with his knife, and tossed it into the cockpit beside the prisoners.

"And there's the evidence, Exhibit A, for the people," Charley continued. "Look it over carefully so that you may identify it in the court-room with the time and place of capture."

And then, in triumph, with no more veering and yawing, we sailed into Benicia, the King of the Greeks bound hard and fast in the cockpit, and for the first time in his life a prisoner of the fish patrol.

WHITE AND YELLOW

SAN FRANCISCO BAY is so large that often its storms are more disastrous to ocean-going craft than is the ocean itself in its violent moments. The waters of the bay contain all manner of fish, wherefore its surface is ploughed by the keels of all manner of fishing boats manned by all manner of fishermen. To protect the fish from this motley floating population many wise laws have been passed, and there is a fish patrol to see that these laws are enforced. Exciting times are the lot of the fish patrol: in its history more than one dead patrolman has marked defeat, and more often dead fishermen across their illegal nets have marked success.

Wildest among the fisher-folk may be accounted the Chinese shrimp-catchers. It is the habit of the shrimp to crawl along the bottom in vast armies till it reaches fresh water, when it turns about and crawls back again to the salt. And where the tide ebbs and flows, the Chinese sink great bag-nets to the bottom, with gaping mouths, into which the shrimp crawls and from which it is transferred to the boiling-pot. This in itself would not be bad, were it not for the small mesh of the nets, so small that the tiniest fishes, little new-hatched things not a quarter of an inch long, cannot pass through. The beautiful beaches of Points Pedro and

Pablo, where are the shrimp-catchers' villages, are made fearful by the stench from myriads of decaying fish, and against this wasteful destruction it has ever been the duty of the fish patrol to act.

When I was a youngster of sixteen, a good sloop-sailor and all-round bay-waterman, my sloop the *Reindeer*, was chartered by the Fish Commission, and I became for the time being a deputy patrolman. After a deal of work among the Greek fishermen of the Upper Bay and rivers, where knives flashed at the beginning of trouble and men permitted themselves to be made prisoners only after a revolver was thrust in their faces, we hailed with delight an expedition to the Lower Bay against the Chinese shrimp-catchers.

There were six of us, in two boats, and to avoid suspicion we ran down after dark and dropped anchor under a projecting bluff of land known as Point Pinole. As the east paled with the first light of dawn we got under way again, and hauled close on the land breeze as we slanted across the bay toward Point Pedro. The morning mists curled and clung to the water so that we could see nothing, but we busied ourselves driving the chill from our bodies with hot coffee. Also we had to devote ourselves to the miserable task of bailing, for in some incomprehensible way the *Reindeer* had sprung a generous leak. Half the night had been spent in overhauling the ballast and exploring the seams, but the labor had been without avail. The water still poured in, and perforce we doubled up in the cockpit and tossed it out again.

After coffee, three of the men withdrew to the other boat, a Columbia River salmon boat, leaving three of us in the *Reindeer*. Then the two craft proceeded in company till the sun showed over the eastern skyline. Its fiery rays dispelled the clinging vapors, and there, before our eyes, like a picture, lay the shrimp fleet, spread out in a great half-moon, the tips of the crescent fully three miles apart, and each junk moored fast to the buoy of a shrimp-net. But there was no stir, no sign of life.

The situation dawned upon us. While waiting for slack water, in which to lift their heavy nets from the bed of the bay, the Chinese had all gone to sleep below. We were elated, and our plan of battle was swiftly formed.

"Throw each of your two men on to a junk," whispered Le Grant to me from the salmon boat. "And you make fast to a third yourself. We'll do the same, and there's no reason in the world why we shouldn't capture six junks at the least."

Then we separated. I put the *Reindeer* about on the other tack, ran up under the lee of a junk, shivered the mainsail into the wind and lost headway, and forged past the stern of the junk so slowly and so near that one of the patrolmen stepped lightly aboard. Then I kept off, filled the mainsail, and bore away for a second junk.

Up to this time there had been no noise, but from the first junk captured by the salmon boat an uproar now broke forth. There was shrill Oriental yelling, a pistol shot, and more yelling.

"It's all up. They're warning the others," said George, the remaining patrolman, as he stood beside me in the cockpit.

By this time we were in the thick of the fleet, and the alarm was spreading with incredible swiftness. The decks were beginning to swarm with half-awakened and half-naked Chinese. Cries and yells of warning and anger were flying over the quiet water, and somewhere a conch shell was being blown with great success. To the right of us I saw the captain of a junk chop away his mooring line with an axe and spring to help his crew at the hoisting of the huge, outlandish lug-sail. But to the left the first heads were popping up from below on another junk, and I rounded up the *Reindeer* alongside long enough for George to spring aboard.

The whole fleet was now under way. In addition to the sails they had gotten out long sweeps, and the bay was being ploughed in every direction by the fleeing junks. I was now alone in the *Reindeer*, seeking feverishly to capture a third prize. The first junk I took after was a clean miss, for it trimmed its sheets and shot away surprisingly into the wind. By fully half a point it outpointed the *Reindeer*, and I began to feel respect for the clumsy craft. Realizing the hopelessness of the pursuit, I filled away, threw out the main-sheet, and drove down before the wind upon the junks to leeward, where I had them at a disadvantage.

The one I had selected wavered indecisively before me, and, as I swung wide to make the boarding gentle, filled suddenly and darted away, the swart Mongols shouting a wild rhythm as they bent to the sweeps. But I had been ready for this. I luffed suddenly. Putting the tiller hard down, and holding it down with my body, I brought the main-sheet in, hand over hand, on the run, so as to retain all possible striking force. The two starboard sweeps of the junk were crumpled up, and then the two boats came together with a crash. The *Reindeer*'s bowsprit, like a monstrous head, reached over and ripped out the junk's chunky mast and towering sail.

This was met by a curdling yell of rage. A big Chinaman, remarkably evil-looking, with his head swathed in a yellow silk handkerchief and face badly pock-marked, planted a pike-pole on the *Reindeer*'s bow and began to shove the entangled boats apart. Pausing long enough to let go the jib halyards, and just as the *Reindeer* cleared and began to drift astern, I leaped aboard the junk with a line and made fast. He of the yellow handkerchief and pock-marked face came toward me threateningly, but I put my hand into my hip pocket, and he hesitated. I was unarmed, but the Chinese have learned to be fastidiously careful of American hip pockets, and it was upon this that I depended to keep him and his savage crew at a distance.

I ordered him to drop the anchor at the junk's bow, to which he replied, "No sabbe." The crew responded in like fashion, and though I made my meaning plain by signs, they refused to understand. Realizing the inexpediency of discussing the matter, I went forward myself, overran the line, and let the anchor go.

"Now get aboard, four of you," I said in a loud voice, indicating with my fingers that four of them were to go with me and the fifth was to remain by the junk. The Yellow Handkerchief hesitated; but I repeated the order fiercely (much more fiercely than I felt), at the same time sending my hand to my hip. Again the Yellow Handkerchief was overawed, and with surly looks he led three of his men aboard the *Reindeer*. I cast off at once, and, leaving the jib down, steered a course for George's junk. Here it was easier, for there were two of us, and George had a pistol to fall back on if it came to the worst. And here, as with my junk, four Chinese were transferred to the sloop and one left behind to take care of things.

Four more were added to our passenger list from the third junk. By this time the salmon boat had collected its twelve prisoners and came alongside, badly overloaded. To make matters worse, as it was a small boat, the patrolmen were so jammed in with their prisoners that they would have little chance in case of trouble.

"You'll have to help us out," said Le Grant.

I looked over my prisoners, who had crowded into the cabin and on top of it. "I can take three," I answered.

"Make it four," he suggested, "and I'll take Bill with me." (Bill was the third patrolman.) "We haven't elbow room here, and in case of a scuffle one white to every two of them will be just about the right proportion."

The exchange was made, and the salmon boat got up its sprit-sail and headed down the bay toward the marshes off San Rafael. I ran up the jib and followed with the *Reindeer*. San Rafael, where we were to turn our catch over to the authorities, communicated with the bay by way of a long and tortuous slough, or marshland creek, which could be navigated only when the tide was in. Slack water had come, and, as the ebb was commencing, there was need for hurry if we cared to escape waiting half a day for the next tide.

But the land breeze had begun to die away with the rising sun, and now came only in failing puffs. The salmon boat got out its oars and soon left us far astern. Some of the Chinese stood in the forward part of the cockpit, near the cabin doors, and once, as I leaned over the cockpit rail to flatten down the jib-sheet a bit, I felt some one brush against my hip pocket. I made no sign, but out of the corner of my eye I saw that the Yellow Handkerchief had discovered the emptiness of the pocket which had hitherto overawed him.

To make matters serious, during all the excitement of boarding the junks the *Reindeer* had not been bailed, and the water was beginning to slush over the cockpit floor. The shrimp-catchers pointed at it and looked to me questioningly.

"Yes," I said. "Bime by, allee same dlown, velly quick, you no bail now. Sabbe?"

No, they did not "sabbe," or at least they shook their heads to that effect, though they chattered most comprehendingly to one another in their own lingo. I pulled up three or four of the bottom boards, got a couple of buckets from a locker, and by unmistakable sign-language invited them to fall to. But they laughed, and some crowded into the cabin and some climbed up on top.

Their laughter was not good laughter. There was a hint of menace in it, a maliciousness which their black looks verified. The Yellow Handkerchief, since his discovery of my empty pocket, had become most insolent in his bearing, and he wormed about among the other prisoners, talking to them with great earnestness.

Swallowing my chagrin, I stepped down into the cockpit and began throwing out the water. But hardly had I begun, when the boom swung overhead, the mainsail filled with a jerk, and the *Reindeer* heeled over. The day wind was springing up. George was the veriest of landlubbers, so I was forced to give over bailing and take the tiller. The wind was blowing directly off Point Pedro and the high mountains behind, and because of this was squally and uncertain, half the time bellying the canvas out, and the other half flapping it idly.

George was about the most all-round helpless man I had ever met. Among his other disabilities, he was a consumptive, and I knew that if he attempted to bail, it might bring on a hemorrhage. Yet the rising water warned me that something must be done. Again I ordered the shrimp-catchers to lend a hand with the buckets. They laughed defiantly, and those inside the cabin, the water up to their ankles, shouted back and forth with those on top.

"You'd better get out your gun and make them bail," I said to George.

But he shook his head and showed all too plainly that he was afraid. The Chinese could see the funk he was in as well as I could, and their insolence became insufferable. Those in the cabin broke into the food lockers, and those above scrambled down and joined them in a feast on our crackers and canned goods.

"What do we care?" George said weakly.

I was fuming with helpless anger. "If they get out of hand, it will be too late to care. The best thing you can do is to get them in check right now."

The water was rising higher and higher, and the gusts, forerunners of a steady breeze, were growing stiffer and stiffer. And between the gusts, the prisoners, having gotten away with a week's grub, took to crowding first to one side and then to the other till the *Reindeer* rocked like a cockleshell. Yellow Handkerchief approached me, and, pointing out his village on the Point Pedro beach, gave me to understand that if I turned the *Reindeer* in that direction and put them ashore, they, in turn, would go to bailing. By now the water in the cabin was up to the bunks, and the bedclothes were sopping. It was a foot deep on the cockpit floor. Nevertheless I refused, and I could see by George's face that he was disappointed.

"If you don't show some nerve, they'll rush us and throw us overboard," I said to him. "Better give me your revolver, if you want to be safe."

"The safest thing to do," he chattered cravenly, "is to put them ashore. I, for one, don't want to be drowned for the sake of a handful of dirty Chinamen."

"And I, for another, don't care to give in to a handful of dirty Chinamen to escape drowning," I answered hotly.

"You'll sink the *Reindeer* under us all at this rate," he whined. "And what good that'll do I can't see."

"Every man to his taste," I retorted.

He made no reply, but I could see he was trembling pitifully. Between the threatening Chinese and the rising water he was beside himself with fright; and, more than the Chinese and the water, I feared him and what his fright might impel him to do. I could see him casting long glances at the small skiff towing astern, so in the next calm I hauled the skiff alongside. As I did so his eyes brightened with hope; but before he could guess my intention, I stove the frail bottom through with a hand-axe and the skiff filled to its gunwales.

"It's sink or float together," I said. "And if you'll give me your revolver, I'll have the *Reindeer* bailed out in a jiffy."

"They're too many for us," he whimpered. "We can't fight them all."

I turned my back on him in disgust. The salmon boat had long since passed from sight behind a little archipelago known as the Marin Islands, so no help could be looked for from that quarter. Yellow Handkerchief came up to me in a familiar manner, the water in the cockpit slushing against his legs. I did not like his looks. I felt that beneath the pleasant smile he was trying to put on his face there was an ill purpose. I ordered him back, and so sharply that he obeyed.

"Now keep your distance," I commanded, "and don't you come closer!"

"Wha' fo'?" he demanded indignantly. "I t'ink-um talkee talkee heap good."

"Talkee talkee," I answered bitterly, for I knew now that he had understood all that passed between George and me. "What for talkee talkee? You no sabbe talkee talkee."

He grinned in a sickly fashion. "Yep, I sabbe velly much. I honest Chinaman."

"All right," I answered. "You sabbe talkee talkee, then you bail water plenty plenty. After that we talkee talkee."

He shook his head, at the same time pointing over his shoulder to his comrades. "No can do. Velly bad Chinamen, heap velly bad. I t'ink-um—"

"Stand back!" I shouted, for I had noticed his hand disappear beneath his blouse and his body prepare for a spring.

Disconcerted, he went back into the cabin, to hold a council, apparently, from the way the jabbering broke forth. The *Reindeer* was very deep in the water, and her movements had grown quite loggy. In a rough sea she would have inevitably swamped; but the wind, when it did blow, was off the land, and scarcely a ripple disturbed the surface of the bay.

"I think you'd better head for the beach," George said abruptly, in a manner that told me his fear had forced him to make up his mind to some course of action.

"I think not," I answered shortly.

"I command you," he said in a bullying tone.

"I was commanded to bring these prisoners into San Rafael," was my reply.

Our voices were raised, and the sound of the altercation brought the Chinese out of the cabin.

"Now will you head for the beach?"

This from George, and I found myself looking into the muzzle of his revolver—of the revolver he dared to use on me, but was too cowardly to use on the prisoners.

My brain seemed smitten with a dazzling brightness. The whole situation, in all its bearings, was focussed sharply before me —the shame of losing the prisoners, the worthlessness and cowardice of George, the meeting with Le Grant and the other patrolmen and the lame explanation; and then there was the fight I had fought so hard, victory wrenched from me just as I thought I had it within my grasp. And out of the tail of my eye I could see the Chinese crowding together by the cabin doors and leering triumphantly. It would never do.

I threw my hand up and my head down. The first act elevated the muzzle, and the second removed my head from the path of the bullet which went whistling past. One hand closed on George's wrist, the other on the revolver. Yellow Handkerchief and his gang sprang toward me. It was now or never. Putting all my strength into a sudden effort, I swung George's body forward to meet them. Then I pulled back with equal suddenness, ripping the revolver out of his fingers and jerking him off his feet. He fell against Yellow Handkerchief's knees, who stumbled over him, and the pair wallowed in the bailing hole where the cockpit floor was torn open. The next instant I was covering them with my revolver, and the wild shrimp-catchers were cowering and cringing away.

But I swiftly discovered that there was all the difference in the world between shooting men who are attacking and men who are doing nothing more than simply refusing to obey. For obey they would not when I ordered them into the bailing hole. I threatened them with the revolver, but they sat stolidly in the flooded cabin and on the roof and would not move.

Fifteen minutes passed, the *Reindeer* sinking deeper and deeper, her mainsail flapping in the calm. But from off the Point Pedro shore I saw a dark line form on the water and travel toward us. It was the steady breeze I had been expecting so long. I called to the Chinese and pointed it out. They hailed it with exclamations. Then I pointed to the sail and to the water in the *Reindeer*, and indicated by signs that when the wind reached the sail, what of the water aboard we would capsize. But they jeered defiantly, for they knew it was in my power to luff the helm and let go the main-sheet, so as to spill the wind and escape damage.

But my mind was made up. I hauled in the main-sheet a foot or two, took a turn with it, and bracing my feet, put my back against the tiller. This left me one hand for the sheet and one for the revolver. The dark line drew nearer, and I could see them looking from me to it and back again with an apprehension they could not successfully conceal.. My brain and will and endurance were pitted against theirs, and the problem was which could stand the strain of imminent death the longer and not give in.

Then the wind struck us. The main-sheet tautened with a brisk rattling of the blocks, the boom uplifted, the sail bellied out, and the *Reindeer* heeled over—over, and over, till the lee-rail went under, the deck went under, the cabin windows went under, and the bay began to pour in over the cockpit rail. So violently had she heeled over, that the men in the cabin had been thrown on top of one another into the lee bunk, where they squirmed and twisted and were washed about, those underneath being perilously near to drowning.

The wind freshened a bit, and the *Reindeer* went over farther than ever. For the moment I thought she was gone, and I knew that another puff like that and she surely would go. While I pressed her under and debated whether I should give up or not, the Chinese cried for mercy. I think it was the sweetest sound I have ever heard. And then, and not until then, did I luff up and ease out the main-sheet. The *Reindeer* righted very slowly, and when she was on an even keel was so much awash that I doubted if she could be saved.

But the Chinese scrambled madly into the cockpit and fell to bailing with buckets, pots, pans, and everything they could lay their hands on. It was a beautiful sight to see that water flying over the side! And when the *Reindeer* was high and proud on the water once more, we dashed away with the breeze on our quarter, and at the last possible moment crossed the mud flats and entered the slough.

The spirit of the Chinese was broken, and so docile did they become that ere we made San Rafael they were out with the tow-rope, Yellow Handkerchief at the head of the line. As for George, it was his last trip with the fish patrol. He did not care for that sort of thing, he explained, and he thought a clerkship ashore was good enough for him. And we thought so, too.

DEMETRIOS CONTOS

IT must not be thought, from what I have told of the Greek fishermen, that they were altogether bad. Far from it. But they were rough men, gathered together in isolated communities and fighting with the elements for a livelihood. They lived far away from the law and its workings, did not understand it, and thought it tyranny. Especially did the fish laws seem tyrannical. And because of this, they looked upon the men of the fish patrol as their natural enemies.

We menaced their lives, or their living, which is the same thing, in many ways. We confiscated illegal traps and nets, the materials of which had cost them considerable sums and the making of which required weeks of labor. We prevented them from catching fish at many times and seasons, which was equivalent to preventing them from making as good a living as they might have made had we not been in existence. And when we captured them, they were brought into the courts of law, where heavy cash fines were collected from them. As a result, they hated us vindictively. As the dog is the natural enemy of the cat, the snake of man, so were we of the fish patrol the natural enemies of the fishermen.

But it is to show that they could act generously as well as hate bitterly that this story of Demetrios Contos is told. Demetrios Contos lived in Vallejo. Next to Big Alec, he was the largest, bravest, and most influential man among the Greeks. He had given us no trouble, and I doubt if he would ever have clashed with us had he not invested in a new salmon boat. This boat was the cause of all the trouble. He had had it built upon his own model, in which the lines of the general salmon boat were somewhat modified.

To his high elation he found his new boat very fast—in fact, faster than any other boat on the bay or rivers. Forthwith he grew proud and boastful: and, our raid with the *Mary Rebecca* on the Sunday salmon fishers having wrought fear in their hearts, he sent a challenge up to Benicia. One of the local fishermen conveyed it to us; it was to the effect that Demetrios Contos would sail up from Vallejo on the following Sunday, and in the plain sight of Benicia set his net and catch salmon, and that Charley Le Grant, patrolman, might come and get him if he could. Of course Charley and I had heard nothing of the new boat. Our own boat was pretty fast, and we were not afraid to have a brush with any other that happened along.

Sunday came. The challenge had been bruited abroad, and the fishermen and seafaring folk of Benicia turned out to a man, crowding Steamboat Wharf till it looked like the grand stand at a football match. Charley and I had been sceptical, but the fact of the crowd convinced us that there was something in Demetrios Contos's dare.

In the afternoon, when the sea-breeze had picked up in strength, his sail hove into view as he bowled along before the wind. He tacked a score of feet from the wharf, waved his hand theatrically, like a knight about to enter the lists, received a hearty cheer in return, and stood away into the Straits for a couple of hundred yards. Then he lowered sail, and, drifting the boat sidewise by means of the wind, proceeded to set his net. He did not set much of it, possibly fifty feet; yet Charley and I were thunderstruck at the man's effrontery. We did not know at the time, but we learned afterward, that the net he used was old and worthless. It *could* catch fish, true; but a catch of any size would have torn it to pieces.

Charley shook his head and said:

"I confess, it puzzles me. What if he has out only fifty feet? He could never get it in if we once started for him. And why does he come here anyway, flaunting his lawbreaking in our faces? Right in our home town, too."

Charley's voice took on an aggrieved tone, and he continued for some minutes to inveigh against the brazenness of Demetrios Contos.

In the meantime, the man in question was lolling in the stern of his boat and watching the net floats. When a large fish is meshed in a gill-net, the floats by their agitation advertise the fact. And they evidently advertised it to Demetrios, for he pulled in about a dozen feet of net, and held aloft for a moment, before he flung it into the bottom of the boat, a big, glistening salmon. It was greeted by the audience on the wharf with round after round of cheers. This was more than Charley could stand.

"Come on, lad," he called to me; and we lost no time jumping into our salmon boat and getting up sail.

The crowd shouted warning to Demetrios, and as we darted out from the wharf we saw him slash his worthless net clear with a long knife. His sail was all ready to go up, and a moment later it fluttered in the sunshine. He ran aft, drew in the sheet, and filled on the long tack toward the Contra Costa Hills.

By this time we were not more than thirty feet astern. Charley was jubilant. He knew our boat was fast, and he knew, further, that in fine sailing few men were his equals. He was confident that we should surely catch Demetrios, and I shared his confidence. But somehow we did not seem to gain.

It was a pretty sailing breeze. We were gliding sleekly through the water, but Demetrios was slowly sliding away from us. And not only was he going faster, but he was eating into the wind a fraction of a point closer than we. This was sharply impressed upon us when he went about under the Contra Costa Hills and passed us on the other tack fully one hundred feet dead to windward.

"Whew!" Charley exclaimed. "Either that boat is a daisy, or we've got a five-gallon coal-oil can fast to our keel!"

It certainly looked it one way or the other. And by the time Demetrios made the Sonoma Hills, on the other side of the Straits, we were so hopelessly outdistanced that Charley told me to slack off the sheet, and we squared away for Benicia. The fishermen on Steamboat Wharf showered us with ridicule when we returned and tied up. Charley and I got out and walked away, feeling rather sheepish, for it is a sore stroke to one's pride when he thinks he has a good boat and knows how to sail it, and another man comes along and beats him.

Charley mooned over it for a couple of days; then word was brought to us, as before, that on the next Sunday Demetrios Contos would repeat his performance. Charley roused himself. He had our boat out of the water, cleaned and repainted its bottom, made a trifling alteration about the centre-board, overhauled the running gear, and sat up nearly all of Saturday night sewing on a new and much larger sail. So large did he make it, in fact, that additional ballast was imperative, and we stowed away nearly five hundred extra pounds of old railroad iron in the bottom of the boat.

Sunday came, and with it came Demetrios Contos, to break the law defiantly in open day. Again we had the afternoon sea-breeze, and again Demetrios cut loose some forty or more feet of his rotten net, and got up sail and under way under our very noses. But he had anticipated Charley's move, and his own sail peaked higher than ever, while a whole extra cloth had been added to the after leech.

It was nip and tuck across to the Contra Costa Hills, neither of us seeming to gain or to lose. But by the time we had made the return tack to the Sonoma Hills, we could see that, while we footed it at about equal speed, Demetrios had eaten into the wind the least bit more than we. Yet Charley was sailing our boat as finely and delicately as it was possible to sail it, and getting more out of it than he ever had before.

Of course, he could have drawn his revolver and fired at Demetrios; but we had long since found it contrary to our natures to shoot at a fleeing man guilty of only a petty offence. Also a sort of tacit agreement seemed to have been reached between the patrolmen and the fishermen. If we did not shoot while they ran away, they, in turn, did not fight if we once laid hands on them. Thus Demetrios Contos ran away from us, and we did no more than try our best to overtake him; and, in turn, if our boat proved faster than his, or was sailed better, he would, we knew, make no resistance when we caught up with him.

With our large sails and the healthy breeze romping up the Carquinez Straits, we found that our sailing was what is called "ticklish." We had to be constantly on the alert to avoid a capsize, and while Charley steered I held the main-sheet in my hand with but a single turn round a pin, ready to let go at any moment. Demetrios, we could see, sailing his boat alone, had his hands full.

But it was a vain undertaking for us to attempt to catch him. Out of his inner consciousness he had evolved a boat that was better than ours. And though Charley sailed fully as well, if not the least bit better, the boat he sailed was not so good as the Greek's.

"Slack away the sheet," Charley commanded; and as our boat fell off before the wind, Demetrios's mocking laugh floated down to us.

Charley shook his head, saying, "It's no use. Demetrios has the better boat. If he tries his performance again, we must meet it with some new scheme."

This time it was my imagination that came to the rescue.

"What's the matter," I suggested, on the Wednesday following, "with my chasing Demetrios in the boat next Sunday, while you wait for him on the wharf at Vallejo when he arrives?"

Charley considered it a moment and slapped his knee.

"A good idea! You're beginning to use that head of yours. A credit to your teacher, I must say."

"But you mustn't chase him too far," he went on, the next moment, "or he'll head out into San Pablo Bay instead of running home to Vallejo, and there I'll be, standing lonely on the wharf and waiting in vain for him to arrive."

On Thursday Charley registered an objection to my plan.

"Everybody'll know I've gone to Vallejo, and you can depend upon it that Demetrios will know, too. I'm afraid we'll have to give up the idea."

This objection was only too valid, and for the rest of the day I struggled under my disappointment. But that night a new way seemed to open to me, and in my eagerness I awoke Charley from a sound sleep.

"Well," he grunted, "what's the matter? House afire?"

"No," I replied, "but my head is. Listen to this. On Sunday you and I will be around Benicia up to the very moment Demetrios's sail heaves into sight. This will lull everybody's suspicions. Then, when Demetrios's sail does heave in sight, do you stroll leisurely away and up-town. All the fishermen will think you're beaten and that you know you're beaten."

"So far, so good," Charley commented, while I paused to catch breath.

"And very good indeed," I continued proudly. "You stroll carelessly up-town, but when you're once out of sight you leg it for all you're worth for Dan Maloney's. Take the little mare of his, and strike out on the county road for Vallejo. The road's in fine condition, and you can make it in quicker time than Demetrios can beat all the way down against the wind."

"And I'll arrange right away for the mare, first thing in the morning," Charley said, accepting the modified plan without hesitation.

"But, I say," he said, a little later, this time waking *me* out of a sound sleep.

I could hear him chuckling in the dark.

"I say, lad, isn't it rather a novelty for the fish patrol to be taking to horseback?"

"Imagination," I answered. "It's what you're always preaching—'keep thinking one thought ahead of the other fellow, and you're bound to win out.'"

"He! he!" he chuckled. "And if one thought ahead, including a mare, doesn't take the other fellow's breath away this time, I'm not your humble servant, Charley Le Grant."

"But can you manage the boat alone?" he asked, on Friday. "Remember, we've a ripping big sail on her."

I argued my proficiency so well that he did not refer to the matter again till Saturday, when he suggested removing one whole cloth from the after leech. I guess it was the disappointment written on my face that made him desist; for I, also, had a pride in my boat-sailing abilities, and I was almost wild to get out alone with the big sail and go tearing down the Carquinez Straits in the wake of the flying Greek.

As usual, Sunday and Demetrios Contos arrived together. It

had become the regular thing for the fishermen to assemble on Steamboat Wharf to greet his arrival and to laugh at our discomfiture. He lowered sail a couple of hundred yards out and set his customary fifty feet of rotten net.

"I suppose this nonsense will keep up as long as his old net holds out," Charley grumbled, with intention, in the hearing of several of the Greeks.

"Den I give-a heem my old-a net-a," one of them spoke up, promptly and maliciously.

"I don't care," Charley answered. "I've got some old net myself he can have—if he'll come around and ask for it."

They all laughed at this, for they could afford to be sweet-tempered with a man so badly outwitted as Charley was.

"Well, so long, lad," Charley called to me a moment later. "I think I'll go up-town to Maloney's."

"Let me take the boat out?" I asked.

"If you want to," was his answer, as he turned on his heel and walked slowly away.

Demetrios pulled two large salmon out of his net, and I jumped into the boat. The fishermen crowded around in a spirit of fun, and when I started to get up sail overwhelmed me with all sorts of jocular advice. They even offered extravagant bets to one another that I would surely catch Demetrios, and two of them, styling themselves the committee of judges, gravely asked permission to come along with me to see how I did it.

But I was in no hurry. I waited to give Charley all the time I could, and I pretended dissatisfaction with the stretch of the sail and slightly shifted the small tackle by which the huge sprit forces up the peak. It was not until I was sure that Charley had reached Dan Maloney's and was on the little mare's back, that I cast off from the wharf and gave the big sail to the wind. A stout puff filled it and suddenly pressed the lee gunwale down till a couple of buckets of water came inboard. A little thing like this will happen to the best small-boat sailors, and yet, though I instantly let go of the sheet and righted, I was cheered sarcastically, as though I had been guilty of a very awkward blunder.

When Demetrios saw only one person in the fish patrol boat, and that one a boy, he proceeded to play with me. Making a short tack out, with me not thirty feet behind, he returned, with his sheet a little free, to Steamboat Wharf. And there he made short tacks, and turned and twisted and ducked around, to the great delight of his sympathetic audience. I was right behind him all the time, and I dared to do whatever he did, even when he squared away before the wind and jibed his big sail over—a most dangerous trick with such a sail in such a wind.

He depended upon the brisk sea breeze and the strong ebb tide, which together kicked up a nasty sea, to bring me to grief. But I was on my mettle, and never in all my life did I sail a boat better than on that day. I was keyed up to concert pitch, my brain was working smoothly and quickly, my hands never fumbled once, and it seemed that I almost divined the thousand little things which a small-boat sailor must be taking into consideration every second.

It was Demetrios who came to grief instead. Something went wrong with his centre-board, so that it jammed in the case and would not go all the way down. In a moment's breathing space, which he had gained from me by a clever trick, I saw him working impatiently with the centre-board, trying to force it down. I gave him little time, and he was compelled quickly to return to the tiller and sheet.

The centre-board made him anxious. He gave over playing with me, and started on the long beat to Vallejo. To my joy, on the first long tack across, I found that I could eat into the wind just a little bit closer than he. Here was where another man in the boat would have been of value to him; for, with me but a few feet astern, he did not dare let go the tiller and run amidships to try to force down the centre-board.

Unable to hang on as close in the eye of the wind as formerly, he proceeded to slack his sheet a trifle and to ease off a bit, in order to outfoot me. This I permitted him to do till I had worked to windward, when I bore down upon him. As I drew close, he feinted at coming about. This led me to shoot into the wind to forestall him. But it was only a feint, cleverly executed, and he held back to his course while I hurried to make up lost ground.

He was undeniably smarter than I when it came to manœuvring. Time after time I all but had him, and each time he tricked me and escaped. Besides, the wind was freshening constantly, and each of us had his hands full to avoid capsizing. As for my boat, it could not have been kept afloat but for the extra ballast. I sat cocked over the weather gunwale, tiller in one hand and sheet in the other; and the sheet, with a single turn around a pin, I was very often forced to let go in the severer puffs. This allowed the sail to spill the wind, which was equivalent to taking off so much driving power, and of course I lost ground. My consolation was that Demetrios was as often compelled to do the same thing.

The strong ebb-tide, racing down the Straits in the teeth of the wind, caused an unusually heavy and spiteful sea, which dashed aboard continually. I was dripping wet, and even the sail was wet half-way up the after leech. Once I did succeed in outmanœuvring Demetrios, so that my bow bumped into him amidships. Here was where I should have had another man. Before I could run forward and leap aboard, he shoved the boats apart with an oar, laughing mockingly in my face as he did so.

We were now at the mouth of the Straits, in a bad stretch of water. Here the Vallejo Straits and the Carquinez Straits rushed directly at each other. Through the first flowed all the water of Napa River and the great tide-lands; through the second flowed all the water of Suisun Bay and the Sacramento and San Joaquin rivers. And where such immense bodies of water, flowing swiftly, clashed together, a terrible tide-rip was produced. To make it worse, the wind howled up San Pablo Bay for fifteen miles and drove in a tremendous sea upon the tide-rip.

Conflicting currents tore about in all directions, colliding, forming whirlpools, sucks, and boils, and shooting up spitefully into hollow waves which fell aboard as often from leeward as from windward. And through it all, confused, driven into a madness of motion, thundered the great smoking seas from San Pablo Bay.

I was as wildly excited as the water. The boat was behaving splendidly, leaping and lurching through the welter like a race-horse. I could hardly contain myself with the joy of it. The huge sail, the howling wind, the driving seas, the plunging boat—I, a pygmy, a mere speck in the midst of it, was mastering the elemental strife, flying through it and over it, triumphant and victorious.

And just then, as I roared along like a conquering hero, the boat received a frightful smash and came instantly to a dead stop. I was flung forward and into the bottom. As I sprang up I caught a fleeting glimpse of a greenish, barnacle-covered object, and knew it at once for what it was, that terror of navigation, a sunken pile.

No man may guard against such a thing. Water-logged and float-ing just beneath the surface, it was impossible to sight it in the troubled water in time to escape.

The whole bow of the boat must have been crushed in, for in a few seconds the boat was half full. Then a couple of seas filled it, and it sank straight down, dragged to bottom by the heavy ballast. So quickly did it all happen that I was entangled in the sail and drawn under. When I fought my way to the surface, suffocating, my lungs almost bursting, I could see nothing of the oars. They must have been swept away by the chaotic currents. I saw Deme-trios Contos looking back from his boat, and heard the vindictive and mocking tones of his voice as he shouted exultantly. He held steadily on his course, leaving me to perish.

There was nothing to do but to swim for it, which, in that wild confusion, was at the best a matter of but a few moments. Hold-ing my breath and working with my hands, I managed to get off my heavy sea-boots and my jacket. Yet there was very little breath I could catch to hold, and I swiftly discovered that it was not so much a matter of swimming as of breathing.

I was beaten and buffeted, smashed under by the great San Pablo whitecaps, and strangled by the hollow tide-rip waves which flung themselves into my eyes, nose, and mouth. Then the strange sucks would grip my legs and drag me under, to spout me up in some fierce boiling, where, even as I tried to catch my breath, a great whitecap would crash down upon my head.

It was impossible to survive any length of time. I was breathing more water than air, and drowning all the time. My senses began to leave me, my head to whirl around. I struggled on, spas-modically, instinctively, and was barely half conscious when I felt myself caught by the shoulders and hauled over the gunwale of a boat.

For some time I lay across a seat where I had been flung, face downward, and with the water running out of my mouth. After a while, still weak and faint, I turned around to see who was my res-cuer. And there, in the stern, sheet in one hand and tiller in the other, grinning and nodding good-naturedly, sat Demetrios Contos. He had intended to leave me to drown,—he said so after-ward,—but his better self had fought the battle, conquered, and sent him back to me.

"You all-a right?" he asked.

I managed to shape a "yes" on my lips, though I could not yet speak.

"You sail-a de boat verr-a good-a," he said. "So good-a as a man."

A compliment from Demetrios Contos was a compliment indeed, and I keenly appreciated it, though I could only nod my head in acknowledgment.

We held no more conversation, for I was busy recovering and he was busy with the boat. He ran in to the wharf at Vallejo, made the boat fast, and helped me out. Then it was, as we both stood on the wharf, that Charley stepped out from behind a net-rack and put his hand on Demetrios Contos's arm.

"He saved my life, Charley," I protested; "and I don't think he ought to be arrested."

A puzzled expression came into Charley's face, which cleared immediately after, in a way it had when he made up his mind.

"I can't help it, lad," he said kindly. "I can't go back on my duty, and it's plain duty to arrest him. To-day is Sunday; there are two salmon in his boat which he caught to-day. What else can I do?"

"But he saved my life," I persisted, unable to make any other argument.

Demetrios Contos's face went black with rage when he learned Charley's judgment. He had a sense of being unfairly treated. The better part of his nature had triumphed, he had performed a generous act and saved a helpless enemy, and in return the enemy was taking him to jail.

Charley and I were out of sorts with each other when we went back to Benicia. I stood for the spirit of the law and not the letter; but by the letter Charley made his stand. As far as he could see, there was nothing else for him to do. The law said distinctly that no salmon should be caught on Sunday. He was a patrolman, and it was his duty to enforce that law. That was all there was to it. He had done his duty, and his conscience was clear. Nevertheless, the whole thing seemed unjust to me, and I felt very sorry for Demetrios Contos.

Two days later we went down to Vallejo to the trial. I had to go along as a witness, and it was the most hateful task that I ever performed in my life when I testified on the witness stand to seeing Demetrios catch the two salmon Charley had captured him with.

Demetrios had engaged a lawyer, but his case was hopeless. The jury was out only fifteen minutes, and returned a verdict of guilty. The judge sentenced Demetrios to pay a fine of one hundred dollars or go to jail for fifty days.

Charley stepped up to the clerk of the court. "I want to pay that fine," he said, at the same time placing five twenty-dollar gold pieces on the desk. "It—it was the only way out of it, lad," he stammered, turning to me.

The moisture rushed into my eyes as I seized his hand. "I want to pay—" I began.

"To pay your half?" he interrupted. "I certainly shall expect you to pay it."

In the meantime Demetrios had been informed by his lawyer that his fee likewise had been paid by Charley.

Demetrios came over to shake Charley's hand, and all his warm Southern blood flamed in his face. Then, not to be outdone in generosity, he insisted on paying his fine and lawyer's fee himself, and flew half-way into a passion because Charley refused to let him.

More than anything else we ever did, I think, this action of Charley's impressed upon the fishermen the deeper significance of the law. Also Charley was raised high in their esteem, while I came in for a little share of praise as a boy who knew how to sail a boat. Demetrios Contos not only never broke the law again, but he became a very good friend of ours, and on more than one occasion he ran up to Benicia to have a gossip with us.

THE LOST POACHER

"BUT they won't take excuses. You're across the line, and that's enough. They'll take you. In you go, Siberia and the salt-mines. And as for Uncle Sam, why, what's he to know about it? Never a word will get back to the States. 'The *Mary Thomas,*' the papers will say, 'the *Mary Thomas* lost with all hands. Probably in a typhoon in the Japanese seas.' That's what the papers will say, and people, too. In you go, Siberia and the salt-mines. Dead to the world and kith and kin, though you live fifty years."

In such manner John Lewis, commonly known as the "sea-lawyer," settled the matter out of hand.

It was a serious moment in the forecastle of the *Mary Thomas.* No sooner had the watch below begun to talk the trouble over, than the watch on deck came down and joined them. As there was no wind, every hand could be spared with the exception of the man at the wheel, and he remained only for the sake of discipline. Even "Bub" Russell, the cabinboy, had crept forward to hear what was going on.

However, it was a serious moment, as the grave faces of the sailors bore witness. For the three preceding months the *Mary Thomas* sealing schooner, had hunted the seal pack along the coast of Japan and north to Bering Sea. Here, on the Asiatic side of the sea, they were forced to give over the chase, or rather, to go no farther; for beyond, the Russian cruisers patrolled forbidden ground, where the seals might breed in peace.

A week before she had fallen into a heavy fog accompanied by calm. Since then the fog-bank had not lifted, and the only wind had been light airs and catspaws. This in itself was not so bad, for the sealing schooners are never in a hurry so long as they are in the midst of the seals; but the trouble lay in the fact that the current at this point bore heavily to the north. Thus the *Mary Thomas* had unwittingly drifted across the line, and every hour she was penetrating, unwillingly, farther and farther into the dangerous waters where the Russian bear kept guard.

How far she had drifted no man knew. The sun had not been visible for a week, nor the stars, and the captain had been unable to take observations in order to determine his position. At any moment a cruiser might swoop down and hale the crew away to Siberia. The fate of other poaching seal-hunters was too well known to the men of the *Mary Thomas*, and there was cause for grave faces.

"Mine friends," spoke up a German boat-steerer, "it vas a pad piziness. Shust as ve make a big catch, und all honest, somedings go wrong, und der Russians nab us, dake our skins and our schooner, und send us mit der anarchists to Siberia. Ach! a pretty pad piziness!"

"Yes, that's where it hurts," the sea-lawyer went on. "Fifteen hundred skins in the salt piles, and all honest, a big pay-day coming to every man Jack of us, and then to be captured and lose it all! It'd be different if we'd been poaching, but it's all honest work in open water."

"But if we haven't done anything wrong, they can't do anything to us, can they?" Bub queried.

"It strikes me as 'ow it ain't the proper thing for a boy o' your age shovin' in when 'is elders is talkin'," protested an English sailor, from over the edge of his bunk.

"Oh, that's all right, Jack," answered the sea-lawyer. "He's a perfect right to. Ain't he just as liable to lose his wages as the rest of us?"

"Wouldn't give thruppence for them!" Jack sniffed back. He

had been planning to go home and see his family in Chelsea when he was paid off, and he was now feeling rather blue over the highly possible loss, not only of his pay, but of his liberty.

"How are they to know?" the sea-lawyer asked in answer to Bub's previous question. "Here we are in forbidden water. How do they know but what we came here of our own accord? Here we are, fifteen hundred skins in the hold. How do they know whether we got them in open water or in the closed sea? Don't you see, Bub, the evidence is all against us. If you caught a man with his pockets full of apples like those which grow on your tree, and if you caught him in your tree besides, what'd you think if he told you he couldn't help it, and had just been sort of blown there, and that anyway those apples came from some other tree—what'd you think, eh?"

Bub saw it clearly when put in that light, and shook his head despondently.

"You'd rather be dead than go to Siberia," one of the boat-pullers said. "They put you into the salt-mines and work you till you die. Never see daylight again. Why, I've heard tell of one fellow that was chained to his mate, and that mate died. And they were both chained together! And if they send you to the quicksilver mines you get salivated. I'd rather be hung than salivated."

"Wot's salivated?" Jack asked, suddenly sitting up in his bunk at the hint of fresh misfortunes.

"Why, the quicksilver gets into your blood; I think that's the way. And your gums all swell like you had the scurvy, only worse, and your teeth get loose in your jaws. And big ulcers form, and then you die horrible. The strongest man can't last long a-mining quicksilver."

"A pad piziness," the boat-steerer reiterated, dolorously, in the silence which followed. "A pad piziness. I vish I was in Yokohama. Eh? Vot vas dot?"

The vessel had suddenly heeled over. The decks were aslant. A tin pannikin rolled down the inclined plane, rattling and banging. From above came the slapping of canvas and the quivering rat-tat-tat of the after leech of the loosely stretched foresail. Then the mate's voice sang down the hatch, "All hands on deck and make sail!"

Never had such summons been answered with more enthusiasm. The calm had broken. The wind had come which was to carry them south into safety. With a wild cheer all sprang on deck. Working with mad haste, they flung out topsails, flying jibs and staysails. As they worked, the fog-bank lifted and the black vault of heaven, bespangled with the old familiar stars, rushed into view. When all was ship-shape, the *Mary Thomas* was lying gallantly over on her side to a beam wind and plunging ahead due south.

"Steamer's lights ahead on the port bow, sir!" cried the lookout from his station on the forecastle-head. There was excitement in the man's voice.

The captain sent Bub below for his night-glasses. Everybody crowded to the lee-rail to gaze at the suspicious stranger, which already began to loom up vague and indistinct. In those unfrequented waters the chance was one in a thousand that it could be anything else than a Russian patrol. The captain was still anxiously gazing through the glasses, when a flash of flame left the stranger's side, followed by the loud report of a cannon. The worst fears were confirmed. It was a patrol, evidently firing across the bows of the *Mary Thomas* in order to make her heave to.

"Hard down with your helm!" the captain commanded the steersman, all the life gone out of his voice. Then to the crew, "Back over the jib and foresail! Run down the flying jib! Clew up the foretopsail! And aft here and swing on to the main-sheet!"

The *Mary Thomas* ran into the eye of the wind, lost headway, and fell to courtesying gravely to the long seas rolling up from the west.

The cruiser steamed a little nearer and lowered a boat. The sealers watched in heart-broken silence. They could see the white bulk of the boat as it was slacked away to the water, and its crew sliding aboard. They could hear the creaking of the davits and the commands of the officers. Then the boat sprang away under the impulse of the oars, and came toward them. The wind had been rising, and already the sea was too rough to permit the frail craft to lie alongside the tossing schooner; but watching their chance, and taking advantage of the boarding ropes thrown to them, an officer and a couple of men clambered aboard. The boat then sheered off into safety and lay to its oars, a young midshipman, sitting in the stern and holding the yoke-lines, in charge.

The officer, whose uniform disclosed his rank as that of second lieutenant in the Russian navy, went below with the captain of the *Mary Thomas* to look at the ship's papers. A few minutes later he emerged, and upon his sailors removing the hatch-covers, passed down into the hold with a lantern to inspect the salt piles. It was a goodly heap which confronted him—fifteen hundred fresh skins, the season's catch; and under the circumstances he could have had but one conclusion.

"I am very sorry," he said, in broken English to the sealing captain, when he again came on deck, "but it is my duty, in the name of the tsar, to seize your vessel as a poacher caught with fresh skins in the closed sea. The penalty, as you may know, is confiscation and imprisonment."

The captain of the *Mary Thomas* shrugged his shoulders in seeming indifference, and turned away. Although they may restrain all outward show, strong men, under unmerited misfortune, are sometimes very close to tears. Just then the vision of his little California home, and of the wife and two yellow-haired boys, was strong upon him, and there was a strange, choking sensation in his throat, which made him afraid that if he attempted to speak he would sob instead.

And also there was upon him the duty he owed his men. No weakness before them, for he must be a tower of strength to sustain them in misfortune. He had already explained to the second lieutenant, and knew the hopelessness of the situation. As the sea-lawyer had said, the evidence was all against him. So he turned aft, and fell to pacing up and down the poop of the vessel over which he was no longer commander.

The Russian officer now took temporary charge. He ordered more of his men aboard, and had all the canvas clewed up and furled snugly away. While this was being done, the boat plied back and forth between the two vessels, passing a heavy hawser, which was made fast to the great towing-bitts on the schooner's forecastle-head. During all this work the sealers stood about in sullen groups. It was madness to think of resisting, with the guns of a man-of-war not a biscuit-toss away; but they refused to lend a hand, preferring instead to maintain a gloomy silence.

Having accomplished his task, the lieutenant ordered all but four of his men back into the boat. Then the midshipman, a lad of sixteen, looking strangely mature and dignified in his uniform and sword, came aboard to take command of the captured sealer. Just as the lieutenant prepared to depart, his eyes chanced to alight upon Bub. Without a word of warning, he seized him by the arm and dropped him over the rail into the waiting boat; and then, with a parting wave of his hand, he followed him.

It was only natural that Bub should be frightened at this unexpected happening. All the terrible stories he had heard of the Russians served to make him fear them, and now returned to his mind with double force. To be captured by them was bad enough, but to be carried off by them, away from his comrades, was a fate of which he had not dreamed.

"Be a good boy, Bub," the captain called to him, as the boat drew away from the *Mary Thomas*'s side, "and tell the truth!"

"Aye, aye, sir!" he answered, bravely enough by all outward appearance. He felt a certain pride of race, and was ashamed to be a coward before these strange enemies, these wild Russian bears.

"Und be politeful!" the German boat-steerer added, his rough voice lifting across the water like a fog-horn.

Bub waved his hand in farewell, and his mates clustered along the rail as they answered with a cheering shout. He found room in the stern-sheets, where he fell to regarding the lieutenant. He didn't look so wild or bearish, after all—very much like other men, Bub concluded, and the sailors were much the same as all other man-of-war's men he had ever known. Nevertheless, as his feet struck the steel deck of the cruiser, he felt as if he had entered the portals of a prison.

For a few minutes he was left unheeded. The sailors hoisted the boat up, and swung it in on the davits. Then great clouds of black smoke poured out of the funnels, and they were under way—to Siberia, Bub could not help but think. He saw the *Mary Thomas* swing abruptly into line as she took the pressure from the hawser, and her side-lights, red and green, rose and fell as she was towed through the sea.

Bub's eyes dimmed at the melancholy sight, but—but just then the lieutenant came to take him down to the commander, and he straightened up and set his lips firmly, as if this were a very commonplace affair and he were used to being sent to Siberia every day in the week. The cabin in which the commander sat was like a palace compared to the humble fittings of the *Mary Thomas*, and the commander himself, in gold lace and dignity, was a most august personage, quite unlike the simple man who navigated his schooner on the trail of the seal pack.

Bub now quickly learned why he had been brought aboard, and in the prolonged questioning which followed, told nothing but the plain truth. The truth was harmless; only a lie could have injured his cause. He did not know much, except that they had been sealing far to the south in open water, and that when the calm and fog came down upon them, being close to the line, they had drifted across. Again and again he insisted that they had not lowered a boat or shot a seal in the week they had been drifting about in the forbidden sea; but the commander chose to consider all that he said to be a tissue of falsehoods, and adopted a bullying tone in an effort to frighten the boy. He threatened and cajoled by turns, but failed in the slightest to shake Bub's statements, and at last ordered him out of his presence.

By some oversight, Bub was not put in anybody's charge, and wandered up on deck unobserved. Sometimes the sailors, in passing, bent curious glances upon him, but otherwise he was left strictly alone. Nor could he have attracted much attention, for he was small, the night dark, and the watch on deck intent on its own business. Stumbling over the strange decks, he made his way aft where he could look upon the side-lights of the *Mary Thomas*, following steadily in the rear.

For a long while he watched, and then lay down in the darkness close to where the hawser passed over the stern to the captured schooner. Once an officer came up and examined the straining rope to see if it were chafing, but Bub cowered away in the shadow undiscovered. This, however, gave him an idea which concerned the lives and liberties of twenty-two men, and which was to avert crushing sorrow from more than one happy home many thousand miles away.

In the first place, he reasoned, the crew were all guiltless of any crime, and yet were being carried relentlessly away to imprisonment in Siberia—a living death, he had heard, and he believed it implicitly. In the second place, he was a prisoner, hard and fast, with no chance of escape. In the third, it was possible for the twenty-two men on the *Mary Thomas* to escape. The only thing which bound them was a four-inch hawser. They dared not cut it at their end, for a watch was sure to be maintained upon it by their Russian captors; but at this end, ah! at his end——

Bub did not stop to reason further. Wriggling close to the hawser, he opened his jackknife and went to work. The blade was not very sharp, and he sawed away, rope-yarn by rope-yarn, the awful picture of the solitary Siberian exile he must endure growing clearer and more terrible at every stroke. Such a fate was bad enough to undergo with one's comrades, but to face it alone seemed frightful. And besides, the very act he was performing was sure to bring greater punishment upon him.

In the midst of such somber thoughts, he heard footsteps approaching. He wriggled away into the shadow. An officer stopped where he had been working, half-stooped to examine the hawser, then changed his mind and straightened up. For a few minutes he stood there, gazing at the lights of the captured schooner, and then went forward again.

Now was the time! Bub crept back and went on sawing. Now two parts were severed. Now three. But one remained. The tension upon this was so great that it readily yielded. Splash! The freed end went overboard. He lay quietly, his heart in his mouth, listening. No one on the cruiser but himself had heard.

He saw the red and green lights of the *Mary Thomas* grow dimmer and dimmer. Then a faint hallo came over the water from the Russian prize crew. Still nobody heard. The smoke continued to pour out of the cruiser's funnels, and her propellers throbbed as mightily as ever.

What was happening on the *Mary Thomas?* Bub could only surmise; but of one thing he was certain: his comrades would assert themselves and overpower the four sailors and the midshipman. A few minutes later he saw a small flash, and straining his ears heard the very faint report of a pistol. Then, oh joy! both the red and green lights suddenly disappeared. The *Mary Thomas* was retaken!

Just as an officer came aft, Bub crept forward, and hid away in one of the boats. Not an instant too soon. The alarm was given. Loud voices rose in command. The cruiser altered her course. An electric search-light began to throw its white rays across the sea, here, there, everywhere; but in its flashing path no tossing schooner was revealed.

Bub went to sleep soon after that, nor did he wake till the gray of dawn. The engines were pulsing monotonously, and the water, splashing noisily, told him the decks were being washed down. One sweeping glance, and he saw that they were alone on the expanse of ocean. The *Mary Thomas* had escaped. As he lifted his head, a roar of laughter went up from the sailors. Even the officer, who ordered him taken below and locked up, could not quite conceal the laughter in his eyes. Bub thought often in the days of confinement which followed, that they were not very angry with him for what he had done.

He was not far from right. There is a certain innate nobility deep down in the hearts of all men, which forces them to admire a brave act, even if it is performed by an enemy. The Russians were in nowise different from other men. True, a boy had outwitted them; but they could not blame him, and they were sore puzzled as to what to do with him. It would never do to take a little mite like him in to represent all that remained of the lost poacher.

So, two weeks later, a United States man-of-war, steaming out of the Russian port of Vladivostok, was signaled by a Russian cruiser. A boat passed between the two ships, and a small boy dropped over the rail upon the deck of the American vessel. A week later he was put ashore at Hakodate, and after some telegraphing, his fare was paid on the railroad to Yokohama.

From the depot he hurried through the quaint Japanese streets to the harbor, and hired a *sampan* boatman to put him aboard a certain vessel whose familiar rigging had quickly caught his eye. Her gaskets were off, her sails unfurled; she was just starting back to the United States. As he came closer, a crowd of sailors sprang upon the forecastle head, and the windlass-bars rose and fell as the anchor was torn from its muddy bottom.

"'Yankee ship come down the ribber!'" the sea-lawyer's voice rolled out as he led the anchor song.

"'Pull, my bully boys, pull!'" roared back the old familiar chorus, the men's bodies lifting and bending to the rhythm.

Bub Russell paid the boatman and stepped on deck. The

anchor was forgotten. A mighty cheer went up from the men, and almost before he could catch his breath he was on the shoulders of the captain, surrounded by his mates, and endeavoring to answer twenty questions to the second.

The next day a schooner hove to off a Japanese fishing village, sent ashore four sailors and a little midshipman, and sailed away. These men did not talk English, but they had money and quickly made their way to Yokohama. From that day the Japanese village folk never heard anything more about them, and they are still a much-talked-of mystery. As the Russian government never said anything about the incident, the United States is still ignorant of the whereabouts of the lost poacher, nor has she ever heard, officially, of the way in which some of her citizens "shanghaied" five subjects of the tsar. Even nations have secrets sometimes.

SECTION TWO

"CARMEN won't last more than a couple of days." Mason spat out a chunk of ice and surveyed the poor animal ruefully, then put her foot in his mouth and proceeded to bite out the ice which clustered cruelly between the toes.

"I never saw a dog with a highfalutin' name that ever was worth a rap," he said, as he concluded his task and shoved her aside. "They just fade away and die under the responsibility. Did ye ever see one go wrong with a sensible name like Cassiar, Siwash, or Husky? No, sir! Take a look at Shookum here, he's——"

Snap! The lean brute flashed up, the white teeth just missing Mason's throat.

"Ye will, will ye?" A shrewd clout behind the ear with the butt of the dog whip stretched the animal in the snow, quivering softly, a yellow slaver dripping from its fangs.

"As I was saying, just look at Shookum here—he's got the spirit. Bet ye he eats Carmen before the week's out."

"I'll bank another proposition against that," replied Malemute Kid, reversing the frozen bread placed before the fire to thaw. "We'll eat Shookum before the trip is over. What d'ye say, Ruth?"

The Indian woman settled the coffee with a piece of ice, glanced from Malemute Kid to her husband, then at the dogs, but vouchsafed no reply. It was such a palpable truism that none was necessary. Two hundred miles of unbroken trail in prospect, with a scant six days' grub for themselves and none for the dogs, could admit no other alternative. The two men and the woman grouped about the fire and began their meager meal. The dogs lay in their harnesses, for it was a midday halt, and watched each mouthful enviously.

"No more lunches after today," said Malemute Kid. "And we've got to keep a close eye on the dogs—they're getting vicious. They'd just as soon pull a fellow down as not, if they get a chance."

"And I was president of an Epworth once, and taught in the Sunday school." Having irrelevantly delivered himself of this, Mason fell into a dreamy contemplation of his steaming moccasins, but was aroused by Ruth filling his cup. "Thank God, we've got slathers of tea! I've seen it growing, down in Tennessee. What wouldn't I give for a hot corn pone just now! Never mind, Ruth; you won't starve much longer, nor wear moccasins either."

The woman threw off her gloom at this, and in her eyes welled up a great love for her white lord—the first white man she had ever seen—the first man whom she had known to treat a woman as something better than a mere animal or beast of burden.

"Yes, Ruth," continued her husband, having recourse to the macaronic jargon in which it was alone possible for them to understand each other; "wait till we clean up and pull for the Outside. We'll take the White Man's canoe and go to the Salt Water. Yes, bad water, rough water—great mountains dance up and down all the time. And so big, so far, so far away—you travel ten sleep, twenty sleep, forty sleep"—he graphically enumerated the days on his fingers—"all the time water, bad water. Then you come to great village, plenty people, just the same mosquitoes next summer. Wigwams oh, so high—ten, twenty pines. Hi-yu skookum!"

He paused impotently, cast an appealing glance at Malemute Kid, then laboriously placed the twenty pines, end on end, by sign language. Malemute Kid smiled with cheery cynicism; but Ruth's eyes were wide with wonder, and with pleasure; for she half believed he was joking, and such condescension pleased her poor woman's heart.

"And then you step into a—a box, and pouf! up you go." He tossed his empty cup in the air by way of illustration and, as he deftly caught it, cried: "And biff! down you come. Oh, great medicine men! You go Fork Yukon, I go Arctic City—twenty-five sleep—bit string, all the time—I catch him string—I say, "Hello, Ruth! How are ye?'—and you say, 'Is that my good husband?'— and I say, 'Yes'—and you say, 'No can bake good bread, no more soda'—then I say, 'Look in cache, under flour; good-by,' You look and catch plenty soda. All the time you Fort Yukon, me Arctic City. Hi-yu medicine man!"

Ruth smiled so ingenuously at the fairy story that both men burst into laughter. A row among the dogs cut short the wonders of the Outside, and by the time the snarling combatants were separated, she had lashed the sleds and all was ready for the trail.

"Mush! Baldy! Hi! Mush on!" Mason worked his whip smartly and, as the dogs whined low in the traces, broke out the sled with the gee pole. Ruth followed with the second team, leaving Malemute Kid, who had helped her start, to bring up the rear. Strong man, brute that he was, capable of felling an ox at a blow, he could not bear to beat the poor animals, but humored them as a dog driver rarely does—nay, almost wept with them in their misery.

"Come, mush on there, you poor sore-footed brutes!" he murmured, after several ineffectual attempts to start the load. But his patience was at last rewarded, and though whimpering with pain, they hastened to join their fellows.

No more conversation; the toil of the trail will not permit such extravagance. And of all deadening labors, that of the Northland trail is the worst. Happy is the man who can weather a day's travel at the price of silence, and that on a beaten track.

And of all heartbreaking labors, that of breaking trail is the worst. At every step the great webbed shoe sinks till the snow is level with the knee. Then up, straight up, the deviation of a fraction of an inch being a certain precursor of disaster, the snowshoe must be lifted till the surface is cleared; then forward, down, and the other foot is raised perpendicularly for the matter of half a yard. He who tries this for the first time, if haply he avoids bringing his shoes in dangerous propinquity and measures not his length on the treacherous footing, will give up exhausted at the end of a hundred yards; he who can keep out of the way of the dogs for a whole day may well crawl into his sleeping bag with a clear conscience and a pride which passeth all understanding; and he who travels twenty sleeps on the Long Trail is a man whom the gods may envy.

The afternoon wore on, and with the awe, born of the White Silence, the voiceless travelers bent to their work. Nature has many tricks wherewith she convinces man of his finity—the ceaseless flow of the tides, the fury of the storm, the shock of the earthquake, the long roll of heaven's artillery—but the most tremendous, the most stupefying of all, is the passive phase of the White Silence. All movement ceases, the sky clears, the heavens are as brass; the slightest whisper seems sacrilege, and man becomes timid, affrighted at the sound of his own voice. Sole speck of life journeying across the ghostly wastes of a dead world, he trembles at his audacity, realizes that his is a maggot, life, nothing more. Strange thoughts arise unsummoned, and the mystery of all things strives for utterance. And the fear of death, of God, of the universe, comes over him—the hope of the Resurrection and the Life, the yearning for immortality, the vain striving of the imprisoned essence—it is then, if ever, man walks alone with God.

So wore the day away. The river took a great bend, and Mason headed his team for the cutoff across the narrow neck of land. But the dogs balked at the high bank. Again and again, though Ruth and Malemute Kid were shoving on the sled, they slipped back. Then came the concerted effort. The miserable creatures, weak from hunger, exerted their last strength. Up—up—the sled poised on the top of the bank; but the leader swung the string of dogs behind him to the right, fouling Mason's snowshoes. The result was grievous. Mason was whipped off his feet; one of the dogs fell in the traces; and the sled toppled back, dragging everything to the bottom again.

Slash! the whip fell among the dogs savagely, especially upon the one which had fallen.

"Don't, Mason," entreated Malemute Kid; "the poor devil's on its last legs. Wait and we'll put my team on."

Mason deliberately withheld the whip till the last word had fallen, then out flashed the long lash, completely curling about the offending creature's body. Carmen—for it was Carmen—cowered in the snow, cried piteously, then rolled over on her side.

It was a tragic moment, a pitiful incident of the trail—a dying dog, two comrades in anger. Ruth glanced solicitously from man to man. But Malemute Kid restrained himself, though there was a world of reproach in his eyes, and, bending over the dog, cut the traces. No word was spoken. The teams were double-spanned and the difficulty overcome; the sleds were under way again, the dying dog dragging herself along in the rear. As long as an animal can travel, it is not shot, and this last chance is accorded it—the crawling into camp, if it can, in the hope of a moose being killed.

Already penitent for his angry action, but too stubborn to make amends, Mason toiled on at the head of the cavalcade, little dreaming that danger hovered in the air. The timber clustered thick in the sheltered bottom, and through this they threaded their way. Fifty feet or more from the trail towered a lofty pine. For generations it had stood there, and for generations destiny had had this one end in view—perhaps the same had been decreed of Mason.

He stooped to fasten the loosened thong of his moccasin. The sleds came to a halt, and the dogs lay down in the snow without a whimper. The stillness was weird; not a breath rustled the frost-encrusted forest; the cold and silence of outer space had chilled the heart and smote the trembling lips of nature. A sigh pulsed through the air—they did not seem to actually hear it, but rather felt it, like the premonition of movement in a motionless void. Then the great tree, burdened with its weight of years and snow, played its last part in the tragedy of life. He heard the warning crash and attempted to spring up but, almost erect, caught the blow squarely on the shoulder.

The sudden danger, the quick death—how often had Malemute Kid faced it! The pine needles were still quivering as he gave his commands and sprang into action. Nor did the Indian girl faint or raise her voice in idle wailing, as might many of her white sisters. At his order, she threw her weight on the end of a quickly extemporized handspike, easing the pressure and listening to her husband's groans, while Malemute Kid attacked the tree with his ax.

The steel rang merrily as it bit into the frozen trunk, each stroke being accompanied by a forced, audible respiration, the "Huh!" "Huh!" of the woodsman.

At last the Kid laid the pitiable thing that was once a man in the snow. But worse than his comrade's pain was the dumb anguish in the woman's face, the blended look of hopeful, hopeless query. Little was said; those of the Northland are early taught the futility of words and the inestimable value of deeds. With the temperature at sixty-five below zero, a man cannot lie many minutes in the snow and live. So the sled lashings were cut, and the sufferer, rolled in furs, laid on a couch of boughs. Before him roared a fire, built of the very wood which wrought the mishap. Behind and partially over him was stretched the primitive fly—a piece of canvas, which caught the radiating heat and threw it back and down upon him—a trick which men may know who study physics at the fount.

And men who have shared their bed with death know when the call is sounded. Mason was terribly crushed. The most cursory examination revealed it. His right arm, leg, and back were broken; his limbs were paralyzed from the hips; and the likelihood of internal injuries was large. An occasional moan was his only sign of life.

No hope; nothing to be done. The pitiless night crept slowly by —Ruth's portion, the despairing stoicism of her race, and Malemute Kid adding new lines to his face of bronze. In fact, Mason suffered least of all, for he spent his time in eastern Tennessee, in the Great Smoky Mountains, living over the scenes of his childhood. And most pathetic was the melody of his long-forgotten Southern vernacular, as he raved of swimming holes and coon hunts and watermelon raids. It was as Greek to Ruth, but the Kid understood and felt—felt as only one can feel who has been shut out for years from all that civilization means.

Morning brought consciousness to the stricken man, and Malemute Kid bent closer to catch his whispers.

"You remember when we foregathered on the Tanana, four years come next ice run? I didn't care so much for her then. It was more like she was pretty, and there was a smack of excitement about it, I think. But d'ye know, I've come to think a heap of her. She's been a good wife to me, always at my shoulder in the pinch.

And when it comes to trading, you know there isn't her equal. D'ye recollect the time she shot the Moosehorn Rapids to pull you and me off that rock, the bullets whipping the water like hailstones?—and the time of the famine at Nuklukyeto?—or when she raced the ice run to bring the news? Yes, she's been a good wife to me, better'n that other one. Didn't know I'd been there? Never told you, eh? Well, I tried it once, down in the States. That's why I'm here. Been raised together, too. I came away to give her a chance for divorce. She got it.

"But that's got nothing to do with Ruth. I had thought of cleaning up and pulling for the Outside next year—her and I—but it's too late. Don't send her back to her people, Kid. It's beastly hard for a woman to go back. Think of it!—nearly four years on our bacon and beans and flour and dried fruit, and then to go back to her fish and caribou. It's not good for her to have tried our ways, to come to know they're better'n her people's, and then return to them. Take care of her, Kid—why don't you—but no, you always fought shy of them—and you never told me why you came to this country. Be kind to her, and send her back to the States as soon as you can. But fix it so she can come back—liable to get homesick, you know.

"And the youngster—it's drawn us closer, Kid. I only hope it is a boy. Think of it!—flesh of my flesh, Kid. He mustn't stop in this country. And if it's a girl, why, she can't. Sell my furs; they'll fetch at least five thousand, and I've got as much more with the company. And handle my interests with yours. I think that bench claim will show up. See that he gets a good schooling; and, Kid, above all, don't let him come back. This country was not made for white men.

"I'm a gone man, Kid. Three or four sleeps at the best. You've got to go on. You must go on! Remember, it's my wife, it's my boy—O God! I hope it's a boy! You can't stay by me—and I charge you, a dying man, to pull on."

"Give me three days," pleaded Malemute Kid. "You may change for the better; something may turn up."

"No."

"Just three days."

"You must pull on."

"Two days."

"It's my wife and my boy, Kid. You would not ask it."

"One day."

"No, no! I charge——"

"Only one day. We can shave it through on the grub, and I might knock over a moose."

"No—all right; one day, but not a minute more. And, Kid, don't—don't leave me to face it alone. Just a shot, one pull on the trigger. You understand. Think of it! Think of it! Flesh of my flesh, and I'll never live to see him!

"Send Ruth here. I want to say good-by and tell her that she must think of the boy and not wait till I'm dead. She might refuse to go with you if I didn't. Good-by, old man; good-by.

"Kid! I say—a—sink a hole above the pup, next to the slide. I panned out forty cents on my shovel there.

"And, Kid!" He stooped lower to catch the last faint words, the dying man's surrender of his pride. "I'm sorry—for—you know—Carmen."

Leaving the girl crying softly over her man, Malemute Kid slipped into his parka and snowshoes, tucked his rifle under his arm, and crept away into the forest. He was no tyro in the stern sorrows of the Northland, but never had he faced so stiff a problem as this. In the abstract, it was a plain, mathematical proposition—three possible lives as against one doomed one. But now he hesitated. For five years, shoulder to shoulder, on the rivers and trails, in the camps and mines, facing death by field and flood and famine, had they knitted the bonds of their comradeship. So close was the tie that he had often been conscious of a vague jealousy of Ruth, from the first time she had come between. And now it must be severed by his own hand.

Though he prayed for a moose, just one moose, all game seemed to have deserted the land, and nightfall found the exhausted man crawling into camp, light-handed, heavyhearted. An uproar from the dogs and shrill cries from Ruth hastened him.

Bursting into the camp, he saw the girl in the midst of the snarling pack, laying about her with an ax. The dogs had broken the iron rule of their masters and were rushing the grub. He joined the issue with his rifle reversed, and the hoary game of natural selection was played out with all the ruthlessness of its primeval environment. Rifle and ax went up and down, hit or missed with monotonous regularity; lithe bodies flashed, with wild eyes and dripping fangs; and man and beast fought for supremacy to the bitterest conclusion. Then the beaten brutes crept to the edge of the firelight, licking their wounds, voicing their misery to the stars.

The whole stock of dried salmon had been devoured, and perhaps five pounds of flour remained to tide them over two hundred miles of wilderness. Ruth returned to her husband, while Malemute Kid cut up the warm body of one of the dogs, the skull of which had been crushed by the ax. Every portion was carefully put away, save the hide and offal, which were cast to his fellows of the moment before.

Morning brought fresh trouble. The animals were turning on each other. Carmen, who still clung to her slender thread of life, was downed by the pack. The lash fell among them unheeded. They cringed and cried under the blows, but refused to scatter till the last wretched bit had disappeared—bones, hide, hair, everything.

Malemute Kid went about his work, listening to Mason, who was back in Tennessee, delivering tangled discourses and wild exhortations to his brethren of other days.

Taking advantage of neighboring pines, he worked rapidly, and Ruth watched him make a cache similar to those sometimes used by hunters to preserve their meat from the wolverines and dogs. One after the other, he bent the tops of two small pines toward each other and nearly to the ground, making them fast with thongs of moosehide. Then he beat the dogs into submission and harnessed them to two of the sleds, loading the same with everything but the furs which enveloped Mason. These he wrapped and lashed tightly about him, fastening either end of the robes to the bent pines. A single stroke of his hunting knife would release them and send the body high in the air.

Ruth had received her husband's last wishes and made no struggle. Poor girl, she had learned the lesson of obedience well. From a child, she had bowed, and seen all women bow, to the lords of creation, and it did not seem in the nature of things for woman to resist. The Kid permitted her one outburst of grief, as she kissed her husband—her own people had no such custom—then led her to the foremost sled and helped her into her snowshoes. Blindly, instinctively, she took the gee pole and whip, and "mushed" the dogs out on the trail. Then he returned to Mason, who had fallen into a coma, and long after she was out of sight crouched by the fire, waiting, hoping, praying for his comrade to die.

It is not pleasant to be alone with painful thoughts in the White Silence. The silence of gloom is merciful, shrouding one as with protection and breathing a thousand intangible sympathies, but the bright White Silence, clear and cold, under steely skies, is pitiless.

An hour passed—two hours—but the man would not die. At high noon the sun, without raising its rim above the southern horizon, threw a suggestion of fire athwart the heavens, then quickly drew it back. Malemute Kid roused and dragged himself to his comrade's side. He cast one glance about him. The White Silence seemed to sneer, and a great fear came upon him. There was a sharp report; Mason swung into his aerial sepulcher, and Malemute Kid lashed the dogs into a wild gallop as he fled across the snow.

AN ODYSSEY OF THE NORTH

THE sleds were singing their eternal lament to the creaking of the harnesses and the tinkling bells of the leaders; but the men and dogs were tired and made no sound. The trail was heavy with new-fallen snow, and they had come far, and the runners, burdened with flintlike quarters of frozen moose, clung tenaciously to the unpacked surface and held back with a stubbornness almost human. Darkness was coming on, but there was no camp to pitch that night. The snow fell gently through the pulseless air, not in flakes, but in tiny frost crystals of delicate design. It was very warm—barely ten below zero—and the men did not mind. Meyers and Bettles had raised their ear flaps, while Malemute Kid had even taken off his mittens.

The dogs had been fagged out early in the afternoon, but they now began to show new vigor. Among the more astute there was a certain restlessness—an impatience at the restraint of the traces, an indecisive quickness of movement, a sniffing of snouts and pricking of ears. These became incensed at their more phlegmatic brothers, urging them on with numerous sly nips on their hinder quarters. Those, thus chidden, also contracted and helped spread the contagion. At last the leader of the foremost sled uttered a sharp whine of satisfaction, crouching lower in the snow and throwing himself against the collar. The rest followed suit. There was an ingathering of back bands, a tightening of traces; the sleds leaped forward, and the men clung to the gee poles, violently accelerating the uplift of their feet that they might escape going under the runners. The weariness of the day fell from them, and they whooped encouragement to the dogs. The animals responded with joyous yelps. They were swinging through the gathering darkness at a rattling gallop.

"Gee! Gee!" the men cried, each in turn, as their sleds abruptly left the main trail, heeling over on single runners like luggers on the wind.

Then came a hundred yards' dash to the lighted parchment window, which told its own story of the home cabin, the roaring Yukon stove, and the steaming pots of tea. But the home cabin had been invaded. Threescore huskies chorused defiance, and as many furry forms precipitated themselves upon the dogs which drew the first sled. The door was flung open, and a man, clad in the scarlet tunic of the Northwest Police, waded knee-deep among the furious brutes, calmly and impartially dispensing soothing justice with the butt end of a dog whip. After that the men shook hands; and in this wise was Malemute Kid welcomed to his own cabin by a stranger.

Stanley Prince, who should have welcomed him, and who was responsible for the Yukon stove and hot tea aforementioned, was busy with his guests. There were a dozen or so of them, as nondescript a crowd as ever served the Queen in the enforcement of her laws or the delivery of her mails. They were of many breeds, but their common life had formed of them a certain type—a lean and wiry type, with trail-hardened muscles, and sun-browned faces, and untroubled souls which gazed frankly forth, clear-eyed and steady. They drove the dogs of the Queen, wrought fear in the hearts of her enemies, ate of her meager fare, and were happy. They had seen life, and done deeds, and lived romances; but they did not know it.

And they were very much at home. Two of them were sprawled upon Malemute Kid's bunk, singing chansons which their French forebears sang in the days when first they entered the Northwest land and mated with its Indian women. Bettles' bunk had suffered a similar invasion, and three or four lusty *voyageurs* worked their toes among its blankets as they listened to the tale of one who had served on the boat brigade with Wolseley when he fought his way to Khartoum. And when he tired, a cowboy told of courts and kings and lords and ladies he had seen when Buffalo Bill toured the capitals of Europe. In a corner two half-breeds, ancient comrades in a lost campaign, mended harnesses and talked of the days when the Northwest flamed with insurrection and Louis Riel was king.

Rough jests and rougher jokes went up and down, and great hazards by trail and river were spoken of in the light of commonplaces, only to be recalled by virtue of some grain of humor or ludicrous happening. Prince was led away by these uncrowned heroes who had seen history made, who regarded the great and the romantic as but the ordinary and the incidental in the routine of life. He passed his precious tobacco among them with lavish disregard, and rusty chains of reminiscence were loosened, and forgotten odysseys resurrected for his especial benefit.

When conversation dropped and the travelers filled the last pipes and unlashed their tight-rolled sleeping furs, Prince fell back upon his comrade for further information.

"Well, you know what the cowboy is," Malemute Kid answered, beginning to unlace his moccasins; "and it's not hard to guess the British blood in his bed partner. As for the rest, they're all children of the *coureurs du bois*, mingled with God knows how many other bloods. The two turning in by the door are the regulation 'breeds' or *Boisbrûles*. That lad with the worsted breech scarf —notice his eyebrows and the turn of his jaw—shows a Scotchman wept in his mother's smoky tepee. And that handsome-looking fellow putting the capote under his head is a French half-breed—you heard him talking; he doesn't like the two Indians turning in next to him. You see, when the 'breeds' rose under Riel the full-bloods kept the peace, and they've not lost much love for one another since."

"But I say, what's that glum-looking fellow by the stove? I'll swear he can't talk English. He hasn't opened his mouth all night."

"You're wrong. He knows English well enough. Did you follow his eyes when he listened? I did. But he's neither kith nor kin to the others. When they talked their own patois you could see he didn't understand. I've been wondering myself what he is. Let's find out."

"Fire a couple of sticks into the stove!" Malemute Kid commanded, raising his voice and looking squarely at the man in question.

He obeyed at once.

"Had discipline knocked into him somewhere," Prince commented in a low tone.

Malemute Kid nodded, took off his socks, and picked his way among recumbent men to the stove. There he hung his damp footgear among a score or so of mates.

"When do you expect to get to Dawson?" he asked tentatively.

The man studied him a moment before replying. "They say seventy-five mile. So? Maybe two days."

The very slightest accent was perceptible, while there was no awkward hesitancy or groping for words.

"Been in the country before?"

"No."

"Northwest Territory?"

"Yes."

"Born there?"

"No."

"Well, where the devil were you born? You're none of these." Malemute Kid swept his hand over the dog drivers, even including the two policemen who had turned into Prince's bunk. "Where did you come from? I've seen faces like yours before, though I can't remember just where."

"I know you," he irrelevantly replied, at once turning the drift of Malemute Kid's questions.

"Where? Ever see me?"

"No; your partner, him priest, Pastilik, long time ago. Him ask me if I see you, Malemute Kid. Him give me grub. I no stop long. You hear him speak 'bout me?"

"Oh! you're the fellow that traded the otter skins for the dogs?"

The man nodded, knocked out his pipe, and signified his disinclination for conversation by rolling up in his furs. Malemute Kid blew out the slush lamp and crawled under the blankets with Prince.

"Well, what is he?"

"Don't know—turned me off, somehow, and then shut up like a clam. But he's a fellow to whet your curiosity. I've heard of him. All the coast wondered about him eight years ago. Sort of mysterious, you know. He came down out of the North, in the dead of winter, many a thousand miles from here, skirting Bering Sea and traveling as though the devil were after him. No one ever learned where he came from, but he must have come far. He was badly travel-worn when he got food from the Swedish missionary on Golovin Bay and asked the way south. We heard of this afterward. Then he abandoned the shore line, heading right across Norton Sound. Terrible weather, snowstorms and high winds, but he pulled through where a thousand other men would have died, missing St. Michael's and making the land at Pastilik. He'd lost all but two dogs, and was nearly gone with starvation.

"He was so anxious to go on that Father Roubeau fitted him out with grub; but he couldn't let him have any dogs for he was only waiting my arrival to go on a trip himself. Mr. Ulysses knew too much to start on without animals, and fretted around for several days. He had on his sled a bunch of beautifully cured otter skins, sea otters, you know, worth their weight in gold. There was also at Pastilik an old Shylock of a Russian trader, who had dogs to kill. Well, they didn't dicker very long, but when the Strange One headed south again, it was in the rear of a spanking dog team. Mr. Shylock, by the way, had the otter skins. I saw them, and they were magnificent. We figured it up and found the dogs brought him at least five hundred apiece. And it wasn't as if the Strange One didn't know the value of sea otter; he was an Indian of some sort, and what little he talked showed he'd been among white men.

"After the ice passed out of the sea, word came up from Nunivak Island that he'd done in there for grub. Then he dropped from sight, and this is the first heard of him in eight years. Now where did he come from? and what was he doing there? and why did he come from there? He's Indian, he's been nobody knows where, and he's had discipline, which is unusual for an Indian. Another mystery of the North for you to solve, Prince."

"Thanks awfully, but I've got too many on hand as it is," he replied.

Malemute Kid was already breathing heavily; but the young mining engineer gazed straight up through the thick darkness, waiting for the strange orgasm which stirred his blood to die away. And when he did sleep, his brain worked on, and for the nonce he, too, wandered through the white unknown, struggled with the dogs on endless trails, and saw men live, and toil, and die like men.

The next morning, hours before daylight, the dog drivers and policemen pulled out for Dawson. But the powers that saw to Her Majesty's interests and ruled the destinies of her lesser creatures gave the mailmen little rest, for a week later they appeared at Stuart River, heavily burdened with letters for Salt Water. However, their dogs had been replaced by fresh ones; but, then, they were dogs.

The men had expected some sort of a layover in which to rest up; besides, this Klondike was a new section of the Northland, and they had wished to see a little something of the Golden City where dust flowed like water and dance halls rang with never-ending revelry. But they dried their socks and smoked their evening pipes with much the same gusto as on their former visit, though one or two bold spirits speculated on desertion and the possibility of crossing the unexplored Rockies to the east, and thence, by the Mackenzie Valley, of gaining their old stamping grounds in the Chippewyan country. Two or three even decided to return to their homes by that route when their terms of service had expired, and they began to lay plans forthwith, looking forward to the hazardous undertaking in much the same way a city-bred man would to a day's holiday in the woods.

He of the Otter Skins seemed very restless, though he took little interest in the discussion, and at last he drew Malemute Kid to one side and talked for some time in low tones. Prince cast curious eyes in their direction, and the mystery deepened when they put on caps and mittens and went outside. When they returned, Malemute Kid placed his gold scales on the table, weighed out the matter of sixty ounces, and transferred them to the Strange One's sack. Then the chief of the dog drivers joined the conclave, and certain business was transacted with him. The next day the gang went on upriver, but He of the Otter Skins took several pounds of grub and turned his steps back toward Dawson.

"Didn't know what to make of it," said Malemute Kid in response to Prince's queries; "but the poor beggar wanted to be quit of the service for some reason or other—at least it seemed a most important one to him, though he wouldn't let on what. You see, it's just like the army: he signed for two years, and the only way to get free was to buy himself out. He couldn't desert and then stay here, and he was just wild to remain in the country. Made up his mind when he got to Dawson, he said; but no one knew him, hadn't a cent, and I was the only one he'd spoken two words with. So he talked it over with the lieutenant-governor, and made arrangements in case he could get the money from me—loan, you know. Said he'd pay back in the year, and, if I wanted, would put me onto something rich. Never'd seen it, but knew it was rich.

"And talk! why, when he got me outside he was ready to weep. Begged and pleaded; got down in the snow to me till I hauled him out of it. Palavered around like a crazy man. Swore he's worked to this very end for years and years, and couldn't bear to be disappointed now. Asked him what end, but he wouldn't say. Said they might keep him on the other half of the trail and he wouldn't get to Dawson in two years, and then it would be too late. Never saw a man take on so in my life. And when I said I'd let him have it, had to yank him out of the snow again. Told him to consider it in the light of a grubstake. Think he'd have it? No sir! Swore he'd give me all he found, make me rich beyond the dreams of avarice, and all such stuff. Now a man who puts his life and time against a grubstake ordinarily finds it hard enough to turn over half of what he finds. Something behind all this, Prince; just you make a note of it. We'll hear of him if he stays in the country——"

"And if he doesn't?"

"Then my good nature gets a shock, and I'm sixty some odd ounces out."

The cold weather had come on with the long nights, and the sun had begun to play his ancient game of peekaboo along the southern snow line ere aught was heard of Malemute Kid's grub-

stake. And then, one bleak morning in early January, a heavily
laden dog train pulled into his cabin below Stuart River. He of
the Otter Skins was there, and with him walked a man such as
the gods have almost forgotten how to fashion. Men never talked
of luck and pluck and five-hundred-dollar dirt without bringing in
the name of Axel Gunderson; nor could tales of nerve or strength
or daring pass up and down the campfire without the summoning
of his presence. And when the conversation flagged, it blazed
anew at mention of the woman who shared his fortunes.

As has been noted, in the making of Axel Gunderson the gods
had remembered their old-time cunning and cast him after the
manner of men who were born when the world was young. Full
seven feet he towered in his picturesque costume which marked a
king of Eldorado. His chest, neck, and limbs were those of a giant.
To bear his three hundred pounds of bone and muscle, his snowshoes were greater by a generous yard than those of other men.
Rough-hewn, with rugged brow and massive jaw and unflinching
eyes of palest blue, his face told the tale of one who knew but the
law of might. Of the yellow of ripe corn silk, his frost-incrusted
hair swept like day across the night and fell far down his coat of
bearskin. A vague tradition of the sea seemed to cling about him
as he swung down the narrow trail in advance of the dogs; and he
brought the butt of his dog whip against Malemute Kid's door as
a Norse sea rover, on southern foray, might thunder for admit-
tance at the castle gate.

Prince bared his womanly arms and kneaded sour-dough bread,
casting, as he did so, many a glance at the three guests—three
guests the like of which might never come under a man's roof in a
lifetime. The Strange One, whom Malemute Kid had surnamed
Ulysses, still fascinated him; but his interest chiefly gravitated between Axel Gunderson and Axel Gunderson's wife. She felt the
day's journey, for she had softened in comfortable cabins during
the many days since her husband mastered the wealth of frozen
pay streaks, and she was tired. She rested against his great breast
like a slender flower against a wall, replying lazily to Malemute
Kid's good-natured banter, and stirring Prince's blood strangely
with an occasional sweep of her deep, dark eyes. For Prince was a
man, and healthy, and had seen few women in many months.
And she was older than he, and an Indian besides. But she was

different from all native wives he had met: she had traveled—had been in his country among others, he gathered from the conversation; and she knew most of the things the women of his own race knew, and much more that it was not in the nature of things for them to know. She could make a meal of sun-dried fish or a bed in the snow; yet she teased them with tantalizing details of many-course dinners, and caused strange internal dissensions to arise at the mention of various quondam dishes which they had well-nigh forgotten. She knew the ways of the moose, the bear, and the little blue fox, and of the wild amphibians of the Northern seas; she was skilled in the lore of the woods and the streams, and the tale writ by man and bird and beast upon the delicate snow crust was to her an open book; yet Prince caught the appreciative twinkle in her eye as she read the Rules of the Camp. These rules had been fathered by the Unquenchable Bettles at a time when his blood ran high, and were remarkable for the terse simplicity of their humor. Prince always turned them to the wall before the arrival of ladies; but who could suspect that this native wife—— Well, it was too late now.

This, then, was the wife of Axel Gunderson, a woman whose name and fame had traveled with her husband's, hand in hand, through all the Northland. At table, Malemute Kid baited her with the assurance of an old friend, and Prince shook off the shyness of first acquaintance and joined in. But she held her own in the unequal contest, while her husband, slower in wit, ventured naught but applause. And he was very proud of her; his every look and action revealed the magnitude of the place she occupied in his life. He of the Otter Skins ate in silence, forgotten in the merry battle; and long ere the others were done he pushed back from the table and went out among the dogs. Yet all too soon his fellow travelers drew on their mittens and parkas and followed him.

There had been no snow for many days, and the sleds slipped along the hard-packed Yukon trail as easily as if it had been glare ice. Ulysses led the first sled; with the second came Prince and Axel Gunderson's wife; while Malemute Kid and the yellow-haired giant brought up the third.

"It's only a hunch, Kid," he said, "but I think it's straight. He's never been there, but he tells a good story, and shows a map I heard of when I was in the Kootenay country years ago. I'd like to have you go along; but he's a strange one, and swore point-blank to throw it up if anyone was brought in. But when I come back you'll get first tip, and I'll stake you next to me, and give you a half share in the town site besides.

"No, no!" he cried, as the other strove to interrupt. "I'm running this, and before I'm done it'll need two heads. If it's all right, why, it'll be a second Cripple Creek, man; do you hear?—a second Cripple Creek! It's quartz, you know, not placer; and if we work it right we'll corral the whole thing—millions upon millions. I've heard of the place before, and so have you. We'll build a town—thousands of workmen—good waterways—steamship lines —big carrying trade—light-draught steamers for head reaches— survey a railroad, perhaps—sawmills—electric-light plant—do our own banking—commercial company—syndicate—— Say! just you hold your hush till I get back!"

The sleds came to a halt where the trail crossed the mouth of Stuart River. An unbroken sea of frost, its wide expanse stretched away into the unknown east. The snowshoes were withdrawn from the lashings of the sleds. Axel Gunderson shook hands and stepped to the fore, his great webbed shoes sinking a fair half yard into the feathery surface and packing the snow so the dogs should not wallow. His wife fell in behind the last sled, betraying long practice in the art of handling the awkward footgear. The stillness was broken with cheery farewells; the dogs whined; and He of the Otter Skins talked with his whip to a recalcitrant wheeler.

An hour later the train had taken on the likeness of a black pencil crawling in a long, straight line across a mighty sheet of foolscap.

II

One night, many weeks later, Malemute Kid and Prince fell to solving chess problems from the torn page of an ancient magazine. The Kid had just returned from his Bonanza properties and was resting up preparatory to a long moose hunt. Prince, too, had been on creek and trail nearly all winter, and had grown hungry for a blissful week of cabin life.

"Interpose the black knight, and force the king. No, that won't do. See, the next move——"

"Why advance the pawn two squares? Bound to take in transit, and with the bishop out of the way——"

"But hold on! That leaves a hole, and——"

"No; it's protected. Go ahead! You'll see it works."

It was very interesting. Somebody knocked at the door a second time before Malemute Kid said, "Come in." The door swung open. Something staggered in. Prince caught one square look and sprang to his feet. The horror in his eyes caused Malemute Kid to whirl about; and he, too, was startled, though he had seen bad things before. The thing tottered blindly toward them. Prince edged away till he reached the nail from which hung his Smith & Wesson.

"My God! what is it?" he whispered to Malemute Kid.

"Don't know. Looks like a case of freezing and no grub," replied the Kid, sliding away in the opposite direction. "Watch out! It may be mad," he warned, coming back from closing the door.

The thing advanced to the table. The bright flame of the slush lamp caught its eye. It was amused, and gave voice to eldritch cackles which betokened mirth. Then, suddenly, he—for it was a man—swayed back, with a hitch to his skin trousers, and began to sing a chantey, such as men lift when they swing around the capstan circle and the sea snorts in their ears:

> "Yan-kee ship come down de ri-ib-er,
>   Pull! my bully boys! Pull!
> D'yeh want—to know de captain ru-uns her?
>   Pull! my bully boys! Pull!
> Jon-a-than Jones ob South Caho-li-in-a,
>   Pull! my bully—"

He broke off abruptly, tottered with a wolfish snarl to the meat shelf, and before they could intercept was tearing with his teeth at a chunk of raw bacon. The struggle was fierce between him and Malemute Kid; but his mad strength left him as suddenly as it had come, and he weakly surrendered the spoil. Between them they got him upon a stool, where he sprawled with half his body across the table. A small dose of whiskey strengthened him, so that he could dip a spoon into the sugar caddy which Malemute

Kid placed before him. After his appetite had been somewhat cloyed, Prince, shuddering as he did so, passed him a mug of weak beef tea.

The creature's eyes were alight with a somber frenzy, which blazed and waned with every mouthful. There was very little skin to the face. The face, for that matter, sunken and emaciated, bore little likeness to human countenance. Frost after frost had bitten deeply, each depositing its stratum of scab upon the half-healed scar that went before. This dry, hard surface was of a bloody-black color, serrated by grievous cracks wherein the raw red flesh peeped forth. His skin garments were dirty and in tatters, and the fur of one side was singed and burned away, showing where he had lain upon his fire.

Malemute Kid pointed to where the sun-tanned hide had been cut away, strip by strip—the grim signature of famine.

"Who—are—you?" slowly and distinctly enunciated the Kid.

The man paid no heed.

"Where do you come from?"

"Yan-kee ship come down de ri-ib-er," was the quavering response.

"Don't doubt the beggar came down the river," the Kid said, shaking him in an endeavor to start a more lucid flow of talk.

But the man shrieked at the contact, clapping a hand to his side in evident pain. He rose slowly to his feet, half leaning on the table.

"She laughed at me—so—with the hate in her eye; and she—would—not—come."

His voice died away, and he was sinking back when Malemute Kid gripped him by the wrist and shouted, "Who? Who would not come?"

"She, Unga. She laughed, and struck at me, so, and so. And then——"

"Yes?"

"And then——"

"And then what?"

"And then he lay very still in the snow a long time. He is—still in—the—snow."

The two men looked at each other helplessly.

"Who is in the snow?"

"She, Unga. She looked at me with the hate in her eye, and then——"

"Yes, yes."

"And then she took the knife, so; and once, twice—she was weak. I traveled very slow. And there is much gold in that place, very much gold."

"Where is Unga?" For all Malemute Kid knew, she might be dying a mile away. He shook the man savagely, repeating again and again, "Where is Unga? Who is Unga?"

"She—is—in—the—snow."

"Go on!" The Kid was pressing his wrist cruelly.

"So—I—would—be—in—the—snow—but—I—had—a—debt—to—pay. It—was—heavy—I—had—a—debt—to—pay—a—debt—to—pay—I—had——" The faltering monosyllables ceased as he fumbled in his pouch and drew forth a buckskin sack. "A—debt—to—pay—five—pounds—of—gold—grub—stake—Mal—e—mute—Kid—I——" The exhausted head dropped upon the table; nor could Malemute Kid rouse it again.

"It's Ulysses," he said quietly, tossing the bag of dust on the table. "Guess it's all day with Axel Gunderson and the woman. Come on, let's get him between the blankets. He's Indian; he'll pull through and tell a tale besides."

As they cut his garments from him, near his right breast could be seen two unhealed, hard-lipped knife thrusts.

III

"I will talk of the things which were in my own way; but you will understand. I will begin at the beginning, and tell of myself and the woman, and, after that, of the man."

He of the Otter Skins drew over to the stove as do men who have been deprived of fire and are afraid the Promethean gift may vanish at any moment. Malemute Kid pricked up the slush lamp and placed it so its light might fall upon the face of the narrator. Prince slid his body over the edge of the bunk and joined them.

"I am Naass, a chief, and the son of a chief, born between a sunset and a rising, on the dark seas, in my father's oomiak. All of a night the men toiled at the paddles, and the women cast out the waves which threw in upon us, and we fought with the storm. The salt spray froze upon my mother's breast till her breath passed with the passing of the tide. But I—I raised my voice with the wind and the storm, and lived.

"We dwelt in Akatan——"

"Where?" asked Malemute Kid.

"Akatan, which is in the Aleutians; Akatan, beyond Chignik, beyond Kardalak, beyond Unimak. As I say, we dwelt in Akatan, which lies in the midst of the sea on the edge of the world. We farmed the salt seas for the fish, the seal, and the otter; and our homes shouldered about one another on the rocky strip between the rim of the forest and the yellow beach where our kayaks lay. We were not many, and the world was very small. There were strange lands to the east—islands like Akatan; so we thought all the world was islands and did not mind.

"I was different from my people. In the sands of the beach were the crooked timbers and wave-warped planks of a boat such as my people never built; and I remember on the point of the island which overlooked the ocean three ways there stood a pine tree which never grew there, smooth and straight and tall. It is said the two men came to that spot, turn about, through many days, and watched with the passing of the light. These two men came from out of the sea in the boat which lay in pieces on the beach. And they were white like you, and weak as the little children when the seal have gone away and the hunters come home empty. I know of these things from the old men and the old women, who got them from their fathers and mothers before them. These strange white men did not take kindly to our ways at first, but they grew strong, what of the fish and the oil, and fierce. And they built them each his own house, and took the pick of our women, and in time children came. Thus he was born who was to become the father of my father's father.

"As I said, I was different from my people, for I carried the strong, strange blood of this white man who came out of the sea. It is said we had other laws in the days before these men; but they were fierce and quarrelsome, and fought with our men till there were no more left who dared to fight. Then they made themselves chiefs, and took away our old laws and gave us new ones, insomuch that the man was the son of his father, and not his mother, as our way had been. They also ruled that the son, first-born, should have all things which were his father's before him, and that the brothers and sisters should shift for themselves. And they gave us other laws. They showed us new ways in the catching of fish and the killing of bear which were thick in the woods; and they taught us to lay bigger stores for the time of famine. And these things were good.

"But when they had become chiefs, and there were no more men to face their anger, they fought, these strange white men, each with the other. And the one whose blood I carry drove his seal spear the length of an arm through the other's body. Their children took up the fight, and their children's children; and there was great hatred between them, and black doings, even to my time, so that in each family but one lived to pass down the blood of them that went before. Of my blood I was alone; of the other man's there was but a girl, Unga, who lived with her mother. Her father and my father did not come back from the fishing one night; but afterward they washed up to the beach on the big tides, and they held very close to each other.

"The people wondered, because of the hatred between the houses, and the old men shook their heads and said the fight would go on when children were born to her and children to me. They told me this as a boy, till I came to believe, and to look upon Unga as a foe, who was to be the mother of children which were to fight with mine. I thought of these things day by day, and when I grew to a stripling I came to ask why this should be so. And they answered, 'We do not know, but that in such way your fathers did.' And I marveled that those which were to come should fight the battles of those that were gone, and in it I could see no right. But the people said it must be, and I was only a stripling.

"And they said I must hurry, that my blood might be the older and grow strong before hers. This was easy, for I was head man, and the people looked up to me because of the deeds and the laws of my fathers, and the wealth which was mine. Any maiden would come to me, but I found none to my liking. And the old men and the mothers of maidens told me to hurry, for even then were the hunters bidding high to the mother of Unga; and should her children grow strong before mine, mine would surely die.

"Nor did I find a maiden till one night coming back from the fishing. The sunlight was lying, so, low and full in the eyes, the wind free, and the kayaks racing with the white seas. Of a sudden the kayak of Unga came driving past me, and she looked upon me, so, with her black hair flying like a cloud of night and the spray wet on her cheek. As I say, the sunlight was full in the eyes, and I was a stripling; but somehow it was all clear, and I knew it to be the call of kind to kind. As she whipped ahead she looked back within the space of two strokes—looked as only the woman Unga could look—and again I knew it as the call of kind. The people shouted as we ripped past the lazy oomiaks and left them far behind. But she was quick at the paddle, and my heart was like the belly of a sail, and I did not gain. The wind freshened, the sea whitened, and, leaping like the seals on the windward breech, we roared down the golden pathway of the sun."

Naass was crouched half out of his stool, in the attitude of one driving a paddle, as he ran the race anew. Somewhere across the stove he beheld the tossing kayak and the flying hair of Unga. The voice of the wind was in his ears, and its salt beat fresh upon his nostrils.

"But she made the shore, and ran up the sand, laughing, to the house of her mother. And a great thought came to me that night —a thought worthy of him that was chief over all the people of Akatan. So, when the moon was up, I went down to the house of her mother, and looked upon the goods of Yash-Noosh, which were piled by the door—the goods of Yash-Noosh, a strong hunter who had it in mind to be the father of the children of Unga. Other young men had piled their goods there and taken them away again; and each young man had made a pile greater than the one before.

"And I laughed to the moon and the stars, and went to my own house where my wealth was stored. And many trips I made, till my pile was greater by the fingers of one hand than the pile of Yash-Noosh. There were fish, dried in the sun and smoked; and forty hides of the hair seal, and half as many of the fur, and each hide was tied at the mouth and big bellied with oil; and ten skins of bear which I killed in the woods when they came out in the spring. And there were beads and blankets and scarlet cloths, such as I got in trade from the people who lived to the east, and who got them in trade from the people who lived still beyond in the east. And I looked upon the pile of Yash-Noosh and laughed, for

I was head man in Akatan, and my wealth was greater than the wealth of all my young men, and my fathers had done deeds, and given laws, and put their names for all time in the mouths of the people.

"So, when the morning came, I went down to the beach, casting out of the corner of my eye at the house of the mother of Unga. My offer yet stood untouched. And the women smiled, and said sly things one to the other. I wondered, for never had such a price been offered; and that night I added more to the pile, and put beside it a kayak of well-tanned skins which never yet had swam in the sea. But in the day it was yet there, open to the laughter of all men. The mother of Unga was crafty, and I grew angry at the shame in which I stood before my people. So that night I added till it became a great pile, and I hauled up my oomiak, which was of the value of twenty kayaks. And in the morning there was no pile.

"Then made I preparation for the wedding, and the people that lived even to the east came for the food of the feast and the potlatch token. Unga was older than I by the age of four suns in the way we reckoned the years. I was only a stripling; but then I was a chief, and the son of a chief, and it did not matter.

"But a ship shoved her sails above the floor of the ocean, and grew larger with the breath of the wind. From her scuppers she ran clear water, and the men were in haste and worked hard at the pumps. On the bow stood a mighty man, watching the depth of the water and giving commands with a voice of thunder. His eyes were of the pale blue of the deep waters, and his head was maned like that of a sea lion. And his hair was yellow, like the straw of a southern harvest or the manila rope yarns which sailormen plait.

"Of late years we had seen ships from afar, but this was the first to come to the beach of Akatan. The feast was broken, and the women and children fled to the houses, while we men strung our bows and waited with spears in hand. But when the ship's forefoot smelled the beach the strange men took no notice of us, being busy with their own work. With the falling of the tide they careened the schooner and patched a great hole in her bottom. So the women crept back, and the feast went on.

"When the tide rose, the sea wanderers kedged the schooner to deep water and then came among us. They bore presents and were friendly; so I made room for them, and out of the largeness of my heart gave them tokens such as I gave all the guests, for it was my wedding day, and I was head man in Akatan. And he with the mane of the sea lion was there, so tall and strong that one looked to see the earth shake with the fall of his feet. He looked much and straight at Unga, with his arms folded, so, and stayed till the sun went away and the stars came out. Then he went down to his ship. After that I took Unga by the hand and led her to my own house. And there was singing and great laughter, and the women said sly things, after the manner of women at such times. But we did not care. Then the people left us alone and went home.

"The last noise had not died away when the chief of the sea wanderers came in by the door. And he had with him black bottles, from which we drank and made merry. You see, I was only a stripling, and had lived all my days on the edge of the world. So my blood became as fire, and my heart as light as the froth that flies from the surf to the cliff. Unga sat silent among the skins in the corner, her eyes wide, for she seemed to fear. And he with the mane of the sea lion looked upon her straight and long. Then his men came in with bundles of goods, and he piled before me wealth such as was not in all Akatan. There were guns, both large and small, and powder and shot and shell, and bright axes and knives of steel, and cunning tools, and strange things the like of which I had never seen. When he showed me by sign that it was all mine, I thought him a great man to be so free; but he showed me also that Unga was to go away with him in his ship. Do you understand?—that Unga was to go away with him in his ship. The blood of my fathers flamed hot on the sudden, and I made to drive him through with my spear. But the spirit of the bottles had stolen the life from my arm, and he took me by the neck, so, and knocked my head against the wall of the house. And I was made weak like a newborn child, and my legs would no more stand under me. Unga screamed, and she laid hold of the things of the house with her hands, till they fell all about as he dragged her to the door. Then he took her in his great arms, and when she tore at his yellow hair laughed with a sound like that of the big bull seal in the rut.

"I crawled to the beach and called upon my people, but they were afraid. Only Yash-Noosh was a man, and they struck him on the head with an oar, till he lay with his face in the sand and did not move. And they raised the sails to the sound of their songs, and the ship went away on the wind.

"The people said it was good, for there would be no more war of the bloods in Akatan; but I said never a word, waiting till the time of the full moon, when I put fish and oil in my kayak and went away to the east. I saw many islands and many people, and I, who had lived on the edge, saw that the world was very large. I talked by signs; but they had not seen a schooner nor a man with the mane of a sea lion, and they pointed always to the east. And I slept in queer places, and ate odd things, and met strange faces. Many laughed, for they thought me light of head; but sometimes old men turned my face to the light and blessed me, and the eyes of the young women grew soft as they asked me of the strange ship, and Unga, and the men of the sea.

"And in this manner, through rough seas and great storms, I came to Unalaska. There were two schooners there, but neither was the one I sought. So I passed on to the east, with the world growing ever larger, and in the island of Unamok there was no word of the ship, nor in Kadiak, nor in Atognak. And so I came one day to a rocky land, where men dug great holes in the mountain. And there was a schooner, but not my schooner, and men loaded upon it the rocks which they dug. This I thought childish, for all the world was made of rocks; but they gave me food and set me to work. When the schooner was deep in the water, the captain gave me money and told me to go; but I asked which way he went, and he pointed south. I made signs that I would go with him, and he laughed at first, but then, being short of men, took me to help work the ship. So I came to talk after their manner, and to heave on ropes, and to reef the stiff sails in sudden squalls, and to take my turn at the wheel. But it was not strange, for the blood of my fathers was the blood of the men of the sea.

"I had thought it an easy task to find him I sought, once I got among his own people; and when we raised the land one day, and passed between a gateway of the sea to a port, I looked for perhaps as many schooners as there were fingers to my hands. But the ships lay against the wharves for miles, packed like so many little fish; and when I went among them to ask for a man with the mane of a sea lion, they laughed, and answered me in the tongues of many peoples. And I found that they hailed from the uttermost parts of the earth.

"And I went into the city to look upon the face of every man. But they were like the cod when they run thick on the banks, and I could not count them. And the noise smote upon me till I could not hear, and my head was dizzy with much movement. So I went on and on, through the lands which sang in the warm sunshine; where the harvests lay rich on the plains; and where great cities were fat with men that lived like women, with false words in their mouths and their hearts black with the lust of gold. And all the while my people of Akatan hunted and fished, and were happy in the thought that the world was small.

"But the look in the eyes of Unga coming home from the fishing was with me always, and I knew I would find her when the time was met. She walked down quiet lanes in the dusk of the evening, or led me chases across the thick fields wet with the morning dew, and there was a promise in her eyes such as only the woman Unga could give.

"So I wandered through a thousand cities. Some were gentle and gave me food, and others laughed, and still others cursed; but I kept my tongue between my teeth, and went strange ways and saw strange sights. Sometimes I, who was a chief and the son of a chief, toiled for men—men rough of speech and hard as iron, who wrung gold from the sweat and sorrow of their fellow men. Yet no word did I get of my quest till I came back to the sea like a homing seal to the rookeries. But this was at another port, in another country which lay to the north. And there I heard dim tales of the yellow-haired sea wanderer, and I learned that he was a hunter of seals, and that even then he was abroad on the ocean.

"So I shipped on a seal schooner with the lazy Siwashes, and followed his trackless trail to the north where the hunt was then warm. And we were away weary months, and spoke many of the fleet, and heard much of the wild doings of him I sought; but never once did we raise him above the sea. We went north, even to the Pribilofs, and killed the seals in herds on the beach, and brought their warm bodies aboard till our scuppers ran grease and blood and no man could stand upon the deck. Then were we chased by a ship of slow steam, which fired upon us with great guns. But we put on sail till the sea was over our decks and washed them clean, and lost ourselves in a fog.

"It is said, at this time, while we fled with fear at our hearts, that the yellow-haired sea wanderer put in to the Pribilofs, right to the factory, and while the part of his men held the servants of the company, the rest loaded ten thousand green skins from the salt houses. I say it is said, but I believe; for in the voyages I made on the coast with never a meeting the northern seas rang with his wildness and daring, till the three nations which have lands there sought him with their ships. And I heard of Unga, for the captains sang loud in her praise, and she was always with him. She had learned the ways of his people, they said, and was happy. But I knew better—knew that her heart harked back to her own people by the yellow beach of Akatan.

"So, after a long time, I went back to the port which is by a gateway of the sea, and there I learned that he had gone across the girth of the great ocean to hunt for the seal to the east of the warm land which runs south from the Russian Seas. And I, who was become a sailorman, shipped with men of his own race, and went after him in the hunt of the seal. And there were few ships off that new land; but we hung on the flank of the seal pack and harried it north through all the spring of the year. And when the cows were heavy with pup and crossed the Russian line, our men grumbled and were afraid. For there was much fog, and every day men were lost in the boats. They would not work, so the captain turned the ship back toward the way it came. But I knew the yellow-haired sea wanderer was unafraid, and would hang by the pack, even to the Russian Isles, where few men go. So I took a boat, in the black of night, when the lookout dozed on the fo'c'slehead, and went alone to the warm, long land. And I journeyed south to meet the men by Yeddo Bay, who are wild and unafraid. And the Yoshiwara girls were small, and bright like steel, and good to look upon; but I could not stop, for I knew that Unga rolled on the tossing floor by the rookeries of the north.

"The men by Yeddo Bay had met from the ends of the earth, and had neither gods nor homes, sailing under the flag of the Japanese. And with them I went to the rich beaches of Copper Island, where our salt piles became high with skins. And in that silent sea we saw no man till we were ready to come away. Then one day the fog lifted on the edge of a heavy wind, and there jammed down upon us a schooner, with close in her wake the cloudy funnels of a Russian man-of-war. We fled away on the beam of the wind, with the schooner jamming still closer and plunging ahead three feet to our two. And upon her poop was the man with the mane of the sea lion, pressing the rails under with the canvas and laughing in his strength of life. And Unga was there—I knew her on the moment—but he sent her below when the cannons began to talk across the sea. As I say, with three feet to our two, till we saw the rudder lift green at every jump—and I swinging on to the wheel and cursing, with my back to the Russian shot. For we knew he had it in mind to run before us, that he might get away while we were caught. And they knocked our masts out of us till we dragged into the wind like a wounded gull; but he went on over the edge of the sky line—he and Unga.

"What could we? The fresh hides spoke for themselves. So they took us to a Russian port, and after that to a lone country, where they set us to work in the mines to dig salt. And some died, and—and some did not die."

Naass swept the blanket from his shoulders, disclosing the gnarled and twisted flesh, marked with the unmistakable striation of the knout. Prince hastily covered him, for it was not nice to look upon.

"We were there a weary time and sometimes men got away to the south, but they always came back. So, when we who hailed from Yeddo Bay rose in the night and took the guns from the guards, we went to the north. And the land was very large, with plains, soggy with water, and great forests. And the cold came, with much snow on the ground, and no man knew the way. Weary months we journeyed through the endless forest—I do not remember, now, for there was little food and often we lay down to die. But at last we came to the cold sea, and but three were left to look upon it. One had shipped from Yeddo as captain, and he knew in his head the lay of the great lands, and of the place where men may cross from one to the other on the ice. And he led us—I do not know, it was so long—till there were but two. When we came to that place we found five of the strange people which live in that country, and they had dogs and skins, and we were very poor. We fought in the snow till they died, and the captain died, and the dogs and skins were mine. Then I crossed on the ice, which was broken, and once I drifted till a gale from the west put me upon the shore. And after that, Golovin Bay, Pastilik, and the priest. Then south, south, to the warm sunlands where first I wandered.

"But the sea was no longer fruitful, and those who went upon it after the seal went to little profit and great risk. The fleets scattered, and the captains and the men had no word of those I sought. So I turned away from the ocean which never rests, and went among the lands, where the trees, the houses, and the mountains sit always in one place and do not move. I journeyed far, and came to learn many things, even to the way of reading and writing from books. It was well I should do this, for it came upon me that Unga must know these things, and that someday, when the time was met—we—you understand, when the time was met.

"So I drifted, like those little fish which raise a sail to the wind but cannot steer. But my eyes and my ears were open always, and I went among men who traveled much, for I knew they had but to see those I sought to remember. At last there came a man, fresh from the mountains, with pieces of rock in which the free gold stood to the size of peas, and he had heard, he had met, he knew them. They were rich, he said, and lived in the place where they drew the gold from the ground.

"It was in a wild country, and very far away; but in time I came to the camp, hidden between the mountains, where men worked night and day, out of the sight of the sun. Yet the time was not come. I listened to the talk of the people. He had gone away— they had gone away—to England, it was said, in the matter of bringing men with much money together to form companies. I saw the house they had lived in; more like a palace, such as one sees in the old countries. In the nighttime I crept in through a window that I might see in what manner he treated her. I went from room to room, and in such way thought kings and queens must live, it was all so very good. And they all said he treated her like a queen, and many marveled as to what breed of woman she was for there was other blood in her veins, and she was different from the women of Akatan, and no one knew her for what she was. Aye, she was a queen; but I was a chief, and the son of a chief, and I had paid for her an untold price of skin and boat and bead.

"But why so many words? I was a sailorman, and knew the way of the ships on the seas. I followed to England, and then to other countries. Sometimes I heard of them by word of mouth, sometimes I read of them in the papers; yet never once could I come by them, for they had much money, and traveled fast, while I was a poor man. Then came trouble upon them, and their wealth slipped away one day like a curl of smoke. The papers were full of it at the time; but after that nothing was said, and I knew they had gone back where more gold could be got from the ground.

"They had dropped out of the world, being now poor, and so I wandered from camp to camp, even north to the Kootenay country, where I picked up the cold scent. They had come and gone, some said this way, and some said that, and still others that they had gone to the country of the Yukon. And I went this way, and I went that, ever journeying from place to place, till it seemed I must grow weary of the world which was so large. But in the Kootenay I traveled a bad trail, and a long trail, with a breed of the Northwest, who saw fit to die when the famine pinched. He had been to the Yukon by an unknown way over the mountains, and when he knew his time was near gave me the map and the secret of a place where he swore by his gods there was much gold.

"After that all the world began to flock into the north. I was a poor man; I sold myself to be a driver of dogs. The rest you know. I met him and her in Dawson. She did not know me, for I was only a stripling, and her life had been large, she had no time to remember the one who had paid for her an untold price.

"So? You bought me from my term of service. I went back to bring things about in my own way, for I had waited long, and now that I had my hand upon him was in no hurry. As I say, I had it in mind to do my own way, for I read back in my life, through all I had seen and suffered, and remembered the cold and hunger of the endless forest by the Russian Seas. As you know, I led him into the east—him and Unga—into the east where many have gone and few returned. I led them to the spot where the bones and the curses of men lie with the gold which they may not have.

"The way was long and the trail unpacked. Our dogs were

many and ate much; nor could our sleds carry till the break of
spring. We must come back before the river ran free. So here and
there we cached grub, that our sleds might be lightened and there
be no chance of famine on the back trip. At the McQuestion
there were three men, and near them we built a cache, as also did
we at the Mayo, where was a hunting camp of a dozen Pellys
which had crossed the divide from the south. After that, as we
went on into the east, we saw no men; only the sleeping river, the
moveless forest, and the White Silence of the North. As I say, the
way was long and the trail unpacked. Sometimes, in a day's toil,
we made no more than eight miles, or ten, and at night we slept
like dead men. And never once did they dream that I was Naass,
head man of Akatan, the righter of wrongs.

"We now made smaller caches, and in the nighttime it was a
small matter to go back on the trail we had broken and change
them in such way that one might deem the wolverines the
thieves. Again there be places where there is a fall to the river,
and the water is unruly, and the ice makes above and is eaten
away beneath. In such a spot the sled I drove broke through, and
the dogs; and to him and Unga it was ill luck, but no more. And
there was much grub on that sled, and the dogs the strongest. But
he laughed, for he was strong of life, and gave the dogs that were
left little grub till we cut them from the harnesses one by one and
fed them to their mates. We would go home light, he said, traveling and eating from cache to cache, with neither dogs nor sleds;
which was true, for our grub was very short, and the last dog died
in the traces the night we came to the gold and the bones and the
curses of men.

"To reach that place—and the map spoke true—in the heart of
the great mountains, we cut ice steps against the wall of a divide.
One looked for a valley beyond, but there was no valley; the snow
spread away, level as the great harvest plains, and here and there
about us mighty mountains shoved their white heads among the
stars. And midway on that strange plain which should have been a
valley the earth and the snow fell away, straight down toward the
heart of the world. Had we not been sailormen our heads would
have swung round with the sight, but we stood on the dizzy edge
that we might see a way to get down. And on one side, and one
side only, the wall had fallen away till it was like the slope of the

decks in a topsail breeze. I do not know why this thing should be so, but it was so. 'It is the mouth of hell,' he said; 'Let us go down.' And we went down.

"And on the bottom there was a cabin, built by some man, of logs which he had cast down from above. It was a very old cabin, for men had died there alone at different times, and on pieces of birch bark which were there we read their last words and their curses. One had died of scurvy; another's partner had robbed him of his last grub and powder and stolen away; a third had been mauled by a bald-face grizzly; a fourth had hunted for game and starved—and so it went, and they had been loath to leave the gold, and had died by the side of it in one way or another. And the worthless gold they had gathered yellowed the floor of the cabin like in a dream.

"But his soul was steady, and his head clear, this man I had led thus far. 'We have nothing to eat,' he said, 'and we will only look upon this gold, and see whence it comes and how much there be. Then we will go away quick, before it gets into our eyes and steals away our judgment. And in this way we may return in the end, with more grub, and possess it all.' So we looked upon the great vein, which cut the wall of the pit as a true vein should, and we measured it, and traced it from above and below, and drove the stakes of the claims and blazed the trees in token of our rights. Then, our knees shaking with lack of food, and a sickness in our bellies, and our hearts chugging close to our mouths, we climbed the mighty wall for the last time and turned our faces to the back trip.

"The last stretch we dragged Unga between us, and we fell often, but in the end we made the cache. And lo, there was no grub. It was well done, for he thought it the wolverines, and damned them and his gods in the one breath. But Unga was brave, and smiled, and put her hand in his, till I turned away that I might hold myself. 'We will rest by the fire,' she said, 'till morning, and we will gather strength from our moccasins.' So we cut the tops of our moccasins in strips, and boiled them half of the night, that we might chew them and swallow them. And in the morning we talked of our chance. The next cache was five days' journey; we could not make it. We must find game.

" 'We will go forth and hunt,' he said.

" 'Yes,' said I, 'we will go forth and hunt.'

"And he ruled that Unga stay by the fire and save her strength. And we went forth, he in quest of the moose and I to the cache I had changed. But I ate little, so they might not see in me much strength. And in the night he fell many times as he drew into camp. And I, too, made to suffer great weakness, stumbling over my snowshoes as though each step might be my last. And we gathered strength from our moccasins.

"He was a great man. His soul lifted his body to the last; nor did he cry aloud, save for the sake of Unga. On the second day I followed him, that I might not miss the end. And he lay down to rest often. That night he was near gone; but in the morning he swore weakly and went forth again. He was like a drunken man, and I looked many times for him to give up, but his was the strength of the strong, and his soul the soul of a giant, for he lifted his body through all the weary day. And he shot two ptarmigan, but would not eat them. He needed no fire; they meant life; but his thought was for Unga, and he turned toward camp. He no longer walked, but crawled on hand and knee through the snow. I came to him, and read death in his eyes. Even then it was not too late to eat of the ptarmigan. He cast away his rifle and carried the birds in his mouth like a dog. I walked by his side, upright. And he looked at me during the moments he rested, and wondered that I was so strong. I could see it, though he no longer spoke; and when his lips moved, they moved without sound. As I say, he was a great man, and my heart spoke for softness; but I read back in my life, and remembered the cold and hunger of the endless forest by the Russian Seas. Besides, Unga was mine, and I had paid for her an untold price of skin and boat and bead.

"And in this manner we came through the white forest, with the silence heavy upon us like a damp sea mist. And the ghosts of the past were in the air and all about us; and I saw the yellow beach of Akatan, and the kayaks racing home from the fishing, and the houses on the rim of the forest. And the men who had made themselves chiefs were there, the lawgivers whose blood I bore and whose blood I had wedded in Unga. Aye, and Yash-Noosh walked with me, the wet sand in his hair, and his war spear, broken as he fell upon it, still in his hand. And I knew the time was met, and saw in the eyes of Unga the promise.

"As I say, we came thus through the forest, till the smell of the camp smoke was in our nostrils. And I bent above him, and tore the ptarmigan from his teeth. He turned on his side and rested, the wonder mounting in his eyes, and the hand which was under slipping slow toward the knife at his hip. But I took it from him, smiling close in his face. Even then he did not understand. So I made to drink from black bottles, and to build high upon the snow a pile of goods, and to live again the things which happened on the night of my marriage. I spoke no word, but he understood. Yet he was unafraid. There was a sneer to his lips, and cold anger, and he gathered new strength with the knowledge. It was not far, but the snow was deep, and he dragged himself very slow. Once he lay so long I turned him over and gazed into his eyes. And sometimes he looked forth, and sometimes death. And when I loosed him he struggled on again. In this way we came to the fire. Unga was at his side on the instant. His lips moved without sound; then he pointed at me, that Unga might understand. And after that he lay in the snow, very still, for a long while. Even now is he there in the snow.

"I said no word till I had cooked the ptarmigan. Then I spoke to her, in her own tongue, which she had not heard in many years. She straightened herself, so, and her eyes were wonder-wide, and she asked who I was, and where I had learned that speech.

"'I am Naass,' I said.

"'You?' she said. 'You?' And she crept close that she might look upon me.

"'Yes,' I answered; 'I am Naass, head man of Akatan, the last of the blood, as you are the last of the blood.'

"And she laughed. By all the things I have seen and the deeds I have done may I never hear such a laugh again. It put the chill to my soul, sitting there in the White Silence, alone with death and this woman who laughed.

"'Come!' I said, for I thought she wandered. 'Eat of the food and let us be gone. It is a far fetch from here to Akatan.'

"But she shoved her face in his yellow mane, and laughed till it seemed the heavens must fall about our ears. I had thought she would be overjoyed at the sight of me, and eager to go back to the memory of old times, but this seemed a strange form to take.

"'Come!' I cried, taking her strong by the hand. 'The way is long and dark. Let us hurry!'

"'Where?' she asked, sitting up, and ceasing from her strange mirth.

"'To Akatan,' I answered, intent on the light to grow on her face at the thought. But it became like his, with a sneer to the lips, and cold anger.

"'Yes,' she said; 'we will go, hand in hand, to Akatan, you and I. And we will live in the dirty huts, and eat of the fish and oil, and bring forth a spawn—a spawn to be proud of all the days of our life. We will forget the world and be happy, very happy. It is good, most good. Come! Let us hurry. Let us go back to Akatan.'

"And she ran her hand through his yellow hair, and smiled in a way which was not good. And there was no promise in her eyes.

"I sat silent, and marveled at the strangeness of woman. I went back to the night when he dragged her from me and she screamed and tore at his hair—at his hair which now she played with and would not leave. Then I remembered the price and the long years of waiting; and I gripped her close, and dragged her away as he had done. And she held back, even as on that night, and fought like a she-cat for its whelp. And when the fire was between us and the man, I loosed her, and she sat and listened. And I told her of all that lay between, of all that had happened to me on strange seas, of all that I had done in strange lands; of my weary quest, and the hungry years, and the promise which had been mine from the first. Aye, I told all, even to what had passed that day between the man and me, and in the days yet young. And as I spoke I saw the promise grow in her eyes, full and large like the break of dawn. And I read pity there, the tenderness of woman, the love, the heart and the soul of Unga. And I was a stripling again, for the look was the look of Unga as she ran up the beach, laughing, to the home of her mother. The stern unrest was gone, and the hunger, and the weary waiting. The time was met. I felt the call of her breast, and it seemed there I must pillow my head and forget. She opened her arms to me, and I came against her. Then, sudden, the hate flamed in her eye, her hand was at my hip. And once, twice, she passed the knife.

"'Dog!' she sneered, as she flung me into the snow. 'Swine!'

And then she laughed till the silence cracked, and went back to her dead.

"As I say, once she passed the knife, and twice; but she was weak with hunger, and it was not meant that I should die. Yet was I minded to stay in that place, and to close my eyes in the last long sleep with those whose lives had crossed with mine and led my feet on unknown trails. But there lay a debt upon me which would not let me rest.

"And the way was long, the cold bitter, and there was little grub. The Pellys had found no moose, and had robbed my cache. And so had the three white men, but they lay thin and dead in their cabin as I passed. After that I do not remember, till I came here, and found food and fire—much fire."

As he finished, he crouched closely, even jealously, over the stove. For a long while the slush-lamp shadows played tragedies upon the wall.

"But Unga!" cried Prince, the vision still strong upon him.

"Unga? She would not eat of the ptarmigan. She lay with her arms about his neck, her face deep in his yellow hair. I drew the fire close, that she might not feel the frost, but she crept to the other side. And I built a fire there; yet it was little good, for she would not eat. And in this manner they still lie up there in the snow."

"And you?" asked Malemute Kid.

"I do not know; but Akatan is small, and I have little wish to go back and live on the edge of the world. Yet is there small use in life. I can go to Constantine, and he will put irons upon me, and one day they will tie a piece of rope, so, and I will sleep good. Yet—no; I do not know."

"But, Kid," protested Prince, "this is murder!"

"Hush!" commanded Malemute Kid. "There be things greater than our wisdom, beyond our justice. The right and the wrong of this we cannot say, and it is not for us to judge."

Naass drew yet closer to the fire. There was a great silence, and in each man's eyes many pictures came and went.

GRIT OF WOMEN

A WOLFISH head, wistful-eyed and frost-rimed, thrust aside the tent-flaps.

"Hi! Chook! Siwash! Chook, you limb of Satan!" chorused the protesting inmates. Bettles rapped the dog sharply with a tin plate, and it withdrew hastily. Louis Savoy refastened the flaps, kicked a frying-pan over against the bottom, and warmed his hands. It was very cold without. Forty-eight hours gone, the spirit thermometer had burst at sixty-eight below, and since that time it had grown steadily and bitterly colder. There was no telling when the snap would end. And it is poor policy, unless the gods will it, to venture far from a stove at such times, or to increase the quantity of cold atmosphere one must breathe. Men sometimes do it, and sometimes they chill their lungs. This leads up to a dry, hacking cough, noticeably irritable when bacon is being fried. After that, somewhere along in the spring or summer, a hole is burned in the frozen muck. Into this a man's carcass is dumped, covered over with moss, and left with the assurance that it will rise on the crack of Doom, wholly and frigidly intact. For those of little faith, sceptical of material integration on that fateful day, no fitter country than the Klondike can be recommended to die in. But it is not to be inferred from this that it is a fit country for living purposes.

It was very cold without, but it was not over-warm within. The only article which might be designated furniture was the stove, and for this the men were frank in displaying their preference. Upon half of the floor pine boughs had been cast; above this were spread the sleeping-furs, beneath lay the winter's snowfall. The remainder of the floor was moccasin-packed snow, littered with pots and pans and the general *impedimenta* of an Arctic camp. The stove was red and roaring hot, but only a bare three feet away lay a block of ice, as sharp-edged and dry as when first quarried from the creek bottom. The pressure of the outside cold forced the inner heat upward. Just above the stove, where the pipe penetrated the roof, was a tiny circle of dry canvas; next, with the pipe always as centre, a circle of steaming canvas; next a damp and moisture-exuding ring; and finally, the rest of the tent, sidewalls and top, coated with a half-inch of dry, white, crystal-encrusted frost.

"*Oh,* Oн! OH!" A young fellow, lying asleep in the furs, bearded and wan and weary, raised a moan of pain, and without waking increased the pitch and intensity of his anguish. His body half-lifted from the blankets, and quivered and shrank spasmodically, as though drawing away from a bed of nettles.

"Roll'm over!" ordered Bettles. "He's crampin'."

And thereat, with pitiless good-will, he was pitched upon and rolled and thumped and pounded by half-a-dozen willing comrades.

"Damn the trail," he muttered softly, as he threw off the robes and sat up. "I've run across country, played quarter three seasons hand-running, and hardened myself in all manner of ways; and then I pilgrim it into this God-forsaken land and find myself an effeminate Athenian without the simplest rudiments of manhood!" He hunched up to the fire and rolled a cigarette. "Oh, I'm not whining. I can take my medicine all right, all right; but I'm just decently ashamed of myself, that's all. Here I am, on top of a dirty thirty miles, as knocked up and stiff and sore as a pink-tea degenerate after a five-mile walk on a country turnpike. Bah! It makes me sick! Got a match?"

"Don't git the tantrums, youngster." Bettles passed over the required fire-stick and waxed patriarchal. "Ye've gotter 'low some

for the breakin'-in. Sufferin' cracky! don't I recollect the first time
I hit the trail! Stiff? I've seen the time it'd take me ten minutes to
git my mouth from the waterhole an' come to my feet—every jint
crackin' an' kickin' fit to kill. Cramp? In sech knots it'd take the
camp half a day to untangle me. You're all right, for a cub, an'
ye've the true sperrit. Come this day year, you'll walk all us old
bucks into the ground any time. An' best in your favor, you hain't
got that streak of fat in your make-up which has sent many a
husky man to the bosom of Abraham afore his right and proper
time."

"Streak of fat?"

"Yep. Comes along of bulk. 'T ain't the big men as is the best
when it comes to the trail."

"Never heard of it."

"Never heered of it, eh? Well, it's a dead straight, open-an'-shut
fact, an' no gittin' round. Bulk's all well enough for a mighty big
effort, but 'thout stayin' powers it ain't worth a continental
whoop; an' stayin' powers an' bulk ain't runnin' mates. Takes the
small, wiry fellows when it comes to gittin' right down an' hangin'
on like a lean-jowled dog to a bone. Why, hell's fire, the big men
they ain't in it!"

"By gar!" broke in Louis Savoy, "dat is no, vot you call, josh! I
know one mans, so vaire beeg like ze buffalo. Wit him, on ze
Sulphur Creek stampede, go one small mans, Lon McFane. You
know dat Lon McFane, dat leetle Irisher wit ze red hair and ze
grin. An' dey walk an' walk an' walk, all ze day long an' ze night
long. And beeg mans, him become vaire tired, an' lay down
mooch in ze snow. And leetle mans keek beeg mans, an' him cry
like, vot you call—ah! vot you call ze kid. And leetle mans keek
an' keek an' keek, an' bime by, long time, long way, keek beeg
mans into my cabin. Tree days 'fore him crawl out my blankets.
Nevaire I see beeg squaw like him. No nevaire. Him haf vot you
call ze streak of fat. You bet."

"But there was Axel Gunderson," Prince spoke up. The great
Scandinavian, with the tragic events which shadowed his passing,
had made a deep mark on the mining engineer. "He lies up there,
somewhere." He swept his hand in the vague direction of the mysterious east.

"Biggest man that ever turned his heels to Salt Water or run a moose down with sheer grit," supplemented Bettles; "but he's the prove-the-rule exception. Look at his woman, Unga,—tip the scales at a hundred an' ten, clean meat an' nary ounce to spare. She'd bank grit 'gainst his for all there was in him, an' see him, an' go him better if it was possible. Nothing over the earth, or in it, or under it, she wouldn't 'a' done."

"But she loved him," objected the engineer.

"'T ain't that. It—"

"Look you, brothers," broke in Sitka Charley from his seat on the grub-box. "Ye have spoken of the streak of fat that runs in big men's muscles, of the grit of women and the love, and ye have spoken fair; but I have in mind things which happened when the land was young and the fires of men apart as the stars. It was then I had concern with a big man, and a streak of fat, and a woman. And the woman was small; but her heart was greater than the beef-heart of the man, and she had grit. And we traveled a weary trail, even to the Salt Water, and the cold was bitter, the snow deep, the hunger great. And the woman's love was a mighty love —no more can man say than this."

He paused, and with the hatchet broke pieces of ice from the large chunk beside him. These he threw into the gold pan on the stove, where the drinking-water thawed. The men drew up closer, and he of the cramps sought greater comfort vainly for his stiffened body.

"Brothers, my blood is red with Siwash, but my heart is white. To the faults of my fathers I owe the one, to the virtues of my friends the other. A great truth came to me when I was yet a boy. I learned that to your kind and you was given the earth; that the Siwash could not withstand you, and like the caribou and the bear, must perish in the cold. So I came into the warm and sat among you, by your fires, and behold, I became one of you. I have seen much in my time. I have known strange things, and bucked big, on big trails, with men of many breeds. And because of these things, I measure deeds after your manner, and judge men, and think thoughts. Wherefore, when I speak harshly of one of your own kind, I know you will not take it amiss; and when I speak high of one of my father's people, you will not take it upon you to say, 'Sitka Charley is Siwash, and there is a crooked light in his eyes and small honor to his tongue.' Is it not so?"

Deep down in throat, the circle vouchsafed its assent.

"The woman was Passuk. I got her in fair trade from her people, who were of the Coast and whose Chilcat totem stood at the head of a salt arm of the sea. My heart did not go out to the woman, nor did I take stock of her looks. For she scarce took her eyes from the ground, and she was timid and afraid, as girls will be when cast into a stranger's arms whom they have never seen before. As I say, there was no place in my heart for her to creep, for I had a great journey in mind, and stood in need of one to feed my dogs and to lift a paddle with me through the long river days. One blanket would cover the twain; so I chose Passuk.

"Have I not said I was a servant to the Government? If not, it is well that ye know. So I was taken on a warship, sleds and dogs and evaporated foods, and with me came Passuk. And we went north, to the winter ice-rim of Bering Sea, where we were landed, —myself, and Passuk, and the dogs. I was also given moneys of the Government, for I was its servant, and charts of lands which the eyes of man had never dwelt upon, and messages. These messages were sealed, and protected shrewdly from the weather, and I was to deliver them to the whale-ships of the Arctic, icebound by the great Mackenzie. Never was there so great a river, forgetting only our own Yukon, the Mother of all Rivers.

"All of which is neither here nor there, for my story deals not with the whale-ships, nor the berg-bound winter I spent by the Mackenzie. Afterward, in the spring, when the days lengthened and there was a crust to the snow, we came south, Passuk and I, to the Country of the Yukon. A weary journey, but the sun pointed out the way of our feet. It was a naked land then, as I have said, and we worked up the current, with pole and paddle, till we came to Forty Mile. Good it was to see white faces once again, so we put into the bank. And that winter was a hard winter. The darkness and the cold drew down upon us, and with them the famine. To each man the agent of the Company gave forty pounds of flour and twenty of bacon. There were no beans. And the dogs howled always, and there were flat bellies and deep-lined faces, and strong men became weak, and weak men died. There was also much scurvy.

"Then came we together in the store one night, and the empty shelves made us feel our own emptiness the more. We talked low, by the light of the fire, for the candles had been set aside for those who might yet gasp in the spring. Discussion was held, and it was said that a man must go forth to the Salt Water and tell to the world our misery. At this all eyes turned to me, for it was understood that I was a great traveler. 'It is seven hundred miles,' said I, 'to Haines Mission by the sea, and every inch of it snowshoe work. Give me the pick of your dogs and the best of your grub, and I will go. And with me shall go Passuk.'

"To this they were agreed. But there arose one, Long Jeff, a Yankee-man, big-boned and big-muscled. Also his talk was big. He, too, was a mighty traveler, he said, born to the snowshoe and bred up on buffalo milk. He would go with me, in case I fell by the trail, that he might carry the word on to the Mission. I was young, and I knew not Yankee-men. How was I to know that big talk betokened the streak of fat, or that Yankee-men who did great things kept their teeth together? So we took the pick of the dogs and the best of the grub, and struck the trail, we three,—Passuk, Long Jeff, and I.

"Well, ye have broken virgin snow, labored at the gee-pole, and are not unused to the packed river-jams; so I will talk little of the toil, save that on some days we made ten miles, and on others thirty, but more often ten. And the best of the grub was not good, while we went on stint from the start. Likewise the pick of the dogs was poor, and we were hard put to keep them on their legs. At the White River our three sleds became two sleds, and we had only come two hundred miles. But we lost nothing; the dogs that left the traces went into the bellies of those that remained.

"Not a greeting, not a curl of smoke, till we made Pelly. Here I had counted on grub; and here I had counted on leaving Long Jeff, who was whining and trail-sore. But the factor's lungs were wheezing, his eyes bright, his cache nigh empty; and he showed us the empty cache of the missionary, also his grave with the rocks piled high to keep off the dogs. There was a bunch of Indians there, but babies and old men there were none, and it was clear that few would see the spring.

"So we pulled on, light-stomached and heavy-hearted, with half a thousand miles of snow and silence between us and Haines Mission by the sea. The darkness was at its worst, and at midday the sun could not clear the sky-line to the south. But the ice-jams were smaller, the going better; so I pushed the dogs hard and traveled late and early. As I said at Forty Mile, every inch of it was snowshoe work. And the shoes made great sores on our feet, which cracked and scabbed but would not heal. And every day these sores grew more grievous, till in the morning, when we girded on the shoes, Long Jeff cried like a child. I put him at the fore of the light sled to break trail, but he slipped off the shoes for comfort. Because of this the trail was not packed, his moccasins made great holes, and into these holes the dogs wallowed. The bones of the dogs were ready to break through their hides, and this was not good for them. So I spoke hard words to the man, and he promised, and broke his word. Then I beat him with the dog-whip, and after that the dogs wallowed no more. He was a child, what of the pain and the streak of fat.

"But Passuk. While the man lay by the fire and wept, she cooked, and in the morning helped lash the sleds, and in the evening to unlash them. And she saved the dogs. Ever was she to the fore, lifting the webbed shoes and making the way easy. Passuk—how shall I say?—I took it for granted that she should do these things, and thought no more about it. For my mind was busy with other matters, and besides, I was young in years and knew little of woman. It was only on looking back that I came to understand.

"And the man became worthless. The dogs had little strength in them, but he stole rides on the sled when he lagged behind. Passuk said she would take the one sled, so the man had nothing to do. In the morning I gave him his fair share of grub and started him on the trail alone. Then the woman and I broke camp, packed the sleds, and harnessed the dogs. By midday, when the sun mocked us, we would overtake the man, with the tears frozen on his cheeks, and pass him. In the night we made camp, set aside his fair share of grub, and spread his furs. Also we made a big fire, that he might see. And hours afterward he would come limping in, and eat his grub with moans and groans, and sleep. He was not sick, this man. He was only trail-sore and tired, and weak with hunger. But Passuk and I were trail-sore and tired, and weak with hunger; and we did all the work and he did none. But he had the streak of fat of which our brother Bettles has spoken. Further, we gave the man always his fair share of grub.

"Then one day we met two ghosts journeying through the Silence. They were a man and a boy, and they were white. The ice had opened on Lake Le Barge, and through it had gone their main outfit. One blanket each carried about his shoulders. At night they built a fire and crouched over it till morning. They had a little flour. This they stirred in warm water and drank. The man showed me eight cups of flour—all they had, and Pelly, stricken with famine, two hundred miles away. They said, also, that there was an Indian behind; that they had whacked fair, but that he could not keep up. I did not believe they had whacked fair, else would the Indian have kept up. But I could give them no grub. They strove to steal a dog—the fattest, which was very thin—but I shoved my pistol in their faces and told them begone. And they went away, like drunken men, through the Silence toward Pelly.

"I had three dogs now, and one sled, and the dogs were only bones and hair. When there is little wood, the fire burns low and the cabin grows cold. So with us. With little grub the frost bites sharp, and our faces were black and frozen till our own mothers would not have known us. And our feet were very sore. In the morning, when I hit the trail, I sweated to keep down the cry when the pain of the snowshoes smote me. Passuk never opened her lips, but stepped to the fore to break the way. The man howled.

"The Thirty Mile was swift, and the current ate away the ice from beneath, and there were many air-holes and cracks, and much open water. One day we came upon the man, resting, for he had gone ahead, as was his wont, in the morning. But between us was open water. This he had passed around by taking to the rim-ice where it was too narrow for a sled. So we found an icebridge. Passuk weighed little, and went first, with a long pole crosswise in her hands in chance she broke through. But she was light, and her shoes large, and she passed over. Then she called the dogs. But they had neither poles nor shoes, and they broke through and were swept under by the water. I held tight to the sled from behind, till the traces broke and the dogs went on down under the ice. There was little meat to them, but I had counted on them for a week's grub, and they were gone.

"The next morning I divided all the grub, which was little, into three portions. And I told Long Jeff that he could keep up with us, or not, as he saw fit; for we were going to travel light and fast. But he raised his voice and cried over his sore feet and his troubles, and said harsh things against comradeship. Passuk's feet were sore, and my feet were sore—ay, sorer than his, for we had worked with the dogs; also, we looked to see. Long Jeff swore he would die before he hit the trail again; so Passuk took a fur robe, and I a cooking pot and an axe, and we made ready to go. But she looked on the man's portion, and said, 'It is wrong to waste good food on a baby. He is better dead.' I shook my head and said no—that a comrade once was a comrade always. Then she spoke of the men of Forty Mile; that they were many men and good; and that they looked to me for grub in the spring. But when I still said no, she snatched the pistol from my belt, quick, and as our brother Bettles has spoken, Long Jeff went to the bosom of Abraham before his time. I chided Passuk for this; but she showed no sorrow, nor was she sorrowful. And in my heart I knew she was right."

Sitka Charley paused and threw pieces of ice into the gold pan on the stove. The men were silent, and their backs chilled to the sobbing cries of the dogs as they gave tongue to their misery in the outer cold. "And day by day we passed in the snow the sleeping-places of the two ghosts—Passuk and I—and we knew we would be glad for such ere we made Salt Water. Then we came to the Indian, like another ghost, with his face set toward Pelly. They had not whacked up fair, the man and the boy, he said, and he had had no flour for three days. Each night he boiled pieces of his moccasins in a cup, and ate them. He did not have much moccasins left. And he was a Coast Indian, and told us these things through Passuk, who talked his tongue. He was a stranger in the Yukon, and he knew not the way, but his face was set to Pelly. How far was it? Two sleeps? ten? a hundred?—he did not know, but he was going to Pelly. It was too far to turn back; he could only keep on.

"He did not ask for grub, for he could see we, too, were hard put. Passuk looked at the man, and at me, as though she were of two minds, like a mother partridge whose young are in trouble. So I turned to her and said, 'This man has been dealt unfair. Shall I give him of our grub a portion?' I saw her eyes light, as with quick pleasure; but she looked long at the man and at me, and her mouth drew close and hard, and she said, 'No. The Salt Water is afar off, and Death lies in wait. Better it is that he take this stranger man and let my man Charley pass.' So the man went away in the Silence toward Pelly. That night she wept. Never had I seen her weep before. Nor was it the smoke of the fire, for the wood was dry wood. So I marveled at her sorrow, and thought her woman's heart had grown soft at the darkness of the trail and the pain.

"Life is a strange thing. Much have I thought on it, and pondered long, yet daily the strangeness of it grows not less, but more. Why this longing for Life? It is a game which no man wins. To live is to toil hard, and to suffer sore, till Old Age creeps heavily upon us and we throw down our hands on the cold ashes of dead fires. It is hard to live. In pain the babe sucks his first breath, in pain the old man gasps his last, and all his days are full of trouble and sorrow; yet he goes down to the open arms of Death, stumbling, falling, with head turned backward, fighting to the last. And Death is kind. It is only Life, and the things of Life that hurt. Yet we love Life, and we hate Death. It is very strange.

"We spoke little, Passuk and I, in the days which came. In the night we lay in the snow like dead people, and in the morning we went on our way, walking like dead people. And all things were dead. There were no ptarmigan, no squirrels, no snowshoe rabbits, —nothing. The river made no sound beneath its white robes. The sap was frozen in the forest. And it became cold, as now; and in the night the stars drew near and large, and leaped and danced; and in the day the sun-dogs mocked us till we saw many suns, and all the air flashed and sparkled, and the snow was diamond dust. And there was no heat, no sound, only the bitter cold and the Silence. As I say, we walked like dead people, as in a dream, and we kept no count of time. Only our faces were set to Salt Water, our souls strained for Salt Water, and our feet carried us toward Salt Water. We camped by the Tahkeena, and knew it not. Our eyes looked upon the White Horse, but we saw it not. Our feet trod the portage of the Canyon, but they felt it not. We felt nothing. And we fell often by the way, but we fell, always, with our faces toward Salt Water.

"Our last grub went, and we had shared fair, Passuk and I, but she fell more often, and at Caribou Crossing her strength left her. And in the morning we lay beneath the one robe and did not take the trail. It was in my mind to stay there and meet Death hand-in-hand with Passuk; for I had grown old, and had learned the love of woman. Also, it was eighty miles to Haines Mission, and the great Chilcoot, far above the timber-line, reared his storm-swept head between. But Passuk spoke to me, low, with my ear against her lips that I might hear. And now, because she need not fear my anger, she spoke her heart, and told me of her love, and of many things which I did not understand.

"And she said: 'You are my man, Charley, and I have been a good woman to you. And in all the days I have made your fire, and cooked your food, and fed your dogs, and lifted paddle or broken trail, I have not complained. Nor did I say that there was more warmth in the lodge of my father, or that there was more grub on the Chilcat. When you have spoken, I have listened. When you have ordered, I have obeyed. Is it not so, Charley?'

"And I said: 'Ay, it is so.'

"And she said: 'When first you came to the Chilcat, nor looked upon me, but bought me as a man buys a dog, and took me away, my heart was hard against you and filled with bitterness and fear. But that was long ago. For you were kind to me, Charley, as a good man is kind to his dog. Your heart was cold, and there was no room for me; yet you dealt me fair and your ways were just. And I was with you when you did bold deeds and led great ventures, and I measured you against the men of other breeds, and I saw you stood among them full of honor, and your word was wise, your tongue true. And I grew proud of you, till it came that you filled all my heart, and all my thought was of you. You were as the midsummer sun, when its golden trail runs in a circle and never leaves the sky. And whatever way I cast my eyes I beheld the sun. But your heart was ever cold, Charley, and there was no room.'

"And I said: 'It is so. It was cold, and there was no room. But that is past. Now my heart is like the snowfall in the spring, when the sun has come back. There is a great thaw and a bending, a sound of running waters, and a budding and sprouting of green things. And there is drumming of partridges, and songs of robins, and great music, for the winter is broken, Passuk, and I have learned the love of woman.'

"She smiled and moved for me to draw her closer. And she said,

'I am glad.' After that she lay quiet for a long time, breathing softly, her head upon my breast. Then she whispered: 'The trail ends here, and I am tired. But first I would speak of other things. In the long ago, when I was a girl on the Chilcat, I played alone among the skin bales of my father's lodge; for the men were away on the hunt, and the women and boys were dragging in the meat. It was in the spring, and I was alone. A great brown bear, just awake from his winter's sleep, hungry, his fur hanging to the bones in flaps of leanness, shoved his head within the lodge and said, "Oof!" My brother came running back with the first sled of meat. And he fought the bear with burning sticks from the fire, and the dogs in their harnesses, with the sled behind them, fell upon the bear. There was a great battle and much noise. They rolled in the fire, the skin bales were scattered, the lodge overthrown. But in the end the bear lay dead, with the fingers of my brother in his mouth and the marks of his claws upon my brother's face. Did you mark the Indian by the Pelly trail, his mitten which had no thumb, his hand which he warmed by our fire? He was my brother. And I said he should have no grub. And he went away in the Silence without grub.'

"This, my brothers, was the love of Passuk, who died in the snow, by the Caribou Crossing. It was a mighty love, for she denied her brother for the man who led her away on weary trails to a bitter end. And, further, such was this woman's love, she denied herself. Ere her eyes closed for the last time she took my hand and slipped it under her squirrel-skin *parka* to her waist. I felt there a well-filled pouch, and learned the secret of her lost strength. Day by day we had shared fair, to the last least bit; and day by day but half her share had she eaten. The other half had gone into the well-filled pouch.

"And she said: 'This is the end of the trail for Passuk; but your trail, Charley, leads on and on, over the great Chilcoot, down to Haines Mission and the sea. And it leads on and on, by the light of many suns, over unknown lands and strange waters, and it is full of years and honors and great glories. It leads you to the lodges of many women, and good women, but it will never lead you to a greater love than the love of Passuk.'

"And I knew the woman spoke true. But a madness came upon me, and I threw the well-filled pouch from me, and swore that my trail had reached an end, till her tired eyes grew soft with tears, and she said: 'Among men has Sitka Charley walked in honor, and ever has his word been true. Does he forget that honor now, and talk vain words by the Caribou Crossing? Does he remember no more the men of Forty Mile, who gave him of their grub the best, of their dogs the pick? Ever has Passuk been proud of her man. Let him lift himself up, gird on his snowshoes, and begone, that she may still keep her pride.'

"And when she grew cold in my arms I arose, and sought out the well-filled pouch, and girt on my snowshoes, and staggered along the trail; for there was a weakness in my knees, and my head was dizzy, and in my ears there was a roaring, and a flashing of fire upon my eyes. The forgotten trails of boyhood came back to me. I sat by the full pots of the *potlach* feast, and raised my voice in song, and danced to the chanting of the men and maidens and the booming of the walrus drums. And Passuk held my hand and walked by my side. When I laid down to sleep, she waked me. When I stumbled and fell, she raised me. When I wandered in the deep snow, she led me back to the trail. And in this wise, like a man bereft of reason, who sees strange visions and whose thoughts are light with wine, I came to Haines Mission by the sea."

Sitka Charley threw back the tent-flaps. It was midday. To the south, just clearing the bleak Henderson Divide, poised the cold-disked sun. On either hand the sun-dogs blazed. The air was a gossamer of glittering frost. In the foreground, beside the trail, a wolf-dog, bristling with frost, thrust a long snout heavenward and mourned.

"DUMP it in."

"But I say, Kid, isn't that going it a little too strong? Whisky and alcohol's bad enough; but when it comes to brandy and pepper sauce and——"

"Dump it in. Who's making this punch, anyway?" And Malemute Kid smiled benignantly through the clouds of steam. "By the time you've been in this country as long as I have, my son, and lived on rabbit tracks and salmon belly, you'll learn that Christmas comes only once per annum. And a Christmas without punch is sinking a hole to bedrock with nary a pay streak."

"Stack up on that fer a high cyard," approved Big Jim Belden, who had come down from his claim on Mazy May to spend Christmas, and who, as everyone knew, had been living the two months past on straight moose meat. "Hain't fergot the hooch we-uns made on the Tanana, hev yeh?"

"Well, I guess yes. Boys, it would have done your hearts good to see that whole tribe fighting drunk—and all because of a glorious ferment of sugar and sour dough. That was before your time," Malemute Kid said as he turned to Stanley Prince, a young mining expert who had been in two years. "No white women in the country then, and Mason wanted to get married. Ruth's father was chief of the Tananas, and objected, like the rest of the tribe. Stiff? Why, I used my last pound of sugar; finest work in that line I ever did in my life. You should have seen the chase, down the river and across the portage."

"But the squaw?" asked Louis Savoy, the tall French Canadian, becoming interested; for he had heard of this wild deed when at Forty Mile the preceding winter.

Then Malemute Kid, who was a born raconteur, told the unvarnished tale of the Northland Lochinvar. More than one rough adventurer of the North felt his heartstrings draw closer and experienced vague yearnings for the sunnier pastures of the Southland, where life promised something more than a barren struggle with cold and death.

"We struck the Yukon just behind the first ice run," he concluded, "and the tribe only a quarter of an hour behind. But that saved us; for the second run broke the jam above and shut them out. When they finally got into Nuklukyeto, the whole post was ready for them. And as to the forgathering, ask Father Roubeau here: he performed the ceremony."

The Jesuit took the pipe from his lips but could only express his gratification with patriarchal smiles, while Protestant and Catholic vigorously applauded.

"By gar!" ejaculated Louis Savoy, who seemed overcome by the romance of it. "*La petite* squaw; *mon* Mason *brav*. By gar!"

Then, as the first tin cups of punch went round, Bettles the Unquenchable sprang to his feet and struck up his favorite drinking song:

> "There's Henry Ward Beecher
> And Sunday-school teachers,
>   All drink of the sassafras root;
> But you bet all the same,
> If it had its right name,
>   It's the juice of the forbidden fruit."

> "Oh, the juice of the forbidden fruit,"

roared out the bacchanalian chorus,

"Oh, the juice of the forbidden fruit;
But you bet all the same,
If it had its right name,
It's the juice of the forbidden fruit."

Malemute Kid's frightful concoction did its work; the men of the camps and trails unbent in its genial glow, and jest and song and tales of past adventure went round the board. Aliens from a dozen lands, they toasted each and all. It was the Englishman, Prince, who pledged "Uncle Sam, the precocious infant of the New World"; the Yankee, Bettles, who drank to "The Queen, God bless her"; and together, Savoy and Meyers, the German trader, clanged their cups to Alsace and Lorraine.

Then Malemute Kid arose, cup in hand, and glanced at the greased-paper window, where the frost stood full three inches thick. "A health to the man on trail this night; may his grub hold out; may his dogs keep their legs; may his matches never miss fire."

Crack! Crack! They heard the familiar music of the dog whip, the whining howl of the Malemutes, and the crunch of a sled as it drew up to the cabin. Conversation languished while they waited the issue.

"An old-timer; cares for his dogs and then himself," whispered Malemute Kid to Prince as they listened to the snapping jaws and the wolfish snarls and yelps of pain which proclaimed to their practiced ears that the stranger was beating back their dogs while he fed his own.

Then came the expected knock, sharp and confident, and the stranger entered. Dazzled by the light, he hesitated a moment at the door, giving to all a chance for scrutiny. He was a striking personage, and a most picturesque one, in his Arctic dress of wool and fur. Standing six foot two or three, with proportionate breadth of shoulders and depth of chest, his smooth-shaven face nipped by the cold to a gleaming pink, his long lashes and eyebrows white with ice, and the ear and neck flaps of his great wolfskin cap loosely raised, he seemed, of a verity, the Frost King, just stepped in out of the night. Clasped outside his Mackinaw jacket, a beaded belt held two large Colt's revolvers and a hunting knife, while he carried, in addition to the inevitable dog whip, a smokeless rifle of the largest bore and latest pattern. As he came forward, for all his step was firm and elastic, they could see that fatigue bore heavily upon him.

An awkward silence had fallen, but his hearty "What cheer, my lads?" put them quickly at ease, and the next instant Malemute Kid and he had gripped hands. Though they had never met, each had heard of the other, and the recognition was mutual. A sweeping introduction and a mug of punch were forced upon him before he could explain his errand.

"How long since that basket sled, with three men and eight dogs, passed?" he asked.

"An even two days ahead. Are you after them?"

"Yes; my team. Run them off under my very nose, the cusses. I've gained two days on them already—pick them up on the next run."

"Reckon they'll show spunk?" asked Belden, in order to keep up the conversation, for Malemute Kid already had the coffeepot on and was busily frying bacon and moose meat.

The stranger significantly tapped his revolvers.

"When'd yeh leave Dawson?"

"Twelve o'clock."

"Last night?"—as a matter of course.

"Today."

A murmur of surprise passed round the circle. And well it might; for it was just midnight, and seventy-five miles of rough river trail was not to be sneered at for a twelve hours' run.

The talk soon became impersonal, however, harking back to the trails of childhood. As the young stranger ate of the rude fare Malemute Kid attentively studied his face. Nor was he long in deciding that it was fair, honest, and open, and that he liked it. Still youthful, the lines had been firmly traced by toil and hardship. Though genial in conversation, and mild when at rest, the blue eyes gave promise of the hard steel-glitter which comes when called into action, especially against odds. The heavy jaw and square-cut chin demonstrated rugged pertinacity and indomitability. Nor, though the attributes of the lion were there, was there wanting the certain softness, the hint of womanliness, which bespoke the emotional nature.

"So thet's how me an' the ol' woman got spliced," said Belden, concluding the exciting tale of his courtship. " 'Here we be, Dad,' sez she. 'An' may yeh be damned,' sez he to her, an' then to me, 'Jim, yeh—yeh git outen them good duds o' yourn; I want a right peart slice o' thet forty acre plowed 'fore dinner.' An' then he turns on her an' sez, 'An' yeh, Sal; yeh sail inter them dishes.' An' then he sort o' sniffled an' kissed her. An' I was thet happy—but he seen me an' roars out, 'Yeh, Jim!' An' yeh bet I dusted fer the barn."

"Any kids waiting for you back in the States?" asked the stranger.

"Nope; Sal died 'fore any come. Thet's why I'm here." Belden abstractedly began to light his pipe, which had failed to go out, and then brightened up with, "How 'bout yerself, stranger—married man?"

For reply, he opened his watch, slipped it from the thong which served for a chain, and passed it over. Belden pricked up the slush lamp, surveyed the inside of the case critically, and, swearing admiringly to himself, handed it over to Louis Savoy. With numerous "By gars!" he finally surrendered it to Prince, and they noticed that his hands trembled and eyes took on a peculiar softness. And so it passed from horny hand to horny hand—the pasted photograph of a woman, the clinging kind that such men fancy, with a babe at the breast. Those who had not yet seen the wonder were keen with curiosity; those who had became silent and retrospective. They could face the pinch of famine, the grip of scurvy, or the quick death by field or flood; but the pictured semblance of a stranger woman and child made women and children of them all.

"Never have seen the youngster yet—he's a boy, she says, and two years old," said the stranger as he received the treasure back. A lingering moment he gazed upon it, then snapped the case and turned away, but not quick enough to hide the restrained rush of tears.

Malemute Kid led him to a bunk and bade him turn in.

"Call me at four sharp. Don't fail me," were his last words, and a moment later he was breathing in the heaviness of exhausted sleep.

"By Jove! He's a plucky chap," commented Prince. "Three

hours' sleep after seventy-five miles with the dogs, and then the trail again. Who is he, Kid?"

"Jack Westondale. Been in going on three years, with nothing but the name of working like a horse, and any amount of bad luck to his credit. I never knew him, but Sitka Charley told me about him."

"It seems hard that a man with a sweet young wife like his should be putting in his years in this Godforsaken hole, where every year counts two on the outside."

"The trouble with him is clean grit and stubbornness. He's cleaned up twice with a stake, but lost it both times."

Here the conversation was broken off by an uproar from Bettles, for the effect had begun to wear away. And soon the bleak years of monotonous grub and deadening toil were being forgotten in rough merriment. Malemute Kid alone seemed unable to lose himself, and cast many an anxious look at his watch. Once he put on his mittens and beaver-skin cap, and, leaving the cabin, fell to rummaging about in the cache.

Nor could he wait the hour designated; for he was fifteen minutes ahead of time in rousing his guest. The young giant had stiffened badly, and brisk rubbing was necessary to bring him to his feet. He tottered painfully out of the cabin, to find his dogs harnessed and everything ready for the start. The company wished him good luck and a short chase, while Father Roubeau, hurriedly blessing him, led the stampede for the cabin; and small wonder, for it is not good to face seventy-four degrees below zero with naked ears and hands.

Malemute Kid saw him to the main trail, and there, gripping his hand heartily, gave him advice.

"You'll find a hundred pounds of salmon eggs on the sled," he said. "The dogs will go as far on that as with one hundred and fifty of fish, and you can't get dog food at Pelly, as you probably expected." The stranger started, and his eyes flashed, but he did not interrupt. "You can't get an ounce of food for dog or man till you reach Five Fingers, and that's a stiff two hundred miles. Watch out for open water on the Thirty Mile River, and be sure you take the big cutoff above Le Barge."

"How did you know it? Surely the news can't be ahead of me already?"

"I don't know it; and what's more, I don't want to know it. But you never owned that team you're chasing. Sitka Charley sold it to them last spring. But he sized you up to me as square once, and I believe him. I've seen your face; I like it. And I've seen—why, damn you, hit the high places for salt water and that wife of yours, and ——" Here the Kid unmittened and jerked out his sack.

"No; I don't need it," and the tears froze on his cheeks as he convulsively gripped Malemute Kid's hand.

"Then don't spare the dogs; cut them out of the traces as fast as they drop; buy them, and think they're cheap at ten dollars a pound. You can get them at Five Fingers, Little Salmon, and Hootalinqua. And watch out for wet feet," was his parting advice. "Keep a-traveling up to twenty-five, but if it gets below that, build a fire and change your socks."

Fifteen minutes had barely elapsed when the jingle of bells announced new arrivals. The door opened, and a mounted policeman of the Northwest Territory entered, followed by two half-breed dog drivers. Like Westondale, they were heavily armed and showed signs of fatigue. The half-breeds had been born to the trail and bore it easily; but the young policeman was badly exhausted. Still, the dogged obstinacy of his race held him to the pace he had set, and would hold him till he dropped in his tracks.

"When did Westondale pull out?" he asked. "He stopped here, didn't he?" This was supererogatory, for the tracks told their own tale too well.

Malemute Kid had caught Belden's eye, and he, scenting the wind, replied evasively, "A right peart while back."

"Come, my man; speak up," the policeman admonished.

"Yeh seem to want him right smart. Hez he ben gittin' cantankerous down Dawson way?"

"Held up Harry McFarland's for forty thousand; exchanged it at the P. C. store for a check on Seattle; and who's to stop the cashing of it if we don't overtake him? When did he pull out?"

Every eye suppressed its excitement, for Malemute Kid had given the cue, and the young officer encountered wooden faces on every hand.

Striding over to Prince, he put the question to him. Though it hurt him, gazing into the frank, earnest face of his fellow countryman, he replied inconsequentially on the state of the trail.

Then he espied Father Roubeau, who could not lie. "A quarter of an hour ago," the priest answered; "but he had four hours' rest for himself and dogs."

"Fifteen minutes' start, and he's fresh! My God!" The poor fellow staggered back, half fainting from exhaustion and disappointment, murmuring something about the run from Dawson in ten hours and the dogs being played out.

Malemute Kid forced a mug of punch upon him; then he turned for the door, ordering the dog drivers to follow. But the warmth and promise of rest were too tempting, and they objected strenuously. The Kid was conversant with their French patois, and followed it anxiously.

They swore that the dogs were gone up; that Siwash and Babette would have to be shot before the first mile was covered; that the rest were almost as bad; and that it would be better for all hands to rest up.

"Lend me five dogs?" he asked, turning to Malemute Kid.

But the Kid shook his head.

"I'll sign a check on Captain Constantine for five thousand—here's my papers—I'm authorized to draw at my own discretion."

Again the silent refusal.

"Then I'll requisition them in the name of the Queen."

Smiling incredulously, the Kid glanced at his well-stocked arsenal and the Englishman, realizing his impotency, turned for the door. But the dog drivers still objecting, he whirled upon them fiercely, calling them women and curs. The swart face of the older half-breed flushed angrily as he drew himself up and promised in good, round terms that he would travel his leader off his legs, and would then be delighted to plant him in the snow.

The young officer—and it required his whole will—walked steadily to the door, exhibiting a freshness he did not possess. But they all knew and appreciated his proud effort; nor could he veil the twinges of agony that shot across his face. Covered with frost, the dogs were curled up in the snow, and it was almost impossible to get them to their feet. The poor brutes whined under the stinging lash, for the dog drivers were angry and cruel; nor till Babette, the leader, was cut from the traces, could they break out the sled and get under way.

"A dirty scoundrel and a liar!" "By gar! Him no good!" "A thief!" "Worse than an Indian!" It was evident that they were angry—first at the way they had been deceived; and second at the outraged ethics of the Northland, where honesty, above all, was man's prime jewel. "An' we gave the cuss a hand, after knowin' what he'd did." All eyes turned accusingly upon Malemute Kid, who rose from the corner where he had been making Babette comfortable, and silently emptied the bowl for a final round of punch.

"It's a cold night, boys—a bitter cold night," was the irrelevant commencement of his defense. "You've all traveled trail, and know what that stands for. Don't jump a dog when he's down. You've only heard one side. A whiter man than Jack Westondale never ate from the same pot nor stretched blanket with you or me. Last fall he gave his whole clean-up, forty thousand, to Joe Castrell, to buy in on Dominion. Today he'd be a millionaire. But while he stayed behind at Circle City, taking care of his partner with the scurvy, what does Castrell do? Goes into McFarland's, jumps the limit, and drops the whole sack. Found him dead in the snow the next day. And poor Jack laying his plans to go out this winter to his wife and the boy he's never seen. You'll notice he took exactly what his partner lost—forty thousand. Well, he's gone out; and what are you going to do about it?"

The Kid glanced round the circle of his judges, noted the softening of their faces, then raised his mug aloft. "So a health to the man on trail this night; may his grub hold out; may his dogs keep their legs; may his matches never miss fire. God prosper him; good luck go with him; and——"

"Confusion to the Mounted Police!" cried Bettles, to the crash of the empty cups.

THE LAW OF LIFE

OLD Koskoosh listened greedily. Though his sight had long since faded, his hearing was still acute, and the slightest sound penetrated to the glimmering intelligence which yet abode behind the withered forehead, but which no longer gazed forth upon the things of the world. Ah! That was Sit-cum-to-ha, shrilly anathematizing the dogs as she cuffed and beat them into the harnesses. Sit-cum-to-ha was his daughter's daughter, but she was too busy to waste a thought upon her broken grandfather, sitting alone there in the snow, forlorn and helpless. Camp must be broken. The long trail waited while the short day refused to linger. Life called her, and the duties of life, not death. And he was very close to death now.

The thought made the old man panicky for the moment, and he stretched forth a palsied hand which wandered tremblingly over the small heap of dry wood beside him. Reassured that it was indeed there, his hand returned to the shelter of his mangy furs, and he again fell to listening. The sulky crackling of half-frozen hides told him that the chief's moose-skin lodge had been struck, and even then was being rammed and jammed into portable compass. The chief was his son, stalwart and strong, headman of the tribesmen, and a mighty hunter. As the women toiled with the camp luggage, his voice rose, chiding them for their slowness. Old Koskoosh strained his ears. It was the last time he would hear that voice. There went Geehow's lodge! And Tusken's! Seven, eight, nine; only the shaman's could be still standing. There! They were at work upon it now. He could hear the shaman grunt as he piled it on the sled. A child whimpered, and a woman soothed it with soft, crooning gutturals. Little Koo-tee, the old man thought, a fretful child, and not overstrong. It would die soon, perhaps, and they would burn a hole through the frozen tundra and pile rocks above to keep the wolverines away. Well, what did it matter? A few years at best, and as many an empty belly as a full one. And in the end, Death waited, ever-hungry and hungriest of them all.

What was that? Oh, the men lashing the sleds and drawing tight the thongs. He listened, who would listen no more. The whiplashes snarled and bit among the dogs. Hear them whine! How they hated the work and the trail! They were off! Sled after sled churned slowly away into the silence. They were gone. They had passed out of his life, and he faced the last bitter hour alone. No. The snow crunched beneath a moccasin; a man stood beside him; upon his head a hand rested gently. His son was good to do this thing. He remembered other old men whose sons had not waited after the tribe. But his son had. He wandered away into the past, till the young man's voice brought him back.

"It is well with you?" he asked.

And the old man answered, "It is well."

"There be wood beside you," the younger man continued, "and the fire burns bright. The morning is gray, and the cold has broken. It will snow presently. Even now it is snowing."

"Aye, even now is it snowing."

"The tribesmen hurry. Their bales are heavy and their bellies flat with lack of feasting. The trail is long and they travel fast. I go now. It is well?"

"It is well. I am as a last year's leaf, clinging lightly to the stem. The first breath that blows, and I fall. My voice is become like an old woman's. My eyes no longer show me the way of my feet, and my feet are heavy, and I am tired. It is well."

He bowed his head in content till the last noise of the complaining snow had died away, and he knew his son was beyond recall. Then his hand crept out in haste to the wood. It alone stood between him and the eternity that yawned in upon him. At last the measure of his life was a handful of faggots. One by one they would go to feed the fire, and just so, step by step, death would creep upon him. When the last stick had surrendered up its heat, the frost would begin to gather strength. First his feet would yield, then his hands; and the numbness would travel, slowly, from the extremities to the body. His head would fall forward upon his knees, and he would rest. It was easy. All men must die.

He did not complain. It was the way of life, and it was just. He had been born close to the earth, close to the earth had he lived, and the law thereof was not new to him. It was the law of all flesh. Nature was not kindly to the flesh. She had no concern for that concrete thing called the individual. Her interest lay in the species, the race. This was the deepest abstraction old Koskoosh's barbaric mind was capable of, but he grasped it firmly. He saw it exemplified in all life. The rise of the sap, the bursting greenness of the willow bud, the fall of the yellow leaf—in this alone was told the whole history. But one task did Nature set the individual. Did he not perform it, he died. Did he perform it, it was all the same, he died. Nature did not care; there were plenty who were obedient, and it was only the obedience in this matter, not the obedient, which lived and lived always. The tribe of Koskoosh was very old. The old men he had known when a boy had known old men before them. Therefore it was true that the tribe lived, that it stood for the obedience of all its members, way down into the forgotten past, whose very resting places were unremembered. They did not count; they were episodes. They had passed away like clouds from a summer sky. He also was an episode and would pass away. Nature did not care. To life she set one task, gave one law. To perpetuate was the task of life, its law was death. A maiden was a good creature to look upon, full-breasted and strong, with spring to her step and light in her eyes. But her task was yet before her. The light in her eyes brightened, her step quickened, she was now bold with the young men, now timid, and she gave them of her own unrest. And ever she grew fairer and yet fairer to look upon, till some hunter, able no longer to withhold himself, took her to his lodge to cook and toil for him and to become the mother of his children. And with the coming of her offspring her looks left her. Her limbs dragged and shuffled, her eyes dimmed and bleared, and only the little children found joy against the withered cheek of the old squaw by the fire. Her task was done. But a little while, on the first pinch of famine or the first long trail, and she would be left, even as he had been left, in the snow, with a little pile of wood. Such was the law.

He placed a stick carefully upon the fire and resumed his meditations. It was the same everywhere, with all things. The mosquitoes vanished with the first frost. The little tree squirrel crawled away to die. When age settled upon the rabbit it became slow and heavy and could no longer outfoot its enemies. Even the big bald-face grew clumsy and blind and quarrelsome, in the end to be dragged down by a handful of yelping huskies. He remembered how he had abandoned his own father on an upper reach of the Klondike one winter, the winter before the missionary came with his talk books and his box of medicines. Many a time had Koskoosh smacked his lips over the recollection of that box, though now his mouth refused to moisten. The "painkiller" had been especially good. But the missionary was a bother after all, for he brought no meat into the camp, and he ate heartily, and the hunters grumbled. But he chilled his lungs on the divide by the Mayo, and the dogs afterward nosed the stones away and fought over his bones.

Koskoosh placed another stick on the fire and harked back deeper into the past. There was the time of the great famine, when the old men crouched empty-bellied to the fire, and let fall from their lips dim traditions of the ancient day when the Yukon ran wide open for three winters, and then lay frozen for three summers. He had lost his mother in that famine. In the summer the salmon run had failed, and the tribe looked forward to the winter and the coming of the caribou. Then the winter came, but with it there were no caribou. Never had the like been known, not even in the lives of the old men. But the caribou did not come, and it was the seventh year, and the rabbits had not replenished, and the dogs were naught but bundles of bones. And through the long darkness the children wailed and died, and the women, and the old men; and not one in ten of the tribe lived to meet the sun when it came back in the spring. That *was* a famine!

But he had seen times of plenty, too, when the meat spoiled on their hands, and the dogs were fat and worthless with overeating —times when they let the game go unkilled, and the women were fertile, and the lodges were cluttered with sprawling men-children and women-children. Then it was the men became high-stomached, and revived ancient quarrels, and crossed the divides to the south to kill the Pellys, and to the west that they might sit by the dead fires of the Tananas. He remembered, when a boy, during a time of plenty, when he saw a moose pulled down by the wolves. Zing-ha lay with him in the snow and watched—Zing-ha, who later became the craftiest of hunters, and who, in the end, fell through an air hole on the Yukon. They found him, a month afterward, just as he had crawled halfway out and frozen stiff to the ice.

But the moose. Zing-ha and he had gone out that day to play at hunting after the manner of their fathers. On the bed of the creek they struck the fresh track of a moose, and with it the tracks of many wolves. "An old one," Zing-ha, who was quicker at reading the sign, said, "an old one who cannot keep up with the herd. The wolves have cut him out from his brothers, and they will never leave him." And it was so. It was their way. By day and by night, never resting, snarling on his heels, snapping at his nose, they would stay by him to the end. How Zing-ha and he felt the blood lust quicken! The finish would be a sight to see!

Eager-footed, they took the trail, and even he, Koskoosh, slow of sight and an unversed tracker, could have followed it blind, it was so wide. Hot were they on the heels of the chase, reading the grim tragedy, fresh-written, at every step. Now they came to where the moose had made a stand. Thrice the length of a grown man's body, in every direction, had the snow been stamped about and uptossed. In the midst were the deep impressions of the splay-hoofed game, and all about, everywhere, were the lighter foot-marks of the wolves. Some, while their brothers harried the kill, had lain to one side and rested. The full-stretched impress of their bodies in the snow was as perfect as though made the moment be-fore. One wolf had been caught in a wild lunge of the maddened victim and trampled to death. A few bones, well picked, bore wit-ness.

Again, they ceased the uplift of their snowshoes at a second stand. Here the great animal had fought desperately. Twice had he been dragged down, as the snow attested, and twice had he shaken his assailants clear and gained footing once more. He had done his task long since, but none the less was life dear to him. Zing-ha said it was a strange thing, a moose once down to get free again; but this one certainly had. The shaman would see signs and wonders in this when they told him.

And yet again, they come to where the moose had made to mount the bank and gain the timber. But his foes had laid on from behind, till he reared and fell back upon them, crushing two deep into the snow. It was plain the kill was at hand, for their brothers had left them untouched. Two more stands were hurried past, brief in time length and very close together. The trail was red now, and the clean stride of the great beast had grown short and slovenly. Then they heard the first sounds of the battle—not the full-throated chorus of the chase, but the short, snappy bark which spoke of close quarters and teeth to flesh. Crawling up the wind, Zing-ha bellied it through the snow, and with him crept he, Koskoosh, who was to be chief of the tribesmen in the years to come. Together they shoved aside the underbranches of a young spruce and peered forth. It was the end they saw.

The picture, like all of youth's impressions, was still strong with him, and his dim eyes watched the end played out as vividly as in that far-off time. Koskoosh marveled at this, for in the days which followed, when he was a leader of men and a head of councilors, he had done great deeds and made his name a curse in the mouths of the Pellys, to say naught of the strange white man he had killed, knife to knife, in open fight.

For long he pondered on the days of his youth, till the fire died down and the frost bit deeper. He replenished it with two sticks this time, and gauged his grip on life by what remained. If Sit-cum-to-ha had only remembered her grandfather, and gathered a larger armful, his hours would have been longer. It would have been easy. But she was ever a careless child, and honored not her ancestors from the time the Beaver, son of the son of Zing-ha, first cast eyes upon her. Well, what mattered it? Had he not done like-wise in his own quick youth? For a while he listened to the silence. Perhaps the heart of his son might soften, and he would come back with the dogs to take his old father on with the tribe to where the caribou ran thick and the fat hung heavy upon them.

He strained his ears, his restless brain for the moment stilled. Not a stir, nothing. He alone took breath in the midst of the great silence. It was very lonely. Hark! What was that? A chill passed over his body. The familiar, long-drawn howl broke the void, and it was close at hand. Then on his darkened eyes was projected the vision of the moose—the old bull moose—the torn flanks and bloody sides, the riddled mane, and the great branching horns, down low and tossing to the last. He saw the flashing forms of gray, the gleaming eyes, the lolling tongues, the slavered fangs. And he saw the inexorable circle close in till it became a dark point in the midst of the stamped snow.

A cold muzzle thrust against his cheek, and at its touch his soul leaped back to the present. His hand shot into the fire and dragged out a burning faggot. Overcome for the nonce by his hereditary fear of man, the brute retreated, raising a prolonged call to his brothers; and greedily they answered, till a ring of crouching, jaw-slobbered gray was stretched round about. The old man listened to the drawing in of this circle. He waved his brand wildly, and sniffs turned to snarls; but the panting brutes refused to scatter. Now one wormed his chest forward, dragging his haunches after, now a second, now a third; but never a one drew back. Why should he cling to life? he asked, and dropped the blazing stick into the snow. It sizzled and went out. The circle grunted uneasily but held its own. Again he saw the last stand of the old bull moose, and Koskoosh dropped his head wearily upon his knees. What did it matter after all? Was it not the law of life?

THE GREAT INTERROGATION

I

TO say the least, Mrs. Sayther's career in Dawson was meteoric. She arrived in the spring, with dog sleds and French-Canadian *voyageurs*, blazed gloriously for a brief month, and departed up the river as soon as it was free of ice. Now womanless Dawson never quite understood this hurried departure, and the local Four Hundred felt aggrieved and lonely till the Nome strike was made and old sensations gave way to new. For it had delighted in Mrs. Sayther, and received her wide-armed. She was pretty, charming, and, moreover, a widow. And because of this she at once had at heel any number of Eldorado Kings, officials, and adventuring younger sons, whose ears were yearning for the frou-frou of a woman's skirts.

The mining engineers revered the memory of her husband, the late Colonel Sayther, while the syndicate and promoter representatives spoke awesomely of his deals and manipulations; for he was known down in the States as a great mining man, and as even a greater one in London. Why his widow, of all women, should have come into the country, was the great interrogation. But they were a practical breed, the men of the Northland, with a wholesome disregard for theories and a firm grip on facts. And to not a few of them Karen Sayther was a most essential fact. That she did not regard the matter in this light, is evidenced by the neatness and celerity with which refusal and proposal tallied off during her four weeks' stay. And with her vanished the fact, and only the interrogation remained.

To the solution, Chance vouchsafed one clew. Her last victim, Jack Coughran, having fruitlessly laid at her feet both his heart and a five-hundred-foot creek claim on Bonanza, celebrated the misfortune by walking all of a night with the gods. In the midwatch of this night he happened to rub shoulders with Pierre Fontaine, none other than head man of Karen Sayther's *voyageurs*. This rubbing of shoulders led to recognition and drinks, and ultimately involved both men in a common muddle of inebriety.

"Heh?" Pierre Fontaine later on gurgled thickly. "Vot for Madame Sayther mak visitation to thees country? More better you spik wit her. I know no t'ing 'tall, only all de tam her ask one man's name. 'Pierre,' her spik wit me; 'Pierre, you moos' find thees mans, and I gif you mooch—one thousand dollar you find thees mans.' Thees mans? Ah, *oui*. Thees man's name—vot you call—Daveed Payne. *Oui*, m'sieu, Daveed Payne. All de tam her spik das name. And all de tam I look rount vaire mooch, work lak hell, but no can find das dam mans, and no get one thousand dollar 'tall. By dam!

"Heh? Ah, *oui*. One tam dose mens vot come from Circle City, dose mens know thees mans. Him Birch Creek, dey spik. And madame? Her say '*Bon!*' and look happy lak anyt'ing. And her spik wit me. 'Pierre,' her spik, 'harness de dogs. We go queek. We find thees mans I gif you one thousand dollar more.' And I say, '*Oui*, queek! *Allons, madame!*'

"For sure, I t'ink, das two thousand dollar mine. Bully boy! Den more mens come from Circle City, and dey say no, das thees mans, Daveed Payne, come Dawson leel tam back. So madame and I go not 'tall.

"*Oui*, m'sieu. Thees day madame spik. 'Pierre,' her spik, and gif me five hundred dollar, 'go buy poling-boat. To-morrow we go up de river.' Ah, *oui*, to-morrow, up de river, and das dam Sitka Charley mak me pay for de poling-boat five hundred dollar. Dam!"

Thus it was, when Jack Coughran unburdened himself next

day, that Dawson fell to wondering who was this David Payne, and in what way his existence bore upon Karen Sayther's. But that very day, as Pierre Fontaine had said, Mrs. Sayther and her barbaric crew of *voyageurs* towed up the east bank to Klondike City, shot across to the west bank to escape the bluffs, and disappeared amid the maze of islands to the south.

II

"*Oui, madame*, thees is de place. One, two, t'ree island below Stuart River. Thees is t'ree island."

As he spoke, Pierre Fontaine drove his pole against the bank and held the stern of the boat against the current. This thrust the bow in, till a nimble breed climbed ashore with the painter and made fast.

"One leel tam, madame, I go look see."

A chorus of dogs marked his disappearance over the edge of the bank, but a minute later he was back again.

"*Oui, madame*, thees is de cabin. I mak investigation. No can find mans at home. But him no go vaire far, vaire long, or him no leave dogs. Him come queek, you bet!"

"Help me out, Pierre. I'm tired all over from the boat. You might have made it softer, you know."

From a nest of furs amidships, Karen Sayther rose to her full height of slender fairness. But if she looked lily-frail in her elemental environment, she was belied by the grip she put upon Pierre's hand, by the knotting of her woman's biceps as it took the weight of her body, by the splendid effort of her limbs as they held her out from the perpendicular bank while she made the ascent. Though shapely flesh clothed delicate frame, her body was a seat of strength.

Still, for all the careless ease with which she had made the landing, there was a warmer color than usual to her face, and a perceptibly extra beat to her heart. But then, also, it was with a certain reverent curiousness that she approached the cabin, while the flush on her cheek showed a yet riper mellowness.

"Look, see!" Pierre pointed to the scattered chips by the woodpile. "Him fresh—two, t'ree day, no more."

Mrs. Sayther nodded. She tried to peer through the small window, but it was made of greased parchment which admitted light while it blocked vision. Failing this, she went round to the door, half lifted the rude latch to enter, but changed her mind and let it fall back into place. Then she suddenly dropped on one knee and kissed the rough-hewn threshold. If Pierre Fontaine saw, he gave no sign, and the memory in the time to come was never shared. But the next instant, one of the boatmen, placidly lighting his pipe, was startled by an unwonted harshness in his captain's voice.

"Hey! You! Le Goire! You mak 'm soft more better," Pierre commanded. "Plenty bear-skin; plenty blanket. Dam!"

But the nest was soon after disrupted, and the major portion tossed up to the crest of the shore, where Mrs. Sayther lay down to wait in comfort. Reclining on her side, she looked out and over the wide-stretching Yukon. Above the mountains which lay beyond the further shore, the sky was murky with the smoke of unseen forest fires, and through this the afternoon sun broke feebly, throwing a vague radiance to earth, and unreal shadows. To the sky-line of the four quarters—spruce-shrouded islands, dark waters, and ice-scarred rocky ridges—stretched the immaculate wilderness. No sign of human existence broke the solitude; no sound the stillness. The land seemed bound under the unreality of the unknown, wrapped in the brooding mystery of great spaces.

Perhaps it was this which made Mrs. Sayther nervous; for she changed her position constantly, now to look up the river, now down, or to scan the gloomy shores for the half-hidden mouths of back channels. After an hour or so the boatmen were sent ashore to pitch camp for the night, but Pierre remained with his mistress to watch.

"Ah! him come thees tam," he whispered, after a long silence, his gaze bent up the river to the head of the island.

A canoe, with a paddle flashing on either side, was slipping down the current. In the stern a man's form, and in the bow a woman's, swung rhythmically to the work. Mrs. Sayther had no eyes for the woman till the canoe drove in closer and her bizarre beauty peremptorily demanded notice. A close-fitting blouse of moose-skin, fantastically beaded, outlined faithfully the well-rounded lines of her body, while a silken kerchief, gay of color and picturesquely draped, partly covered great masses of blue-black hair. But it was the face, cast belike in copper bronze, which caught and held Mrs. Sayther's fleeting glance. Eyes, piercing and black and large, with a traditionary hint of obliqueness, looked forth from under clear-stencilled, clean-arching brows. Without suggesting cadaverousness, though high-boned and prominent, the cheeks fell away and met in a mouth, thin-lipped and softly strong. It was a face which advertised the dimmest trace of ancient Mongol blood, a reversion, after long centuries of wandering, to the parent stem. This effect was heightened by the delicately aquiline nose with its thin trembling nostrils, and by the general air of eagle wildness which seemed to characterize not only the face but the creature herself. She was, in fact, the Tartar type modified to idealization, and the tribe of Red Indian is lucky that breeds such a unique body once in a score of generations.

Dipping long strokes and strong, the girl, in concert with the man, suddenly whirled the tiny craft about against the current and brought it gently to the shore. Another instant and she stood at the top of the bank, heaving up by rope, hand under hand, a quarter of fresh-killed moose. Then the man followed her, and together, with a swift rush, they drew up the canoe. The dogs were in a whining mass about them, and as the girl stooped among them caressingly, the man's gaze fell upon Mrs. Sayther, who had arisen. He looked, brushed his eyes unconsciously as though his sight were deceiving him, and looked again.

"Karen," he said simply, coming forward and extending his hand, "I thought for the moment I was dreaming. I went snow-blind for a time, this spring, and since then my eyes have been playing tricks with me."

Mrs. Sayther, whose flush had deepened and whose heart was urging painfully, had been prepared for almost anything save this coolly extended hand; but she tactfully curbed herself and grasped it heartily with her own.

"You know, Dave, I threatened often to come, and I would have, too, only—only—"

"Only I didn't give the word." David Payne laughed and watched the Indian girl disappearing into the cabin.

"Oh, I understand, Dave, and had I been in your place I'd most probably have done the same. But I have come—now."

"Then come a little bit farther, into the cabin and get something to eat," he said genially, ignoring or missing the feminine suggestion of appeal in her voice. "And you must be tired too. Which way are you travelling? Up? Then you wintered in Dawson, or came in on the last ice. Your camp?" He glanced at the *voyageurs* circled about the fire in the open and held back the door for her to enter.

"I came up on the ice from Circle City last winter," he continued, "and settled down here for a while. Am prospecting some on Henderson Creek, and if that fails, have been thinking of trying my hand this fall up at the Stuart River."

"You aren't changed much, are you?" she asked irrelevantly, striving to throw the conversation upon a more personal basis.

"A little less flesh, perhaps, and a little more muscle. How did *you* mean?"

But she shrugged her shoulders and peered through the dim light at the Indian girl, who had lighted the fire and was frying great chunks of moose meat, alternated with thin ribbons of bacon.

"Did you stop in Dawson long?" The man was whittling a stave of birchwood into a rude axe-handle, and asked the question without raising his head.

"Oh, a few days," she answered, following the girl with her eyes, and hardly hearing. "What were you saying? In Dawson? A month, in fact, and glad to get away. The arctic male is elemental, you know, and somewhat strenuous in his feelings."

"Bound to be when he gets right down to the soil. He leaves convention with the spring bed at home. But you were wise in your choice of time for leaving. You'll be out of the country before mosquito season, which is a blessing your lack of experience will not permit you to appreciate."

"I suppose not. But tell me about yourself, about your life. What kind of neighbors have you? Or have you any?"

While she queried she watched the girl grinding coffee in the corner of a flower sack upon the hearthstone. With a steadiness and skill which predicated nerves as primitive as the method, she crushed the imprisoned berries with a heavy fragment of quartz. David Payne noted his visitor's gaze, and the shadow of a smile drifted over his lips.

"I did have some," he replied. "Missourian chaps, and a couple of Cornishmen, but they went down to Eldorado to work at wages for a grubstake."

Mrs. Sayther cast a look of speculative regard upon the girl. "But of course there are plenty of Indians about?"

"Every mother's son of them down to Dawson long ago. Not a native in the whole country, barring Winapie here, and she's a Koyokuk lass,—comes from a thousand miles or so down the river."

Mrs. Sayther felt suddenly faint; and though the smile of interest in no wise waned, the face of the man seemed to draw away to a telescopic distance, and the tiered logs of the cabin to whirl drunkenly about. But she was bidden draw up to the table, and during the meal discovered time and space in which to find herself. She talked little, and that principally about the land and weather, while the man wandered off into a long description of the difference between the shallow summer diggings of the Lower Country and the deep winter diggings of the Upper Country.

"You do not ask why I came north?" she asked. "Surely you know." They had moved back from the table, and David Payne had returned to his axe-handle. "Did you get my letter?"

"A last one? No, I don't think so. Most probably it's trailing around the Birch Creek Country or lying in some trader's shack on the Lower River. The way they run the mails in here is shameful. No order, no system, no—"

"Don't be wooden, Dave! Help me!" She spoke sharply now, with an assumption of authority which rested upon the past. "Why don't you ask me about myself? About those we knew in the old times? Have you no longer any interest in the world? Do you know that my husband is dead?"

"Indeed, I am sorry. How long—"

"David!" She was ready to cry with vexation, but the reproach she threw into her voice eased her.

"Did you get any of my letters? You must have got some of them, though you never answered."

"Well, I didn't get the last one, announcing, evidently, the death of your husband, and most likely others went astray; but I did get some. I—er—read them aloud to Winapie as a warning—that is, you know, to impress upon her the wickedness of her white sisters. And I—er—think she profited by it. Don't you?"

She disregarded the sting, and went on. "In the last letter, which you did not receive, I told, as you have guessed, of Colonel Sayther's death. That was a year ago. I also said that if you did not come out to me, I would go in to you. And as I had often promised, I came."

"I know of no promise."

"In the earlier letters?"

"Yes, you promised, but as I neither asked nor answered, it was unratified. So I do not know of any such promise. But I do know of another, which you, too, may remember. It was very long ago." He dropped the axe-handle to the floor and raised his head. "It was so very long ago, yet I remember it distinctly, the day, the time, every detail. We were in a rose garden, you and I,—your mother's rose garden. All things were budding, blossoming, and the sap of spring was in our blood. And I drew you over—it was the first—and kissed you full on the lips. Don't you remember?"

"Don't go over it, Dave, don't! I know every shameful line of it. How often have I wept! If you only knew how I have suffered—"

"You promised me then—ay, and a thousand times in the sweet days that followed. Each look of your eyes, each touch of your hand, each syllable that fell from your lips, was a promise. And then—how shall I say?—there came a man. He was old—old enough to have begotten you—and not nice to look upon, but as the world goes, clean. He had done no wrong, followed the letter of the law, was respectable. Further, and to the point, he possessed some several paltry mines,—a score; it does not matter: and he owned a few miles of lands, and engineered deals, and clipped coupons. He—"

"But there were other things," she interrupted, "I told you. Pressure—money matters—want—my people—trouble. You understood the whole sordid situation. I could not help it. It was not my will. I was sacrificed, or I sacrificed, have it as you wish. But, my God! Dave, I gave you up! You never did *me* justice. Think what I have gone through!"

"It was not your will? Pressure? Under high heaven there was no thing to will you to this man's bed or that."

"But I cared for you all the time," she pleaded.

"I was unused to your way of measuring love. I am still unused. I do not understand."

"But now! now!"

"We were speaking of this man you saw fit to marry. What manner of man was he? Wherein did he charm your soul? What potent virtues were his? True, he had a golden grip,—an almighty golden grip. He knew the odds. He was versed in cent per cent. He had a narrow wit and excellent judgment of the viler parts, whereby he transferred this man's money to his pockets, and that man's money, and the next man's. And the law smiled. In that it did not condemn, our Christian ethics approved. By social measure he was not a bad man. But by your measure, Karen, by mine, by ours of the rose garden, what was he?"

"Remember, he is dead."

"The fact is not altered thereby. What was he? A great, gross, material creature, deaf to song, blind to beauty, dead to the spirit. He was fat with laziness, and flabby-cheeked, and the round of his belly witnessed his gluttony—"

"But he is dead. It is we who are now—now! now! Don't you hear? As you say, I have been inconstant. I have sinned. Good. But should not you, too, cry *peccavi?* If I have broken promises, have not you? Your love of the rose garden was of all time, or so you said. Where is it now?"

"It is here! now!" he cried, striking his breast passionately with clenched hand. "It has always been."

"And your love was a great love; there was none greater," she continued; "or so you said in the rose garden. Yet it is not fine enough, large enough, to forgive me here, crying now at your feet?"

The man hesitated. His mouth opened; words shaped vainly on his lips. She had forced him to bare his heart and speak truths which he had hidden from himself. And she was good to look upon, standing there in a glory of passion, calling back old associations and warmer life. He turned away his head that he might not see, but she passed around and fronted him.

"Look at me, Dave! Look at me! I am the same, after all. And so are you, if you would but see. We are not changed."

Her hand rested on his shoulder, and his had half-passed, roughly, about her, when the sharp crackle of a match startled him to himself. Winapie, alien to the scene, was lighting the slow wick of the slush lamp. She appeared to start out against a background of utter black, and the flame, flaring suddenly up, lighted her bronze beauty to royal gold.

"You see, it is impossible," he groaned, thrusting the fair-haired woman gently from him. "It is impossible," he repeated. "It is impossible."

"I am not a girl, Dave, with a girl's illusions," she said softly, though not daring to come back to him. "It is as a woman that I understand. Men are men. A common custom of the country. I am not shocked. I divined it from the first. But—ah!—it is only a marriage of the country—not a real marriage?"

"We do not ask such questions in Alaska," he interposed feebly.

"I know, but—"

"Well, then, it is only a marriage of the country—nothing else."

"And there are no children?"

"No."

"Nor—"

"No, no; nothing—but it is impossible."

"But it is not." She was at his side again, her hand touching lightly, caressingly, the sunburned back of his. "I know the custom of the land too well. Men do it every day. They do not care to remain here, shut out from the world, for all their days; so they give an order on the P. C. C. Company for a year's provisions, some money in hand, and the girl is content. By the end of that time, a man—" She shrugged her shoulders. "And so with the girl here. We will give her an order upon the company, not for a year, but for life. What was she when you found her? A raw, meat-eating savage; fish in summer, moose in winter, feasting in plenty, starving in famine. But for you that is what she would have remained. For your coming she was happier; for your going, surely, with a life of comparative splendor assured, she will be happier than if you had never been."

"No, no," he protested. "It is not right."

"Come, Dave, you must see. She is not your kind. There is no race affinity. She is an aborigine, sprung from the soil, yet close to the soil, and impossible to lift from the soil. Born savage, savage she will die. But we—you and I—the dominant, evolved race— the salt of the earth and the masters thereof! We are made for

each other. The supreme call is of kind, and we are of kind.
Reason and feeling dictate it. Your very instinct demands it. That
you cannot deny. You cannot escape the generations behind you.
Yours is an ancestry which has survived for a thousand centuries,
and for a hundred thousand centuries, and your line must not
stop here. It cannot. Your ancestry will not permit it. Instinct is
stronger than the will. The race is mightier than you. Come,
Dave, let us go. We are young yet, and life is good. Come."

Winapie, passing out of the cabin to feed the dogs, caught his
attention and caused him to shake his head and weakly to reiter-
ate. But the woman's hand slipped about his neck, and her cheek
pressed to his. His bleak life rose up and smote him,—the vain
struggle with pitiless forces; the dreary years of frost and famine;
the harsh and jarring contact with elemental life; the aching void
which mere animal existence could not fill. And there, seduction
by his side, whispering of brighter, warmer lands, of music, light,
and joy, called the old times back again. He visioned it unconsciously. Faces rushed in upon him; glimpses of forgotten scenes,
memories of merry hours; strains of song and trills of laughter—

"Come, Dave, come. I have for both. The way is soft." She
looked about her at the bare furnishings of the cabin. "I have for
both. The world is at our feet, and all joy is ours. Come! come!"

She was in his arms, trembling, and he held her tightly. He rose
to his feet. . . . But the snarling of hungry dogs, and the shrill
cries of Winapie bringing about peace between the combatants,
came muffled to his ear through the heavy logs. And another
scene flashed before him. A struggle in the forest,—a bald-face
grizzly, broken-legged, terrible; the snarling of the dogs and the
shrill cries of Winapie as she urged them to the attack; himself in
the midst of the crush, breathless, panting, striving to hold off red
death; broken-backed, entrail-ripped dogs howling in impotent anguish and desecrating the snow; the virgin white running scarlet
with the blood of man and beast; the bear, ferocious, irresistible,
crunching, crunching down to the core of his life; and Winapie,
at the last, in the thick of the frightful muddle, hair flying, eyes
flashing, fury incarnate, passing the long hunting knife again and
again— Sweat started to his forehead. He shook off the clinging
woman and staggered back to the wall. And she, knowing that the

moment had come, but unable to divine what was passing within him, felt all she had gained slipping away.

"Dave! Dave!" she cried. "I will not give you up! I will not give you up! If you do not wish to come, we will stay. I will stay with you. The world is less to me than are you. I will be a Northland wife to you. I will cook your food, feed your dogs, break trail for you, lift a paddle with you. I can do it. Believe me, I am strong."

Nor did he doubt it, looking upon her and holding her off from him; but his face had grown stern and gray, and the warmth had died out of his eyes.

"I will pay off Pierre and the boatmen, and let them go. And I will stay with you, priest or no priest, minister or no minister; go with you, now, anywhere! Dave! Dave! Listen to me! You say I did you wrong in the past—and I did—let me make up for it, let me atone. If I did not rightly measure love before, let me show that I can now."

She sank to the floor and threw her arms about his knees, sobbing. "And you *do* care for me. You *do* care for me. Think! The long years I have waited, suffered! You can never know!"

He stooped and raised her to her feet.

"Listen," he commanded, opening the door and lifting her bodily outside. "It cannot be. We are not alone to be considered. You must go. I wish you a safe journey. You will find it tougher work when you get up by the Sixty Mile, but you have the best boatmen in the world, and will get through all right. Will you say good-by?"

Though she already had herself in hand, she looked at him hopelessly. "If—if—if Winapie should—" She quavered and stopped.

But he grasped the unspoken thought, and answered, "Yes." Then struck with the enormity of it, "It cannot be conceived. There is no likelihood. It must not be entertained."

"Kiss me," she whispered, her face lighting. Then she turned and went away.

"Break camp, Pierre," she said to the boatman, who alone had remained awake against her return. "We must be going."

By the firelight his sharp eyes scanned the woe in her face, but he received the extraordinary command as though it were the most usual thing in the world. "*Oui, madame,*" he assented. "Which way? Dawson?"

"No," she answered, lightly enough; "up; out; Dyea."

Whereat he fell upon the sleeping *voyageurs,* kicking them, grunting, from their blankets, and buckling them down to the work, the while his voice, vibrant with action, shrilling through all the camp. In a trice Mrs. Sayther's tiny tent had been struck, pots and pans were being gathered up, blankets rolled, and the men staggering under the loads to the boat. Here, on the banks, Mrs. Sayther waited till the luggage was made shipshape and her nest prepared.

"We line up to de head of de island," Pierre explained to her while running out the long tow rope. "Den we tak to das back channel, where de water not queek, and I t'ink we mak good tam."

A scuffling and pattering of feet in the last year's dry grass caught his quick ear, and he turned his head. The Indian girl, circled by a bristling ring of wolf dogs, was coming toward them. Mrs. Sayther noted that the girl's face, which had been apathetic throughout the scene in the cabin, had now quickened into blazing and wrathful life.

"What you do my man?" she demanded abruptly of Mrs. Sayther. "Him lay on bunk, and him look bad all the time. I say, 'What the matter, Dave? You sick?' But him no say nothing. After that him say, 'Good girl Winapie, go way. I be all right bimeby.' What you do my man, eh? I think you bad woman."

Mrs. Sayther looked curiously at the barbarian woman who shared the life of this man, while she departed alone in the darkness of night.

"I think you bad woman," Winapie repeated in the slow, methodical way of one who gropes for strange words in an alien tongue. "I think better you go way, no come no more. Eh? What you think? I have one man. I Indian girl. You 'Merican woman. You good to see. You find plenty men. Your eyes blue like the sky. Your skin so white, so soft."

Coolly she thrust out a brown forefinger and pressed the soft cheek of the other woman. And to the eternal credit of Karen Sayther, she never flinched. Pierre hesitated and half stepped forward; but she motioned him away, though her heart welled to him with secret gratitude. "It's all right, Pierre," she said. "Please go away."

He stepped back respectfully out of earshot, where he stood grumbling to himself and measuring the distance in springs.

"Um white, um soft, like baby." Winapie touched the other cheek and withdrew her hand. "Bimeby mosquito come. Skin get sore in spot; um swell, oh, so big; um hurt, oh, so much. Plenty mosquito; plenty spot. I think better you go now before mosquito come. This way," pointing down the stream, "you go St. Michael's; that way," pointing up, "you go Dyea. Better you go Dyea. Good-by."

And that which Mrs. Sayther then did, caused Pierre to marvel greatly. For she threw her arms around the Indian girl, kissed her, and burst into tears.

"Be good to him," she cried. "Be good to him."

Then she slipped half down the face of the bank, called back "Good-by," and dropped into the boat amidships. Pierre followed her and cast off. He shoved the steering oar into place and gave the signal. Le Goire lifted an old French *chanson*; the men, like a row of ghosts in the dim starlight, bent their backs to the tow line; the steering oar cut the black current sharply, and the boat swept out into the night.

THE WISDOM OF THE TRAIL

SITKA CHARLEY had achieved the impossible. Other Indians might have known as much of the wisdom of the trail as did he; but he alone knew the white man's wisdom, the honor of the trail, and the law. But these things had not come to him in a day. The aboriginal mind is slow to generalize, and many facts, repeated often, are required to compass an understanding. Sitka Charley, from boyhood, had been thrown continually with white men, and as a man he had elected to cast his fortunes with them, expatriating himself, once and for all, from his own people. Even then, respecting, almost venerating their power, and pondering over it, he had yet to divine its secret essence—the honor and the law. And it was only by the cumulative evidence of years that he had finally come to understand. Being an alien, when he did know, he knew it better than the white man himself; being an Indian, he had achieved the impossible.

And of these things had been bred a certain contempt for his own people—a contempt which he had made it a custom to conceal, but which now burst forth in a polyglot whirlwind of curses upon the heads of Kah-Chucte and Gowhee. They cringed before him like a brace of snarling wolf dogs, too cowardly to spring, too wolfish to cover their fangs. They were not handsome creatures. Neither was Sitka Charley. All three were frightful-looking. There was no flesh to their faces; their cheekbones were massed with hideous scabs which had cracked and frozen alternately under the intense frost; while their eyes burned luridly with the light which is born of desperation and hunger. Men so situated, beyond the pale of the honor and the law, are not to be trusted. Sitka Charley knew this; and this was why he had forced them to abandon their rifles with the rest of the camp outfit ten days before. His rifle and Captain Eppingwell's were the only ones that remained.

"Come, get a fire started," he commanded, drawing out the precious matchbox with its attendant strips of dry birchbark.

The two Indians fell sullenly to the task of gathering dead branches and underwood. They were weak and paused often, catching themselves, in the act of stooping with giddy motions, or staggering to the center of operations with their knees shaking like castanets. After each trip they rested for a moment, as though sick and deadly weary. At times their eyes took on the patient stoicism of dumb suffering; and again the ego seemed almost bursting forth with its wild cry, "I, I, I want to exist!"—the dominant note of the whole living universe.

A light breath of air blew from the south, nipping the exposed portions of their bodies and driving the frost, in needles of fire, through fur and flesh to the bones. So, when the fire had grown lusty and thawed a damp circle in the snow about it, Sitka Charley forced his reluctant comrades to lend a hand in pitching a fly. It was a primitive affair, merely a blanket stretched parallel with the fire and to windward of it, at an angle of perhaps forty-five degrees. This shut out the chill wind and threw the heat backward and down upon those who were to huddle in its shelter. Then a layer of green spruce boughs was spread, that their bodies might not come in contact with the snow. When this task was completed, Kah-Chucte and Gowhee proceeded to take care of their feet. Their icebound moccasins were sadly worn by much travel, and the sharp ice of the river jams had cut them to rags. Their Siwash socks were similarly conditioned, and when these had been thawed and removed, the dead-white tips of the toes, in the various stages of mortification, told their simple tale of the trail.

Leaving the two to the drying of their footgear, Sitka Charley turned back over the course he had come. He, too, had a mighty longing to sit by the fire and tend his complaining flesh, but the honor and the law forbade. He toiled painfully over the frozen field, each step a protest, every muscle in revolt. Several times, where the open water between the jams had recently crusted, he was forced to miserably accelerate his movements as the fragile footing swayed and threatened beneath him. In such places death was quick and easy; but it was not his desire to endure no more.

His deepening anxiety vanished as two Indians dragged into view round a bend in the river. They staggered and panted like men under heavy burdens; yet the packs on their backs were a matter of but few pounds. He questioned them eagerly, and their replies seemed to relieve him. He hurried on. Next came two white men, supporting between them a woman. They also behaved as though drunken, and their limbs shook with weakness. But the woman leaned lightly upon them, choosing to carry herself forward with her own strength. At sight of her a flash of joy cast its fleeting light across Sitka Charley's face. He cherished a very great regard for Mrs. Eppingwell. He had seen many white women, but this was the first to travel the trail with him. When Captain Eppingwell proposed the hazardous undertaking and made him an offer for his services, he had shaken his head gravely; for it was an unknown journey through the dismal vastnesses of the Northland, and he knew it to be of the kind that try to the uttermost the souls of men. But when he learned that the captain's wife was to accompany them, he had refused flatly to have anything further to do with it. Had it been a woman of his own race he would have harbored no objections; but these women of the Southland—no, no, they were too soft, too tender, for such enterprises.

Sitka Charley did not know this kind of woman. Five minutes before, he did not even dream of taking charge of the expedition; but when she came to him with her wonderful smile and her straight clean English, and talked to the point, without pleading or persuading, he had incontinently yielded. Had there been a softness and appeal to mercy in the eyes, a tremble to the voice, a taking advantage of sex, he would have stiffened to steel; instead her clear-searching eyes and clear-ringing voice, her utter frankness and tacit assumption of equality, had robbed him of his reason.

He felt, then, that this was a new breed of woman; and ere they had been trail mates for many days he knew why the sons of such women mastered the land and the sea, and why the sons of his own womankind could not prevail against them. *Tender and soft!* Day after day he watched her, muscle-weary, exhausted, indomitable, and the words beat in upon him in a perennial refrain. *Tender and soft!* He knew her feet had been born to easy paths and sunny lands, strangers to the moccasined pain of the North, unkissed by the chill lips of the frost, and he watched and marveled at them twinkling ever through the weary day.

She had always a smile and a word of cheer, from which not even the meanest packer was excluded. As the way grew darker she seemed to stiffen and gather greater strength, and when Kah-Chucte and Gowhee, who had bragged that they knew every landmark of the way as a child did the skin bails of the tepee, acknowledged that they knew not where they were, it was she who raised a forgiving voice amid the curses of the men. She had sung to them that night till they felt the weariness fall from them and were ready to face the future with fresh hope. And when the food failed and each scant stint was measured jealously, she it was who rebelled against the machinations of her husband and Sitka Charley, and demanded and received a share neither greater nor less than that of the others.

Sitka Charley was proud to know this woman. A new richness, a greater breadth, had come into his life with her presence. Hitherto he had been his own mentor, had turned to right or left at no man's beck; he had molded himself according to his own dictates, nourished his manhood regardless of all save his own opinion. For the first time he had felt a call from without for the best that was in him. Just a glance of appreciation from the clear-searching eyes, a word of thanks from the clear-ringing voice, just a slight wreathing of the lips in the wonderful smile, and he walked with the gods for hours to come. It was a new stimulant to his manhood; for the first time he thrilled with a conscious pride in his wisdom of the trail; and between the twain they ever lifted the sinking hearts of their comrades.

The faces of the two men and the woman brightened as they saw him, for after all he was the staff they leaned upon. But Sitka

Charley, rigid as was his wont, concealing pain and pleasure impartially beneath an iron exterior, asked them the welfare of the rest, told the distance to the fire, and continued on the back-trip. Next he met a single Indian, unburdened, limping, lips compressed, and eyes set with the pain of a foot in which the quick fought a losing battle with the dead. All possible care had been taken of him, but in the last extremity the weak and unfortunate must perish, and Sitka Charley deemed his days to be few. The man could not keep up for long, so he gave him rough cheering words. After that came two more Indians, to whom he had allotted the task of helping along Joe, the third white man of the party. They had deserted him. Sitka Charley saw at a glance the lurking spring in their bodies, and knew they had at last cast off his mastery. So he was not taken unawares when he ordered them back in quest of their abandoned charge, and saw the gleam of the hunting knives that they drew from the sheaths. A pitiful spectacle, three weak men lifting their puny strength in the face of the mighty vastness; but the two recoiled under the fierce rifle blows of the one and returned like beaten dogs to the leash. Two hours later, with Joe reeling between them and Sitka Charley bringing up the rear, they came to the fire, where the remainder of the expedition crouched in the shelter of the fly.

"A few words, my comrades, before we sleep," Sitka Charley said after they had devoured their slim rations of unleavened bread. He was speaking to the Indians, in their own tongue, having already given the import to the whites. "A few words, my comrades, for your own good, that ye may yet perchance live. I shall give you the law; on his own head be the death of him that breaks it. We have passed the Hills of Silence, and we now travel the head reaches of the Stuart. It may be one sleep, it may be several, it may be many sleeps, but in time we shall come among the men of the Yukon, who have much grub. It were well that we look to the law. Today Kah-Chucte and Gowhee, whom I commanded to break trail, forgot they were men, and like frightened children ran away. True, they forgot; so let us forget. But hereafter let them remember. If it should happen they do not . . ." He touched his rifle carelessly, grimly. "Tomorrow they shall carry the flour and see that the white man Joe lies not down by the trail. The cups of flour are counted; should so much as an ounce be wanting at nightfall . . . Do ye understand? Today there were others that forgot. Moose Head and Three Salmon left the white man Joe to lie in the snow. Let them forget no more. With the light of day shall they go forth and break trail. Ye have heard the law. Look well, lest ye break it."

Sitka Charley found it beyond him to keep the line close up. From Moose Head and Three Salmon, who broke trail in advance, to Kah-Chucte, Gowhee, and Joe, it straggled out over a mile. Each staggered, fell, or rested as he saw fit. The line of march was a progression through a chain of irregular halts. Each drew upon the last remnant of his strength and stumbled onward till it was expended, but in some miraculous way there was always another last remnant. Each time a man fell it was with the firm belief that he would rise no more; yet he did rise, and again, and again. The flesh yielded, the will conquered; but each triumph was a tragedy. The Indian with the frozen foot, no longer erect, crawled forward on hand and knee. He rarely rested, for he knew the penalty exacted by the frost. Even Mrs. Eppingwell's lips were at last set in a stony smile, and her eyes, seeing, saw not. Often she stopped, pressing a mittened hand to her heart, gasping and dizzy.

Joe, the white man, had passed beyond the stage of suffering. He no longer begged to be let alone, prayed to die; but was soothed and content under the anodyne of delirium. Kah-Chucte and Gowhee dragged him on roughly, venting upon him many a savage glance or blow. To them it was the acme of injustice. Their hearts were bitter with hate, heavy with fear. Why should they cumber their strength with his weakness? To do so meant death; not to do so—and they remembered the law of Sitka Charley, and the rifle.

Joe fell with greater frequency as the daylight waned, and so hard was he to raise that they dropped farther and farther behind. Sometimes all three pitched into the snow, so weak had the Indians become. Yet on their backs was life, and strength, and warmth. Within the flour sacks were all the potentialities of existence. They could not but think of this, and it was not strange, that which came to pass. They had fallen by the side of a great timber jam where a thousand cords of firewood waited the match.

Near by was an air hole through the ice. Kah-Chucte looked on the wood and the water, as did Gowhee; then they looked on each other. Never a word was spoken. Gowhee struck a fire; Kah-Chucte filled a tin cup with water and heated it; Joe babbled of things in another land, in a tongue they did not understand. They mixed flour with the warm water till it was a thin paste, and of this they drank many cups. They did not offer any to Joe; but he did not mind. He did not mind anything, not even his moccasins, which scorched and smoked among the coals.

A crystal mist of snow fell about them, softly, caressingly, wrapping them in clinging robes of white. And their feet would have yet trod many trails had not destiny brushed the clouds aside and cleared the air. Nay, ten minutes' delay would have been salvation. Sitka Charley, looking back, saw the pillared smoke of their fire, and guessed. And he looked ahead at those who were faithful, and at Mrs. Eppingwell.

"So, my good comrades, ye have again forgotten that you were men? Good. Very good. There will be fewer bellies to feed."

Sitka Charley retied the flour as he spoke, strapping the pack to the one on his own back. He kicked Joe till the pain broke through the poor devil's bliss and brought him doddering to his feet. Then he shoved him out upon the trail and started him on his way. The two Indians attempted to slip off.

"Hold, Gowhee! And thou, too, Kah-Chucte! Hath the flour given such strength to thy legs that they may outrun the swift-winged lead? Think not to cheat the law. Be men for the last time, and be content that ye die full-stomached. Come, step up, back to the timber, shoulder to shoulder. Come!"

The two men obeyed, quietly, without fear; for it is the future which presses upon the man, not the present.

"Thou, Gowhee, hast a wife and children and a deerskin lodge in the Chipewyan. What is thy will in the matter?"

"Give thou her of the goods which are mine by the word of the captain—the blankets, the beads, the tobacco, the box which makes strange sounds after the manner of the white men. Say that I did die on the trail, but say not how."

"And thou, Kah-Chucte, who hast nor wife nor child?"

"Mine is a sister, the wife of the factor at Koshim. He beats her, and she is not happy. Give thou her the goods which are mine by the contract, and tell her it were well she go back to her own people. Shouldst thou meet the man, and be so minded, it were a good deed that he should die. He beats her, and she is afraid."

"Are ye content to die by the law?"

"We are."

"Then good-by, my good comrades. May ye sit by the well-filled pot, in warm lodges, ere the day is done."

As he spoke he raised his rifle, and many echoes broke the silence. Hardly had they died away when other rifles spoke in the distance. Sitka Charley started. There had been more than one shot, yet there was but one other rifle in the party. He gave a fleeting glance at the men who lay so quietly, smiled viciously at the wisdom of the trail, and hurried on to meet the men of the Yukon.

SECTION THREE

MOON-FACE

JOHN CLAVERHOUSE was a moon-faced man. You know the kind, cheek-bones wide apart, chin and forehead melting into the cheeks to complete the perfect round, and the nose, broad and pudgy, equidistant from the circumference, flattened against the very centre of the face like a dough-ball upon the ceiling. Perhaps that is why I hated him, for truly he had become an offence to my eyes, and I believed the earth to be cumbered with his presence. Perhaps my mother may have been superstitious of the moon and looked upon it over the wrong shoulder at the wrong time.

Be that as it may, I hated John Claverhouse. Not that he had done me what society would consider a wrong or an ill turn. Far from it. The evil was of a deeper, subtler sort; so elusive, so intangible, as to defy clear, definite analysis in words. We all experience such things at some period in our lives. For the first time we see a certain individual, one who the very instant before we did not dream existed; and yet, at the first moment of meeting, we say: "I do not like that man." Why do we not like him? Ah, we do not know why; we know only that we do not. We have taken a dislike, that is all. And so I with John Claverhouse.

What right had such a man to be happy? Yet he was an optimist. He was always gleeful and laughing. All things were always all right, curse him! Ah! how it grated on my soul that he should be so happy! Other men could laugh, and it did not bother me. I even used to laugh myself—before I met John Claverhouse.

But his laugh! It irritated me, maddened me, as nothing else under the sun could irritate or madden me. It haunted me, gripped hold of me, and would not let me go. It was a huge, Gargantuan laugh. Waking or sleeping it was always with me, whirring and jarring across my heart-strings like an enormous rasp. At break of day it came whooping across the fields to spoil my pleasant morning revery. Under the aching noonday glare, when the green things drooped and the birds withdrew to the depths of the forest, and all nature drowsed, his great "Ha! ha!" and "Ho! ho!" rose up to the sky and challenged the sun. And at black midnight, from the lonely cross-roads where he turned from town into his own place, came his plaguey cachinnations to rouse me from my sleep and make me writhe and clench my nails into my palms.

I went forth privily in the night-time, and turned his cattle into his fields, and in the morning heard his whooping laugh as he drove them out again. "It is nothing," he said; "the poor, dumb beasties are not to be blamed for straying into fatter pastures."

He had a dog he called "Mars," a big, splendid brute, part deer-hound and part blood-hound, and resembling both. Mars was a great delight to him, and they were always together. But I bided my time, and one day, when opportunity was ripe, lured the animal away and settled for him with strychnine and beefsteak. It made positively no impression on John Claverhouse. His laugh was as hearty and frequent as ever, and his face as much like the full moon as it always had been.

Then I set fire to his haystacks and his barn. But the next morning, being Sunday, he went forth blithe and cheerful.

"Where are you going?" I asked him, as he went by the cross-roads.

"Trout," he said, and his face beamed like a full moon. "I just dote on trout!"

Was there ever such an impossible man! His whole harvest had gone up in his haystacks and barn. It was uninsured, I knew. And yet, in the face of famine and the rigorous winter, he went out gayly in quest of a mess of trout, forsooth, because he "doted" on them! Had gloom but rested, no matter how lightly, on his brow, or had his bovine countenance grown long and serious and less like the moon, or had he removed that smile but once from off his face, I am sure I could have forgiven him for existing. But no, he grew only more cheerful under misfortune.

I insulted him. He looked at me in slow and smiling surprise.

"I fight you? Why?" he asked slowly. And then he laughed. "You are so funny! Ho! ho! You'll be the death of me! He! he! he! Oh! Ho! ho! ho!"

What would you? It was past endurance. By the blood of Judas, how I hated him! Then there was that name—Claverhouse! What a name! Wasn't it absurd? Claverhouse! Merciful heaven, *why* Claverhouse? Again and again I asked myself that question. I should not have minded Smith, or Brown, or Jones—but *Claverhouse!* I leave it to you. Repeat it to yourself—Claverhouse. Just listen to the ridiculous sound of it—Claverhouse! Should a man live with such a name? I ask of you. "No," you say. And "No" said I.

But I bethought me of his mortgage. What of his crops and barn destroyed, I knew he would be unable to meet it. So I got a shrewd, close-mouthed, tight-fisted money-lender to get the mortgage transferred to him. I did not appear, but through this agent I forced the foreclosure, and but few days (no more, believe me, than the law allowed) were given John Claverhouse to remove his goods and chattels from the premises. Then I strolled down to see how he took it, for he had lived there upward of twenty years. But he met me with his saucer-eyes twinkling, and the light glowing and spreading in his face till it was as a full-risen moon.

"Ha! ha! ha!" he laughed. "The funniest tike, that youngster of mine! Did you ever hear the like? Let me tell you. He was down playing by the edge of the river when a piece of the bank caved in and splashed him. 'O papa!' he cried; 'a great big puddle flewed up and hit me.'"

He stopped and waited for me to join him in his infernal glee.

"I don't see any laugh in it," I said shortly, and I know my face went sour.

He regarded me with wonderment, and then came the damnable light, glowing and spreading, as I have described it, till his face shone soft and warm, like the summer moon, and then the laugh—"Ha! ha! That's funny! You don't see it, eh? He! he! Ho! ho! ho! He doesn't see it! Why, look here. You know a puddle—"

But I turned on my heel and left him. That was the last. I could stand it no longer. The thing must end right there, I thought, curse him! The earth should be quit of him. As I went over the hill, I could hear his monstrous laugh reverberating against the sky.

Now, I pride myself on doing things neatly, and when I resolved to kill John Claverhouse I had it in mind to do so in such fashion that I should not look back upon it and feel ashamed. I hate bungling, and I hate brutality. To me there is something repugnant in merely striking a man with one's naked fist—faugh! it is sickening! So, to shoot, or stab, or club John Claverhouse (oh, that name!) did not appeal to me. And not only was I impelled to do it neatly and artistically, but also in such manner that not the slightest possible suspicion could be directed against me.

To this end I bent my intellect, and, after a week of profound incubation, I hatched the scheme. Then I set to work. I bought a water spaniel bitch, five months old, and devoted my whole attention to her training. Had any one spied upon me, they would have remarked that this training consisted entirely of one thing—*retrieving*. I taught the dog, which I called "Bellona," to fetch sticks I threw into the water, and not only to fetch, but to fetch at once, without mouthing or playing with them. The point was that she was to stop for nothing, but to deliver the stick in all haste. I made a practice of running away and leaving her to chase me, with the stick in her mouth, till she caught me. She was a bright animal, and took to the game with such eagerness that I was soon content.

After that, at the first casual opportunity, I presented Bellona to John Claverhouse. I knew what I was about, for I was aware of a little weakness of his, and of a little private sinning of which he was regularly and inveterately guilty.

"No," he said, when I placed the end of the rope in his hand. "No, you don't mean it." And his mouth opened wide and he grinned all over his damnable moon-face.

"I—I kind of thought, somehow, you didn't like me," he explained. "Wasn't it funny for me to make such a mistake?" And at the thought he held his sides with laughter.

"What is her name?" he managed to ask between paroxysms.

"Bellona," I said.

"He! he!" he tittered. "What a funny name!"

I gritted my teeth, for his mirth put them on edge, and snapped out between them, "She was the wife of Mars, you know."

Then the light of the full moon began to suffuse his face, until he exploded with: "That was my other dog. Well, I guess she's a widow now. Oh! Ho! ho! E! he! he! Ho!" he whooped after me, and I turned and fled swiftly over the hill.

The week passed by, and on Saturday evening I said to him, "You go away Monday, don't you?"

He nodded his head and grinned.

"Then you won't have another chance to get a mess of those trout you just 'dote' on."

But he did not notice the sneer. "Oh, I don't know," he chuckled. "I'm going up to-morrow to try pretty hard."

Thus was assurance made doubly sure, and I went back to my house hugging myself with rapture.

Early next morning I saw him go by with a dipnet and gunnysack, and Bellona trotting at his heels. I knew where he was bound, and cut out by the back pasture and climbed through the underbrush to the top of the mountain. Keeping carefully out of sight, I followed the crest along for a couple of miles to a natural amphitheatre in the hills, where the little river raced down out of a gorge and stopped for breath in a large and placid rock-bound pool. That was the spot! I sat down on the croup of the mountain, where I could see all that occurred, and lighted my pipe.

Ere many minutes had passed, John Claverhouse came plodding up the bed of the stream. Bellona was ambling about him, and they were in high feather, her short, snappy barks mingling with his deeper chest-notes. Arrived at the pool, he threw down the dip-net and sack, and drew from his hip-pocket what looked like a large, fat candle. But I knew it to be a stick of "giant"; for such was his method of catching trout. He dynamited them. He attached the fuse by wrapping the "giant" tightly in a piece of cotton. Then he ignited the fuse and tossed the explosive into the pool.

Like a flash, Bellona was into the pool after it. I could have shrieked aloud for joy. Claverhouse yelled at her, but without avail. He pelted her with clods and rocks, but she swam steadily on till she got the stick of "giant" in her mouth, when she whirled about and headed for shore. Then, for the first time, he realized his danger, and started to run. As foreseen and planned by me, she made the bank and took out after him. Oh, I tell you, it was great! As I have said, the pool lay in a sort of amphitheatre. Above and below, the stream could be crossed on stepping stones. And around and around, up and down and across the stones, raced Claverhouse and Bellona. I could never have believed that such an ungainly man could run so fast. But run he did, Bellona hot-footed after him, and gaining. And then, just as she caught up, he in full stride, and she leaping with nose at his knee, there was a sudden flash, a burst of smoke, a terrific detonation, and where man and dog had been the instant before there was naught to be seen but a big hole in the ground.

"Death from accident while engaged in illegal fishing." That was the verdict of the coroner's jury; and that is why I pride myself on the neat and artistic way in which I finished off John Claverhouse. There was no bungling, no brutality; nothing of which to be ashamed in the whole transaction, as I am sure you will agree. No more does his infernal laugh go echoing among the hills, and no more does his fat moon-face rise up to vex me. My days are peaceful now, and my night's sleep deep.

THE SHADOW AND THE FLASH

WHEN I look back, I realize what a peculiar friendship it was. First, there was Lloyd Inwood, tall, slender, and finely knit, nervous and dark. And then Paul Tichlorne, tall, slender, and finely knit, nervous and blond. Each was the replica of the other in everything except color. Lloyd's eyes were black; Paul's were blue. Under stress of excitement, the blood coursed olive in the face of Lloyd, crimson in the face of Paul. But outside this matter of coloring they were as like as two peas. Both were high-strung, prone to excessive tension and endurance, and they lived at concert pitch.

But there was a trio involved in this remarkable friendship, and the third was short, and fat, and chunky, and lazy, and, loath to say, it was I. Paul and Lloyd seemed born to rivalry with each other, and I to be peacemaker between them. We grew up together, the three of us, and full often have I received the angry blows each intended for the other. They were always competing, striving to outdo each other, and when entered upon some such struggle there was no limit either to their endeavors or passions.

This intense spirit of rivalry obtained in their studies and their games. If Paul memorized one canto of "Marmion," Lloyd memorized two cantos, Paul came back with three, and Lloyd again with four, till each knew the whole poem by heart. I remember an incident that occurred at the swimming hole—an incident tragically significant of the life-struggle between them. The boys had a game of diving to the bottom of a ten-foot pool and holding on by submerged roots to see who could stay under the longest. Paul and Lloyd allowed themselves to be bantered into making the descent together. When I saw their faces, set and determined, disappear in the water as they sank swiftly down, I felt a foreboding of something dreadful. The moments sped, the ripples died away, the face of the pool grew placid and untroubled, and neither black nor golden head broke surface in quest of air. We above grew anxious. The longest record of the longest-winded boy had been exceeded, and still there was no sign. Air bubbles trickled slowly upward, showing that the breath had been expelled from their lungs, and after that the bubbles ceased to trickle upward. Each second became interminable, and, unable longer to endure the suspense, I plunged into the water.

I found them down at the bottom, clutching tight to the roots, their heads not a foot apart, their eyes wide open, each glaring fixedly at the other. They were suffering frightful torment, writhing and twisting in the pangs of voluntary suffocation; for neither would let go and acknowledge himself beaten. I tried to break Paul's hold on the root, but he resisted me fiercely. Then I lost my breath and came to the surface, badly scared. I quickly explained the situation, and half a dozen of us went down and by main strength tore them loose. By the time we got them out, both were unconscious, and it was only after much barrel-rolling and rubbing and pounding that they finally came to their senses. They would have drowned there, had no one rescued them.

When Paul Tichlorne entered college, he let it be generally understood that he was going in for the social sciences. Lloyd Inwood, entering at the same time, elected to take the same course. But Paul had had it secretly in mind all the time to study the natural sciences, specializing on chemistry, and at the last moment he switched over. Though Lloyd had already arranged his year's work and attended the first lectures, he at once followed Paul's lead and went in for the natural sciences and especially for chemistry. Their rivalry soon became a noted thing throughout the university. Each was a spur to the other, and they went into chemistry deeper than did ever students before—so deep, in fact, that ere they took their sheepskins they could have stumped any chemistry or "cow college" professor in the institution, save "old" Moss, head of the department, and even him they puzzled and edified more than once. Lloyd's discovery of the "death bacillus" of the sea toad, and his experiments on it with potassium cyanide, sent his name and that of his university ringing round the world; nor was Paul a whit behind when he succeeded in producing laboratory colloids exhibiting amoeba-like activities, and when he cast new light upon the processes of fertilization through his startling experiments with simple sodium chlorides and magnesium solutions on low forms of marine life.

It was in their undergraduate days, however, in the midst of their profoundest plunges into the mysteries of organic chemistry, that Doris Van Benschoten entered into their lives. Lloyd met her first, but within twenty-four hours Paul saw to it that he also made her acquaintance. Of course, they fell in love with her, and she became the only thing in life worth living for. They wooed her with equal ardor and fire, and so intense became their struggle for her that half the student-body took to wagering wildly on the result. Even "old" Moss, one day, after an astounding demonstration in his private laboratory by Paul, was guilty to the extent of a month's salary of backing him to become the bridegroom of Doris Van Benschoten.

In the end she solved the problem in her own way, to everybody's satisfaction except Paul's and Lloyd's. Getting them together, she said that she really could not choose between them because she loved them both equally well; and that, unfortunately, since polyandry was not permitted in the United States she would be compelled to forego the honor and happiness of marrying either of them. Each blamed the other for this lamentable outcome, and the bitterness between them grew more bitter.

But things came to a head soon enough. It was at my home, after they had taken their degrees and dropped out of the world's sight, that the beginning of the end came to pass. Both were men of means, with little inclination and no necessity for professional life. My friendship and their mutual animosity were the two things that linked them in any way together. While they were very often at my place, they made it a fastidious point to avoid each other on such visits, though it was inevitable, under the circumstances, that they should come upon each other occasionally.

On the day I have in recollection, Paul Tichlorne had been mooning all morning in my study over a current scientific review. This left me free to my own affairs, and I was out among my roses when Lloyd Inwood arrived. Clipping and pruning and tacking the climbers on the porch, with my mouth full of nails, and Lloyd following me about and lending a hand now and again, we fell to discussing the mythical race of invisible people, that strange and vagrant people the traditions of which have come down to us. Lloyd warmed to the talk in his nervous, jerky fashion, and was soon interrogating the physical properties and possibilities of invisibility. A perfectly black object, he contended, would elude and defy the acutest vision.

"Color is a sensation," he was saying. "It has no objective reality. Without light, we can see neither colors nor objects themselves. All objects are black in the dark, and in the dark it is impossible to see them. If no light strikes upon them, then no light is flung back from them to the eye, and so we have no vision-evidence of their being."

"But we see black objects in daylight," I objected.

"Very true," he went on warmly. "And that is because they are not perfectly black. Were they perfectly black, absolutely black, as it were, we could not see them—ay, not in the blaze of a thousand suns could we see them! And so I say, with the right pigments, properly compounded, an absolutely black paint could be produced which would render invisible whatever it was applied to."

"It would be a remarkable discovery," I said non-committally, for the whole thing seemed too fantastic for aught but speculative purposes.

"Remarkable!" Lloyd slapped me on the shoulder. "I should say so. Why, old chap, to coat myself with such a paint would be to put the world at my feet. The secrets of kings and courts would be mine, the machinations of diplomats and politicians, the play of stock-gamblers, the plans of trusts and corporations. I could keep my hand on the inner pulse of things and become the greatest power in the world. And I—" He broke off shortly, then added,

"Well, I have begun my experiments, and I don't mind telling you that I'm right in line for it."

A laugh from the doorway startled us. Paul Tichlorne was standing there, a smile of mockery on his lips.

"You forget, my dear Lloyd," he said.

"Forget what?"

"You forget," Paul went on—"ah, you forget the shadow."

I saw Lloyd's face drop, but he answered sneeringly, "I can carry a sunshade, you know." Then he turned suddenly and fiercely upon him. "Look here, Paul, you'll keep out of this if you know what's good for you."

A rupture seemed imminent, but Paul laughed good-naturedly. "I wouldn't lay fingers on your dirty pigments. Succeed beyond your most sanguine expectations, yet you will always fetch up against the shadow. You can't get away from it. Now I shall go on the very opposite tack. In the very nature of my proposition the shadow will be eliminated—"

"Transparency!" ejaculated Lloyd, instantly. "But it can't be achieved."

"Oh, no; of course not." And Paul shrugged his shoulders and strolled off down the brier-rose path.

This was the beginning of it. Both men attacked the problem with all the tremendous energy for which they were noted, and with a rancor and bitterness that made me tremble for the success of either. Each trusted me to the utmost, and in the long weeks of experimentation that followed I was made a party to both sides, listening to their theorizings and witnessing their demonstrations. Never, by word or sign, did I convey to either the slightest hint of the other's progress, and they respected me for the seal I put upon my lips.

Lloyd Inwood, after prolonged and unintermittent application, when the tension upon his mind and body became too great to bear, had a strange way of obtaining relief. He attended prize fights. It was at one of these brutal exhibitions, whither he had dragged me in order to tell his latest results, that his theory received striking confirmation.

"Do you see that red-whiskered man?" he asked, pointing across the ring to the fifth tier of seats on the opposite side. "And do you see the next man to him, the one in the white hat? Well, there is quite a gap between them, is there not?"

"Certainly," I answered. "They are a seat apart. The gap is the unoccupied seat."

He leaned over to me and spoke seriously. "Between the red-whiskered man and the white-hatted man sits Ben Wasson. You have heard me speak of him. He is the cleverest pugilist of his weight in the country. He is also a Caribbean negro, full-blooded, and the blackest in the United States. He has on a black overcoat buttoned up. I saw him when he came in and took that seat. As soon as he sat down he disappeared. Watch closely; he may smile."

I was for crossing over to verify Lloyd's statement, but he restrained me. "Wait," he said.

I waited and watched, till the red-whiskered man turned his head as though addressing the unoccupied seat; and then, in that empty space, I saw the rolling whites of a pair of eyes and the white double-crescent of two rows of teeth, and for the instant I could make out a negro's face. But with the passing of the smile his visibility passed, and the chair seemed vacant as before.

"Were he perfectly black, you could sit alongside him and not see him," Lloyd said; and I confess the illustration was apt enough to make me well-nigh convinced.

I visited Lloyd's laboratory a number of times after that, and found him always deep in his search after the absolute black. His experiments covered all sorts of pigments, such as lamp-blacks, tars, carbonized vegetable matters, soots of oils and fats, and the various carbonized animal substances.

"White light is composed of the seven primary colors," he argued to me. "But it is itself, of itself, invisible. Only by being reflected from objects do it and the objects become visible. But only that portion of it that is reflected becomes visible. For instance, here is a blue tobacco-box. The white light strikes against it, and, with one exception, all its component colors—violet, indigo, green, yellow, orange, and red—are absorbed. The one exception is *blue*. It is not absorbed but reflected. Wherefore the tobacco-box gives us a sensation of blueness. We do not see the other colors because they are absorbed. We see only the blue. For the same reason grass is *green*. The green waves of white light are thrown upon our eyes."

"When we paint our houses, we do not apply color to them," he said at another time. "What we do is to apply certain substances that have the property of absorbing from white light all the colors except those that we would have our houses appear. When a substance reflects all the colors to the eye, it seems to us white. When it absorbs all the colors, it is black. But, as I said before, we have as yet no perfect black. *All* the colors are not absorbed. The perfect black, guarding against high lights, will be utterly and absolutely invisible. Look at that, for example."

He pointed to the palette lying on his work-table. Different shades of black pigments were brushed on it. One, in particular, I could hardly see. It gave my eyes a blurring sensation, and I rubbed them and looked again.

"That," he said impressively, "is the blackest black you or any mortal man ever looked upon. But just you wait, and I'll have a black so black that no mortal man will be able to look upon it— *and see it!*"

On the other hand, I used to find Paul Tichlorne plunged as deeply into the study of light polarization, diffraction, and interference, single and double refraction, and all manner of strange organic compounds.

"Transparency: a state or quality of body which permits all rays of light to pass through," he defined for me. "That is what I am seeking. Lloyd blunders up against the shadow with his perfect opaqueness. But I escape it. A transparent body casts no shadow; neither does it reflect light-waves—that is, the perfectly transparent does not. So, avoiding high lights, not only will such a body cast no shadow, but, since it reflects no light, it will also be invisible."

We were standing by the window at another time. Paul was engaged in polishing a number of lenses, which were ranged along the sill. Suddenly, after a pause in the conversation, he said, "Oh! I've dropped a lens. Stick your head out, old man, and see where it went to."

Out I started to thrust my head, but a sharp blow on the forehead caused me to recoil. I rubbed my bruised brow and gazed with reproachful inquiry at Paul, who was laughing in gleeful, boyish fashion.

"Well?" he said.

"Well?" I echoed.

"Why don't you investigate?" he demanded. And investigate I did. Before thrusting out my head, my senses, automatically active, had told me there was nothing there, that nothing intervened between me and out-of-doors, that the aperture of the window opening was utterly empty. I stretched forth my hand and felt a hard object, smooth and cool and flat, which my touch, out of its experience, told me to be glass. I looked again, but could see positively nothing.

"White quartzose sand," Paul rattled off, "sodic carbonate, slaked lime, cullet, manganese peroxide—there you have it, the finest French plate glass, made by the great St. Gobain Company, who made the finest plate glass in the world, and this is the finest piece they ever made. It cost a king's ransom. But look at it! You can't see it. You don't know it's there till you run your head against it.

"Eh, old boy! That's merely an object-lesson—certain elements, in themselves opaque, yet so compounded as to give a resultant body which is transparent. But that is a matter of inorganic chemistry, you say. Very true. But I dare to assert, standing here on my two feet, that in the organic I can duplicate whatever occurs in the inorganic.

"Here!" he held a test-tube between me and the light, and I noted the cloudy or muddy liquid it contained. He emptied the contents of another test-tube into it, and almost instantly it became clear and sparkling.

"Or here!" With quick, nervous movements among his array of test-tubes, he turned a white solution to a wine color, and a light yellow solution to a dark brown. He dropped a piece of litmus paper into an acid, when it changed instantly to red, and on floating it in an alkali it turned as quickly to blue.

"The litmus paper is still the litmus paper," he enunciated in the formal manner of the lecturer. "I have not changed it into something else. Then what did I do? I merely changed the arrangement of its molecules. Where, at first, it absorbed all colors from the light but red, its molecular structure was so changed that it absorbed red and all colors except blue. And so it goes, *ad infinitum*. Now, what I purpose to do is this." He paused for a space. I purpose to seek—ay, and to find—the proper reagents, which, acting upon the living organism, will bring about molecular changes analogous to those you have just witnessed. But these reagents, which I shall find, and for that matter, upon which I already have my hands, will not turn the living body to blue or red or black, but they will turn it to transparency. All light will pass through it. It will be invisible. It will cast no shadow."

A few weeks later I went hunting with Paul. He had been promising me for some time that I should have the pleasure of shooting over a wonderful dog—the most wonderful dog, in fact, that ever man shot over, so he averred, and continued to aver till my curiosity was aroused. But on the morning in question I was disappointed, for there was no dog in evidence.

"Don't see him about," Paul remarked unconcernedly, and we set off across the fields.

I could not imagine, at the time, what was ailing me, but I had a feeling of some impending and deadly illness. My nerves were all awry, and, from the astounding tricks they played me, my senses seemed to have run riot. Strange sounds disturbed me. At times I heard the swish-swish of grass being shoved aside, and once the patter of feet across a patch of stony ground.

"Did you hear anything, Paul?" I asked once.

But he shook his head, and thrust his feet steadily forward.

While climbing a fence, I heard the low, eager whine of a dog, apparently from within a couple of feet of me; but on looking about me I saw nothing.

I dropped to the ground, limp and trembling.

"Paul," I said, "we had better return to the house. I am afraid I am going to be sick."

"Nonsense, old man," he answered. "The sunshine has gone to your head like wine. You'll be all right. It's famous weather."

But, passing along a narrow path through a clump of cotton-woods, some object brushed against my legs and I stumbled and nearly fell. I looked with sudden anxiety at Paul.

"What's the matter?" he asked. "Tripping over your own feet?"

I kept my tongue between my teeth and plodded on, though sore perplexed and thoroughly satisfied that some acute and mysterious malady had attacked my nerves. So far my eyes had escaped; but, when we got to the open fields again, even my vision went back on me. Strange flashes of vari-colored, rainbow light began to appear and disappear on the path before me. Still, I managed to keep myself in hand, till the vari-colored lights persisted for a space of fully twenty seconds, dancing and flashing in continuous play. Then I sat down, weak and shaky.

"It's all up with me," I gasped, covering my eyes with my hands. "It has attacked my eyes. Paul, take me home."

But Paul laughed long and loud. "What did I tell you?—the most wonderful dog, eh? Well, what do you think?"

He turned partly from me and began to whistle. I heard the patter of feet, the panting of a heated animal, and the unmistakable yelp of a dog. Then Paul stooped down and apparently fondled the empty air.

"Here! Give me your fist."

And he rubbed my hand over the cold nose and jowls of a dog. A dog it certainly was, with the shape and the smooth, short coat of a pointer.

Suffice to say, I speedily recovered my spirits and control. Paul put a collar about the animal's neck and tied his handkerchief to its tail. And then was vouchsafed us the remarkable sight of an empty collar and a waving handkerchief cavorting over the fields. It was something to see that collar and handkerchief pin a bevy of quail in a clump of locusts and remain rigid and immovable till we had flushed the birds.

Now and again the dog emitted the vari-colored light-flashes I have mentioned. The one thing, Paul explained, which he had not anticipated and which he doubted could be overcome.

"They're a large family," he said, "these sun dogs, wind dogs, rainbows, halos, and parhelia. They are produced by refraction of light from mineral and ice crystals, from mist, rain, spray, and no end of things; and I am afraid they are the penalty I must pay for transparency. I escaped Lloyd's shadow only to fetch up against the rainbow flash."

A couple of days later, before the entrance to Paul's laboratory, I encountered a terrible stench. So overpowering was it that it was easy to discover the source—a mass of putrescent matter on the doorstep which in general outlines resembled a dog.

Paul was startled when he investigated my find. It was his invisible dog, or rather, what had been his invisible dog, for it was now plainly visible. It had been playing about but a few minutes before in all health and strength. Closer examination revealed that the skull had been crushed by some heavy blow. While it was strange that the animal should have been killed, the inexplicable thing was that it should so quickly decay.

"The reagents I injected into its system were harmless," Paul explained. "Yet they were powerful, and it appears that when death comes they force practically instantaneous disintegration. Remarkable! Most remarkable! Well, the only thing is not to die. They do not harm so long as one lives. But I do wonder who smashed in that dog's head."

Light, however, was thrown upon this when a frightened housemaid brought the news that Gaffer Bedshaw had that very morning, not more than an hour back, gone violently insane, and was strapped down at home, in the huntsman's lodge, where he raved of a battle with a ferocious and gigantic beast that he had encountered in the Tichlorne pasture. He claimed that the thing, whatever it was, was invisible, that with his own eyes he had seen that it was invisible; wherefore his tearful wife and daughters shook their heads, and wherefore he but waxed the more violent, and the gardener and the coachman tightened the straps by another hole.

Nor, while Paul Tichlorne was thus successfully mastering the problem of invisibility, was Lloyd Inwood a whit behind. I went over in answer to a message of his to come and see how he was getting on. Now his laboratory occupied an isolated situation in the midst of his vast grounds. It was built in a pleasant little glade, surrounded on all sides by a dense forest growth, and was to be gained by way of a winding and erratic path. But I had travelled that path so often as to know every foot of it, and conceive my surprise when I came upon the glade and found no laboratory. The quaint shed structure with its red sandstone chimney was not. Nor did it look as if it ever had been. There were no signs of ruin, no débris, nothing.

I started to walk across what had once been its site. "This," I said to myself, "should be where the step went up to the door." Barely were the words out of my mouth when I stubbed my toe on some obstacle, pitched forward, and butted my head into something that *felt* very much like a door. I reached out my hand. It *was* a door. I found the knob and turned it. And at once, as the door swung inward on its hinges, the whole interior of the laboratory impinged upon my vision. Greeting Lloyd, I closed the door and backed up the path a few paces. I could see nothing of the building. Returning and opening the door, at once all the furniture and every detail of the interior were visible. It was indeed startling, the sudden transition from void to light and form and color.

"What do you think of it, eh?" Lloyd asked, wringing my hand. "I slapped a couple of coats of absolute black on the outside yesterday afternoon to see how it worked. How's your head? You bumped it pretty solidly, I imagine."

"Never mind that," he interrupted my congratulations. "I've something better for you to do."

While he talked he began to strip, and when he stood naked before me he thrust a pot and brush into my hand and said, "Here, give me a coat of this."

It was an oily, shellac-like stuff, which spread quickly and easily over the skin and dried immediately.

"Merely preliminary and precautionary," he explained when I had finished; "but now for the real stuff."

I picked up another pot he indicated, and glanced inside, but could see nothing.

"It's empty," I said.

"Stick your finger in it."

I obeyed, and was aware of a sensation of cool moistness. On withdrawing my hand I glanced at the forefinger, the one I had immersed, but it had disappeared. I moved it, and knew from the alternate tension and relaxation of the muscles that I moved it, but it defied my sense of sight. To all appearances I had been shorn of a finger; nor could I get any visual impression of it till I extended it under the skylight and saw its shadow plainly blotted on the floor.

Lloyd chuckled. "Now spread it on, and keep your eyes open."

I dipped the brush into the seemingly empty pot, and gave him a long stroke across his chest. With the passage of the brush the living flesh disappeared from beneath. I covered his right leg, and he was a one-legged man defying all laws of gravitation. And so, stroke by stroke, member by member, I painted Lloyd Inwood into nothingness. It was a creepy experience, and I was glad when naught remained in sight but his burning black eyes, poised apparently unsupported in mid-air.

"I have a refined and harmless solution for them," he said. "A fine spray with an air-brush, and presto! I am not."

This deftly accomplished, he said, "Now I shall move about, and do you tell me what sensations you experience."

"In the first place, I cannot see you," I said, and I could hear his gleeful laugh from the midst of the emptiness. "Of course," I continued, "you cannot escape your shadow, but that was to be expected. When you pass between my eye and an object, the object disappears, but so unusual and incomprehensible is its disappearance that it seems to me as though my eyes had blurred. When you move rapidly, I experience a bewildering succession of blurs. The blurring sensation makes my eyes ache and my brain tired."

"Have you any other warnings of my presence?" he asked.

"No, and yes," I answered. "When you are near me I have feelings similar to those produced by dank warehouses, gloomy crypts, and deep mines. And as sailors feel the loom of the land on dark nights, so I think I feel the loom of your body. But it is all very vague and intangible."

Long we talked that last morning in his laboratory; and when I turned to go, he put his unseen hand in mine with nervous grip, and said, "Now I shall conquer the world!" And I could not dare to tell him of Paul Tichlorne's equal success.

At home I found a note from Paul, asking me to come up immediately, and it was high noon when I came spinning up the driveway on my wheel. Paul called me from the tennis court, and I dismounted and went over. But the court was empty. As I stood there, gaping open-mouthed, a tennis ball struck me on the arm, and as I turned about, another whizzed past my ear. For aught I could see of my assailant, they came whirling at me from out of space, and right well was I peppered with them. But when the balls already flung at me began to come back for a second whack, I realized the situation. Seizing a racquet and keeping my eyes open, I quickly saw a rainbow flash appearing and disappearing and darting over the ground. I took out after it, and when I laid the racquet upon it for a half-dozen stout blows, Paul's voice rang out:

"Enough! Enough! Oh! Ouch! Stop! You're landing on my naked skin, you know! Ow! O-w-w! I'll be good! I'll be good! I only wanted you to see my metamorphosis," he said ruefully, and I imagined he was rubbing his hurts.

A few minutes later we were playing tennis—a handicap on my part, for I could have no knowledge of his position save when all the angles between himself, the sun, and me, were in proper conjunction. Then he flashed, and only then. But the flashes were more brilliant than the rainbow—purest blue, most delicate violet, brightest yellow, and all the intermediary shades, with the scintillant brilliancy of the diamond, dazzling, blinding, iridescent.

But in the midst of our play I felt a sudden cold chill, reminding me of deep mines and gloomy crypts, such a chill as I had experienced that very morning. The next moment, close to the net, I saw a ball rebound in mid-air and empty space, and at the same instant, a score of feet away, Paul Tichlorne emitted a rainbow flash. It could not be he from whom the ball had rebounded, and with sickening dread I realized that Lloyd Inwood had come upon the scene. To make sure, I looked for his shadow, and there it was, a shapeless blotch the girth of his body, (the sun was overhead), moving along the ground. I remembered his threat, and felt sure that all the long years of rivalry were about to culminate in uncanny battle.

I cried a warning to Paul, and heard a snarl as of a wild beast, and an answering snarl. I saw the dark blotch move swiftly across the court, and a brilliant burst of vari-colored light moving with equal swiftness to meet it; and then shadow and flash came together and there was the sound of unseen blows. The net went down before my frightened eyes. I sprang toward the fighters, crying:

"For God's sake!"

But their locked bodies smote against my knees, and I was overthrown.

"You keep out of this, old man!" I heard the voice of Lloyd Inwood from out of the emptiness. And then Paul's voice crying, "Yes, we've had enough of peacemaking!"

From the sound of their voices I knew they had separated. I could not locate Paul, and so approached the shadow that represented Lloyd. But from the other side came a stunning blow on the point of my jaw, and I heard Paul scream angrily, "Now will you keep away?"

Then they came together again, the impact of their blows, their groans and gasps, and the swift flashings and shadow-movings telling plainly of the deadliness of the struggle.

I shouted for help, and Gaffer Bedshaw came running into the court. I could see, as he approached, that he was looking at me strangely, but he collided with the combatants and was hurled headlong to the ground. With despairing shriek and a cry of "O Lord, I've got 'em!" he sprang to his feet and tore madly out of the court.

I could do nothing, so I sat up, fascinated and powerless, and watched the struggle. The noonday sun beat down with dazzling brightness on the naked tennis court. And it *was* naked. All I could see was the blotch of shadow and the rainbow flashes, the dust rising from the invisible feet, the earth tearing up from beneath the straining foot-grips, and the wire screen bulge once or twice as their bodies hurled against it. That was all, and after a time even that ceased. There were no more flashes, and the shadow had become long and stationary; and I remembered their set boyish faces when they clung to the roots in the deep coolness of the pool.

They found me an hour afterward. Some inkling of what had happened got to the servants and they quitted the Tichlorne service in a body. Gaffer Bedshaw never recovered from the second shock he received, and is confined in a madhouse, hopelessly incurable. The secrets of their marvellous discoveries died with Paul and Lloyd, both laboratories being destroyed by grief-stricken relatives. As for myself, I no longer care for chemical research, and science is a tabooed topic in my household. I have returned to my roses. Nature's colors are good enough for me.

AMATEUR NIGHT

THE elevator boy smiled knowingly to himself. When he took her up, he had noted the sparkle in her eyes, the color in her cheeks. His little cage had quite warmed with the glow of her repressed eagerness. And now, on the down trip, it was glacier-like. The sparkle and the color were gone. She was frowning, and what little he could see of her eyes was cold and steel-gray. Oh, he knew the symptoms, he did. He was an observer, and he knew it, too, and some day, when he was big enough, he was going to be a reporter, sure. And in the meantime he studied the procession of life as it streamed up and down eighteen sky-scraper floors in his elevator car. He slid the door open for her sympathetically and watched her trip determinedly out into the street.

There was a robustness in her carriage which came of the soil rather than of the city pavement. But it was a robustness in a finer than the wonted sense, a vigorous daintiness, it might be called, which gave an impression of virility with none of the womanly left out. It told of a heredity of seekers and fighters, of people that worked stoutly with head and hand, of ghosts that reached down out of the misty past and moulded and made her to be a doer of things.

But she was a little angry, and a great deal hurt. "I can guess what you would tell me," the editor had kindly but firmly interrupted her lengthy preamble in the long-looked-forward-to interview just ended. "And you have told me enough," he had gone on (heartlessly, she was sure, as she went over the conversation in its freshness). "You have done no newspaper work. You are undrilled, undisciplined, unhammered into shape. You have received a high-school education, and possibly topped it off with normal school or college. You have stood well in English. Your friends have all told you how cleverly you write, and how beautifully, and so forth and so forth. You think you can do newspaper work, and you want me to put you on. Well, I am sorry, but there are no openings. If you knew how crowded—"

"But if there are no openings," she had interrupted, in turn, "how did those who are in, get in? How am I to show that I am eligible to get in?"

"They made themselves indispensable," was the terse response. "Make yourself indispensable."

"But how can I, if I do not get the chance?"

"Make your chance."

"But how?" she had insisted, at the same time privately deeming him a most unreasonable man.

"How? That is your business, not mine," he said conclusively, rising in token that the interview was at an end. "I must inform you, my dear young lady, that there have been at least eighteen other aspiring young ladies here this week, and that I have not the time to tell each and every one of them how. The function I perform on this paper is hardly that of instructor in a school of journalism."

She caught an outbound car, and ere she descended from it she had conned the conversation over and over again. "But how?" she repeated to herself, as she climbed the three flights of stairs to the rooms where she and her sister "bach'ed." "But how?" And so she continued to put the interrogation, for the stubborn Scotch blood, though many times removed from Scottish soil, was still strong in her. And, further, there was need that she should learn how. Her sister Letty and she had come up from an interior town to the city to make their way in the world. John Wyman was land-poor. Disastrous business enterprises had burdened his acres and forced his two girls Edna and Letty, into doing something for themselves. A year of school-teaching and of night-study of short-hand and typewriting had capitalized their city project and fitted them for the venture, which same venture was turning out anything but successful. The city seemed crowded with inexperienced stenographers and typewriters, and they had nothing but their own inexperience to offer. Edna's secret ambition had been journalism; but she had planned a clerical position first, so that she might have time and space in which to determine where and on what line of journalism she would embark. But the clerical position had not been forthcoming, either for Letty or her, and day by day their little hoard dwindled, though the room rent remained normal and the stove consumed coal with undiminished voracity. And it was a slim little hoard by now.

"There's Max Irwin," Letty said, talking it over. "He's a journalist with a national reputation. Go and see him, Ed. He knows how, and he should be able to tell you how."

"But I don't know him," Edna objected.

"No more than you knew the editor you saw to-day."

"Y-e-s," (long and judicially), "but that's different."

"Not a bit different from the strange men and women you'll interview when you've learned how," Letty encouraged.

"I hadn't looked at it in that light," Edna conceded. "After all, where's the difference between interviewing Mr. Max Irwin for some paper, or interviewing Mr. Max Irwin for myself? It will be practice, too. I'll go and look him up in the directory."

"Letty, I know I can write if I get the chance," she announced decisively a moment later. "I just *feel* that I have the feel of it, if you know what I mean."

And Letty knew and nodded. "I wonder what he is like?" she asked softly.

"I'll make it my business to find out," Edna assured her; "and I'll let you know inside forty-eight hours."

Letty clapped her hands. "Good! That's the newspaper spirit! Make it twenty-four hours, and you are perfect!"

"—and I am sorry to trouble you," she concluded the statement of her case to Max Irwin, famous war correspondent and veteran journalist.

"Not at all," he answered, with a deprecatory wave of the hand. "If you don't do your own talking, who's to do it for you? Now I understand your predicament precisely. You want to get on the *Intelligencer*, you want to get on at once, and you have had no previous experience. In the first place, then, have you any pull? There are a dozen men in the city, a line from whom would be an open-sesame. After that you would stand or fall by your own ability. There's Senator Longbridge, for instance, and Claus Inskeep the street-car magnate, and Lane, and McChesney—" He paused, with voice suspended.

"I am sure I know none of them," she answered despondently.

"It's not necessary. Do you know any one that knows them? or any one that knows any one else that knows them?"

Edna shook her head.

"Then we must think of something else," he went on, cheerfully. "You'll have to do something yourself. Let me see."

He stopped and thought for a moment, with closed eyes and wrinkled forehead. She was watching him, studying him intently, when his blue eyes opened with a snap and his face suddenly brightened.

"I have it! But no, wait a minute."

And for a minute it was his turn to study her. And study her he did, till she could feel her cheeks flushing under his gaze.

"You'll do, I think, though it remains to be seen," he said enigmatically. "It will show the stuff that's in you, besides, and it will be a better claim upon the *Intelligencer* people than all the lines from all the senators and magnates in the world. The thing for you is to do Amateur Night at the Loops."

"I—I hardly understand," Edna said, for his suggestion conveyed no meaning to her. "What are the 'Loops'? and what is 'Amateur Night'?"

"I forgot you said you were from the interior. But so much the better, if you've only got the journalistic grip. It will be a first impression, and first impressions are always unbiased, unprejudiced, fresh, vivid. The Loops are out on the rim of the city, near the Park,—a place of diversion. There's a scenic railway, a water toboggan slide, a concert band, a theatre, wild animals, moving pictures, and so forth and so forth. The common people go there to look at the animals and enjoy themselves, and the other people go there to enjoy themselves by watching the common people enjoy themselves. A democratic, fresh-air-breathing, frolicking affair, that's what the Loops are.

"But the theatre is what concerns you. It's vaudeville. One turn follows another—jugglers, acrobats, rubber-jointed wonders, fire-dancers, coon-song artists, singers, players, female impersonators, sentimental soloists and so forth and so forth. These people are professional vaudevillists. They make their living that way. Many are excellently paid. Some are free rovers, doing a turn wherever they can get an opening, at the Obermann, the Orpheus, the Alcatraz, the Louvre, and so forth and so forth. Others cover circuit pretty well all over the country. An interesting phase of life, and the pay is big enough to attract many aspirants.

"Now the management of the Loops, in its bid for popularity, instituted what is called 'Amateur Night'; that is to say, twice a week, after the professionals have done their turns, the stage is given over to the aspiring amateurs. The audience remains to criticise. The populace becomes the arbiter of art—or it thinks it does, which is the same thing; and it pays its money and is well pleased with itself, and Amateur Night is a paying proposition to the management.

"But the point of Amateur Night, and it is well to note it, is that these amateurs are not really amateurs. They are paid for doing their turn. At the best, they may be termed 'professional amateurs.' It stands to reason that the management could not get people to face a rampant audience for nothing, and on such occasions the audience certainly goes mad. It's great fun—for the audience. But the thing for you to do, and it requires nerve, I assure you, is to go out, make arrangements for two turns, (Wednesday and Saturday nights, I believe), do your two turns, and write it up for the *Sunday Intelligencer*."

"But—but," she quavered, "I—I—" and there was a suggestion of disappointment and tears in her voice.

"I see," he said kindly. "You were expecting something else, something different, something better. We all do at first. But remember the admiral of the Queen's Na-vee, who swept the floor and polished up the handle of the big front door. You must face the drudgery of apprenticeship or quit right now. What do you say?"

The abruptness with which he demanded her decision startled her. As she faltered, she could see a shade of disappointment beginning to darken his face.

"In a way it must be considered a test," he added encouragingly. "A severe one, but so much the better. Now is the time. Are you game?"

"I'll try," she said faintly, at the same time making a note of the directness, abruptness, and haste of these city men with whom she was coming in contact.

"Good! Why, when I started in, I had the dreariest, deadliest details imaginable. And after that, for a weary time, I did the police and divorce courts. But it all came well in the end and did me good. You are luckier in making your start with Sunday work. It's not particularly great. What of it? Do it. Show the stuff you're made of, and you'll get a call for better work—better class and better pay. Now you go out this afternoon to the Loops, and engage to do two turns."

"But what kind of turns can I do?" Edna asked dubiously.

"Do? That's easy. Can you sing? Never mind, don't need to sing. Screech, do anything—that's what you're paid for, to afford amusement, to give bad art for the populace to howl down. And when you do your turn, take some one along for chaperon. Be afraid of no one. Talk up. Move about among the amateurs waiting their turn, pump them, study them, photograph them in your brain. Get the atmosphere, the color, strong color, lots of it. Dig right in with both hands, and get the essence of it, the spirit, the significance. What does it mean? Find out what it means. That's what you're there for. That's what the readers of the *Sunday Intelligencer* want to know.

"Be terse in style, vigorous of phrase, apt, concretely apt, in similitude. Avoid platitudes and commonplaces. Exercise selection. Seize upon things salient, eliminate the rest, and you have pictures. Paint those pictures in words and the *Intelligencer* will have you. Get hold of a few back numbers, and study the *Sunday Intelligencer* feature story. Tell it all in the opening paragraph as advertisement of contents, and in the contents tell it all over again. Then put a snapper at the end, so if they're crowded for space they can cut off your contents anywhere, re-attach the snapper, and the story will still retain form. There, that's enough. Study the rest out for yourself."

They both rose to their feet, Edna quite carried away by his enthusiasm and his quick, jerky sentences, bristling with the things she wanted to know.

"And remember, Miss Wyman, if you're ambitious, that the aim and end of journalism is not the feature article. Avoid the rut. The feature is a trick. Master it, but don't let it master you. But master it you must; for if you can't learn to do a feature well, you can never expect to do anything better. In short, put your whole self into it, and yet, outside of it, above it, remain yourself, if you follow me. And now good luck to you."

They had reached the door and were shaking hands.

"And one thing more," he interrupted her thanks, "let me see your copy before you turn it in. I may be able to put you straight here and there."

Edna found the manager of the Loops a full-fleshed, heavy-jowled man, bushy of eyebrow and generally belligerent of aspect, with an absent-minded scowl on his face and a black cigar stuck in the midst thereof. Symes was his name, she had learned, Ernst Symes.

"Whatcher turn?" he demanded, ere half her brief application had left her lips.

"Sentimental soloist, soprano," she answered promptly, remembering Irwin's advice to talk up.

"Whatcher name?" Mr. Symes asked, scarcely deigning to glance at her.

She hesitated. So rapidly had she been rushed into the adventure that she had not considered the question of a name at all.

"Any name? Stage name?" he bellowed impatiently.

"Nan Bellayne," she invented on the spur of the moment. "B-e-l-l-a-y-n-e. Yes, that's it."

He scribbled it into a notebook. "All right. Take your turn Wednesday and Saturday."

"How much do I get?" Edna demanded.

"Two-an'-a-half a turn. Two turns, five. Getcher pay first Monday after second turn."

And without the simple courtesy of "Good day," he turned his back on her and plunged into the newspaper he had been reading when she entered.

Edna came early on Wednesday evening, Letty with her, and in a telescope basket her costume—a simple affair. A plaid shawl borrowed from the washerwoman, a ragged scrubbing skirt borrowed from the charwoman, and a gray wig rented from a costumer for twenty-five cents a night, completed the outfit; for Edna had elected to be an old Irishwoman singing broken-heartedly after her wandering boy.

Though they had come early, she found everything in uproar. The main performance was under way, the orchestra was playing and the audience intermittently applauding. The infusion of the amateurs clogged the working of things behind the stage, crowded the passages, dressing rooms, and wings, and forced everybody into everybody else's way. This was particularly distasteful to the professionals, who carried themselves as befitted those of a higher caste, and whose behavior toward the pariah amateurs was marked by hauteur and even brutality. And Edna, bullied and elbowed and shoved about, clinging desperately to her basket and seeking a dressing room, took note of it all.

A dressing room she finally found, jammed with three other amateur "ladies," who were "making up" with much noise, high-pitched voices, and squabbling over a lone mirror. Her own make-up was so simple that it was quickly accomplished, and she left the trio of ladies holding an armed truce while they passed judgment upon her. Letty was close at her shoulder, and with patience and persistence they managed to get a nook in one of the wings which commanded a view of the stage.

A small, dark man, dapper and debonair, swallow-tailed and top-hatted, was waltzing about the stage with dainty, mincing steps, and in a thin little voice singing something or other about somebody or something evidently pathetic. As his waning voice neared the end of the lines, a large woman, crowned with an amazing wealth of blond hair, thrust rudely past Edna, trod heavily on her toes, and shoved her contemptuously to the side. "Bloomin' hamateur!" she hissed as she went past, and the next instant she was on the stage, graciously bowing to the audience, while the small, dark man twirled extravagantly about on his tip-toes.

"Hello, girls!"

This greeting, drawled with an inimitable vocal caress in every syllable, close in her ear, caused Edna to give a startled little jump. A smooth-faced, moon-faced young man was smiling at her good-naturedly. His "make-up" was plainly that of the stock tramp of the stage, though the inevitable whiskers were lacking.

"Oh, it don't take a minute to slap 'm on," he explained, divining the search in her eyes and waving in his hand the adornment in question. "They make a feller sweat," he explained further. And then, "What's yer turn?"

"Soprano—sentimental," she answered, trying to be offhand and at ease.

"Whata you doin' it for?" he demanded directly.

"For fun; what else?" she countered.

"I just sized you up for that as soon as I put eyes on you. You ain't graftin' for a paper, are you?"

"I never met but one editor in my life," she replied evasively, "and I, he—well, we didn't get on very well together."

"Hittin' 'm for a job?"

Edna nodded carelessly, though inwardly anxious and cudgelling her brains for something to turn the conversation.

"What 'd he say?"

"That eighteen other girls had already been there that week."

"Gave you the icy mit, eh?" The moon-faced young man laughed and slapped his thighs. "You see, we're kind of suspicious. The Sunday papers'd like to get Amateur Night done up brown in a nice little package, and the manager don't see it that way. Gets wild-eyed at the thought of it."

"And what's your turn?" she asked.

"Who? me? Oh, I'm doin' the tramp act tonight. I'm Charley Welsh, you know."

She felt that by the mention of his name he intended to convey to her complete enlightenment, but the best she could do was to say politely, "Oh, is that so?"

She wanted to laugh at the hurt disappointment which came into his face, but concealed her amusement.

"Come, now," he said brusquely, "you can't stand there and tell me you've never heard of Charley Welsh? Well, you must be young. Why, I'm an Only, the Only amateur at that. Sure, you must have seen me. I'm everywhere. I could be a professional, but I get more dough out of it by doin' the amateur."

"But what's an 'Only'?" she queried. "I want to learn."

"Sure," Charley Welsh said gallantly. "I'll put you wise. An 'Only' is a nonpareil, the feller that does one kind of a turn better'n any other feller. He's the Only, see?"

And Edna saw.

"To get a line on the biz," he continued, "throw yer lamps on me. I'm the Only all-round amateur. To-night I make a bluff at the tramp act. It's harder to bluff it than to really do it, but then it's acting, it's amateur, it's art. See? I do everything, from Sheeny monologue to team song and dance and Dutch comedian. Sure, I'm Charley Welsh, the Only Charley Welsh."

And in this fashion, while the thin, dark man and the large, blond woman warbled dulcetly out on the stage and the other professionals followed in their turns, did Charley Welsh put Edna wise, giving her much miscellaneous and superfluous information and much that she stored away for the *Sunday Intelligencer.*

"Well, tra la loo," he said suddenly. "There's his highness chasin' you up. Yer first on the bill. Never mind the row when you go on. Just finish yer turn like a lady."

It was at that moment that Edna felt her journalistic ambition departing from her, and was aware of an overmastering desire to be somewhere else. But the stage manager, like an ogre, barred her retreat. She could hear the opening bars of her song going up from the orchestra and the noises of the house dying away to the silence of anticipation.

"Go ahead," Letty whispered, pressing her hand; and from the other side came the peremptory "Don't flunk!" of Charley Welsh.

But her feet seemed rooted to the floor, and she leaned weakly against a shift scene. The orchestra was beginning over again, and a lone voice from the house piped with startling distinctness:

"Puzzle picture! Find Nannie!"

A roar of laughter greeted the sally, and Edna shrank back. But the strong hand of the manager descended on her shoulder, and with a quick, powerful shove propelled her out on to the stage. His hand and arm had flashed into full view, and the audience, grasping the situation, thundered its appreciation. The orchestra was drowned out by the terrible din, and Edna could see the bows scraping away across the violins, apparently without sound. It was impossible for her to begin in time, and as she patiently waited, arms akimbo and ears straining for the music, the house let loose again (a favorite trick, she afterward learned, of confusing the amateur by preventing him or her from hearing the orchestra).

But Edna was recovering her presence of mind. She became aware, pit to dome, of a vast sea of smiling and fun-distorted faces, of vast roars of laughter, rising wave on wave, and then her Scotch blood went cold and angry. The hard-working but silent orchestra gave her the cue, and, without making a sound, she began to move her lips, stretch forth her arms, and sway her body, as though she were really singing. The noise in the house redoubled in the attempt to drown her voice, but she serenely went on with her pantomime. This seemed to continue an interminable time, when the audience, tiring of its prank and in order to hear, suddenly stilled its clamor, and discovered the dumb show she had been making. For a moment all was silent, save for the orchestra, her lips moving on without a sound, and then the audience realized that it had been sold, and broke out afresh, this time with genuine applause in acknowledgment of her victory. She chose this as the happy moment for her exit, and with a bow and backward retreat, she was off the stage in Letty's arms.

The worst was past, and for the rest of the evening she moved about among the amateurs and professionals, talking, listening, observing, finding out what it meant and taking mental notes of it all. Charley Welsh constituted himself her preceptor and guardian angel, and so well did he perform the self-allotted task that when it was all over she felt fully prepared to write her article. But the proposition had been to do two turns, and her native pluck forced her to live up to it. Also, in the course of the intervening days, she discovered fleeting impressions that required verification; so, on Saturday, she was back again, with her telescope basket and Letty.

The manager seemed looking for her, and she caught an expression of relief in his eyes when he first saw her. He hurried up, greeted her, and bowed with a respect ludicrously at variance with his previous ogre-like behavior. And as he bowed, across his shoulders she saw Charley Welsh deliberately wink.

But the surprise had just begun. The manager begged to be introduced to her sister, chatted entertainingly with the pair of them, and strove greatly and anxiously to be agreeable. He even went so far as to give Edna a dressing room to herself, to the unspeakable envy of the three other amateur ladies of previous acquaintance. Edna was nonplussed, and it was not till she met Charley Welsh in the passage that light was thrown on the mystery.

"Hello!" he greeted her. "On Easy Street, eh? Everthing slidin' your way."

She smiled brightly.

"Thinks yer a female reporter, sure. I almost split when I saw 'm layin' himself out sweet an' pleasin'. Honest, now, that ain't yer graft, is it?"

"I told you my experience with editors," she parried. "And honest now, it was honest, too."

But the Only Charley Welsh shook his head dubiously. "Not that I care a rap," he declared. "And if you are, just gimme a couple of lines of notice, the right kind, good ad, you know. And if yer not, why yer all right anyway. Yer not our class, that's straight."

After her turn, which she did this time with the nerve of an old campaigner, the manager returned to the charge; and after saying nice things and being generally nice himself, he came to the point.

"You'll treat us well, I hope," he said insinuatingly. "Do the right thing by us, and all that?"

"Oh," she answered innocently, "you couldn't persuade me to do another turn; I know I seemed to take and that you'd like to have me, but I really, really can't."

"You know what I mean," he said, with a touch of his old bulldozing manner.

"No, I really won't," she persisted. "Vaudeville's too—too wearing on the nerves, my nerves, at any rate."

Whereat he looked puzzled and doubtful, and forbore to press the point further.

But on Monday morning, when she came to his office to get her pay for the two turns, it was he who puzzled her.

"You surely must have mistaken me," he lied glibly. "I remember saying something about paying your car fare. We always do this, you know, but we never, never pay amateurs. That would take the life and sparkle out of the whole thing. No, Charley Welsh was stringing you. He gets paid nothing for his turns. No amateur gets paid. The idea is ridiculous. However, here's fifty cents. It will pay your sister's car fare also. And,"—very suavely,—"speaking for the Loops, permit me to thank you for the kind and successful contribution of your services."

That afternoon, true to her promise to Max Irwin, she placed her typewritten copy into his hands. And while he ran over it, he nodded his head from time to time, and maintained a running fire of commendatory remarks: "Good!—that's it!—that's the stuff!—psychology's all right!—the very idea!—you've caught it!—excellent!—missed it a bit here, but it'll go—that's vigorous!—strong!—vivid!—pictures! pictures!—excellent!—most excellent!"

And when he had run down to the bottom of the last page, holding out his hand: "My dear Miss Wyman, I congratulate you. I must say you have exceeded my expectations, which, to say the least, were large. You are a journalist, a natural journalist. You've got the grip, and you're sure to get on. The *Intelligencer* will take it, without doubt, and take you too. They'll have to take you. If they don't, some of the other papers will get you."

"But what's this?" he queried, the next instant, his face going serious. "You've said nothing about receiving the pay for your turns, and that's one of the points of the feature. I expressly mentioned it, if you'll remember."

"It will never do," he said, shaking his head ominously, when she had explained. "You simply must collect that money somehow. Let me see. Let me think a moment."

"Never mind, Mr. Irwin," she said. "I've bothered you enough. Let me use your 'phone, please, and I'll try Mr. Ernst Symes again."

He vacated his chair by the desk, and Edna took down the receiver.

"Charley Welsh is sick," she began, when the connection had been made. "What? No! I'm not Charley Welsh. Charley Welsh is sick, and his sister wants to know if she can come out this afternoon and draw his pay for him?"

"Tell Charley Welsh's sister that Charley Welsh was out this morning, and drew his own pay," came back the manager's familiar tones, crisp with asperity.

"All right," Edna went on. "And now Nan Bellayne wants to know if she and her sister can come out this afternoon and draw Nan Bellayne's pay?"

"What'd he say? What'd he say?" Max Irwin cried excitedly, as she hung up.

"That Nan Bellayne was too much for him, and that she and her sister could come out and get her pay and the freedom of the Loops, to boot."

"One thing more," he interrupted her thanks at the door, as on her previous visit. "Now that you've shown the stuff you're made of, I should esteem it, ahem, a privilege to give you a line myself to the *Intelligencer* people."

A RELIC OF THE PLIOCENE

I WASH my hands of him at the start. I cannot father his tales, nor will I be responsible for them. I make these preliminary reservations, observe, as a guard upon my own integrity. I possess a certain definite position in a small way, also a wife; and for the good name of the community that honors my existence with its approval, and for the sake of her posterity and mine, I cannot take the chances I once did, nor foster probabilities with the careless improvidence of youth. So, I repeat, I wash my hands of him, this Nimrod, this mighty hunter, this homely, blue-eyed, freckle-faced Thomas Stevens.

Having been honest to myself, and to whatever prospective olive branches my wife may be pleased to tender me, I can now afford to be generous. I shall not criticise the tales told me by Thomas Stevens, and, further, I shall withold my judgment. If it be asked why, I can only add that judgment I have none. Long have I pondered, weighed, and balanced, but never have my conclusions been twice the same—forsooth! because Thomas Stevens is a greater man than I. If he have told truths, well and good; if untruths, still well and good. For who can prove? or who disprove? I eliminate myself from the proposition, while those of little faith may do as I have done—go find the said Thomas Stevens, and discuss to his face the various matters which, if fortune serve, I shall relate. As to where he may be found? The directions are simple: anywhere between 53 north latitude and the Pole, on the one hand; and, on the other, the likeliest hunting grounds that lie between the east coast of Siberia and farthermost Labrador. That he is there, somewhere, within that clearly defined territory, I pledge the word of an honorable man whose expectations entail straight speaking and right living.

Thomas Stevens may have toyed prodigiously with truth, but when we first met (it were well to mark this point), he wandered into my camp when I thought myself a thousand miles beyond the outermost post of civilization. At the sight of his human face, the first in weary months, I could have sprung forward and folded him in my arms (and I am not by any means a demonstrative man); but to him his visit seemed the most casual thing under the sun. He just strolled into the light of my camp, passed the time of day after the custom of men on beaten trails, threw my snowshoes the one way and a couple of dogs the other, and so made room for himself by the fire. Said he'd just dropped in to borrow a pinch of soda and to see if I had any decent tobacco. He plucked forth an ancient pipe, loaded it with painstaking care, and, without as much as by your leave, whacked half the tobacco of my pouch into his. Yes, the stuff was fairly good. He sighed with the contentment of the just, and literally absorbed the smoke from the crisping yellow flakes, and it did my smoker's heart good to behold him.

Hunter? Trapper? Prospector? He shrugged his shoulders No; just sort of knocking round a bit. Had come up from the Great Slave some time since, and was thinking of trapsing over into the Yukon country. The Factor of Koshim had spoken about the discoveries on the Klondike, and he was of a mind to run over for a peep. I noticed that he spoke of the Klondike in the archaic vernacular, calling it the Reindeer River—a conceited custom that the Old Timers employ against the *che-cha-quas* and all tenderfeet in general. But he did it so naïvely and as such a matter of course, that there was no sting, and I forgave him. He also had it in view, he said, before he crossed the divide into the Yukon, to make a little run up Fort o' Good Hope way.

Now Fort o' Good Hope is a far journey to the north, over and beyond the Circle, in a place where the feet of few men have trod; and when a nondescript ragamuffin comes in out of the night, from nowhere in particular, to sit by one's fire and discourse on such in terms of "trapsing" and "a little run," it is fair time to rouse up and shake off the dream. Wherefore I looked about me; saw the fly, and, underneath, the pine boughs spread for the sleeping furs; saw the grub sacks, the camera, the frosty breaths of the dogs circling on the edge of the light; and, above, a great streamer of the aurora bridging the zenith from southeast to northwest. I shivered. There is a magic in the Northland night, that steals in on one like fevers from malarial marshes. You are clutched and downed before you are aware. Then I looked to the snowshoes, lying prone and crossed where he had flung them. Also I had an eye to my tobacco pouch. Half, at least, of its goodly store had vamosed. That settled it. Fancy had not tricked me after all.

Crazed with suffering, I thought, looking steadfastly at the man —one of those wild stampeders, strayed far from his bearings and wandering like a lost soul through great vastnesses and unknown deeps. Oh, well, let his moods slip on, until, mayhap, he gathers his tangled wits together. Who knows?—the mere sound of a fellow-creature's voice may bring all straight again.

So I led him on in talk, and soon I marvelled, for he talked of game and the ways thereof. He had killed the Siberian wolf of westernmost Alaska, and the chamois in the secret Rockies. He averred he knew the haunts where the last buffalo still roamed; that he had hung on the flanks of the caribou when they ran by the hundred thousand, and slept in the Great Barrens on the musk-ox's winter trail.

And I shifted my judgment accordingly (the first revision, but by no account the last), and deemed him a monumental effigy of truth. Why it was I know not, but the spirit moved me to repeat a tale told to me by a man who had dwelt in the land too long to know better. It was of the great bear that hugs the steep slopes of St. Elias, never descending to the levels of the gentler inclines. Now God so constituted this creature for its hillside habitat that the legs of one side are all of a foot longer than those of the other. This is mighty convenient, as will be readily admitted. So I hunted this rare beast in my own name, told it in the first person, present tense, painted the requisite locale, gave it the necessary garnishings and touches of verisimilitude, and looked to see the man stunned by the recital.

Not he. Had he doubted, I could have forgiven him. Had he objected, denying the dangers of such a hunt by virtue of the animal's inability to turn about and go the other way—had he done this, I say, I could have taken him by the hand for the true sportsman that he was. Not he. He sniffed, looked on me, and sniffed again; then gave my tobacco due praise, thrust one foot into my lap, and bade me examine the gear. It was a *mucluc* of the Innuit pattern, sewed together with sinew threads, and devoid of beads or furbelows. But it was the skin itself that was remarkable. In that it was all of half an inch thick, it reminded me of walrus-hide; but there the resemblance ceased, for no walrus ever bore so marvellous a growth of hair. On the side and ankles this hair was well-nigh worn away, what of friction with underbrush and snow; but around the top and down the more sheltered back it was coarse, dirty black, and very thick. I parted it with difficulty and looked beneath for the fine fur that is common with northern animals, but found it in this case to be absent. This, however, was compensated for by the length. Indeed, the tufts that had survived wear and tear measured all of seven or eight inches.

I looked up into the man's face, and he pulled his foot down and asked, "Find hide like that on your St. Elias bear?"

I shook my head. "Nor on any other creature of land or sea," I answered candidly. The thickness of it, and the length of the hair, puzzled me.

"That," he said, and said without the slightest hint of impressiveness, "that came from a mammoth."

"Nonsense!" I exclaimed, for I could not forbear the protest of my unbelief. "The mammoth, my dear sir, long ago vanished from the earth. We know it once existed by the fossil remains that we have unearthed, and by a frozen carcass that the Siberian sun saw fit to melt from out the bosom of a glacier; but we also know that no living specimen exists. Our explorers—"

At this word he broke in impatiently. "Your explorers? Pish! A weakly breed. Let us hear no more of them. But tell me, O man, what you may know of the mammoth and his ways."

Beyond contradiction, this was leading to a yarn; so I baited my hook by ransacking my memory for whatever data I possessed on the subject in hand. To begin with, I emphasized that the animal was prehistoric, and marshalled all my facts in support of this. I mentioned the Siberian sand bars that abounded with ancient mammoth bones; spoke of the large quantities of fossil ivory purchased from the Innuits by the Alaska Commercial Company; and acknowledged having myself mined six- and eight-foot tusks from the pay gravel of the Klondike creeks. "All fossils," I concluded, "found in the midst of débris deposited through countless ages."

"I remember when I was a kid," Thomas Stevens sniffed (he had a most confounded way of sniffing), "that I saw a petrified watermelon. Hence, though mistaken persons sometimes delude themselves into thinking that they are really raising or eating them, there are no such things as extant watermelons."

"But the question of food," I objected, ignoring his point, which was puerile and without bearing. "The soil must bring forth vegetable life in lavish abundance to support so monstrous creations. Nowhere in the North is the soil so prolific. Ergo, the mammoth cannot exist."

"I pardon your ignorance concerning many matters of this Northland, for you are a young man and have travelled little; but, at the same time, I am inclined to agree with you on one thing. The mammoth no longer exists. How do I know? I killed the last one with my own right arm."

Thus spake Nimrod, the Mighty Hunter. I threw a stick of firewood at the dogs and bade them quit their unholy howling, and waited. Undoubtedly this liar of singular felicity would open his mouth and requite me for my St. Elias bear.

"It was this way," he at last began, after the appropriate silence had intervened. "I was in camp one day—"

"Where?" I interrupted.

He waved his hand vaguely in the direction of the northeast, where stretched a terra incognita into which vastness few men have strayed and fewer emerged. "I was in camp one day with Klooch. Klooch was as handsome a little *kamooks* as ever whined betwixt the traces or shoved nose into a camp kettle. Her father was a full-blood Malemute from Russian Pastilik on Bering Sea, and I bred her, and with understanding, out of a clean-legged bitch of the Hudson Bay stock. I tell you, O man, she was a corker combination. And now, on this day I have in mind, she was brought to pup through a pure wild wolf of the woods—gray, and long of limb, with big lungs and no end of staying powers. Say! Was there ever the like? It was a new breed of dog I had started, and I could look forward to big things.

"As I have said, she was brought neatly to pup, and safely delivered. I was squatting on my hams over the litter—seven sturdy, blind little beggars—when from behind came a bray of trumpets and crash of brass. There was a rush, like the wind-squall that kicks the heels of the rain, and I was midway to my feet when knocked flat on my face. At the same instant I heard Klooch sigh, very much as a man does when you've planted your fist in his belly. You can stake your sack I lay quiet, but I twisted my head around and saw a huge bulk swaying above me. Then the blue sky flashed into view and I got to my feet. A hairy mountain of flesh was just disappearing in the underbrush on the edge of the open. I caught a rear-end glimpse, with a stiff tail, as big in girth as my body, standing out straight behind. The next second only a tremendous hole remained in the thicket, though I could still hear the sounds as of a tornado dying quickly away, underbrush ripping and tearing, and trees snapping and crashing.

"I cast about for my rifle. It had been lying on the ground with the muzzle against a log; but now the stock was smashed, the barrel out of line, and the working-gear in a thousand bits. Then I looked for the slut, and—and what do you suppose?"

I shook my head.

"May my soul burn in a thousand hells if there was anything left of her! Klooch, the seven sturdy, blind little beggars—gone, all gone. Where she had stretched was a slimy, bloody depression in the soft earth, all of a yard in diameter, and around the edges a few scattered hairs."

I measured three feet on the snow, threw about it a circle, and glanced at Nimrod.

"The beast was thirty long and twenty high," he answered, "and its tusks scaled over six times three feet. I couldn't believe, myself, at the time, for all that it had just happened. But if my senses had played me, there was the broken gun and the hole in the brush. And there was—or, rather, there was not—Klooch and the pups. O man, it makes me hot all over now when I think of it. Klooch! Another Eve! The mother of a new race! And a rampaging, ranting, old bull mammoth, like a second flood, wiping them, root and branch, off the face of the earth! Do you wonder that the blood-soaked earth cried out to high God? Or that I grabbed the hand-axe and took the trail?"

"The hand-axe?" I exclaimed, startled out of myself by the picture. "The hand-axe, and a big bull mammoth, thirty feet long, twenty feet—"

Nimrod joined me in my merriment, chuckling gleefully. "Wouldn't it kill you?" he cried. "Wasn't it a beaver's dream? Many's the time I've laughed about it since, but at the time it was no laughing matter, I was that danged mad, what of the gun and Klooch. Think of it, O man! A brand-new, unclassified, uncopyrighted breed, and wiped out before ever it opened its eyes or took out its intention papers! Well, so be it. Life's full of disappointments, and rightly so. Meat is best after a famine, and bed soft after a hard trail.

"As I was saying, I took out after the beast with the hand-axe, and hung to its heels down the valley; but when he circled back toward the head, I was left winded at the lower end. Speaking of grub, I might as well stop long enough to explain a couple of points. Up thereabouts, in the midst of the mountains, is an almighty curious formation. There is no end of little valleys, each like the other much as peas in a pod, and all neatly tucked away with straight, rocky walls rising on all sides. And at the lower ends are always small openings where the drainage or glaciers must have broken out. The only way in is through these mouths, and they are all small, and some smaller than others. As to grub— you've slushed around on the rain-soaked islands of the Alaskan coast down Sitka way, most likely, seeing as you're a traveller. And you know how stuff grows there—big, and juicy, and jungly. Well, that's the way it was with those valleys. Thick, rich soil, with ferns and grasses and such things in patches higher than your head. Rain three days out of four during the summer months; and food in them for a thousand mammoths, to say nothing of small game for man.

"But to get back. Down at the lower end of the valley I got winded and gave over. I began to speculate, for when my wind left me my dander got hotter and hotter, and I knew I'd never know peace of mind till I dined on roasted mammoth-foot. And I knew, also, that that stood for *skookum mamook pukapuk*—excuse Chinook, I mean there was a big fight coming. Now the mouth of my valley was very narrow, and the walls steep. High up on one side was one of those big pivot rocks, or balancing, rocks, as some call them, weighing all of a couple of hundred tons. Just the thing. I hit back for camp, keeping an eye open so the bull couldn't slip past, and got my ammunition. It wasn't worth anything with the rifle smashed; so I opened the shells, planted the powder under the rock, and touched it off with slow fuse. Wasn't much of a charge, but the old boulder tilted up lazily and dropped down into place, with just space enough to let the creek drain nicely. Now I had him."

"But how did you have him?" I queried. "Who ever heard of a man killing a mammoth with a hand-axe? And, for that matter, with anything else?"

"O man, have I not told you I was mad?" Nimrod replied, with a slight manifestation of sensitiveness. "Mad clean through, what of Klooch and the gun? Also, was I not a hunter? And was this not new and most unusual game? A hand-axe? Pish! I did not need it. Listen, and you shall hear of a hunt, such as might have happened in the youth of the world when caveman rounded up the kill with hand-axe of stone. Such would have served me as well. Now is it not a fact that man can outwalk the dog or horse? That he can wear them out with the intelligence of his endurance?"

I nodded.

"Well?"

The light broke in on me, and I bade him continue.

"My valley was perhaps five miles around. The mouth was closed. There was no way to get out. A timid beast was that bull mammoth, and I had him at my mercy. I got on his heels again, hollered like a fiend, pelted him with cobbles, and raced him around the valley three times before I knocked off for supper. Don't you see? A race-course! A man and a mammoth! A hippodrome, with sun, moon, and stars to referee!

"It took me two months to do it, but I did it. And that's no beaver dream. Round and round I ran him, me travelling on the inner circle, eating jerked meat and salmon berries on the run, and snatching winks of sleep between. Of course, he'd get desperate at times and turn. Then I'd head for soft ground where the creek spread out, and lay anathema upon him and his ancestry, and dare him to come on. But he was too wise to bog in a mud puddle. Once he pinned me in against the walls, and I crawled back into a deep crevice and waited. Whenever he felt for me with his trunk, I'd belt him with the hand-axe till he pulled out, shrieking fit to split my ear drums, he was that mad. He knew he had me and didn't have me, and it near drove him wild. But he was no man's fool. He knew he was safe as long as I stayed in the crevice, and he made up his mind to keep me there. And he was dead right, only he hadn't figured on the commissary. There was neither grub nor water around that spot, so on the face of it he couldn't keep up the siege. He'd stand before the opening for hours, keeping an eye on me and flapping mosquitoes away with his big blanket ears. Then the thirst would come on him and he'd ramp round and roar till the earth shook, calling me every name he could lay tongue to. This was to frighten me, of course; and when he thought I was sufficiently impressed, he'd back away softly and try to make a sneak for the creek. Sometimes I'd let him get almost there—only a couple of hundred yards away it was —when out I'd pop and back he'd come, lumbering along like the old landslide he was. After I'd done this a few times, and he'd figured it out, he changed his tactics. Grasped the time element, you see. Without a word of warning, away he'd go, tearing for the water like mad, scheming to get there and back before I ran away. Finally, after cursing me most horribly, he raised the siege and deliberately stalked off to the water hole.

"That was the only time he penned me,—three days of it,—but after that the hippodrome never stopped. Round, and round, and round, like a six days' go-as-I-please, for he never pleased. My clothes went to rags and tatters, but I never stopped to mend, till at last I ran naked as a son of earth, with nothing but the old hand-axe in one hand and a cobble in the other. In fact, I never stopped, save for peeps of sleep in the crannies and ledges of the cliffs. As for the bull, he got perceptibly thinner and thinner— must have lost several tons at least—and as nervous as a schoolmarm on the wrong side of matrimony. When I'd come up with him and yell, or lam him with a rock at long range, he'd jump like a skittish colt and tremble all over. Then he'd pull out on the run, tail and trunk waving stiff, head over one shoulder and wicked eyes blazing, and the way he'd swear at me was something dreadful. A most immoral beast he was, a murderer, and a blasphemer.

"But toward the end he quit all this, and fell to whimpering and crying like a baby. His spirit broke and he became a quivering jelly-mountain of misery. He'd get attacks of palpitation of the heart, and stagger around like a drunken man, and fall down and bark his shins. And then he'd cry, but always on the run. O man, the gods themselves would have wept with him, and you yourself or any other man. It was pitiful, and there was so much of it, but I only hardened my heart and hit up the pace. At last I wore him clean out, and he lay down, broken-winded, broken-hearted, hungry, and thirsty. When I found he wouldn't budge, I hamstrung him, and spent the better part of the day wading into him with the hand-axe, he a sniffing and sobbing till I worked in far enough to shut him off. Thirty feet long he was, and twenty high, and a man could sling a hammock between his tusks and sleep comfortably. Barring the fact that I had run most of the juices out of him, he was fair eating, and his four feet, alone, roasted whole, would have lasted a man a twelvemonth. I spent the winter there myself."

"And where is this valley?" I asked.

He waved his hand in the direction of the northeast, and said: "Your tobacco is very good. I carry a fair share of it in my pouch, but I shall carry the recollection of it until I die. In token of my appreciation, and in return for the moccasins on your own feet, I will present to you these *muclucs*. They commemorate Klooch and the seven blind little beggars. They are also souvenirs of an unparalleled event in history, namely, the destruction of the oldest breed of animal on earth, and the youngest. And their chief virtue lies in that they will never wear out."

Having effected the exchange, he knocked the ashes from his pipe, gripped my hand good night, and wandered off through the snow. Concerning this tale, for which I have already disclaimed responsibility, I would recommend those of little faith to make a visit to the Smithsonian Institute. If they bring the requisite credentials and do not come in vacation time, they will undoubtedly gain an audience with Professor Dolvidson. The *muclucs* are in his possession, and he will verify, not the manner in which they were obtained, but the material of which they are composed. When he states that they are made from the skin of the mammoth, the scientific world accepts his verdict. What more would you have?

SEMPER IDEM

DOCTOR BICKNELL was in a remarkably gracious mood. Through a minor accident, a slight bit of carelessness, that was all, a man who might have pulled through had died the preceding night. Though it had been only a sailorman, one of the innumerable unwashed, the steward of the receiving hospital had been on the anxious seat all the morning. It was not that the man had died that gave him discomfort, he knew the Doctor too well for that, but his distress lay in the fact that the operation had been done so well. One of the most delicate in surgery, it had been as successful as it was clever and audacious. All had then depended upon the treatment, the nurses, the steward. And the man had died. Nothing much, a bit of carelessness, yet enough to bring the professional wrath of Doctor Bicknell about his ears and to perturb the working of the staff and nurses for twenty-four hours to come.

But, as already stated, the Doctor was in a remarkably gracious mood. When informed by the steward, in fear and trembling, of the man's unexpected take-off, his lips did not so much as form one syllable of censure; nay, they were so pursed that snatches of rag-time floated softly from them, to be broken only by a pleasant query after the health of the other's eldest-born. The steward, deeming it impossible that he could have caught the gist of the case, repeated it.

"Yes, yes," Doctor Bicknell said impatiently; "I understand. But how about Semper Idem? Is he ready to leave?"

"Yes. They're helping him dress now," the steward answered, passing on to the round of his duties, content that peace still reigned within the iodine-saturated walls.

It was Semper Idem's recovery which had so fully compensated Doctor Bicknell for the loss of the sailorman. Lives were to him as nothing, the unpleasant but inevitable incidents of the profession, but cases, ah, cases were everything. People who knew him were prone to brand him a butcher, but his colleagues were at one in the belief that a bolder and yet a more capable man never stood over the table. He was not an imaginative man. He did not possess, and hence had no tolerance for, emotion. His nature was accurate, precise, scientific. Men were to him no more than pawns, without individuality or personal value. But as cases it was different. The more broken a man was, the more precarious his grip on life, the greater his significance in the eyes of Doctor Bicknell. He would as readily forsake a poet laureate suffering from a common accident for a nameless, mangled vagrant who defied every law of life by refusing to die, as would a child forsake a Punch and Judy for a circus.

So it had been in the case of Semper Idem. The mystery of the man had not appealed to him, nor had his silence and the veiled romance which the yellow reporters had so sensationally and so fruitlessly exploited in divers Sunday editions. But Semper Idem's throat had been cut. That was the point. That was where his interest had centred. Cut from ear to ear, and not one surgeon in a thousand to give a snap of the fingers for his chance of recovery. But, thanks to the swift municipal ambulance service and to Doctor Bicknell, he had been dragged back into the world he had sought to leave. The Doctor's co-workers had shaken their heads when the case was brought in. Impossible, they said. Throat, windpipe, jugular, all but actually severed, and the loss of blood frightful. As it was such a foregone conclusion, Doctor Bicknell had employed methods and done things which made them, even in their professional capacities, to shudder. And lo! the man had recovered.

So, on this morning that Semper Idem was to leave the hospital, hale and hearty, Doctor Bicknell's geniality was in nowise disturbed by the steward's report, and he proceeded cheerfully to bring order out of the chaos of a child's body which had been ground and crunched beneath the wheels of an electric car.

As many will remember, the case of Semper Idem aroused a vast deal of unseemly yet highly natural curiosity. He had been found in a slum lodging, with throat cut as aforementioned, and blood dripping down upon the inmates of the room below and disturbing their festivities. He had evidently done the deed standing, with head bowed forward that he might gaze his last upon a photograph which stood on the table propped against a candlestick. It was this attitude which had made it possible for Doctor Bicknell to save him. So terrific had been the sweep of the razor that had he had his head thrown back, as he should have done to have accomplished the act properly, with his neck stretched and the elastic vascular walls distended, he would have of a certainty well nigh decapitated himself.

At the hospital, during all the time he travelled the repugnant road back to life, not a word had left his lips. Nor could anything be learned of him by the sleuths detailed by the chief of police. Nobody knew him, nor had ever seen or heard of him before. He was strictly, uniquely, of the present. His clothes and surroundings were those of the lowest laborer, his hands the hands of a gentleman. But not a shred of writing was discovered, nothing, save in one particular, which would serve to indicate his past or his position in life.

And that one particular was the photograph. If it were at all a likeness, the woman who gazed frankly out upon the onlooker from the cardmount must have been a striking creature indeed. It was an amateur production, for the detectives were baffled in that no professional photographer's signature or studio was appended. Across a corner of the mount, in delicate feminine tracery, was written: "*Semper idem; semper fidelis.*" And she looked it. As many recollect, it was a face one could never forget. Clever halftones, remarkably like, were published in all the leading papers at the time; but such procedure gave rise to nothing but the uncontrollable public curiosity and interminable copy to the space writers.

For want of a better name, the rescued suicide was known to the hospital attendants, and to the world, as Semper Idem. And Semper Idem he remained. Reporters, detectives, and nurses gave him up in despair. Not one word could he be persuaded to utter; yet the flitting conscious light of his eyes showed that his ears heard and his brain grasped every question put to him.

But this mystery and romance played no part in Doctor Bicknell's interest when he paused in the office to have a parting word with his patient. He, the Doctor, had performed a prodigy in the matter of this man, done what was virtually unprecedented in the annals of surgery. He did not care who or what the man was, and it was highly improbable that he should ever see him again; but, like the artist gazing upon a finished creation, he wished to look for the last time upon the work of his hand and brain.

Semper Idem still remained mute. He seemed anxious to be gone. Not a word could the Doctor extract from him, and little the Doctor cared. He examined the throat of the convalescent carefully, idling over the hideous scar with the lingering, half-caressing fondness of a parent. It was not a particularly pleasing sight. An angry line circled the throat,—for all the world as though the man had just escaped the hangman's noose, and,—disappearing below the ear on either side, had the appearance of completing the fiery periphery at the nape of the neck.

Maintaining his dogged silence, yielding to the other's examination in much the manner of a leashed lion, Semper Idem betrayed only his desire to drop from out of the public eye.

"Well, I'll not keep you," Doctor Bicknell finally said, laying a hand on the man's shoulder and stealing a last glance at his own handiwork. "But let me give you a bit of advice. Next time you try it on, hold your chin up, so. Don't snuggle it down and butcher yourself like a cow. Neatness and despatch, you know. Neatness and despatch."

Semper Idem's eyes flashed in token that he heard, and a moment later the hospital door swung to on his heel.

It was a busy day for Doctor Bicknell, and the afternoon was well along when he lighted a cigar preparatory to leaving the table upon which it seemed the sufferers almost clamored to be laid.

But the last one, an old rag-picker with a broken shoulder-blade, had been disposed of, and the first fragrant smoke wreaths had begun to curl about his head, when the gong of a hurrying ambulance came through the open window from the street, followed by the inevitable entry of the stretcher with its ghastly freight.

"Lay it on the table," the Doctor directed, turning for a moment to place his cigar in safety. "What is it?"

"Suicide—throat cut," responded one of the stretcher bearers. "Down on Morgan Alley. Little hope, I think, sir. He's 'most gone."

"Eh? Well, I'll give him a look, anyway." He leaned over the man at the moment when the quick made its last faint flutter and succumbed.

"It's Semper Idem come back again," the steward said.

"Ay," replied Doctor Bicknell, "and gone again. No bungling this time. Properly done, upon my life, sir, properly done. Took my advice to the letter. I'm not required here. Take it along to the morgue."

Doctor Bicknell secured his cigar and relighted it. "That," he said between the puffs, looking at the steward, "that evens up for the one you lost last night. We're quits now."

THEIR ALCOVE

HE crumpled each dainty note with a steadfastness of purpose that surprised him. He had not thought it would be so easy. In fact, he felt a sort of passive elation as he laid them carefully upon the hearth, side by side and in intermingled tiers. He began to take a curious pleasure in the task, and his habitual neatness asserted itself till the pile began to assume architectural proportions. How like a pedestal, he mused. He regarded it critically. One little missive—her latest and last—protested with the lusty strength of youth at such untimely incineration. It bulged forth distressingly, ruining the lines of the parallelogram. A few gentle pokes and it subsided among its fellows.

How like a shrine, an altar, it was and he, apostate to the gentle Hymen, officiating as high priest. The fancy pleased him; there was a hint of poesy about it. After all, this was the better way. He was glad she had been so sensible about it. Paugh! this giddy return of trinkets and tokens! What right had she to her letters, or he to his? A senseless custom at best. And how readily she had acquiesced when he mentioned it! He confessed to a momentary pang at this; he had expected some show of sentiment, of womanly weakness: but no, she had merely nodded her head and smiled. Why, it was very plain that she had grown tired. Of course, she had not said as much to him, but it was clear, even clearer now that it was over. And it was to be admitted he had behaved splendidly; even she must acknowledge that. If aught were said it was he who must bear it. How the fellows would cod him! And at teas and numerous other feminine functions sly whispers and little giggles and significant nods—well, he was a man, and he could bear it.

He was glad that he had done this, for in no way could there be reproach, while there was much to admire about his conduct. In after-years it would endear him to her, and her memory of him could not but be sweet. Certainly she would marry, and perhaps the thought of all this would come to her some day and she would know what she had lost. He would take up his work with new vigor, and with the ripening years his name would be respected, admired and often on the lips of men; and then he would go to her and they would be friends, merely friends; she would see all that was best in him—those sterling qualities he knew she did not now appreciate—and she would perhaps feel sorrow that things had not been different. The thought of the regret that would be hers when she saw into what manner of man time and his efforts had wrought him bore to him a sweet satisfaction. But as in his reverie he saw himself in the days to come, when time should have white-lined his hair and brought him fame, looking down upon her and speaking calmly, he knew that he would not have had his life shaped otherwise. Yet, withal, it was sweet to feel that perhaps the years that would give to her another for husband would leave with her also regret.

He made little journeys between the fireplace and various portions of the room. How vacant the wall seemed! He must get something to replace it, he thought, as he knelt before the altar he had reared and placed upon it a photograph—her photograph. And before it he laid a glove, once white but now soiled with much carriage in coat breast-pocket. How foolish he had been! Then he added a lock of hair, nut-brown and curly, to the sacrifice; and beside it a withered bunch of violets. Why, once he would have staked his hopes of heaven on those fragile tokens; and now—and now he touched a vesta to the altar's base, humming as he did so, "Love like ours can never die."

He drew up his lounging-chair and settled back comfortably. He felt a boyish curiousness as to the behavior of the different articles, and which would succumb first to the destroyer. The tiny flame mounted and spread till a diminutive conflagration roared at his feet. The violets burst into a brilliant evanescence, their stems lingering like fire-spun filaments of steel, tense and quivering with heat. The glove glowed somberly against the bright background of flaming paper; while the photograph, like the tower of a lordly castle, sent aloft black columns of smoke, then tottered, swayed for a moment indecisively, and crashed into the fiery embers beneath. Slowly the glow of life went out of the sunken pyre as light leaves a drying eye; soon the little nothings—yesterday they were everything—that to him had been pledges upon the future for his happiness were only a dead heap of black and gray ash shivering on the hearth.

It was all over. He was free now, free as the wind. A short month past he would have deemed it impossible to break the gyves so easily. Yet emancipation—he would have called it banishment then—had come without effort, without that strange orgasm of the blood, that fiery tumult of the emotions one would so naturally expect.

Over the charred fetters he could sit there and think of her calmly; there was not an extra beat to his pulse; he was perfectly normal. Well, it showed on the face of it how transitory had been the fancy.

Yes, it was fancy; mere fancy—that was the word. It could not have been genuine love, else the separation of their paths of life could have brought to him but one emotion—a sense of agonizing loss. But he felt no loss; he was as easy in mind now that she had gone out of his life as he had been in the old days before she had made entry into it. And now he was free; free to go back to the old life, the old ways. It was early yet. The several little arrangements attendant on departure had been seen to, and the train was not scheduled till midnight. He would dine down town and look up some of the fellows for old sake's sake.

Free, free as the wind! There was an exhilaration to the phrase. It obtruded itself among his thoughts like some pleasant refrain. He had never been in sympathy with the simple little word, he thought, as he came down the steps, never understood its strength before. And she? No doubt she was pleased at the termination, and could already look back pleasantly upon the episode. That was all it was, an episode. And she would marry, as a matter of course, and be happy ever after.

He wondered what the husband might be like, and tried to pick him from all the eligibles he could think of. But he could conjure no harmonious union; now their tastes ran counter, now their temperaments; perhaps the lucky fellow still lay in the lap of the future. Yes, lucky fellow! There was no denying she was a nice girl: and yet "nice" did not rightfully convey the sense of her choiceness. It told but half the tale. Certainly there was room for improvement in the vernacular.

He followed his many-mirrored fancy through endless turnings, and before he knew it came to himself at the entrance of the "Grotto." He pulled out his watch. It was absurd to eat at such an hour, but he was hungry and went in. He fell to planning for his new life; but the waiter, pausing for his order, reminded him of the day they had dined there—the day when the volunteers marched through the streets and the city went dizzy with enthusiastic patriotism. He realized the trend of his mind with a start. He must put her away. That was past and done with. It was an episode. He must concern himself with the days to come, and in them she had no place. But a woman's laughter floated across from the other side and wove itself into his fancy as her laughter. How happy they had been that day! What silly nonsense they had prattled in burlesque seriousness; and then how they had laughed at the graver things, the austerities of life! What a thoroughly wholesome creature she was, meeting mood with mood in a way which was not given to many women!

He remembered a thousand and one little incidents—trivial events, so unimportant at the time, but now fair mile-stones to look back upon. It began to dawn upon him how large a place she had filled in his life. For the time he had lived his days in her, and now—to-morrow? The future loomed before him like a blank wall. He had no wish to contemplate it. There were the fellows—but the fellows would not understand. The old equality could never be the same. He felt so much broader, stronger than they. She had led his feet in paths they little dreamed of, and, through her, life had taken upon itself a significance which they might never come to know. The secret of woman! He had caught glimmerings of it; he knew there was yet more for him to learn; but they—they were deep in outer darkness. Could he go back to them, and forget all this? What would he do to-morrow, and the next day, and the next? The emptiness of the immediate future pressed against him. He must remodel his life, look about him, get some new interest into it.

After all, he did not care to eat. It was too early. He strayed up the street in an absent fashion. A sudden distaste for the fellows came upon him. He would not look them up. He wished it were train-time, and knew already the promised dullness of the night. He felt strangely solitary among the shop-people hurrying home from their work. Any other evening he would have gone to her. What was she doing now? The vision of the tea-table came to him vividly, and with it her sweet face and her mother's, and the paneled roses which hung opposite his accustomed seat just over her head. He remembered the smallest details; even the napkin-rings were in his mind as perfectly as had he designed them himself. And there were to be no more such evenings! Well, he was a man; she would see that he could stand it. He glanced up to the library clock. Yes, it was just tea-time. No, he was not sentimental; he drew back from such nonsense and thanked his gods frequently that he had escaped such affectation of exquisite feeling. It was only that he was going away, and the familiar atmosphere of the books appealed to him. He entered the library. At this hour, save for the noiseless attendants and certain weird creatures that infest such places, it was deserted. He passed by the shelves, whose transient occupants came and went unceasingly. In the upper galleries they rarely left their peaceful abode, and were consulted at infrequent periods by musty antiquarians and eager, hungry-looking collectors of worthless facts and figures. In these alcoves pale-faced students were wont to study, and, it must be confessed, sometimes to doze over the weary text.

Turn after turn he ascended the spiral staircase, fine-ribbed of steel, like a gigantic cork-screw. At last he came to "their" alcove, and drew a stool to its farthest recess. The lights had not yet been turned on and the day was growing dim. Yes, "their" alcove! He remembered the days when he had coached her there through the Elizabethan period, and the time they lost themselves among the metaphysical subtleties of "Alastor." "Their" alcove—why, all the habitués of the library acknowledged their ownership; and he smiled at the recollection of the young student they had found there one day, and his embarrassment, conscious of having trespassed, and his apologetic manner as he glided away. And their post-office, too! And parcels delivery! He nodded knowingly at a short, fat volume sandwiched between two ponderous tomes on an upper shelf. Come to think of it, the letter, the last letter, must be there yet. He had left it there that morning before—before it all happened. Of course, she would never come for it now. Should he take it? He had his own ideas on such things, but this was an unlooked-for contingency. Was it his or hers? Should it lie there until resurrected on some problematic cleaning-day by an attendant, who perhaps would remember the romance of the alcove when it was "theirs"? He debated the question with great seriousness. No, he was not sentimental.

Somebody paused on the gallery—a woman—then entered. He felt irritated at the intrusion. He barely noticed her. She would go away soon, he hoped, and leave him alone. She reached hesitatingly toward the short, fat volume. This was desecration, he thought; and how had others come to know the secret of "their" alcove? She turned in his direction, kissing the letter as she did so. In the failing light he noticed in her sweet eyes a moistness he had never seen before. He cried her name softly and sprang toward her.

The soft-footed attendant forgot to turn on the light before "their" alcove. Later, when a long-haired, elderly gentleman asked for Mechnu's "Mirror of Alchemy" he informed him that it was out. The "Mirror of Alchemy" was the short, fat volume.

THE MINIONS OF MIDAS

WADE ATSHELER is dead—dead by his own hand. To say that this was entirely unexpected by the small coterie which knew him, would be to say an untruth; and yet never once had we, his intimates, ever canvassed the idea. Rather had we been prepared for it in some incomprehensible subconscious way. Before the perpetration of the deed, its possibility was remotest from our thoughts; but when we did know that he was dead, it seemed, somehow, that we had understood and looked forward to it all the time. This, by retrospective analysis, we could easily explain by the fact of his great trouble. I use "great trouble" advisedly. Young, handsome, with an assured position as the right-hand man of Eben Hale, the great street-railway magnate, there could be no reason for him to complain of fortune's favors. Yet we had watched his smooth brow furrow and corrugate as under some carking care or devouring sorrow. We had watched his thick, black hair thin and silver as green grain under brazen skies and parching drought. Who can forget, in the midst of the hilarious scenes he toward the last sought with greater and greater avidity—who can forget, I say, the deep abstractions and black moods into which he fell? At such times, when the fun rippled and soared from height to height, suddenly, without rhyme or reason, his eyes would turn lacklustre, his brows knit, as with clenched hands and face overshot with spasms of mental pain he wrestled on the edge of the abyss with some unknown danger.

He never spoke of his trouble, nor were we indiscreet enough to ask. But it was just as well; for had we, and had he spoken, our help and strength could have availed nothing. When Eben Hale died, whose confidential secretary he was—nay, well-nigh adopted son and full business partner—he no longer came among us. Not, as I now know, that our company was distasteful to him, but because his trouble had so grown that he could not respond to our happiness nor find surcease with us. Why this should be so we could not at the time understand, for when Eben Hale's will was probated, the world learned that he was sole heir to his employer's many millions, and it was expressly stipulated that this great inheritance was given to him without qualification, hitch, or hindrance in the exercise thereof. Not a share of stock, not a penny of cash, was bequeathed to the dead man's relatives. As for his direct family, one astounding clause expressly stated that Wade Atsheler was to dispense to Eben Hale's wife and sons and daughters whatever moneys his judgment dictated, at whatever times he deemed advisable. Had there been any scandal in the dead man's family, or had his sons been wild or undutiful, then there might have been a glimmering of reason in this most unusual action; but Eben Hale's domestic happiness had been proverbial in the community, and one would have to travel far and wide to discover a cleaner, saner, wholesomer progeny of sons and daughters. While his wife—well, by those who knew her best she was endearingly termed "The Mother of the Gracchi." Needless to state, this inexplicable will was a nine days' wonder; but the expectant public was disappointed in that no contest was made.

It was only the other day that Eben Hale was laid away in his stately marble mausoleum. And now Wade Atsheler is dead. The news was printed in this morning's paper. I have just received through the mail a letter from him, posted, evidently, but a short hour before he hurled himself into eternity. This letter, which lies before me, is a narrative in his own handwriting, linking together numerous newspaper clippings and facsimiles of letters. The original correspondence, he has told me, is in the hands of the police. He has begged me, also, as a warning to society against a most frightful and diabolical danger which threatens its very existence, to make public the terrible series of tragedies in which he has been innocently concerned. I herewith append the text in full:

It was in August, 1899, just after my return from my summer vacation, that the blow fell. We did not know it at the time; we had not yet learned to school our minds to such awful possibilities. Mr. Hale opened the letter, read it, and tossed it upon my desk with a laugh. When I had looked it over, I also laughed, saying, "Some ghastly joke, Mr. Hale, and one in very poor taste." Find here, my dear John, an exact duplicate of the letter in question.

OFFICE OF THE M. OF M.,
August 17, 1899.

MR. EBEN HALE, Money Baron:

Dear Sir,—We desire you to realize upon whatever portion of your vast holdings is necessary to obtain, *in cash*, twenty millions of dollars. This sum we require you to pay over to us, or to our agents. You will note we do not specify any given time, for it is not our wish to hurry you in this matter. You may even, if it be easier for you, pay us in ten, fifteen, or twenty instalments; but we will accept no single instalment of less than a million.

Believe us, dear Mr. Hale, when we say that we embark upon this course of action utterly devoid of animus. We are members of that intellectual proletariat, the increasing numbers of which mark in red lettering the last days of the nineteenth century. We have, from a thorough study of economics, decided to enter upon this business. It has many merits, chief among which may be noted that we can indulge in large and lucrative operations without capital. So far, we have been fairly successful, and we hope our dealings with you may be pleasant and satisfactory.

Pray attend while we explain our views more fully. At the base of the present system of society is to be found the property right. And this right of the individual to hold property is demonstrated, in the last analysis, to rest solely and wholly upon *might*. The mailed gentlemen of William the Conqueror divided and apportioned England amongst themselves with the naked sword. This, we are sure you will grant, is true of all feudal possessions. With the invention of steam and the Industrial Revolution there came into existence the Capitalist Class, in the modern sense of the word. These capitalists quickly towered above the ancient nobility. The captains of industry have virtually dispossessed the descendants of the captains of war. Mind, and not muscle, wins in to-day's struggle for existence. But this state of affairs is none the less based upon might. The change has been qualitative. The old-time Feudal Baronage ravaged the world with fire and sword; the modern Money Baronage exploits the world by mastering and applying the world's economic forces. Brain, and not brawn, endures; and those best fitted to survive are the intellectually and commercially powerful.

We, the M. of M., are not content to become wage slaves. The great trusts and business combinations (with which you have your rating) prevent us from rising to the place among you which our intellects qualify us to occupy. Why? Because we are without capital. We are of the unwashed, but with this difference: our brains are of the best, and we have no foolish ethical nor social scruples. As wage slaves, toiling early and late, and living abstemiously, we could not save in threescore years—nor in twenty times threescore years—a sum of money sufficient successfully to cope with the great aggregations of massed capital which now exist. Nevertheless, we have entered the arena. We now throw down the gage to the capital of the world. Whether it wishes to fight or not, it shall have to fight.

Mr. Hale, our interests dictate us to demand of you twenty millions of dollars. While we are considerate enough to give you reasonable time in which to carry out your share of the transaction, please do not delay too long. When you have agreed to our terms, insert a suitable notice in the agony column of the "Morning Blazer." We shall then acquaint you with our plan for transferring the sum mentioned. You had better do this some time prior to October 1st. If you do not, in order to show that we are in earnest we shall on that date kill a man on East Thirty-ninth

Street. He will be a workingman. This man you do not know; nor do we. You represent a force in modern society; we also represent a force—a new force. Without anger or malice, we have closed in battle. As you will readily discern, we are simply a business proposition. You are the upper, and we the nether, millstone; this man's life shall be ground out between. You may save him if you agree to our conditions and act in time.

There was once a king cursed with a golden touch. His name we have taken to do duty as our official seal. Some day, to protect ourselves against competitors, we shall copyright it.

We beg to remain,
THE MINIONS OF MIDAS.

I leave it to you, dear John, why should we not have laughed over such a preposterous communication? The idea, we could not but grant, was well conceived, but it was too grotesque to be taken seriously. Mr. Hale said he would preserve it as a literary curiosity, and shoved it away in a pigeonhole. Then we promptly forgot its existence. And as promptly, on the 1st of October, going over the morning mail, we read the following:

OFFICE OF THE M. OF M.,
October 1, 1899.

MR. EBEN HALE, Money Baron:
Dear Sir,—Your victim has met his fate. An hour ago, on East Thirty-ninth Street, a workingman was thrust through the heart with a knife. Ere you read this his body will be lying at the Morgue. Go and look upon your handiwork.

On October 14th, in token of our earnestness in this matter, and in case you do not relent, we shall kill a policeman on or near the corner of Polk Street and Clermont Avenue.

Very cordially,
THE MINIONS OF MIDAS.

Again Mr. Hale laughed. His mind was full of a prospective deal with a Chicago syndicate for the sale of all his street railways in that city, and so he went on dictating to the stenographer, never giving it a second thought. But somehow, I know not why, a heavy depression fell upon me. What if it were not a joke, I asked myself, and turned involuntarily to the morning paper. There it was, as befitted an obscure person of the lower classes, a paltry half-dozen lines tucked away in a corner, next a patent medicine advertisement:

Shortly after five o'clock this morning, on East Thirty-ninth Street, a laborer named Pete Lascalle, while on his way to work, was stabbed to the heart by an unknown assailant, who escaped by running. The police have been unable to discover any motive for the murder.

"Impossible!" was Mr. Hale's rejoinder, when I had read the item aloud; but the incident evidently weighed upon his mind, for late in the afternoon, with many epithets denunciatory of his foolishness, he asked me to acquaint the police with the affair. I had the pleasure of being laughed at in the Inspector's private office, although I went away with the assurance that they would look into it and that the vicinity of Polk and Clermont would be doubly patrolled on the night mentioned. There it dropped, till the two weeks had sped by, when the following note came to us through the mail:

> OFFICE OF THE M. OF M.,
> October 15, 1899.

MR. EBEN HALE, Money Baron:

Dear Sir,—Your second victim has fallen on schedule time. We are in no hurry; but to increase the pressure we shall henceforth kill weekly. To protect ourselves against police interference we shall hereafter inform you of the event but a little prior to or simultaneously with the deed. Trusting this finds you in good health,

> We are,
> THE MINIONS OF MIDAS.

This time Mr. Hale took up the paper, and after a brief search, read to me this account:

A DASTARDLY CRIME

Joseph Donahue, assigned only last night to special patrol duty in the Eleventh Ward, at midnight was shot through the brain and instantly killed. The tragedy was enacted in the full glare of the street lights on the corner of Polk Street and Clermont Avenue. Our society is indeed unstable when the custodians of its peace are thus openly and wantonly shot down. The police have so far been unable to obtain the slightest clue.

Barely had he finished this when the police arrived—the Inspector himself and two of his keenest sleuths. Alarm sat upon their faces, and it was plain that they were seriously perturbed. Though the facts were so few and simple, we talked long, going over the affair again and again. When the Inspector went away, he confidently assured us that everything would soon be straightened out and the assassins run to earth. In the meantime he thought it well to detail guards for the protection of Mr. Hale and myself, and several more to be constantly on the vigil about the house and grounds. After the lapse of a week, at one o'clock in the afternoon, this telegram was received:

OFFICE OF THE M. OF M.,
October 21, 1899.

MR. EBEN HALE, Money Baron:

Dear Sir,—We are sorry to note how completely you have misunderstood us. You have seen fit to surround yourself and household with armed guards, as though, forsooth, we were common criminals, apt to break in upon you and wrest away by force your twenty millions. Believe us, this is farthest from our intention.

You will readily comprehend, after a little sober thought, that your life is dear to us. Do not be afraid. We would not hurt you for the world. It is our policy to cherish you tenderly and protect you from all harm. Your death means nothing to us. If it did, rest assured that we would not hesitate a moment in destroying you. Think this over, Mr. Hale. When you have paid us our price, there will be need of retrenchment. Dismiss your guards now, and cut down your expenses.

Within ten minutes of the time you receive this a nurse-girl will have been choked to death in Brentwood Park. The body may be found in the shrubbery lining the path which leads off to the left from the band-stand.

Cordially yours,

THE MINIONS OF MIDAS.

The next instant Mr. Hale was at the telephone, warning the Inspector of the impending murder. The Inspector excused himself in order to call up Police Sub-station F and despatch men to the scene. Fifteen minutes later he rang us up and informed us that the body had been discovered, yet warm, in the place indicated. That evening the papers teemed with glaring Jack-the-Strangler headlines, denouncing the brutality of the deed and complaining about the laxity of the police. We were also closeted with the Inspector, who begged us by all means to keep the affair secret. Success, he said, depended upon silence.

As you know, John, Mr. Hale was a man of iron. He refused to surrender. But, oh, John, it was terrible, nay, horrible—this awful something, this blind force in the dark. We could not fight, could not plan, could do nothing save hold our hands and wait. And week by week, as certain as the rising of the sun, came the notification and death of some person, man or woman, innocent of evil, but just as much killed by us as though we had done it with our own hands. A word from Mr. Hale and the slaughter would have ceased. But he hardened his heart and waited, the lines deepening, the mouth and eyes growing sterner and firmer, and the face aging with the hours. It is needless for me to speak of my own suffering during that frightful period. Find here the letters and telegrams of the M. of M., and the newspaper accounts, etc., of the various murders.

You will notice also the letters warning Mr. Hale of certain machinations of commercial enemies and secret manipulations of stock. The M. of M. seemed to have its hand on the inner pulse of the business and financial world. They possessed themselves of and forwarded to us information which our agents could not obtain. One timely note from them, at a critical moment in a certain deal, saved all of five millions to Mr. Hale. At another time they sent us a telegram which probably was the means of prevent-

ing an anarchist crank from taking my employer's life. We captured the man on his arrival and turned him over to the police,
who found upon him enough of a new and powerful explosive to
sink a battleship.

We persisted. Mr. Hale was grit clear through. He disbursed at
the rate of one hundred thousand per week for secret service. The
aid of the Pinkertons and of countless private detective agencies
was called in, and in addition to this thousands were upon our
payroll. Our agents swarmed everywhere, in all guises, penetrating
all classes of society. They grasped at a myriad clues; hundreds of
suspects were jailed, and at various times thousands of suspicious
persons were under surveillance, but nothing tangible came to
light. With its communications the M. of M. continually changed
its method of delivery. And every messenger they sent us was
arrested forthwith. But these inevitably proved to be innocent individuals, while their descriptions of the persons who had employed them for the errand never tallied. On the last day of December we received this notification:

Office of the M. of M.,
December 31, 1899.

Mr. Eben Hale, Money Baron:

Dear Sir,—Pursuant of our policy, with which we flatter ourselves you are already well versed, we beg to state that we shall
give a passport from this Vale of Tears to Inspector Bying, with
whom, because of our attentions, you have become so well
acquainted. It is his custom to be in his private office at this hour.
Even as you read this he breathes his last.

Cordially yours,
The Minions of Midas.

I dropped the letter and sprang to the telephone. Great was my
relief when I heard the Inspector's hearty voice. But, even as he
spoke, his voice died away in the receiver to a gurgling sob, and I
heard faintly the crash of a falling body. Then a strange voice
hello'd me, sent me the regards of the M. of M., and broke the
switch. Like a flash I called up the public office of the Central
Police, telling them to go at once to the Inspector's aid in his private office. I then held the line, and a few minutes later received
the intelligence that he had been found bathed in his own blood

and breathing his last. There were no eyewitnesses, and no trace was discoverable of the murderer.

Whereupon Mr. Hale immediately increased his secret service till a quarter of a million flowed weekly from his coffers. He was determined to win out. His graduated rewards aggregated over ten millions. You have a fair idea of his resources and you can see in what manner he drew upon them. It was the principle, he affirmed, that he was fighting for, not the gold. And it must be admitted that his course proved the nobility of his motive. The police departments of all the great cities coöperated, and even the United States Government stepped in, and the affair became one of the highest questions of state. Certain contingent funds of the nation were devoted to the unearthing of the M. of M., and every government agent was on the alert. But all in vain. The Minions of Midas carried on their damnable work unhampered. They had their way and struck unerringly.

But while he fought to the last, Mr. Hale could not wash his hands of the blood with which they were dyed. Though not technically a murderer, though no jury of his peers would ever have convicted him, none the less the death of every individual was due to him. As I said before, a word from him and the slaughter would have ceased. But he refused to give that word. He insisted that the integrity of society was assailed; that he was not sufficiently a coward to desert his post; and that it was manifestly just that a few should be martyred for the ultimate welfare of the many. Nevertheless this blood was upon his head, and he sank into deeper and deeper gloom. I was likewise whelmed with the guilt of an accomplice. Babies were ruthlessly killed, children, aged men; and not only were these murders local, but they were distributed over the country. In the middle of February, one evening, as we sat in the library, there came a sharp knock at the door. On responding to it I found, lying on the carpet of the corridor, the following missive:

OFFICE OF THE M. OF M.,
February 15, 1900.

MR. EBEN HALE, Money Baron:

Dear Sir,—Does not your soul cry out upon the red harvest it is reaping? Perhaps we have been too abstract in conducting our business. Let us now be concrete. Miss Adelaide Laidlaw is a talented young woman, as good, we understand, as she is beautiful. She is the daughter of your old friend, Judge Laidlaw, and we happen to know that you carried her in your arms when she was an infant. She is your daughter's closest friend, and at present is visiting her. When your eyes have read thus far her visit will have terminated.

Very cordially,
THE MINIONS OF MIDAS.

My God! did we not instantly realize the terrible import! We rushed through the day-rooms—she was not there—and on to her own apartments. The door was locked, but we crashed it down by hurling ourselves against it. There she lay, just as she had finished dressing for the opera, smothered with pillows torn from the couch, the flush of life yet on her flesh, the body still flexible and warm. Let me pass over the rest of this horror. You will surely remember, John, the newspaper accounts.

Late that night Mr. Hale summoned me to him, and before God did pledge me most solemnly to stand by him and not to compromise, even if all kith and kin were destroyed.

The next day I was surprised at his cheerfulness. I had thought he would be deeply shocked by this last tragedy—how deep I was soon to learn. All day he was light-hearted and high-spirited, as though at last he had found a way out of the frightful difficulty. The next morning we found him dead in his bed, a peaceful smile upon his careworn face—asphyxiation. Through the connivance of the police and the authorities, it was given out to the world as heart disease. We deemed it wise to withhold the truth; but little good has it done us, little good has anything done us.

Barely had I left that chamber of death, when—but too late— the following extraordinary letter was received:

OFFICE OF THE M. OF M.,
February 17, 1900.

MR. EBEN HALE, Money Baron:

Dear Sir,—You will pardon our intrusion, we hope, so closely upon the sad event of day before yesterday; but what we wish to say may be of the utmost importance to you. It is in our mind that you may attempt to escape us. There is but one way, apparently, as you have ere this doubtless discovered. But we wish to inform you that even this one way is barred. You may die, but you die failing and acknowledging your failure. Note this: *We are part and parcel of your possessions. With your millions we pass down to your heirs and assigns forever.*

We are the inevitable. We are the culmination of industrial and social wrong. We turn upon the society that has created us. We are the successful failures of the age, the scourges of a degraded civilization.

We are the creatures of a perverse social selection. We meet force with force. Only the strong shall endure. We believe in the survival of the fittest. You have crushed your wage slaves into the dirt and you have survived. The captains of war, at your command, have shot down like dogs your employees in a score of bloody strikes. By such means you have endured. We do not grumble at the result, for we acknowledge and have our being in the same natural law. And now the question has arisen: *Under the present social environment, which of us shall survive?* We believe we are the fittest. You believe you are the fittest. We leave the eventuality to time and law.

Cordially yours,
THE MINIONS OF MIDAS.

John, do you wonder now that I shunned pleasure and avoided friends? But why explain? Surely this narrative will make everything clear. Three weeks ago Adelaide Laidlaw died. Since then I have waited in hope and fear. Yesterday the will was probated and made public. To-day I was notified that a woman of the middle class would be killed in Golden Gate Park, in far-away San Francisco. The despatches in to-night's papers give the details of the brutal happening—details which correspond with those furnished me in advance.

It is useless. I cannot struggle against the inevitable. I have been faithful to Mr. Hale and have worked hard. Why my faithfulness should have been thus rewarded I cannot understand. Yet I cannot be false to my trust, nor break my word by compromising. Still, I have resolved that no more deaths shall be upon my head. I have willed the many millions I lately received to their rightful owners. Let the stalwart sons of Eben Hale work out their own salvation. Ere you read this I shall have passed on. The Minions of Midas are all-powerful. The police are impotent. I have learned from them that other millionnaires have been likewise mulcted or persecuted—how many is not known, for when one yields to the M. of M., his mouth is thenceforth sealed. Those who have not yielded are even now reaping their scarlet harvest. The grim game is being played out. The Federal Government can do nothing. I also understand that similar branch organizations have made their appearance in Europe. Society is shaken to its foundations. Principalities and powers are as brands ripe for the burning. Instead of the masses against the classes, it is a class against the classes. We, the guardians of human progress, are being singled out and struck down. Law and order have failed.

The officials have begged me to keep this secret. I have done so, but can do so no longer. It has become a question of public import, fraught with the direst consequences, and I shall do my duty before I leave this world by informing it of its peril. Do you, John, as my last request, make this public. Do not be frightened. The fate of humanity rests in your hand. Let the press strike off millions of copies; let the electric currents sweep it round the world; wherever men meet and speak, let them speak of it in fear and trembling. And then, when thoroughly aroused, let society arise in its might and cast out this abomination.

Yours, in long farewell,
WADE ATSHELER.

SECTION FOUR

TO BUILD A FIRE

DAY had broken cold and gray, exceedingly cold and gray, when the man turned aside from the main Yukon trail and climbed the high earth-bank, where a dim and little-travelled trail led eastward through the fat spruce timberland. It was a steep bank, and he paused for breath at the top, excusing the act to himself by looking at his watch. It was nine o'clock. There was no sun nor hint of sun, though there was not a cloud in the sky. It was a clear day, and yet there seemed an intangible pall over the face of things, a subtle gloom that made the day dark, and that was due to the absence of sun. This fact did not worry the man. He was used to the lack of sun. It had been days since he had seen the sun, and he knew that a few more days must pass before that cheerful orb, due south, would just peep above the sky line and dip immediately from view.

The man flung a look back along the way he had come. The Yukon lay a mile wide and hidden under three feet of ice. On top of this ice were as many feet of snow. It was all pure white, rolling in gentle undulations where the ice jams of the freeze-up had formed. North and south, as far as his eye could see, it was unbroken white, save for a dark hairline that curved and twisted from around the spruce-covered island to the south, and that curved and twisted away into the north, where it disappeared behind another spruce-covered island. This dark hairline was the trail—the main trail—that led south five hundred miles to the Chilcoot Pass, Dyea, and salt water; and that led north seventy miles to Dawson, and still on to the north a thousand miles to Nulato, and finally to St. Michael, on Bering Sea, a thousand miles and half a thousand more.

But all this—the mysterious, far-reaching hairline trail, the absence of sun from the sky, the tremendous cold, and the strangeness and weirdness of it all—made no impression on the man. It was not because he was long used to it. He was a newcomer in the land, a *chechaquo*, and this was his first winter. The trouble with him was that he was without imagination. He was quick and alert in the things of life, but only in the things, and not in the significances. Fifty degrees below zero meant eighty-odd degrees of frost. Such fact impressed him as being cold and uncomfortable, and that was all. It did not lead him to meditate upon his frailty as a creature of temperature, and upon man's frailty in general, able only to live within certain narrow limits of heat and cold; and from there on it did not lead him to the conjectural field of immortality and man's place in the universe. Fifty degrees below zero stood for a bite of frost that hurt and that must be guarded against by the use of mittens, ear flaps, warm moccasins, and thick socks. Fifty degrees below zero was to him just precisely fifty degrees below zero. That there should be anything more to it than that was a thought that never entered his head.

As he turned to go on, he spat speculatively. There was a sharp, explosive crackle that startled him. He spat again. And again, in the air, before it could fall to the snow, the spittle crackled. He knew that at fifty below spittle crackled on the snow, but this spittle had crackled in the air. Undoubtedly it was colder than fifty below—how much colder he did not know. But the temperature did not matter. He was bound for the old claim on the left fork of Henderson Creek, where the boys were already. They had come over across the divide from the Indian Creek country, while he had come the roundabout way to take a look at the possibilities of getting out logs in the spring from the islands in the Yukon. He would be in to camp by six o'clock; a bit after dark, it was true, but the boys would be there, a fire would be going, and a hot supper would be ready. As for lunch, he pressed his hand against the protruding bundle under his jacket. It was also under his shirt, wrapped up in a handkerchief and lying against the naked skin. It was the only way to keep the biscuits from freezing. He smiled agreeably to himself as he thought of those biscuits, each cut open and sopped in bacon grease, and each enclosing a generous slice of fried bacon.

He plunged in among the big spruce trees. The trail was faint. A foot of snow had fallen since the last sled had passed over, and he was glad he was without a sled, travelling light. In fact, he carried nothing but the lunch wrapped in the handkerchief. He was surprised, however, at the cold. It certainly was cold, he concluded, as he rubbed his numb nose and cheekbones with his mittened hand. He was a warm-whiskered man, but the hair on his face did not protect the high cheekbones and the eager nose that thrust itself aggressively into the frosty air.

At the man's heels trotted a dog, a big native husky, the proper wolf dog, gray-coated and without any visible or temperamental difference from its brother, the wild wolf. The animal was depressed by the tremendous cold. It knew that it was no time for travelling. Its instinct told it a truer tale than was told to the man by the man's judgment. In reality, it was not merely colder than fifty below zero; it was colder than sixty below, than seventy below. It was seventy-five below zero. Since the freezing point is thirty-two above zero, it meant that one hundred and seven degrees of frost obtained. The dog did not know anything about thermometers. Possibly in its brain there was no sharp consciousness of a condition of very cold such as was in the man's brain. But the brute had its instinct. It experienced a vague but menacing apprehension that subdued it and made it slink along at the man's heels, and that made it question eagerly every unwonted movement of the man as if expecting him to go into camp or to seek shelter somewhere and build a fire. The dog had learned fire, and it wanted fire, or else to burrow under the snow and cuddle its warmth away from the air.

The frozen moisture of its breathing had settled on its fur in a fine powder of frost, and especially were its jowls, muzzle, and eyelashes whitened by its crystalled breath. The man's red beard and mustache were likewise frosted, but more solidly, the deposit taking the form of ice and increasing with every warm, moist breath he exhaled. Also, the man was chewing tobacco, and the muzzle of ice held his lips so rigidly that he was unable to clear his chin when he expelled the juice. The result was that a crystal beard of the color and solidity of amber was increasing its length on his chin. If he fell down it would shatter itself, like glass, into brittle fragments. But he did not mind the appendage. It was the penalty all tobacco chewers paid in that country, and he had been out before in two cold snaps. They had not been so cold as this, he knew, but by the spirit thermometer at Sixty Mile he knew they had been registered at fifty below and at fifty-five.

He held on through the level stretch of woods for several miles, crossed a wide flat of nigger heads, and dropped down a bank to the frozen bed of a small stream. This was Henderson Creek, and he knew he was ten miles from the forks. He looked at his watch. It was ten o'clock. He was making four miles an hour, and he calculated that he would arrive at the forks at half-past twelve. He decided to celebrate that event by eating his lunch there.

The dog dropped in again at his heels, with a tail drooping discouragement, as the man swung along the creek bed. The furrow of the old sled trail was plainly visible, but a dozen inches of snow covered the marks of the last runners. In a month no man had come up or down that silent creek. The man held steadily on. He was not much given to thinking, and just then particularly he had nothing to think about save that he would eat lunch at the forks and that at six o'clock he would be in camp with the boys. There was nobody to talk to; and, had there been, speech would have been impossible because of the ice muzzle on his mouth. So he continued monotonously to chew tobacco and to increase the length of his amber beard.

Once in a while the thought reiterated itself that it was very cold and that he had never experienced such cold. As he walked along he rubbed his cheekbones and nose with the back of his mittened hand. He did this automatically, now and again changing hands. But, rub as he would, the instant he stopped his cheekbones went numb, and the following instant the end of his nose went numb. He was sure to frost his cheeks; he knew that, and experienced a pang of regret that he had not devised a nose strap of the sort Bud wore in cold snaps. Such a strap passed across the cheeks, as well, and saved them. But it didn't matter much, after all. What were frosted cheeks? A bit painful, that was all; they were never serious.

Empty as the man's mind was of thoughts, he was keenly observant, and he noticed the changes in the creek, the curves and bends and timber jams, and always he sharply noted where he placed his feet. Once, coming around a bend, he shied abruptly, like a startled horse, curved away from the place where he had been walking, and retreated several paces back along the trail. The creek he knew was frozen clear to the bottom—no creek could contain water in that arctic winter—but he knew also that there were springs that bubbled out from the hillsides and ran along under the snow and on top the ice of the creek. He knew that the coldest snaps never froze these springs, and he knew likewise their danger. They were traps. They hid pools of water under the snow that might be three inches deep, or three feet. Sometimes a skin of ice half an inch thick covered them, and in turn was covered by the snow. Sometimes there were alternate layers of water and ice skin, so that when one broke through he kept on breaking through for a while, sometimes wetting himself to the waist.

That was why he had shied in such panic. He had felt the give under his feet and heard the crackle of a snow-hidden ice skin. And to get his feet wet in such a temperature meant trouble and danger. At the very least it meant delay, for he would be forced to stop and build a fire, and under its protection to bare his feet while he dried his socks and moccasins. He stood and studied the creek bed and its banks, and decided that the flow of water came from the right. He reflected awhile, rubbing his nose and cheeks, then skirted to the left, stepping gingerly and testing the footing for each step. Once clear of the danger, he took a fresh chew of tobacco and swung along at his four-mile gait.

In the course of the next two hours he came upon several similar traps. Usually the snow above the hidden pools had a sunken, candied appearance that advertised the danger. Once again, however, he had a close call; and once, suspecting danger, he compelled the dog to go on in front. The dog did not want to go. It hung back until the man shoved it forward, and then it went quickly across the white, unbroken surface. Suddenly it broke through, floundered to one side, and got away to firmer footing. It had wet its forefeet and legs, and almost immediately the water that clung to it turned to ice. It made quick efforts to lick the ice off its legs, then dropped down in the snow and began to bite out the ice that had formed between the toes. This was a matter of instinct. To permit the ice to remain would mean sore feet. It did not know this. It merely obeyed the mysterious prompting that arose from the deep crypts of its being. But the man knew, having achieved a judgment on the subject, and he removed the mitten from his right hand and helped tear out the ice particles. He did not expose his fingers more than a minute, and was astonished at the swift numbness that smote them. It certainly was cold. He pulled on the mitten hastily, and beat the hand savagely across his chest.

At twelve o'clock the day was at its brightest. Yet the sun was too far south on its winter journey to clear the horizon. The bulge of the earth intervened between it and Henderson Creek, where the man walked under a clear sky at noon and cast no shadow. At half-past twelve, to the minute, he arrived at the forks of the creek. He was pleased at the speed he had made. If he kept it up, he would certainly be with the boys by six. He unbuttoned his jacket and shirt and drew forth his lunch. The action consumed no more than a quarter of a minute, yet in that brief moment the numbness laid hold of the exposed fingers. He did not put the mitten on, but, instead, struck the fingers a dozen sharp smashes against his leg. Then he sat down on a snow-covered log to eat. The sting that followed upon the striking of his fingers against his leg ceased so quickly that he was startled. He had had no chance to take a bite of biscuit. He struck the fingers repeatedly and returned them to the mitten, baring the other hand for the purpose of eating. He tried to take a mouthful, but the ice muzzle prevented. He had forgotten to build a fire and thaw out. He chuckled at his foolishness, and as he chuckled he noted the numbness creeping into the exposed fingers. Also, he noted that the stinging which had first come to his toes when he sat down was already passing away. He wondered whether the toes were warm or numb. He moved them inside the moccasins and decided that they were numb.

He pulled the mitten on hurriedly and stood up. He was a bit frightened. He stamped up and down until the stinging returned into the feet. It certainly was cold, was his thought. That man from Sulphur Creek had spoken the truth when telling how cold it sometimes got in the country. And he had laughed at him at the time! That showed one must not be too sure of things. There was no mistake about it, it *was* cold. He strode up and down, stamping his feet and threshing his arms, until reassured by the returning warmth. Then he got out matches and proceeded to make a fire. From the undergrowth, where high water of the previous spring had lodged a supply of seasoned twigs, he got his firewood. Working carefully from a small beginning, he soon had a roaring fire, over which he thawed the ice from his face and in the protection of which he ate his biscuits. For the moment the cold of space was outwitted. The dog took satisfaction in the fire, stretching out close enough for warmth and far enough away to escape being singed.

When the man had finished, he filled his pipe and took his comfortable time over a smoke. Then he pulled on his mittens, settled the ear flaps of his cap firmly about his ears, and took the creek trail up the left fork. The dog was disappointed and yearned back toward the fire. This man did not know cold. Possibly all the generations of his ancestry had been ignorant of cold, of real cold, of cold one hundred and seven degrees below freezing point. But the dog knew; all its ancestry knew, and it had inherited the knowledge. And it knew that it was not good to walk abroad in such fearful cold. It was the time to lie snug in a hole in the snow and wait for a curtain of cloud to be drawn across the face of outer space whence this cold came. On the other hand, there was no keen intimacy between the dog and the man. The one was the toil slave of the other, and the only caresses it had ever received were the caresses of the whip lash and of harsh and menacing throat sounds that threatened the whip lash. So the dog made no effort to communicate its apprehension to the man. It was not concerned in the welfare of the man; it was for its own sake that it yearned back toward the fire. But the man whistled, and spoke to it with the sound of whip lashes, and the dog swung in at the man's heels and followed after.

The man took a chew of tobacco and proceeded to start a new amber beard. Also, his moist breath quickly powdered with white his mustache, eyebrows, and lashes. There did not seem to be so many springs on the left fork of the Henderson, and for half an hour the man saw no signs of any. And then it happened. At a place where there were no signs, where the soft, unbroken snow seemed to advertise solidity beneath, the man broke through. It was not deep. He wet himself halfway to the knees before he floundered out to the firm crust.

He was angry, and cursed his luck aloud. He had hoped to get into camp with the boys at six o'clock, and this would delay him an hour, for he would have to build a fire and dry out his footgear. This was imperative at that low temperature—he knew that much; and he turned aside to the bank, which he climbed. On top, tangled in the underbrush about the trunks of several small spruce trees, was a high-water deposit of dry firewood—sticks and twigs, principally, but also larger portions of seasoned branches and fine, dry, last year's grasses. He threw down several large pieces on top of the snow. This served for a foundation and prevented the young flame from drowning itself in the snow it otherwise would melt. The flame he got by touching a match to a small shred of birch bark that he took from his pocket. This burned even more readily than paper. Placing it on the foundation, he fed the young flame with wisps of dry grass and with the tiniest dry twigs.

He worked slowly and carefully, keenly aware of his danger. Gradually, as the flame grew stronger, he increased the size of the twigs with which he fed it. He squatted in the snow, pulling the twigs out from their entanglement in the brush and feeding directly to the flame. He knew there must be no failure. When it is seventy-five below zero, a man must not fail in his first attempt to build a fire—that is, if his feet are wet. If his feet are dry, and he fails, he can run along the trail for half a mile and restore his circulation. But the circulation of wet and freezing feet cannot be restored by running when it is seventy-five below. No matter how fast he runs, the wet feet will freeze the harder.

All this the man knew. The old-timer on Sulphur Creek had told him about it the previous fall, and now he was appreciating the advice. Already all sensation had gone out of his feet. To build the fire he had been forced to remove his mittens, and the fingers had quickly gone numb. His pace of four miles an hour had kept his heart pumping blood to the surface of his body and to all the extremities. But the instant he stopped, the action of the pump eased down. The cold of space smote the unprotected tip of the planet, and he, being on that unprotected tip, received the full force of the blow. The blood of his body recoiled before it. The blood was alive, like the dog, and like the dog it wanted to hide away and cover itself up from the fearful cold. So long as he walked four miles an hour, he pumped that blood, willy-nilly, to the surface; but now it ebbed away and sank down into the recesses of his body. The extremities were the first to feel its absence. His wet feet froze the faster, and his exposed fingers numbed the faster, though they had not yet begun to freeze. Nose and cheeks were already freezing, while the skin of all his body chilled as it lost its blood.

But he was safe. Toes and nose and cheeks would be only touched by the frost, for the fire was beginning to burn with strength. He was feeding it with twigs the size of his finger. In another minute he would be able to feed it with branches the size of his wrist, and then he could remove his wet footgear, and while it dried, he could keep his naked feet warm by the fire, rubbing them at first, of course, with snow. The fire was a success. He was safe. He remembered the advice of the old-timer on Sulphur Creek, and smiled. The old-timer had been very serious in laying down the law that no man must travel alone in the Klondike after fifty below. Well, here he was; he had had the accident; he was alone; and he had saved himself. Those old-timers were rather womanish, some of them, he thought. All a man had to do was to keep his head, and he was all right. Any man who was a man could travel alone. But it was surprising, the rapidity with which his cheeks and nose were freezing. And he had not thought his fingers could go lifeless in so short a time. Lifeless they were, for he could scarcely make them move together to grip a twig, and they seemed remote from his body and from him. When he touched a twig, he had to look and see whether or not he had hold of it. The wires were pretty well down between him and his finger ends.

All of which counted for little. There was the fire, snapping and crackling and promising life with every dancing flame. He started to untie his moccasins. They were coated with ice; the thick German socks were like sheaths of iron halfway to the knees; and the moccasin strings were like rods of steel all twisted and knotted as by some conflagration. For a moment he tugged with his numb fingers, then, realizing the folly of it, he drew his sheath knife.

But before he could cut the strings, it happened. It was his own fault or, rather, his mistake. He should not have built the fire under the spruce tree. He should have built it in the open. But it had been easier to pull the twigs from the brush and drop them directly on the fire. Now the tree under which he had done this carried a weight of snow on its boughs. No wind had blown for weeks, and each bough was fully freighted. Each time he had pulled a twig he had communicated a slight agitation to the tree —an imperceptible agitation, so far as he was concerned, but an agitation sufficient to bring about the disaster. High up in the tree one bough capsized its load of snow. This fell on the boughs beneath, capsizing them. This process continued, spreading out and involving the whole tree. It grew like an avalanche, and it descended without warning upon the man and the fire, and the fire was blotted out! Where it had burned was a mantle of fresh and disordered snow.

The man was shocked. It was as though he had just heard his own sentence of death. For a moment he sat and stared at the spot where the fire had been. Then he grew very calm. Perhaps the old-timer on Sulphur Creek was right. If he had only had a trail mate he would have been in no danger now. The trail mate could have built the fire. Well, it was up to him to build the fire over again, and this second time there must be no failure. Even if he succeeded, he would most likely lose some toes. His feet must be badly frozen by now, and there would be some time before the second fire was ready.

Such were his thoughts, but he did not sit and think them. He was busy all the time they were passing through his mind. He made a new foundation for a fire, this time in the open, where no treacherous tree could blot it out. Next he gathered dry grasses and tiny twigs from the high-water flotsam. He could not bring his fingers together to pull them out, but he was able to gather them by the handful. In this way he got many rotten twigs and bits of green moss that were undesirable, but it was the best he could do. He worked methodically, even collecting an armful of the larger branches to be used later when the fire gathered strength. And all the while the dog sat and watched him, a certain yearning wistfulness in its eyes, for it looked upon him as the fire provider, and the fire was slow in coming.

When all was ready, the man reached in his pocket for a second piece of birch bark. He knew the bark was there, and, though he could not feel it with his fingers, he could hear its crisp rustling as he fumbled for it. Try as he would, he could not clutch hold of it. And all the time, in his consciousness, was the knowledge that each instant his feet were freezing. This thought tended to put him in a panic, but he fought against it and kept calm. He pulled on his mittens with his teeth, and threshed his arms back and forth, beating his hands with all his might against his sides. He did this sitting down, and he stood up to do it; and all the while the dog sat in the snow, its wolf brush of a tail curled around warmly over its forefeet, its sharp wolf ears pricked forward intently as it watched the man. And the man, as he beat and threshed with his arms and hands, felt a great surge of envy as he regarded the creature that was warm and secure in its natural covering.

After a time he was aware of the first faraway signals of sensation in his beaten fingers. The faint tingling grew stronger till it evolved into a stinging ache that was excruciating, but which the man hailed with satisfaction. He stripped the mitten from his right hand and fetched forth the birch bark. The exposed fingers were quickly going numb again. Next he brought out his bunch of sulphur matches. But the tremendous cold had already driven the life out of his fingers. In his effort to separate one match from the others, the whole bunch fell in the snow. He tried to pick it out of the snow, but failed. The dead fingers could neither touch nor clutch. He was very careful. He drove the thought of his freezing feet, and nose, and cheeks, out of his mind, devoting his whole soul to the matches. He watched, using the sense of vision in place of that of touch, and when he saw his fingers on each side the bunch, he closed them—that is, he willed to close them, for the wires were down, and the fingers did not obey. He pulled the mitten on the right hand, and beat it fiercely against his knee. Then, with both mittened hands, he scooped the bunch of matches, along with much snow, into his lap. Yet he was no better off.

After some manipulation he managed to get the bunch between the heels of his mittened hands. In this fashion he carried it to his mouth. The ice crackled and snapped when by a violent effort he opened his mouth. He drew the lower jaw in, curled the upper lip out of the way, and scraped the bunch with his upper teeth in order to separate a match. He succeeded in getting one, which he dropped on his lap. He was no better off. He could not pick it up. Then he devised a way. He picked it up in his teeth and scratched it on his leg. Twenty times he scratched before he succeeded in lighting it. As it flamed he held it with his teeth to the birch bark. But the burning brimstone went up his nostrils and into his lungs, causing him to cough spasmodically. The match fell into the snow and went out.

The old-timer on Sulphur Creek was right, he thought in the moment of controlled despair that ensued: after fifty below, a man should travel with a partner. He beat his hands, but failed in exciting any sensation. Suddenly he bared both hands, removing the mittens with his teeth. He caught the whole bunch between the heels of his hands. His arm muscles not being frozen enabled him to press the hand heels tightly against the matches. Then he scratched the bunch along his leg. It flared into flame, seventy sulphur matches at once! There was no wind to blow them out. He kept his head to one side to escape the strangling fumes, and held the blazing bunch to the birch bark. As he so held it, he became aware of sensation in his hand. His flesh was burning. He could smell it. Deep down below the surface he could feel it. The sensation developed into pain that grew acute. And still he endured it, holding the flame of the matches clumsily to the bark that would not light readily because his own burning hands were in the way, absorbing most of the flame.

At last, when he could endure no more, he jerked his hands apart. The blazing matches fell sizzling into the snow, but the birch bark was alight. He began laying dry grasses and the tiniest twigs on the flame. He could not pick and choose, for he had to lift the fuel between the heels of his hands. Small pieces of rotten wood and green moss clung to the twigs, and he bit them off as well as he could with his teeth. He cherished the flame carefully and awkwardly. It meant life, and it must not perish. The withdrawal of blood from the surface of his body now made him begin to shiver, and he grew more awkward. A large piece of green moss fell squarely on the little fire. He tried to poke it out with his fingers, but his shivering frame made his poke too far, and he disrupted the nucleus of the little fire, the burning grasses and tiny twigs separating and scattering. He tried to poke them together again, but in spite of the tenseness of the effort, his shivering got away with him, and the twigs were hopelessly scattered. Each twig gushed a puff of smoke and went out. The fire provider had failed. As he looked apathetically about him, his eyes chanced on the dog, sitting across the ruins of the fire from him, in the snow, making restless, hunching movements, slightly lifting one forefoot and then the other, shifting its weight back and forth on them with wistful eagerness.

The sight of the dog put a wild idea into his head. He remembered the tale of the man, caught in a blizzard, who killed a steer and crawled inside the carcass, and so was saved. He would kill the dog and bury his hands in the warm body until the numbness went out of them. Then he could build another fire. He spoke to the dog, calling it to him; but in his voice was a strange note of fear that frightened the animal, who had never known the man to speak in such way before. Something was the matter, and its suspicious nature sensed danger—it knew not what danger, but somewhere, somehow, in its brain arose an apprehension of the man. It flattened its ears down at the sound of the man's voice, and its restless, hunching movements and the liftings and shiftings of its forefeet became more pronounced; but it would not come to the man. He got on his hands and knees and crawled toward the dog. This unusual posture again excited suspicion, and the animal sidled mincingly away.

The man sat up in the snow for a moment and struggled for calmness. Then he pulled on his mittens, by means of teeth, and got upon his feet. He glanced down at first in order to assure himself that he was really standing up, for the absence of sensation in his feet left him unrelated to the earth. His erect position in itself started to drive the webs of suspicion from the dog's mind; and when he spoke peremptorily, with the sound of whip lashes in his voice, the dog rendered its customary allegiance and came to him.

As it came within reaching distance, the man lost his control. His arms flashed out to the dog, and he experienced genuine surprise when he discovered that his hands could not clutch, that there was neither bend nor feeling in the fingers. He had forgotten for the moment that they were frozen and that they were freezing more and more. All this happened quickly, and before the animal could get away, he encircled its body with his arms. He sat down in the snow, and in this fashion held the dog, while it snarled and whined and struggled.

But it was all he could do, hold its body encircled in his arms and sit there. He realized that he could not kill the dog. There was no way to do it. With his helpless hands he could neither draw nor hold his sheath knife nor throttle the animal. He released it, and it plunged wildly away, with tail between its legs, and still snarling. It halted forty feet away and surveyed him curiously, with ears sharply pricked forward.

The man looked down at his hands in order to locate them, and found them hanging on the ends of his arms. It struck him as curious that one should have to use his eyes in order to find out where his hands were. He began threshing his arms back and forth, beating the mittened hands against his sides. He did this for five minutes, violently, and his heart pumped enough blood up to the surface to put a stop to his shivering. But no sensation was aroused in the hands. He had an impression that they hung like weights on the ends of his arms, but when he tried to run the impression down, he could not find it.

A certain fear of death, dull and oppressive, came to him. This fear quickly became poignant as he realized that it was no longer a mere matter of freezing his fingers and toes, or of losing his hands and feet, but that it was a matter of life and death with the chances against him. This threw him into a panic, and he turned and ran up the creek bed along the old, dim trail. The dog joined in behind and kept up with him. He ran blindly, without intention, in fear such as he had never known in his life. Slowly, as he plowed and floundered through the snow, he began to see things again—the banks of the creek, the old timber jams, the leafless aspens, and the sky. The running made him feel better. He did not shiver. Maybe, if he ran on, his feet would thaw out; and, anyway, if he ran far enough, he would reach camp and the boys.

Without doubt he would lose some fingers and toes and some of his face; but the boys would take care of him, and save the rest of him when he got there. And at the same time there was another thought in his mind that said he would never get to the camp and the boys; that it was too many miles away, that the freezing had too great a start on him, and that he would soon be stiff and dead. This thought he kept in the background and refused to consider. Sometimes it pushed itself forward and demanded to be heard, but he thrust it back and strove to think of other things.

It struck him as curious that he could run at all on feet so frozen that he could not feel them when they struck the earth and took the weight of his body. He seemed to himself to skim along above the surface, and to have no connection with the earth. Somewhere he had once seen a winged Mercury, and he wondered if Mercury felt as he felt when skimming over the earth.

His theory of running until he reached camp and the boys had one flaw in it: he lacked the endurance. Several times he stumbled. and finally he tottered, crumpled up, and fell. When he tried to rise, he failed. He must sit and rest, he decided, and next time he would merely walk and keep on going. As he sat and regained his breath, he noted that he was feeling quite warm and comfortable. He was not shivering, and it even seemed that a warm glow had come to his chest and trunk. And yet, when he touched his nose or cheeks, there was no sensation. Running would not thaw them out. Nor would it thaw out his hands and feet. Then the thought came to him that the frozen portions of his body must be extending. He tried to keep this thought down, to forget it, to think of something else; he was aware of the panicky feeling that it caused, and he was afraid of the panic. But the thought asserted itself, and persisted, until it produced a vision of his body totally frozen. This was too much, and he made another wild run along the trail. Once he slowed down to a walk, but the thought of the freezing extending itself made him run again.

And all the time the dog ran with him, at his heels. When he fell down a second time, it curled its tail over its forefeet and sat in front of him, facing him, curiously eager and intent. The warmth and security of the animal angered him, and he cursed it till it flattened down its ears appeasingly. This time the shivering came more quickly upon the man. He was losing in his battle with the frost. It was creeping into his body from all sides. The thought of it drove him on, but he ran no more than a hundred feet, when he staggered and pitched headlong. It was his last panic. When he had recovered his breath and control, he sat up and entertained in his mind the conception of meeting death with dignity. However, the conception did not come to him in such terms. His idea of it was that he had been making a fool of himself, running around like a chicken with its head cut off—such was the simile that occurred to him. Well, he was bound to freeze anyway, and he might as well take it decently. With this new-found peace of mind came the first glimmerings of drowsiness. A good idea, he thought, to sleep off to death. It was like taking an anesthetic. Freezing was not so bad as people thought. There were lots worse ways to die.

He pictured the boys finding his body next day. Suddenly he found himself with them, coming along the trail and looking for himself. And, still with them, he came around a turn in the trail and found himself lying in the snow. He did not belong with himself any more, for even then he was out of himself, standing with the boys and looking at himself in the snow. It certainly was cold, was his thought. When he got back to the States he could tell the folks what real cold was. He drifted on from this to a vision of the old-timer on Sulphur Creek. He could see him quite clearly, warm and comfortable, and smoking a pipe.

"You were right, old hoss; you were right," the man mumbled to the old-timer of Sulphur Creek.

Then the man drowsed off into what seemed to him the most comfortable and satisfying sleep he had ever known. The dog sat facing him and waiting. The brief day drew to a close in a long, slow twilight. There were no signs of a fire to be made, and, besides, never in the dog's experience had it known a man to sit like that in the snow and make no fire. As the twilight drew on, its eager yearning for the fire mastered it, and with a great lifting and shifting of forefeet, it whined softly, then flattened its ears down in anticipation of being chidden by the man. But the man remained silent. Later the dog whined loudly. And still later it crept close to the man and caught the scent of death. This made the animal bristle and back away. A little longer it delayed, howling under the stars that leaped and danced and shone brightly in the cold sky. Then it turned and trotted up the trail in the direction of the camp it knew, where were the other food providers and fire providers.

BÂTARD

BÂTARD was a devil. This was recognized throughout the Northland. "Hell's Spawn" he was called by many men, but his master, Black Leclère, chose for him the shameful name "Bâtard." Now Black Leclère was also a devil, and the twain were well matched. There is a saying that when two devils come together, hell is to pay. This is to be expected, and this certainly was to be expected when Bâtard and Black Leclère came together. The first time they met, Bâtard was a part-grown puppy, lean and hungry, with bitter eyes; and they met with snap and snarl, and wicked looks, for Leclère's upper lip had a wolfish way of lifting and showing the white, cruel teeth. And it lifted then, and his eyes glinted viciously, as he reached for Bâtard and dragged him out from the squirming litter. It was certain that they divined each other, for on the instant Bâtard had buried his puppy fangs in Leclère's hand, and Leclère, thumb and finger, was coolly choking his young life out of him.

"*Sacredam*," the Frenchman said softly, flirting the quick blood from his bitten hand and gazing down on the little puppy choking and gasping in the snow.

Leclère turned to John Hamlin, storekeeper of the Sixty Mile

Post. "Dat fo' w'at Ah lak heem. 'Ow moch, eh, you, *M'sieu'*? 'Ow moch? Ah buy heem, now; Ah buy heem queek."

And because he hated him with an exceeding bitter hate, Leclère bought Bâtard and gave him his shameful name. And for five years the twain adventured across the Northland, from St. Michael's and the Yukon delta to the head-reaches of the Pelly and even so far as the Peace River, Athabasca, and the Great Slave. And they acquired a reputation for uncompromising wickedness, the like of which never before attached itself to man and dog.

Bâtard did not know his father,—hence his name,—but, as John Hamlin knew, his father was a great gray timber wolf. But the mother of Bâtard, as he dimly remembered her, was snarling, bickering, obscene, husky, full-fronted and heavy-chested, with a malign eye, a cat-like grip on life, and a genius for trickery and evil. There was neither faith nor trust in her. Her treachery alone could be relied upon, and her wild-wood amours attested her general depravity. Much of evil and much of strength were there in these, Bâtard's progenitors, and, bone and flesh of their bone and flesh, he had inherited it all. And then came Black Leclère, to lay his heavy hand on the bit of pulsating puppy life, to press and prod and mould till it became a big bristling beast, acute in knavery, overspilling with hate, sinister, malignant, diabolical. With a proper master Bâtard might have made an ordinary, fairly efficient sled-dog. He never got the chance: Leclère but confirmed him in his congenital iniquity.

The history of Bâtard and Leclère is a history of war—of five cruel, relentless years, of which their first meeting is fit summary. To begin with, it was Leclère's fault, for he hated with understanding and intelligence, while the long-legged, ungainly puppy hated only blindly, instinctively, without reason or method. At first there were no refinements of cruelty (these were to come later), but simple beatings and crude brutalities. In one of these Bâtard had an ear injured. He never regained control of the riven muscles, and ever after the ear drooped limply down to keep keen the memory of his tormentor. And he never forgot.

His puppyhood was a period of foolish rebellion. He was always worsted, but he fought back because it was his nature to fight back. And he was unconquerable. Yelping shrilly from the pain of lash and club, he none the less contrived always to throw in the defiant snarl, the bitter vindictive menace of his soul which fetched without fail more blows and beatings. But his was his mother's tenacious grip on life. Nothing could kill him. He flourished under misfortune, grew fat with famine, and out of his terrible struggle for life developed a preternatural intelligence. His were the stealth and cunning of the husky, his mother, and the fierceness and valor of the wolf, his father.

Possibly it was because of his father that he never wailed. His puppy yelps passed with his lanky legs, so that he became grim and taciturn, quick to strike, slow to warn. He answered curse with snarl, and blow with snap, grinning the while his implacable hatred; but never again, under the extremest agony, did Leclère bring from him the cry of fear nor of pain. This unconquerableness but fanned Leclère's wrath and stirred him to greater deviltries.

Did Leclère give Bâtard half a fish and to his mates whole ones, Bâtard went forth to rob other dogs of their fish. Also he robbed cachés and expressed himself in a thousand rogueries, till he became a terror to all dogs and masters of dogs. Did Leclère beat Bâtard and fondle Babette,—Babette who was not half the worker he was,—why, Bâtard threw her down in the snow and broke her hind leg in his heavy jaws, so that Leclère was forced to shoot her. Likewise, in bloody battles, Bâtard mastered all his team-mates, set them the law of trail and forage, and made them live to the law he set.

In five years he heard but one kind word, received but one soft stroke of a hand, and then he did not know what manner of things they were. He leaped like the untamed thing he was, and his jaws were together in a flash. It was the missionary at Sunrise, a newcomer in the country, who spoke the kind word and gave the soft stroke of the hand. And for six months after, he wrote no letters home to the States, and the surgeon at McQuestion travelled two hundred miles on the ice to save him from blood-poisoning.

Men and dogs looked askance at Bâtard when he drifted into their camps and posts. The men greeted him with feet threateningly lifted for the kick, the dogs with bristling manes and bared fangs. Once a man did kick Bâtard, and Bâtard, with quick wolf snap, closed his jaws like a steel trap on the man's calf and crunched down to the bone. Whereat the man was determined to have his life, only Black Leclère, with ominous eyes and naked hunting-knife, stepped in between. The killing of Bâtard—ah, *sacredam, that* was a pleasure Leclère reserved for himself. Some day it would happen, or else—bah! who was to know? Anyway, the problem would be solved.

For they had become problems to each other. The very breath each drew was a challenge and a menace to the other. Their hate bound them together as love could never bind. Leclère was bent on the coming of the day when Bâtard should wilt in spirit and cringe and whimper at his feet. And Bâtard—Leclère knew what was in Bâtard's mind, and more than once had read it in Bâtard's eyes. And so clearly had he read, that when Bâtard was at his back, he made it a point to glance often over his shoulder.

Men marvelled when Leclère refused large money for the dog. "Some day you'll kill him and be out his price," said John Hamlin once, when Bâtard lay panting in the snow where Leclère had kicked him, and no one knew whether his ribs were broken, and no one dared look to see.

"Dat," said Leclère, dryly, "dat is my biz'ness, *M'sieu'*."

And the men marvelled that Bâtard did not run away. They did not understand. But Leclère understood. He was a man who lived much in the open, beyond the sound of human tongue, and he had learned the voices of wind and storm, the sigh of night, the whisper of dawn, the clash of day. In a dim way he could hear the green things growing, the running of the sap, the bursting of the bud. And he knew the subtle speech of the things that moved, of the rabbit in the snare, the moody raven beating the air with hollow wing, the baldface shuffling under the moon, the wolf like a gray shadow gliding betwixt the twilight and the dark. And to him Bâtard spoke clear and direct. Full well he understood why Bâtard did not run away, and he looked more often over his shoulder.

When in anger, Bâtard was not nice to look upon, and more than once had he leapt for Leclère's throat, to be stretched quivering and senseless in the snow, by the butt of the ever ready dogwhip. And so Bâtard learned to bide his time. When he reached his full strength and prime of youth, he thought the time had come. He was broad-chested, powerfully muscled, of far more than ordinary size, and his neck from head to shoulders was a mass of bristling hair—to all appearances a full-blooded wolf. Leclère was lying asleep in his furs when Bâtard deemed the time to be ripe. He crept upon him stealthily, head low to earth and lone ear laid back, with a feline softness of tread. Bâtard breathed gently, very gently, and not till he was close at hand did he raise his head. He paused for a moment, and looked at the bronzed bull throat, naked and knotty, and swelling to a deep and steady pulse. The slaver dripped down his fangs and slid off his tongue at the sight, and in that moment he remembered his drooping ear, his uncounted blows and prodigious wrongs, and without a sound sprang on the sleeping man.

Leclère awoke to the pang of the fangs in his throat, and, perfect animal that he was, he awoke clear-headed and with full comprehension. He closed on Bâtard's windpipe with both his hands, and rolled out of his furs to get his weight uppermost. But the thousands of Bâtard's ancestors had clung at the throats of unnumbered moose and caribou and dragged them down, and the wisdom of those ancestors was his. When Leclère's weight came on top of him, he drove his hind legs upward and in, and clawed down chest and abdomen, ripping and tearing through skin and muscle. And when he felt the man's body wince above him and lift, he worried and shook at the man's throat. His team-mates closed around in a snarling circle, and Bâtard, with failing breath and fading sense, knew that their jaws were hungry for him. But that did not matter—it was the man, the man above him, and he ripped and clawed, and shook and worried, to the last ounce of his strength. But Leclère choked him with both his hands, till Bâtard's chest heaved and writhed for the air denied, and his eyes glazed and set, and his jaws slowly loosened, and his tongue protruded black and swollen.

"Eh? *Bon*, you devil!" Leclère gurgled, mouth and throat clogged with his own blood, as he shoved the dizzy dog from him.

And then Leclère cursed the other dogs off as they fell upon Bâtard. They drew back into a wider circle, squatting alertly on their haunches and licking their chops, the hair on every neck bristling and erect.

Bâtard recovered quickly, and at sound of Leclère's voice, tottered to his feet and swayed weakly back and forth.

"A-h-ah! You beeg devil!" Leclère spluttered. "Ah fix you; Ah fix you plentee, by *Gar!*"

Bâtard, the air biting into his exhausted lungs like wine, flashed full into the man's face, his jaws missing and coming together with a metallic clip. They rolled over and over on the snow, Leclère striking madly with his fists. Then they separated, face to face, and circled back and forth before each other. Leclère could have drawn his knife. His rifle was at his feet. But the beast in him was up and raging. He would do the thing with his hands— and his teeth. Bâtard sprang in, but Leclère knocked him over with a blow of the fist, fell upon him, and buried his teeth to the bone in the dog's shoulder.

It was a primordial setting and a primordial scene, such as might have been in the savage youth of the world. An open space in a dark forest, a ring of grinning wolf-dogs, and in the centre two beasts, locked in combat, snapping and snarling, raging madly about, panting, sobbing, cursing, straining, wild with passion in a fury of murder, ripping and tearing and clawing in elemental brutishness.

But Leclère caught Bâtard behind the ear, with a blow from his fist, knocking him over, and, for the instant, stunning him. Then Leclère leaped upon him with his feet, and sprang up and down, striving to grind him into the earth. Both Bâtard's hind legs were broken ere Leclère ceased that he might catch breath.

"A-a-ah! A-a-ah!" he screamed, incapable of speech, shaking his fist, through sheer impotence of throat and larynx.

But Bâtard was indomitable. He lay there in a helpless welter, his lip feebly lifting and writhing to the snarl he had not the strength to utter. Leclère kicked him, and the tired jaws closed on the ankle, but could not break the skin.

Then Leclère picked up the whip and proceeded almost to cut him to pieces, at each stroke of the lash crying: "Dis taim Ah break you! Eh? By *Gar!* Ah break you!"

In the end, exhausted, fainting from loss of blood, he crumpled up and fell by his victim, and when the wolf-dogs closed in to take their vengeance, with his last consciousness dragged his body on top Bâtard to shield him from their fangs.

This occurred not far from Sunrise, and the missionary, opening the door to Leclère a few hours later, was surprised to note the absence of Bâtard from the team. Nor did his surprise lessen when Leclère threw back the robes from the sled, gathered Bâtard into his arms, and staggered across the threshold. It happened that the surgeon of McQuestion, who was something of a gadabout, was up on a gossip, and between them they proceeded to repair Leclère.

"*Merci, non,*" said he, "Do you fix firs' de dog. To die? *Non.* Eet is not good. Becos' heem Ah mus' yet break. Dat fo' w'at he mus' not die."

The surgeon called it a marvel, the missionary a miracle, that Leclère pulled through at all; and so weakened was he, that in the spring the fever got him, and he went on his back again. Bâtard had been in even worse plight, but his grip on life prevailed, and the bones of his hind legs knit, and his organs righted themselves, during the several weeks he lay strapped to the floor. And by the time Leclère, finally convalescent, sallow and shaky, took the sun by the cabin door, Bâtard had reasserted his supremacy among his kind, and brought not only his own team-mates but the missionary's dogs into subjection.

He moved never a muscle, nor twitched a hair, when for the first time, Leclère tottered out on the missionary's arm, and sank down slowly and with infinite caution on the three-legged stool.

"*Bon!*" he said. "*Bon!* De good sun!" And he stretched out his wasted hands and washed them in the warmth.

Then his gaze fell on the dog, and the old light blazed back in his eyes. He touched the missionary lightly on the arm. "*Mon père,* dat is one beeg devil, dat Bâtard. You will bring me one pistol, so, dat Ah drink de sun in peace."

And thenceforth for many days he sat in the sun before the cabin door. He never dozed, and the pistol lay always across his knees. Bâtard had a way, the first thing each day, of looking for the weapon in its wonted place. At sight of it he would lift his lip faintly in token that he understood, and Leclère would lift his own lip in an answering grin. One day the missionary took note of the trick.

"Bless me!" he said. "I really believe the brute comprehends."

Leclère laughed softly. "Look you, *mon père.* Dat w'at Ah now spik, to dat does he lissen."

As if in confirmation, Bâtard just perceptibly wriggled his lone ear up to catch the sound.

"Ah say 'keel.'"

Bâtard growled deep down in his throat, the hair bristled along his neck, and every muscle went tense and expectant.

"Ah lift de gun, so, like dat." And suiting action to word, he sighted the pistol at Bâtard.

Bâtard, with a single leap, sideways, landed around the corner of the cabin out of sight.

"Bless me!" he repeated at intervals.

Leclère grinned proudly.

"But why does he not run away?"

The Frenchman's shoulders went up in the racial shrug that means all things from total ignorance to infinite understanding.

"Then why do you not kill him?"

Again the shoulders went up.

"*Mon père*," he said after a pause, "de taim is not yet. He is one beeg devil. Some taim Ah break heem, so, an' so, all to leetle bits. Hey? Some taim. *Bon!*"

A day came when Leclère gathered his dogs together and floated down in a bateau to Forty Mile, and on to the Porcupine, where he took a commission from the P. C. Company, and went exploring for the better part of a year. After that he poled up the Koyokuk to deserted Arctic City, and later came drifting back, from camp to camp, along the Yukon. And during the long months Bâtard was well lessoned. He learned many tortures, and, notably, the torture of hunger, the torture of thirst, the torture of fire, and, worst of all, the torture of music.

Like the rest of his kind, he did not enjoy music. It gave him exquisite anguish, racking him nerve by nerve, and ripping apart every fibre of his being. It made him howl, long and wolf-like, as when the wolves bay the stars on frosty nights. He could not help howling. It was his one weakness in the contest with Leclère, and it was his shame. Leclère, on the other hand, passionately loved music—as passionately as he loved strong drink. And when his soul clamored for expression, it usually uttered itself in one or the other of the two ways, and more usually in both ways. And when he had drunk, his brain a-lilt with unsung song and the devil in him aroused and rampant, his soul found its supreme utterance in torturing Bâtard.

"Now we will haf a leetle museek," he would say. "Eh? W'at you t'ink, Bâtard?"

It was only an old and battered harmonica, tenderly treasured and patiently repaired; but it was the best that money could buy, and out of its silver reeds he drew weird vagrant airs that men had never heard before. Then Bâtard, dumb of throat, with teeth tight clenched, would back away, inch by inch, to the farthest cabin corner. And Leclère, playing, playing, a stout club tucked under his arm, followed the animal up, inch by inch, step by step, till there was no further retreat.

At first Bâtard would crowd himself into the smallest possible space, grovelling close to the floor; but as the music came nearer and nearer, he was forced to uprear, his back jammed into the logs, his fore legs fanning the air as though to beat off the rippling waves of sound. He still kept his teeth together, but severe muscular contractions attacked his body, strange twitching and jerkings, till he was all a-quiver and writhing in silent torment. As he lost control, his jaws spasmodically wrenched apart, and deep throaty vibrations issued forth, too low in the register of sound for human ear to catch. And then, nostrils distended, eyes dilated, hair bristling in helpless rage, arose the long wolf howl. It came with a slurring rush upward, swelling to a great heart-breaking burst of sound, and dying away in sadly cadenced woe—then the next rush upward, octave upon octave; the bursting heart; and the infinite sorrow and misery, fainting, fading, falling, and dying slowly away.

It was fit for hell. And Leclère, with fiendish ken, seemed to divine each particular nerve and heartstring, and with long wails and tremblings and sobbing minors to make it yield up its last shred of grief. It was frightful, and for twenty-four hours after, Bâtard was nervous and unstrung, starting at common sounds, tripping over his own shadow, but, withal, vicious and masterful with his team-mates. Nor did he show signs of a breaking spirit. Rather did he grow more grim and taciturn, biding his time with an inscrutable patience that began to puzzle and weigh upon Leclère. The dog would lie in the firelight, motionless, for hours, gazing straight before him at Leclère, and hating him with his bitter eyes.

Often the man felt that he had bucked against the very essence of life—the unconquerable essence that swept the hawk down out of the sky like a feathered thunderbolt, that drove the great gray goose across the zones, that hurled the spawning salmon through two thousand miles of boiling Yukon flood. At such times he felt impelled to express his own unconquerable essence; and with strong drink, wild music, and Bâtard, he indulged in vast orgies, wherein he pitted his puny strength in the face of things, and challenged all that was, and had been, and was yet to be.

"Dere is somet'ing dere," he affirmed, when the rhythmed vagaries of his mind touched the secret chords of Bâtard's being and brought forth the long lugubrious howl. "Ah pool eet out wid bot' my han's, so, an' so. Ha! Ha! Eet is fonee! Eet is ver' fonee! De priest chant, de womans pray, de mans swear, de lettle bird go *peep-peep*, Bâtard, heem go *yow-yow*—an' eet is all de ver' same t'ing. Ha! Ha!"

Father Gautier, a worthy priest, once reproved him with instances of concrete perdition. He never reproved him again.

"Eet may be so, *mon père*," he made answer. "An' Ah t'ink Ah go troo hell a'snappin', lak de hemlock troo de fire. Eh, *mon père?*"

But all bad things come to an end as well as good, and so with Black Leclère. On the summer low water, in a poling boat, he left McDougall for Sunrise. He left McDougall in company with Timothy Brown, and arrived at Sunrise by himself. Further, it was known that they had quarrelled just previous to pulling out; for the *Lizzie*, a wheezy ten-ton sternwheeler, twenty-four hours behind, beat Leclère in by three days. And when he did get in, it was with a clean-drilled bullet-hole through his shoulder muscle, and a tale of ambush and murder.

A strike had been made at Sunrise, and things had changed considerably. With the infusion of several hundred gold-seekers, a deal of whiskey, and half a dozen equipped gamblers, the missionary had seen the page of his years of labor with the Indians wiped clean. When the squaws became preoccupied with cooking beans and keeping the fire going for the wifeless miners, and the bucks with swapping their warm furs for black bottles and broken timepieces, he took to his bed, said "bless me" several times, and departed to his final accounting in a rough-hewn, oblong box. Whereupon the gamblers moved their roulette and faro tables into the mission house, and the click of chips and clink of glasses went up from dawn till dark and to dawn again.

Now Timothy Brown was well beloved among these adventurers of the north. The one thing against him was his quick temper and ready fist,—a little thing, for which his kind heart and forgiving hand more than atoned. On the other hand, there was nothing to atone for Black Leclère. He was "black," as more than one remembered deed bore witness, while he was as well hated as the other was beloved. So the men of Sunrise put an antiseptic dressing on his shoulder and haled him before Judge Lynch.

It was a simple affair. He had quarrelled with Timothy Brown at McDougall. With Timothy Brown he had left McDougall. Without Timothy Brown he had arrived at Sunrise. Considered in the light of his evilness, the unanimous conclusion was that he had killed Timothy Brown. On the other hand, Leclère acknowledged their facts, but challenged their conclusion, and gave his own explanation. Twenty miles out of Sunrise he and Timothy Brown were poling the boat along the rocky shore. From that shore two rifle-shots rang out. Timothy Brown pitched out of the boat and went down bubbling red, and that was the last of Timothy Brown. He, Leclère, pitched into the bottom of the boat with a stinging shoulder. He lay very quiet, peeping at the shore. After a time two Indians stuck up their heads and came out to the water's edge, carrying between them a birch-bark canoe. As they launched it, Leclère let fly. He potted one, who went over the side after the manner of Timothy Brown. The other dropped into the bottom of the canoe, and then canoe and poling boat went down the stream in a drifting battle. After that they hung up on a split current, and the canoe passed on one side of an island, the poling boat on the other. That was the last of the canoe, and he came on into Sunrise. Yes, from the way the Indian in the canoe jumped, he was sure he had potted him. That was all.

This explanation was not deemed adequate. They gave him ten hours' grace while the *Lizzie* steamed down to investigate. Ten hours later she came wheezing back to Sunrise. There had been nothing to investigate. No evidence had been found to back up his statements. They told him to make his will, for he possessed a fifty-thousand-dollar Sunrise claim, and they were a law-abiding as well as a law-giving breed.

Leclère shrugged his shoulder. "Bot one t'ing," he said; "a leetle, w'at you call, favor—a leetle favor, dat is eet. I gif my feefty t'ousan' dollair to de church. I gif my husky dog, Bâtard, to de devil. De leetle favor? Firs' you hang heem, an' den you hang me. Eet is good, eh?"

Good it was, they agreed, that Hell's Spawn should break trail for his master across the last divide, and the court was adjourned down to the river bank, where a big spruce tree stood by itself. Slackwater Charley put a hangman's knot in the end of a hauling-line, and the noose was slipped over Leclère's head and pulled tight around his neck. His hands were tied behind his back, and he was assisted to the top of a cracker box. Then the running end of the line was passed over an overhanging branch, drawn taut, and made fast. To kick the box out from under would leave him dancing on the air.

"Now for the dog," said Webster Shaw, sometime mining engineer. "You'll have to rope him, Slackwater."

Leclère grinned. Slackwater took a chew of tobacco, rove a running noose, and proceeded leisurely to coil a few turns in his hand. He paused once or twice to brush particularly offensive mosquitoes from off his face. Everybody was brushing mosquitoes, except Leclère, about whose head a small cloud was visible. Even Bâtard, lying full-stretched on the ground, with his forepaws rubbed the pests away from eyes and mouth.

But while Slackwater waited for Bâtard to lift his head, a faint call came down the quiet air, and a man was seen waving his arms and running across the flat from Sunrise. It was the storekeeper.

"C-call 'er off, boys," he panted, as he came in among them.

"Little Sandy and Bernadotte's jes' got in," he explained with returning breath. "Landed down below an' come up by the short cut. Got the Beaver with 'm. Picked 'm up in his canoe, stuck in the back channel, with a couple of bullet holes in 'm. Other buck was Klok-Kutz, the one that knocked spots out of his squaw and dusted."

"Eh? W'at Ah say? Eh?" Leclère cried exultantly. "Dat de one fo' sure! Ah know. Ah spik true."

"The thing to do is teach these damned Siwashes a little manners," spoke Webster Shaw. "They're getting fat and sassy, and we'll have to bring them down a peg. Round in all the bucks and string up the Beaver for an object lesson. That's the programme. Come on and let's see what he's got to say for himself."

"Heh, M'sieu'!" Leclère called, as the crowd began to melt away through the twilight in the direction of Sunrise. "Ah lak ver' moch to see de fon."

"Oh, we'll turn you loose when we come back," Webster Shaw shouted over his shoulder. "In the meantime meditate on your sins and the way of providence. It will do you good, so be grateful."

As is the way with men who are accustomed to great hazards, whose nerves are healthy and trained to patience, so it was with Leclère, who settled himself to the long wait—which is to say that he reconciled his mind to it. There was no settling of the body, for the taut rope forced him to stand rigidly erect. The least relaxation of the leg muscles pressed the rough-fibred noose into his neck, while the upright position caused him much pain in his wounded shoulder. He projected his under lip and expelled his breath upward along his face to blow the mosquitoes away from his eyes. But the situation had its compensation. To be snatched from the maw of death was well worth a little bodily suffering, only it was unfortunate that he should miss the hanging of the Beaver.

And so he mused, till his eyes chanced to fall upon Bâtard, head between fore paws and stretched on the ground asleep. And then Leclère ceased to muse. He studied the animal closely, striving to sense if the sleep were real or feigned. Bâtard's sides were heaving regularly, but Leclère felt that the breath came and went a shade too quickly; also he felt that there was a vigilance or alertness to every hair that belied unshackling sleep. He would have given his Sunrise claim to be assured that the dog was not awake, and once, when one of his joints cracked, he looked quickly and guiltily at Bâtard to see if he roused. He did not rouse then, but a few minutes later he got up slowly and lazily, stretched, and looked carefully about him.

"*Sacredam*," said Leclère, under his breath.

Assured that no one was in sight or hearing, Bâtard sat down, curled his upper lip almost into a smile, looked up at Leclère, and licked his chops.

"Ah see my feenish," the man said, and laughed sardonically aloud.

Bâtard came nearer, the useless ear wabbling, the good ear cocked forward with devilish comprehension. He thrust his head on one side quizzically, and advanced with mincing, playful steps. He rubbed his body gently against the box till it shook and shook again. Leclère teetered carefully to maintain his equilibrium.

"Bâtard," he said calmly, "look out. Ah keel you."

Bâtard snarled at the word, and shook the box with greater force. Then he upreared, and with his fore paws threw his weight against it higher up. Leclère kicked out with one foot, but the rope bit into his neck and checked so abruptly as nearly to overbalance him.

"Hi, ya! *Chook! Mush-on!*" he screamed.

Bâtard retreated, for twenty feet or so, with a fiendish levity in his bearing that Leclère could not mistake. He remembered the dog often breaking the scum of ice on the water hole, by lifting up and throwing his weight upon it; and, remembering, he understood what he now had in mind. Bâtard faced about and paused. He showed his white teeth in a grin, which Leclère answered; and then hurled his body through the air, in full charge, straight for the box.

Fifteen minutes later, Slackwater Charley and Webster Shaw, returning, caught a glimpse of a ghostly pendulum swinging back and forth in the dim light. As they hurriedly drew in closer, they made out the man's inert body, and a live thing that clung to it, and shook and worried, and gave to it the swaying motion.

"Hi, ya! *Chook!* you Spawn of Hell," yelled Webster Shaw.

But Bâtard glared at him, and snarled threateningly, without loosing his jaws.

Slackwater Charley got out his revolver, but his hand was shaking, as with a chill, and he fumbled.

"Here, you take it," he said, passing the weapon over.

Webster Shaw laughed shortly, drew a sight between the gleaming eyes, and pressed the trigger. Bâtard's body twitched with the shock, threshed the ground spasmodically for a moment, and went suddenly limp. But his teeth still held fast locked.

THE STORY OF JEES UCK

THERE have been renunciations and renunciations. But in its essence renunciation is ever the same. And the paradox of it is that men and women forego the dearest thing in the world for something dearer. It was never otherwise. Thus it was when Abel brought of the firstlings of his flock and of the fat thereof. The firstlings and the fat thereof were to him the dearest things in the world; yet he gave them over that he might be on good terms with God. So it was with Abraham when he prepared to offer up his son Isaac on a stone. Isaac was very dear to him; but God, in incomprehensible ways, was yet dearer. It may be that Abraham feared the Lord. But whether that be true or not, it has since been determined by a few billion people that he loved the Lord and desired to serve Him.

And since it has been determined that love is service, and since to renounce is to serve, then Jees Uck, who was merely a woman of a swart-skinned breed, loved with a great love. She was unversed in history, having learned to read only the signs of weather and of game; so she had never heard of Abel nor of Abraham; nor, having escaped the good sisters at Holy Cross, had she been told the story of Ruth, the Moabitess, who renounced her very God for the sake of a stranger woman from a strange land. Jees Uck had learned only one way of renouncing, and that was with a club as the dynamic factor, in much the same manner as a dog is made to renounce a stolen marrowbone. Yet when the time came she proved herself capable of rising to the height of the fair-faced royal races and of renouncing in right regal fashion.

So this is the story of Jees Uck, which is also the story of Neil Bonner, and Kitty Bonner, and a couple of Neil Bonner's progeny. Jees Uck was of a swart-skinned breed, it is true, but she was not an Indian; nor was she an Eskimo; nor even an Innuit. Going backward into mouth tradition, there appears the figure of one Skolkz, a Toyaat Indian of the Yukon who journeyed down in his youth to the Great Delta where dwell the Innuits, and where he forgathered with a woman remembered as Olillie. Now the woman Olillie had been bred from an Eskimo mother by an Innuit man. And from Skolkz and Olillie came Halie, who was one half Toyaat Indian, one quarter Innuit, and one quarter Eskimo. And Halie was the grandmother of Jees Uck.

Now Halie, in whom three stocks had been bastardized, who cherished no prejudice against further admixture, mated with a Russian fur trader called Shpack, also known in his time as the Big Fat. Shpack is herein classed Russian for lack of a more adequate term; for Shpack's father, a Slavonic convict from the Lower Provinces, had escaped from the quicksilver mines into northern Siberia, where he knew Zimba, who was a woman of the Deer People and who became the mother of Shpack, who became the grandfather of Jees Uck.

Now had not Shpack been captured in his boyhood by the Sea People, who fringe the rim of the Arctic Sea with their misery, he would not have become the grandfather of Jees Uck and there would be no story at all. But he *was* captured by the Sea People, from whom he escaped to Kamchatka, and thence, on a Norwegian whaleship, to the Baltic. Not long after that he turned up in St. Petersburg, and the years were not many till he went drifting east over the same weary road his father had measured with blood and groans a half century before. But Shpack was a free man, in the employ of the great Russian Fur Company. And in that employ he fared farther and farther east, until he crossed Bering Sea into Russian America; and at Pastilik, which is hard by the Great Delta of the Yukon, became the husband of Halie, who was the grandmother of Jees Uck. Out of this union came the woman-child, Tukesan.

Shpack, under the orders of the company, made a canoe voyage of a few hundred miles up the Yukon to the post of Nulato. With him he took Halie and the babe Tukesan. This was in 1850, and in 1850 it was that the river Indians fell upon Nulato and wiped if from the face of the earth. And that was the end of Shpack and Halie. On that terrible night Tukesan disappeared. To this day the Toyaats aver they had no hand in the trouble; but, be that as it may, the fact remains that the babe Tukesan grew up among them.

Tukesan was married successively to two Toyaat brothers, to both of whom she was barren. Because of this, other women shook their heads, and no third Toyaat man could be found to dare matrimony with the childless widow. But at this time, many hundred miles above, at Fort Yukon was a man, Spike O'Brien. Fort Yukon was a Hudson's Bay Company post, and Spike O'Brien one of the company's servants. He was a good servant, but he achieved an opinion that the service was bad, and in the course of time vindicated that opinion by deserting. It was a year's journey, by the chain of posts, back to York Factory on Hudson Bay. Further, being company posts, he knew he could not evade the company's clutches. Nothing remained but to go down the Yukon. It was true no white man had ever gone down the Yukon, and no white man knew whether the Yukon emptied into the Arctic Ocean or Bering Sea; but Spike O'Brien was a Celt, and the promise of danger was a lure he had ever followed.

A few weeks later, somewhat battered, rather famished, and about dead with river fever, he drove the nose of his canoe into the earth bank by the village of the Toyaats and promptly fainted away. While getting his strength back, in the weeks that followed, he looked upon Tukesan and found her good. Like the father of Shpack, who lived to a ripe old age among the Siberian Deer People, Spike O'Brien might have left his aged bones with the Toyaats. But romance gripped his heartstrings and would not let him stay. As he had journeyed from York Factory to Fort Yukon, so, first among men, might he journey from Fort Yukon to the sea and win the honor of being the first man to make the Northwest

Passage by land. So he departed down the river, won the honor, and was unannaled and unsung. In after years he ran a sailors' boardinghouse in San Francisco, where he became esteemed a most remarkable liar by virtue of the gospel truths he told. But a child was born to Tukesan, who had been childless. And this child was Jees Uck. Her lineage has been traced at length to show that she was neither Indian, nor Eskimo, nor Innuit, nor much of anything else; also to show what waifs of the generations we are, all of us, and the strange meanderings of the seed from which we spring.

What with the vagrant blood in her and the heritage compounded of many races, Jees Uck developed a wonderful young beauty. Bizarre perhaps, it was, and oriental enough to puzzle any passing ethnologist. A lithe and slender grace characterized her. Beyond a quickened lilt to the imagination, the contribution of the Celt was in no wise apparent. It might possibly have put the warm blood under her skin, which made her face less swart and her body fairer; but that, in turn, might have come from Shpack, the Big Fat, who inherited the color of his Slavonic father. And, finally, she had great, blazing black eyes—the half-caste eye, round, full-orbed, and sensuous, which marks the collision of the dark races with the light. Also the white blood in her, combined with her knowledge that it was in her, made her, in a way, ambitious. Otherwise, by upbringing and in outlook on life, she was wholly and utterly a Toyaat Indian.

One winter, when she was a young woman, Neil Bonner came into her life. But he came into her life, as he had come into the country, somewhat reluctantly. In fact it was very much against his will, coming into the country. Between a father who clipped coupons and cultivated roses, and a mother who loved the social round, Neil Bonner had gone rather wild. He was not vicious, but a man with meat in his belly and without work in the world has to expend his energy somehow, and Neil Bonner was such a man. And he expended his energy in such fashion and to such extent that when the inevitable climax came his father, Neil Bonner, Sr., crawled out of his roses in a panic and looked on his son with a wondering eye. Then he hied himself away to a crony of kindred pursuits, with whom he was wont to confer over coupons and roses, and between the two the destiny of young Neil Bonner was made manifest. He must go away, on probation, to live down his harmless follies in order that he might live up to their own excellent standard.

This determined upon, and young Neil a little repentant and a great deal ashamed, the rest was easy. The cronies were heavy stockholders in the P. C. Company. The P. C. Company owned fleets of river steamers and ocean-going craft, and, in addition to farming the sea, exploited a hundred thousand square miles or so of the land that, on the maps of geographers, usually occupies the white spaces. So the P. C. Company sent young Neil Bonner north, where the white spaces are, to do its work and to learn to be good like his father. "Five years of simplicity, close to the soil and far from temptation, will make a man of him," said old Neil Bonner, and forthwith crawled back among his roses. Young Neil set his jaw, pitched his chin at the proper angle, and went to work. As an underling he did his work well and gained the commendation of his superiors. Not that he delighted in the work, but that it was the one thing that prevented him from going mad.

The first year he wished he was dead. The second year he cursed God. The third year he was divided between the two emotions, and in the confusion quarreled with a man in authority. He had the best of the quarrel, though the man in authority had the last word—a word that sent Neil Bonner into an exile that made his old billet appear as paradise. But he went without a whimper, for the North had succeeded in making him into a man.

Here and there, on the white spaces on the map, little circlets like the letter o are to be found, and, appended to these circlets, on one side or the other, are names such as "Fort Hamilton," "Yanana Station," "Twenty Mile," thus leading one to imagine that the white spaces are plentifully besprinkled with towns and villages. But it is a vain imagining. Twenty Mile, which is very like the rest of the posts, is a log building the size of a corner grocery with rooms to let upstairs. A long-legged cache on stilts may be found in the back yard; also a couple of outhouses. The back yard is unfenced and extends to the sky line and an unascertainable bit beyond. There are no other houses in sight, though the Toyaats sometimes pitch a winter camp a mile or two down the Yukon. And this is Twenty Mile, one tentacle of the many-tentacled P. C. Company. Here the agent, with an assistant, barters with the Indians for their furs and does an erratic trade on a gold-dust basis with the wandering miners. Here, also, the agent and his assistant yearn all winter for the spring and, when the spring comes, camp blasphemously on the roof while the Yukon washes out the establishment. And here, also, in the fourth year of his sojourn in the land, came Neil Bonner to take charge.

He had displaced no agent; for the man that previously ran the post had made away with himself; "because of the rigors of the place," said the assistant, who still remained; though the Toyaats, by their fires, had another version. The assistant was a shrunken-shouldered, hollow-chested man with a cadaverous face and cavernous cheeks that his sparse black beard could not hide. He coughed much, as though consumption gripped his lungs, while his eyes had that mad, fevered light common to consumptives in the last stage. Pentley was his name, Amos Pentley, and Bonner did not like him, though he felt a pity for the forlorn and hopeless devil. They did not get along together, these two men who, of all men, should have been on good terms in the face of the cold and silence and darkness of the long winter.

In the end Bonner concluded that Amos was partly demented, and left him alone, doing all the work himself except the cooking. Even then Amos had nothing but bitter looks and an undisguised hatred for him. This was a great loss to Bonner; for the smiling face of one of his own kind, the cheery word, the sympathy of comradeship shared with misfortune—these things meant much; and the winter was yet young when he began to realize the added reasons, with such an assistant, that the previous agent had found to impel his own hand against his life.

It was very lonely at Twenty Mile. The bleak vastness stretched away on every side to the horizon. The snow, which was really frost, flung its mantle over the land and buried everything in the silence of death. For days it was clear and cold, the thermometer steadily recording forty to fifty degrees below zero. Then a change came over the face of things. What little moisture had oozed into the atmosphere gathered into dull gray, formless clouds; it became quite warm, the thermometer rising to twenty below; and the moisture fell out of the sky in hard frost granules that hissed like dry sugar or driving sand when kicked underfoot. After that it became clear and cold again, until enough moisture had gathered to blanket the earth from the cold of outer space. That was all. Nothing happened. No storms, no churning waters and threshing forests, nothing but the machinelike precipitation of accumulated moisture. Possibly the most notable thing that occurred through the weary weeks was the gliding of the temperature up to the unprecedented height of fifteen below. To atone for this, outer space smote the earth with its cold till the mercury froze and the spirit thermometer remained more than seventy below for a fortnight, when it burst. There was no telling how much colder it was after that. Another occurrence, monotonous in its regularity, was the lengthening of the nights, till day became a mere blink of light between the darknesses.

Neil Bonner was a social animal. The very follies for which he was doing penance had been bred of his excessive sociability. And here, in the fourth year of his exile, he found himself in company —which were to travesty the word—with a morose and speechless creature in whose sombre eyes smoldered a hatred as bitter as it was unwarranted. And Bonner, to whom speech and fellowship were as the breath of life, went about as a ghost might go, tantalized by the gregarious revelries of some former life. In the day his lips were compressed, his face stern; but in the night he clenched his hands, rolled about in his blankets, and cried aloud like a little child. And he would remember a certain man in authority and curse him through the long hours. Also he cursed God. But God understands. He cannot find it in His heart to blame weak mortals who blaspheme in Alaska.

And here, to the post of Twenty Mile, came Jees Uck, to trade for flour and bacon, and beads, and bright scarlet cloths for her fancywork. And further, and unwittingly, she came to the post of Twenty Mile to make a lonely man more lonely, make him reach out empty arms in his sleep. For Neil Bonner was only a man. When she first came into the store he looked at her long, as a thirsty man may look at a flowing well. And she, with the heritage bequeathed her by Spike O'Brien, imagined daringly and smiled up into his eyes, not as the swart-skinned peoples should smile at the royal races, but as a woman smiles at a man. The thing was inevitable; only he did not see it, and fought against her as fiercely and passionately as he was drawn toward her. And she? She was

Jees Uck, by upbringing wholly and utterly a Toyaat Indian woman.

She came often to the post to trade. And often she sat by the big wood stove and chatted in broken English with Neil Bonner. And he came to look for her coming; and on the days she did not come he was worried and restless. Sometimes he stopped to think, and then she was met coldly, with a reserve that perplexed and piqued her, and which, she was convinced, was not sincere. But more often he did not dare to think, and then all went well and there were smiles and laughter. And Amos Pentley, gasping like a stranded catfish, his hollow cough a-reek with the grave, looked upon it all and grinned. He, who loved life, could not live, and it rankled his soul that others should be able to live. Wherefore he hated Bonner, who was so very much alive and into whose eyes sprang joy at the sight of Jees Uck. As for Amos, the very thought of the girl was sufficient to send his blood pounding up into a hemorrhage.

Jees Uck, whose mind was simple, who thought elementally and was unused to weighing life in its subtler quantities, read Amos Pentley like a book. She warned Bonner, openly and bluntly, in few words; but the complexities of higher existence confused the situation to him, and he laughed at her evident anxiety. To him, Amos was a poor, miserable devil, tottering desperately into the grave. And Bonner, who had suffered much, found it easy to forgive greatly.

But one morning, during a bitter snap, he got up from the breakfast table and went into the store. Jees Uck was already there, rosy from the trail, to buy a sack of flour. A few minutes later he was out in the snow lashing the flour on her sled. As he bent over he noticed a stiffness in his neck and felt a premonition of impending physical misfortune. And as he put the last half hitch into the lashing and attempted to straighten up a quick spasm seized him and he sank into the snow. Tense and quivering, head jerked back, limbs extended, back arched and mouth twisted and distorted, he appeared as though being racked limb from limb. Without cry or sound, Jees Uck was in the snow beside him; but he clutched both her wrists spasmodically, as long as the convulsion endured she was helpless. In a few moments the spasm relaxed and he was left weak and fainting, his forehead beaded with sweat, his lips flecked with foam.

"Quick!" he muttered in a strange, hoarse voice. "Quick! Inside!"

He started to crawl on hands and knees, but she raised him up, and, supported by her young arm, he made faster progress. As he entered the store the spasm seized him again, and his body writhed irresistibly away from her and rolled and curled on the floor. Amos Pentley came and looked on with curious eyes.

"Oh, Amos!" she cried in an agony of apprehension and helplessness. "Him die, you think?" But Amos shrugged his shoulders and continued to look on.

Bonner's body went slack, the tense muscles easing down and an expression of relief coming into his face. "Quick!" he gritted between his teeth, his mouth twisting with the oncoming of the next spasm and with his effort to control it. "Quick, Jees Uck! The medicine! Never mind! Drag me!"

She knew where the medicine chest stood, at the rear of the room beyond the stove, and thither, by the legs, she dragged the struggling man. As the spasm passed he began, very faint and very sick, to overhaul the chest. He had seen dogs die exhibiting symptoms similar to his own, and he knew what should be done. He held up a vial of chloral hydrate, but his fingers were too weak and nerveless to draw the cork. This Jees Uck did for him, while he was plunged into another convulsion. As he came out of it he found the open bottle proffered him and looked into the great black eyes of the woman and read what men have always read in the mate-woman's eyes. Taking a full dose of the stuff, he sank back until another spasm had passed. Then he raised himself limply on his elbow.

"Listen, Jees Uck!" he said very slowly, as though aware of the necessity for haste and yet afraid to hasten. "Do what I say. Stay by my side but do not touch me. I must be very quiet, but you must not go away." His jaw began to set and his face to quiver and distort with the forerunning pangs, but he gulped and struggled to master them. "Do not go away. And do not let Amos go away. Understand! Amos must stay right here."

She nodded her head, and he passed off into the first of many convulsions, which gradually diminished in force and frequency.

Jees Uck hung over him, remembering his injunction and not daring to touch him. Once Amos grew restless and made as though to go into the kitchen; but a quick blaze from her eyes quelled him, and after that, save for his labored breathing and charnel cough, he was very quiet.

Bonner slept. The blink of light that marked the day disappeared. Amos, followed about by the woman's eyes, lighted the kerosene lamps. Evening came on. Through the north window the heavens were emblazoned with an auroral display which flamed and flared and died down into blackness. Some time after that Neil Bonner roused. First he looked to see that Amos was still there, then smiled at Jees Uck and pulled himself up. Every muscle was stiff and sore, and he smiled ruefully, pressing and prodding himself as if to ascertain the extent of the ravage. Then his face went stern and businesslike.

"Jees Uck," he said, "take a candle. Go into the kitchen. There is food on the table—biscuits and beans and bacon; also coffee in the pot on the stove. Bring it here on the counter. Also bring tumblers and water and whisky, which you will find on the top shelf of the locker. Do not forget the whisky."

Having swallowed a stiff glass of the whisky, he went carefully through the medicine chest, now and again putting aside, with definite purpose, certain bottles and vials. Then he set to work on the food, attempting a crude analysis. He had not been unused to the laboratory in his college days and was possessed of sufficient imagination to achieve results with his limited materials. The condition of tetanus, which had marked his paroxysms, simplified matters, and he made but one test. The coffee yielded nothing; nor did the beans. To the biscuits he devoted the utmost care. Amos, who knew nothing of chemistry, looked on with steady curiosity. But Jees Uck, who had boundless faith in the white man's wisdom, and especially in Neil Bonner's wisdom, and who not only knew nothing but knew that she knew nothing, watched his face rather than his hands.

Step by step he eliminated possibilities, until he came to the final test. He was using a thin medicine vial for a tube, and this he held between him and the light, watching the slow precipitation of a salt through the solution contained in the tube. He said nothing, but he saw what he had expected to see. And Jees Uck, her eyes riveted on his face, saw something too—something that made her spring like a tigress upon Amos and with splendid suppleness and strength bend his body back across her knee. Her knife was out of its sheath and uplifted, glinting in the lamplight. Amos was snarling; but Bonner intervened ere the blade could fall.

"That's a good girl, Jees Uck. But never mind. Let him go!"

She dropped the man obediently, though with protest writ large on her face; and his body thudded to the floor. Bonner nudged him with his moccasined foot.

"Get up, Amos!" he commanded. "You've got to pack an outfit yet tonight and hit the trail."

"You don't mean to say—" Amos blurted savagely.

"I mean to say that you tried to kill me," Neil went on in cold, even tones. "I mean to say that you killed Birdsall, for all the company believes he killed himself. You used strychnine in my case. God knows with what you fixed him. Now I can't hang you. You're too near dead as it is. But Twenty Mile is too small for the pair of us, and you've got to mush. It's two hundred miles to Holy Cross. You can make it if you're careful not to overexert. I'll give you grub, a sled, and three dogs. You'll be as safe as if you were in jail, for you can't get out of the country. And I'll give you one chance. You're almost dead. Very well. I shall send no word to the company until the spring. In the meantime the thing for you to do is to die. Now *mush!*"

"You go to bed!" Jees Uck insisted when Amos had churned away into the night toward Holy Cross. "You sick man yet, Neil."

"And you're a good girl, Jees Uck," he answered. "And here's my hand on it. But you must go home."

"You don't like me," she said simply.

He smiled, helped her on with her parka, and led her to the door. "Only too well, Jees Uck," he said softly, "only too well."

After that the pall of the Arctic night fell deeper and blacker on the land. Neil Bonner discovered that he had failed to put proper valuation upon even the sullen face of the murderous and death-stricken Amos. It became very lonely at Twenty Mile. "For the love of God, Prentiss, send me a man," he wrote to the agent at Fort Hamilton, three hundred miles upriver. Six weeks later the

Indian messenger brought back a reply. It was characteristic: "Hell. Both feet frozen. Need him myself—Prentiss."

To make matters worse, most of the Toyaats were in the back country on the flanks of a caribou herd, and Jees Uck was with them. Removing to a distance seemed to bring her closer than ever, and Neil Bonner found himself picturing her, day by day, in camp and on trail. It is not good to be alone. Often he went out of the quiet store, bareheaded and frantic, and shook his fist at the blink of day that came over the southern sky line. And on still, cold nights he left his bed and stumbled into the frost, where he assaulted the silence at the top of his lungs, as though it were some tangible, sentient thing that he might arouse; or he shouted at the sleeping dogs till they howled and howled again. One shaggy brute he brought into the post, playing that it was the new man sent by Prentiss. He strove to make it sleep decently under the blankets at night and to sit at table and eat as a man should; but the beast, mere domesticated wolf that it was, rebelled, and sought out dark corners and snarled and bit him in the leg, and was finally beaten and driven forth.

Then the trick of personification seized upon Neil Bonner and mastered him. All the forces of his environment metamorphosed into living, breathing entities and came to live with him. He re-created the primitive pantheon; reared an altar to the sun and burned candle fat and bacon grease thereon; and in the unfenced yard, by the long-legged cache, made a frost devil, which he was wont to make faces at and mock when the mercury oozed down into the bulb. All this in play, of course. He said to himself that it was in play, and repeated it over and over to make sure, unaware that madness is ever prone to express itself in make-believe and play.

One midwinter day Father Champreau, a Jesuit missionary, pulled into Twenty Mile. Bonner fell upon him and dragged him into the post, and clung to him and wept, until the priest wept with him from sheer compassion. Then Bonner became madly hilarious and made lavish entertainment, swearing valiantly that his guest should not depart. But Father Champreau was pressing to Salt Water on urgent business for his order, and pulled out next morning, with Bonner's blood threatened on his head.

And the threat was in a fair way toward realization, when the

Toyaats returned from their long hunt to the winter camp. They had many furs, and there was much trading and stir at Twenty Mile. Also Jees Uck came to buy beads and scarlet cloths and things, and Bonner began to find himself again. He fought for a week against her. Then the end came one night when she rose to leave. She had not forgotten her repulse, and the pride that drove Spike O'Brien on to complete the Northwest Passage by land was her pride.

"I go now," she said; "good night, Neil."

But he came up behind her. "Nay, it is not well," he said.

And as she turned her face toward his with a sudden joyful flash he bent forward, slowly and gravely, as it were a sacred thing, and kissed her on the lips. The Toyaats had never taught her the meaning of a kiss upon the lips, but she understood and was glad.

With the coming of Jees Uck, at once things brightened up. She was regal in her happiness, a source of unending delight. The elemental workings of her mind and her naïve little ways made an immense sum of pleasurable surprise to the overcivilized man that had stooped to catch her up. Not alone was she solace to his loneliness, but her primitiveness rejuvenated his jaded mind. It was as though, after long wandering, he had returned to pillow his head in the lap of Mother Earth. In short, in Jees Uck he found the youth of the world—the youth and the strength and the joy.

And to fill the full round of his need, and that they might not see overmuch of each other, there arrived at Twenty Mile one Sandy MacPherson, as companionable a man as ever whistled along the trail or raised a ballad by a campfire. A Jesuit priest had run into his camp, a couple of hundreds miles up the Yukon, in the nick of time to say a last word over the body of Sandy's partner. And on departing, the priest had said, "My son, you will be lonely now." And Sandy had bowed his head brokenly. "At Twenty Mile," the priest added, "there is a lonely man. You have need of each other, my son."

So it was that Sandy became a welcome third at the post, brother to the man and woman that resided there. He took Bonner moose hunting and wolf trapping; and in return Bonner resurrected a battered and wayworn volume and made him friends with Shakespeare, till Sandy declaimed iambic pentameters to his sled dogs whenever they waxed mutinous. And of the long evenings they played cribbage and talked and disagreed about the universe, the while Jees Uck rocked matronly in an easy chair and darned their moccasins and socks.

Spring came. The sun shot up out of the south. The land exchanged its austere robes for the garb of a smiling wanton. Everywhere light laughed and life invited. The days stretched out their balmy length and the nights passed from blinks of darkness to no darkness at all. The river bared its bosom, and snorting steamboats challenged the wilderness. There were stir and bustle, new faces, and fresh facts. An assistant arrived at Twenty Mile, and Sandy MacPherson wandered off with a bunch of prospectors to invade the Koyukuk country. And there were newspapers and magazines and letters for Neil Bonner. And Jees Uck looked on in worriment, for she knew his kindred talked with him across the world.

Without much shock it came to him that his father was dead. There was a sweet letter of forgiveness, dictated in his last hours. There were official letters from the company, graciously ordering him to turn the post over to the assistant and permitting him to depart at his earliest pleasure. A long, legal affair from the lawyers informed him of interminable lists of stocks and bonds, real estate, rents, and chattels that were his by his father's will. And a dainty bit of stationery, sealed and monogrammed, implored dear Neil's return to his heartbroken and loving mother.

Neil Bonner did some swift thinking, and when the *Yukon Belle* coughed in to the bank on her way down to Bering Sea he departed—departed with the ancient lie of quick return young and blithe on his lips.

"I'll come back, dear Jees Uck, before the first snow flies," he promised her between the last kisses at the gangplank.

And not only did he promise, but, like the majority of men under the same circumstances, he really meant it. To John Thompson, the new agent, he gave orders for the extension of unlimited credit to his wife, Jees Uck. Also, with his last look from the deck of the *Yukon Belle*, he saw a dozen men at work rearing the logs that were to make the most comfortable house along a thousand miles of river front—the house of Jees Uck, and likewise the house of Neil Bonner—ere the first flurry of snow. For he fully and fondly meant to come back. Jees Uck was dear to him, and, further, a golden future awaited the North. With his father's money he intended to verify that future. An ambitious dream allured him. With his four years of experience, and aided by the friendly co-operation of the P. C. Company, he would return to become the Rhodes of Alaska. And he would return, fast as steam could drive, as soon as he had put into shape the affairs of his father, whom he had never known, and comforted his mother, whom he had forgotten.

There was much ado when Neil Bonner came back from the Arctic. The fires were lighted and the fleshpots slung, and he took of it all and called it good. Not only was he bronzed and creased, but he was a new man under his skin, with a grip on things and a seriousness and control. His old companions were amazed when he declined to hit up the pace in the good old way, while his father's crony rubbed hands gleefully and became an authority upon the reclamation of wayward and idle youth.

For four years Neil Bonner's mind had lain fallow. Little that was new had been added to it, but it had undergone a process of selection. It had, so to say, been purged of the trivial and superfluous. He had lived quick years down in the world; and up in the wilds time had been given him to organize the confused mass of his experiences. His superficial standards had been flung to the winds and new standards erected on deeper and broader generalizations. Concerning civilization, he had gone away with one set of values, had returned with another set of values. Aided, also, by the earth smells in his nostrils and the earth sights in his eyes, he laid hold of the inner significance of civilization, beholding with clear vision its futilities and powers. It was a simple little philosophy he evolved. Clean living was the way to grace. Duty performed was sanctification. One must live clean and do his duty in order that he might work. Work was salvation. And to work toward life abundant, and more abundant, was to be in line with the scheme of things and the will of God.

Primarily he was of the city. And his fresh earth grip and virile conception of humanity gave him a finer sense of civilization and endeared civilization to him. Day by day the people of the city clung closer to him and the world loomed more colossal. And day by day Alaska grew more remote and less real. And then he met

Kitty Sharon—a woman of his own flesh and blood and kind; a woman who put her hand into his hand and drew him to her, till he forgot the day and hour and the time of the year the first snow flies on the Yukon.

Jees Uck moved into her grand log house and dreamed away three golden summer months. Then came the autumn, posthaste before the downrush of winter. The air grew thin and sharp, the days thin and short. The river ran sluggishly, and skin ice formed in the quiet eddies. All migratory life departed south, and silence fell upon the land. The first snow flurries came, and the last homing steamboat bucked desperately into the running mush ice. Then came the hard ice, solid cakes and sheets, till the Yukon ran level with its banks. And when all this ceased the river stood still and the blinking days lost themselves in the darkness.

John Thompson, the new agent, laughed; but Jees Uck had faith in the mischances of sea and river. Neil Bonner might be frozen in anywhere between Chilkoot Pass and St. Michael's, for the last travelers of the year are always caught by the ice, when they exchange boat for sled and dash on through the long hours behind the flying dogs.

But no flying dogs came up the trail nor down the trail to Twenty Mile. And John Thompson told Jees Uck, with a certain gladness ill concealed, that Bonner would never come back again. Also, and brutally, he suggested his own eligibility. Jees Uck laughed in his face and went back to her grand log house. But when midwinter came, when hope dies down and life is at its lowest ebb, Jees Uck found she had no credit at the store. This was Thompson's doing, and he rubbed his hands, and walked up and down, and came to his door and looked up at Jees Uck's house, and waited. And he continued to wait. She sold her dog team to a party of miners and paid cash for her food. And when Thompson refused to honor even her coin, Toyaat Indians made her purchases and sledded them up to her house in the dark.

In February the first post came in over the ice, and John Thompson read in the society column of a five-months-old paper of the marriage of Neil Bonner and Kitty Sharon. Jees Uck held the door ajar and him outside while he imparted the information; and, when he had done, laughed pridefully and did not believe. In March, and all alone, she gave birth to a man-child, a brave bit of new life at which she marveled. And at that hour, a year later, Neil Bonner sat by another bed, marveling at another bit of new life that had fared into the world.

The snow went off the ground and the ice broke out of the Yukon. The sun journeyed north and journeyed south again; and, the money from the dogs being spent, Jees Uck went back to her own people. Oche Ish, a shrewd hunter, proposed to kill the meat for her and her babe, and catch the salmon, if she would marry him. And Imego and Hah Yo and Wy Nooch, husky young hunters all, made similar proposals. But she elected to live alone and seek her own meat and fish. She sewed moccasins and parkas and mittens—warm, serviceable things, and pleasing to the eye, withal, what of the ornamental hair tufts and beadwork. These she sold to the miners, who were drifting faster into the land each year. And not only did she win food that was good and plentiful, but she laid money by, and one day took passage on the *Yukon Belle* down the river.

At St. Michael's she washed dishes in the kitchen of the post. The servants of the company wondered at the remarkable woman with the remarkable child, though they asked no questions and she vouchsafed nothing. But just before Bering Sea closed in for the year she bought a passage south on a strayed sealing schooner. That winter she cooked for Captain Markheim's household at Unalaska, and in the spring continued south to Sitka on a whisky sloop. Later she appeared at Metlakahtla, which is near to St. Mary's on the end of the Panhandle, where she worked in the cannery through the salmon season. When autumn came and the Siwash fishermen prepared to return to Puget Sound, she embarked with a couple of families in a big cedar canoe; and with them she threaded the hazardous chaos of the Alaskan and Canadian coasts, till the strait of Juan de Fuca was passed and she led her boy by the hand up the hard pave of Seattle.

There she met Sandy MacPherson, on a windy corner, very much surprised and, when he had heard her story, very wroth—not so wroth as he might have been, had he known of Kitty Sharon; but of her Jees Uck breathed no word, for she had never believed. Sandy, who read commonplace and sordid desertion into the circumstance, strove to dissuade her from her trip to San Francisco, where Neil Bonner was supposed to live when he was at home. And, having striven, he made her comfortable, bought her tickets, and saw her off, the while smiling in her face and muttering "Damshame" into his beard.

With roar and rumble, through daylight and dark, swaying and lurching between the dawns, soaring into the winter snows and sinking to summer valleys, skirting depths, leaping chasms, piercing mountains, Jees Uck and her boy were hurled south. But she had no fear of the iron stallion; nor was she stunned by this masterful civilization of Neil Bonner's people. It seemed, rather, that she saw with greater clearness the wonder that a man of such godlike race had held her in his arms. The screaming medley of San Francisco, with its restless shipping, belching factories, and thundering traffic, did not confuse her; instead she comprehended swiftly the pitiful sordidness of Twenty Mile and the skin-lodged Toyaat village. And she looked down at the boy that clutched her hand and wondered that she had borne him by such a man.

She paid the hack driver five prices and went up the stone steps to Neil Bonner's front door. A slant-eyed Japanese parleyed with her for a fruitless space, then led her inside and disappeared. She remained in the hall, which to her simple fancy seemed to be the guest room—the show place wherein were arrayed all the household treasures with the frank purpose of parade and dazzlement. The walls and ceiling were of oiled and paneled redwood. The floor was more glassy than glare ice, and she sought standing place on one of the great skins that gave a sense of security to the polished surface. A huge fireplace—an extravagant fireplace, she deemed it—yawned in the farther wall. A flood of light, mellowed by stained glass, fell across the room, and from the far end came the white gleam of a marble figure.

This much she saw, and more, when the slant-eyed servant led the way past another room—of which she caught a fleeting glance —and into a third, both of which dimmed the brave show of the entrance hall. And to her eyes the great house seemed to hold out a promise of endless similar rooms. There was such length and breadth to them, and the ceilings were so far away! For the first time since her advent into the white man's civilization a feeling of awe laid hold of her. Neil, her Neil, lived in this house, breathed the air of it, and lay down at night and slept! It was beautiful, all this that she saw, and it pleased her; but she felt, also, the wisdom and master behind. It was the concrete expression of power in terms of beauty, and it was the power that she unerringly divined.

And then came a woman, queenly tall, crowned with a glory of hair that was like a golden sun. She seemed to come toward Jees Uck as a ripple of music across still water, her sweeping garment itself a song, her body playing rhythmically beneath. Jees Uck was herself a man-compeller. There were Oche Ish and Imego and Hah Yo and Wy Nooch, to say nothing of Neil Bonner and John Thompson and other white men that had looked upon her and felt her power. But she gazed upon the wide blue eyes and rose-white skin of this woman that advanced to meet her, and she measured her with woman's eyes looking through man's eyes; and as a man-compeller she felt herself diminish and grow insignificant before this radiant and flashing creature.

"You wish to see my husband?" the woman asked; and Jees Uck gasped at the liquid silver of a voice that had never sounded harsh cries at snarling wolf dogs, nor molded itself to a guttural speech, nor toughened in storm and frost and camp smoke.

"No," Jees Uck answered slowly and gropingly, in order that she might do justice to her English. "I come to see Neil Bonner."

"He is my husband," the woman laughed.

Then it was true! John Thompson had not lied that bleak February day when she laughed pridefully and shut the door in his face. As once she had thrown Amos Pentley across her knee and ripped her knife into the air, so now she felt impelled to spring upon this woman and bear her back and down, and tear the life out of her fair body. But Jees Uck was thinking quickly and gave no sign, and Kitty Bonner little dreamed how intimately she had for an instant been related with sudden death.

Jees Uck nodded her head that she understood, and Kitty Bonner explained that Neil was expected at any moment. Then they sat down on ridiculously comfortable chairs, and Kitty sought to entertain her strange visitor, and Jees Uck strove to help her.

"You knew my husband in the North?" Kitty asked once.

"Sure. I wash um clothes," Jees Uck had answered, her English abruptly beginning to grow atrocious.

"And this is your boy? I have a little girl."

Kitty caused her daughter to be brought, and while the children, after their manner, struck an acquaintance, the mothers indulged in the talk of mothers and drank tea from cups so fragile that Jees Uck feared lest hers should crumble to pieces between her fingers. Never had she seen such cups, so delicate and dainty. In her mind she compared them with the woman who poured the tea, and there uprose in contrast the gourds and pannikins of the Toyaat village and the clumsy mugs of Twenty Mile, to which she likened herself. She was beaten. There was a woman other than herself better fitted to bear and upbring Neil Bonner's children. Just as his people exceeded her people, so did his womenkind exceed her. They were the man-compellers, as their men were the world-compellers. She looked at the rose-white tenderness of Kitty Bonner's skin and remembered the sun-beat on her own face. Likewise she looked from brown hand to white—the one, workworn and hardened by whip handle and paddle, the other as guiltless of toil and soft as a newborn babe's. And for all the obvious softness and apparent weakness, Jees Uck looked into the blue eyes and saw the mastery she had seen in Neil Bonner's eyes and in the eyes of Neil Bonner's people.

"Why, it's Jees Uck!" Neil Bonner said when he entered. He said it calmly, with even a ring of joyful cordiality, coming over to her and shaking both her hands, but looking into her eyes with a worry in his own that she understood.

"Hello, Neil!" she said. "You look much good."

"Fine, fine, Jees Uck," he answered heartily, though secretly studying Kitty for some sign of what had passed between the two. Yet he knew his wife too well to expect, even though the worst had passed, such a sign.

"Well, I can't say how glad I am to see you," he went on. "What's happened? Did you strike a mine? And when did you get in?"

"Oo-a, I get in today," she replied, her voice instinctively seeking its guttural parts. "I no strike it, Neil. You know Cap'n Markheim, Unalaska? I cook, his house, long time. No spend money. Bime-by, plenty. Pretty good, I think, go down and see White Man's Land. Very fine, White Man's Land, very fine," she added. Her English puzzled him, for Sandy and he had sought, constantly, to better her speech, and she had proved an apt pupil. Now it seemed that she had sunk back into her race. Her face was guileless, stolidly guileless, giving no cue. Kitty's untroubled brow likewise baffled him. What had happened? How much had been said? And how much guessed?

While he wrestled with these questions and while Jees Uck wrestled with her problem—never had he looked so wonderful and great—a silence fell.

"To think that you knew my husband in Alaska!" Kitty said softly.

Knew him! Jees Uck could not forbear a glance at the boy she had borne him, and his eyes followed hers mechanically to the window where played the two children. An iron band seemed to tighten across his forehead. His knees went weak and his heart leaped up and pounded like a fist against his breast. His boy! He had never dreamed it!

Little Kitty Bonner, fairylike in gauzy lawn, with pinkest of cheeks and bluest of dancing eyes, arms outstretched and lips puckered in invitation, was striving to kiss the boy. And the boy, lean and lithe, sun-beaten and browned, skin-clad and in hair-fringed and hair-tufted *muclucs* that showed the wear of the sea and rough work, coolly withstood her advances, his body straight and stiff with the peculiar erectness common to children of savage people. A stranger in a strange land, unabashed and unafraid, he appeared more like an untamed animal, silent and watchful, his black eyes flashing from face to face, quiet so long as quiet endured, but prepared to spring and fight and tear and scratch for life at the first sign of danger.

The contrast between boy and girl was striking but not pitiful. There was too much strength in the boy for that, waif that he was of the generations of Shpack, Spike O'Brien, and Bonner. In his features, clean-cut as a cameo and almost classic in their severity, there were the power and achievement of his father, and his grandfather, and the one known as the Big Fat, who was captured by the Sea People and escaped to Kamchatka.

Neil Bonner fought his emotion down, swallowed it down, and choked over it, though his face smiled with good humor and the joy with which one meets a friend.

"Your boy, eh, Jees Uck?" he said. And then, turning to Kitty: "Handsome fellow! He'll do something with those two hands of his in this our world."

Kitty nodded concurrence. "What is your name?" she asked.

The young savage flashed his quick eyes upon her and dwelt over her for a space, seeking out, as it were, the motive beneath the question.

"Neil," he answered deliberately when the scrutiny had satisfied him.

"Injun talk," Jees Uck interposed, glibly manufacturing languages on the spur of the moment. "Him Injun talk, *nee-al,* all the same 'cracker.' Him baby, him like cracker; him cry for cracker. Him say, '*Nee-al, nee-al,*' all time him say, '*Nee-al.*' Then I say that um name. So um name all time Nee-al."

Never did sound more blessed fall upon Neil Bonner's ear than that lie from Jees Uck's lips. It was the cue, and he knew there was reason for Kitty's untroubled brow.

"And his father?" Kitty asked. "He must be a fine man."

"Oo-a, yes," was the reply. "Um father fine man. Sure!"

"Did you know him, Neil?" queried Kitty.

"Know him? Most intimately," Neil answered, and harked back to dreary Twenty Mile and the man alone in the silence with his thoughts.

And here might well end the story of Jees Uck, but for the crown she put upon her renunciation. When she returned to the North to dwell in her grand log house, John Thompson found that the P. C. Company could make a shift somehow to carry on its business without his aid. Also the new agent and the succeeding agents received instructions that the woman Jees Uck should be given whatsoever goods and grub she desired, in whatsoever quantities she ordered, and that no charge should be placed upon the books. Further, the company paid yearly to the woman Jees Uck a pension of five thousand dollars.

When he had attained suitable age, Father Champreau laid hands upon the boy, and the time was not long when Jees Uck received letters regularly from the Jesuit college in Maryland. Later on these letters came from Italy, and still later from France. And in the end there returned to Alaska one Father Neil, a man mighty for good in the land, who loved his mother and who ultimately went into a wider field and rose to high authority in the order.

Jees Uck was a young woman when she went back into the North, and men still looked upon her and yearned. But she lived straight, and no breath was ever raised save in commendation. She stayed for a while with the good sisters at Holy Cross, where she learned to read and write and became versed in practical medicine and surgery. After that she returned to her grand log house and gathered about her the young girls of the Toyaat village, to show them the way of their feet in the world. It is neither Protestant nor Catholic, this school in the house built by Neil Bonner for Jees Uck, his wife; but the missionaries of all the sects look upon it with equal favor. The latchstring is always out, and tired prospectors and trail-weary men turn aside from the flowing river or frozen trail to rest there for a space and be warm by her fire. And, down in the States, Kitty Bonner is pleased at the interest her husband takes in Alaskan education and the large sums he devotes to that purpose; and though she often smiles and chaffs, deep down and secretly she is but the prouder of him.

THE LEAGUE OF THE OLD MEN

AT the barracks a man was being tried for his life. He was an old man, a native from the Whitefish River, which empties into the Yukon below Lake Le Barge. All Dawson was wrought up over the affair, and likewise the Yukon dwellers for a thousand miles up and down. It has been the custom of the land-robbing and sea-robbing Anglo-Saxon to give the law to conquered peoples, and ofttimes this law is harsh. But in the case of Imber the law for once seemed inadequate and weak. In the mathematical nature of things, equity did not reside in the punishment to be accorded him. The punishment was a foregone conclusion, there could be no doubt of that; and though it was capital, Imber had but one life, while the tale against him was one of scores.

In fact the blood of so many was upon his hands that the killings attributed to him did not permit of precise enumeration. Smoking a pipe by the trailside or lounging around the stove, men made rough estimates of the numbers that had perished at his hand. They had been whites, all of them, these poor murdered people, and they had been slain singly, in pairs, and in parties. And so purposeless and wanton had been these killings that they had long been a mystery to the mounted police, even in the time

of the captains, and later, when the creeks realized and a governor
came from the Dominion to make the land pay for its prosperity.

But more mysterious still was the coming of Imber to Dawson
to give himself up. It was in the late spring, when the Yukon was
growling and writhing under its ice, that the old Indian climbed
painfully up the bank from the river trail and stood blinking on
the main street. Men who had witnessed his advent noted that he
was weak and tottery, and that he staggered over to a heap of
cabin logs and sat down. He sat there a full day, staring straight
before him at the unceasing tide of white men that flooded past.
Many a head jerked curiously to the side to meet his stare, and
more than one remark was dropped anent the old Siwash with so
strange a look upon his face. No end of men remembered afterward that they had been struck by his extraordinary figure, and
forever afterward prided themselves upon their swift discernment
of the unusual.

But it remained for Dickensen, Little Dickensen, to be the hero
of the occasion. Little Dickensen had come into the land with
great dreams and a pocketful of cash; but with the cash the
dreams vanished, and to earn his passage back to the States he
had accepted a clerical position with the brokerage firm of
Holbrook and Mason. Across the street from the office of Holbrook and Mason was the heap of cabin logs upon which Imber
sat. Dickensen looked out of the window at him before he went
to lunch; and when he came back from lunch he looked out of
the window, and the old Siwash was still there.

Dickensen continued to look out of the window, and he, too,
forever afterward prided himself upon his swiftness of discernment. He was a romantic little chap, and he likened the immobile
old heathen to the genius of the Siwash race, gazing calm-eyed
upon the hosts of the invading Saxon. The hours swept along, but
Imber did not vary his posture, did not by a hairsbreadth move a
muscle; and Dickensen remembered the man who once sat upright on a sled in the main street where men passed to and fro.
They thought the man was resting, but later, when they touched
him, they found him stiff and cold, frozen to death in the midst
of the busy street. To undouble him, that he might fit into a
coffin, they had been forced to lug him to a fire and thaw him out
a bit. Dickensen shivered at the recollection.

Later on Dickensen went out on the sidewalk to smoke a cigar and cool off; and a little later Emily Travis happened along. Emily Travis was dainty and delicate and rare, whether in London or Klondike she gowned herself as befitted the daughter of a millionaire mining engineer. Little Dickensen deposited his cigar on an outside window ledge where he could find it again, and lifted his hat.

They chatted for ten minutes or so, when Emily Travis, glancing past Dickensen's shoulder, gave a startled little scream. Dickensen turned about to see, and was startled too. Imber had crossed the street and was standing there, a gaunt and hungry-looking shadow, his gaze riveted upon the girl.

"What do you want?" Little Dickensen demanded, tremulously plucky.

Imber grunted and stalked up to Emily Travis. He looked her over, keenly and carefully, every square inch of her. Especially did he appear interested in her silky brown hair and in the color of her cheek, faintly sprayed and soft, like the downy bloom of a butterfly wing. He walked around her, surveying her with the calculating eye of a man who studies the lines upon which a horse or a boat is builded. In the course of his circuit the pink shell of her ear came between his eye and the westering sun, and he stopped to contemplate its rosy transparency. Then he returned to her face and looked long and intently into her blue eyes. He grunted and laid a hand on her arm midway between the shoulder and elbow. With his other hand he lifted her forearm and doubled it back. Disgust and wonder showed in his face, and he dropped her arm with a contemptuous grunt. Then he muttered a few guttural syllables, turned his back upon her, and addressed himself to Dickensen.

Dickensen could not understand his speech, and Emily Travis laughed. Imber turned from one to the other, frowning, but both shook their heads. He was about to go away, when she called out:

"Oh, Jimmy! Come here!"

Jimmy came from the other side of the street. He was a big, hulking Indian clad in approved white-man style, with an Eldorado king's sombrero on his head. He talked with Imber, haltingly, with throaty spasms. Jimmy was a Sitkan, possessed of no more than a passing knowledge of the interior dialects.

"Him Whitefish man," he said to Emily Travis. "Me savve um talk no very much. Him want to look see chief white man."

"The governor," suggested Dickensen.

Jimmy talked some more with the Whitefish man, and his face went grave and puzzled.

"I t'ink um want Cap'n Alexander," he explained. "Him say um kill white man, white woman, white boy, plenty kill um white people. Him want to die."

"Insane, I guess," said Dickensen.

"What you call dat?" queried Jimmy.

Dickensen thrust a finger figuratively inside his head and imparted a rotary motion thereto.

"Mebbe so, mebbe so," said Jimmy, returning to Imber, who still demanded the chief man of the white men.

A mounted policeman (unmounted for Klondike service) joined the group and heard Imber's wish repeated. He was a stalwart young fellow, broad-shouldered, deep-chested, legs cleanly built and stretched wide apart, and tall though Imber was, he towered above him by half a head. His eyes were cool and gray and steady, and he carried himself with the peculiar confidence of power that is bred of blood and tradition. His splendid masculinity was emphasized by his excessive boyishness—he was a mere lad—and his smooth cheek promised a blush as willingly as the cheek of a maid.

Imber was drawn to him at once. The fire leaped into his eyes at sight of a saber slash that scarred his cheek. He ran a withered hand down the young fellow's leg and caressed the swelling thew. He smote the broad chest with his knuckles, and pressed and prodded the thick muscle pads that covered the shoulders like a cuirass. The group had been added to by curious passers-by—husky miners, mountaineers, and frontiersmen, sons of the long-legged and broad-shouldered generations. Imber glanced from one to another, then he spoke aloud in the Whitefish tongue.

"What did he say?" asked Dickensen.

"Him say um all the same one man, dat p'liceman," Jimmy interpreted.

Little Dickensen was little, and what of Miss Travis? He felt sorry for having asked the question.

The policeman was sorry for him and stepped into the breach.

"I fancy there may be something in his story. I'll take him up to the captain for examination. Tell him to come along with me, Jimmy."

Jimmy indulged in more throaty spasms, and Imber grunted and looked satisfied.

"But ask him what he said, Jimmy, and what he meant when he took hold of my arm."

So spoke Emily Travis, and Jimmy put the question and received the answer.

"Him say you no afraid," said Jimmy.

Emily Travis looked pleased.

"Him say you no *skookum*, no strong, all the same very soft like little baby. Him break you, in um two hands, to little pieces. Him t'ink much funny, very strange, how you can be mother of men so big, so strong, like dat p'liceman."

Emily Travis kept her eyes up and unfaltering, but her cheeks were sprayed with scarlet. Little Dickensen blushed and was quite embarrassed. The policeman's face blazed with his boy's blood.

"Come along, you," he said gruffly, setting his shoulder to the crowd and forcing a way.

Thus it was that Imber found his way to the barracks, where he made full and voluntary confession, and from the precincts of which he never emerged.

Imber looked very tired. The fatigue of hopelessness and age was in his face. His shoulders drooped depressingly, and his eyes were lackluster. His mop of hair should have been white, but sun and weather had burned and bitten it so that it hung limp and lifeless and colorless. He took no interest in what went on around him. The courtroom was jammed with the men of the creeks and trails, and there was an ominous note in the rumble and grumble of their low-pitched voices, which came to his ears like the growl of the sea from deep caverns.

He sat close by a window, and his apathetic eyes rested now and again on the dreary scene without. The sky was overcast, and a gray drizzle was falling. It was floodtime on the Yukon. The ice was gone, and the river was up in the town. Back and forth on the main street, in canoes and poling boats, passed the people that never rested. Often he saw these boats turn aside from the street and enter the flooded square that marked the barracks' parade ground. Sometimes they disappeared beneath him, and he heard them jar against the house logs and their occupants scramble in through the window. After that came the slush of water against men's legs as they waded across the lower room and mounted the stairs. Then they appeared in the doorway, with doffed hats and dripping sea boots, and added themselves to the waiting crowd.

And while they centered their looks on him, and in grim anticipation enjoyed the penalty he was to pay, Imber looked at them and mused on their ways, and on their law that never slept, but went on unceasing, in good times and bad, in flood and famine, through trouble and terror and death, and which would go unceasing, it seemed to him, to the end of time.

A man rapped sharply on a table, and the conversation droned away into silence. Imber looked at the man. He seemed one in authority, yet Imber divined the square-browed man who sat by a desk farther back to be the one chief over them all and over the man who had rapped. Another man by the same table uprose and began to read aloud from many fine sheets of paper. At the top of each sheet he cleared his throat, at the bottom moistened his fingers. Imber did not understand his speech, but the others did, and he knew that it made them angry. Sometimes it made them very angry, and once a man cursed him, in single syllables, stinging and tense, till a man at the table rapped him to silence.

For an interminable period the man read. His monotonous, sing-song utterance lured Imber to dreaming, and he was dreaming deeply when the man ceased. A voice spoke to him in his own Whitefish tongue, and he roused up, without surprise, to look upon the face of his sister's son, a young man who had wandered away years agone to make his dwelling with the whites.

"Thou dost not remember me," he said by way of greeting.

"Nay," Imber answered. "Thou art Howkan who went away. Thy mother be dead."

"She was an old woman," said Howkan.

But Imber did not hear, and Howkan, with hand upon his shoulder, roused him again.

"I shall speak to thee what the man has spoken, which is the tale of the troubles thou hast done and which thou hast told, O fool, to the Captain Alexander. And thou shalt understand and say if it be true talk or talk not true. It is so commanded."

Howkan had fallen among the mission folk and been taught by them to read and write. In his hands he held the many fine sheets from which the man had read aloud, and which had been taken down by a clerk when Imber first made confession, through the mouth of Jimmy, to Captain Alexander. Howkan began to read. Imber listened for a space, when a wonderment rose up in his face and he broke in abruptly.

"That be my talk, Howkan. Yet from thy lips it comes when thy ears have not heard."

Howkan smirked with self-appreciation. His hair was parted in the middle. "Nay, from the paper it comes, O Imber. Never have my ears heard. From the paper it comes, through my eyes, into my head, and out of my mouth to thee. Thus it comes."

"Thus it comes? It be there in the paper?" Imber's voice sank in whisperful awe as he crackled the sheets 'twixt thumb and finger and stared at the charactery scrawled thereon. "It be a great medicine, Howkan, and thou art a worker of wonders."

"It be nothing, it be nothing," the young man responded carelessly and pridefully. He read at hazard from the document: "In that year, before the break of the ice, came an old man, and a boy who was lame of one foot. These also did I kill, and the old man made much noise——"

"It be true," Imber interrupted breathlessly. "He made much noise and would not die for a long time. But how dost thou know, Howkan? The chief man of the white men told thee, mayhap? No one beheld me, and him alone have I told."

Howkan shook his head with impatience. "Have I not told thee it be there in the paper, O fool?"

Imber stared hard at the ink-scrawled surface. "As the hunter looks upon the snow and says, 'Here but yesterday there passed a rabbit; and here by the willow scrub it stood and listened, and heard, and was afraid; and here it turned upon its trail; and here it went with great swiftness, leaping wide; and here, with greater swiftness and wider leapings, came a lynx; and here, where the claws cut deep into the snow, the lynx made a very great leap; and here it struck, with the rabbit under and rolling belly up; and here leads off the trail of the lynx alone, and there is no more rabbit'——

as the hunter looks upon the markings of the snow and says thus and so and here, dost thou, too, look upon the paper and say thus and so and here be the things old Imber hath done?"

"Even so," said Howkan. "And now do thou listen, and keep thy woman's tongue between thy teeth till thou art called upon for speech."

Thereafter, and for a long time, Howkan read to him the confession, and Imber remained musing and silent. At the end he said:

"It be my talk, and true talk, but I am grown old, Howkan, and forgotten things come back to me which were well for the head man there to know. First, there was the man who came over the Ice Mountains, with cunning traps made of iron, who sought the beaver of the Whitefish. Him I slew. And there were three men seeking gold on the Whitefish long ago. Them also I slew, and left them to the wolverines. And at the Five Fingers there was a man with a raft and much meat."

At the moments when Imber paused to remember, Howkan translated and a clerk reduced to writing. The courtroom listened stolidly to each unadorned little tragedy, till Imber told of a red-haired man whose eyes were crossed and whom he had killed with a remarkably long shot.

"Hell," said a man in the forefront of the onlookers. He said it soulfully and sorrowfully. He was red-haired. "Hell," he repeated. "That was my brother Bill." And at regular intervals throughout the session, his solemn "Hell" was heard in the courtroom; nor did his comrades check him, nor did the man at the table rap him to order.

Imber's head drooped once more, and his eyes went dull, as though a film rose up and covered them from the world. And he dreamed as only age can dream upon the colossal futility of youth.

Later Howkan roused him again, saying: "Stand up, O Imber. It be commanded that thou tellest why you did these troubles, and slew these people, and at the end journeyed here seeking the law."

Imber rose feebly to his feet and swayed back and forth. He began to speak in a low and faintly rumbling voice, but Howkan interrupted him.

"This old man, he is damn crazy," he said in English to the square-browed man. "His talk is foolish and like that of a child."

"We will hear his talk which is like that of a child," said the square-browed man. "And we will hear it, word for word, as he speaks it. Do you understand?"

Howkan understood, and Imber's eyes flashed, for he had witnessed the play between his sister's son and the man in authority. And then began the story, the epic of a bronze patriot which might well itself be wrought into bronze for the generations unborn. The crowd fell strangely silent, and the square-browed judge leaned head on hand and pondered his soul and the soul of his race. Only was heard the deep tones of Imber, rhythmically alternating with the shrill voice of the interpreter, and now and again, like the bell of the Lord, the wondering and meditative "Hell" of the red-haired man.

"I am Imber of the Whitefish people." So ran the interpretation of Howkan, whose inherent barbarism gripped hold of him, and who lost his mission culture and veneered civilization as he caught the savage ring and rhythm of old Imber's tale. "My father was Otsbaok, a strong man. The land was warm with sunshine and gladness when I was a boy. The people did not hunger after strange things, nor hearken to new voices, and the ways of their fathers were their ways. The women found favor in the eyes of the young men, and the young men looked upon them with content. Babes hung at the breasts of the women, and they were heavy-hipped with increase of the tribe. Men were men in those days. In peace and plenty, and in war and famine, they were men.

"At that time there was more fish in the water than now, and more meat in the forest. Our dogs were wolves, warm with thick hides and hard to the frost and storm. And as with our dogs so with us, for we were likewise hard to the frost and storm. And when the Pellys came into our land we slew them and were slain. For we were men, we Whitefish, and our fathers and our fathers' fathers had fought against the Pellys and determined the bounds of the land.

"As I say, with our dogs so with us. And one day came the first white man. He dragged himself, so, on hand and knee, in the snow. And his skin was stretched tight, and his bones were sharp beneath. Never was such a man, we thought, and we wondered of what strange tribe he was, and of its land. And he was weak, most weak, like a little child, so that we gave him a place by the fire, and warm furs to lie upon, and we gave him food as little children are given food.

"And with him was a dog, large as three of our dogs, and very weak. The hair of this dog was short, and not warm, and the tail was frozen so that the end fell off. And this strange dog we fed, and bedded by the fire, and fought from it our dogs, which else would have killed him. And what of the moose meat and the sun-dried salmon, the man and dog took strength to themselves; and what of the strength they became big and unafraid. And the man spoke loud words and laughed at the old men and young men, and looked boldly upon the maidens. And the dog fought with our dogs, and for all of this short hair and softness slew three of them in one day.

"When we asked the man concerning his people, he said, 'I have many brothers,' and laughed in a way that was not good. And when he was in his full strength he went away, and with him went Noda, daughter to the chief. First, after that, was one of our bitches brought to pup. And never was there such a breed of dogs —big-headed, thick-jawed, and short-haired, and helpless. Well do I remember my father, Otsbaok, a strong man. His face was black with anger at such helplessness, and he took a stone, so, and so, and there was no more helplessness. And two summers after that came Noda back to us with a man-child in the hollow of her arm.

"And that was the beginning. Came a second white man, with short-haired dogs, which he left behind him when he went. And with him went six of our strongest dogs, for which, in trade, he had given Koo-So-Tee, my mother's brother, a wonderful pistol that fired with great swiftness six times. And Koo-So-Tee was very big, what of the pistol, and laughed at our bows and arrows. 'Woman's things,' he called them, and went forth against the bald-face grizzly, with the pistol in his hand. Now it be known that it is not good to hunt the bald-face with a pistol, but how were we to know? And how was Koo-So-Tee to know? So he went against the bald-face, very brave, and fired the pistol with great swiftness six times; and the bald-face but grunted and broke in his breast like it were an egg, and like honey from a bee's nest dripped the brains of Koo-So-Tee upon the ground. He was a good hunter, and there was no one to bring meat to his squaw and children. And we were bitter, and we said, 'That which for the white man is well, is for us not well.' And this be true. There be many white men and fat, but their ways have made us few and lean.

"Came the third white man, with great wealth of all manner of wonderful foods and things. And twenty of our strongest dogs he took from us in trade. Also, what of presents and great promises, ten of our young hunters did he take with him on a journey which fared no man knew where. It is said they died in the snow of the Ice Mountains where man has never been, or in the Hills of Silence which are beyond the edge of the earth. Be that as it may, dogs and young hunters were seen never again by the Whitefish people.

"And more white men came with the years, and ever, with pay and presents, they led the young men away with them. And sometimes the young men came back with strange tales of dangers and toils in the lands beyond the Pellys, and sometimes they did not come back. And we said: 'If they be unafraid of life, these white men, it is because they have many lives; but we be few by the Whitefish, and the young men shall go away no more.' But the young men did go away; and the young women went also; and we were very wroth.

"It be true, we ate flour, and salt pork, and drank tea which was a great delight; only, when we could not get tea, it was very bad and we became short of speech and quick of anger. So we grew to hunger for the things the white men brought in trade. Trade! Trade! All the time was it trade! One winter we sold our meat for clocks that would not go, and watches with broken guts, and files worn smooth, and pistols without cartridges and worthless. And then came famine, and we were without meat, and twoscore died ere the break of spring.

" 'Now we are grown weak,' we said; 'and the Pellys will fall upon us, and our bounds be overthrown.' But as it fared with us, so had it fared with the Pellys, and they were too weak to come against us.

"My father, Otsbaok, a strong man, was now old and very wise. And he spoke to the chief, saying: 'Behold, our dogs be worthless. No longer are they thick-furred and strong, and they die in the frost and harness. Let us go into the village and kill them, saving only the wolf ones, and these let us tie out in the night that they may mate with the wild wolves of the forest. Thus shall we have dogs warm and strong again.'

"And his word was harkened to, and we Whitefish became known for our dogs, which were the best in the land. But known we were not for ourselves. The best of our young men and women had gone away with the white men to wander on trail and river to far places. And the young women came back old and broken, as Noda had come, or they came not at all. And the young men came back to sit by our fires for a time, full of ill speech and rough ways, drinking evil drinks and gambling through long nights and days, with a great unrest always in their hearts, till the call of the white men came to them and they went away again to the unknown places. And they were without honor and respect, jeering the old-time customs and laughing in the faces of chief and shamans.

"As I say, we were become a weak breed, we Whitefish. We sold our warm skins and furs for tobacco and whisky and thin cotton things that left us shivering in the cold. And the coughing sickness came upon us, and men and women coughed and sweated through the long nights, and the hunters on trail spat blood upon the snow. And now one and now another bled swiftly from the mouth and died. And the women bore few children, and those they bore were weak and given to sickness. And other sicknesses came to us from the white men, the like of which we had never known and could not understand. Smallpox, likewise measles, have I heard these sicknesses named, and we died of them as die the salmon in the still eddies when in the fall their eggs are spawned and there is no longer need for them to live.

"And yet—and here be the strangeness of it—the white men come as the breath of death; all their ways lead to death, their nostrils are filled with it; and yet they do not die. Theirs the whisky and tobacco and short-haired dogs; theirs the many sicknesses, the smallpox and measles, the coughing and mouth-bleeding; theirs the white skin, and softness to the frost and storm; and theirs the pistols that shoot six times very swift and are worthless. And yet they grow fat on their many ills, and prosper, and lay a heavy hand all over the world and tread mightily upon its peoples.

And their women, too, are soft as little babes, most breakable and never broken, the mothers of men. And out of all this softness and sickness and weakness come strength and power and authority. They be gods or devils, as the case may be. I do not know. What do I know—I, old Imber of the Whitefish? Only do I know that they are past understanding, these white men, far-wanderers and fighters over the earth that they be.

"As I say, the meat in the forest became less and less. It be true, the white man's gun is most excellent and kills a long way off; but of what worth the gun, when there is no meat to kill? When I was a boy on the Whitefish there was moose on every hill, and each year came the caribou uncountable. But now the hunter may take the trail ten days and not one moose gladden his eyes, while the caribou uncountable come no more at all. Small worth the gun, I say, killing a long way off, when there be nothing to kill.

"And I, Imber, pondered upon these things, watching the while the Whitefish, and the Pellys, and all the tribes of the land, perishing as perished the meat of the forest. Long I pondered. I talked with the shamans and the old men who were wise. I went apart that the sounds of the village might not disturb me, and I ate no meat so that my belly should not press upon me and make me slow of eye and ear. I sat long and sleepless in the forest, wide-eyed for the sign, my ears patient and keen for the word that was to come. And I wandered alone in the blackness of night to the river bank, where was wind-moaning and sobbing of water, and where I sought wisdom from the ghosts of old shamans in the trees and dead and gone.

"And in the end, as in a vision, came to me the short-haired and detestable dogs, and the way seemed plain. By the wisdom of Otsbaok, my father and a strong man, had the blood of our own wolf dogs been kept clean, wherefore they had remained warm of hide and strong in the harness. So I returned to my village and made oration to the men. 'This be a tribe, these white men,' I said. 'A very large tribe, and doubtless there is no longer meat in their land, and they are come among us to make a new land for themselves. But they weaken us, and we die. They are a very hungry folk. Already has our meat gone from us, and it were well, if we would live, that we deal by them as we have dealt by their dogs.'

"And further oration I made, counseling fight. And the men of the Whitefish listened, and some said one thing, and some another, and some spoke of other and worthless things, and no man made brave talks of deeds and war. But while the young men were weak as water and afraid, I watched that the old men sat silent, and that in their eyes fires came and went. And later, when the village slept and no one knew, I drew the old men away into the forest and made more talk. And now we were agreed, and we remembered the good young days, and the free land, and the times of plenty, and the gladness and sunshine; and we called ourselves brothers, and swore great secrecy, and a mighty oath to cleanse the land of the evil breed that had come upon it. It be plain we were fools, but how were we to know, we old men of the Whitefish?

"And to hearten the others, I did the first deed. I kept guard upon the Yukon till the first canoe came down. In it were two white men, and when I stood upright upon the bank and raised my hand they changed their course and drove in to me. And as the man in the bow lifted his head, so, that he might know wherefore I wanted him, my arrow sang through the air straight to his throat, and he knew. The second man, who held paddle in the stern, had his rifle half to his shoulder when the first of my three spear casts smote him.

" 'These be the first,' I said when the old men had gathered to me. 'Later we will bind together all the old men of all the tribes, and after that the young men who remain strong, and the work will become easy.'

"And then the two dead white men we cast into the river. And of the canoe, which was a very good canoe, we made a fire, and a fire, also, of the things within the canoe. But first we looked at the things, and they were pouches of leather which we cut open with our knives. And inside these pouches were many papers, like that from which thou hast read, O Howkan, with markings on them which we marveled at and could not understand. Now I am become wise, and I know them for the speech of men as thou hast told me."

A whisper and buzz went around the courtroom when Howkan finished interpreting the affair of the canoe, and one man's voice spoke up: "That was the lost '91 mail, Peter James and Delaney bringing it in and last spoken at Le Barge by Matthews going out." The clerk scratched steadily away, and another paragraph was added to the history of the North.

"There be little more," Imber went on slowly. "It be there on the paper, the things we did. We were old men, and we did not understand. Even I, Imber, do not now understand. Secretly we slew, and continued to slay, for with our years we were crafty and we had learned the swiftness of going without haste. When white men came among us with black looks and rough words, and took away six of the young men with irons binding them helpless, we knew we must slay wider and farther. And one by one we old men departed upriver and down to the unknown lands. It was a brave thing. Old we were, and unafraid, but the fear of far places is a terrible fear to men who are old.

"So we slew, without haste and craftily. On the Chilcoot and in the Delta we slew, from the passes to the sea, wherever the white men camped or broke their trails. It be true, they died, but it was without worth. Ever did they come over the mountains, ever did they grow and grow, while we, being old, became less and less. I remember, by the Caribou Crossing, the camp of a white man. He was a very little white man, and three of the old men came upon him in his sleep. And the next day I came upon the four of them. The white man alone still breathed, and there was breath in him to curse me once and well before he died.

"And so it went, now one old man, and now another. Sometimes the word reached us long after of how they died, and sometimes it did not reach us. And the old men of the other tribes were weak and afraid, and would not join with us. As I say, one by one, till I alone was left. I am Imber, of the Whitefish people. My father was Otsbaok, a strong man. There are no Whitefish now. Of the old men I am the last. The young men and young women are gone away, some to live with the Pellys, some with the Salmons, and more with the white men. I am very old and very tired, and it being vain fighting the law, as thou sayest, Howkan, I am come seeking the law."

"O Imber, thou art indeed a fool," said Howkan.

But Imber was dreaming. The square-browed judge likewise dreamed, and all his race rose up before him in a mighty phantasmagoria—his steel-shod, mail-clad race, the lawgiver and world-maker among the families of men. He saw it dawn red-flickering across the dark forests and sullen seas; he saw it blaze, bloody and red, to full and triumphant noon; and down the shaded slope he saw the blood-red sands dropping into night. And through it all he observed the law, pitiless and potent, ever unswerving and ever ordaining, greater than the motes of men who fulfilled it or were crushed by it, even as it was greater than he, his heart speaking for softness.

LOVE OF LIFE

This out of all will remain—
   They have lived and have tossed:
So much of the game will be gain,
   Though the gold of the dice has been lost.

THEY limped painfully down the bank, and once the foremost of the two men staggered among the rough-strewn rocks. They were tired and weak, and their faces had the drawn expression of patience which comes of hardship long endured. They were heavily burdened with blanket packs which were strapped to their shoulders. Head straps, passing across the forehead, helped support these packs. Each man carried a rifle. They walked in a stooped posture, the shoulders well forward, the head still farther forward, the eyes bent upon the ground.

"I wish we had just about two of them cartridges that's layin' in that cache of ourn," said the second man.

His voice was utterly and drearily expressionless. He spoke without enthusiasm; and the first man, limping into the milky stream that foamed over the rocks, vouchsafed no reply.

The other man followed at his heels. They did not remove their footgear, though the water was icy cold—so cold that their ankles ached and their feet went numb. In places the water dashed against their knees, and both men staggered for footing.

The man who followed slipped on a smooth boulder, nearly fell, but recovered himself with a violent effort, at the same time uttering a sharp exclamation of pain. He seemed faint and dizzy and put out his free hand while he reeled, as though seeking support against the air. When he had steadied himself he stepped forward, but reeled again and nearly fell. Then he stood still and looked at the other man, who had never turned his head.

The man stood still for fully a minute, as though debating with himself. Then he called out:

"I say, Bill, I've sprained my ankle."

Bill staggered on through the milky water. He did not look around. The man watched him go, and though his face was expressionless as ever, his eyes were like the eyes of a wounded deer.

The other man limped up the farther bank and continued straight on without looking back. The man in the stream watched him. His lips trembled a little, so that the rough thatch of brown hair which covered them was visibly agitated. His tongue even strayed out to moisten them.

"Bill!" he cried out.

It was the pleading cry of a strong man in distress, but Bill's head did not turn. The man watched him go, limping grotesquely and lurching forward with stammering gait up the slow slope toward the soft sky line of the low-lying hill. He watched him go till he passed over the crest and disappeared. Then he turned his gaze and slowly took in the circle of the world that remained to him now that Bill was gone.

Near the horizon the sun was smoldering dimly, almost obscured by formless mists and vapors, which gave an impression of mass and density without outline or tangibility. The man pulled out his watch, the while resting his weight on one leg. It was four o'clock, and as the season was near the last of July or first of August—he did not know the precise date within a week or two— he knew that the sun roughly marked the northwest. He looked to the south and knew that somewhere beyond those bleak hills lay the Great Bear Lake; also he knew that in that direction the Arctic Circle cut its forbidding way across the Canadian Barrens. This stream in which he stood was a feeder to the Coppermine River, which in turn flowed north and emptied into Coronation Gulf and the Arctic Ocean. He had never been there, but he had seen it, once, on a Hudson's Bay Company chart.

Again his gaze completed the circle of the world about him. It was not a heartening spectacle. Everywhere was soft sky line. The hills were all low-lying. There were no trees, no shrubs, no grasses —naught but a tremendous and terrible desolation that sent fear swiftly dawning into his eyes.

"Bill!" he whispered, once and twice; "Bill!"

He cowered in the midst of the milky water, as though the vastness were pressing in upon him with overwhelming force brutally crushing him with its complacent awfulness. He began to shake as with an ague fit, till the gun fell from his hand with a splash. This served to rouse him. He fought with his fear and pulled himself together, groping in the water and recovering the weapon. He hitched his pack farther over on his left shoulder, so as to take a portion of its weight from off the injured ankle. Then he proceeded, slowly and carefully, wincing with pain, to the bank.

He did not stop. With a desperation that was madness, unmindful of the pain, he hurried up the slope to the crest of the hill over which his comrade had disappeared—more grotesque and comical by far than that limping, jerking comrade. But at the crest he saw a shallow valley, empty of life. He fought with his fear again, overcame it, hitched the pack still farther over on his left shoulder, and lurched on down the slope.

The bottom of the valley was soggy with water, which the thick moss held, spongelike, close to the surface. This water squirted out from under his feet at every step, and each time he lifted a foot the action culminated in a sucking sound as the wet moss reluctantly released its grip. He picked his way from muskeg to muskeg, and followed the other man's footsteps along and across the rocky ledges which thrust like islets through the sea of moss.

Though alone, he was not lost. Farther on, he knew, he would come to where dead spruce and fir, very small and wizened, bordered the shore of a little lake, the *titchin-nichilie*, in the tongue of the country, the "land of little sticks." And into that lake flowed a small stream, the water of which was not milky. There was rush grass on that stream—this he remembered well—but no timber, and he would follow it till its first trickle ceased at a divide. He would cross this divide to the first trickle of another stream, flowing to the west, which he would follow until it emptied into the river Dease, and here he would find a cache under an upturned canoe and piled over with many rocks. And in this cache would be ammunition for his empty gun, fishhooks and lines, a small net—all the utilities for the killing and snaring of food. Also he would find flour—not much—a piece of bacon, and some beans.

Bill would be waiting for him there, and they would paddle away south down the Dease to the Great Bear Lake. And south across the lake they would go, ever south, till they gained the Mackenzie. And south, still south, they would go, while the winter raced vainly after them, and the ice formed in the eddies, and the days grew chill and crisp, south to some warm Hudson's Bay Company post, where timber grew tall and generous and there was grub without end.

These were the thoughts of the man as he strove onward. But hard as he strove with his body, he strove equally hard with his mind, trying to think that Bill had not deserted him, that Bill would surely wait for him at the cache. He was compelled to think this thought, or else there would not be any use to strive, and he would have lain down and died. And as the dim ball of the sun sank slowly into the northwest he covered every inch— and many times—of his and Bill's flight south before the down-coming winter. And he conned the grub of the cache and the grub of the Hudson's Bay Company post over and over again. He had not eaten for two days; for a far longer time he had not had all he wanted to eat. Often he stooped and picked pale muskeg berries, put them into his mouth, and chewed and swallowed them. A muskeg berry is a bit of seed enclosed in a bit of water. In the mouth the water melts away and the seed chews sharp and bitter. The man knew there was no nourishment in the berries, but he chewed them patiently with a hope greater than knowl-edge and defying experience.

At nine o'clock he stubbed his toe on a rocky ledge, and from sheer weariness and weakness staggered and fell. He lay for some time, without movement, on his side. Then he slipped out of the pack straps and clumsily dragged himself into a sitting posture. It was not yet dark, and in the lingering twilight he groped about among the rocks for shreds of dry moss. When he had gathered a heap he built a fire—a smoldering, smudgy fire—and put a tin pot of water on to boil.

He unwrapped his pack and the first thing he did was to count his matches. There were sixty-seven. He counted them three times to make sure. He divided them into several portions, wrapping them in oil paper, disposing of one bunch in his empty tobacco pouch, of another bunch in the inside band of his battered hat, of a third bunch under his shirt on the chest. This accomplished, a panic came upon him, and he unwrapped them all and counted them again. There were still sixty-seven.

He dried his wet footgear by the fire. The moccasins were in soggy shreds. The blanket socks were worn through in places, and his feet were raw and bleeding. His ankle was throbbing, and he gave it an examination. It had swollen to the size of his knee. He tore a long strip from one of his two blankets and bound the ankle tightly. He tore other strips and bound them about his feet to serve for both moccasins and socks. Then he drank the pot of water, steaming hot, wound his watch, and crawled between his blankets.

He slept like a dead man. The brief darkness around midnight came and went. The sun arose in the northeast—at least the day dawned in that quarter, for the sun was hidden by gray clouds.

At six o'clock he awoke, quietly lying on his back. He gazed straight up into the gray sky and knew that he was hungry. As he rolled over on his elbow he was startled by a loud snort, and saw a bull caribou regarding him with alert curiosity. The animal was not more than fifty feet away, and instantly in the man's mind leaped the vision and the savor of a caribou steak sizzling and frying over a fire. Mechanically he reached for the empty gun, drew a bead, and pulled the trigger. The bull snorted and leaped away, his hoofs rattling and clattering as he fled across the ledges.

The man cursed and flung the empty gun from him. He groaned aloud as he started to drag himself to his feet. It was a slow and arduous task. His joints were like rusty hinges. They worked harshly in their sockets, with much friction, and each bending or unbending was accomplished only through a sheer exertion of will. When he finally gained his feet, another minute or so was consumed in straightening up, so that he could stand erect as a man should stand.

He crawled up a small knoll and surveyed the prospect. There were no trees, no bushes, nothing but a gray sea of moss scarcely diversified by gray rocks, gray lakelets, and gray streamlets. The sky was gray. There was no sun nor hint of sun. He had no idea of north, and he had forgotten the way he had come to this spot the night before. But he was not lost. He knew that. Soon he would come to the land of the little sticks. He felt that it lay off to the left somewhere, not far—possibly just over the next low hill.

He went back to put his pack into shape for traveling. He assured himself of the existence of his three separate parcels of matches, though he did not stop to count them. But he did linger, debating, over a squat moose-hide sack. It was not large. He could hide it under his two hands. He knew that it weighed fifteen pounds—as much as all the rest of the pack—and it worried him. He finally set it to one side and proceeded to roll the pack. He paused to gaze at the squat moose-hide sack. He picked it up hastily with a defiant glance about him, as though the desolation were trying to rob him of it; and when he rose to his feet to stagger on into the day, it was included in the pack on his back.

He bore away to the left, stopping now and again to eat muskeg berries. His ankle had stiffened, his limp was more pronounced, but the pain of it was as nothing compared with the pain of his stomach. The hunger pangs were sharp. They gnawed and gnawed until he could not keep his mind steady on the course he must pursue to gain the land of little sticks. The muskeg berries did not allay this gnawing, while they made his tongue and the roof of his mouth sore with their irritating bite.

He came upon a valley where rock ptarmigan rose on whirring wings from the ledges and muskegs. "Ker—ker—ker" was the cry they made. He threw stones at them but could not hit them. He placed his pack on the ground and stalked them as a cat stalks a sparrow. The sharp rocks cut through his pants legs till his knees left a trail of blood; but the hurt was lost in the hurt of his hunger. He squirmed over the wet moss, saturating his clothes and chilling his body; but he was not aware of it, so great was his fever for food. And always the ptarmigan rose, whirring, before him, till their "Ker—ker—ker" became a mock to him, and he cursed them and cried aloud at them with their own cry.

Once he crawled upon one that must have been asleep. He did not see it till it shot up in his face from its rocky nook. He made a clutch as startled as was the rise of the ptarmigan, and there remained in his hand three tail feathers. As he watched its flight he hated it, as though it had done him some terrible wrong. Then he returned and shouldered his pack.

As the day wore along he came into valleys or swales where game was more plentiful. A band of caribou passed by, twenty and odd animals, tantalizingly within rifle range. He felt a wild desire to run after them, a certitude that he could run them down. A black fox came toward him, carrying a ptarmigan in his mouth. The man shouted. It was a fearful cry, but the fox, leaping away in fright, did not drop the ptarmigan.

Late in the afternoon he followed a stream, milky with lime, which ran through sparse patches of rush grass. Grasping these rushes firmly near the root, he pulled up what resembled a young onion sprout no larger than a shingle nail. It was tender, and his teeth sank into it with a crunch that promised deliciously of food. But its fibers were tough. It was composed of stringy filaments saturated with water, like the berries, and devoid of nourishment. He threw off his pack and went into the rush grass on hands and knees, crunching and munching, like some bovine creature.

He was very weary and often wished to rest—to lie down and sleep; but he was continually driven on, not so much by his desire to gain the land of little sticks as by his hunger. He searched little ponds for frogs and dug up the earth with his nails for worms, though he knew in spite that neither frogs nor worms existed so far north.

He looked into every pool of water vainly, until, as the long twilight came on, he discovered a solitary fish, the size of a minnow, in such a pool. He plunged his arm in up to the shoulder, but it eluded him. He reached for it with both hands and stirred up the milky mud at the bottom. In his excitement he fell in, wetting himself to the waist. Then the water was too muddy to admit of his seeing the fish, and he was compelled to wait until the sediment had settled.

The pursuit was renewed, till the water was again muddied. But he could not wait. He unstrapped the tin bucket and began to bail the pool. He bailed wildly at first, splashing himself and flinging the water so short a distance that it ran back into the pool. He worked more carefully, striving to be cool, though his heart was pounding against his chest and his hands were trembling. At the end of half an hour the pool was nearly dry. Not a cupful of water remained. And there was no fish. He found a hidden crevice among the stones through which it had escaped to the adjoining and larger pool—a pool which he could not empty in a night and a day. Had he known of the crevice, he could have closed it with a rock at the beginning and the fish would have been his.

Thus he thought, and crumpled up and sank down upon the wet earth. At first he cried softly to himself, then he cried loudly to the pitiless desolation that ringed him around; and for a long time after he was shaken by great dry sobs.

He built a fire and warmed himself by drinking quarts of hot water, and made camp on a rocky ledge in the same fashion he had the night before. The last thing he did was to see that his matches were dry and to wind his watch. The blankets were wet and clammy. His ankle pulsed with pain. But he knew only that he was hungry, and through his restless sleep he dreamed of feasts and banquets and of food served and spread in all imaginable ways.

He awoke chilled and sick. There was no sun. The gray of earth and sky had become deeper, more profound. A raw wind was blowing, and the first flurries of snow were whitening the hilltops. The air about him thickened and grew white while he made a fire and boiled more water. It was wet snow, half rain, and the flakes were large and soggy. At first they melted as soon as they came in contact with the earth, but ever more fell, covering the ground, putting out the fire, spoiling his supply of moss fuel.

This was a signal for him to strap on his pack and stumble onward, he knew not where. He was not concerned with the land of little sticks, nor with Bill and the cache under the upturned canoe by the river Dease. He was mastered by the verb "to eat." He was hunger-mad. He took no heed of the course he pursued, so long as that course led him through the swale bottoms. He felt his way through the wet snow to the watery muskeg berries, and went by feel as he pulled up the rush grass by the roots. But it was tasteless stuff and did not satisfy. He found a weed that tasted sour and he ate all he could find of it, which was not much, for it was a creeping growth, easily hidden under the several inches of snow.

He had no fire that night, nor hot water, and crawled under his blanket to sleep the broken hunger sleep. The snow turned into a cold rain. He awakened many times to feel it falling on his up-

turned face. Day came—a gray day and no sun. It had ceased rain-
ing. The keenness of his hunger had departed. Sensibility, as far as
concerned the yearning for food, had been exhausted. There was a
dull, heavy ache in his stomach, but it did not bother him so
much. He was more rational, and once more he was chiefly interested in the land of little sticks and the cache by the river Dease.

He ripped the remnant of one of his blankets into strips and
bound his bleeding feet. Also he recinched the injured ankle and
prepared himself for a day of travel. When he came to his pack he
paused long over the squat moose-hide sack, but in the end it
went with him.

The snow had melted under the rain, and only the hilltops
showed white. The sun came out, and he succeeded in locating
the points of the compass, though he knew now that he was lost.
Perhaps, in his previous days' wanderings, he had edged away too
far to the left. He now bore off to the right to counteract the possible deviation from his true course.

Though the hunger pangs were no longer so exquisite, he realized that he was weak. He was compelled to pause for frequent
rests, when he attacked the muskeg berries and rush-grass patches.
His tongue felt dry and large, as though covered with a fine hairy
growth, and it tasted bitter in his mouth. His heart gave him a
great deal of trouble. When he had traveled a few minutes it
would begin a remorseless thump, thump, thump, and then leap
up and away in a painful flutter of beats that choked him and
made him go faint and dizzy.

In the middle of the day he found two minnows in a large pool.
It was impossible to bail it, but he was calmer now and managed
to catch them in his tin bucket. They were no longer than his little finger, but he was not particularly hungry. The dull ache in his
stomach had been growing duller and fainter. It seemed almost
that his stomach was dozing. He ate the fish raw, masticating with
painstaking care, for the eating was an act of pure reason. While
he had no desire to eat, he knew that he must eat to live.

In the evening he caught three more minnows, eating two and
saving the third for breakfast. The sun had dried stray shreds of
moss, and he was able to warm himself with hot water. He had
not covered more than ten miles that day; and the next day, traveling whenever his heart permitted him, he covered no more than

five miles. But his stomach did not give him the slightest uneasiness. It had gone to sleep. He was in a strange country, too, and the caribou were growing more plentiful, also the wolves. Often their yelps drifted across the desolation, and once he saw three of them slinking away before his path.

Another night; and in the morning, being more rational, he untied the leather string that fastened the squat moose-hide sack. From its open mouth poured a yellow stream of coarse gold dust and nuggets. He roughly divided the gold in halves, caching one half on a prominent ledge, wrapped in a piece of blanket, and returning the other half to the sack. He also began to use strips of the one remaining blanket for his feet. He still clung to his gun, for there were cartridges in that cache by the river Dease.

This was a day of fog, and this day hunger awoke in him again. He was very weak and was afflicted with a giddiness which at times blinded him. It was no uncommon thing now for him to stumble and fall; and stumbling once, he fell squarely into a ptarmigan nest. There were four newly hatched chicks, a day old—little specks of pulsating life no more than a mouthful; and he ate them ravenously, thrusting them alive into his mouth and crunching them like eggshells between his teeth. The mother ptarmigan beat about him with great outcry. He used his gun as a club with which to knock her over, but she dodged out of reach. He threw stones at her and with one chance shot broke a wing. Then she fluttered away, running, trailing the broken wing, with him in pursuit.

The little chicks had no more than whetted his appetite. He hopped and bobbed clumsily along on his injured ankle, throwing stones and screaming hoarsely at times; at other times hopping and bobbing silently along, picking himself up grimly and patiently when he fell, or rubbing his eyes with his hand when the giddiness threatened to overpower him.

The chase led him across swampy ground in the bottom of the valley, and he came upon footprints in the soggy moss. They were not his own—he could see that. They must be Bill's. But he could not stop, for the mother ptarmigan was running on. He would catch her first, then he would return and investigate.

He exhausted the mother ptarmigan; but he exhausted himself. She lay panting on her side. He lay panting on his side, a dozen feet away, unable to crawl to her. And as he recovered she recovered, fluttering out of reach as his hungry hand went out to her. The chase was resumed. Night settled down and she escaped. He stumbled from weakness and pitched head foremost on his face, cutting his cheek, his pack upon his back. He did not move for a long while; then he rolled over on his side, wound his watch, and lay there until morning.

Another day of fog. Half of his last blanket had gone into foot-wrappings. He failed to pick up Bill's trail. It did not matter. His hunger was driving him too compellingly—only—only he wondered if Bill, too, were lost. By midday the irk of his pack became too oppressive. Again he divided the gold, this time merely spilling half of it on the ground. In the afternoon he threw the rest of it away, there remaining to him only the half blanket, the tin bucket, and the rifle.

A hallucination began to trouble him. He felt confident that one cartridge remained to him. It was in the chamber of the rifle and he had overlooked it. On the other hand, he knew all the time that the chamber was empty. But the hallucination persisted. He fought it off for hours, then threw his rifle open and was confronted with emptiness. The disappointment was as bitter as though he had really expected to find the cartridge.

He plodded on for half an hour, when the hallucination arose again. Again he fought it, and still it persisted, till for very relief he opened his rifle to unconvince himself. At times his mind wandered farther afield, and he plodded on, a mere automaton, strange conceits and whimsicalities gnawing at his brain like worms. But these excursions out of the real were of brief duration, for ever the pangs of the hunger bite called him back. He was jerked back abruptly once from such an excursion by a sight that caused him nearly to faint. He reeled and swayed, doddering like a drunken man to keep from falling. Before him stood a horse. A horse! He could not believe his eyes. A thick mist was in them, intershot with sparkling points of light. He rubbed his eyes savagely to clear his vision, and beheld not a horse but a great brown bear. The animal was studying him with bellicose curiosity.

The man had brought his gun halfway to his shoulder before he realized. He lowered it and drew his hunting knife from its beaded sheath at his hip. Before him was meat and life. He ran his thumb along the edge of his knife. It was sharp. The point was sharp. He would fling himself upon the bear and kill it. But his heart began its warning thump, thump, thump. Then followed the wild upward leap and tattoo of flutters, the pressing as of an iron band about his forehead, the creeping of the dizziness into his brain.

His desperate courage was evicted by a great surge of fear. In his weakness, what if the animal attacked him? He drew himself up to his most imposing stature, gripping the knife and staring hard at the bear. The bear advanced clumsily a couple of steps, reared up, and gave vent to a tentative growl. If the man ran, he would run after him; but the man did not run. He was animated now with the courage of fear. He, too, growled, savagely, terribly, voicing the fear that is to life germane and that lies twisted about life's deepest roots.

The bear edged away to one side, growling menacingly, himself appalled by this mysterious creature that appeared upright and unafraid. But the man did not move. He stood like a statue till the danger was past, when he yielded to a fit of trembling and sank down into the wet moss.

He pulled himself together and went on, afraid now in a new way. It was not the fear that he should die passively from lack of food, but that he should be destroyed violently before starvation had exhausted the last particle of the endeavor in him that made toward surviving. There were the wolves. Back and forth across the desolation drifted their howls, weaving the very air into a fabric of menace that was so tangible that he found himself, arms in the air, pressing it back from him as it might be the walls of a wind-blown tent.

Now and again the wolves, in packs of two and three, crossed his path. But they sheered clear of him. They were not in sufficient numbers, and besides, they were hunting the caribou, which did not battle, while this strange creature that walked erect might scratch and bite.

In the late afternoon he came upon shattered bones where the wolves had made a kill. The debris had been a caribou calf an hour before, squawking and running and very much alive. He contemplated the bones, clean-picked and polished, pink with the cell life in them which had not yet died. Could it possibly be that he

might be that ere the day was done! Such was life, eh? A vain and
fleeting thing. It was only life that pained. There was no hurt in
death. To die was to sleep. It meant cessation, rest. Then why was
he not content to die?

But he did not moralize long. He was squatting in the moss, a
bone in his mouth, sucking at the shreds of life that still dyed it
faintly pink. The sweet meaty taste, thin and elusive almost as a
memory, maddened him. He closed his jaws on the bones and
crunched. Sometimes it was the bone that broke, sometimes his
teeth. Then he crushed the bones between rocks, pounded them
to a pulp, and swallowed them. He pounded his fingers, too, in his
haste, and yet found a moment in which to feel surprise at the
fact that his fingers did not hurt much when caught under the descending rock.

Came frightful days of snow and rain. He did not know when
he made camp, when he broke camp. He traveled in the night as
much as in the day. He rested wherever he fell, crawled on whenever the dying life in him flickered up and burned less dimly. He,
as a man, no longer strove. It was the life in him, unwilling to die,
that drove him on. He did not suffer. His nerves had become
blunted, numb, while his mind was filled with weird visions and
delicious dreams.

But ever he sucked and chewed on the crushed bones of the caribou calf, the least remnants of which he had gathered up and
carried with him. He crossed no more hills or divides, but automatically followed a large stream which flowed through a wide
and shallow valley. He did not see this stream nor this valley. He
saw nothing save visions. Soul and body walked or crawled side by
side, yet apart, so slender was the thread that bound them.

He awoke in his right mind, lying on his back on a rocky
ledge. The sun was shining bright and warm. Afar off he heard
the squawking of caribou calves. He was aware of vague memories
of rain and wind and snow, but whether he had been beaten by
the storm for two days or two weeks he did not know.

For some time he lay without movement, the genial sunshine
pouring upon him and saturating his miserable body with its
warmth. A fine day, he thought. Perhaps he could manage to
locate himself. By a painful effort he rolled over on his side.
Below him flowed a wide and sluggish river. Its unfamiliarity

puzzled him. Slowly he followed it with his eyes, winding in wide sweeps among the bleak, bare hills, bleaker and barer and lower-lying than any hills he had yet encountered. Slowly, deliberately, without excitement or more than the most casual interest, he followed the course of the strange stream toward the sky line and saw it emptying into a bright and shining sea. He was still unexcited. Most unusual, he thought, a vision or a mirage—more likely a vision, a trick of his disordered mind. He was confirmed in this by sight of a ship lying at anchor in the midst of the shining sea. He closed his eyes for a while, then opened them. Strange how the vision persisted! Yet not strange. He knew there were no seas or ships in the heart of the barren lands, just as he had known there was no cartridge in the empty rifle.

He heard a snuffle behind him—a half-choking gasp or cough. Very slowly, because of his exceeding weakness and stiffness, he rolled over on his other side. He could see nothing near at hand, but he waited patiently. Again came the snuffle and cough, and outlined between two jagged rocks not a score of feet away he made out the gray head of a wolf. The sharp ears were not pricked so sharply as he had seen them on other wolves; the eyes were bleared and bloodshot, the head seemed to droop limply and forlornly. The animal blinked continually in the sunshine. It seemed sick. As he looked it snuffled and coughed again.

This, at least, was real, he thought, and turned on the other side so that he might see the reality of the world which had been veiled from him before by the vision. But the sea still shone in the distance and the ship was plainly discernible. Was it reality after all? He closed his eyes for a long while and thought, and then it came to him. He had been making north by east, away from the Dease Divide and into the Coppermine Valley. This wide and sluggish river was the Coppermine. That shining sea was the Arctic Ocean. That ship was a whaler, strayed east, far east, from the mouth of the Mackenzie, and it was lying at anchor in Coronation Gulf. He remembered the Hudson's Bay Company chart he had seen long ago, and it was all clear and reasonable to him.

He sat up and turned his attention to immediate affairs. He had worn through the blanket wrappings, and his feet were shapeless lumps of raw meat. His last blanket was gone. Rifle and knife were both missing. He had lost his hat somewhere, with the bunch of matches in the band, but the matches against his chest were safe and dry inside the tobacco pouch and oil paper. He looked at his watch. It marked eleven o'clock and was still running. Evidently he had kept it wound.

He was calm and collected. Though extremely weak, he had no sensation of pain. He was not hungry. The thought of food was not even pleasant to him, and whatever he did was done by his reason alone. He ripped off his pants legs to the knees and bound them about his feet. Somehow he had succeeded in retaining the tin bucket. He would have some hot water before he began what he foresaw was to be a terrible journey to the ship.

His movements were slow. He shook as with a palsy. When he started to collect dry moss he found he could not rise to his feet. He tried again and again, then contented himself with crawling about on hands and knees. Once he crawled near to the sick wolf. The animal dragged itself reluctantly out of his way, licking its chops with a tongue which seemed hardly to have the strength to curl. The man noticed that the tongue was not the customary healthy red. It was a yellowish brown and seemed coated with a rough and half-dry mucus.

After he had drunk a quart of hot water the man found he was able to stand, and even walk as well as a dying man might be supposed to walk. Every minute or so he was compelled to rest. His steps were feeble and uncertain, just as the wolf's that trailed him were feeble and uncertain; and that night, when the shining sea was blotted out by blackness, he knew he was nearer to it by no more than four miles.

Throughout the night he heard the cough of the sick wolf, and now and then the squawking of the caribou calves. There was life all around him, but it was strong life, very much alive and well, and he knew the sick wolf clung to the sick man's trail in the hope that the man would die first. In the morning, on opening his eyes, he beheld it regarding him with a wistful and hungry stare. It stood crouched, with tail between its legs, like a miserable and woebegone dog. It shivered in the chill morning wind and grinned dispiritedly when the man spoke to it in a voice that achieved no more than a hoarse whisper.

The sun rose brightly, and all morning the man tottered and fell toward the ship on the shining sea. The weather was perfect.

It was the brief Indian summer of the high latitudes. It might last a week. Tomorrow or next day it might be gone.

In the afternoon the man came upon a trail. It was of another man, who did not walk, but who dragged himself on all fours. The man thought it might be Bill, but he thought in a dull, uninterested way. He had no curiosity. In fact sensation and emotion had left him. He was no longer susceptible to pain. Stomach and nerves had gone to sleep. Yet the life that was in him drove him on. He was very weary, but it refused to die. It was because it refused to die that he still ate muskeg berries and minnows, drank his hot water, and kept a wary eye on the sick wolf.

He followed the trail of the other man who dragged himself along, and soon came to the end of it—a few fresh-picked bones where the soggy moss was marked by the foot pads of many wolves. He saw a squat moose-hide sack, mate to his own, which had been torn by sharp teeth. He picked it up, though its weight was almost too much for his feeble fingers. Bill had carried it to the last. Ha-ha! He would have the laugh on Bill. He would survive and carry it to the ship in the shining sea. His mirth was hoarse and ghastly, like a raven's croak, and the sick wolf joined him, howling lugubriously. The man ceased suddenly. How could he have the laugh on Bill if that were Bill; if those bones, so pinky-white and clean, were Bill?

He turned away. Well, Bill had deserted him; but he would not take the gold, nor would he suck Bill's bones. Bill would have, though, had it been the other way around, he mused as he staggered on.

He came to a pool of water. Stooping over in quest of minnows, he jerked his head back as though he had been stung. He had caught sight of his reflected face. So horrible was it that sensibility awoke long enough to be shocked. There were three minnows in the pool, which was too large to drain; and after several ineffectual attempts to catch them in the tin bucket he forbore. He was afraid, because of his great weakness, that he might fall in and drown. It was for this reason that he did not trust himself to the river astride one of the many drift logs which lined its sandspits.

That day he decreased the distance between him and the ship by three miles; the next day by two—for he was crawling now as Bill had crawled; and the end of the fifth day found the ship still seven miles away and him unable to make even a mile a day. Still the Indian summer held on, and he continued to crawl and faint, turn and turn about; and ever the sick wolf coughed and wheezed at his heels. His knees had become raw meat like his feet, and though he padded them with the shirt from his back it was a red track he left behind him on the moss and stones. Once, glancing back, he saw the wolf licking hungrily his bleeding trail, and he saw sharply what his own end might be—unless—unless he could get the wolf. Then began as grim a tragedy of existence as was ever played—a sick man that crawled, a sick wolf that limped, two creatures dragging their dying carcasses across the desolation and hunting each other's lives.

Had it been a well wolf, it would not have mattered so much to the man; but the thought of going to feed the maw of that loathsome and all but dead thing was repugnant to him. He was finicky. His mind had begun to wander again and to be perplexed by hallucinations, while his lucid intervals grew rarer and shorter.

He was awakened once from a faint by a wheeze close in his ear. The wolf leaped lamely back, losing its footing and falling in its weakness. It was ludicrous, but he was not amused. Nor was he even afraid. He was too far gone for that. But his mind was for the moment clear, and he lay and considered. The ship was no more than four miles away. He could see it quite distinctly when he rubbed the mists out of his eyes, and he could see the white sail of a small boat cutting the water of the shining sea. But he could never crawl those four miles. He knew that, and was very calm in the knowledge. He knew that he could not crawl half a mile. And yet he wanted to live. It was unreasonable that he should die after all he had undergone. Fate asked too much of him. And, dying, he declined to die. It was stark madness, perhaps, but in the very grip of death he defied death and refused to die.

He closed his eyes and composed himself with infinite precaution. He steeled himself to keep above the suffocating languor that lapped like a rising tide through all the wells of his being. It was very like a sea, this deadly languor that rose and rose and drowned his consciousness bit by bit. Sometimes he was all but submerged, swimming through oblivion with a faltering stroke;

and again, by some strange alchemy of soul, he would find another shred of will and strike out more strongly.

Without movement he lay on his back, and he could hear, slowly drawing near and nearer, the wheezing intake and output of the sick wolf's breath. It drew closer, ever closer, through an infinitude of time, and he did not move. It was at his ear. The harsh dry tongue grated like sandpaper against his cheek. His hands shot out—or at least he willed them to shoot out. The fingers were curved like talons, but they closed on empty air. Swiftness and certitude require strength, and the man had not this strength.

The patience of the wolf was terrible. The man's patience was no less terrible. For half a day he lay motionless, fighting off unconsciousness and waiting for the thing that was to feed upon him and upon which he wished to feed. Sometimes the languid sea rose over him and he dreamed long dreams; but ever through it all, waking and dreaming, he waited for the wheezing breath and the harsh caress of the tongue.

He did not hear the breath, and he slipped slowly from some dream to the feel of the tongue along his hand. He waited. The fangs pressed softly; the pressure increased; the wolf was exerting its last strength in an effort to sink teeth in the food for which it had waited so long. But the man had waited long, and the lacerated hand closed on the jaw. Slowly, while the wolf struggled feebly and the hand clutched feebly, the other hand crept across to a grip. Five minutes later the whole weight of the man's body was on top of the wolf. The hands had not sufficient strength to choke the wolf, but the face of the man was pressed close to the throat of the wolf and the mouth of the man was full of hair. At the end of half an hour the man was aware of a warm trickle in his throat. It was not pleasant. It was like molten lead being forced into his stomach, and it was forced by his will alone. Later the man rolled over on his back and slept.

There were some members of a scientific expedition on the whaleship *Bedford*. From the deck they remarked a strange object on the shore. It was moving down the beach toward the water. They were unable to classify it, and, being scientific men, they climbed into the whaleboat alongside and went ashore to see. And they saw something that was alive but which could hardly be called a man. It was blind, unconscious. It squirmed along the ground like some monstrous worm. Most of its efforts were ineffectual, but it was persistent, and it writhed and twisted and went ahead perhaps a score of feet an hour.

Three weeks afterward the man lay in a bunk on the whaleship *Bedford*, and with tears streaming down his wasted cheeks told who he was and what he had undergone. He also babbled incoherently of his mother, of sunny southern California, and a home among the orange groves and flowers.

The days were not many after that when he sat at table with the scientific men and ship's officers. He gloated over the spectacle of so much food, watching it anxiously as it went into the mouths of others. With the disappearance of each mouthful an expression of deep regret came into his eyes. He was quite sane, yet he hated those men at mealtime. He was haunted by a fear that the food would not last. He inquired of the cook, the cabin boy, the captain, concerning the food stores. They reassured him countless times; but he could not believe them, and pried cunningly about the lazaret to see with his own eyes.

It was noticed that the man was getting fat. He grew stouter with each day. The scientific men shook their heads and theorized. They limited the man at his meals, but still his girth increased and he swelled prodigiously under his shirt.

The sailors grinned. They knew. And when the scientific men set a watch on the man they knew. They saw him slouch for'ard after breakfast, and, like a mendicant, with outstretched palm, accost a sailor. The sailor grinned and passed him a fragment of sea biscuit. He clutched it avariciously, looked at it as a miser looks at gold, and thrust it into his shirt bosom. Similar were the donations from other grinning sailors.

The scientific men were discreet. They let him alone. But they privily examined his bunk. It was lined with hardtack; the mattress was stuffed with hardtack; every nook and cranny was filled with hardtack. Yet he was sane. He was taking precautions against another possible famine—that was all. He would recover from it, the scientific men said; and he did, ere the *Bedford's* anchor rumbled down in San Francisco Bay.

ALL GOLD CANYON

IT was the green heart of the canyon, where the walls swerved back from the rigid plan and relieved their harshness of line by making a little sheltered nook and filling it to the brim with sweetness and roundness and softness. Here all things rested. Even the narrow stream ceased its turbulent downrush long enough to form a quiet pool. Knee-deep in the water, with drooping head and half-shut eyes, drowsed a red-coated, many-antlered buck.

On one side, beginning at the very lip of the pool, was a tiny meadow, a cool, resilient surface of green that extended to the base of the frowning wall. Beyond the pool a gentle slope of earth ran up and up to meet the opposing wall. Fine grass covered the slope—grass that was spangled with flowers, with here and there patches of color, orange and purple and golden. Below, the canyon was shut in. There was no view. The walls leaned together abruptly and the canyon ended in a chaos of rocks, moss-covered and hidden by a green screen of vines and creepers and boughs of trees. Up the canyon rose far hills and peaks, the big foothills, pine-covered and remote. And far beyond, like clouds upon the border of the sky, towered minarets of white, where the Sierra's eternal snows flashed austerely the blazes of the sun.

There was no dust in the canyon. The leaves and flowers were clean and virginal. The grass was young velvet. Over the pool three cottonwoods sent their snowy fluffs fluttering down the quiet air. On the slope the blossoms of the wine-wooded manzanita filled the air with springtime odors, while the leaves, wise with experience, were already beginning their vertical twist against the coming aridity of summer. In the open spaces on the slope, beyond the farthest shadow-reach of the manzanita, poised the mariposa lilies, like so many flights of jeweled moths suddenly arrested and on the verge of trembling into flight again. Here and there that woods harlequin, the madroña, permitting itself to be caught in the act of changing its pea-green trunk to madder red, breathed its fragrance into the air from great clusters of waxen bells. Creamy white were these bells, shaped like lilies of the valley, with the sweetness of perfume that is of the springtime.

There was not a sigh of wind. The air was drowsy with its weight of perfume. It was a sweetness that would have been cloying had the air been heavy and humid. But the air was sharp and thin. It was as starlight transmuted into atmosphere, shot through and warmed by sunshine, and flower-drenched with sweetness.

An occasional butterfly drifted in and out through the patches of light and shade. And from all about rose the low and sleepy hum of mountain bees—feasting sybarites that jostled one another good-naturedly at the board, nor found time for rough discourtesy. So quietly did the little stream drip and ripple its way through the canyon that it spoke only in faint and occasional gurgles. The voice of the stream was as a drowsy whisper, ever interrupted by dozings and silences, ever lifted again in the awakenings.

The motion of all things was a drifting in the heart of the canyon. Sunshine and butterflies drifted in and out among the trees. The hum of the bees and the whisper of the stream were a drifting of sound. And the drifting sound and drifting color seemed to weave together in the making of a delicate and intangible fabric which was the spirit of the place. It was a spirit of peace that was not of death, but of smooth-pulsing life, of quietude that was not silence, of movement that was not action, of repose that was quick with existence without being violent with struggle and travail. The spirit of the place was the spirit of the peace of the living, somnolent with the easement and content of prosperity, and undisturbed by rumors of far wars.

The red-coated, many-antlered buck acknowledged the lordship of the spirit of the place and dozed knee-deep in the cool, shaded pool. There seemed no flies to vex him and he was languid with rest. Sometimes his ears moved when the stream awoke and whispered; but they moved lazily, with foreknowledge that it was merely the stream grown garrulous at discovery that it had slept.

But there came a time when the buck's ears lifted and tensed with swift eagerness for sound. His head was turned down the canyon. His sensitive, quivering nostrils scented the air. His eyes could not pierce the green screen through which the stream rippled away, but to his ears came the voice of a man. It was a steady, monotonous, singsong voice. Once the buck heard the harsh clash of metal upon rock. At the sound he snorted with a sudden start that jerked him through the air from water to meadow, and his feet sank into the young velvet, while he pricked his ears and again scented the air. Then he stole across the tiny meadow, pausing once and again to listen, and faded away out of the canyon like a wraith, soft-footed and without sound.

The clash of steel-shod soles against the rocks began to be heard, and the man's voice grew louder. It was raised in a sort of chant and became distinct with nearness, so that the words could be heard:

> "Tu'n around an' tu'n yo' face
> Untoe them sweet hills of grace.
> (D' pow'rs of sin yo' am scornin'!)
> Look about an' look aroun',
> Fling yo' sin pack on d' groun'.
> (Yo' will meet wid d' Lord in d' mornin'!)"

A sound of scrambling accompanied the song, and the spirit of the place fled away on the heels of the red-coated buck. The green screen was burst asunder, and a man peered out at the meadow and the pool and the sloping sidehill. He was a deliberate sort of man. He took in the scene with one embracing glance, then ran his eyes over the details to verify the general impression. Then, and not until then, did he open his mouth in vivid and solemn approval:

"Smoke of life an' snakes of purgatory! Will you just look at that! Wood an' water an' grass an' a sidehill! A pocket hunter's delight an' a cayuse's paradise! Cool green for tired eyes! Pink pills for pale people ain't in it. A secret pasture for prospectors and a resting place for tired burros, by damn!"

He was a sandy-complexioned man in whose face geniality and humor seemed the salient characteristics. It was a mobile face, quick-changing to inward mood and thought. Thinking was in him a visible process. Ideas chased across his face like windflaws across the surface of a lake. His hair, sparse and unkempt of growth, was as indeterminate and colorless as his complexion. It would seem that all the color of his frame had gone into his eyes, for they were startlingly blue. Also they were laughing and merry eyes, within them much of the naïveté and wonder of the child; and yet, in an unassertive way, they contained much of calm self-reliance and strength of purpose founded upon self-experience and experience of the world.

From out the screen of vines and creepers he flung ahead of him a miner's pick and shovel and gold pan. Then he crawled out himself into the open. He was clad in faded overalls and black cotton shirt, with hobnailed brogans on his feet, and on his head a hat whose shapelessness and stains advertised the rough usage of wind and rain and sun and camp smoke. He stood erect, seeing wide-eyed the secrecy of the scene and sensuously inhaling the warm, sweet breath of the canyon garden through nostrils that dilated and quivered with delight. His eyes narrowed to laughing slits of blue, his face wreathed itself in joy, and his mouth curled in a smile as he cried aloud:

"Jumping dandelions and happy hollyhocks, but that smells good to me! Talk about your attar o' roses an' cologne factories! They ain't in it!"

He had the habit of soliloquy. His quick-changing facial expressions might tell every thought and mood, but the tongue, perforce, ran hard after, repeating, like a second Boswell.

The man lay down on the lip of the pool and drank long and deep of its water. "Tastes good to me," he murmured, lifting his head and gazing across the pool at the sidehill, while he wiped his mouth with the back of his hand. The sidehill attracted his attention. Still lying on his stomach, he studied the hill formation long and carefully. It was a practiced eye that traveled up the slope to the crumbling canyon wall and back and down again to the edge of the pool. He scrambled to his feet and favored the sidehill with a second survey.

"Looks good to me," he concluded, picking up his pick and shovel and gold pan.

He crossed the stream below the pool, stepping agilely from stone to stone. Where the sidehill touched the water he dug up a shovelful of dirt and put it into the gold pan. He squatted down, holding the pan in his two hands, and partly immersing it in the stream. Then he imparted to the pan a deft circular motion that sent the water sluicing in and out through the dirt and gravel. The larger and the lighter particles worked to the surface, and these, by a skillful dipping movement of the pan, he spilled out and over the edge. Occasionally, to expedite matters, he rested the pan and with his fingers raked out the large pebbles and pieces of rock.

The contents of the pan diminished rapidly until only fine dirt and the smallest bits of gravel remained. At this stage he began to work very deliberately and carefully. It was fine washing, and he washed fine and finer, with a keen scrutiny and delicate and fastidious touch. At last the pan seemed empty of everything but water; but with a quick semicircular flirt that sent the water flying over the shallow rim into the stream he disclosed a layer of black sand on the bottom of the pan. So thin was this layer that it was like a streak of paint. He examined it closely. In the midst of it was a tiny golden speck. He dribbled a little water in over the depressed edge of the pan. With a quick flirt he sent the water sluicing across the bottom, turning the grains of black sand over and over. A second tiny golden speck rewarded his effort.

The washing had now become very fine—fine beyond all need of ordinary placer mining. He worked the black sand, a small portion at a time, up the shallow rim of the pan. Each small portion he examined sharply, so that his eyes saw every grain of it before he allowed it to slide over the edge and away. Jealously, bit by bit, he let the black sand slip away. A golden speck, no larger than a pin point, appeared on the rim, and by his manipulation of the water it returned to the bottom of the pan. And in such fashion another speck was disclosed, and another. Great was his care of them. Like a shepherd he herded his flock of golden specks so that not one should be lost. At last, of the pan of dirt nothing remained but his golden herd. He counted it, and then, after all his labor, sent it flying out of the pan with one final swirl of water.

But his blue eyes were shining with desire as he rose to his feet. "Seven," he muttered aloud, asserting the sum of the specks for which he had toiled so hard and which he had so wantonly thrown away. "Seven," he repeated, with the emphasis of one trying to impress a number on his memory.

He stood still a long while, surveying the hillside. In his eyes was a curiosity, new-aroused and burning. There was an exultance about his bearing and a keenness like that of a hunting animal catching the fresh scent of game.

He moved down the stream a few steps and took a second panful of dirt.

Again came the careful washing, the jealous herding of the golden specks, and the wantonness with which he sent them flying into the stream when he had counted their number.

"Five," he muttered, and repeated, "five."

He could not forbear another survey of the hill before filling the pan farther down the stream. His golden herds diminished. "Four, three, two, two, one," were his memory tabulations as he moved down the stream. When but one speck of gold rewarded his washing he stopped and built a fire of dry twigs. Into this he thrust the gold pan and burned it till it was blue-black. He held up the pan and examined it critically. Then he nodded approbation. Against such a color background he could defy the tiniest yellow speck to elude him.

Still moving down the stream, he panned again. A single speck was his reward. A third pan contained no gold at all. Not satisfied with this, he panned three times again, taking his shovels of dirt within a foot of one another. Each pan proved empty of gold, and the fact, instead of discouraging him, seemed to give him satisfaction. His elation increased with each barren washing, until he arose, exclaiming jubilantly:

"If it ain't the real thing, may God knock off my head with sour apples!"

Returning to where he had started operations, he began to pan up the stream. At first his golden herds increased—increased prodigiously. "Fourteen, eighteen, twenty-one, twenty-six," ran his memory tabulations. Just above the pool he struck his richest pan —thirty-five colors.

"Almost enough to save," he remarked regretfully as he allowed the water to sweep them away.

The sun climbed to the top of the sky. The man worked on. Pan by pan he went up the stream, the tally of results steadily decreasing.

"It's just booful, the way it peters out," he exulted when a shovelful of dirt contained no more than a single speck of gold.

And when no specks at all were found in several pans he straightened up and favored the hillside with a confident glance.

"Aha! Mr. Pocket!" he cried out as though to an auditor hidden somewhere above him beneath the surface of the slope. "Aha! Mr. Pocket! I'm a-comin', I'm a-comin', an' I'm shorely gwine to get yer! You heah me, Mr. Pocket? I'm gwine to get yer as shore as punkins ain't cauliflowers!"

He turned and flung a measuring glance at the sun poised above him in the azure of the cloudless sky. Then he went down the canyon, following the line of shovel holes he had made in filling the pans. He crossed the stream below the pool and disappeared through the green screen. There was little opportunity for the spirit of the place to return with its quietude and repose, for the man's voice, raised in ragtime song, still dominated the canyon with possession.

After a time, with a greater clashing of steel-shod feet on rock, he returned. The green screen was tremendously agitated. It surged back and forth in the throes of a struggle. There was a loud grating and clanging of metal. The man's voice leaped to a higher pitch and was sharp with imperativeness. A large body plunged and panted. There was a snapping and ripping and rending, and amid a shower of falling leaves a horse burst through the screen. On its back was a pack, and from this trailed broken vines and torn creepers. The animal gazed with astonished eyes at the scene into which it had been precipitated, then dropped its head to the grass and began contentedly to graze. A second horse scrambled into view, slipping once on the mossy rocks and regaining equilibrium when its hoofs sank into the yielding surface of the meadow. It was riderless, though on its back was a high-horned Mexican saddle, scarred and discolored by long usage.

The man brought up the rear. He threw off pack and saddle, with an eye to camp location, and gave the animals their freedom to graze. He unpacked his food and got out frying pan and coffeepot. He gathered an armful of dry wood, and with a few stones made a place for his fire.

"My," he said, "but I've got an appetite! I could scoff iron filings an' horseshoe nails an' thank you kindly, ma'am, for a second helpin'."

He straightened up, and while he reached for matches in the pocket of his overalls his eyes traveled across the pool to the sidehill. His fingers had clutched the matchbox, but they relaxed their hold and the hand came out empty. The man wavered perceptibly. He looked at his preparations for cooking and he looked at the hill.

"Guess I'll take another whack at her," he concluded, starting to cross the stream.

"They ain't no sense in it, I know," he mumbled apologetically. "But keepin' grub back an hour ain't goin' to hurt none, I reckon."

A few feet back from his first line of test pans he started a second line. The sun dropped down the western sky, the shadows lengthened, but the man worked on. He began a third line of test pans. He was crosscutting the hillside, line by line, as he ascended. The center of each line produced the richest pans, while the ends came where no colors showed in the pan. And as he ascended the hillside the lines grew perceptibly shorter. The regularity with which their length diminished served to indicate that somewhere up the slope the last line would be so short as to have scarcely length at all, and that beyond could come only a point. The design was growing into an inverted V. The converging sides of this V marked the boundaries of the gold-bearing dirt.

The apex of the V was evidently the man's goal. Often he ran his eye along the converging sides and on up the hill, trying to divine the apex, the point where the gold-bearing dirt must cease.

Here resided "Mr. Pocket"—for so the man familiarly addressed the imaginary point above him on the slope, crying out:

"Come down out o' that, Mr. Pocket! Be right smart an' agreeable, an' come down!"

"All right," he would add later, in a voice resigned to determination. "All right, Mr. Pocket. It's plain to me I got to come right up an' snatch you out bald-headed. An' I'll do it! I'll do it!" he would threaten still later.

Each pan he carried down to the water to wash, and as he went higher up the hill the pans grew richer, until he began to save the gold in an empty baking-powder can which he carried carelessly in his lap pocket. So engrossed was he in his toil that he did not notice the long twilight of oncoming night. It was not until he tried vainly to see the gold colors in the bottom of the pan that he realized the passage of time. He straightened up abruptly. An expression of whimsical wonderment and awe overspread his face as he drawled:

"Gosh darn my buttons, if I didn't plumb forget dinner!"

He stumbled across the stream in the darkness and lighted his long-delayed fire. Flapjacks and bacon and warmed-over beans constituted his supper. Then he smoked a pipe by the smoldering coals, listening to the night noises and watching the moonlight stream through the canyon. After that he unrolled his bed, took off his heavy shoes, and pulled the blankets up to his chin. His face showed white in the moonlight, like the face of a corpse. But it was a corpse that knew its resurrection, for the man rose suddenly on one elbow and gazed across at his hillside.

"Good night, Mr. Pocket," he called sleepily. "Good night."

He slept through the early gray of morning until the direct rays of the sun smote his closed eyelids, when he awoke with a start and looked about him until he had established the continuity of his existence and identified his present self with the days previously lived.

To dress, he had merely to buckle on his shoes. He glanced at his fireplace and at his hillside, wavered, but fought down the temptation and started the fire.

"Keep yer shirt on, Bill; keep yer shirt on," he admonished himself. "What's the good of rushin'? No use in gettin' all het up an' sweaty. Mr. Pocket'll wait for you. He ain't a-runnin' away before you can get yer breakfast. Now what you want, Bill, is something fresh in yer bill o' fare. So it's up to you to go an' get it."

He cut a short pole at the water's edge and drew from one of his pockets a bit of line and a draggled fly that had once been a royal coachman.

"Mebbe they'll bite in the early morning," he muttered as he made his first cast into the pool. And a moment later he was gleefully crying: "What'd I tell you, eh? What'd I tell you?"

He had no reel nor any inclination to waste time, and by main strength, and swiftly, he drew out of the water a flashing ten-inch trout. Three more, caught in rapid succession, furnished his break-fast. When he came to the steppingstones on his way to his hill-side, he was struck by a sudden thought, and paused.

"I'd just better take a hike downstream a ways," he said. "There's no tellin' what cuss may be snoopin' around."

But he crossed over on the stones, and with a "I really oughter take that hike" the need of the precaution passed out of his mind and he fell to work.

At nightfall he straightened up. The small of his back was stiff from stooping toil, and as he put his hand behind him to soothe the protesting muscles he said:

"Now what d'ye think of that, by damn? I clean forgot my din-ner again! If I don't watch out I'll sure be degeneratin' into a two-meal-a-day crank."

"Pockets is the damnedest things I ever see for makin' a man absent-minded," he communed that night as he crawled into his blankets. Nor did he forget to call up the hillside, "Good night, Mr. Pocket! Good night!"

Rising with the sun, and snatching a hasty breakfast, he was early at work. A fever seemed to be growing in him, nor did the increasing richness of the test pans allay this fever. There was a flush in his cheek other than that made by the heat of the sun, and he was oblivious to fatigue and the passage of time. When he filled a pan with dirt he ran down the hill to wash it; nor could he forbear running up the hill again, panting and stumbling pro-fanely, to refill the pan.

He was now a hundred yards from the water, and the inverted

V was assuming definite proportions. The width of the pay dirt steadily decreased, and the man extended in his mind's eye the sides of the V to their meeting place far up the hill. This was his goal, the apex of the V, and he panned many times to locate it.

"Just about two yards above that manzanita bush an' a yard to the right," he finally concluded.

Then the temptation seized him. "As plain as the nose on your face," he said as he abandoned his laborious crosscutting and climbed to the indicated apex. He filled a pan and carried it down the hill to wash. It contained no trace of gold. He dug deep, and he dug shallow, filling and washing a dozen pans, and was unrewarded even by the tiniest golden speck. He was enraged at having yielded to the temptation, and cursed himself blasphemously and pridelessly. Then he went down the hill and took up the crosscutting.

"Slow an' certain, Bill; slow an' certain," he crooned. "Short cuts to fortune ain't in your line, an' it's about time you know it. Get wise, Bill; get wise. Slow an' certain's the only hand you can play; so go to it, an' keep to it, too."

As the crosscuts decreased, showing that the sides of the V were converging, the depth of the V increased. The gold trace was dipping into the hill. It was only at thirty inches beneath the surface that he could get colors in his pan. The dirt he found at twenty-five inches from the surface, and at thirty-five inches, yielded barren pans. At the base of the V, by the water's edge, he had found the gold colors at the grass roots. The higher he went up the hill, the deeper the gold dipped. To dig a hole three feet deep in order to get one test pan was a task of no mean magnitude; while between the man and the apex intervened an untold number of such holes to be dug. "An' there's no tellin' how much deeper it'll pitch," he sighed in a moment's pause, while his fingers soothed his aching back.

Feverish with desire, with aching back and stiffening muscles, with pick and shovel gouging and mauling the soft brown earth, the man toiled up the hill. Before him was the smooth slope, spangled with flowers and made sweet with their breath. Behind him was devastation. It looked like some terrible eruption breaking out on the smooth skin of the hill. His slow progress was like that of a slug, befouling beauty with a monstrous trail.

Though the dipping gold trace increased the man's work, he found consolation in the increasing richness of the pans. Twenty cents, thirty cents, fifty cents, sixty cents, were the values of the gold found in the pans, and at nightfall he washed his banner pan, which gave him a dollar's worth of gold dust from a shovelful of dirt.

"I'll just bet it's my luck to have some inquisitive cuss come buttin' in here on my pasture," he mumbled sleepily that night as he pulled the blankets up to his chin.

Suddenly he sat upright. "Bill!" he called sharply. "Now listen to me, Bill; d'ye hear! It's up to you, tomorrow mornin', to mosey round an' see what you can see. Understand? Tomorrow morning, an' don't you forget it!"

He yawned and glanced across at his sidehill. "Good night, Mr. Pocket," he called.

In the morning he stole a march on the sun, for he had finished breakfast when its first rays caught him, and he was climbing the wall of the canyon where it crumbled away and gave footing. From the outlook at the top he found himself in the midst of loneliness. As far as he could see, chain after chain of mountains heaved themselves into his vision. To the east his eyes, leaping the miles between range and range and between many ranges, brought up at last against the white-peaked Sierras—the main crest, where the backbone of the Western world reared itself against the sky. To the north and south he could see more distinctly the cross systems that broke through the main trend of the sea of mountains. To the west the ranges fell away, one behind the other, diminishing and fading into the gentle foothills that, in turn, descended into the great valley which he could not see.

And in all that mighty sweep of earth he saw no sign of man nor of the handiwork of man—save only the torn bosom of the hillside at his feet. The man looked long and carefully. Once, far down his own canyon, he thought he saw in the air a faint hint of smoke. He looked again and decided that it was the purple haze of the hills made dark by a convolution of the canyon wall at its back.

"Hey, you, Mr. Pocket!" he called down into the canyon. "Stand out from under! I'm a-comin', Mr. Pocket! I'm a-comin'!"

The heavy brogans on the man's feet made him appear clumsy-footed, but he swung down from the giddy height as lightly and airily as a mountain goat. A rock, turning under his foot on the edge of the precipice, did not disconcert him. He seemed to know the precise time required for the turn to culminate in disaster, and in the meantime he utilized the false footing itself for the momentary earth contact necessary to carry him on into safety. Where the earth sloped so steeply that it was impossible to stand for a second upright, the man did not hesitate. His foot pressed the impossible surface for but a fraction of the fatal second and gave him the bound that carried him onward. Again, where even the fraction of a second's footing was out of the question, he would swing his body past by a moment's handgrip on a jutting knob of rock, a crevice, or a precariously rooted shrub. At last, with a wild leap and yell, he exchanged the face of the wall for an earth slide and finished the descent in the midst of several tons of sliding earth and gravel.

His first pan of the morning washed out over two dollars in coarse gold. It was from the center of the V. To either side the diminution in the values of the pans was swift. His lines of cross-cutting holes were growing very short. The converging sides of the inverted V were only a few yards apart. Their meeting point was only a few yards above him. But the pay streak was dipping deeper and deeper into the earth. By early afternoon he was sinking the test holes five feet before the pans could show the gold trace.

For that matter the gold trace had become something more than a trace; it was a placer mine in itself, and the man resolved to come back after he had found the pocket and work over the ground. But the increasing richness of the pans began to worry him. By late afternoon the worth of the pans had grown to three and four dollars. The man scratched his head perplexedly and looked a few feet up the hill at the manzanita bush that marked approximately the apex of the V. He nodded his head and said oracularly:

"It's one o' two things, Bill; one o' two things. Either Mr. Pocket's spilled himself all out an' down the hill, or else Mr. Pocket's that damned rich you maybe won't be able to carry him all away with you. And that'd be hell, wouldn't it, now?" He chuckled at contemplation of so pleasant a dilemma.

Nightfall found him by the edge of the stream, his eyes wrestling with the gathering darkness over the washing of a five-dollar pan.

"Wisht I had an electric light to go on working," he said.

He found sleep difficult that night. Many times he composed himself and closed his eyes for slumber to overtake him; but his blood pounded with too strong desire, and as many times his eyes opened and he murmured wearily, "Wisht it was sunup."

Sleep came to him in the end, but his eyes were open with the first paling of the stars, and the gray of dawn caught him with breakfast finished and climbing the hillside in the direction of the secret abiding place of Mr. Pocket.

The first crosscut the man made, there was space for only three holes, so narrow had become the pay streak and so close was he to the fountainhead of the golden stream he had been following for four days.

"Be ca'm, Bill; be ca'm," he admonished himself as he broke ground for the final hole where the sides of the V had at last come together in a point.

"I've got the almighty cinch on you, Mr. Pocket, an' you can't lose me," he said many times as he sank the hole deeper and deeper.

Four feet, five feet, six feet, he dug his way down into the earth. The digging grew harder. His pick grated on broken rock. He examined the rock. "Rotten quartz," was his conclusion as, with the shovel, he cleared the bottom of the hole of loose dirt. He attacked the crumbling quartz with the pick, bursting the disintegrating rock asunder with every stroke.

He thrust his shovel into the loose mass. His eye caught a gleam of yellow. He dropped the shovel and squatted suddenly on his heels. As a farmer rubs the clinging earth from fresh-dug potatoes, so the man, a piece of rotten quartz held in both hands, rubbed the dirt away.

"Sufferin' Sardanopolis!" he cried. "Lumps an' chunks of it! Lumps an' chunks of it!"

It was only half rock he held in his hand. The other half was virgin gold. He dropped it into his pan and examined another piece. Little yellow was to be seen, but with his strong fingers he crumbled the rotten quartz away till both hands were filled with glowing yellow. He rubbed the dirt away from fragment after fragment, tossing them into the gold pan. It was a treasure hole. So much had the quartz rotted away that there was less of it than there was of gold. Now and again he found a piece to which no rock clung—a piece that was all gold. A chunk, where the pick had laid open the heart of the gold, glittered like a handful of yellow jewels, and he cocked his head at it and slowly turned it around and over to observe the rich play of the light upon it.

"Talk about yer Too Much Gold diggin's!" the man snorted contemptuously. "Why, this diggin'd make it look like thirty cents. This diggin' is all gold. An' right here an' now I name this yere canyon 'All Gold Canyon,' b' gosh!"

Still squatting on his heels, he continued examining the fragments and tossing them into the pan. Suddenly there came to him a premonition of danger. It seemed a shadow had fallen upon him. But there was no shadow. His heart had given a great jump up into his throat and was choking him. Then his blood slowly chilled and he felt the sweat of his shirt cold against his flesh.

He did not spring up nor look around. He did not move. He was considering the nature of the premonition he had received, trying to locate the source of the mysterious force that had warned him, striving to sense the imperative presence of the unseen thing that threatened him. There is an aura of things hostile, made manifest by messengers too refined for the senses to know; and this aura he felt, but knew not how he felt it. His was the feeling as when a cloud passes over the sun. It seemed that between him and life had passed something dark and smothering and menacing; a gloom, as it were, that swallowed up life and made for death—his death.

Every force of his being impelled him to spring up and confront the unseen danger, but his soul dominated the panic, and he remained squatting on his heels, in his hands a chunk of gold. He did not dare to look around, but he knew by now that there was something behind him and above him. He made believe to be interested in the gold in his hand. He examined it critically, turned it over and over, and rubbed the dirt from it. And all the time he knew that something behind him was looking at the gold over his shoulder.

Still feigning interest in the chunk of gold in his hand, he listened intently and he heard the breathing of the thing behind him. His eyes searched the ground in front of him for a weapon, but they saw only the uprooted gold, worthless to him now in his extremity. There was his pick, a handy weapon on occasion; but this was not such an occasion. The man realized his predicament. He was in a narrow hole that was seven feet deep. His head did not come to the surface of the ground. He was in a trap.

He remained squatting on his heels. He was quite cool and collected; but his mind, considering every factor, showed him only his helplessness. He continued rubbing the dirt from the quartz fragments and throwing the gold into the pan. There was nothing else for him to do. Yet he knew that he would have to rise up, sooner or later, and face the danger that breathed at his back. The minutes passed, and with the passage of each minute he knew that by so much he was nearer the time when he must stand up or else—and his wet shirt went cold against his flesh again at the thought—or else he might receive death as he stooped there over his treasure.

Still he squatted on his heels, rubbing dirt from gold and debating in just what manner he should rise up. He might rise up with a rush and claw his way out of the hole to meet whatever threatened on the even footing aboveground. Or he might rise up slowly and carelessly, and feign casually to discover the thing that breathed at his back. His instinct and every fighting fiber of his body favored the mad, clawing rush to the surface. His intellect, and the craft thereof, favored the slow and cautious meeting with the thing that menaced and which he could not see. And while he debated, a loud, crashing noise burst on his ear. At the same instant he received a stunning blow on the left side of the back, and from the point of impact felt a rush of flame through his flesh. He sprang up in the air, but halfway to his feet collapsed. His body crumpled in like a leaf withered in sudden heat, and he came down, his chest across his pan of gold, his face in the dirt and rock, his legs tangled and twisted because of the restricted space at the bottom of the hole. His legs twitched convulsively several times. His body was shaken as with a mighty ague. There was a slow expansion of the lungs, accompanied by a deep sigh. Then the air was slowly, very slowly, exhaled, and his body as slowly flattened itself down into inertness.

Above, revolver in hand, a man was peering down over the edge of the hole. He peered for a long time at the prone and motionless body beneath him. After a while the stranger sat down on the edge of the hole so that he could see into it, and rested the revolver on his knee. Reaching his hand into a pocket, he drew out a wisp of brown paper. Into this he dropped a few crumbs of tobacco. The combination became a cigarette, brown and squat, with the ends turned in. Not once did he take his eyes from the body at the bottom of the hole. He lighted the cigarette and drew its smoke into his lungs with a caressing intake of the breath. He smoked slowly. Once the cigarette went out and he relighted it. And all the while he studied the body beneath him.

In the end he tossed the cigarette stub away and rose to his feet. He moved to the edge of the hole. Spanning it, a hand resting on each edge, and with the revolver still in the right hand, he muscled his body down into the hole. While his feet were yet a yard from the bottom he released his hands and dropped down.

At the instant his feet struck bottom he saw the pocket miner's arm leap out, and his own legs knew a swift, jerking grip that overthrew him. In the nature of the jump his revolver hand was above his head. Swiftly as the grip had flashed about his legs, just as swiftly he brought the revolver down. He was still in the air, his fall in process of completion, when he pulled the trigger. The explosion was deafening in the confined space. The smoke filled the hole so that he could see nothing. He struck the bottom on his back, and like a cat's the pocket miner's body was on top of him. Even as the miner's body passed on top, the stranger crooked in his right arm to fire; and even in that instant the miner, with a quick thrust of elbow, struck his wrist. The muzzle was thrown up and the bullet thudded into the dirt of the side of the hole.

The next instant the stranger felt the miner's hand grip his wrist. The struggle was now for the revolver. Each man strove to turn it against the other's body. The smoke in the hole was clearing. The stranger, lying on his back, was beginning to see dimly. But suddenly he was blinded by a handful of dirt deliberately flung into his eyes by his antagonist. In that moment of shock his grip on the revolver was broken. In the next moment he felt a smashing darkness descend upon his brain, and in the midst of the darkness even the darkness ceased.

But the pocket miner fired again and again, until the revolver was empty. Then he tossed it from him and, breathing heavily, sat down on the dead man's legs.

The miner was sobbing and struggling for breath. "Measly skunk!" he panted; "a-campin' on my trail an' lettin' me do the work, an' then shootin' me in the back!"

He was half crying from anger and exhaustion. He peered at the face of the dead man. It was sprinkled with loose dirt and gravel, and it was difficult to distinguish the features.

"Never laid eyes on him before," the miner concluded his scrutiny. "Just a common an' ordinary thief, damn him! An' he shot me in the back! He shot me in the back!"

He opened his shirt and felt himself, front and back, on his left side.

"Went clean through, and no harm done!" he cried jubilantly. "I'll bet he aimed all right, all right; but he drew the gun over when he pulled the trigger—the cuss! But I fixed 'm! Oh, I fixed 'm!"

His fingers were investigating the bullet hole in his side, and a shade of regret passed over his face. "It's goin' to be stiffer'n hell," he said. "An' it's up to me to get mended an' get out o' here."

He crawled out of the hole and went down the hill to his camp. Half an hour later he returned, leading his pack horse. His open shirt disclosed the rude bandages with which he had dressed his wound. He was slow and awkward with his left-hand movements, but that did not prevent his using the arm.

The bight of the pack rope under the dead man's shoulders enabled him to heave the body out of the hole. Then he set to work gathering up his gold. He worked steadily for several hours, pausing often to rest his stiffening shoulder and to exclaim:

"He shot me in the back, the measly skunk! He shot me in the back!"

When his treasure was quite cleaned up and wrapped securely into a number of blanket-covered parcels, he made an estimate of its value.

"Four hundred pounds, or I'm a Hottentot," he concluded. "Say two hundred in quartz an' dirt—that leaves two hundred pounds of gold. Bill! Wake up! Two hundred pounds of gold! Forty thousand dollars! An' it's yourn—all yourn!"

He scratched his head delightedly and his fingers blundered into an unfamiliar groove. They quested along it for several inches. It was a crease through his scalp where the second bullet had plowed.

He walked angrily over to the dead man.

"You would, would you?" he bullied. "You would, eh? Well, I fixed you good an' plenty, an' I'll give you decent burial, too. That's more'n you'd have done for me."

He dragged the body to the edge of the hole and toppled it in. It struck the bottom with a dull crash, on its side, the face twisted up to the light. The miner peered down at it.

"An' you shot me in the back!" he said accusingly.

With pick and shovel he filled the hole. Then he loaded the gold on his horse. It was too great a load for the animal, and when he had gained his camp he transferred part of it to his saddle horse. Even so, he was compelled to abandon a portion of his outfit—pick and shovel and gold pan, extra food and cooking utensils, and divers odd and ends.

The sun was at the zenith when the man forced the horses at the screen of vines and creepers. To climb the huge boulders the animals were compelled to uprear and struggle blindly through the tangled mass of vegetation. Once the saddle horse fell heavily and the man removed the pack to get the animal on its feet. After it started on its way again the man thrust his head out from among the leaves and peered up at the hillside.

"The measly skunk!" he said, and disappeared.

There was a ripping and tearing of vines and boughs. The trees surged back and forth, marking the passage of the animals through the midst of them. There was a clashing of steel-shod hoofs on stone, and now and again an oath or a sharp cry of command. Then the voice of the man was raised in song:

> *"Tu'n around an' tu'n yo' face*
> *Untoe them sweet hills of grace.*
> *(D' pow'rs of sin yo' am scornin'!)*
> *Look about an' look aroun',*
> *Fling yo' sin pack on d' groun'.*
> *(Yo' will meet wid d' Lord in d' mornin'!)"*

The song grew faint and fainter, and through the silence crept back the spirit of the place. The stream once more drowsed and whispered; the hum of the mountain bees rose sleepily. Down through the perfume-weighted air fluttered the snowy fluffs of the cottonwoods. The butterflies drifted in and out among the trees, and over all blazed the quiet sunshine. Only remained the hoof-marks in the meadow and the torn hillside to mark the boisterous trail of the life that had broken the peace of the place and passed on.

THE ONE THOUSAND DOZEN

DAVID RASMUNSEN was a hustler, and, like many a greater man, a man of the one idea. Wherefore, when the clarion call of the North rang on his ear, he conceived an adventure in eggs and bent all his energy to its achievement. He figured briefly and to the point, and the adventure became iridescent-hued, splendid. That eggs would sell at Dawson for five dollars a dozen was a safe working premise. Whence it was incontrovertible that one thousand dozen would bring, in the Golden Metropolis, five thousand dollars.

On the other hand, expense was to be considered, and he considered it well, for he was a careful man, keenly practical, with a hard head and a heart that imagination never warmed. At fifteen cents a dozen, the initial cost of his thousand dozen would be one hundred and fifty dollars, a mere bagatelle in face of the enormous profit. And suppose, just suppose, to be wildly extravagant for once, that transportation for himself and eggs should run up eight hundred and fifty more; he would still have four thousand clear cash and clean when the last egg was disposed of and the last dust had rippled into his sack.

"You see, Alma,"—he figured it over with his wife, the cosy dining room submerged in a sea of maps, government surveys, guide-books, and Alaskan itineraries,—"you see, expenses don't really begin till you make Dyea—fifty dollars'll cover it with a first-class passage thrown in. Now from Dyea to Lake Linderman, Indian packers take your goods over for twelve cents a pound, twelve dollars a hundred, or one hundred and twenty dollars a thousand. Say I have fifteen hundred pounds, it'll cost one hundred and eighty dollars—call it two hundred and be safe. I am creditably informed by a Klondiker just come out that I can buy a boat for three hundred. But the same man says I'm sure to get a couple of passengers for one hundred and fifty each, which will give me the boat for nothing, and, further, they can help me manage it. And . . . that's all; I put my eggs ashore from the boat at Dawson. Now let me see how much is that?"

"Fifty dollars from San Francisco to Dyea, two hundred from Dyea to Linderman, passengers pay for the boat—two hundred and fifty all told," she summed up swiftly.

"And a hundred for my clothes and personal outfit," he went on happily; "that leaves a margin of five hundred for emergencies. And what possible emergencies can arise?"

Alma shrugged her shoulders and elevated her brows. If that vast Northland was capable of swallowing up a man and a thousand dozen eggs, surely there was room and to spare for whatever else he might happen to possess. So she thought, but she said nothing. She knew David Rasmunsen too well to say anything.

"Doubling the time because of chance delays, I should make the trip in two months. Think of it, Alma! Four thousand in two months! Beats the paltry hundred a month I'm getting now. Why, we'll build further out where we'll have more space, gas in every room, and a view, and the rent of the cottage'll pay taxes, insurance, and water, and leave something over. And then there's always the chance of my striking it and coming out a millionnaire. Now tell me, Alma, don't you think I'm very moderate?"

And Alma could hardly think otherwise. Besides, had not her own cousin,—though a remote and distant one to be sure, the black sheep, the harum-scarum, the ne'er do-well,—had not he come down out of that weird North country with a hundred thousand in yellow dust, to say nothing of a half-ownership in the hole from which it came?

David Rasmunsen's grocer was surprised when he found him weighing eggs in the scales at the end of the counter, and Rasmunsen himself was more surprised when he found that a dozen eggs weighed a pound and a half—fifteen hundred pounds for his thousand dozen! There would be no weight left for his clothes, blankets, and cooking utensils, to say nothing of the grub he must necessarily consume by the way. His calculations were all thrown out, and he was just proceeding to recast them when he hit upon the idea of weighing small eggs. "For whether they be large or small, a dozen eggs is a dozen eggs," he observed sagely to himself; and a dozen small ones he found to weigh but a pound and a quarter. Thereat the city of San Francisco was overrun by anxious-eyed emissaries, and commission houses and dairy associations were startled by a sudden demand for eggs running not more than twenty ounces to the dozen.

Rasmunsen mortgaged the little cottage for a thousand dollars, arranged for his wife to make a prolonged stay among her own people, threw up his job, and started North. To keep within his schedule he compromised on a second-class passage, which, because of the rush, was worse than steerage; and in the late summer, a pale and wabbly man, he disembarked with his eggs on the Dyea beach. But it did not take him long to recover his land legs and appetite. His first interview with the Chilkoot packers straightened him up and stiffened his backbone. Forty cents a pound they demanded for the twenty-eight-mile portage, and while he caught his breath and swallowed, the price went up to forty-three. Fifteen husky Indians put the straps on his packs at forty-five, but took them off at an offer of forty-seven from a Skaguay Crœsus in dirty shirt and ragged overalls who had lost his horses on the White Pass Trail and was now making a last desperate drive at the country by way of Chilkoot.

But Rasmunsen was clean grit, and at fifty cents found takers, who, two days later, set his eggs down intact at Linderman. But fifty cents a pound is a thousand dollars a ton, and his fifteen hundred pounds had exhausted his emergency fund and left him stranded at the Tantalus point where each day he saw the fresh-whipsawed boats departing for Dawson. Further, a great anxiety brooded over the camp where the boats were built. Men worked frantically, early and late, at the height of their endurance, calking, nailing, and pitching in a frenzy of haste for which adequate explanation was not far to seek. Each day the snow-line crept farther down the bleak, rock-shouldered peaks, and gale followed gale, with sleet and slush and snow, and in the eddies and quiet places young ice formed and thickened through the fleeting hours. And each morn, toil-stiffened men turned wan faces across the lake to see if the freeze-up had come. For the freeze-up heralded the death of their hope—the hope that they would be floating down the swift river ere navigation closed on the chain of lakes.

To harrow Rasmunsen's soul further, he discovered three competitors in the egg business. It was true that one, a little German, had gone broke and was himself forlornly back-tripping the last pack of the portage; but the other two had boats nearly completed and were daily supplicating the god of merchants and traders to stay the iron hand of winter for just another day. But the iron hand closed down over the land. Men were being frozen in the blizzard, which swept Chilkoot, and Rasmunsen frosted his toes ere he was aware. He found a chance to go passenger with his freight in a boat just shoving off through the rubble, but two hundred, hard cash, was required, and he had no money.

"Ay tank you yust wait one leedle w'ile," said the Swedish boat-builder, who had struck his Klondike right there and was wise enough to know it—"one leedle w'ile und I make you a tam fine skiff boat, sure Pete."

With this unpledged word to go on, Rasmunsen hit the back trail to Crater Lake, where he fell in with two press correspondents whose tangled baggage was strewn from Stone House, over across the Pass, and as far as Happy Camp.

"Yes," he said with consequence. "I've a thousand dozen eggs at Linderman, and my boat's just about got the last seam calked. Consider myself in luck to get it. Boats are at a premium, you know, and none to be had."

Whereupon and almost with bodily violence the correspondents clamored to go with him, fluttered greenbacks before his eyes, and spilled yellow twenties from hand to hand. He could not hear of it, but they overpersuaded him, and he reluctantly consented to take them at three hundred apiece. Also they pressed upon him the passage money in advance. And while they wrote to their respective journals concerning the good Samaritan with the thousand dozen eggs, the good Samaritan was hurrying back to the Swede at Linderman.

"Here, you! Gimme that boat!" was his salutation, his hand jingling the correspondents' gold pieces and his eyes hungrily bent upon the finished craft.

The Swede regarded him stolidly and shook his head.

"How much is the other fellow paying? Three hundred? Well, here's four. Take it."

He tried to press it upon him, but the man backed away.

"Ay tank not. Ay say him get der skiff boat. You yust wait—"

"Here's six hundred. Last call. Take it or leave it. Tell'm it's a mistake."

The Swede wavered. "Ay tank yes," he finally said, and the last Rasmunsen saw of him his vocabulary was going to wreck in a vain effort to explain the mistake to the other fellows.

The German slipped and broke his ankle on the steep hogback above Deep Lake, sold out his stock for a dollar a dozen, and with the proceeds hired Indian packers to carry him back to Dyea. But on the morning Rasmunsen shoved off with his correspondents, his two rivals followed suit.

"How many you got?" one of them, a lean little New Englander, called out.

"One thousand dozen," Rasmunsen answered proudly.

"Huh! I'll go you even stakes I beat you in with my eight hundred."

The correspondents offered to lend him the money; but Rasmunsen declined, and the Yankee closed with the remaining rival, a brawny son of the sea and sailor of ships and things, who promised to show them all a wrinkle or two when it came to cracking on. And crack on he did, with a large tarpaulin squaresail which pressed the bow half under at every jump. He was the first to run out of Linderman, but, disdaining the portage, piled his loaded boat on the rocks in the boiling rapids. Rasmunsen and the Yankee, who likewise had two passengers, portaged across on their backs and then lined their empty boats down through the bad water to Bennett.

Bennett was a twenty-five-mile lake, narrow and deep, a funnel between the mountains through which storms ever romped. Rasmunsen camped on the sand-pit at its head, where were many men and boats bound north in the teeth of the Arctic winter. He awoke in the morning to find a piping gale from the south, which caught the chill from the whited peaks and glacial valleys and blew as cold as north wind ever blew. But it was fair, and he also found the Yankee staggering past the first bold headland with all sail set. Boat after boat was getting under way, and the correspondents fell to with enthusiasm.

"We'll catch him before Cariboo Crossing," they assured Rasmunsen, as they ran up the sail and the *Alma* took the first icy spray over her bow.

Now Rasmunsen all his life had been prone to cowardice on water, but he clung to the kicking steering-oar with set face and determined jaw. His thousand dozen were there in the boat before his eyes, safely secured beneath the correspondents' baggage, and somehow, before his eyes, were the little cottage and the mortgage for a thousand dollars.

It was bitter cold. Now and again he hauled in the steering-sweep and put out a fresh one while his passengers chopped the ice from the blade. Wherever the spray struck, it turned instantly to frost, and the dipping broom of the spritsail was quickly fringed with icicles. The *Alma* strained and hammered through the big sails till the seams and butts began to spread, but in lieu of bailing the correspondents chopped ice and flung it overboard. There was no let-up. The mad race with winter was on, and the boats tore along in a desperate string.

"W-w-we can't stop to save our souls!" one of the correspondents chattered, from cold, not fright.

"That's right! Keep her down the middle, old man!" the other encouraged.

Rasmunsen replied with an idiotic grin. The iron-bound shores were in a lather of foam, and even down the middle the only hope was to keep running away from the big seas. To lower sail was to be overtaken and swamped. Time and again they passed boats pounding among the rocks, and once they saw one on the edge of the breakers about to strike. A little craft behind them, with two men, jibed over and turned bottom up.

"W-w-watch out, old man!" cried he of the chattering teeth.

Rasmunsen grinned and tightened his aching grip on the sweep. Scores of times had the send of the sea caught the big square stern of the *Alma* and thrown her off from dead before it till the after leach of the spritsail fluttered hollowly, and each time, and only with all his strength, had he forced her back. His grin by then had become fixed, and it disturbed the correspondents to look at him.

They roared down past an isolated rock a hundred yards from shore. From its wave-drenched top a man shrieked wildly, for the instant cutting the storm with his voice. But the next instant the *Alma* was by, and the rock growing a black speck in the troubled froth.

"That settles the Yankee! Where's the sailor?" shouted one of his passengers.

Rasmunsen shot a glance over his shoulder at a black squaresail. He had seen it leap up out of the gray to windward, and for an hour, off and on, had been watching it grow. The sailor had evidently repaired damages and was making up for lost time.

"Look at him come!"

Both passengers stopped chopping ice to watch. Twenty miles of Bennett were behind them—room and to spare for the sea to toss up its mountains toward the sky. Sinking and soaring like a storm god, the sailor drove by them. The huge sail seemed to grip the boat from the crests of the waves, to tear it bodily out of the water, and fling it crashing and smothering down into the yawning troughs.

"The sea'll never catch him!"

"But he'll r-r-run her nose under!"

Even as they spoke, the black tarpaulin swooped from sight behind a big comber. The next wave rolled over the spot, and the next, but the boat did not reappear. The *Alma* rushed by the place. A little riffraff of oars and boxes was seen. An arm thrust up and a shaggy head broke surface a score of yards away.

For a time there was silence. As the end of the lake came in sight, the waves began to leap aboard with such steady recurrence that the correspondents no longer chopped ice but flung the water out with buckets. Even this would not do, and, after a shouted conference with Rasmunsen, they attacked the baggage. Flour, bacon, beans, blankets, cooking stove, ropes, odds and ends, everything they could get hands on, flew overboard. The boat acknowledged it at once, taking less water and rising more buoyantly.

"That'll do!" Rasmunsen called sternly, as they applied themselves to the top layer of eggs.

"The h-hell it will!" answered the shivering one, savagely. With the exception of their notes, films, and cameras, they had sacrificed their outfit. He bent over, laid hold of an egg-box, and began to worry it out from under the lashing.

"Drop it! Drop it, I say!"

Rasmunsen had managed to draw his revolver, and with the crook of his arm over the sweep head was taking aim. The correspondent stood up on the thwart, balancing back and forth, his face twisted with menace and speechless anger.

"My God!"

So cried his brother correspondent, hurling himself, face downward, into the bottom of the boat. The *Alma*, under the divided attention of Rasmunsen, had been caught by a great mass of water and whirled around. The after leach hollowed, the sail emptied and jibed, and the boom, sweeping with terrific force across the boat, carried the angry correspondent overboard with a broken back. Mast and sail had gone over the side as well. A drenching sea followed, as the boat lost headway, and Rasmunsen sprang to the bailing bucket.

Several boats hurtled past them in the next half-hour,—small boats, boats of their own size, boats afraid, unable to do aught but run madly on. Then a ten-ton barge, at imminent risk of destruction, lowered sail to windward and lumbered down upon them.

"Keep off! Keep off!" Rasmunsen screamed.

But his low gunwale ground against the heavy craft, and the remaining correspondent clambered aboard. Rasmunsen was over the eggs like a cat and in the bow of the *Alma*, striving with numb fingers to bend the hauling-lines together.

"Come on!" a red-whiskered man yelled at him.

"I've a thousand dozen eggs here," he shouted back. "Gimme a tow! I'll pay you!"

"Come on!" they howled in chorus.

A big whitecap broke just beyond, washing over the barge and leaving the *Alma* half swamped. The men cast off, cursing him as they ran up their sail. Rasmunsen cursed back and fell to bailing. The mast and sail, like a sea anchor, still fast by the halyards, held the boat head on to wind and sea and gave him a chance to fight the water out.

Three hours later, numbed, exhausted, blathering like a lunatic, but still bailing, he went ashore on an ice-strewn beach near Cariboo Crossing. Two men, a government courier and a half-breed voyageur, dragged him out of the surf, saved his cargo, and beached the *Alma*. They were paddling out of the country in a Peterborough, and gave him shelter for the night in their storm-bound camp. Next morning they departed, but he elected to stay by his eggs. And thereafter the name and fame of the man with the thousand dozen eggs began to spread through the land. Gold-seekers who made in before the freeze-up carried the news of his coming. Grizzled old-timers of Forty Mile and Circle City, sour doughs with leathern jaws and bean-calloused stomachs, called up dream memories of chickens and green things at mention of his name. Dyea and Skaguay took an interest in his being, and questioned his progress from every man who came over the passes, while Dawson—golden, omeletless Dawson—fretted and worried, and waylaid every chance arrival for word of him.

But of this, Rasmunsen knew nothing. The day after the wreck he patched up the *Alma* and pulled out. A cruel east wind blew in his teeth from Tagish, but he got the oars over the side and bucked manfully into it, though half the time he was drifting backward and chopping ice from the blades. According to the custom of the country, he was driven ashore at Windy Arm; three times on Tagish saw him swamped and beached; and Lake Marsh held him at the freeze-up. The *Alma* was crushed in the jamming of the floes, but the eggs were intact. These he back-tripped two miles across the ice to the shore, where he built a caché, which stood for years after and was pointed out by men who knew.

Half a thousand frozen miles stretched between him and Dawson, and the waterway was closed. But Rasmunsen, with a peculiar tense look in his face, struck back up the lakes on foot. What he suffered on that lone trip, with naught but a single blanket, an axe, and a handful of beans, is not given to ordinary mortals to know. Only the Arctic adventurer may understand. Suffice that he was caught in a blizzard on Chilkoot and left two of his toes with the surgeon at Sheep Camp. Yet he stood on his feet and washed dishes in the scullery of the *Pawona* to the Puget Sound, and from there passed coal on a P.S. boat to San Francisco.

It was a haggard, unkempt man who limped across the shining office floor to raise a second mortgage from the bank people. His hollow cheeks betrayed themselves through the scraggly beard, and his eyes seemed to have retired into deep caverns where they burned with cold fires. His hands were grained from exposure and hard work, and the nails were rimmed with tight-packed dirt and coal dust. He spoke vaguely of eggs and ice-packs, winds and tides; but when they declined to let him have more than a second thousand, his talk became incoherent, concerning itself chiefly with the price of dogs and dog-food, and such things as snowshoes and moccasins and winter trails. They let him have fifteen hundred, which was more than the cottage warranted, and breathed easier when he scrawled his signature and passed out the door.

Two weeks later he went over Chilkoot with three dog sleds of five dogs each. One team he drove, the two Indians with him driving the others. At Lake Marsh they broke out the caché and loaded up. But there was no trail. He was the first in over the ice, and to him fell the task of packing the snow and hammering away through the rough river jams. Behind him he often observed a camp-fire smoke trickling thinly up through the quiet air, and he wondered why the people did not overtake him. For he was a stranger to the land and did not understand. Nor could he understand his Indians when they tried to explain. This they conceived to be a hardship, but when they balked and refused to break camp of mornings, he drove them to their work at pistol point.

When he slipped through an ice bridge near the White Horse and froze his foot, tender yet and oversensitive from the previous freezing, the Indians looked for him to lie up. But he sacrificed a blanket, and, with his foot incased in an enormous moccasin, big as a water-bucket, continued to take his regular turn with the front sled. Here was the cruelest work, and they respected him, though on the side they rapped their foreheads with their knuckles and significantly shook their heads. One night they tried to run away, but the zip-zip of his bullets in the snow brought them back, snarling but convinced. Whereupon, being only savage Chilkat men, they put their heads together to kill him; but he slept like a cat, and, waking or sleeping, the chance never came.

Often they tried to tell him the import of the smoke wreath in the rear, but he could not comprehend and grew suspicious of them. And when they sulked or shirked, he was quick to let drive at them between the eyes, and quick to cool their heated souls with sight of his ready revolver.

And so it went—with mutinous men, wild dogs, and a trail that broke the heart. He fought the men to stay with him, fought the dogs to keep them away from the eggs, fought the ice, the cold, and the pain of his foot, which would not heal. As fast as the young tissue renewed, it was bitten and seared by the frost, so that a running sore developed, into which he could almost shove his fist. In the mornings, when he first put his weight upon it, his head went dizzy, and he was near to fainting from the pain; but later on in the day it usually grew numb, to recommence when he crawled into his blankets and tried to sleep. Yet he, who had been a clerk and sat at a desk all his days, toiled till the Indians were exhausted, and even outworked the dogs. How hard he worked, how much he suffered, he did not know. Being a man of the one idea, now that the idea had come, it mastered him. In the foreground of his consciousness was Dawson, in the background his thousand dozen eggs, and midway between the two his ego fluttered, striving alway to draw them together to a glittering golden point. This golden point was the five thousand dollars, the consummation of the idea and the point of departure for whatever new idea might present itself. For the rest, he was a mere automaton. He was unaware of other things, seeing them as through a glass darkly, and giving them no thought. The work of his hands he did with machine-like wisdom; likewise the work of his head. So the look on his face grew very tense, till even the Indians were afraid of it, and marvelled at the strange white man who had made them slaves and forced them to toil with such foolishness.

Then came a snap on Lake Le Barge, when the cold of outer space smote the tip of the planet, and the frost ranged sixty and odd degrees below zero. Here, laboring with open mouth that he might breathe more freely, he chilled his lungs, and for the rest of the trip he was troubled with a dry, hacking cough, especially irritable in smoke of camp or under stress of undue exertion. On the Thirty Mile river he found much open water, spanned by precarious ice bridges and fringed with narrow rim ice, tricky and uncer-

tain. The rim ice was impossible to reckon on, and he dared it
without reckoning, falling back on his revolver when his drivers
demurred. But on the ice bridges, covered with snow though they
were, precautions could be taken. These they crossed on their
snowshoes, with long poles, held crosswise in their hands, to
which to cling in case of accident. Once over, the dogs were
called to follow. And on such a bridge, where the absence of the
centre ice was masked by the snow, one of the Indians met his
end. He went through as quickly and as neatly as a knife through
thin cream, and the current swept him from view down under the
stream ice.

That night his mate fled away through the pale moonlight, Rasmunsen futilely puncturing the silence with his revolver—a thing
that he handled with more celerity than cleverness. Thirty-six
hours later the Indian made a police camp on the Big Salmon.

"Um—um—um funny mans—what you call?—top um head all
loose," the interpreter explained to the puzzled captain. "Eh?
Yep, clazy, much clazy mans. Eggs, eggs, all a time eggs—savvy?
Come bime-by."

It was several days before Rasmunsen arrived, the three sleds
lashed together, and all the dogs in a single team. It was awkward,
and where the going was bad he was compelled to back-trip it sled
by sled, though he managed most of the time, through herculean
efforts, to bring all along on the one haul. He did not seem moved
when the captain of police told him his man was hitting the high
places for Dawson, and was by that time, probably, halfway between Selkirk and Stewart. Nor did he appear interested when informed that the police had broken the trail as far as Pelly; for he
had attained to a fatalistic acceptance of all natural dispensations,
good or ill. But when they told him that Dawson was in the bitter
clutch of famine, he smiled, threw the harness on his dogs, and
pulled out.

But it was at his next halt that the mystery of the smoke was
explained. With the word at Big Salmon that the trail was broken
to Pelly, there was no longer any need for the smoke wreath to
linger in his wake; and Rasmunsen, crouching over his lonely fire,
saw a motley string of sleds go by. First came the courier and the
half-breed who had hauled him out from Bennett; then mail-car-
riers for Circle City, two sleds of them, and a mixed following of

ingoing Klondikers. Dogs and men were fresh and fat, while Rasmunsen and his brutes were jaded and worn down to the skin and bone. They of the smoke wreath had travelled one day in three, resting and reserving their strength for the dash to come when broken trail was met with; while each day he had plunged and floundered forward, breaking the spirit of his dogs and robbing them of their mettle.

As for himself, he was unbreakable. They thanked him kindly for his efforts in their behalf, those fat, fresh men,—thanked him kindly, with broad grins and ribald laughter; and now, when he understood, he made no answer. Nor did he cherish silent bitterness. It was immaterial. The idea—the fact behind the idea—was not changed. Here he was and his thousand dozen; there was Dawson; the problem was unaltered.

At the Little Salmon, being short of dog food, the dogs got into his grub, and from there to Selkirk he lived on beans—coarse, brown beans, big beans, grossly nutritive, which griped his stomach and doubled him up at two-hour intervals. But the Factor at Selkirk had a notice on the door of the Post to the effect that no steamer had been up the Yukon for two years, and in consequence grub was beyond price. He offered to swap flour, however, at the rate of a cupful for each egg, but Rasmunsen shook his head and hit the trail. Below the Post he managed to buy frozen horse hide for the dogs, the horses having been slain by the Chilkat cattle men, and the scraps and offal preserved by the Indians. He tackled the hide himself, but the hair worked into the bean sores of his mouth, and was beyond endurance.

Here at Selkirk, he met the forerunners of the hungry exodus of Dawson, and from there on they crept over the trail, a dismal throng. "No grub!" was the song they sang. "No grub, and had to go." "Everbody holding candles for a rise in the spring." "Flour dollar'n a half a pound, and no sellers."

"Eggs?" one of them answered. "Dollar apiece, but they ain't none."

Rasmunsen made a rapid calculation. "Twelve thousand dollars," he said aloud.

"Hey?" the man asked.

"Nothing," he answered, and *mushed* the dogs along.

When he arrived at Stewart River, seventy miles from Dawson, five of his dogs were gone, and the remainder were falling in the traces. He, also, was in the traces, hauling with what little strength was left in him. Even then he was barely crawling along ten miles a day. His cheek-bones and nose, frostbitten again and again, were turned bloody-black and hideous. The thumb, which was separated from the fingers by the gee-pole, had likewise been nipped and gave him great pain. The monstrous moccasin still incased his foot, and strange pains were beginning to rack the leg. At Sixty Mile, the last beans, which he had been rationing for some time, were finished; yet he steadfastly refused to touch the eggs. He could not reconcile his mind to the legitimacy of it, and staggered and fell along the way to Indian River. Here a fresh-killed moose and an open-handed old-timer gave him and his dogs new strength, and at Ainslie's he felt repaid for it all when a stampede, ripe from Dawson in five hours, was sure he could get a dollar and a quarter for every egg he possessed.

He came up the steep bank by the Dawson barracks with fluttering heart and shaking knees. The dogs were so weak that he was forced to rest them, and, waiting, he leaned limply against the gee-pole. A man, an eminently decorous-looking man, came sauntering by in a great bearskin coat. He glanced at Rasmunsen curiously, then stopped and ran a speculative eye over the dogs and the three lashed sleds.

"What you got?" he asked.

"Eggs," Rasmunsen answered huskily, hardly able to pitch his voice above a whisper.

"Eggs! Whoopee! Whoopee!" He sprang up into the air, gyrated madly, and finished with half a dozen war steps. "You don't say—all of 'em?"

"All of 'em."

"Say, you must be the Egg Man." He walked around and viewed Rasmunsen from the other side. "Come, now, ain't you the Egg Man?"

Rasmunsen didn't know, but supposed he was, and the man sobered down a bit.

"What d'ye expect to get for 'em?" he asked cautiously.

Rasmunsen became audacious. "Dollar'n a half," he said.

"Done!" the man came back promptly. "Gimme a dozen."

"I—I mean a dollar'n a half apiece," Rasmunsen hesitatingly explained.

"Sure. I heard you. Make it two dozen. Here's the dust."

The man pulled out a healthy gold sack the size of a small sausage and knocked it negligently against the gee-pole. Rasmunsen felt a strange trembling in the pit of his stomach, a tickling of the nostrils, and an almost overwhelming desire to sit down and cry. But a curious, wide-eyed crowd was beginning to collect, and man after man was calling out for eggs. He was without scales, but the man with the bearskin coat fetched a pair and obligingly weighed in the dust while Rasmunsen passed out the goods. Soon there was a pushing and shoving and shouldering, and a great clamor. Everybody wanted to buy and to be served first. And as the excitement grew, Rasmunsen cooled down. This would never do. There must be something behind the fact of their buying so eagerly. It would be wiser if he rested first and sized up the market. Perhaps eggs were worth two dollars apiece. Anyway, whenever he wished to sell, he was sure of a dollar and a half. "Stop!" he cried, when a couple of hundred had been sold. "No more now. I'm played out. I've got to get a cabin, and then you can come and see me."

A groan went up at this, but the man with the bearskin coat approved. Twenty-four of the frozen eggs went rattling in his capacious pockets and he didn't care whether the rest of the town ate or not. Besides, he could see Rasmunsen was on his last legs.

"There's a cabin right around the second corner from the Monte Carlo," he told him—"the one with the sody-bottle window. It ain't mine, but I've got charge of it. Rents for ten a day and cheap for the money. You move right in, and I'll see you later. Don't forget the sody-bottle window."

"Tra-la-loo!" he called back a moment later. "I'm goin' up the hill to eat eggs and dream of home."

On his way to the cabin, Rasmunsen recollected he was hungry and bought a small supply of provisions at the N. A. T. & T. store —also a beefsteak at the butcher shop and dried salmon for the dogs. He found the cabin without difficulty and left the dogs in the harness while he started the fire and got the coffee under way.

"A dollar'n a half apiece—one thousand dozen—eighteen thousand dollars!" He kept muttering it to himself, over and over, as he went about his work.

As he flopped the steak into the frying-pan the door opened. He turned. It was the man with the bearskin coat. He seemed to come in with determination, as though bound on some explicit errand, but as he looked at Rasmunsen an expression of perplexity came into his face.

"I say—now I say—" he began, then halted.

Rasmunsen wondered if he wanted the rent.

"I say, damn it, you know, them eggs is bad."

Rasmunsen staggered. He felt as though some one had struck him an astounding blow between the eyes. The walls of the cabin reeled and tilted up. He put out his hand to steady himself and rested it on the stove. The sharp pain and the smell of the burning flesh brought him back to himself.

"I see," he said slowly, fumbling in his pocket for the sack. "You want your money back."

"It ain't the money," the man said, "but hain't you got any eggs—good?"

Rasmunsen shook his head. "You'd better take the money."

But the man refused and backed away. "I'll come back," he said, "when you've taken stock, and get what's comin'."

Rasmunsen rolled the chopping-block into the cabin and carried in the eggs. He went about it quite calmly. He took up the hand-axe, and, one by one, chopped the eggs in half. These halves he examined carefully and let fall to the floor. At first he sampled from the different cases, then deliberately emptied one case at a time. The heap on the floor grew larger. The coffee boiled over and the smoke of the burning beefsteak filled the cabin. He chopped steadfastly and monotonously till the last case was finished.

Somebody knocked at the door, knocked again, and let himself it.

"What a mess!" he remarked, as he paused and surveyed the scene.

The severed eggs were beginning to thaw in the heat of the stove, and a miserable odor was growing stronger.

"Must a-happened on the steamer," he suggested.

Rasmunsen looked at him long and blankly.

"I'm Murray, Big Jim Murray, everybody knows me," the man volunteered. "I'm just hearin' your eggs is rotten, and I'm offerin' you two hundred for the batch. They ain't good as salmon, but still they're fair scoffin's for dogs."

Rasmunsen seemed turned to stone. He did not move. "You go to hell," he said passionlessly.

"Now just consider. I pride myself it's a decent price for a mess like that, and it's better'n nothin'. Two hundred. What you say?"

"You go to hell," Rasmunsen repeated softly, "and get out of here."

Murray gaped with a great awe, then went out carefully, backward, with his eyes fixed on the other's face.

Rasmunsen followed him out and turned the dogs loose. He threw them all the salmon he had bought, and coiled a sled-lashing up in his hand. Then he reëntered the cabin and drew the latch in after him. The smoke from the cindered steak made his eyes smart. He stood on the bunk, passed the lashing over the ridge-pole, and measured the swing-off with his eye. It did not seem to satisfy, for he put the stool on the bunk and climbed upon the stool. He drove a noose in the end of the lashing and slipped his head through. The other end he made fast. Then he kicked the stool out from under.

THE FAITH OF MEN

"TELL you what we'll do; we'll shake for it."

"That suits me," said the second man, turning, as he spoke, to the Indian that was mending snowshoes in a corner of the cabin. "Here, you Billebedam, take a run down to Oleson's cabin like a good fellow and tell him we want to borrow his dice box."

This sudden request in the midst of a council on wages of men, wood, and grub surprised Billebedam. Besides, it was early in the day, and he had never known white men of the caliber of Pentfield and Hutchinson to dice and play till the day's work was done. But his face was impassive as a Yukon Indian's should be, as he pulled on his mittens and went out the door.

Though eight o'clock, it was still dark outside, and the cabin was lighted by a tallow candle thrust into an empty whiskey bottle. It stood on the pine board table in the middle of a disarray of dirty tin dishes. Tallow from innumerable candles had dripped down the long neck of the bottle and hardened into a miniature glacier. The small room, which composed the entire cabin, was as badly littered as the table. While at one end, against the wall, were two bunks, one above the other, with the blankets turned down just as the two men had crawled out in the morning.

Lawrence Pentfield and Corry Hutchinson were millionnaires, though they did not look it. There seemed nothing unusual about them, while they would have passed muster as fair specimens of lumbermen in any Michigan camp. But outside, in the darkness, where holes yawned in the ground, were many men engaged in windlassing muck and gravel and gold from the bottoms of the holes where other men received fifteen dollars per day for scraping it from off the bedrock. Each day thousands of dollars' worth of gold were scraped from bedrock and windlassed to the surface, and it all belonged to Pentfield and Hutchinson, who took their rank among the richest kings of Bonanza.

Pentfield broke the silence that followed on Billebedam's departure by heaping the dirty plates higher on the table and drumming a tattoo on the cleared space with his knuckles. Hutchinson snuffed the smoky candle and reflectively rubbed the soot from the wick between thumb and forefinger.

"By Jove, I wish we could both go out!" he abruptly exclaimed. "That would settle it all."

Pentfield looked at him darkly.

"If it weren't for your cursed obstinacy, it'd be settled anyway. All you have to do is get up and get. I'll look after things, and next year I can go out."

"Why should I go? I've no one waiting for me—"

"Your people," Pentfield broke in roughly.

"Like you have," Hutchinson went on. "A girl, I mean, and you know it."

Pentfield shrugged his shoulders gloomily.

"She can wait, I guess."

"But she's been waiting two years now."

"And another won't age her beyond recognition."

"That'd be three years. Think of it, old man, three years in this end of the earth, this falling-off place for the damned!" Hutchinson threw up his arm in an almost articulate groan.

He was several years younger than his partner, not more than twenty-six, and there was a certain wistfulness in his face that comes into the faces of men when they yearn vainly for the things they have been long denied. This same wistfulness was in Pentfield's face, and the groan of it was articulate in the heave of his shoulders.

"I dreamed last night I was in Zinkand's," he said. "The music playing, glasses clinking, voices humming, women laughing, and I was ordering eggs—yes, sir, eggs, fried and boiled and poached and scrambled, and in all sorts of ways, and downing them as fast as they arrived."

"I'd have ordered salads and green things," Hutchinson criticised hungrily, "with a big, rare porterhouse, and young onions and radishes, the kind your teeth sink into with a crunch."

"I'd have followed the eggs with them, I guess, if I hadn't awakened," Pentfield replied.

He picked up a trail-scarred banjo from the floor and began to strum a few wandering notes. Hutchinson winced and breathed heavily.

"Quit it!" he burst out with sudden fury, as the other struck into a gayly lilting swing. "It drives me mad. I can't stand it."

Pentfield tossed the banjo into a bunk and quoted:—

> "Hear me babble what the weakest won't confess—
> I am Memory and Torment—I am Town!
> I am all that ever went with evening dress!"

The other man winced where he sat and dropped his head forward on the table. Pentfield resumed the monotonous drumming with his knuckles. A loud snap from the door attracted his attention. The frost was creeping up the inside in a white sheet, and he began to hum:—

> "The flocks are folded, boughs are bare,
> The salmon takes the sea;
> And oh, my fair, would I somewhere
> Might house my heart with thee."

Silence fell and was not again broken till Billebedam arrived and threw the dice box on the table.

"Um much cold," he said. "Oleson um speak to me, um say um Yukon freeze last night."

"Hear that, old man!" Pentfield cried, slapping Hutchinson on the shoulder. "Whoever wins can be hitting the trail for God's country this time to-morrow morning!"

He picked up the box, briskly rattling the dice.

"What'll it be?"

"Straight poker dice," Hutchinson answered. "Go on and roll them out."

Pentfield swept the dishes from the table with a crash, and rolled out the five dice. Both looked eagerly. The shake was without a pair and five-spot high.

"A stiff!" Pentfield groaned.

After much deliberating Pentfield picked up all the five dice and put them in the box.

"I'd shake to the five if I were you," Hutchinson suggested.

"No, you wouldn't, not when you see this," Pentfield replied, shaking out the dice.

Again they were without a pair, running this time in unbroken sequence from two to six.

"A second stiff!" he groaned. "No use your shaking, Corry. You can't lose."

The other man gathered up the dice without a word, rattled them, rolled them out on the table with a flourish, and saw that he had likewise shaken a six-high stiff.

"Tied you, anyway, but I'll have to do better than that," he said, gathering in four of them and shaking to the six. "And here's what beats you."

But they rolled out deuce, tray, four, and five,—a stiff still and no better nor worse than Pentfield's throw.

Hutchinson sighed.

"Couldn't happen once in a million times," he said.

"Nor in a million lives," Pentfield added, catching up the dice and quickly throwing them out. Three fives appeared, and, after much delay, he was rewarded by a fourth five on the second shake. Hutchinson seemed to have lost his last hope.

But three sixes turned up on his first shake. A great doubt rose in the other's eyes, and hope returned into his. He had one more shake. Another six and he would go over the ice to salt water and the states.

He rattled the dice in the box, made as though to cast them, hesitated, and continued to rattle them.

"Go on! Go on! Don't take all night about it!" Pentfield cried sharply, bending his nails on the table, so tight was the clutch with which he strove to control himself.

The dice rolled forth, an upturned six meeting their eyes. Both men sat staring at it. There was a long silence. Hutchinson shot a covert glance at his partner, who, still more covertly, caught it, and pursed up his lips in an attempt to advertise his unconcern.

Hutchinson laughed as he got up on his feet. It was a nervous, apprehensive laugh. It was a case where it was more awkward to win than lose. He walked over to his partner, who whirled upon him fiercely:

"Now you just shut up, Corry! I know all you're going to say—that you'd rather stay in and let me go, and all that; so don't say it. You've your own people in Detroit to see, and that's enough. Besides, you can do for me the very thing I expected to do if I went out."

"And that is—?"

Pentfield read the full question in his partner's eyes, and answered:—

"Yes, that very thing. You can bring her in to me. The only difference will be a Dawson wedding instead of a San Franciscan one."

"But man alive!" Corry Hutchinson objected. "How under the sun can I bring her in? We're not exactly brother and sister, seeing that I have not even met her, and it wouldn't be just the proper thing, you know, for us to travel together. Of course, it would be all right—you and I know that; but think of the looks of it, man!"

Pentfield swore under his breath, consigning the looks of it to a less frigid region than Alaska.

"Now, if you'll just listen and not get astride that high horse of yours so blamed quick," his partner went on, "you'll see that the only fair thing under the circumstances is for me to let you go out this year. Next year is only a year away, and then I can take my fling."

Pentfield shook his head, though visibly swayed by the temptation.

"It won't do, Corry, old man. I appreciate your kindness and all that, but it won't do. I'd be ashamed every time I thought of you slaving away in here in my place."

A thought seemed suddenly to strike him. Burrowing into his bunk and disrupting it in his eagerness, he secured a writing pad and pencil, and sitting down at the table, began to write with swiftness and certitude.

"Here," he said, thrusting the scrawled letter into his partner's hand. "You just deliver that and everything'll be all right."

Hutchinson ran his eye over it and laid it down.

"How do you know the brother will be willing to make that beastly trip in here?" he demanded.

"Oh, he'll do it for me—and for his sister," Pentfield replied. "You see, he's tenderfoot, and I wouldn't trust her with him alone. But with you along it will be an easy trip and a safe one. As soon as you get out, you'll go to her and prepare her. Then you can take your run East to your own people, and in the spring she and her brother'll be ready to start with you. You'll like her, I know, right from the jump; and from that, you'll know her as soon as you lay eyes on her."

So saying he opened the back of his watch and exposed a girl's photograph pasted on the inside of the case. Corry Hutchinson gazed at it with admiration welling up in his eyes.

"Mabel is her name," Pentfield went on. "And it's just as well you should know how to find the house. Soon as you strike 'Frisco, take a cab and just say, 'Holmes's place, Myrdon Avenue' —I doubt if the Myrdon Avenue is necessary. The cabby'll know where Judge Holmes lives.

"And say," Pentfield continued, after a pause, "it won't be a bad idea for you to get me a few little things which—a—er—"

"A married man should have in his business," Hutchinson blurted out with a grin.

Pentfield grinned back.

"Sure, napkins and tablecloths and sheets and pillowslips, and such things. And you might get a good set of china. You know it'll come hard for her to settle down to this sort of thing. You can freight them in by steamer around by Bering Sea. And, I say, what's the matter with a piano?"

Hutchinson seconded the idea heartily. His reluctance had vanished, and he was warming up to his mission.

"By Jove! Lawrence," he said at the conclusion of the council, as they both rose to their feet, "I'll bring back that girl of yours in style. I'll do the cooking and take care of the dogs, and all that brother'll have to do will be to see to her comfort and do for her whatever I've forgotten. And I'll forget damn little, I can tell you."

The next day Lawrence Pentfield shook hands with him for the last time and watched him, running with his dogs, disappear up the frozen Yukon on his way to salt water and the world. Pentfield went back to his Bonanza mine, which was many times more dreary than before, and faced resolutely into the long winter. There was work to be done, men to superintend, and operations to direct in burrowing after the erratic pay streak; but his heart was not in the work. Nor was his heart in any work till the tiered logs of a new cabin began to rise on the hill behind the mine. It was a grand cabin, warmly built and divided into three comfortable rooms. Each log was hand-hewed and squared—an expensive whim when the axemen received a daily wage of fifteen dollars; but to him nothing could be too costly for the home in which Mabel Holmes was to live.

So he went about with the building of the cabin, singing, "And oh, my fair, would I somewhere might house my heart with thee!" Also, he had a calendar pinned on the wall above the table, and his first act each morning was to check off the day and to count the days that were left ere his partner would come booming down the Yukon ice in the spring. Another whim of his was to permit no one to sleep in the new cabin on the hill. It must be as fresh for her occupancy as the square-hewed wood was fresh; and when it stood complete, he put a padlock on the door. No one entered save himself, and he was wont to spend long hours there, and to come forth with his face strangely radiant and in his eyes a glad, warm light.

In December he received a letter from Corry Hutchinson. He had just seen Mabel Holmes. She was all she ought to be, to be Lawrence Pentfield's wife, he wrote. He was enthusiastic, and his letter sent the blood tingling through Pentfield's veins. Other letters followed, one on the heels of another and sometimes two or three together when the mail lumped up. And they were all in the same tenor. Corry had just come from Myrdon Avenue; Corry was just going to Myrdon Avenue; or Corry was at Myrdon Avenue.

And he lingered on and on in San Francisco, nor even mentioned his trip to Detroit.

Lawrence Pentfield began to think that his partner was a great deal in the company of Mabel Holmes for a fellow who was going East to see his people. He even caught himself worrying about it at times, though he would have worried more had he not known Mabel and Corry so well. Mabel's letters, on the other hand, had a great deal to say about Corry. Also, a thread of timidity that was near to disinclination ran through them concerning the trip in over the ice and the Dawson marriage. Pentfield wrote back heartily, laughing at her fears, which he took to be the mere physical ones of danger and hardship rather than those bred of maidenly reserve.

But the long winter and tedious wait, following upon the two previous long winters, were telling upon him. The superintendence of the men and the pursuit of the pay streak could not break the irk of the daily round, and the end of January found him making occasional trips to Dawson, where he could forget his identity for a space at the gambling tables. Because he could afford to lose, he won, and "Pentfield's luck" became a stock phrase among the faro players.

His luck ran with him till the second week in February. How much farther it might have run is conjectural; for, after one big game, he never played again.

It was in the Opera House that it occurred, and for an hour it had seemed that he could not place his money on a card without making the card a winner. In the lull at the end of a deal, while the game keeper was shuffling the deck, Nick Inwood, the owner of the game, remarked, apropos of nothing:—

"I say, Pentfield, I see that partner of yours has been cutting up monkeyshines on the outside."

"Trust Corry to have a good time," Pentfield had answered; "especially when he has earned it."

"Every man to his taste," Nick Inwood laughed; "but I should scarcely call getting married a good time."

"Corry married!" Pentfield cried, incredulous and yet surprised out of himself for the moment.

"Sure," Inwood said. "I saw it in the 'Frisco paper that came in over the ice this morning."

"Well, and who's the girl?" Pentfield demanded, somewhat with the air of patient fortitude with which one takes the bait of a catch and is aware at the time of the large laugh bound to follow at his expense.

Nick Inwood pulled the newspaper from his pocket and began looking it over, saying:—

"I haven't a remarkable memory for names, but it seems to me it's something like Mabel—Mabel—oh, yes, here it is—'Mabel Holmes, daughter of Judge Holmes'—whoever he is."

Lawrence Pentfield never turned a hair, though he wondered how any man in the North could know her name. He glanced coolly from face to face to note any vagrant signs of the game that was being played upon him, but beyond a healthy curiosity the faces betrayed nothing. Then he turned to the gambler and said in cold, even tones:—

"Inwood, I've got an even five hundred here that says the print of what you have just said is not in that paper."

The gambler looked at him in quizzical surprise.

"Go 'way, child. I don't want your money."

"I thought so," Pentfield sneered, returning to the game and laying a couple of bets.

Nick Inwood's face flushed, and, as though doubting his senses, he ran careful eyes over the print of a quarter of a column. Then he turned on Lawrence Pentfield.

"Look here, Pentfield," he said, in quick, nervous manner; "I can't allow that, you know."

"Allow what?" Pentfield demanded brutally.

"You implied that I lied."

"Nothing of the sort," came the reply. "I merely implied that you were trying to be clumsily witty."

"Make your bets, gentlemen," the dealer protested.

"But I tell you it's true," Nick Inwood insisted.

"And I have told you I've five hundred that says it's not in that paper," Pentfield answered, at the same time throwing a heavy sack of dust on the table.

"I am sorry to take your money," was the retort, as Inwood thrust the newspaper into Pentfield's hand.

Pentfield saw, though he could not quite bring himself to believe. Glancing through the headline, "Young Lochinvar came out of the North," and skimming the article until the names of Mabel Holmes and Corry Hutchinson, coupled together, leaped squarely before his eyes, he turned to the top of the page. It was a San Francisco paper.

"The money's yours, Inwood," he remarked, with a short laugh. "There's no telling what that partner of mine will do when he gets started."

Then he returned to the article and read it word for word, very slowly and very carefully. He could no longer doubt. Beyond dispute, Corry Hutchinson had married Mabel Holmes. "One of the Bonanza kings," it described him, "a partner with Lawrence Pentfield (whom San Francisco society has not yet forgotten), and interested with that gentleman in other rich Klondike properties." Further, and at the end, he read, "It is whispered that Mr. and Mrs. Hutchinson will, after a brief trip east to Detroit, make their real honeymoon journey into the fascinating Klondike country."

"I'll be back again; keep my place for me," Pentfield said, rising to his feet and taking his sack, which meantime had hit the blower and came back lighter by five hundred dollars.

He went down the street and bought a Seattle paper. It contained the same facts, though somewhat condensed. Corry and Mabel were indubitably married. Pentfield returned to the Opera House and resumed his seat in the game. He asked to have the limit removed.

"Trying to get action," Nick Inwood laughed, as he nodded assent to the dealer. "I was going down to the A. C. store, but now I guess I'll stay and watch you do your worst."

This Lawrence Pentfield did at the end of two hours' plunging, when the dealer bit the end off a fresh cigar and struck a match as he announced that the bank was broken. Pentfield cashed in for forty thousand, shook hands with Nick Inwood, and stated that it was the last time he would ever play at his game or at anybody else's.

No one knew nor guessed that he had been hit, much less hit hard. There was no apparent change in his manner. For a week he went about his work much as he had always done, when he read an account of the marriage in a Portland paper. Then he called in a friend to take charge of his mine and departed up the Yukon behind his dogs. He held to the Salt Water trail till White River was reached, into which he turned. Five days later he came upon a hunting camp of the White River Indians. In the evening there was a feast, and he sat in honor beside the chief; and next morning he headed his dogs back toward the Yukon. But he no longer travelled alone. A young squaw fed his dogs for him that night and helped to pitch camp. She had been mauled by a bear in her childhood and suffered from a slight limp. Her name was Lashka, and she was diffident at first with the strange white man that had come out of the Unknown, married her with scarcely a look or word, and now was carrying her back with him into the Unknown.

But Lashka's was better fortune than falls to most Indian girls that mate with white men in the Northland. No sooner was Dawson reached than the barbaric marriage that had joined them was resolemnized, in the white man's fashion, before a priest. From Dawson, which to her was all a marvel and a dream, she was taken directly to the Bonanza claim and installed in the square-hewed cabin on the hill.

The nine days' wonder that followed arose not so much out of the fact of the squaw whom Lawrence Pentfield had taken to bed and board as out of the ceremony that had legalized the tie. The properly sanctioned marriage was the one thing that passed the community's comprehension. But no one bothered Pentfield about it. So long as a man's vagaries did no special hurt to the community, the community let the man alone, nor was Pentfield barred from the cabins of men who possessed white wives. The marriage ceremony removed him from the status of squaw-man and placed him beyond moral reproach, though there were men that challenged his taste where women were concerned.

No more letters arrived from the outside. Six sledloads of mail had been lost at the Big Salmon. Besides, Pentfield knew that Corry and his bride must by that time have started in over the trail. They were even then on their honeymoon trip—the honeymoon trip he had dreamed of for himself through two dreary years. His lip curled with bitterness at the thought; but beyond being kinder to Lashka he gave no sign.

March had passed and April was nearing its end, when, one spring morning, Lashka asked permission to go down the creek several miles to Siwash Pete's cabin. Pete's wife, a Stewart River woman, had sent up word that something was wrong with her baby, and Lashka, who was preëminently a mother-woman and who held herself to be truly wise in the matter of infantile troubles, missed no opportunity of nursing the children of other women as yet more fortunate than she.

Pentfield harnessed his dogs, and with Lashka behind took the trail down the creek bed of Bonanza. Spring was in the air. The sharpness had gone out of the bite of the frost, and though snow still covered the land, the murmur and trickling of water told that the iron grip of winter was relaxing. The bottom was dropping out of the trail, and here and there a new trail had been broken around open holes. At such a place, where there was not room for two sleds to pass, Pentfield heard the jingle of approaching bells and stopped his dogs.

A team of tired-looking dogs appeared around the narrow bend, followed by a heavily loaded sled. At the gee-pole was a man who steered in a manner familiar to Pentfield, and behind the sled walked two women. His glance returned to the man at the gee-pole. It was Corry. Pentfield got on his feet and waited. He was glad that Lashka was with him. The meeting could not have come about better had it been planned, he thought. And as he waited he wondered what they would say, what they would be able to say. As for himself there was no need to say anything. The explaining was all on their side, and he was ready to listen to them.

As they drew in abreast, Corry recognized him and halted the dogs. With a "Hello, old man," he held out his hand.

Pentfield shook it, but without warmth or speech. By this time the two women had come up, and he noticed that the second one was Dora Holmes. He doffed his fur cap, the flaps of which were flying, shook hands with her, and turned toward Mabel. She swayed forward, splendid and radiant, but faltered before his outstretched hand. He had intended to say, "How do you do, Mrs. Hutchinson?"—but somehow, the Mrs. Hutchinson had choked him, and all he had managed to articulate was the "How do you do?"

There was all the constraint and awkwardness in the situation he could have wished. Mabel betrayed the agitation appropriate to her position, while Dora, evidently brought along as some sort of peacemaker, was saying:—

"Why, what is the matter, Lawrence?"

Before he could answer, Corry plucked him by the sleeve and drew him aside.

"See here, old man, what's this mean?" Corry demanded in a low tone, including Lashka with his eyes.

"I can hardly see, Corry, where you can have any concern in the matter," Pentfield answered mockingly.

But Corry drove straight to the point.

"What is that squaw doing on your sled? A nasty job you've given me to explain all this away. I only hope it can be explained away. Who is she? Whose squaw is she?"

Then Lawrence Pentfield delivered his stroke, and he delivered it with a certain calm elation of spirit that seemed somewhat to compensate for the wrong that had been done him.

"She is my squaw," he said; "Mrs. Pentfield, if you please."

Corry Hutchinson gasped, and Pentfield left him and returned to the two women. Mabel, with a worried expression on her face, seemed holding herself aloof. He turned to Dora and asked, quite genially, as though all the world was sunshine:—

"How did you stand the trip, anyway? Have any trouble to sleep warm?"

"And how did Mrs. Hutchinson stand it?" he asked next, his eyes on Mabel.

"Oh, you dear ninny!" Dora cried, throwing her arms around him and hugging him. "Then you saw it, too! I thought something was the matter, you were acting so strangely."

"I—I hardly understand," he stammered.

"It was corrected in next day's paper," Dora chattered on. "We did not dream you would see it. All the other papers had it correctly, and of course that one miserable paper was the very one you saw!"

"Wait a moment! What do you mean?" Pentfield demanded, a sudden fear at his heart, for he felt himself on the verge of a great gulf.

But Dora swept volubly on.

"Why, when it became known that Mabel and I were going to

Klondike, *Every Other Week* said that when we were gone, it would be lovely on Myrdon Avenue, meaning, of course, lonely."

"Then—"

"I am Mrs. Hutchinson," Dora answered. "And you thought it was Mabel all the time."

"Precisely the way of it," Pentfield replied slowly. "But I can see now. The reporter got the names mixed. The Seattle and Portland papers copied."

He stood silently for a minute. Mabel's face was turned toward him again, and he could see the glow of expectancy in it. Corry was deeply interested in the ragged toe of one of his moccasins, while Dora was stealing sidelong glances at the immobile face of Lashka sitting on the sled. Lawrence Pentfield stared straight out before him into a dreary future, through the gray vistas of which he saw himself riding on a sled behind running dogs with lame Lashka by his side.

Then he spoke, quite simply, looking Mabel in the eyes.

"I am very sorry. I did not dream it. I thought you had married Corry. That is Mrs. Pentfield sitting on the sled over there."

Mabel Holmes turned weakly toward her sister, as though all the fatigue of her great journey had suddenly descended on her. Dora caught her around the waist. Corry Hutchinson was still occupied with his moccasins. Pentfield glanced quickly from face to face, then turned to his sled.

"Can't stop here all day, with Pete's baby waiting," he said to Lashka.

The long whip-lash hissed out, the dogs sprang against the breast bands, and the sled lurched and jerked ahead.

"Oh, I say, Corry," Pentfield called back, "you'd better occupy the old cabin. It's not been used for some time. I've built a new one on the hill."

SECTION FIVE

THE APOSTATE

Now I wake me up to work;
I pray the Lord I may not shirk.
If I should die before the night,
I pray the Lord my work's all right.

Amen.

"IF you don't git up, Johnny, I won't give you a bite to eat!"

The threat had no effect on the boy. He clung stubbornly to sleep, fighting for its oblivion as the dreamer fights for his dream. The boy's hands loosely clenched themselves, and he made feeble, spasmodic blows at the air. These blows were intended for his mother, but she betrayed practised familiarity in avoiding them as she shook him roughly on the shoulder.

"Lemme 'lone!"

It was a cry that began, muffled, in the deeps of sleep, that swiftly rushed upward, like a wail, into passionate belligerence, and that died away and sank down into an inarticulate whine. It was a bestial cry, as of a soul in torment, filled with infinite protest and pain.

But she did not mind. She was a sad-eyed, tired-faced woman, and she had grown used to this task, which she repeated every day of her life. She got a grip on the bedclothes and tried to strip them down; but the boy, ceasing his punching, clung to them desperately. In a huddle, at the foot of the bed, he still remained covered. Then she tried dragging the bedding to the floor. The boy opposed her. She braced herself. Hers was the superior weight, and the boy and bedding gave, the former instinctively following the latter in order to shelter against the chill of the room that bit into his body.

As he toppled on the edge of the bed it seemed that he must fall head-first to the floor. But consciousness fluttered up in him. He righted himself and for a moment perilously balanced. Then he struck the floor on his feet. On the instant his mother seized him by the shoulders and shook him. Again his fists struck out, this time with more force and directness. At the same time his eyes opened. She released him. He was awake.

"All right," he mumbled.

She caught up the lamp and hurried out, leaving him in darkness.

"You'll be docked," she warned back to him.

He did not mind the darkness. When he had got into his clothes, he went out into the kitchen. His tread was very heavy for so thin and light a boy. His legs dragged with their own weight, which seemed unreasonable because they were such skinny legs. He drew a broken-bottom chair to the table.

"Johnny!" his mother called sharply.

He arose as sharply from the chair, and, without a word, went to the sink. It was a greasy, filthy sink. A smell came up from the outlet. He took no notice of it. That a sink should smell was to him part of the natural order, just as it was a part of the natural order that the soap should be grimy with dish-water and hard to lather. Nor did he try very hard to make it lather. Several splashes of the cold water from the running faucet completed the function. He did not wash his teeth. For that matter he had never seen a toothbrush, nor did he know that there existed beings in the world who were guilty of so great a foolishness as tooth washing.

"You might wash yourself wunst a day without bein' told," his mother complained.

She was holding a broken lid on the pot as she poured two cups of coffee. He made no remark, for this was a standing quarrel between them, and the one thing upon which his mother was hard as adamant. "Wunst" a day it was compulsory that he should wash his face. He dried himself on a greasy towel, damp and dirty and ragged, that left his face covered with shreds of lint.

"I wish we didn't live so far away," she said, as he sat down. "I try to do the best I can. You know that. But dollar on the rent is such a savin', an' we've more room here. You know that."

He scarcely followed her. He had heard it all before, many times. The range of her thought was limited, and she was ever harkening back to the hardship worked upon them by living so far from the mills.

"A dollar means more grub," he remarked sententiously. "I'd sooner do the walkin' an' git the grub."

He ate hurriedly, half chewing the bread and washing the unmasticated chunks down with coffee. The hot and muddy liquid went by the name of coffee. Johnny thought it was coffee—and excellent coffee. That was one of the few of life's illusions that remained to him. He had never drunk real coffee in his life.

In addition to the bread, there was a small piece of cold pork. His mother refilled his cup with coffee. As he was finishing the bread, he began to watch if more was forthcoming. She intercepted his questioning glance.

"Now, don't be hoggish, Johnny," was her comment. "You've had your share. Your brothers an' sisters are smaller'n you."

He did not answer the rebuke. He was not much of a talker. Also, he ceased his hungry glancing for more. He was uncomplaining, with a patience that was as terrible as the school in which it had been learned. He finished his coffee, wiped his mouth on the back of his hand, and started to rise.

"Wait a second," she said hastily. "I guess the loaf kin stand you another slice—a thin un."

There was legerdemain in her actions. With all the seeming of cutting a slice from the loaf for him, she put loaf and slice back in the bread box and conveyed to him one of her own two slices. She believed she had deceived him, but he had noted her sleight-of-hand. Nevertheless, he took the bread shamelessly. He had a philosophy that his mother, what of her chronic sickliness, was not much of an eater anyway.

She saw that he was chewing the bread dry, and reached over and emptied her coffee cup into his.

"Don't set good somehow on my stomach this morning," she explained.

A distant whistle, prolonged and shrieking, brought both of

them to their feet. She glanced at the tin alarm-clock on the shelf. The hands stood at half-past five. The rest of the factory world was just arousing from sleep. She drew a shawl about her shoulders, and on her head put a dingy hat, shapeless and ancient.

"We've got to run," she said, turning the wick of the lamp and blowing down the chimney.

They groped their way out and down the stairs. It was clear and cold, and Johnny shivered at the first contact with the outside air. The stars had not yet begun to pale in the sky, and the city lay in blackness. Both Johnny and his mother shuffled their feet as they walked. There was no ambition in the leg muscles to swing the feet clear of the ground.

After fifteen silent minutes, his mother turned off to the right.

"Don't be late," was her final warning from out of the dark that was swallowing her up.

He made no response, steadily keeping on his way. In the factory quarter, doors were opening everywhere, and he was soon one of a multitude that pressed onward through the dark. As he entered the factory gate the whistle blew again. He glanced at the east. Across a ragged sky-line of housetops a pale light was beginning to creep. This much he saw of the day as he turned his back upon it and joined his work gang.

He took his place in one of many long rows of machines. Before him, above a bin filled with small bobbins, were large bobbins revolving rapidly. Upon these he wound the jute twine of the small bobbins. The work was simple. All that was required was celerity. The small bobbins were emptied so rapidly, and there were so many large bobbins that did the emptying, that there were no idle moments.

He worked mechanically. When a small bobbin ran out, he used his left hand for a brake, stopping the large bobbin and at the same time, with thumb and forefinger, catching a flying end of twine. Also, at the same time, with his right hand, he caught up the loose twine-end of a small bobbin. These various acts with both hands were performed simultaneously and swiftly. Then there would come a flash of his hands as he looped the weaver's knot and released the bobbin. There was nothing difficult about weaver's knots. He once boasted he could tie them in his sleep.

And for that matter, he sometimes did, toiling centuries long in a single night at tying an endless succession of weaver's knots.

Some of the boys shirked, wasting time and machinery by not replacing the small bobbins when they ran out. And there was an overseer to prevent this. He caught Johnny's neighbor at the trick, and boxed his ears.

"Look at Johnny there—why ain't you like him?" the overseer wrathfully demanded.

Johnny's bobbins were running full blast, but he did not thrill at the indirect praise. There had been a time . . . but that was long ago, very long ago. His apathetic face was expressionless as he listened to himself being held up as a shining example. He was the perfect worker. He knew that. He had been told so, often. It was a commonplace, and besides it didn't seem to mean anything to him any more. From the perfect worker he had evolved into the perfect machine. When his work went wrong, it was with him as with the machine, due to faulty material. It would have been as possible for a perfect nail-die to cut imperfect nails as for him to make a mistake.

And small wonder. There had never been a time when he had not been in intimate relationship with machines. Machinery had almost been bred into him, and at any rate he had been brought up on it. Twelve years before, there had been a small flutter of excitement in the loom room of this very mill. Johnny's mother had fainted. They stretched her out on the floor in the midst of the shrieking machines. A couple of elderly women were called from their looms. The foreman assisted. And in a few minutes there was one more soul in the loom room than had entered by the doors. It was Johnny, born with the pounding, crashing roar of the looms in his ears, drawing with his first breath the warm, moist air that was thick with flying lint. He had coughed that first day in order to rid his lungs of the lint; and for the same reason he had coughed ever since.

The boy alongside of Johnny whimpered and sniffed. The boy's face was convulsed with hatred for the overseer who kept a threatening eye on him from a distance; but every bobbin was running full. The boy yelled terrible oaths into the whirling bobbins before him; but the sound did not carry half a dozen feet, the roaring of the room holding it in and containing it like a wall.

Of all this Johnny took no notice. He had a way of accepting things. Besides, things grow monotonous by repetition, and this particular happening he had witnessed many times. It seemed to him as useless to oppose the overseer as to defy the will of a machine. Machines were made to go in certain ways and to perform certain tasks. It was the same with the overseer.

But at eleven o'clock there was excitement in the room. In an apparently occult way the excitement instantly permeated everywhere. The one-legged boy who worked on the other side of Johnny bobbed swiftly across the floor to a bin truck that stood empty. Into this he dived out of sight, crutch and all. The superintendent of the mill was coming along, accompanied by a young man. He was well dressed and wore a starched shirt—a gentleman, in Johnny's classification of men, and also, "the Inspector."

He looked sharply at the boys as he passed along. Sometimes he stopped and asked questions. When he did so, he was compelled to shout at the top of his lungs, at which moments his face was ludicrously contorted with the strain of making himself heard. His quick eye noted the empty machine alongside of Johnny's, but he said nothing. Johnny also caught his eye, and he stopped abruptly. He caught Johnny by the arm to draw him back a step from the machine; but with an exclamation of surprise he released the arm.

"Pretty skinny," the superintendent laughed anxiously.

"Pipe stems," was the answer. "Look at those legs. The boy's got the rickets—incipient, but he's got them. If epilepsy doesn't get him in the end, it will be because tuberculosis gets him first."

Johnny listened, but did not understand. Furthermore he was not interested in future ills. There was an immediate and more serious ill that threatened him in the form of the inspector.

"Now, my boy, I want you to tell me the truth," the inspector said, or shouted, bending close to the boy's ear to make him hear. "How old are you?"

"Fourteen," Johnny lied, and he lied with the full force of his lungs. So loudly did he lie that it started him off in a dry, hacking cough that lifted the lint which had been settling in his lungs all morning.

"Looks sixteen at least," said the superintendent.

"Or sixty," snapped the inspector.

"He's always looked that way."

"How long?" asked the inspector, quickly.

"For years. Never gets a bit older."

"Or younger, I dare say. I suppose he's worked here all those years?"

"Off and on—but that was before the new law was passed," the superintendent hastened to add.

"Machine idle?" the inspector asked, pointing at the unoccupied machine beside Johnny's, in which the part-filled bobbins were flying like mad.

"Looks that way." The superintendent motioned the overseer to him and shouted in his ear and pointed at the machine. "Machine's idle," he reported back to the inspector.

They passed on, and Johnny returned to his work, relieved in that the ill had been averted. But the one-legged boy was not so fortunate. The sharp-eyed inspector haled him out at arm's length from the bin truck. His lips were quivering, and his face had all the expression of one upon whom was fallen profound and irremediable disaster. The overseer looked astounded, as though for the first time he had laid eyes on the boy, while the superintendent's face expressed shock and displeasure.

"I know him," the inspector said. "He's twelve years old. I've had him discharged from three factories inside the year. This makes the fourth."

He turned to the one-legged boy. "You promised me, word and honor, that you'd go to school."

The one-legged boy burst into tears. "Please, Mr. Inspector, two babies died on us, and we're awful poor."

"What makes you cough that way?" the inspector demanded, as though charging him with crime.

And as in denial of guilt, the one-legged boy replied: "It ain't nothin'. I jes' caught a cold last week, Mr. Inspector, that's all."

In the end the one-legged boy went out of the room with the inspector, the latter accompanied by the anxious and protesting superintendent. After that monotony settled down again. The long morning and the longer afternoon wore away and the whistle blew for quitting time. Darkness had already fallen when Johnny passed out through the factory gate. In the interval the sun had made a golden ladder of the sky, flooded the world with its gracious warmth, and dropped down and disappeared in the west behind a ragged sky-line of housetops.

Supper was the family meal of the day—the one meal at which Johnny encountered his younger brothers and sisters. It partook of the nature of an encounter, to him, for he was very old, while they were distressingly young. He had no patience with their excessive and amazing juvenility. He did not understand it. His own childhood was too far behind him. He was like an old and irritable man, annoyed by the turbulence of their young spirits that was to him arrant silliness. He glowered silently over his food, finding compensation in the thought that they would soon have to go to work. That would take the edge off them and make them sedate and dignified—like him. Thus it was, after the fashion of the human, that Johnny made of himself a yardstick with which to measure the universe.

During the meal, his mother explained in various ways and with infinite repetition that she was trying to do the best she could; so that it was with relief, the scant meal ended, that Johnny shoved back his chair and arose. He debated for a moment between bed and the front door, and finally went out the latter. He did not go far. He sat down on the stoop, his knees drawn up and his narrow shoulders drooping forward, his elbows on his knees and the palms of his hands supporting his chin.

As he sat there, he did no thinking. He was just resting. So far as his mind was concerned, it was asleep. His brothers and sisters came out, and with other children played noisily about him. An electric globe on the corner lighted their frolics. He was peevish and irritable, that they knew; but the spirit of adventure lured them into teasing him. They joined hands before him, and, keeping time with their bodies, chanted in his face weird and uncomplimentary doggerel. At first he snarled curses at them—curses he had learned from the lips of various foremen. Finding this futile, and remembering his dignity, he relapsed into dogged silence.

His brother Will, next to him in age, having just passed his tenth birthday, was the ringleader. Johnny did not possess particularly kindly feelings toward him. His life had early been embittered by continual giving over and giving way to Will. He had a definite feeling that Will was greatly in his debt and was ungrateful about it. In his own playtime, far back in the dim past, he had been robbed of a large part of that playtime by being compelled to take care of Will. Will was a baby then, and then, as now, their mother had spent her days in the mills. To Johnny had fallen the part of little father and little mother as well.

Will seemed to show the benefit of the giving over and the giving way. He was well-built, fairly rugged, as tall as his elder brother and even heavier. It was as though the life-blood of the one had been diverted into the other's veins. And in spirits it was the same. Johnny was jaded, worn out, without resilience, while his younger brother seemed bursting and spilling over with exuberance.

The mocking chant rose louder and louder. Will leaned closer as he danced, thrusting out his tongue. Johnny's left arm shot out and caught the other around the neck. At the same time he rapped his bony fist to the other's nose. It was a pathetically bony fist, but that it was sharp to hurt was evidenced by the squeal of pain it produced. The other children were uttering frightened cries, while Johnny's sister, Jennie, had dashed into the house.

He thrust Will from him, kicked him savagely on the shins, then reached for him and slammed him face downward in the dirt. Nor did he release him till the face had been rubbed into the dirt several times. Then the mother arrived, an anaemic whirlwind of solicitude and maternal wrath.

"Why can't he leave me alone?" was Johnny's reply to her upbraiding. "Can't he see I'm tired?"

"I'm as big as you," Will raged in her arms, his face a mess of tears, dirt, and blood. "I'm as big as you now, an' I'm goin' to get bigger. Then I'll lick you—see if I don't."

"You ought to be to work, seein' how big you are," Johnny snarled. "That's what's the matter with you. You ought to be to work. An' it's up to your ma to put you to work."

"But he's too young," she protested. "He's only a little boy."

"I was youngern' him when I started to work."

Johnny's mouth was open, further to express the sense of unfairness that he felt, but the mouth closed with a snap. He turned gloomily on his heel and stalked into the house and to bed. The door of his room was open to let in warmth from the kitchen. As he undressed in the semi-darkness he could hear his mother talking with a neighbor woman who had dropped in. His mother was crying, and her speech was punctuated with spiritless sniffles.

"I can't make out what's gittin' into Johnny," he could hear her say. "He didn't used to be this way. He was a patient little angel.

"An' he *is* a good boy," she hastened to defend. "He's worked faithful, an' he did go to work too young. But it wasn't my fault. I do the best I can, I'm sure."

Prolonged sniffling from the kitchen, and Johnny murmured to himself as his eyelids closed down, "You betcher life I've worked faithful."

The next morning he was torn bodily by his mother from the grip of sleep. Then came the meager breakfast, the tramp through the dark, and the pale glimpse of day across the housetops as he turned his back on it and went in through the factory gate. It was another day, of all the days, and all the days were alike.

And yet there had been variety in his life—at the times he changed from one job to another, or was taken sick. When he was six, he was little mother and father to Will and the other children still younger. At seven he went into the mills—winding bobbins. When he was eight, he got work in another mill. His new job was marvellously easy. All he had to do was to sit down with a little stick in his hand and guide a stream of cloth that flowed past him. This stream of cloth came out of the maw of a machine, passed over a hot roller, and went on its way elsewhere. But he sat always in the one place, beyond the reach of daylight, a gas-jet flaring over him, himself part of the mechanism.

He was very happy at that job, in spite of the moist heat, for he was still young and in possession of dreams and illusions. And wonderful dreams he dreamed as he watched the steaming cloth streaming endlessly by. But there was no exercise about the work, no call upon his mind, and he dreamed less and less, while his mind grew torpid and drowsy. Nevertheless, he earned two dollars a week, and two dollars represented the difference between acute starvation and chronic underfeeding.

But when he was nine, he lost his job. Measles was the cause of it. After he recovered, he got work in a glass factory. The pay was better, and the work demanded skill. It was piece-work, and the more skilful he was, the bigger wages he earned. Here was incentive. And under this incentive he developed into a remarkable worker.

It was simple work, the tying of glass stoppers into small bottles. At his waist he carried a bundle of twine. He held the bottles between his knees so that he might work with both hands. Thus, in a sitting position and bending over his own knees, his narrow shoulders grew humped and his chest was contracted for ten hours each day. This was not good for the lungs, but he tied three hundred dozen bottles a day.

The superintendent was very proud of him, and brought visitors to look at him. In ten hours three hundred dozen bottles passed through his hands. This meant that he had attained machine-like perfection. All waste movements were eliminated. Every motion of his thin arms, every movement of a muscle in the thin fingers, was swift and accurate. He worked at high tension, and the result was that he grew nervous. At night his muscles twitched in his sleep, and in the daytime he could not relax and rest. He remained keyed up and his muscles continued to twitch. Also he grew sallow and his lint-cough grew worse. Then pneumonia laid hold of the feeble lungs within the contracted chest, and he lost his job in the glass-works.

Now he had returned to the jute mills where he had first begun with winding bobbins. But promotion was waiting for him. He was a good worker. He would next go on the starcher, and later he would go into the loom room. There was nothing after that except increased efficiency.

The machinery ran faster than when he had first gone to work, and his mind ran slower. He no longer dreamed at all, though his earlier years had been full of dreaming. Once he had been in love. It was when he first began guiding the cloth over the hot roller, and it was with the daughter of the superintendent. She was much older than he, a young woman, and he had seen her at a distance only a paltry half-dozen times. But that made no difference. On the surface of the cloth stream that poured past him, he pictured radiant futures wherein he performed prodigies of toil, invented miraculous machines, won to the mastership of the mills, and in the end took her in his arms and kissed her soberly on the brow.

But that was all in the long ago, before he had grown too old and tired to love. Also, she had married and gone away, and his mind had gone to sleep. Yet it had been a wonderful experience, and he often used to look back upon it as other men and women look back upon the time they believed in fairies. He had never believed in fairies nor Santa Claus; but he had believed implicitly in the smiling future his imagination had wrought into the steaming cloth stream.

He had become a man very early in life. At seven, when he drew his first wages, began his adolescence. A certain feeling of independence crept up in him, and the relationship between him and his mother changed. Somehow, as an earner and breadwinner, doing his own work in the world, he was more like an equal with her. Manhood, full-blown manhood, had come when he was eleven, at which time he had gone to work on the night shift for six months. No child works on the night shift and remains a child.

There had been several great events in his life. One of these had been when his mother bought some California prunes. Two others had been the two times when she cooked custard. Those had been events. He remembered them kindly. And at that time his mother had told him of a blissful dish she would sometime make—"floating island," she had called it, "better than custard." For years he had looked forward to the day when he would sit down to the table with floating island before him, until at last he had relegated the idea of it to the limbo of unattainable ideals.

Once he found a silver quarter lying on the sidewalk. That, also, was a great event in his life, withal a tragic one. He knew his duty on the instant the silver flashed on his eyes, before even he had picked it up. At home, as usual, there was not enough to eat, and home he should have taken it as he did his wages every Saturday night. Right conduct in this case was obvious; but he never had any spending of his money, and he was suffering from candy hunger. He was ravenous for the sweets that only on red-letter days he had ever tasted in his life.

He did not attempt to deceive himself. He knew it was sin, and deliberately he sinned when he went on a fifteen-cent candy debauch. Ten cents he saved for a future orgy; but not being accustomed to the carrying of money, he lost the ten cents. This occurred at the time when he was suffering all the torments of conscience, and it was to him an act of divine retribution. He had a frightened sense of the closeness of an awful and wrathful God. God had seen, and God had been swift to punish, denying him even the full wages of sin.

In memory he always looked back upon that event as the one great criminal deed of his life, and at the recollection his conscience always awoke and gave him another twinge. It was the one skeleton in his closet. Also, being so made and circumstanced, he looked back upon the deed with regret. He was dissatisfied with the manner in which he had spent the quarter. He could have invested it better, and, out of his later knowledge of the quickness of God, he would have beaten God out by spending the whole quarter at one fell swoop. In retrospect he spent the quarter a thousand times, and each time to better advantage.

There was one other memory of the past, dim and faded, but stamped into his soul everlasting by the savage feet of his father. It was more like a nightmare than a remembered vision of a concrete thing—more like the race-memory of man that makes him fall in his sleep and that goes back to his arboreal ancestry.

This particular memory never came to Johnny in broad daylight when he was wide awake. It came at night, in bed, at the moment that his consciousness was sinking down and losing itself in sleep. It always aroused him to frightened wakefulness, and for the moment, in the first sickening start, it seemed to him that he lay crosswise on the foot of the bed. In the bed were the vague forms of his father and mother. He never saw what his father looked like. He had but one impression of his father, and that was that he had savage and pitiless feet.

His earlier memories lingered with him, but he had no late memories. All days were alike. Yesterday or last year were the same as a thousand years—or a minute. Nothing ever happened. There were no events to mark the march of time. Time did not march. It stood always still. It was only the whirling machines that moved, and they moved nowhere—in spite of the fact that they moved faster.

When he was fourteen, he went to work on the starcher. It was a colossal event. Something had at last happened that could be remembered beyond a night's sleep or a week's pay-day. It marked an era. It was a machine Olympiad, a thing to date from. "When I went to work on the starcher," or "after," or "before I went to work on the starcher," were sentences often on his lips.

He celebrated his sixteenth birthday by going into the loom room and taking a loom. Here was an incentive again, for it was piece-work. And he excelled, because the clay of him had been moulded by the mills into the perfect machine. At the end of three months he was running two looms, and, later three and four.

At the end of his second year at the looms he was turning out more yards than any other weaver, and more than twice as much as some of the less skilful ones. And at home things began to prosper as he approached the full stature of his earning power. Not, however, that his increased earnings were in excess of need. The children were growing up. They ate more. And they were going to school, and school-books cost money. And somehow, the faster he worked, the faster climbed the prices of things. Even the rent went up, though the house had fallen from bad to worse disrepair.

He had grown taller; but with his increased height he seemed leaner than ever. Also, he was more nervous. With the nervousness increased his peevishness and irritability. The children had learned by many bitter lessons to fight shy of him. His mother respected him for his earning power, but somehow her respect was tinctured with fear.

There was no joyousness in life for him. The procession of the days he never saw. The nights he slept away in twitching unconsciousness. The rest of the time he worked, and his consciousness was machine consciousness. Outside this his mind was a blank. He had no ideals, and but one illusion; namely, that he drank excellent coffee. He was a work-beast. He had no mental life whatever; yet deep down in the crypts of his mind, unknown to him, were being weighed and sifted every hour of his toil, every movement of his hands, every twitch of his muscles, and preparations were making for a future course of action that would amaze him and all his little world.

It was in the late spring that he came home from work one night aware of unusual tiredness. There was a keen expectancy in the air as he sat down to the table, but he did not notice. He went through the meal in moody silence, mechanically eating what was before him. The children um'd and ah'd and made smacking noises with their mouths. But he was deaf to them.

"D'ye know what you're eatin'?" his mother demanded at last, desperately.

He looked vacantly at the dish before him, and vacantly at her.

"Floatin' island," she announced triumphantly.

"Oh," he said.

"Floating island!" the children chorused loudly.

"Oh," he said. And after two or three mouthfuls, he added, "I guess I ain't hungry to-night."

He dropped the spoon, shoved back his chair, and arose wearily from the table.

"An' I guess I'll go to bed."

His feet dragged more heavily than usual as he crossed the kitchen floor. Undressing was a Titan's task, a monstrous futility, and he wept weakly as he crawled into bed, one shoe still on. He was aware of a rising, swelling something inside his head that made his brain thick and fuzzy. His lean fingers felt as big as his wrist, while in the ends of them was a remoteness of sensation vague and fuzzy like his brain. The small of his back ached intolerably. All his bones ached. He ached everywhere. And in his head began the shrieking, pounding, crashing, roaring of a million looms. All space was filled with flying shuttles. They darted in and out, intricately, amongst the stars. He worked a thousand looms himself, and ever they speeded up, faster and faster, and his brain unwound, faster and faster, and became the thread that fed the thousand flying shuttles.

He did not go to work next morning. He was too busy weaving colossally on the thousand looms that ran inside his head. His mother went to work, but first she sent for the doctor. It was a severe attack of la grippe, he said. Jennie served as nurse and carried out his instructions.

It was a very severe attack, and it was a week before Johnny dressed and tottered feebly across the floor. Another week, the doctor said, and he would be fit to return to work. The foreman of the loom room visited him on Sunday afternoon, the first day of his convalescence. The best weaver in the room, the foreman told his mother. His job would be held for him. He could come back to work a week from Monday.

"Why don't you thank 'im, Johnny?" his mother asked anxiously.

"He's ben that sick he ain't himself yet," she explained apologetically to the visitor.

Johnny sat hunched up and gazing steadfastly at the floor. He sat in the same position long after the foreman had gone. It was warm outdoors, and he sat on the stoop in the afternoon. Sometimes his lips moved. He seemed lost in endless calculations.

Next morning, after the day grew warm, he took his seat on the stoop. He had pencil and paper this time with which to continue his calculations, and he calculated painfully and amazingly.

"What comes after millions?" he asked at noon, when Will came home from school. "An' how d'ye work 'em?"

That afternoon finished his task. Each day, but without paper and pencil, he returned to the stoop. He was greatly absorbed in the one tree that grew across the street. He studied it for hours at a time, and was unusually interested when the wind swayed its branches and fluttered its leaves. Throughout the week he seemed lost in a great communion with himself. On Sunday, sitting on the stoop, he laughed aloud, several times, to the perturbation of his mother, who had not heard him laugh in years.

Next morning, in the early darkness, she came to his bed to rouse him. He had had his fill of sleep all week, and awoke easily. He made no struggle, nor did he attempt to hold on to the bedding when she stripped it from him. He lay quietly, and spoke quietly.

"It ain't no use, ma."

"You'll be late," she said, under the impression that he was still stupid with sleep.

"I'm awake, ma, an' I tell you it ain't no use. You might as well lemme alone. I ain't goin' to git up."

"But you'll lose your job!" she cried.

"I ain't goin' to git up," he repeated in a strange, passionless voice.

She did not go to work herself that morning. This was sickness beyond any sickness she had ever known. Fever and delirium she could understand; but this was insanity. She pulled the bedding up over him and sent Jennie for the doctor.

When that person arrived, Johnny was sleeping gently, and gently he awoke and allowed his pulse to be taken.

"Nothing the matter with him," the doctor reported. "Badly debilitated, that's all. Not much meat on his bones."

"He's always been that way," his mother volunteered.

"Now go 'way, ma, an' let me finish my snooze."

Johnny spoke sweetly and placidly, and sweetly and placidly he rolled over on his side and went to sleep.

At ten o'clock he awoke and dressed himself. He walked out into the kitchen, where he found his mother with a frightened expression on her face.

"I'm goin' away, ma," he announced, "an' I jes' want to say good-by."

She threw her apron over her head and sat down suddenly and wept. He waited patiently.

"I might a-known it," she was sobbing.

"Where?" she finally asked, removing the apron from her head and gazing up at him with a stricken face in which there was little curiosity.

"I don't know—anywhere."

As he spoke, the tree across the street appeared with dazzling brightness on his inner vision. It seemed to lurk just under his eyelids, and he could see it whenever he wished.

"An' your job?" she quavered.

"I ain't never goin' to work again."

"My God, Johnny!" she wailed, "don't say that!"

What he had said was blasphemy to her. As a mother who hears her child deny God, was Johnny's mother shocked by his words.

"What's got into you, anyway?" she demanded, with a lame attempt at imperativeness.

"Figures," he answered. "Jes' figures. I've ben doin' a lot of figurin' this week, an' it's most surprisin'."

"I don't see what that's got to do with it," she sniffled.

Johnny smiled patiently, and his mother was aware of a distinct shock at the persistent absence of his peevishness and irritability.

"I'll show you," he said. "I'm plum' tired out. What makes me tired? Moves. I've been movin' ever since I was born. I'm tired of movin', an' I ain't goin' to move any more. Remember when I worked in the glass-house? I used to do three hundred dozen a day. Now I reckon I made about ten different moves to each bottle. That's thirty-six thousan' moves a day. Ten days, three hundred an' sixty thousan' moves a day. One month, one million an' eighty thousan' moves. Chuck out the eighty thousan'—" he spoke with the complacent beneficence of a philanthropist— "chuck out the eighty thousan', that leaves a million moves a month—twelve million moves a year.

"At the looms I'm movin' twic'st as much. That makes twenty-five million moves a year, an' it seems to me I've been a movin' that way 'most a million years.

"Now this week I ain't moved at all. I ain't made one move in hours an' hours. I tell you it was swell, jes' settin' there, hours an' hours, an' doin' nothin'. I ain't never ben happy before. I never had any time. I've been movin' all the time. That ain't no way to be happy. An' I ain't goin' to do it any more. I'm jes' goin' to set, an' set, an' rest, an' rest, and then rest some more."

"But what's goin' to come of Will an' the children?" she asked despairingly.

"That's it, 'Will an' the children,'" he repeated.

But there was no bitterness in his voice. He had long known his mother's ambition for the younger boy, but the thought of it no longer rankled. Nothing mattered any more. Not even that.

"I know, ma, what you've ben plannin' for Will—keepin' him in school to make a bookkeeper out of him. But it ain't no use, I've quit. He's got to go to work."

"An' after I have brung you up the way I have," she wept, starting to cover her head with the apron and changing her mind.

"You never brung me up," he answered with sad kindliness. "I brung myself up, ma, an' I brung up Will. He's bigger'n me, an' heavier, an' taller. When I was a kid, I reckon I didn't git enough to eat. When he come along an' was a kid, I was workin' an' earnin' grub for him too. But that's done with. Will can go to work, same as me, or he can go to hell, I don't care which. I'm tired. I'm goin' now. Ain't you goin' to say good-by?"

She made no reply. The apron had gone over her head again, and she was crying. He paused a moment in the doorway.

"I'm sure I done the best I knew how," she was sobbing.

He passed out of the house and down the street. A wan delight came into his face at the sight of the lone tree. "Jes' ain't goin' to do nothin'," he said to himself, half aloud, in a crooning tone. He glanced wistfully up at the sky, but the bright sun dazzled and blinded him.

It was a long walk he took, and he did not walk fast. It took him past the jutemill. The muffled roar of the loom room came to his ears, and he smiled. It was a gentle, placid smile. He hated no one, not even the pounding, shrieking machines. There was no bitterness in him, nothing but an inordinate hunger for rest.

The houses and factories thinned out and the open spaces increased as he approached the country. At last the city was behind him, and he was walking down a leafy lane beside the railroad track. He did not walk like a man. He did not look like a man. He was a travesty of the human. It was a twisted and stunted and nameless piece of life that shambled like a sickly ape, arms loose-hanging, stoop-shouldered, narrow-chested, grotesque and terrible.

He passed by a small railroad station and lay down in the grass under a tree. All afternoon he lay there. Sometimes he dozed, with muscles that twitched in his sleep. When awake, he lay without movement, watching the birds or looking up at the sky through the branches of the tree above him. Once or twice he laughed aloud, but without relevance to anything he had seen or felt.

After twilight had gone, in the first darkness of the night, a freight train rumbled into the station. When the engine was switching cars on to the side-track, Johnny crept along the side of the train. He pulled open the side-door of an empty box-car and awkwardly and laboriously climbed in. He closed the door. The engine whistled. Johnny was lying down, and in the darkness he smiled.

SECTION SIX

THE CALL OF THE WILD

1. INTO THE PRIMITIVE

"Old longings nomadic leap,
Chafing at custom's chain;
Again from its brumal sleep
Wakens the ferine strain."

BUCK did not read the newspapers, or he would have known that trouble was brewing, not alone for himself, but for every tidewater dog, strong of muscle and with warm, long hair, from Puget Sound to San Diego. Because men, groping in the Arctic darkness, had found a yellow metal, and because steamship and transportation companies were booming the find, thousands of men were rushing into the Northland. These men wanted dogs, and the dogs they wanted were heavy dogs, with strong muscles by which to toil, and furry coats to protect them from the frost.

Buck lived at a big house in the sun-kissed Santa Clara Valley. Judge Miller's place, it was called. It stood back from the road, half hidden among the trees, through which glimpses could be caught of the wide, cool veranda that ran around its four sides. The house was approached by graveled driveways which wound about through wide-spreading lawns and under the interlacing boughs of tall poplars. At the rear things were on even a more spacious scale than at the front. There were great stables, where a dozen grooms and boys held forth, rows of vine-clad servants' cottages, an endless and orderly array of outhouses, long grape arbors, green pastures, orchards, and berry patches. Then there was the pumping plant for the artesian well, and the big cement tank where Judge Miller's boys took their morning plunge and kept cool in the hot afternoon.

And over this great demesne Buck ruled. Here he was born, and here he had lived the four years of his life. It was true, there were other dogs. There could not but be other dogs on so vast a place, but they did not count. They came and went, resided in the populous kennels, or lived obscurely in the recesses of the house after the fashion of Toots, the Japanese pug, or Ysabel, the Mexican hairless—strange creatures that rarely put nose out of doors or set foot to ground. On the other hand, there were the fox terriers, a score of them at least, who yelped fearful promises at Toots and Ysabel looking out of the windows at them and protected by a legion of housemaids armed with brooms and mops.

But Buck was neither house dog nor kennel dog. The whole realm was his. He plunged into the swimming tank or went hunting with the Judge's sons; he escorted Mollie and Alice, the Judge's daughters, on long twilight or early morning rambles; on wintry nights he lay at the Judge's feet before the roaring library fire; he carried the Judge's grandsons on his back, or rolled them in the grass, and guarded their footsteps through wild adventures down to the fountain in the stable yard, and even beyond, where the paddocks were, and the berry patches. Among the terriers he stalked imperiously, and Toots and Ysabel he utterly ignored, for he was king—king over all creeping, crawling, flying things of Judge Miller's place, humans included.

His father, Elmo, a huge St. Bernard, had been the Judge's inseparable companion, and Buck bid fair to follow in the way of his father. He was not so large—he weighed only one hundred and forty pounds—for his mother, Shep, had been a Scotch shepherd dog. Nevertheless, one hundred and forty pounds, to which was added the dignity that comes of good living and universal respect, enabled him to carry himself in right royal fashion. During the four years since his puppyhood he had lived the life of a sated aristocrat; he had a fine pride in himself, was even a trifle egotistical, as country gentlemen sometimes become because of their insular situation. But he had saved himself by not becoming a mere pampered house dog. Hunting and kindred outdoor delights had kept down the fat and hardened his muscles; and to him, as to the cold-tubbing races, the love of water had been a tonic and a health preserver.

And this was the manner of dog Buck was in the fall of 1897, when the Klondike strike dragged men from all the world into the frozen North. But Buck did not read the newspapers, and he did not know that Manuel, one of the gardener's helpers, was an undesirable acquaintance. Manuel had one besetting sin. He loved to play Chinese lottery. Also, in his gambling, he had one besetting weakness—faith in a system: and this made his damnation certain. For to play a system requires money, while the wages of a gardener's helper do not lap over the needs of wife and numerous progeny.

The Judge was at a meeting of the Raisin Growers' Association, and the boys were busy organizing an athletic club, on the memorable night of Manuel's treachery. No one saw him and Buck go off through the orchard on what Buck imagined was merely a stroll. And with the exception of a solitary man, no one saw them arrive at the little flag station known as College Park. This man talked with Manuel, and money chinked between them.

"You might wrap up the goods before you deliver 'm," the stranger said gruffly, and Manuel doubled a piece of stout rope around Buck's neck under the collar.

"Twist it, an' you'll choke 'm plentee," said Manuel, and the stranger grunted a ready affirmative.

Buck had accepted the rope with quiet dignity. To be sure, it was an unwonted performance: but he had learned to trust in men he knew, and to give them credit for a wisdom that outreached his own. But when the ends of the rope were placed in the stranger's hands, he growled menacingly. He had merely intimated his displeasure, in his pride believing that to intimate was to command. But to his surprise the rope tightened around his neck, shutting off his breath. In quick rage he sprang at the man, who met him halfway, grappled him close by the throat, and with a deft twist threw him over on his back. Then the rope tightened mercilessly, while Buck struggled in a fury, his tongue lolling out of his mouth and his great chest panting futilely. Never in all his life had he been so vilely treated, and never in all his life had he been so angry. But his strength ebbed, his eyes glazed, and he knew nothing when the train was flagged and the two men threw him into the baggage car.

The next he knew, he was dimly aware that his tongue was hurting and that he was being jolted along in some kind of a conveyance. The hoarse shriek of a locomotive whistling a crossing told him where he was. He had traveled too often with the Judge not to know the sensation of riding in a baggage car. He opened his eyes, and into them came the unbridled anger of a kidnaped king. The man sprang for his throat, but Buck was too quick for him. His jaws closed on the hand, nor did they relax till his senses were choked out of him once more.

"Yep, has fits," the man said, hiding his mangled hand from the baggageman, who had been attracted by the sounds of struggle. "I'm takin' 'm up for the boss to 'Frisco. A crack dog doctor there thinks that he can cure 'm."

Concerning that night's ride, the man spoke most eloquently for himself, in a little shed back of a saloon on the San Francisco waterfront.

"All I get is fifty for it," he grumbled; "an' I wouldn't do it over for a thousand, cold cash."

His hand was wrapped in a bloody handkerchief, and the right trouser leg was ripped from knee to ankle.

"How much did the other mug get?" the saloonkeeper demanded.

"A hundred," was the reply. "Wouldn't take a sou less, so help me."

"That makes a hundred and fifty," the saloonkeeper calculated; "and he's worth it, or I'm a squarehead."

The kidnaper undid the bloody wrappings and looked at his lacerated hand. "If I don't get the hydrophoby—"

"It'll be because you was born to hang," laughed the saloonkeeper. "Here, lend me a hand before you pull your freight," he added.

Dazed, suffering intolerable pain from throat and tongue, with the life half throttled out of him, Buck attempted to face his tormentors. But he was thrown down and choked repeatedly till they succeeded in filing the heavy brass collar from off his neck. Then the rope was removed, and he was flung into a cagelike crate.

There he lay for the remainder of the weary night, nursing his wrath and wounded pride. He could not understand what it all meant. What did they want with him, these strange men? Why were they keeping him pent up in this narrow crate? He did not know why, but he felt oppressed by the vague sense of inpending calamity. Several times during the night he sprang to his feet when the shed door rattled open, expecting to see the Judge, or the boys at least. But each time it was the bulging face of the saloonkeeper that peered in at him by the sickly light of a tallow candle. And each time the joyful bark that trembled in Buck's throat was twisted into a savage growl.

But the saloonkeeper let him alone, and in the morning four men entered and picked up the crate. More tormentors, Buck decided, for they were evil-looking creatures, ragged and unkempt; and he stormed and raged at them through the bars. They only laughed and poked sticks at him, which he promptly assailed with his teeth till he realized that that was what they wanted. Whereupon he lay down sullenly and allowed the crate to be lifted into a wagon. Then he, and the crate in which he was imprisoned, began a passage through many hands. Clerks in the express office took charge of him; he was carted about in another wagon; a truck carried him, with an assortment of boxes and parcels, upon a ferry steamer; he was trucked off the steamer into a great railway depot, and finally he was deposited in an express car.

For two days and nights this express car was dragged along at the tail of shrieking locomotives; and for two days and nights Buck neither ate nor drank. In his anger he had met the first advances of the express messengers with growls, and they had retaliated by teasing him. When he flung himself against the bars, quivering and frothing, they laughed at him and taunted him. They growled and barked like detestable dogs, mewed, and flapped their arms and crowed. It was all very silly, he knew; but therefore the more outrage to his dignity, and his anger waxed and waxed. He did not mind the hunger so much, but the lack of water caused him severe suffering and fanned his wrath to fever pitch. For that matter, high-strung and finely sensitive, the ill treatment had flung him into a fever, which was fed by the inflammation of his parched and swollen throat and tongue.

He was glad for one thing: the rope was off his neck. That had given them an unfair advantage; but now that it was off, he would show them. They would never get another rope around his neck. Upon that he was resolved. For two days and nights he neither ate nor drank, and during those two days and nights of torment, he accumulated a fund of wrath that boded ill for whoever first fell foul of him. His eyes turned bloodshot, and he was metamorphosed into a raging fiend. So changed was he that the Judge himself would not have recognized him; and the express messengers breathed with relief when they bundled him off the train at Seattle.

Four men gingerly carried the crate from the wagon into a small, high-walled back yard. A stout man, with a red sweater that sagged generously at the neck, came out and signed the book for the driver. That was the man, Buck divined, the next tormentor, and he hurled himself savagely against the bars. The man smiled grimly, and brought a hatchet and a club.

"You ain't going to take him out now?" the driver asked.

"Sure," the man replied, driving the hatchet into the crate for a pry.

There was an instantaneous scattering of the four men who had carried it in, and from safe perches on top of the wall they prepared to watch the performance.

Buck rushed at the splintering wood, sinking his teeth into it, surging and wrestling with it. Wherever the hatchet fell on the outside, he was there on the inside, snarling and growling, as furiously anxious to get out as the man in the red sweater was calmly intent on getting him out.

"Now, you red-eyed devil," he said, when he had made an opening sufficient for the passage of Buck's body. At the same ime he dropped the hatchet and shifted the club to his right hand.

And Buck was truly a red-eyed devil, as he drew himself together for the spring, hair bristling, mouth foaming, a mad glitter in his bloodshot eyes. Straight at the man he launched his hundred and forty pounds of fury, surcharged with the pent passion of two days and nights. In mid-air, just as his jaws were about to close on the man, he received a shock that checked his body and brought his teeth together with an agonizing clip. He whirled over, fetching the ground on his back and side. He had never been struck by a club in his life, and did not understand. With a snarl that was part bark and more scream he was again on his feet and launched into the air. And again the shock came and he was brought crushingly to the ground. This time he was aware that it was the club, but his madness knew no caution. A dozen times he charged, and as often the club broke the charge and smashed him down.

After a particularly fierce blow, he crawled to his feet, too dazed to rush. He staggered limply about, the blood flowing from nose and mouth and ears, his beautiful coat sprayed and flecked with bloody slaver. Then the man advanced and deliberately dealt him a frightful blow on the nose. All the pain he had endured was as nothing compared with the exquisite agony of this. With a roar that was almost lionlike in its ferocity, he again hurled himself at the man. But the man, shifting the club from right to left, coolly caught him by the under jaw, at the same time wrenching downward and backward. Buck described a complete circle in the air, and half of another, then crashed to the ground on his head and chest.

For the last time he rushed. The man struck the shrewd blow he had purposely withheld for so long, and Buck crumpled up and went down, knocked utterly senseless.

"He's no slouch at dog-breakin', that's wot I say," one of the men on the wall cried enthusiastically.

"Druther break cayuses any day, and twice on Sundays," was the reply of the driver, as he climbed on the wagon and started the horses.

Buck's senses came back to him, but not his strength. He lay where he had fallen, and from there he watched the man in the red sweater.

"'Answers to the name of Buck,'" the man soliloquized, quoting from the saloonkeeper's letter, which had announced the consignment of the crate and contents. "Well, Buck, my boy," he went on in a genial voice, "we've had our little ruction, and the best thing we can do is to let it go at that. You've learned your place, and I know mine. Be a good dog and all'll go well and the goose hang high. Be a bad dog, and I'll whale the stuffin' outa you. Understand?"

As he spoke he fearlessly patted the head he had so mercilessly pounded, and though Buck's hair involuntarily bristled at touch of the hand, he endured it without protest. When the man brought him water he drank eagerly, and later bolted a generous meal of raw meat, chunk by chunk, from the man's hand.

He was beaten (he knew that); but he was not broken. He saw, once for all, that he stood no chance against a man with a club. He had learned the lesson, and in all his after life he never forgot it. That club was a revelation. It was his introduction to the reign of primitive law, and he met the introduction halfway. The facts of life took on a fiercer aspect; and while he faced that aspect uncowed, he faced it with all the latent cunning of his nature aroused. As the days went by, other dogs came, in crates and at the ends of ropes, some docilely, and some raging and roaring as he had come; and, one and all, he watched them pass under the dominion of the man in the red sweater. Again and again, as he looked at each brutal performance, the lesson was driven home to Buck: a man with a club was a lawgiver, a master to be obeyed, though not necessarily conciliated. Of this last Buck was never guilty, though he did see beaten dogs that fawned upon the man, and wagged their tails, and licked his hand. Also he saw one dog, that would neither conciliate nor obey, finally killed in the struggle for mastery.

Now and again men came, strangers, who talked excitedly, wheedlingly and in all kinds of fashions to the man in the red sweater. And at such times that money passed between them the strangers took one or more of the dogs away with them. Buck wondered where they went, for they never came back; but the fear of the future was strong upon him, and he was glad each time when he was not selected.

Yet his time came, in the end, in the form of a little weazened man who spat broken English and many strange and uncouth exclamations which Buck could not understand.

"*Sacrédam!*" he cried, when his eyes lit upon Buck. "Dot one dam bully dog! Eh? How moch?"

"Three hundred, and a present at that," was the prompt reply of the man in the red sweater. "And seein' it's government money, you ain't got no kick coming, eh, Perrault?"

Perrault grinned. Considering that the price of dogs had been boomed skyward by the unwonted demand, it was not an unfair sum for so fine an animal. The Canadian Government would be no loser, nor would its dispatches travel the slower. Perrault knew dogs, and when he looked at Buck he knew that he was one in a thousand. "One in ten t'ousand," he commented mentally.

Buck saw money pass between them, and was not surprised when Curly, a good-natured Newfoundland, and he were led away by the little weazened man. That was the last of the man in the red sweater, and as Curly and he looked at receding Seattle from the deck of the *Narwhal,* it was the last he saw of the warm Southland. Curly and he were taken below by Perrault and turned over to a black-faced giant called François. Perrault was a French-Canadian, and swarthy; but François was a French-Canadian half-breed, and twice as swarthy. They were a new kind of men to Buck (of which he was destined to see many more), and while he developed no affection for them, he none the less grew honestly to respect them. He speedily learned that Perrault and François were fair men, calm and impartial in administering justice, and too wise in the ways of dogs to be fooled by dogs.

In the 'tween decks of the *Narwhal,* Buck and Curly joined two other dogs. One of them was a big, snow-white fellow from Spitzbergen who had been brought away by a whaling captain, and who had later accompanied a Geological Survey into the Barrens. He was friendly, in a treacherous sort of way, smiling into one's face the while he meditated some underhand trick, as, for instance, when he stole from Buck's food at the first meal. As Buck sprang to punish him, the lash of François's whip sang through the air, reaching the culprit first; and nothing remained to Buck but to recover the bone. That was fair of François, he decided, and the half-breed began his rise in Buck's estimation.

The other dog made no advances, nor received any; also, he did not attempt to steal from the newcomers. He was a gloomy, morose fellow, and he showed Curly plainly that all he desired was to be left alone, and further, that there would be trouble if he were not left alone. Dave he was called, and he ate and slept, or yawned between times, and took interest in nothing, not even when the *Narwhal* crossed Queen Charlotte Sound and rolled and pitched and bucked like a thing possessed. When Buck and Curly grew excited, half wild with fear, he raised his head as though annoyed, favored them with an incurious glance, yawned, and went to sleep again.

Day and night the ship throbbed to the tireless pulse of the propeller, and though one day was very like another, it was apparent to Buck that the weather was steadily growing colder. At last, one morning, the propeller was quiet, and the *Narwhal* was pervaded with an atmosphere of excitement. He felt it, as did the other dogs, and knew that a change was at hand. François leashed them and brought them on deck. At the first step upon the cold surface, Buck's feet sank into a white mushy something very like mud. He sprang back with a snort. More of this white stuff was falling through the air. He shook himself, but more of it fell upon him. He sniffed it curiously, then licked some up on his tongue. It bit like fire, and the next instant was gone. This puzzled him. He tried it again, with the same result. The onlookers laughed uproariously, and he felt ashamed, he knew not why, for it was his first snow.

2. THE LAW OF CLUB AND FANG

BUCK'S first day on the Dyea beach was like a nightmare. Every hour was filled with shock and surprise. He had been suddenly jerked from the heart of civilization and flung into the heart of things primordial. No lazy, sun-kissed life was this, with nothing to do but loaf and be bored. Here was neither peace, nor rest, nor a moment's safety. All was confusion and action, and every moment life and limb were in peril. There was imperative need to be constantly alert; for these dogs and men were not town dogs and men. They were savages, all of them, who knew no law but the law of club and fang.

He had never seen dogs fight as these wolfish creatures fought, and his first experience taught him an unforgettable lesson. It is true, it was a vicarious experience, else he would not have lived to profit by it. Curly was the victim. They were camped near the log store, where she, in her friendly way, made advances to a husky dog the size of a full-grown wolf, though not half so large as she. There was no warning, only a leap in like a flash, a metallic clip of teeth, a leap out equally swift, and Curly's face was ripped open from eye to jaw.

It was the wolf manner of fighting, to strike and leap away; but there was more to it than this. Thirty or forty huskies ran to the spot and surrounded the combatants in an intent and silent circle. Buck did not comprehend that silent intentness, nor the eager way with which they were licking their chops. Curly rushed her antagonist, who struck again and leaped aside. He met her next rush with his chest, in a peculiar fashion that tumbled her off her feet. She never regained them. This was what the onlooking huskies had waited for. They closed in upon her, snarling and yelping, and she was buried, screaming with agony, beneath the bristling mass of bodies.

So sudden was it, and so unexpected, that Buck was taken aback. He saw Spitz run out his scarlet tongue in a way he had of laughing; and he saw François, swinging an ax, spring into the mess of dogs. Three men with clubs were helping him to scatter them. It did not take long. Two minutes from the time Curly went down, the last of her assailants were clubbed off. But she lay there limp and lifeless in the bloody, trampled snow, almost literally torn to pieces, the swart half-breed standing over her and cursing horribly. The scene often came back to Buck to trouble him in his sleep. So that was the way. No fair play. Once down, that was the end of you. Well, he would see to it that he never went down. Spitz ran out his tongue and laughed again, and from that moment Buck hated him with a bitter and deathless hatred.

Before he had recovered from the shock caused by the tragic passing of Curly, he received another shock. François fastened upon him an arrangement of straps and buckles. It was a harness, such as he had seen the grooms put on the horses at home. And as he had seen horses work, so he was set to work, hauling François on a sled to the forest that fringed the valley, and returning with a load of firewood. Though his dignity was sorely hurt by thus being made a draft animal, he was too wise to rebel. He buckled down with a will and did his best, though it was all new and strange. François was stern, demanding instant obedience, and by virtue of his whip receiving instant obedience; while Dave, who was an experienced wheeler, nipped Buck's hind quarters whenever he was in error. Spitz was the leader, likewise experienced, and while he could not always get at Buck, he growled sharp reproof now and again, or cunningly threw his weight in the traces to jerk Buck into the way he should go. Buck learned easily, and under the combined tuition of his two mates and François made remarkable progress. Ere they returned to camp he knew enough to stop at "ho," to go ahead at "mush," to swing wide on the bends, and to keep clear of the wheeler when the loaded sled shot downhill at their heels.

"T'ree vair' good dogs," François told Perrault. "Dat Buck, heem pool lak hell. I tich heem queek as anyt'ing."

By afternoon, Perrault, who was in a hurry to be on the trail with his dispatches, returned with two more dogs. Billee and Joe he called them, two brothers, and true huskies both. Sons of the one mother though they were, they were as different as day and night. Billee's one fault was his excessive good nature, while Joe was the very opposite, sour and introspective, with a perpetual snarl and a malignant eye. Buck received them in comradely fashion, Dave ignored them, while Spitz proceeded to thrash first one and then the other. Billee wagged his tail appeasingly, turned to run when he saw that appeasement was of no avail, and cried (still appeasingly) when Spitz's sharp teeth scored his flank. But no matter how Spitz circled, Joe whirled around on his heels to face him, mane bristling, ears laid back, lips writhing and snarling, jaws clipping together as fast as he could snap, and eyes diabolically gleaming—the incarnation of belligerent fear. So terrible was his appearance that Spitz was forced to forgo disciplining him; but to cover his own discomfiture he turned upon the inoffensive and wailing Billee and drove him to the confines of the camp.

By evening Perrault secured another dog, an old husky, long and lean and gaunt, with a battle-scarred face and a single eye which flashed a warning of prowess that commanded respect. He was called Sol-leks, which means The Angry One. Like Dave, he asked nothing, gave nothing, expected nothing; and when he marched slowly and deliberately into their midst, even Spitz left him alone. He had one peculiarity which Buck was unlucky enough to discover. He did not like to be approached on his blind side. Of this offense Buck was unwittingly guilty, and the first knowledge he had of his indiscretion was when Sol-leks whirled upon him and slashed his shoulder to the bone for three inches up and down. Forever after Buck avoided his blind side, and to the last of their comradeship had no more trouble. His only apparent ambition, like Dave's, was to be left alone; though, Buck was afterward to learn, each of them possessed one other and even more vital ambition.

That night Buck faced the great problem of sleeping. The tent, illumined by a candle, glowed warmly in the midst of the white plain; and when he, as a matter of course, entered it, both Perrault and François bombarded him with curses and cooking utensils, till he recovered from his consternation and fled ignominiously into the outer cold. A chill wind was blowing that nipped him sharply and bit with especial venom into his wounded shoulder. He lay down on the snow and attempted to sleep, but the frost soon drove him shivering to his feet. Miserable and disconsolate, he wandered about among the many tents, only to find that one place was as cold as another. Here and there savage dogs rushed upon him, but he bristled his neck hair and snarled (for he was learning fast), and they let him go his way unmolested.

Finally an idea came to him. He would return and see how his own teammates were making out. To his astonishment, they had disappeared. Again he wandered about through the great camp, looking for them, and again he returned. Were they in the tent? No, that could not be, else he would not have been driven out. Then where could they possibly be? With drooping tail and shivering body, very forlorn indeed, he aimlessly circled the tent. Suddenly the snow gave way beneath his forelegs and he sank down. Something wriggled under his feet. He sprang back, bristling and snarling, fearful of the unseen and unknown. But a friendly little yelp reassured him, and he went back to investigate. A whiff of warm air ascended to his nostrils, and there, curled up under the snow in a snug ball, lay Billee. He whined placatingly, squirmed and wriggled to show his good will and intentions, and even ventured, as a bribe for peace, to lick Buck's face with his warm, wet tongue.

Another lesson. So that was the way they did it, eh? Buck confidently selected a spot, and with much fuss and waste effort proceeded to dig a hole for himself. In a trice the heat from his body filled the confined space and he was asleep. The day had been long and arduous, and he slept soundly and comfortably, though he growled and barked and wrestled with bad dreams.

Nor did he open his eyes till roused by the noises of the waking camp. At first he did not know where he was. It had snowed during the night and he was completely buried. The snow walls pressed him on every side, and a great surge of fear swept through him—the fear of the wild thing for the trap. It was a token that he was harking back through his own life to the lives of his forebears; he was a civilized dog, an unduly civilized dog, and of his own experience knew no trap and so could not of himself fear it. The muscles of his whole body contracted spasmodically and instinctively, the hair on his neck and shoulders stood on end, and with a ferocious snarl he bounded straight up into the blinding day, the snow flying about him in a flashing cloud. Ere he landed on his feet, he saw the white camp spread out before him and knew where he was and remembered all that had passed from the time he went for a stroll with Manual to the hole he had dug for himself the night before.

A shout from François hailed his appearance. "Wot I say?" the dog driver cried to Perrault. "Dat Buck for sure learn queek as anyt'ing."

Perrault nodded gravely. As courier for the Canadian Government, bearing important dispatches, he was anxious to secure the best dogs, and he was particularly gladdened by the possession of Buck.

Three more huskies were added to the team inside an hour, making a total of nine, and before another quarter of an hour had passed they were in harness and swinging up the trail toward the Dyea Canyon. Buck was glad to be gone, and though the work was hard he found he did not particularly despise it. He was surprised at the eagerness which animated the whole team and which was communicated to him; but still more surprising was the change wrought in Dave and Sol-leks. They were new dogs, utterly transformed by the harness. All passiveness and unconcern had dropped from them. They were alert and active, anxious that the work should go well, and fiercely irritable with whatever, by delay or confusion, retarded that work. The toil of the traces seemed the supreme expression of their being, and all that they lived for and the only thing in which they took delight.

Dave was wheeler or sled dog, pulling in front of him was Buck, then came Sol-leks; the rest of the team was strung out ahead, single file, to the leader, which position was filled by Spitz.

Buck had been purposely placed between Dave and Sol-leks so that he might receive instruction. Apt scholar that he was, they were equally apt teachers, never allowing him to linger long in error, and enforcing their teaching with their sharp teeth. Dave was fair and very wise. He never nipped Buck without cause, and he never failed to nip him when he stood in need of it. As François's whip backed him up, Buck found it to be cheaper to mend his ways than to retaliate. Once, during a brief halt, when he got tangled in the traces and delayed the start, both Dave and Sol-leks flew at him and administered a sound trouncing. The resulting tangle was even worse, but Buck took good care to keep the traces clear thereafter; and ere the day was done, so well had he mastered his work, his mates about ceased nagging him. François's whip snapped less frequently, and Perrault even honored Buck by lifting up his feet and carefully examining them.

It was a hard day's run, up the Canyon, through Sheep Camp, past the Scales and the timber line, across glaciers and snowdrifts hundreds of feet deep, and over the great Chilkoot Divide, which stands between the salt water and the fresh and guards forbiddingly the sad and lonely North. They made good time down the chain of lakes which fills the craters of extinct volcanoes, and late that night pulled into the huge camp at the head of Lake Bennett, where thousands of gold seekers were building boats against the breakup of the ice in the spring. Buck made his hole in the snow and slept the sleep of the exhausted just, but all too early was routed out in the cold darkness and harnessed with his mates to the sled.

That day they made forty miles, the trail being packed; but the next day, and for many days to follow, they broke their own trail, worked harder, and made poorer time. As a rule, Perrault traveled ahead of the team, packing the snow with webbed shoes to make it easier for them. François, guiding the sled at the gee pole, sometimes exchanged places with him, but not often. Perrault was in a hurry, and he prided himself on his knowledge of ice, which knowledge was indispensable, for the fall ice was very thin, and where there was swift water, there was no ice at all.

Day by day, for days unending, Buck toiled in the traces. Always, they broke camp in the dark, and the first gray of dawn found them hitting the trail with fresh miles reeled off behind

them. And always they pitched camp after dark, eating their bit
of fish, and crawling to sleep into the snow. Buck was ravenous.
The pound and a half of sun-dried salmon which was his ration
for each day seemed to go nowhere. He never had enough, and
suffered from perpetual hunger pangs. Yet the other dogs, because
they weighed less and were born to the life, received a pound only
of the fish and managed to keep in good condition.

He swiftly lost the fastidiousness which had characterized his
old life. A dainty eater, he found that his mates, finishing first,
robbed him of his unfinished ration. There was no defending it.
While he was fighting off two or three, it was disappearing down
the throats of the others. To remedy this, he ate as fast as they;
and, so greatly did hunger compel him, he was not above taking
what did not belong to him. He watched and learned. When he
saw Pike, one of the new dogs, a clever malingerer and thief, slyly
steal a slice of bacon when Perrault's back was turned, he duplicated the performance the following day, getting away with the
whole chunk. A great uproar was raised, but he was unsuspected;
while Dub, an awkward blunderer who was always getting caught,
was punished for Buck's misdeed.

This first theft marked Buck as fit to survive in the hostile
Northland environment. It marked his adaptability, his capacity
to adjust himself to changing conditions, the lack of which would
have meant swift and terrible death. It marked, further, the decay
or going to pieces of his moral nature, a vain thing and a handicap in the ruthless struggle for existence. It was all well enough in
the Southland, under the law of love and fellowship, to respect
private property and personal feelings; but in the Northland,
under the law of club and fang, whoso took such things into account was a fool, and in so far as he oberved them he would fail
to prosper.

Not that Buck reasoned it out. He was fit, that was all, and unconsciously he accommodated himself to the new mode of life.
All his days, no matter what the odds, he had never run from a
fight. But the club of the man in the red sweater had beaten into
him a more fundamental and primitive code. Civilized, he could
have died for a moral consideration, say the defense of Judge
Miller's riding whip; but the completeness of his decivilization
was now evidenced by his ability to flee from the defense of a

moral consideration and so save his hide. He did not steal for joy of it, but because of the clamor of his stomach. He did not rob openly, but stole secretly and cunningly, out of respect for club and fang. In short, the things he did were done because it was easier to do them than not to do them.

His development (or retrogression) was rapid. His muscles became hard as iron, and he grew callous to all ordinary pain. He achieved an internal as well as external economy. He could eat anything, no matter how loathsome or indigestible; and, once eaten, the juices of his stomach extracted the last least particle of nutriment; and his blood carried it to the farthest reaches of his body, building it into the toughest and stoutest of tissues. Sight and scent became remarkably keen, while his hearing developed such acuteness that in his sleep he heard the faintest sound and knew whether it heralded peace or peril. He learned to bite the ice out with his teeth when it collected between his toes; and when he was thirsty and there was a thick scum of ice over the water hole, he would break it by rearing and striking it with stiff forelegs. His most conspicuous trait was an ability to scent the wind and forecast it a night in advance. No matter how breathless the air when he dug his nest by a tree or bank, the wind that later blew inevitably found him to leeward, sheltered and snug.

And not only did he learn by experience, but instincts long dead became alive again. The domesticated generations fell from him. In vague ways he remembered back to the youth of the breed, to the time the wild dogs ranged in packs through the primeval forest and killed their meat as they ran it down. It was no task for him to learn to fight with cut and slash and the quick wolf snap. In this manner had fought forgotten ancestors. They quickened the old life within him, and the old tricks which they had stamped into the heredity of the breed were his tricks. They came to him without effort or discovery, as though they had been his always. And when, on the still, cold nights, he pointed his nose at a star and howled long and wolflike, it was his ancestors, dead and dust, pointing nose at star and howling down through the centuries and through him. And his cadences were their cadences, the cadences which voiced their woe and what to them was the meaning of the stillness, and the cold, and dark.

Thus, as a token of what a puppet thing life is, the ancient song surged through him and he came into his own again; and he came because men had found a yellow metal in the North, and because Manuel was a gardener's helper whose wages did not lap over the needs of his wife and divers small copies of himself.

3. THE DOMINANT PRIMORDIAL BEAST

THE dominant primordial beast was strong in Buck, and under the fierce conditions of trail life it grew and grew. Yet it was a secret growth. His newborn cunning gave him poise and control. He was too busy adjusting himself to the new life to feel at ease, and not only did he not pick fights, but he avoided them whenever possible. A certain deliberateness characterized his attitude. He was not prone to rashness and precipitate action; and in the bitter hatred between him and Spitz he betrayed no impatience, shunned all offensive acts.

On the other hand, possibly because he divined in Buck a dangerous rival, Spitz never lost an opportunity of showing his teeth. He even went out of his way to bully Buck, striving constantly to start the fight which could end only in the death of one or the other.

Early in the trip this might have taken place had it not been for an unwonted accident. At the end of this day they made a bleak and miserable camp on the shore of Lake Laberge. Driving snow, a wind that cut like a white-hot knife, and darkness had forced them to grope for a camping place. They could hardly have fared worse. At their backs rose a perpendicular wall of rock, and Perrault and François were compelled to make their fire and spread their sleeping robes on the ice of the lake itself. The tent they had discarded at Dyea in order to travel light. A few sticks of driftwood furnished them with a fire that thawed down through the ice and left them to eat supper in the dark.

Close in under the sheltering rock Buck made his nest. So snug and warm was it, that he was loath to leave it when François distributed the fish which he had first thawed over the fire. But when Buck finished his ration and returned, he found his nest occupied. A warning snarl told him that the trespasser was Spitz. Till now Buck had avoided trouble with his enemy, but this was too much. The beast in him roared. He sprang upon Spitz with a fury which surprised them both, and Spitz particularly, for his whole experience with Buck had gone to teach him that his rival was an unusually timid dog, who managed to hold his own only because of his great weight and size.

François was surprised, too, when they shot out in a tangle from the disrupted nest and he divined the cause of the trouble. "A-a-ah!" he cried to Buck. "Gif it to heem, by Gar! Gif it to heem, the dirty t'eef!"

Spitz was equally willing. He was crying with sheer rage and eagerness as he circled back and forth for a chance to spring in. Buck was no less eager, and no less cautious, as he likewise circled back and forth for the advantage. But it was then that the unexpected happened, the thing which projected their struggle for supremacy far into the future, past many a weary mile of trail and toil.

An oath from Perrault, the resounding impact of a club upon a bony frame, and a shrill yelp of pain heralded the breaking forth of pandemonium. The camp was suddenly discovered to be alive with skulking furry forms—starving huskies, four or five score of them, who had scented the camp from some Indian village. They had crept in while Buck and Spitz were fighting, and when the two men sprang among them with stout clubs they showed their teeth and fought back. They were crazed by the smell of the food. Perrault found one with head buried in the grub box. His club landed heavily on the gaunt ribs, and the grub box was capsized on the ground. On the instant a score of the famished brutes were scrambling for the bread and bacon. The clubs fell upon them unheeded. They yelped and howled under the rain of blows, but struggled none the less madly till the last crumb had been devoured.

In the meantime the astonished team dogs had burst out of their nests only to be set upon by the fierce invaders. Never had Buck seen such dogs. It seemed as though their bones would burst through their skins. They were mere skeletons, draped loosely in draggled hides, with blazing eyes and slavered fangs. But the hunger madness made them terrifying, irresistible. There was no opposing them. The team dogs were swept back against the cliff at the first onset. Buck was beset by three huskies, and in a trice his head and shoulders were ripped and slashed. The din was frightful. Billee was crying as usual. Dave and Sol-leks, dripping blood from a score of wounds, were fighting bravely side by side. Joe was snapping like a demon. Once, his teeth closed on the foreleg of a husky, and he crunched down through the bone. Pike, the malingerer, leaped upon the crippled animal, breaking its neck with a quick flash of teeth and a jerk. Buck got a frothing adversary by the throat, and was sprayed with blood when his teeth sank through the jugular. The warm taste of it in his mouth goaded him to greater fierceness. He flung himself upon another, and at the same time felt teeth sink into his own throat. It was Spitz, treacherously attacking from the side.

Perrault and François, having cleaned out their part of the camp, hurried to save their sled dogs. The wild wave of famished beasts rolled back before them, and Buck shook himself free. But it was only for a moment. The two men were compelled to run back to save the grub, upon which the huskies returned to the attack on the team. Billee, terrified into bravery, sprang through the savage circle and fled away over the ice. Pike and Dub followed on his heels, with the rest of the team behind. As Buck drew himself together to spring after them, out of the tail of his eye he saw Spitz rush upon him with the evident intention of overthrowing him. Once off his feet and under that mass of huskies, there was no hope for him. But he braced himself to the shock of Spitz's charge, then joined the flight out on the lake.

Later, the nine team dogs gathered together and sought shelter in the forest. Though unpursued, they were in a sorry plight. There was not one who was not wounded in four or five places,

while some were wounded grievously. Dub was badly injured in a
hind leg; Dolly, the last husky added to the team at Dyea, had a
badly torn throat; Joe had lost an eye; while Billee, the good-natured, with an ear chewed and rent to ribbons, cried and whimpered throughout the night. At daybreak they limped warily back
to camp, to find the marauders gone and the two men in bad
tempers. Fully half their grub supply was gone. The huskies had
chewed through the sled lashings and canvas coverings. In fact,
nothing, no matter how remotely eatable, had escaped them.
They had eaten a pair of Perrault's moose-hide moccasins, chunks
out of the leather traces, and even two feet of lash from the end
of François's whip. He broke from a mournful contemplation of it
to look over his wounded dogs.

"Ah, my frien's," he said softly, "mebbe it mek you mad dog,
dose many bites. Mebbe all mad dog, *sacrédam!* Wot you t'ink,
eh, Perrault?"

The courier shook his head dubiously. With four hundred miles
of trail between him and Dawson, he could ill afford to have
madness break out among his dogs. Two hours of cursing and exertion got the harnesses into shape and the wound-stiffened team
was under way, struggling painfully over the hardest part of the
trail they had yet encountered, and for that matter, the hardest
between them and Dawson.

The Thirty Mile River was wide open. Its wild water defied the
frost, and it was in the eddies only and in the quiet places that
the ice held at all. Six days of exhausting toil were required to
cover those thirty terrible miles. And terrible they were, for every
foot of them was accomplished at the risk of life to dog and man.
A dozen times Perrault, nosing the way, broke through the ice
bridges, being saved by the long pole he carried, which he so held
that it fell each time across the hole made by his body. But a cold
snap was on, the thermometer registering fifty below zero, and
each time he broke through he was compelled for very life to
build a fire and dry his garments.

Nothing daunted him. It was because nothing daunted him
that he had been chosen for government courier. He took all manner of risks, resolutely thrusting his little weazened face into the
frost and struggling on from dim dawn to dark. He skirted the
frowning shores on rim ice that bent and crackled under foot and

upon which they dared not halt. Once, the sled broke through, with Dave and Buck, and they were half-frozen and all but drowned by the time they were dragged out. The usual fire was necessary to save them. They were coated solidly with ice, and the two men kept them on the run around the fire, sweating and thawing, so close that they were singed by the flames.

At another time Spitz went through, dragging the whole team after him up to Buck, who strained backward with all his strength, his forepaws on the slippery edge and the ice quivering and snapping all around. But behind him was Dave, likewise straining backward, and behind the sled was François, pulling till his tendons cracked.

Again, the rim ice broke away before and behind, and there was no escape except up the cliff. Perrault scaled it by a miracle, while François prayed for just that miracle; and with every thong and sled lashing and the last bit of harness rove into a long rope, the dogs were hoisted, one by one, to the cliff crest. François came up last, after the sled and load. Then came the search for a place to descend, which descent was ultimately made by the aid of the rope, and night found them back on the river with a quarter of a mile to the day's credit.

By the time they made the Hootalinqua and good ice, Buck was played out. The rest of the dogs were in like condition; but Perrault, to make up lost time, pushed them late and early. The first day they covered thirty-five miles to the Big Salmon; the next day thirty-five more to the Little Salmon; the third day forty miles, which brought them well up toward the Five Fingers.

Buck's feet were not so compact and hard as the feet of the huskies. His had softened during the many generations since the day his last wild ancestor was tamed by a cave dweller or river man. All day long he limped in agony, and camp once made, lay down like a dead dog. Hungry as he was, he would not move to receive his ration of fish, which François had to bring to him. Also, the dog driver rubbed Buck's feet for half an hour each night after supper, and sacrificed the tops of his own moccasins to make four moccasins for Buck. This was a great relief, and Buck caused even the weazened face of Perrault to twist itself into a grin one morning, when François forgot the moccasins and Buck lay on his back, his four feet waving appealingly in the air, and refused to budge without them. Later his feet grew hard to the trail, and the worn-out footgear was thrown away.

At the Pelly one morning, as they were harnessing up, Dolly, who had never been conspicuous for anything, went suddenly mad. She announced her condition by a long, heartbreaking wolf howl that sent every dog bristling with fear, then sprang straight for Buck. He had never seen a dog go mad, nor did he have any reason to fear madness; yet he knew that here was horror, and fled away from it in a panic. Straight away he raced, with Dolly, panting and frothing, one leap behind; nor could she gain on him, so great was his terror, nor could he leave her, so great was her madness. He plunged through the wooded breast of the island, flew down to the lower end, crossed a back channel filled with rough ice to another island, gained a third island, curved back to the main river, and in desperation started to cross it. And all the time, though he did not look, he could hear her snarling just one leap behind. François called to him a quarter of a mile away and he doubled back, still one leap ahead, gasping painfully for air and putting all his faith in that François would save him. The dog driver held the ax poised in his hand, and as Buck shot past him the ax crashed down upon mad Dolly's head.

Buck staggered over against the sled, exhausted, sobbing for breath, helpless. This was Spitz's opportunity. He sprang upon Buck, and twice his teeth sank into his unresisting foe and ripped and tore the flesh to the bone. Then François's lash descended, and Buck had the satisfaction of watching Spitz receive the worst whipping as yet administered to any of the team.

"One devil, dat Spitz," remarked Perrault. "Some dam' day heem keel dat Buck."

"Dat Buck two devils," was François's rejoinder. "All de tam I watch dat Buck I know for sure. Lissen: some dam' fine day heem get mad lak hell an' den heem chew dat Spitz all up an' spit heem out on de snow. Sure. I know."

From then on it was war between them. Spitz, as lead dog and acknowledged master of the team, felt his supremacy threatened by this strange Southland dog. And strange Buck was to him, for of the many Southland dogs he had known, not one had shown up worthily in camp and on trail. They were all too soft, dying under the toil, the frost, and starvation. Buck was the exception.

He alone endured and prospered, matching the husky in strength, savagery, and cunning. Then he was a masterful dog, and what made him dangerous was the fact that the club of the man in the red sweater had knocked all blind pluck and rashness out of his desire for mastery. He was pre-eminently cunning, and could bide his time with a patience that was nothing less than primitive.

It was inevitable that the clash for leadership should come. Buck wanted it. He wanted it because it was his nature, because he had been gripped tight by that nameless, incomprehensible pride of the trail and trace—that pride which holds dogs in the toil to the last gasp, which lures them to die joyfully in the harness, and breaks their hearts if they are cut out of the harness. This was the pride of Dave as wheel dog, of Sol-leks as he pulled with all his strength; the pride that laid hold of them at break of camp, transforming them from sour and sullen brutes into straining, eager, ambitious creatures; the pride that spurred them on all day and dropped them at pitch of camp at night, letting them fall back into gloomy unrest and uncontent. This was the pride that bore up Spitz and made him thrash the sled dogs who blundered and shirked in the traces or hid away at harness-up time in the morning. Likewise it was this pride that made him fear Buck as a possible lead dog. And this was Buck's pride, too.

He openly threatened the other's leadership. He came between him and the shirks he should have punished. And he did it deliberately. One night there was a heavy snowfall, and in the morning Pike, the malingerer, did not appear. He was securely hidden in his nest under a foot of snow. François called him and sought him in vain. Spitz was wild with wrath. He raged through the camp, smelling and digging in every likely place, snarling so frightfully that Pike heard and shivered in his hiding place.

But when he was at last unearthed, and Spitz flew at him to punish him, Buck flew, with equal rage, in between. So unexpected was it, and so shrewdly managed, that Spitz was hurled backward and off his feet. Pike, who had been trembling abjectly, took heart at this open mutiny, and sprang upon his overthrown leader. Buck, to whom fair play was a forgotten code, likewise sprang upon Spitz. But François, chuckling at the incident while unswerving the administration of justice, brought his lash down upon Buck with all his might. This failed to drive Buck from his prostrate rival, and the butt of the whip was brought into play. Half-stunned by the blow, Buck was knocked backward and the lash laid upon him again and again, while Spitz soundly punished the many-times-offending Pike.

In the days that followed, as Dawson grew closer and closer, Buck still continued to interfere between Spitz and the culprits; but he did it craftily, when François was not around. With the covert mutiny of Buck, a general insubordination sprang up and increased. Dave and Sol-leks were unaffected, but the rest of the team went from bad to worse. Things no longer went right. There was continual bickering and jangling. Trouble was always afoot, and at the bottom of it was Buck. He kept François busy, for the dog driver was in constant apprehension of the life-and-death struggle between the two which he knew must take place sooner or later; and on more than one night the sounds of quarreling and strife among the other dogs turned him out of his sleeping robe, fearful that Buck and Spitz were at it.

But the opportunity did not present itself, and they pulled into Dawson one dreary afternoon with the great fight still to come. Here were many men, and countless dogs, and Buck found them all at work. It seemed the ordained order of things that dogs should work. All day they swung up and down the main street in long teams, and in the night their jingling bells still went by. They hauled cabin logs and firewood, freighted up to the mines, and did all manner of work that horses did in the Santa Clara Valley. Here and there Buck met Southland dogs, but in the main they were the wild wolf husky breed. Every night, regularly, at nine, at twelve, at three, they lifted a nocturnal song, a weird and eerie chant, in which it was Buck's delight to join.

With the aurora borealis flaming coldly overhead, or the stars leaping in the frost dance, and the land numb and frozen under its pall of snow, this song of the huskies might have been the defiance of life, only it was pitched in minor key, with long-drawn wailings and half-sobs, and was more the pleading of life, the articulate travail of existence. It was an old song, old as the breed itself—one of the first songs of the younger world in a day when songs were sad. It was invested with the woe of unnumbered generations, this plaint by which Buck was so strangely stirred. When he moaned and sobbed, it was with the pain of living that was of old the pain of his wild fathers, and the fear and mystery of the cold and dark that was to them fear and mystery. And that he should be stirred by it marked the completeness with which he harked back through the ages of fire and roof to the raw beginnings of life in the howling ages.

Seven days from the time they pulled into Dawson, they dropped down the steep bank by the Barracks to the Yukon Trail, and pulled for Dyea and Salt Water. Perrault was carrying dispatches if anything more urgent than those he had brought in; also, the travel pride had gripped him, and he purposed to make the record trip of the year. Several things favored him in this. The week's rest had recuperated the dogs and put them in thorough trim. The trail they had broken into the country was packed hard by later journeyers. And further, the police had arranged in two or three places deposits of grub for dog and man, and he was traveling light.

They made Sixty Mile, which is a fifty-mile run, on the first day; and the second day saw them booming up the Yukon well on their way to Pelly. But such splendid running was achieved not without great trouble and vexation on the part of François. The insidious revolt led by Buck had destroyed the solidarity of the team. It no longer was as one dog leaping in the traces. The encouragement Buck gave the rebels led them into all kinds of petty misdemeanors. No more was Spitz a leader greatly to be feared. The old awe departed, and they grew equal to challenging his authority. Pike robbed him of half a fish one night, and gulped it down under the protection of Buck. Another night Dub and Joe fought Spitz and made him forego the punishment they deserved. And even Billee, the good-natured, was less good-natured, and whined not half so placatingly as in former days. Buck never came near Spitz without snarling and bristling menacingly. In fact, his conduct approached that of a bully, and he was given to swaggering up and down before Spitz's very nose.

The breaking down of discipline likewise affected the dogs in their relations with one another. They quarreled and bickered more than ever among themselves, till at times the camp was a howling bedlam. Dave and Sol-leks alone were unaltered, though they were made irritable by the unending squabbling. François swore strange, barbarous oaths, and stamped the snow in futile rage, and tore his hair. His lash was always singing among the dogs, but it was of small avail. Directly his back was turned they were at it again. He backed up Spitz with his whip, while Buck backed up the remainder of the team. François knew he was behind all the trouble, and Buck knew he knew; but Buck was too clever ever again to be caught red-handed. He worked faithfully in the harness, for the toil had become a delight to him; yet it was a greater delight slyly to precipitate a fight amongst his mates and tangle the traces.

At the mouth of the Talkeetna, one night after supper, Dub turned up a snowshoe rabbit, blundered it, and missed. In a second the whole team was in full cry. A hundred yards away was a camp of the Northwest Police, with fifty dogs, huskies all, who joined the chase. The rabbit sped down the river, turned off into a small creek, up the frozen bed of which it held steadily. It ran lightly on the surface of the snow, while the dogs ploughed through by main strength. Buck led the pack, sixty strong, around bend after bend, but he could not gain. He lay down low to the race, whining eagerly, his splendid body flashing forward, leap by leap, in the wan, white moonlight. And leap by leap, like some pale frost wraith, the snowshoe rabbit flashed on ahead.

All that stirring of old instincts which at stated periods drives men out from the sounding cities to forest and plain to kill things by chemically propelled leaden pellets, the blood lust, the joy to kill—all this was Buck's, only it was infinitely more intimate. He was ranging at the head of the pack, running the wild thing down, the living meat, to kill with his own teeth and wash his muzzle to the eyes in warm blood.

There is an ecstasy that marks the summit of life, and beyond which life cannot rise. And such is the paradox of living, this ecstasy comes when one is most alive, and it comes as complete forgetfulness that one is alive. This ecstasy, this forgetfulness of living, comes to the artist, caught up and out of himself in a sheet of flame; it comes to the soldier, war-mad on a stricken field and refusing quarter; and it came to Buck, leading the pack, sounding the old wolf cry, straining after the food that was alive and that fled swiftly before him through the moonlight. He was sounding the deeps of his nature, and of the parts of his nature that were deeper than he, going back into the womb of Time. He was mastered by the sheer surging of life, the tidal wave of being, the perfect joy of each separate muscle, joint, and sinew in that it was everything that was not death, that it was aglow and rampant, expressing itself in movement, flying exultantly under the stars and over the face of dead matter that did not move.

But Spitz, cold and calculating even in his supreme moods, left the pack and cut across a narrow neck of land where the creek made a long bend around. Buck did not know of this, and as he rounded the bend, the frost wraith of a rabbit still flitting before him, he saw another and larger frost wraith leap from the overhanging bank into the immediate path of the rabbit. It was Spitz. The rabbit could not turn, and as the white teeth broke its back in mid-air it shrieked as loudly as a stricken man may shriek. At sound of this, the cry of Life plunging down from Life's apex in the grip of Death, the full pack at Buck's heels raised a hell's chorus of delight.

Buck did not cry out. He did not check himself, but drove in upon Spitz, shoulder to shoulder, so hard that he missed the throat. They rolled over and over in the powdery snow. Spitz gained his feet almost as though he had not been overthrown, slashing Buck down the shoulder and leaping clear. Twice his teeth clipped together, like the steel jaws of a trap, as he backed away for better footing, with lean and lifting lips that writhed and snarled.

In a flash Buck knew it. The time had come. It was to the death. As they circled about, snarling, ears laid back, keenly watchful for the advantage, the scene came to Buck with a sense of familiarity. He seemed to remember it all—the white woods, and earth, and moonlight, and the thrill of battle. Over the whiteness and silence brooded a ghostly calm. There was not the faintest whisper of air—nothing moved, not a leaf quivered, the visible breaths of the dogs rising slowly and lingering in the frosty air. They had made short work of the snowshoe rabbit, these dogs that were ill-tamed wolves; and they were now drawn up in an expectant circle. They, too, were silent, their eyes only gleaming and their breaths drifting slowly upward. To Buck it was nothing new or strange, this scene of old time. It was as though it had always been, the wonted way of things.

Spitz was a practiced fighter. From Spitzbergen through the

Arctic, and across Canada and the Barrens, he had held his own
with all manner of dogs and achieved to mastery over them. Bitter rage was his, but never blind rage. In passion to rend and destroy, he never forgot that his enemy was in like passion to rend
and destroy. He never rushed till he was prepared to receive a
rush; never attacked till he had first defended that attack.

In vain Buck strove to sink his teeth in the neck of the big white
dog. Wherever his fangs struck for the softer flesh, they were
countered by the fangs of Spitz. Fang clashed fang, and lips were
cut and bleeding, but Buck could not penetrate his enemy's
guard. Then he warmed up and enveloped Spitz in a whirlwind of
rushes. Time and time again he tried for the snow-white throat,
where life bubbled near to the surface, and each time and every
time Spitz slashed him and got away. Then Buck took to rushing,
as though for the throat, when, suddenly drawing back his head
and curving in from the side, he would drive his shoulder at the
shoulder of Spitz, as a ram by which to overthrow him. But instead, Buck's shoulder was slashed down each time as Spitz leaped
lightly away.

Spitz was untouched, while Buck was streaming with blood and
panting hard. The fight was growing desperate. And all the while
the silent and wolfish circle waited to finish off whichever dog
went down. As Buck grew winded, Spitz took to rushing, and he
kept him staggering for footing. Once Buck went over, and the
whole circle of sixty dogs started up; but he recovered himself, almost in mid-air, and the circle sank down again and waited.

But Buck possessed a quality that made for greatness—imagination. He fought by instinct, but he could fight by head as well. He
rushed, as though attempting the old shoulder trick, but at the
last instant swept low to the snow and in. His teeth closed on
Spitz's left foreleg. There was a crunch of breaking bone, and the
white dog faced him on three legs. Thrice he tried to knock him
over, then repeated the trick and broke the right foreleg. Despite
the pain and helplessness, Spitz struggled madly to keep up. He
saw the silent circle, with gleaming eyes, lolling tongues, and silvery breaths drifting upward, closing in upon him as he had seen
similar circles close in upon beaten antagonists in the past. Only
this time he was the one who was beaten.

There was no hope for him. Buck was inexorable. Mercy was a

thing reserved for gentler climes. He maneuvered for the final rush. The circle had tightened till he could feel the breaths of the huskies on his flanks. He could see them, beyond Spitz and to either side, half-crouching for the spring, their eyes fixed upon him. A pause seemed to fall. Every animal was motionless as though turned to stone. Only Spitz quivered and bristled as he staggered back and forth, snarling with horrible menace, as though to frighten off impending death. Then Buck sprang in and out; but while he was in, shoulder had at last squarely met shoulder. The dark circle became a dot on the moon-flooded snow as Spitz disappeared from view. Buck stood and looked on, the successful champion, the dominant primordial beast who had made his kill and found it good.

4. WHO HAS WON TO MASTERSHIP

"EH? Wot I say? I spik true w'en I say dat Buck two devils."

This was François's speech next morning when he discovered Spitz missing and Buck covered with wounds. He drew him to the fire and by its light pointed them out.

"Dat Spitz fight lak hell," said Perrault, as he surveyed the gaping rips and cuts.

"An' dat Buck fight lak two hells," was François's answer. "An' now we make good time. No more Spitz, no more trouble, sure."

While Perrault packed the camp outfit and loaded the sled, the dog driver proceeded to harness the dogs. Buck trotted up to the place Spitz would have occupied as leader; but François, not noticing him, brought Sol-leks to the coveted position. In his judgment, Sol-leks was the best lead dog left. Buck sprang upon Sol-leks in a fury, driving him back and standing in his place.

"Eh? eh?" François cried, slapping his thighs gleefully. "Look at dat Buck. Heem keel dat Spitz, heem t'ink to take de job."

"Go 'way, Chook!" he cried, but Buck refused to budge.

He took Buck by the scruff of the neck, and though the dog growled threateningly, dragged him to one side and replaced Sol-leks. The old dog did not like it, and showed plainly that he was afraid of Buck. François was obdurate, but when he turned his back Buck again displaced Sol-leks, who was not at all unwilling to go.

François was angry. "Now, by Gar, I feex you!" he cried, coming back with a heavy club in his hand.

Buck remembered the man in the red sweater, and retreated slowly; nor did he attempt to charge in when Sol-leks was once more brought forward. But he circled just beyond the range of the club, snarling with bitterness and rage; and while he circled he watched the club so as to dodge it if thrown by François, for he was become wise in the way of clubs.

The driver went about his work, and he called to Buck when he was ready to put him in his old place in front of Dave. Buck retreated two or three steps. François followed him up, whereupon he again retreated. After some time of this, François threw down the club, thinking that Buck feared a thrashing. But Buck was in open revolt. He wanted, not to escape a clubbing, but to have the leadership. It was his by right. He had earned it, and he would not be content with less.

Perrault took a hand. Between them they ran him about for the better part of an hour. They threw clubs at him. He dodged. They cursed him, and his fathers and mothers before him, and all his seed to come after him down to the remotest generation, and every hair on his body and drop of blood in his veins; and he answered curse with snarl and kept out of their reach. He did not try to run away, but retreated around and around the camp, advertising plainly that when his desire was met, he would come in and be good.

François sat down and scratched his head. Perrault looked at his watch and swore. Time was flying, and they should have been on the trail an hour gone. François scratched his head again. He shook it and grinned sheepishly at the courier, who shrugged his shoulders in sign that they were beaten. The François went up to where Sol-leks stood and called to Buck. Buck laughed, as dogs laugh, yet kept his distance. François unfastened Sol-lek's traces and put him back in his old place. The team stood harnessed to the sled in an unbroken line, ready for the trail. There was no place for Buck save at the front. Once more François called, and once more Buck laughed and kept away.

"T'row down de club," Perrault commanded.

François complied, whereupon Buck trotted in, laughing triumphantly, and swung around into position at the head of the team. His traces were fastened, the sled broken out, and with both men running they dashed out on to the river trail.

Highly as the dog driver had forevalued Buck, with his two devils, he found, while the day was yet young, that he had undervalued. At a bound Buck took up the duties of leadership; and where judgment was required and quick thinking and quick acting, he showed himself the superior even of Spitz, of whom François had never seen an equal.

But it was in giving the law and making his mates live up to it that Buck excelled. Dave and Sol-leks did not mind the change in leadership. It was none of their business. Their business was to toil, and toil mightily, in the traces. So long as that were not interfered with, they did not care what happened. Billee, the good-natured, could lead for all they cared so long as he kept order. The rest of the team, however, had grown unruly during the last days of Spitz, and their surprise was great now that Buck proceeded to lick them into shape.

Pike, who pulled at Buck's heels, and who never put an ounce more of his weight against the breastband than he was compelled to do, was swiftly and repeatedly shaken for loafing; and ere the first day was done he was pulling more than ever before in his life. The first night in camp, Joe, the sour one, was punished roundly —a thing that Spitz had never succeeded in doing. Buck simply smothered him by virtue of superior weight, and cut him up till he ceased snapping and began to whine for mercy.

The general tone of the team picked up immediately. It recovered its old-time solidarity, and once more the dogs leaped as one dog in the traces. At the Rink Rapids two native huskies, Teek and Koona, were added; and the celerity with which Buck broke them in took away François's breath.

"Nevaire such a dog as dat Buck!" he cried. "No, nevaire! Heem worth one t'ousan' dollair, by Gar! Eh? Wot you say, Perrault?"

And Perrault nodded. He was ahead of the record then, and gaining day by day. The trail was in excellent condition, well packed and hard, and there was no new-fallen snow with which to contend. It was not too cold. The temperature dropped to fifty below zero and remained there the whole trip. The men rode and ran by turn, and the dogs were kept on the jump, with but infrequent stoppages.

The Thirty Mile River was comparatively coated with ice, and they covered in one day going out what had taken them ten days coming in. In one run they made a sixty-mile dash from the foot of Lake Laberge to the Whitehorse Rapids. Across Marsh, Tagish, and Bennett (seventy miles of lakes), they flew so fast that the man whose turn it was to run towed behind the sled at the end of a rope. And on the last night of the second week they topped White Pass and dropped down the sea slope with the lights of Skagway and of the shipping at their feet.

It was a record run. Each day for fourteen days they had averaged forty miles. For three days Perrault and François threw chests up and down the main street of Skagway and were deluged with invitations to drink, while the team was the constant center of a worshipful crowd of dog busters and mushers. Then three or four Western bad men aspired to clean out the town, were riddled like pepperboxes for their pains, and public interest turned to other idols. Next came official orders. François called Buck to him, threw his arms around him, wept over him. And that was the last of François and Perrault. Like other men, they passed out of Buck's life for good.

A Scotch half-breed took charge of him and his mates, and in company with a dozen other dog teams he started back over the weary trail to Dawson. It was no light running now, nor record time, but heavy toil each day, with a heavy load behind; for this was the mail train, carrying word from the world to the men who sought gold under the shadow of the Pole.

Buck did not like it, but he bore up well to the work, taking pride in it after the manner of Dave and Sol-leks, and seeing that his mates, whether they prided in it or not, did their fair share. It was a monotonous life, operating with machine-like regularity. One day was very like another. At a certain time each morning the cooks turned out, fires were built, and breakfast was eaten. Then, while some broke camp, others harnessed the dogs, and they were under way an hour or so before the darkness fell which gave warning of dawn. At night, camp was made. Some pitched the flies, other cut firewood and pine boughs for the beds, and still others carried water or ice for the cooks. Also, the dogs were fed. To them, this was the one feature of the day, though it was good to loaf around, after the fish was eaten, for an hour or so with the other dogs, of which there were fivescore and odd. There were fierce fighters among them, but three battles with the fiercest brought Buck to mastery, so that when he bristled and showed his teeth they got out of his way.

Best of all, perhaps, he loved to lie near the fire, hind legs crouched under him, forelegs stretched out in front, head raised, and eyes blinking dreamily at the flames. Sometimes he thought of Judge Miller's big house in the sun-kissed Santa Clara Valley, and of the cement swimming tank, and Ysabel, the Mexican hairless, and Toots, the Japanese pug; but oftener he remembered the man in the red sweater, the death of Curly, the great fight with Spitz, and the good things he had eaten or would like to eat. He was not homesick. The Sunland was very dim and distant, and such memories had no power over him. Far more potent were the memories of his heredity that gave things he had never seen before a seeming familiarity; the instincts (which were but the memories of his ancestors become habits) which had lapsed in later days, and still later, in him, quickened and became alive again.

Sometimes as he crouched there, blinking dreamily at the flames, it seemed that the flames were of another fire, and that as he crouched by this other fire he saw another and different man from the half-breed cook before him. This other man was shorter of leg and longer of arm, with muscles that were stringy and knotty rather than rounded and swelling. The hair of this man was long and matted, and his head slanted back under it from the eyes. He uttered strange sounds, and seemed very much afraid of the darkness, into which he peered continually, clutching in his hand, which hung midway between knee and foot, a stick with a heavy stone made fast to the end. He was all but naked, a ragged and firescorched skin hanging partway down his back, but on his body there was much hair. In some places, across the chest and shoulders and down the outside of the arms and thighs, it was matted into almost a thick fur. He did no stand erect, but with trunk inclined forward from the hips, on legs that bent at the knees. About his body there was a peculiar springiness, or resiliency, almost catlike, and a quick alertness as of one who lived in perpetual fear of things seen and unseen.

At other times this hairy man squatted by the fire with head between his legs and slept. On such occasions his elbows were on his knees, his hands clasped above his head as though to shed rain by the hairy arms. And beyond that fire, in the circling darkness, Buck could see many gleaming coals, two by two, always two by two, which he knew to be the eyes of great beasts of prey. And he could hear the crashing of their bodies through the undergrowth, and the noises they made in the night. And dreaming there by the Yukon bank, with lazy eyes blinking at the fire, these sounds and sights of another world would make the hair to rise along his back and stand on end across his shoulders and up his neck, till he whimpered low and suppressedly, or growled softly, and the half-breed cook shouted at him, "Hey, you Buck, wake up!" Whereupon the other world would vanish and the real world come into his eyes, and he would get up and yawn and stetch as though he had been asleep.

It was a hard trip, with the mail behind them, and the heavy work wore them down. They were short of weight and in poor condition when they made Dawson, and should have had a ten days' or a week's rest at least. But in two days' time they dropped down the Yukon bank from the Barracks, loaded with letters for the outside. The dogs were tired, the drivers grumbling, and to make matters worse, it snowed every day. This meant a soft trail, greater friction on the runners, and heavier pulling for the dogs; yet the drivers were fair through it all, and did their best for the animals.

Each night the dogs were attended to first. They ate before the drivers ate, and no man sought his sleeping robe till he had seen to the feet of the dogs he drove. Still, their strength went down. Since the beginning of the winter they had traveled eighteen hundred miles, dragging sleds the whole weary distance; and eighteen hundred miles will tell upon life of the toughest. Buck stood it, keeping his mates up to their work and maintaining discipline, though he, too, was very tired. Billee cried and whimpered regularly in his sleep each night. Joe was sourer than ever, and Solleks was unapproachable, blind side or other side.

But it was Dave who suffered most of all. Something had gone wrong with him. He became more morose and irritable, and when camp was pitched at once made his nest, where his driver fed him. Once out of the harness and down, he did not get on his feet again till harness-up time in the morning. Sometimes, in the traces, when jerked by a sudden stoppage of the sled, or by straining to start it, he would cry out with pain. The driver examined him, but could find nothing. All the drivers became interested in his case. They talked it over at mealtime, and over their last pipes before going to bed, and one night they held a consultation. He was brought from his nest to the fire and was pressed and prodded till he cried out many times. Something was wrong inside, but they could locate no broken bones, could not make it out.

By the time Cassiar Bar was reached, he was so weak that he was falling repeatedly in the traces. The Scotch half-breed called a halt and took him out of the team, making the next dog, Sol-leks, fast to the sled. His intention was to rest Dave, letting him run free behind the sled. Sick as he was, Dave resented being taken out, grunting and growling while the traces were unfastened, and whimpering brokenheartedly when he saw Sol-leks in the position he had held and served so long. For the pride of trace and trail was his, and, sick unto death, he could not bear that another dog should do his work.

When the sled started, he floundered in the soft snow alongside the beaten trail attacking Sol-leks with his teeth, rushing against him and trying to thrust him off into the soft snow on the other side, striving to leap inside his traces and get between him and the sled, and all the while whining and yelping and crying with grief and pain. The half-breed tried to drive him away with the whip; but he paid no heed to the stinging lash, and the man had not the heart to strike harder. Dave refused to run quietly on the trail behind the sled, where the going was easy, but continued to flounder alongside in the soft snow, where the going was most difficult, till exhausted. Then he fell, and lay where he fell, howling lugubriously as the long train of sleds churned by.

With the last remnant of his strength he managed to stagger along behind till the train made another stop, when he floundered past the sleds to his own, where he stood alongside Sol-leks. His driver lingered a moment to get a light for his pipe from the man behind. Then he returned and started his dogs. They swung out on the trail with remarkable lack of exertion, turned their heads uneasily, and stopped in surprise. The driver was surprised, too; the sled had not moved. He called his comrades to witness the sight. Dave had bitten through both of Sol-leks's traces, and was standing directly in front of the sled in his proper place.

He pleaded with his eyes to remain there. The driver was perplexed. His comrades talked of how a dog could break its heart through being denied the work that killed it, and recalled instances they had known, where dogs, too old for the toil, or injured, had died because they were cut out of the traces. Also, they held it a mercy, since Dave was to die anyway, that he should die in the traces, heart-easy and content. So he was harnessed in again, and proudly he pulled as of old, though more than once he cried out involuntarily from the bite of his inward hurt. Several times he fell down and was dragged in the traces, and once the sled ran upon him so that he limped thereafter in one of his hind legs.

But he held out till camp was reached, when his driver made a place for him by the fire. Morning found him too weak to travel. At harness-up time he tried to crawl to his driver. By convulsive efforts he got on his feet, staggered, and fell. Then he wormed his way forward slowly toward where the harnesses were being put on his mates. He would advance his forelegs and drag up his body with a sort of hitching movement, when he would advance his forelegs and hitch ahead again for a few more inches. His strength left him, and the last his mates saw of him he lay gasping in the snow and yearning toward them. But they could hear him mournfully howling till they passed out of sight behind a belt of river timber.

Here the train was halted. The Scotch half-breed slowly retraced his steps to the camp they had left. The men ceased talking. A revolver shot rang out. The man came back hurriedly. The whips snapped, the bells tinkled merrily, the sleds churned along the trail; but Buck knew, and every dog knew, what had taken place behind the belt of river trees.

5. THE TOIL OF TRACE AND TRAIL

THIRTY days from the time it left Dawson, the Salt Water Mail, with Buck and his mates at the fore, arrived at Skagway. They were in a wretched state, worn out and worn down. Buck's one hundred and forty pounds had dwindled to one hundred and fifteen. The rest of his mates, though lighter dogs, had relatively lost more weight than he. Pike, the malingerer, who, in his life-time of deceit, had often successfully feigned a hurt leg, was now limping in earnest. Sol-leks was limping, and Dub was suffering from a wrenched shoulder blade.

They were all terribly footsore. No spring or rebound was left in them. Their feet fell heavily on the trail, jarring their bodies and doubling the fatigue of a day's travel. There was nothing the mat-ter with them except that they were dead tired. It was not the dead-tiredness that comes through brief and excessive effort, from which recovery is a matter of hours; but it was the dead-tiredness that comes through the slow and prolonged strength drainage of months of toil. There was no power of recuperation left, no reserve strength to call upon. It had been all used, the last least bit of it. Every muscle, every fiber, every cell, was tired, dead tired. And there was reason for it. In less than five months they had traveled twenty-five hundred miles, during the last eighteen hundred of which they had had but five days' rest. When they arrived at Skagway they were apparently on their last legs. They could barely keep the traces taut, and on the downgrades just managed to keep out of the way of the sled.

"Mush on, poor sore feets," the driver encouraged them as they tottered down the main street of Skagway. "Dis is de las'. Den we get one long res'. Eh? For sure. One bully long res'."

The drivers confidently expected a long stopover. Themselves, they had covered twelve hundred miles with two days' rest, and in the nature of reason and common justice they deserved an interval of loafing. But so many were the men who had rushed into the Klondike, and so many were the sweethearts, wives, and kin that had not rushed in, that the congested mail was taking on Alpine proportions; also, there were official orders. Fresh batches of Hudson Bay dogs were to take the places of those worthless for the trail. The worthless ones were to be got rid of, and, since dogs count for little against dollars, they were to be sold.

Three days passed, by which time Buck and his mates found how really tired and weak they were. Then, on the morning of the fourth day, two men from the States came along and bought them, harness and all, for a song. The men addressed each other as Hal and Charles. Charles was a middle-aged, lightish-colored man, with weak and watery eyes and a mustache that twisted fiercely and vigorously up, giving the lie to the limply drooping lip it concealed. Hal was a youngster of nineteen or twenty, with a big Colt's revolver and a hunting knife strapped about him on a belt that fairly bristled with cartridges. This belt was the most salient thing about him. It advertised his callowness—a callowness sheer and unutterable. Both men were manifestly out of place, and why such as they should adventure the North is part of the mystery of things that passes understanding.

Buck heard the chaffering, saw the money pass between the man and the Government agent, and knew that the Scotch half-breed and the mail-train drivers were passing out of his life on the heels of Perrault and François and the others who had gone before. When driven with his mates to the new owners' camp, Buck saw a slipshod and slovenly affair, tent half-stretched, dishes unwashed, everything in disorder; also, he saw a woman. Mercedes the men called her. She was Charles's wife and Hal's sister—a nice family party.

Buck watched them apprehensively as they proceeded to take down the tent and load the sled. There was a great deal of effort about their manner, but no businesslike method. The tent was rolled into an awkward bundle three times as large as it should have been. The tin dishes were packed away unwashed. Mercedes continually fluttered in the way of her men and kept up an unbroken chattering of remonstrance and advice. When they put a clothes sack on the front of the sled, she suggested it should go on the back; and when they had put it on the back, and covered it over with a couple of other bundles, she discovered overlooked articles which could abide nowhere else but in that very sack, and they unloaded again.

Three men from a neighboring tent came out and looked on, grinning and winking at one another.

"You've got a right smart load as it is," said one of them; "and it's not me should tell you your business, but I wouldn't tote that tent along if I was you."

"Undreamed of!" cried Mercedes, throwing up her hands in dainty dismay. "However in the world could I manage without a tent?"

"It's springtime, and you won't get any more cold weather," the man replied.

She shook her head decidedly, and Charles and Hal put the last odds and ends on top of the mountainous load.

"Think it'll ride?" one of the men asked.

"Why shouldn't it?" Charles demanded rather shortly.

"Oh, that's all right, that's all right," the man hastened meekly to say. "I was just a-wonderin', that is all. It seemed a mite top-heavy."

Charles turned his back and drew the lashings down as well as he could, which was not in the least well.

"An' of course the dogs can hike along all day with that contraption behind them," affirmed a second of the men.

"Certainly," said Hal, with freezing politeness, taking hold of the gee pole with one hand and swinging his whip from the other. "Mush!" he shouted. "Mush on there!"

The dogs sprang against the breastbands, strained hard for a few moments, then relaxed. They were unable to move the sled.

"The lazy brutes, I'll show them," he cried, preparing to lash out at them with the whip.

But Mercedes interfered, crying, "Oh, Hal, you mustn't," as she caught hold of the whip and wrenched it from him. "The poor dears! Now you must promise you won't be harsh with them for the rest of the trip, or I won't go a step."

"Precious lot you know about dogs," her brother sneered; "and I wish you'd leave me alone. They're lazy, I tell you, and you've got to whip them to get anything out of them. That's their way. You ask anyone. Ask one of those men."

Mercedes looked at them imploringly, untold repugnance at sight of pain written in her pretty face.

"They're weak as water, if you want to know," came the reply from one of the men. "Plumb tuckered out, that's what's the matter. They need a rest."

"Rest be blanked," said Hal, with his beardless lips; and Mercedes said, "Oh!" in pain and sorrow at the oath.

But she was a clannish creature, and rushed at once to the defense of her brother. "Never mind that man," she said pointedly. "You're driving our dogs, and you do what you think best with them."

Again Hal's whip fell upon the dogs. They threw themselves against the breastbands, dug their feet into the packed snow, got down low to it, and put forth all their strength. The sled held as though it were an anchor. After two efforts, they stood still, panting. The whip was whistling savagely, when once more Mercedes interfered. She dropped on her knees before Buck, with tears in her eyes, and put her arms around his neck.

"You poor, poor dears," she cried sympathetically, "why don't you pull hard?—then you wouldn't be whipped." Buck did not like her, but he was feeling too miserable to resist her, taking it as part of the day's miserable work.

One of the onlookers, who had been clenching his teeth to suppress hot speech, now spoke up:

"It's not that I care a whoop what becomes of you, but for the dogs' sakes I just want to tell you, you can help them a mighty lot by breaking out that sled. The runners are froze fast. Throw your weight against the gee pole, right and left, and break it out."

A third time the attempt was made, but this time, following the advice. Hal broke out the runners which had been frozen to the snow. The overloaded and unwieldy sled forged ahead, Buck and his mates struggling frantically under the rain of blows. A hundred yards ahead the path turned and sloped steeply into the main street. It would have required an experienced man to keep the top-heavy sled upright, and Hal was not such a man. As they swung on the turn the sled went over, spilling half its load through the loose lashings. The dogs never stopped. The lightened sled bounded on its side behind them. They were angry because of the ill treatment they had received and the unjust load. Buck was raging. He broke into a run, the team following his lead. Hal cried "Whoa! whoa!" but they gave no heed. He tripped and was pulled off his feet. The capsized sled ground over him, and the dogs dashed up the street, adding to the gaiety of Skagway as they scattered the remainder of the outfit along its chief thoroughfare.

Kindhearted citizens caught the dogs and gathered up the scattered belongings. Also, they gave advice. Half the load and twice the dogs, if they ever expected to reach Dawson, was what was said. Hal and his sister and brother-in-law listened unwillingly, pitched tent, and overhauled the outfit. Canned goods were turned out that made men laugh, for canned goods on the Long Trail are a thing to dream about. "Blankets for a hotel," quoth one of the men who laughed and helped. "Half as many is too much; get rid of them. Throw away that tent, and all those dishes —who's going to wash them, anyway? Good Lord, do you think you're traveling on a Pullman?"

And so it went, the inexorable elimination of the superfluous. Mercedes cried when her clothes bags were dumped on the ground and article after article was thrown out. She cried in general, and she cried in particular over each discarded thing. She clasped hands about knees, rocking back and forth broken-heartedly. She averred she would not go an inch, not for a dozen Charleses. She appealed to everybody and to everything, finally wiping her eyes and proceeding to cast out even articles of apparel that were imperative necessaries. And in her zeal, when she had finished with her own, she attacked the belongings of her men and went through them like a tornado.

This accomplished, the outfit, though cut in half, was still a formidable bulk. Charles and Hal went out in the evening and bought six Outside dogs. These, added to the six of the original team, and Teek and Koona, the huskies obtained at the Rink Rapids on the record trip, brought the team up to fourteen. But the Outside dogs, though practically broken in since their landing, did not amount to much. Three were short-haired pointers, one was a Newfoundland, and the other two were mongrels of indeterminate breed. They did not seem to know anything, these newcomers. Buck and his comrades looked upon them with disgust, and though he speedily taught them their places and what not to do, he could not teach them what to do. They did not take kindly to trace and trail. With the exception of the two mongrels, they were bewildered and spirit-broken by the strange, savage environment in which they found themselves and by the ill treatment they had received. The two mongrels were without spirit at all; bones were the only things breakable about them.

With the newcomers hopeless and forlorn, and the old team worn out by twenty-five hundred miles of continuous trail, the outlook was anything but bright. The two men, however, were quite cheerful. And they were proud, too. They were doing the thing in style, with fourteen dogs. They had seen other sleds depart over the Pass for Dawson, or come in from Dawson, but never had they seen a sled with so many as fourteen dogs. In the nature of Arctic travel there was a reason why fourteen dogs should not drag one sled, and that was that one sled could not carry the food for fourteen dogs. But Charles and Hal did not know this. They had worked the trip out with a pencil, so much to a dog, so many dogs, so many days, Q.E.D. Mercedes looked over their shoulders and nodded comprehensively, it was all so very simple.

Late next morning Buck led the long team up the street. There was nothing lively about it, no snap or go in him and his fellows. They were starting dead weary. Four times he had covered the distance between Salt Water and Dawson, and the knowledge that, jaded and tired, he was facing the same trail once more, made him bitter. His heart was not in the work, nor was the heart of any dog. The Outsides were timid and frightened, the Insides without confidence in their masters.

Buck felt vaguely that there was no depending upon these two men and the woman. They did not know how to do anything, and as the days went by it became apparent that they could not learn. They were slack in all things, without order or discipline. It took them half the night to pitch a slovenly camp, and half the morning to break that camp and get the sled loaded in fashion so slovenly that for the rest of the day they were occupied in stopping and rearranging the load. Some days they did not make ten miles. On other days they were unable to get started at all. And on no day did they succeed in making more than half the distance used by the men as a basis in their dog-food computation.

It was inevitable that they should go short on dog food. But they hastened it by overfeeding, bringing the day nearer when underfeeding would commence. The Outside dogs, whose digestions had not been trained by chronic famine to make the most of little, had voracious appetites. And when, in addition to this, the worn-out huskies pulled weakly, Hal decided that the orthodox ration was too small. He doubled it. And to cap it all, when Mercedes, with tears in her pretty eyes and a quaver in her throat, could not cajole him into giving the dogs still more, she stole from the fish sacks and fed them slyly. But it was not food that Buck and the huskies needed, but rest. And though they were making poor time, the heavy load they dragged sapped their strength severely.

Then came the underfeeding. Hal awoke one day to the fact that his dog food was half gone and the distance only quarter covered; further, that for love or money no additional dog food was to be obtained. So he cut down even the orthodox ration and tried to increase the day's travel. His sister and brother-in-law seconded him; but they were frustrated by their heavy outfit and their own incompetence. It was a simple matter to give the dogs less food; but it was impossible to make the dogs travel faster, while their own inability to get under way earlier in the morning prevented them from traveling longer hours. Not only did they not know how to work dogs, but they did not know how to work themselves.

The first to go was Dub. Poor blundering thief that he was, always getting caught and punished, he had none the less been a faithful worker. His wrenched shoulder blade, untreated and unrested, went from bad to worse, till finally Hal shot him with the big Colt's revolver. It is a saying of the country that an Outside dog starves to death on the ration of the husky, so the six Outside dogs under Buck could do no less than die on half the ration of the husky. The Newfoundland went first, followed by the three short-haired pointers, the two mongrels hanging more grittily on to life, but going in the end.

By this time all the amenities and gentlenesses of the Southland had fallen away from the three people. Shorn of its glamour and romance, Arctic travel became to them a reality too harsh for their manhood and womanhood. Mercedes ceased weeping over the dogs, being too occupied with weeping over herself and with quarreling with her husband and brother. To quarrel was the one thing they were never too weary to do. Their irritability arose out of their misery, increased with it, doubled upon it, outdistanced it. The wonderful patience of the trail which comes to men who toil hard and suffer sore, and remain sweet of speech and kindly, did not come to these two men and the woman. They had no inkling of such a patience. They were stiff and in pain; their muscles ached, their bones ached, their very hearts ached; and because of this they became sharp of speech, and hard words were first on their lips in the morning and last at night.

Charles and Hal wrangled whenever Mercedes gave them a chance. It was the cherished belief of each that he did more than his share of the work, and neither forbore to speak this belief at every opportunity. Sometimes Mercedes sided with her husband, sometimes with her brother. The result was a beautiful and unending family quarrel. Starting from a dispute as to which should chop a few sticks for the fire (a dispute which concerned only Charles and Hal), presently would be lugged in the rest of the family, fathers, mothers, uncles, cousins, people thousands of miles away, and some of them dead. That Hal's views on art, or the sort of society plays his mother's brother wrote, should have anything to do with the chopping of a few sticks of firewood, passes comprehension; nevertheless the quarrel was as likely to tend in that direction as in the direction of Charles's political prejudices. And that Charles's sister's tale-bearing tongue should be relevant to the building of a Yukon fire was apparent only to Mercedes, who disburdened herself of copious opinions upon that topic, and incidentally upon a few other traits unpleasantly peculiar to her husband's family. In the meantime the fire remained unbuilt, the camp half pitched, and the dogs unfed.

Mercedes nursed a special grievance—the grievance of sex. She was pretty and soft, and had been chivalrously treated all her days. But the present treatment by her husband and brother was everything save chivalrous. It was her custom to be helpless. They complained. Upon which impeachment of what to her was her most essential sex-prerogative, she made their lives unendurable. She no longer considered the dogs, and because she was sore and tired, she persisted in riding on the sled. She was pretty and soft, but she weighed one hundred and twenty pounds—a lusty last straw to the load dragged by the weak and starving animals. She rode for days, till they fell in the traces and the sled stood still. Charles and Hal begged her to get off and walk, pleaded with her, entreated, the while she wept and importuned Heaven with a recital of their brutality.

On one occasion they took her off the sled by main strength. They never did it again. She let her legs go limp like a spoiled child, and sat down on the trail. They went on their way, but she did not move. After they had traveled three miles they unloaded the sled, came back for her, and by main strength put her on the sled again.

In the excess of their own misery they were callous to the suffering of their animals. Hal's theory, which he practiced on others, was that one must get hardened. He had started out preaching it to his sister and brother-in-law. Failing there, he hammered it into the dogs with a club. At the Five Fingers the dog food gave out, and a toothless old squaw offered to trade them a few pounds of frozen horse hide for the Colt's revolver that kept the big hunting knife company at Hal's hip. A poor substitute for food was this hide, just as it had been stripped from the starved horses of the cattlemen six months back. In its frozen state it was more like strips of galvanized iron, and when a dog wrestled it into his stomach it thawed into thin and innutritious leather strings and into a mass of short hair, irritating and indigestible.

And through it all Buck staggered along at the head of the team as in a nightmare. He pulled when he could; when he could no longer pull, he fell down and remained down till blows from whip or club drove him to his feet again. All the stiffness and gloss had gone out of his beautiful furry coat. The hair hung down, limp and draggled, or matted with dried blood where Hal's club had bruised him. His muscles had wasted away to knotty strings, and the flesh pads had disappeared, so that each rib and every bone in his frame were outlined cleanly through the loose hide that was wrinkled in folds of emptiness. It was heartbreaking, only Buck's heart was unbreakable. The man in the red sweater had proved that.

As it was with Buck, so was it with his mates. They were perambulating skeletons. There were seven altogether, including him. In their very great misery they had become insensible to the bite of the lash or the bruise of the club. The pain of the beating was dull and distant, just as the things their eyes saw and their ears heard seemed dull and distant. They were not half living, or quarter living. They were simply so many bags of bones in which sparks of life fluttered faintly. When a halt was made, they dropped down in the traces like dead dogs, and the spark dimmed and paled and seemed to go out. And when the club or whip fell upon them, the spark fluttered feebly up, and they tottered to their feet and staggered on.

There came a day when Billee, the good-natured, fell and could not rise. Hal had traded off his revolver, so he took the ax and knocked Billee on the head as he lay in the traces, then cut the carcass out of the harness and dragged it to one side. Buck saw, and his mates saw, and they knew that this thing was very close to them. On the next day Koona went, and but five of them remained: Joe, too far gone to be malignant; Pike, crippled and limping, only half conscious and not conscious enough longer to malinger; Sol-leks, the one-eyed, still faithful to the toil of trace and trail, and mournful in that he had so little strength with which to pull; Teek, who had not traveled so far that winter and who was now beaten more than the others because he was fresher; and Buck, still at the head of the team, but no longer enforcing discipline or striving to enforce it, blind with weakness half the time and keeping the trail by the loom of it and by the dim feel of his feet.

It was beautiful spring weather, but neither dogs nor humans were aware of it. Each day the sun rose earlier and set later. It was dawn by three in the morning, and twilight lingered till nine at night. The whole long day was a blaze of sunshine. The ghostly winter silence had given way to the great spring murmur of awakening life. This murmur arose from all the land, fraught with the joy of living. It came from the things that lived and moved again, things which had been as dead and which had not moved during the long months of frost. The sap was rising in the pines. The willows and aspens were bursting out in young buds. Shrubs and vines were putting on fresh garbs of green. Crickets sang in the nights, and in the days all manner of creeping, crawling things rustled forth into the sun. Partridges and woodpeckers were booming and knocking in the forest. Squirrels were chattering, birds singing, and overhead honked the wild fowl driving up from the south in cunning wedges that split the air.

From every hill slope came the trickle of running water, the music of unseen fountains. All things were thawing, bending, snapping. The Yukon was straining to break loose the ice that bound it down. It ate away from beneath; the sun ate from above. Air holes formed, fissures sprang and spread apart, while thin sections of ice fell through bodily into the river. And amid all this bursting, rending, throbbing of awakening life, under the blazing sun and through the soft-sighing breezes, like wayfarers to death, staggered the two men, the woman, and the huskies.

With the dogs falling, Mercedes weeping and riding, Hal swearing innocuously, and Charles's eyes wistfully watering, they staggered into John Thornton's camp at the mouth of White River. When they halted, the dogs dropped down as though they had been struck dead. Mercedes dried her eyes and looked at John Thornton. Charles sat down on a log to rest. He sat down very slowly and painstakingly what of his great stiffness. Hal did the talking. John Thornton was whittling the last touches on an ax handle he had made from a stick of birch. He whittled and listened, gave monosyllabic replies, and, when it was asked, terse advice. He knew the breed, and he gave his advice in the certainty that it would not be followed.

"They told us up above that the bottom was dropping out of the trail and that the best thing for us to do was to lay over," Hal said in response to Thornton's warning to take no more chances on the rotten ice. "They told us we couldn't make White River, and here we are." This last with a sneering ring of triumph in it.

"And they told you true," John Thornton answered. "The bottom's likely to drop out at any moment. Only fools, with the blind luck of fools, could have made it. I tell you straight, I wouldn't risk my carcass on that ice for all the gold in Alaska."

"That's because you're not a fool, I suppose," said Hal. "All the same, we'll go on to Dawson." He uncoiled his whip. "Get up there, Buck! Hi! Get up there! Mush on!"

Thornton went on whittling. It was idle, he knew, to get between a fool and his folly; while two or three fools more or less would not alter the scheme of things.

But the team did not get up at the command. It had long since passed into the stage where blows were required to rouse it. The whip flashed out, here and there, on its merciless errands. John Thornton compressed his lips. Sol-leks was the first to crawl to his feet. Teek followed. Joe came next, yelping with pain. Pike made painful efforts. Twice he fell over, when half up, and on the third attempt managed to rise. Buck made no effort. He lay quietly where he had fallen. The lash bit into him again and again, but he neither whined nor struggled. Several times Thornton started, as though to speak, but changed his mind. A moisture came into his eyes, and, as the whipping continued, he arose and walked irresolutely up and down.

This was the first time Buck had failed, in itself a sufficient reason to drive Hal into a rage. He exchanged the whip for the customary club. Buck refused to move under the rain of heavier blows which now fell upon him. Like his mates, he was barely able to get up, but, unlike them, he had made up his mind not to get up. He had a vague feeling of impending doom. This had been strong upon him when he pulled in to the bank, and it had not departed from him. What with the thin and rotten ice he had felt under his feet all day, it seemed that he sensed disaster close at hand, out there ahead on the ice where his master was trying to drive him. He refused to stir. So greatly had he suffered, and so far gone was he, that the blows did not hurt much. And as they continued to fall upon him, the spark of life within flickered and went down. It was nearly out. He felt strangely numb. As though from a great distance, he was aware that he was being beaten. The last sensations of pain left him. He no longer felt anything, though very faintly he could hear the impact of the club upon his body. But it was no longer his body, it seemed so far away.

And then, suddenly, without warning, uttering a cry that was inarticulate and more like the cry of an animal, John Thornton sprang upon the man who wielded the club. Hal was hurled backward, as though struck by a falling tree. Mercedes screamed. Charles looked on wistfully, wiped his watery eyes, but did not get up because of his stiffness.

John Thornton stood over Buck, struggling to control himself, too convulsed with rage to speak.

"If you strike that dog again, I'll kill you," he at last managed to say in a choking voice.

"It's my dog," Hal replied, wiping the blood from his mouth as he came back. "Get out of my way, or I'll fix you. I'm going to Dawson."

Thornton stood between him and Buck, and evinced no intention of getting out of the way. Hal drew his long hunting knife. Mercedes screamed, cried, laughed, and manifested the chaotic abandonment of hysteria. Thornton rapped Hal's knuckles with the ax handle, knocking the knife to the ground. He rapped his knuckles as he tried to pick it up. Then he stooped, picked it up himself, and with two strokes cut Buck's traces.

Hal had no fight left in him. Besides, his hands were full with his sister, or his arms, rather; while Buck was too near dead to be of further use in hauling the sled. A few minutes later they pulled out from the bank and down the river. Buck heard them go and raised his head to see. Pike was leading, Sol-leks was at the wheel, and between were Joe and Teek. They were limping and staggering. Mercedes was riding the loaded sled. Hal guided at the gee pole, and Charles stumbled along in the rear.

As Buck watched them, Thornton knelt beside him and with rough, kindly hands searched for broken bones. By the time his search had disclosed nothing more than many bruises and a state of terrible starvation, the sled was a quarter of a mile away. Dog and man watched it crawling along over the ice. Suddenly, they saw its back end drop down, as into a rut, and the gee pole, with Hal clinging to it, jerk into the air. Mercedes's scream came to their ears. They saw Charles turn and make one step to run back, and then a whole section of ice gave way and dogs and humans disappeared. A yawning hole was all that was to be seen. The bottom had dropped out of the trail.

John Thornton and Buck looked at each other.

"You poor devil," said John Thornton, and Buck licked his hand.

6. FOR THE LOVE OF A MAN

WHEN John Thornton froze his feet in the previous December, his partners had made him comfortable and left him to get well, going on themselves up the river to get out a raft of saw logs for Dawson. He was still limping slightly at the time he rescued Buck, but with the continued warm weather even the slight limp left him. And here, lying by the river bank through the long spring days, watching the running water, listening lazily to the songs of birds and the hum of nature, Buck slowly won back his strength.

A rest comes very good after one has traveled three thousand miles, and it must be confessed that Buck waxed lazy as his wounds healed, his muscles swelled out, and the flesh came back to cover his bones. For that matter, they were all loafing—Buck, John Thornton, and Skeet and Nig—waiting for the raft to come that was to carry them down to Dawson. Skeet was a little Irish setter who early made friends with Buck, who, in a dying condition, was unable to resent her first advances. She had the doctor trait which some dogs possess; and as a mother cat washes her kittens, so she washed and cleansed Buck's wounds. Regularly, each morning after he had finished his breakfast, she performed her self-appointed task, till he came to look for her ministrations as much as he did for Thornton's. Nig, equally friendly, though less demonstrative, was a huge black dog, half bloodhound and half deerhound, with eyes that laughed and a boundless good nature.

To Buck's surprise these dogs manifested no jealousy toward him. They seemed to share the kindliness and largeness of John Thornton. As Buck grew stronger they enticed him into all sorts of ridiculous games, in which Thornton himself could not forbear to join; and in this fashion Buck romped through his convalescence and into a new existence. Love, genuine passionate love, was his for the first time. This he had never experienced at Judge Miller's down in the sun-kissed Santa Clara Valley. With the Judge's sons, hunting and tramping, it had been a working partnership; with the Judge's grandsons, a sort of pompous guardianship; and with the Judge himself, a stately and dignified friendship. But love that was feverish and burning, that was adoration, that was madness, it had taken John Thornton to arouse.

This man had saved his life, which was something; but, further, he was the ideal master. Other men saw to the welfare of their dogs from a sense of duty and business expediency; he saw to the welfare of his as if they were his own children, because he could not help it. And he saw further. He never forgot a kindly greeting or a cheering word, and to sit down for a long talk with them (gas, he called it) was as much his delight as theirs. He had a way of taking Buck's head roughly between his hands, and resting his own head upon Buck's, of shaking him back and forth, the while calling him ill names that to Buck were love names. Buck knew no greater joy that that rough embrace and the sound of murmured oaths, and at each jerk back and forth it seemed that his heart would be shaken out of his body so great was its ecstasy. And when, released, he sprang to his feet, his mouth laughing, his eyes eloquent, his throat vibrant with unuttered sound, and in that fashion remained without movement, John Thornton would reverently exclaim, "God! you can all but speak!"

Buck had a trick of love expression that was akin to hurt. He would often seize Thornton's hand in his mouth and close so fiercely that the flesh bore the impress of his teeth for some time afterward. And as Buck understood the oaths to be love words, so the man understood this feigned bite for a caress.

For the most part, however, Buck's love was expressed in adoration. While he went wild with happiness when Thornton touched him or spoke to him, he did not seek these tokens. Unlike Skeet, who was wont to shove her nose under Thornton's hand and nudge and nudge till petted, or Nig, who would stalk up and rest his great head on Thornton's knee, Buck was content to adore at a distance. He would lie by the hour, eager, alert, at Thornton's feet, looking up into his face, dwelling upon it, studying it, following with keenest interest each fleeting expression, every movement or change of feature. Or, as chance might have it, he would lie farther away, to the side or rear, watching the outlines of the man and the occasional movements of his body. And often, such was the communion in which they lived, the strength of Buck's gaze would draw John Thornton's head around, and he would return the gaze, without speech, his heart shining out of his eyes as Buck's heart shone out.

For a long time after his rescue, Buck did not like Thornton to get out of his sight. From the moment he left the tent to when he entered it again, Buck would follow at his heels. His transient masters since he had come into the Northland had bred in him a fear that no master could be permanent. He was afraid that Thornton would pass out of his life as Perrault and François and the Scotch half-breed had passed out. Even in the night, in his dreams, he was haunted by this fear. At such times he would shake off sleep and creep through the chill to the flap of the tent, where he would stand and listen to the sound of his master's breathing.

But in spite of this great love he bore John Thornton, which seemed to bespeak the soft, civilizing influence, the strain of the primitive, which the Northland had aroused in him, remained alive and active. Faithfulness and devotion, things born of fire and roof, were his; yet he retained his wildness and wiliness. He was a thing of the wild, come in from the wild to sit by John Thornton's fire, rather than a dog of the soft Southland stamped with the marks of generations of civilization. Because of his very great love, he could not steal from this man, but from any other man, in any other camp, he did not hesitate an instant; while the cunning with which he stole enabled him to escape detection.

His face and body were scored by the teeth of many dogs, and he fought as fiercely as ever and more shrewdly. Skeet and Nig were too good-natured for quarreling—besides, they belonged to John Thornton; but the strange dog, no matter what the breed or valor, swiftly acknowledged Buck's supremacy or found himself struggling for life with a terrible antagonist. And Buck was merciless. He had learned well the law of club and fang, and he never forwent an advantage or drew back from a foe he had started on the way to Death. He had lessoned from Spitz, and from the chief fighting dogs of the police and mail, and knew there was no middle course. He must master or be mastered; while to show mercy was a weakness. Mercy did not exist in the primordial life. It was misunderstood for fear, and such misunderstandings made for death. Kill or be killed, eat or be eaten, was the law; and this mandate, down out of the depths of Time, he obeyed.

He was older than the days he had seen and the breaths he had drawn. He linked the past with the present, and the eternity behind him throbbed through him in a mighty rhythm to which he swayed as the tides and seasons swayed. He sat by John Thornton's fire, a broad-breasted dog, white-fanged and long-furred; but behind him were the shades of all manner of dogs, half wolves and wild wolves, urgent and prompting, tasting the savor of the meat he ate, thirsting for the water he drank, scenting the wind with him, listening with him and telling him the sounds made by the wild life in the forest, dictating his moods, directing his actions, lying down to sleep with him when he lay down, and dreaming with him and beyond him and becoming themselves the stuff of his dreams.

So peremptorily did these shades beckon him, that each day mankind and the claims of mankind slipped farther from him. Deep in the forest a call was sounding, and as often as he heard this call, mysteriously thrilling and luring, he felt compelled to turn his back upon the fire and the beaten earth around it, and to plunge into the forest, and on and on, he knew not where or why; nor did he wonder where or why, the call sounding imperiously, deep in the forest. But as often as he gained the soft unbroken earth and the green shade, the love for John Thornton drew him back to the fire again.

Thornton alone held him. The rest of mankind was as nothing. Chance travelers might praise or pet him; but he was cold under it all, and from a too demonstrative man he would get up and walk away. When Thornton's partners, Hans and Pete, arrived on the long-expected raft, Buck refused to notice them till he learned they were close to Thornton; after that he tolerated them in a passive sort of way, accepting favors from them as though he favored them by accepting. They were of the same large type as Thornton, living close to the earth, thinking simply and seeing clearly; and ere they swung the raft into the big eddy by the sawmill at Dawson, they understood Buck and his ways, and did not insist upon an intimacy such as obtained with Skeet and Nig.

For Thornton, however, his love seemed to grow and grow. He, alone among men, could put a pack upon Buck's back in the summer traveling. Nothing was too great for Buck to do, when Thornton commanded. One day (they had grubstaked themselves from the proceeds of the raft and left Dawson for the headwaters of the Tanana) the men and dogs were sitting on the crest of a cliff which fell away, straight down, to naked bedrock three hundred feet below. John Thornton was sitting near the edge, Buck at his shoulder. A thoughtless whim seized Thornton, and he drew the attention of Hans and Pete to the experiment he had in mind. "Jump, Buck!" he commanded, sweeping his arm out and over the chasm. The next instant he was grappling with Buck on the extreme edge, while Hans and Pete were dragging them back into safety.

"It's uncanny," Pete said, after it was over and they had caught their speech.

Thornton shook his head. "No, it is splendid, and it is terrible, too. Do you know, it sometimes makes me afraid."

"I'm not hankering to be the man that lays hands on you while he's around," Pete announced conclusively, nodding his head toward Buck.

"Py Jingo!" was Hans's contribution. "Not mineself either."

It was at Circle City, ere the year was out, that Pete's apprehensions were realized. "Black" Burton, a man evil-tempered and malicious, had been picking a quarrel with a tenderfoot at the bar, when Thornton stepped good-naturedly between. Buck, as was his custom, was lying in a corner, head on paws, watching his master's every action. Burton struck out, without warning, straight from the shoulder. Thornton was sent spinning, and saved himself from falling only by clutching the rail of the bar.

Those who were looking on heard what was neither bark nor yelp, but a something which is best described as a roar, and they saw Buck's body rise up in the air as he left the floor for Burton's throat. The man saved his life by instinctively throwing out his arm, but was hurled backward to the floor with Buck on top of him. Buck loosed his teeth from the flesh of the arm and drove in again for the throat. This time the man succeeded only in partly blocking, and his throat was torn open. Then the crowd was upon Buck, and he was driven off; but while a surgeon checked the bleeding, he prowled up and down, growling furiously, attempting to rush in, and being forced back by an array of hostile clubs. A "miners' meeting," called on the spot, decided that the dog had sufficient provocation, and Buck was discharged. But his reputation was made, and from that day his name spread through every camp in Alaska.

Later on, in the fall of the year, he saved John Thornton's life in quite another fashion. The three partners were lining a long and narrow poling boat down a bad stretch of rapids on the Forty Mile Creek. Hans and Pete moved along the bank, snubbing with a thin Manila rope from tree to tree, while Thornton remained in the boat, helping its descent by means of a pole, and shouting directions to the shore. Buck, on the bank, worried and anxious, kept abreast of the boat, his eyes never off his master.

At a particularly bad spot, where a ledge of barely submerged rocks jutted out into the river, Hans cast off the rope, and, while Thornton poled the boat out into the stream, ran down the bank with the end in his hand to snub the boat when it had cleared the ledge. This it did, and was flying downstream in a current as swift as a millrace, when Hans checked it with the rope and checked too suddenly. The boat flirted over and snubbed in to the bank bottom up, while Thornton, flung sheer out of it, was carried downstream toward the worst part of the rapids, a stretch of wild water in which no swimmer could live.

Buck had sprung in on the instant; and at the end of three hundred yards, amid a mad swirl of water, he overhauled Thornton. When he felt him grasp his tail, Buck headed for the bank, swimming with all his splendid strength. But the progress shoreward was slow, the process downstream amazingly rapid. From below came the fatal roaring where the wild current went wilder and was rent in shreds and spray by the rocks which thrust through like the teeth of an enormous comb. The suck of the water as it took the beginning of the last steep pitch was frightful, and Thornton knew that the shore was impossible. He scraped furiously over a rock, bruised across a second, and struck a third with crushing force. He clutched its slippery top with both hands, releasing Buck, and above the roar of the churning water shouted: "Go, Buck! Go!"

Buck could not hold his own, and swept on downstream, struggling desperately, but unable to win back. When he heard Thornton's command repeated, he partly reared out of the water, throwing his head high, as though for a last look, then turned obediently toward the bank. He swam powerfully and was dragged ashore by Pete and Hans at the very point where swimming ceased to be possible and destruction began.

They knew that the time a man could cling to a slippery rock in the face of that driving current was a matter of minutes, and they ran as fast as they could up the bank to a point far above where Thornton was hanging on. They attached the line with which they had been snubbing the boat to Buck's neck and shoulders, being careful that it should neither strangle him nor impede his swimming, and launched him into the stream. He struck out boldly, but not straight enough into the stream. He discovered the mistake too late, when Thornton was abreast of him and a bare half-dozen strokes away while he was being carried helplessly past.

Hans promptly snubbed with the rope, as though Buck were a boat. The rope thus tightening on him in the sweep of the current, he was jerked under the surface, and under the surface he remained till his body struck against the bank and he was hauled out. He was half drowned, and Hans and Pete threw themselves upon him, pounding the breath into him and the water out of him. He staggered to his feet and fell down. The faint sound of Thornton's voice came to them, and though they could not make out the words of it, they knew that he was in his extremity. His master's voice acted on Buck like an electric shock. He sprang to his feet and ran up the bank ahead of the men to the point of his previous departure.

Again the rope was attached and he was launched, and again he struck out, but this time straight into the stream. He had miscalculated once, but he would not be guilty of it a second time. Hans paid out the rope, permitting no slack, while Pete kept it clear of coils. Buck held on till he was on a line straight above Thornton; then he turned, and with the speed of an express train headed down upon him. Thornton saw him coming, and, as Buck struck him like a battering-ram, with the whole force of the current behind him, he reached up and closed with both arms around the shaggy neck. Hans snubbed the rope around the tree, and Buck and Thornton were jerked under the water. Strangling, suffocating, sometimes one uppermost and sometimes the other, dragging over the jagged bottom, smashing against rocks and snags, they veered in to the bank.

Thornton came to, belly downward and being violently propelled back and forth across a drift log by Hans and Pete. His first glance was for Buck, over whose limp and apparently lifeless body Nig was setting up a howl, while Skeet was licking the wet face and closed eyes. Thornton was himself bruised and battered, and he went carefully over Buck's body, when he had been brought around, finding three broken ribs.

"That settles it," he announced. "We camp right here." And camp they did, till Buck's ribs knitted and he was able to travel.

That winter, at Dawson, Buck performed another exploit, not so heroic, perhaps, but one that put his name many notches higher on the totem pole of Alaskan fame. This exploit was particularly gratifying to the three men; for they stood in need of the outfit which it furnished, and were enabled to make a long-desired trip into the virgin East, where miners had not yet appeared. It was brought about by a conversation in the Eldorado Saloon, in which men waxed boastful of their favorite dogs. Buck, because of his record, was the target for these men, and Thornton was driven stoutly to defend him. At the end of half an hour one man stated that his dog could start a sled with five hundred pounds and walk off with it; a second bragged six hundred for his dog; and a third, seven hundred.

"Pooh! pooh!" said John Thornton; "Buck can start a thousand pounds."

"And break it out! and walk off with it for a hundred yards?" demanded Matthewson, a Bonanza King, he of the seven hundred vaunt.

"And break it out, and walk off with it for a hundred yards," John Thornton said coolly.

"Well," Matthewson said, slowly and deliberately, so that all could hear, "I've got a thousand dollars that says he can't. And there it is." So saying, he slammed a sack of gold dust of the size of a bologna sausage down upon the bar.

Nobody spoke. Thornton's bluff, if bluff it was, had been called. He could feel a flush of warm blood creeping up his face. His tongue had tricked him. He did not know whether Buck could start a thousand pounds. Half a ton! The enormousness of it appalled him. He had great faith in Buck's strength and had often thought him capable of starting such a load; but never, as now, had he faced the possibility of it, the eyes of a dozen men fixed upon him, silent and waiting. Further, he had no thousand dollars; nor had Hans or Pete.

"I've got a sled standing outside now, with twenty fifty-pound sacks of flour on it," Matthewson went on with brutal directness; "so don't let that hinder you."

Thornton did not reply. He did not know what to say. He glanced from face to face in the absent way of a man who has lost the power of thought and is seeking somewhere to find the thing that will start it going again. The face of Jim O'Brien, a Mastodon King and old-time comrade, caught his eyes. It was as a cue to him, seeming to rouse him to do what he would never have dreamed of doing.

"Can you lend me a thousand?" he asked, almost in a whisper.

"Sure," answered O'Brien, thumping down a plethoric sack by the side of Matthewson's. "Though it's little faith I'm having, John, that the beast can do the trick."

The Eldorado emptied its occupants into the street to see the test. The tables were deserted, and the dealers and gamekeepers came forth to see the outcome of the wager and to lay odds. Several hundred men, furred and mittened, banked around the sled within easy distance. Matthewson's sled, loaded with a thousand pounds of flour, had been standing for a couple of hours, and in the intense cold (it was sixty below zero) the runners had frozen fast to the hard-packed snow. Men offered odds of two to one that Buck could not budge the sled. A quibble arose concerning the phrase "break out." O'Brien contended it was Thornton's privilege to knock the runners loose, leaving Buck to "break it out" from a dead standstill. Matthewson insisted that the phrase included breaking the runners from the frozen grip of the snow. A majority of the men who had witnessed the making of the bet decided in his favor, whereat the odds went up to three to one against Buck.

There were no takers. Not a man believed him capable of the feat. Thornton had been hurried into the wager, heavy with doubt; and now that he looked at the sled itself, the concrete fact, with the regular team of ten dogs curled up in the snow before it, the more impossible the task appeared. Matthewson waxed jubilant.

"Three to one!" he proclaimed. "I'll lay you another thousand at that figure, Thornton. What d'ye say?"

Thornton's doubt was strong in his face, but his fighting spirit was aroused—the fighting spirit that soars above odds, fails to recognize the impossible, and is deaf to all save the clamor for battle. He called Hans and Pete to him. Their sacks were slim, and with his own, the three partners could rake together only two hundred dollars. In the ebb of their fortunes, this sum was their total capital; yet they laid it unhesitatingly against Matthewson's six hundred.

The team of ten dogs was unhitched, and Buck, with his own harness, was put into the sled. He had caught the contagion of the excitement, and he felt that in some way he must do a great thing for John Thornton. Murmurs of admiration at his splendid appearance went up. He was in perfect condition, without an ounce of superfluous flesh, and the one hundred and fifty pounds that he weighed were so many pounds of grit and virility. His furry coat shone with the sheen of silk. Down the neck and across the shoulders, his mane, in repose as it was, half bristled and seemed to lift with every movement, as though excess of vigor made each particular hair alive and active. The great breast and heavy forelegs were no more than in proportion with the rest of the body, where the muscles showed in tight rolls underneath the skin. Men felt these muscles and proclaimed them hard as iron, and the odds went down to two to one.

"Gad, sir! Gad, sir!" stuttered a member of the latest dynasty, a king of the Skookum Benches. "I offer you eight hundred for him, sir, before the test, sir; eight hundred just as he stands."

Thornton shook his head and stepped to Buck's side.

"You must stand off from him," Matthewson protested. "Free play and plenty of room."

The crowd fell silent; only could be heard the voices of the gamblers vainly offering two to one. Everybody acknowledged Buck a magnificent animal, but twenty fifty-pound sacks of flour bulked too large in their eyes for them to loosen their pouch strings.

Thornton knelt down by Buck's side. He took his head in his two hands and rested cheek to cheek. He did not playfully shake him, as was his wont, or murmur soft love curses; but he whispered in his ear. "As you love me, Buck. As you love me," was what he whispered. Buck whined with suppressed eagerness.

The crowd was watching curiously. The affair was growing mysterious. It seemed like a conjuration. As Thornton got to his feet, Buck seized his mittened hand between his jaws, pressing it with his teeth and releasing slowly, half-reluctantly. It was the answer, in terms, not of speech, but of love. Thornton stepped well back.

"Now, Buck," he said.

Buck tightened the traces, then slacked them for a matter of several inches. It was the way he had learned.

"Gee!" Thornton's voice rang out, sharp in the tense silence.

Buck swung to the right, ending the movement in a plunge that took up the slack and with a sudden jerk arrested his one hundred and fifty pounds. The load quivered, and from under the runners arose a crisp crackling.

"Haw!" Thornton commanded.

Buck duplicated the maneuver, this time to the left. The crackling turned into a snapping, the sled pivoting and the runners slipping and grating several inches to the side. The sled was broken out. Men were holding their breaths, intensely unconscious of the fact.

"Now, MUSH!"

Thornton's command cracked out like a pistol shot. Buck threw himself forward, tightening the traces with a jarring lunge. His whole body was gathered compactly together in the tremendous effort, the muscles writhing and knotting like live things under the silky fur. His great chest was low to the ground, his head forward and down, while his feet were flying like mad, the claws scarring the hard-packed snow in parallel grooves. The sled swayed and trembled, half-started forward. One of his feet slipped, and one man groaned aloud. Then the sled lurched ahead in what appeared a rapid succession of jerks, though it never really came to a dead stop again . . . half an inch . . . an inch . . . two inches. . . . The jerks perceptibly diminished; as the sled gained momentum, he caught them up, till it was moving steadily along.

Men gasped and began to breathe again, unaware that for a moment they had ceased to breathe. Thornton was running behind, encouraging Buck with short, cheery words. The distance had been measured off, and as he neared the pile of firewood which marked the end of the hundred yards, a cheer began to grow and grow, which burst into a roar as he passed the firewood and halted at command. Every man was tearing himself loose, even Matthewson. Hats and mittens were flying in the air. Men were shaking hands, it did not matter with whom, and bubbling over in a general incoherent babel.

But Thornton fell on his knees beside Buck. Head was against head, and he was shaking him back and forth. Those who hurried up heard him cursing Buck, and he cursed him long and fervently, and softly and lovingly.

"Gad, sir! Gad, sir!" spluttered the Skookum Bench king. "I'll give you a thousand for him, sir, a thousand, sir—twelve hundred, sir."

Thornton rose to his feet. His eyes were wet. The tears were streaming frankly down his cheeks. "Sir," he said to the Skookum Bench king, "no, sir. You can go to hell, sir. It's the best I can do for you, sir."

Buck seized Thornton's hand in his teeth. Thornton shook him back and forth. As though animated by a common impulse, the onlookers drew back to a respectful distance; nor were they again indiscreet enough to interrupt.

7. THE SOUNDING OF THE CALL

WHEN Buck earned sixteen hundred dollars in five minutes for John Thornton, he made it possible for his master to pay off certain debts and to journey with his partners into the East after a fabled lost mine, the history of which was as old as the history of the country. Many men had sought it; few had found it; and more than a few there were who had never returned from the quest. This lost mine was steeped in tragedy and shrouded in mystery. No one knew of the first man. The oldest tradition stopped before it got back to him. From the beginning there had been an ancient and ramshackle cabin. Dying men had sworn to it, and to the mine the site of which it marked, clinching their testimony with nuggets that were unlike any known grade of gold in the Northland.

But no living man had looted this treasure house, and the dead were dead; wherefore John Thornton and Pete and Hans, with Buck and half a dozen other dogs, faced into the East on an unknown trail to achieve where men and dogs as good as themselves had failed. They sledded seventy miles up the Yukon, swung to the left into the Stewart River, passed the Mayo and the McQuestion, and held on until the Stewart itself became a streamlet, threading the upstanding peaks which marked the backbone of the continent.

John Thornton asked little of man or nature. He was unafraid of the wild. With a handful of salt and a rifle he could plunge into the wilderness and fare wherever he pleased and as long as he pleased. Being in no haste, Indian fashion, he hunted his dinner in the course of the day's travel; and if he failed to find it, like the Indian, he kept on traveling, secure in the knowledge that sooner or later he would come to it. So, on this great journey into the East, straight meat was the bill of fare, ammunition and tools principally made up the load on the sled, and the time card was drawn upon the limitless future.

To Buck it was boundless delight, this hunting, fishing, and indefinite wandering through strange places. For weeks at a time they would hold on steadily, day after day; and for weeks upon end they would camp, here and there, the dogs loafing and the men burning holes through frozen muck and gravel and washing countless pans of dirt by the heat of the fire. Sometimes they went hungry, sometimes they feasted riotously, all according to the abundance of game and the fortune of hunting. Summer arrived, and dogs and men packed on their backs, rafted across blue mountain lakes, and descended or ascended unknown rivers in slender boats whipsawed from the standing forest.

The months came and went, and back and forth they twisted through the uncharted vastness, where no men were and yet where men had been if the Lost Cabin were true. They went across divides in summer blizzards, shivered under the midnight sun on naked mountains between the timber line and the eternal snows, dropped into summer valleys amid swarming gnats and flies, and in the shadows of glaciers picked strawberries and flowers as ripe and fair as any the Southland could boast. In the fall of the year they penetrated a weird lake country, sad and silent, where wild fowl had been, but where then there was no life nor sign of life—only the blowing of chill winds, the forming of ice in sheltered places, and the melancholy rippling of waves on lonely beaches.

And through another winter they wandered on the obliterated trails of men who had gone before. Once, they came upon a path blazed through the forest, an ancient path, and the Lost Cabin seemed very near. But the path began nowhere and ended nowhere, and it remained mystery, as the man who made it and the reason he made it remained mystery. Another time they chanced upon the time-graven wreckage of a hunting lodge, and amid the shreds of rotted blankets John Thornton found a long-barreled flintlock. He knew it for a Hudson Bay Company gun of the young days in the Northwest, when such a gun was worth its height in beaver skins packed flat. And that was all—no hint as to the man who in an early day had reared the lodge and left the gun among the blankets.

Spring came on once more, and at the end of all their wandering they found, not the Lost Cabin, but a shallow placer in a broad valley where the gold showed like yellow butter across the bottom of the washing pan. They sought no farther. Each day they worked earned them thousands of dollars in clean dust and nuggets, and they worked every day. The gold was sacked in moose-hide bags, fifty pounds to the bag, and piled like so much firewood outside the spruce-bough lodge. Like giants they toiled, days flashing on the heels of days like dreams as they heaped the treasure up.

There was nothing for the dogs to do, save the hauling in of meat now and again that Thornton killed, and Buck spent long hours musing by the fire. The vision of the short-legged hairy man came to him more frequently, now that there was little work to be done; and often, blinking by the fire, Buck wandered with him in that other world which he remembered.

The salient thing of this other world seemed fear. When he watched the hairy man sleeping by the fire, head between his knees and hands clasped above, Buck saw that he slept restlessly, with many starts and awakenings, at which times he would peer fearfully into the darkness and fling more wood upon the fire. Did they walk by the beach of a sea, where the hairy man gathered shellfish and ate them as he gathered, it was with eyes that roved everywhere for hidden danger and with legs prepared to run like the wind at its first appearance. Through the forest they crept noiselessly, Buck at the hairy man's heels; and they were alert and vigilant, the pair of them, ears twitching and moving and nostrils quivering, for the man heard and smelled as keenly as Buck. The hairy man could spring up into the trees and travel ahead as fast

as on the ground, swinging by the arms from limb to limb, sometimes a dozen feet apart, letting go and catching, never falling,
never missing his grip. In fact, he seemed as much at home
among the trees as on the ground; and Buck had memories of
nights of vigil spent beneath trees wherein the hairy man roosted,
holding on tightly as he slept.

And closely akin to the visions of the hairy man was the call
still sounding in the depths of the forest. It filled him with a great
unrest and strange desires. It caused him to feel a vague, sweet
gladness, and he was aware of wild yearnings and stirrings for he
knew not what. Sometimes he pursued the call into the forest,
looking for it as though it were a tangible thing, barking softly or
defiantly, as the mood might dictate. He would thrust his nose
into the cool wood moss, or into the black soil where long grasses
grew, and snort with joy at the fat earth smells; or he would
crouch for hours, as if in concealment, behind fungus-covered
trunks of fallen trees, wide-eyed and wide-eared to all that moved
and sounded about him. It might be, lying thus, that he hoped to
surprise this call he could not understand. But he did not know
why he did these various things. He was impelled to do them, and
did not reason about them at all.

Irresistible impulses seized him. He would be lying in camp,
dozing lazily in the heat of the day, when suddenly his head
would lift and his ears cock up, intent and listening, and he would
spring to his feet and dash away, and on and on, for hours,
through the forest aisles and across the open spaces where the nig-
gerheads bunched. He loved to run down dry watercourses, and to
creep and spy upon the bird life in the woods. For a day at a time
he would lie in the underbrush where he could watch the partridges drumming and strutting up and down. But especially he
loved to run in the dim twilight of the summer midnights, listening to the subdued and sleepy murmurs of the forest, reading
signs and sounds as man may read a book, and seeking for the
mysterious something that called—called, waking or sleeping, at
all times, for him to come.

One night he sprang from sleep with a start, eager-eyed, nostrils
quivering and scenting, his mane bristling in recurrent waves.
From the forest came the call (or one note of it, for the call was
many-noted), distinct and definite as never before—a long-drawn

howl, like, yet unlike, any noise made by husky dog. And he knew it, in the old familiar way, as a sound heard before. He sprang through the sleeping camp and in swift silence dashed through the woods. As he drew closer to the cry he went more slowly, with caution in every movement, till he came to an open place among the trees, and looking out saw, erect on haunches, with nose pointed to the sky, a long, lean timber wolf.

He had made no noise, yet it ceased from its howling and tried to sense his presence. Buck stalked into the open, half-crouching, body gathered compactly together, tail straight and stiff, feet falling with unwonted care. Every movement advertised commingled threatening and overture of friendliness. It was the menacing truce that marks the meeting of wild beasts that prey. But the wolf fled at sight of him. He followed, with wild leapings, in a frenzy to overtake. He ran him into a blind channel, in the bed of the creek, where a timber jam barred the way. The wolf whirled about, pivoting on his hind legs after the fashion of Joe and of all cornered husky dogs, snarling and bristling, clipping his teeth together in a continuous and rapid succession of snaps.

Buck did not attack, but circled him about and hedged him in with friendly advances. The wolf was suspicious and afraid; for Buck made three of him in weight, while his head barely reached Buck's shoulder. Watching his chance, he darted away, and the chase was resumed. Time and again he was cornered, and the thing repeated, though he was in poor condition, or Buck could not so easily have overtaken him. He would run till Buck's head was even with his flank, when he would whirl around at bay, only to dash away again at the first opportunity.

But in the end Buck's pertinacity was rewarded; for the wolf, finding that no harm was intended, finally sniffed noses with him. Then they became friendly, and played about in the nervous, half-coy way with which fierce beasts belie their fierceness. After some time of this the wolf started off at an easy lope in a manner that plainly showed he was going somewhere. He made it clear to Buck that he was to come, and they ran side by side through the somber twilight, straight up the creek bed, into the gorge from which it issued, and across the bleak divide where it took its rise.

On the opposite slope of the watershed they came down into a level country where were great stretches of forest and many streams, and through these great stretches they ran steadily, hour after hour, the sun rising higher and the day growing warmer. Buck was wildly glad. He knew he was at last answering the call, running by the side of his wood brother toward the place from where the call surely came. Old memories were coming upon him fast, and he was stirring to them as of old he stirred to the realities of which they were the shadows. He had done this thing before, somewhere in that other and dimly remembered world, and he was doing it again, now, running free in the open, the unpacked earth underfoot, the wide sky overhead.

They stopped by a running stream to drink, and, stopping, Buck remembered John Thornton. He sat down. The wolf started on toward the place from where the call surely came, then returned to him, sniffing noses and making actions as though to encourage him. But Buck turned about and started slowly on the back track. For the better part of an hour the wild brother ran by his side, whining softly. Then he sat down, pointed his nose upward, and howled. It was a mournful howl, and as Buck held steadily on his way he heard it grow faint and fainter until it was lost in the distance.

John Thornton was eating dinner when Buck dashed into camp and sprang upon him in a frenzy of affection, overturning him, scrambling upon him, licking his face, biting his hand—"playing the general tomfool," as John Thornton characterized it, the while he shook Buck back and forth and cursed him lovingly.

For two days and nights Buck never left camp, never let Thornton out of his sight. He followed him about at his work, watched him while he ate, saw him into his blankets at night and out of them in the morning. But after two days the call in the forest began to sound more imperiously than ever. Buck's restlessness came back on him, and he was haunted by recollections of the wild brother, and of the smiling land beyond the divide and the run side by side through the wide forest stretches. Once again he took to wandering in the woods, but the wild brother came no more; and though he listened through long vigils, the mournful howl was never raised.

He began to sleep out at night, staying away from camp for days at a time; and once he crossed the divide at the head of the creek and went down into the land of timber and streams. There he wandered for a week, seeking vainly for fresh sign of the wild brother, killing his meat as he traveled and traveling with the long, easy lope that seems never to tire. He fished for salmon in a broad stream that emptied somewhere into the sea, and by this stream he killed a large black bear, blinded by the mosquitoes while likewise fishing, and raging through the forest helpless and terrible. Even so, it was a hard fight, and it aroused the last latent remnants of Buck's ferocity. And two days later, when he returned to his kill and found a dozen wolverines quarreling over the spoil, he scattered them like chaff; and those that fled left two behind who would quarrel no more.

The blood longing became stronger than ever before. He was a killer, a thing that preyed, living on the things that lived, unaided, alone, by virtue of his own strength and prowess, surviving triumphantly in a hostile environment where only the strong survived. Because of all this he became possessed of a great pride in himself, which communicated itself like a contagion to his physical being. It advertised itself in all his movements, was apparent in the play of every muscle, spoke plainly as speech in the way he carried himself, and made his glorious furry coat if anything more glorious. But for the stray brown on his muzzle and above his eyes, and for the splash of white hair that ran midmost down his chest, he might well have been mistaken for a gigantic wolf, larger than the largest of the breed. From his St. Bernard father he had inherited size and weight, but it was his shepherd mother who had given shape to that size and weight. His muzzle was the long wolf muzzle, save that it was larger than the muzzle of any wolf; and his head, somewhat broader, was the wolf head on a massive scale.

His cunning was wolf cunning, and wild cunning; his intelligence, shepherd intelligence and St. Bernard intelligence; and all this, plus an experience gained in the fiercest of schools, made him as formidable a creature as any that roamed the wild. A carnivorous animal, living on a straight meat diet, he was in full flower, at the high tide of his life, overspilling with vigor and virility. When Thornton passed a caressing hand along his back, a snapping and crackling followed the hand, each hair discharging its pent magnetism at the contact. Every part, brain and body, nerve tissue and fiber, was keyed to the most exquisite pitch; and between all the parts there was a perfect equilibrium or adjustment. To sights and sounds and events which required action, he responded with lightning-like rapidity. Quickly as a husky dog could leap to defend from attack or to attack, he could leap twice as quickly. He saw the movement, or heard sound, and responded in less time than another dog required to compass the mere seeing or hearing. He perceived and determined and responded in the same instant. In point of fact the three actions of perceiving, determining, and responding were sequential; but so infinitesimal were the intervals of time between them that they appeared simultaneous. His muscles were surcharged with vitality, and snapped into play sharply, like steel springs. Life streamed through him in splendid flood, glad and rampant, until it seemed that it would burst him asunder in sheer ecstasy and pour forth generously over the world.

"Never was there such a dog," said John Thornton one day, as the partners watched Buck marching out of camp.

"When he was made, the mold was broke," said Pete.

"Py jingo! I t'ink so mineself," Hans affirmed.

They saw him marching out of camp, but they did not see the instant and terrible transformation which took place as soon as he was within the secrecy of the forest. He no longer marched. At once he became a thing of the wild, stealing along softly, cat-footed, a passing shadow that appeared and disappeared among the shadows. He knew how to take advantage of every cover, to crawl on his belly like a snake, and like a snake to leap and strike. He could take a ptarmigan from its nest, kill a rabbit as it slept, and snap in mid-air the little chipmunks fleeing a second too late for the trees. Fish, in open pools, were not too quick for him; nor were beaver, mending their dams, too wary. He killed to eat, not from wantonness; but he preferred to eat what he killed himself. So a lurking humor ran through his deeds, and it was his delight to steal upon the squirrels, and, when he all but had them, to let them go, chattering in mortal fear to the treetops.

As the fall of the year came on, the moose appeared in greater abundance, moving slowly down to meet the winter in the lower and less rigorous valleys. Buck had already dragged down a stray part-grown calf; but he wished strongly for larger and more formidable quarry, and he came upon it one day on the divide at the head of the creek. A band of twenty moose had crossed over from the land of streams and timber, and chief among them was a great bull. He was in a savage temper, and, standing over six feet from the ground, was as formidable an antagonist as even Buck could desire. Back and forth the bull tossed his great palmated antlers, branching to fourteen points and embracing seven feet within the tips. His small eyes burned with a vicious and bitter light, while he roared with fury at sight of Buck.

From the bull's side, just forward of the flank, protruded a feathered arrow, which accounted for his savageness. Guided by that instinct which came from the old hunting days of the primordial world, Buck proceeded to cut the bull out from the herd. It was no slight task. He would bark and dance about in front of the bull, just out of reach of the great antlers and of the terrible splay hoofs which could have stamped his life out with a single blow. Unable to turn his back on the fanged danger and go on, the bull would be driven into paroxysms of rage. At such moments he charged Buck, who retreated craftily, luring him on by a simulated inability to escape. But when he was thus separated from his fellows, two or three of the younger bulls would charge back upon Buck and enable the wounded bull to rejoin the herd.

There is a patience of the wild—dogged, tireless, persistent as life itself—that holds motionless for endless hours the spider in its web, the snake in its coils, the panther in its ambuscade; this patience belongs peculiarly to life when it hunts its living food; and it belonged to Buck as he clung to the flank of the herd, retarding its march, irritating the young bulls, worrying the cows with their half-grown calves, and driving the wounded bull mad with helpless rage. For half a day this continued. Buck multiplied himself, attacking from all sides, enveloping the herd in a whirlwind of menace, cutting out his victim as fast as it could rejoin its mates, wearing out the patience of creatures preyed upon, which is a lesser patience than that of creatures preying.

As the day wore along and the sun dropped to its bed in the northwest (the darkness had come back and the fall nights were six hours long), the young bulls retraced their steps more and more reluctantly to the aid of their beset leader. The downcoming winter was harrying them on to the lower levels, and it seemed they could never shake off this tireless creature that held them back. Besides, it was not the life of the herd, or the young bulls, that was threatened. The life of only one member was demanded, which was a remoter interest than themselves, and in the end they were content to pay the toll.

As twilight fell the old bull stood with lowered head, watching his mates—the cows he had known, the calves he had fathered, the bulls he had mastered—as they shambled by a rapid pace through the fading light. He could not follow, for before his nose leaped the merciless fanged terror that would not let him go. Three hundredweight more than half a ton he weighed; he had lived a long, strong life, full of fight and rugged, and at the end he faced death at the teeth of a creature whose head did not reach beyond his great knuckled knees.

From then on, night and day, Buck never left his prey, never gave it a moment's rest, never permitted it to browse the leaves of trees or the shoots of young birch and willow. Nor did he give the wounded bull opportunity to slake his burning thirst in the slender trickling streams they crossed. Often, in desperation, he burst into long stretches of flight. At such times Buck did not attempt to stay him, but loped easily at his heels, satisfied with the way the game was played, lying down when the moose stood still, attacking him fiercely when he strove to eat or drink.

The great head drooped more and more under its tree of horns, and the shambling trot grew weaker. He took to standing for long periods, with nose to the ground and dejected ears dropped limply; and Buck found more time in which to get water for himself and in which to rest. At such moments, panting with red lolling tongue and ... coming over the big bull, it appeared to Buck that a change ... land. As the moose were coming He could feel a new ... life were coming in. Forest and into the land, other ... with their presence. The news of stream and air seemed by sight, or sound, or smell, but by it was borne in upon He heard nothing, saw nothing, yet some other and ... different; that through it strange knew that the lang ... and he resolved to investigate after things were afoot ... in hand. he had finished ... fourth day, he pulled the great moose At last, at ... he remained by the kill, eating and down. For a ...

sleeping, turn and turn about. Then, rested, refreshed and strong, he turned his face toward camp and John Thornton. He broke into the long easy lope, and went on, hour after hour, never at loss for the tangled way, heading straight home through strange country with a certitude of direction that put man and his magnetic needle to shame.

As he held on he became more and more conscious of the new stir in the land. There was life abroad in it different from the life which had been there throughout the summer. No longer was this fact borne in upon him in some subtle, mysterious way. The birds talked of it, the squirrels chattered about it, the very breeze whispered of it. Several times he stopped and drew in the fresh morning air in great sniffs, reading a message which made him leap on with greater speed. He was oppressed with a sense of calamity happening, if it were not calamity already happened; and as he crossed the last watershed and dropped down into the valley toward camp, he proceeded with great caution.

Three miles away he came upon a fresh trail that sent his neck hair rippling and bristling. It led straight toward camp and John Thornton. Buck hurried on, swiftly and stealthily, every nerve straining and tense, alert to the multitudinous details which told a story—all but the end. His nose gave him a varying description of the passage of the life on the heels of which he was traveling. He remarked the pregnant silence of the forest. The bird life had flitted. The squirrels were in hiding. One only he saw—a sleek gray fellow, flattened against a gray dead limb so that he seemed a part of it, a woody excrescence upon the wood itself.

As Buck slid along with the obscureness of a gliding shadow, his nose was jerked suddenly to the side as though a positive force had gripped and pulled it. He followed the new scent into a thicket and found Nig. He was lying on his side, dead where he had dragged himself, an arrow protruding, head and feathers, from either side of his body.

A hundred yards farther on, Buck came upon one of the sled dogs Thornton had bought in Dawson. This dog was thrashing about in a death struggle, directly on the trail, and Buck passed around him without stopping. From the camp came the faint sound of many voices, rising and falling in a singsong chant. Bellying forward to the edge of the clearing, he found Hans, lying on his face, feathered with arrows like a porcupine. At the same instant Buck peered out where the spruce-bough lodge had been and saw what made his hair leap straight up on his neck and shoulders. A gust of overpowering rage swept over him. He did not know that he growled, but he growled aloud with a terrible ferocity. For the last time in his life he allowed passion to usurp cunning and reason, and it was because of his great love for John Thornton that he lost his head.

The Yeehats were dancing about the wreckage of the spruce-bough lodge when they heard a fearful roaring and saw rushing upon them an animal the like of which they had never seen before. It was Buck, a live hurricane of fury, hurling himself upon them in a frenzy to destroy. He sprang at the foremost man (it was the chief of the Yeehats), ripping the throat wide open till the rent jugular spouted a fountain of blood. He did not pause to worry the victim, but ripped in passing, with the next bound tearing wide the throat of a second man. There was no withstanding him. He plunged about in their very midst, tearing, rending, destroying, in constant and terrific motion which defied the arrows they discharged at him. In fact, so inconceivably rapid were his movements, and so closely were the Indians tangled together, that they shot one another with the arrows; and one young hunter, hurling a spear at Buck in mid-air, drove it through the chest of another hunter with such force that the point broke through the skin of the back and stood out beyond. Then a panic seized the Yeehats, and they fled in terror to the woods, proclaiming as they fled the advent of the Evil Spirit.

And truly Buck was the Fiend incarnate, raging at their heels and dragging them down like deer as they raced through the trees. It was a fateful day for the Yeehats. They scattered far and wide over the country, and it was not till a week later that the last of the survivors gathered together in a lower valley and counted their losses. As for Buck, wearying of the pursuit, he returned to the desolate camp. He found Pete where he had been killed in his blankets in the first moment of surprise. Thornton's desperate struggle was fresh-written on the earth, and Buck scented every detail of it down to the edge of a deep pool. By the edge, head and forefeet in the water, lay Skeet, faithful to the last. The pool itself, muddy and discolored from the sluice boxes, effectually hid what it contained, and it contained John Thornton; for Buck followed his trace into the water, from which no trace led away.

All day Buck brooded by the pool or roamed restlessly about the camp. Death, as a cessation of movement, as a passing out and away from the lives of the living, he knew, and he knew John Thornton was dead. It left a great void in him, somewhat akin to hunger, but a void which ached and ached, and which food could not fill. At times, when he paused to contemplate the carcasses of the Yeehats, he forgot the pain of it; and at such times he was aware of a great pride in himself—a pride greater than any he had yet experienced. He had killed man, the noblest game of all, and he had killed in the face of the law of club and fang. He sniffed the bodies curiously. They had died so easily. It was harder to kill a husky dog than them. They were no match at all, were it not for their arrows and spears and clubs. Thenceforward he would be unafraid of them except when they bore in their hands their arrows, spears, and clubs.

Night came on, and a full moon rose high over the trees into the sky, lighting the land till it lay bathed in ghostly day. And with the coming of the night, brooding and mourning by the pool, Buck became alive to a stirring of the new life in the forest other than that which the Yeehats had made. He stood up, listening and scenting. From far away drifted a faint, sharp yelp, followed by a chorus of similar sharp yelps. As the moments passed the yelps grew closer and louder. Again Buck knew them as things heard in that other world which persisted in his memory. He walked to the center of the open space and listened. It was the call, the many-noted call, sounding more luringly and compellingly than ever before. And as never before, he was ready to obey. John Thornton was dead. The last tie was broken. Man and the claims of man no longer bound him.

Hunting their living meat, as the Yeehats were hunting it, on the flanks of the migrating moose, the wolf pack had at last crossed over from the land of streams and timber and invaded Buck's valley. Into the clearing where the moonlight streamed, they poured in a silvery flood; and in the center of the clearing stood Buck, motionless as a statue, waiting their coming. They were awed, so still and large he stood, and a moment's pause fell, till the boldest one leaped straight for him. Like a flash Buck struck, breaking the neck. Then he stood, without movement, as before, the stricken wolf rolling in agony behind him. Three others tried it in sharp succession; and one after the other they drew back, streaming blood from slashed throats or shoulders.

This was sufficient to fling the whole pack forward, pell-mell, crowded together, blocked and confused by its eagerness to pull down the prey. Buck's marvelous quickness and agility stood him in good stead. Pivoting on his hind legs, and snapping and gashing, he was everywhere at once, presenting a front which was apparently unbroken so swiftly did he whirl and guard from side to side. But to prevent them from getting behind him, he was forced back, down past the pool and into the creek bed, till he brought up against a high gravel bank. He worked along to a right angle in the bank which the men had made in the course of mining, and in this angle he came to bay, protected on three sides and with nothing to do but face the front.

And so well did he face it, that at the end of half an hour the wolves drew back discomfited. The tongues of all were out and lolling, the white fangs showing cruelly white in the moonlight. Some were lying down with heads raised and ears pricked forward; others stood on their feet, watching him; and still others were lapping water from the pool. One wolf, long and lean and gray, advanced cautiously, in a friendly manner, and Buck recognized the wild brother with whom he had run for a night and a day. He was whining softly, and, as Buck whined, they touched noses.

Then an old wolf, gaunt and battle-scarred, came forward. Buck writhed his lips into the preliminary of a snarl, but sniffed noses with him. Whereupon the old wolf sat down, pointed nose at the moon, and broke out the long wolf howl. The others sat down and howled. And now the call came to Buck in unmistakable accents. He, too, sat down and howled. This over, he came out of his angle and the pack crowded around him, sniffing in half-friendly, half-savage manner. The leaders lifted the yelp of the pack and sprang away into the woods. The wolves swung in behind, yelping in chorus. And Buck ran with them, side by side with the wild brother, yelping as he ran.

And here may well end the story of Buck. The years were not many when the Yeehats noted a change in the breed of timber wolves; for some were seen with splashes of brown on head and muzzle, and with a rift of white centering down the chest. But more remarkable than this, the Yeehats tell of a Ghost Dog that runs at the head of the pack. They are afraid of this Ghost Dog, for it has cunning greater than they, stealing from their camps in fierce winters, robbing their traps, slaying their dogs, and defying their bravest hunters.

Nay, the tale grows worse. Hunters there are who fail to return to the camp, and hunters there have been whom their tribesmen found with throats slashed cruelly open and with wolf prints about them in the snow greater than the prints of any wolf. Each fall, when the Yeehats follow the movement of the moose, there is a certain valley which they never enter. And women there are who become sad when the word goes over the fire of how the Evil Spirit came to select that valley for an abiding place.

In the summers there is one visitor, however, to that valley, of which the Yeehats do not know. It is a great, gloriously coated wolf, like, and yet unlike, all other wolves. He crosses alone from the smiling timber land and comes down into an open space among the trees. Here a yellow stream flows from rotted moose-hide sacks and sinks into the ground, with long grasses growing through it and vegetable mold overrunning it and hiding its yellow from the sun; and here he muses for a time, howling once, long and mournfully, ere he departs.

But he is not always alone. When the long winter nights come on and the wolves follow their meat into the lower valleys, he may be seen running at the head of the pack through the pale moonlight or glimmering borealis, leaping gigantic above his fellows, his great throat a-bellow as he sings a song of the younger world, which is the song of the pack.